A COMMENTARY ON ST. LUKE'S GOSPEL

JESUS AND THE
NEW AGE

Completely revised
and expanded

Frederick W. Danker

D1501460

FORTRESS PRESS   PHILADELPHIA

COPYRIGHT © 1988 BY FORTRESS PRESS

Library of Congress Cataloging-in-Publication Data

Danker, Frederick W.
  Jesus and the new age.

  Bibliography: p.
  1. Bible.   N.T.   Luke—Commentaries.   I. Title.
BS2595.3.D35   1988   226'.407   86–46420
ISBN 0–8006–2045–3

2989H87   Printed in the United States of America   1–2045

To
James and Kathleen

CONTENTS

PART SIX
THE PASSION ACCOUNT
22—23

PREFACE

The first edition of this commentary was titled *Jesus and the New Age*
(= *JANA*, St. Louis: Clayton Publishing House, 1972). It was the first
commentary on Luke to incorporate modern developments in linguistics
and literary criticism and was especially designed to help contemporary
students of Luke's Gospel through a meeting of ancient and modern horizons to appreciate the evangelist's genius as a writer with uncommon
contemporary significance. The title pointed to Luke's main theme: Jesus of
Nazareth, Christ and Lord, Great Benefactor, who is named above all other
names (Acts 4:12).

Responses to that edition were so encouraging that I accepted the invitation of Fortress Press to incorporate some of my research since the first
publication in 1972 in this considerably revised edition that also features
approximately 25 percent more content.

In the course of my work on the revision of the English-language edition
of Walter Bauer's lexicon of New Testament Greek (*A Greek-English Lexicon
of the New Testament and Other Early Christian Literature:* A translation and
adaptation of Walter Bauer's fourth revised and augmented ed. by William F.
Arndt and F. Wilbur Gingrich [= BAG, 1957]; 2d ed. rev. and augmented
by F. Wilbur Gingrich and Frederick W. Danker from Bauer's 5th ed.
Chicago: University of Chicago Press [= BAGD, 1979]), I found myself
most fortunately compelled to reread much of the literature, both formal
and informal, of the Greco-Roman world. At the same time, I found that
the writer of the Third Gospel possessed more of the spirit of Hellenic
culture than I had even suspected when I first prepared *Jesus and the New Age*
for publication in 1972.

Especially conducive to this realization were the historical writings, both
Greek and Roman, and many documents, including epigraphs which were
inscribed on stone. Already in the preparation of *JANA* I had observed that
Luke found in the Greco-Roman world's preoccupation with civic and
private benefactors an opportunity to interpret for a wider audience the
significance of Jesus as Israel's Messiah. This awareness led to exploration in
depth of a large constellation of terms and concepts relating to deities and
persons who were esteemed as possessing exceptional merit especially be-

cause of their generosity. To encourage discussion of the subject I presented my initial findings in a provisional work that was limited for methodological reasons to data in inscriptions: *Benefactor: Epigraphic Study of a Graeco-Roman Semantic Field* (= *Benefactor,* St. Louis: Clayton Publishing House, 1982). A second volume is to contain the texts underlying the translations in *Benefactor.* Since the publication of *Benefactor,* I found that I had been overly cautious in assessing the extent to which Luke showed awareness of his public's interest in this cultural phenomenon. Hence this new edition of *JANA* offers a far more satisfactory accounting, in my judgment, of the unity in Luke's presentation of a variety of motifs and themes.

Because my work on the revision of BAGD required the reading of a large corpus of Greek and Roman authors, I also discovered numerous parallels that had not been noticed by Jakob Wettstein (*Novum Testamentum Graecum,* 2 Vols. [Amsterdam, 1751–52]) or Bauer (BAG). This new edition therefore includes many more references to Greek and Roman authors. My aim in this was not so much to establish parallels, for parallel lines never do meet, but in a small way to re-create for modern readers some of the ancient cultural atmosphere that pervades Luke's work. The many additional references to the Jewish Scriptures—the Old Testament—take more adequate account of the extent to which Luke was able to reach people who were steeped in Jewish traditions. In brief, this new edition of *JANA* offers its users a greater opportunity to note the ways in which Luke's original audience and modern readers can find entry into the meaning of his work. At the same time, more effort has been made to help proclaimers find contemporary humanity in Luke's profound presentation of the principal issues that concern us all.

As to the relation of this work to my volume titled *Luke* in the Proclamation Commentaries series (Philadelphia: Fortress Press, 1987), it is to be noted that the latter is not a verse-by-verse and unit-by-unit commentary, but a discussion at a more technical level of various themes and topics in Luke's Gospel. It thus serves as a helpful introduction to this new edition of *JANA,* which aims to help the reader of Luke's Gospel see it new and whole.

I owe a huge debt of thanks to the Aid Association for Lutherans for a research grant (1978) and a study leave (1979–80) that made it possible for me to engage in study of primary Greco-Roman sources. John A. Hollar of Fortress Press deserves the subtitle of Beneficent Redactor. And I am privileged to note that without the technical assistance of my wife, Lois, this work would have taken much longer to complete. To all my benefactors, *eucharistō.*

February 19, 1987

REFERENCE CODES AND ABBREVIATIONS

OLD TESTAMENT (OT)—THE TANAK

Gen.	Genesis
Exod.	Exodus
Lev.	Leviticus
Num.	Numbers
Deut.	Deuteronomy
Josh.	Joshua
Judg.	Judges
Ruth	
1 and 2 Sam.	1 and 2 Samuel
1 and 2 Kings	
1 and 2 Chron.	1 and 2 Chronicles
Ezra	
Neh.	Nehemiah
Esth.	Esther
Job	
Ps(s).	Psalms
Prov.	Proverbs
Eccl.	Ecclesiastes
Cant.	Song of Solomon
Isa.	Isaiah
Jer.	Jeremiah
Lam.	Lamentations
Ezek.	Ezekiel
Dan.	Daniel
Hos.	Hosea
Joel	
Amos	
Obad.	Obadiah
Jonah	
Mic.	Micah
Nah.	Nahum

Hab.   Habakkuk
Zeph.   Zephaniah
Hag.   Haggai
Zech.   Zechariah
Mal.   Malachi

THE SEPTUAGINT (LXX)

Apart from overlapping with the books as cited above, reference is also made to the following:

Baruch
Dan.   Daniel (additions)
Epistle of Jeremiah
1 Esdras   An "apocryphal" book, which covers, with
                        variations, the content of 2 Chron. 35:1–36:23,
                        Ezra, and Neh. 7:38–8:12, and adds a story
                        about three young men in the court of Darius.
Judith
1 and 2 Kgds.   1 and 2 Kingdoms = 1 and 2 Samuel
1 and 2 Macc.   1 and 2 Maccabees
Sir.   Jesus ben Sirach (Ecclesiasticus)
Tobit
Wisd.   Wisdom of Solomon

Note: References to Psalms and Jeremiah of printed Septuagint editions frequently deviate from the capitulation and versification used in the standard versions.

PSEUDEPIGRAPHA

Ascension of Isaiah
Assumption of Moses
Enoch (= 1 Enoch)
2 Esdras   An apocalyptic work (= 4 Esdras in the
                        Vulgate).
3 Macc.   3 Maccabees
Pss. of Sol.   Psalms of Solomon
Sibylline Oracles
Test. (XII)   *Testaments of the Twelve Patriarchs* Reuben,
                        Simeon, Levi, Judah, Issachar, Zebulun,
                        Naphtali, Dan, Gad, Asher, Joseph, Benjamin

NEW TESTAMENT (NT)

Matt.	Matthew
Mark	
Luke	
John	
Acts	
Rom.	Romans
1 and 2 Cor.	1 and 2 Corinthians
Gal.	Galatians
Eph.	Ephesians
Phil.	Philippians
Col.	Colossians
1 and 2 Thess.	1 and 2 Thessalonians
1 and 2 Tim.	1 and 2 Timothy
Tit.	Titus
Phmn.	Philemon
Heb.	Hebrews
James	
1 and 2 Pet.	1 and 2 Peter
1, 2, and 3 John	
Jude	
Rev.	Revelation

QUMRAN AND OTHER DOCUMENTS

In addition to the Gospel of Peter and the Cairo Geniza Damascus Document (CD), the following scrolls from Qumran are cited:

1QH	*Hodayot,* the *Psalms of Thanksgiving*
1QM	*The War of the Children of Light against the Children of Darkness*
4QNahum	*Commentary on Nahum*
1QS	*The Rule of the Community*

OTHERS

★	The bold asterisk notes the author's biblical translations.
APOT	R. H. Charles. *The Apocrypha and Pseudepigrapha of the Old Testament in English,* 2 vols. (Oxford, 1913). For a complete collection of the pseudepigrapha, see James H. Charlesworth, ed., *The Old Testament Pseudepigrapha.* 2 vols., Garden City, N.Y.: Doubleday, 1983–85.

BAGD

Walter Bauer. *A Greek-English Lexicon of the New Testament and Other Early Christian Literature:* A translation and adaptation of Walter Bauer's fourth revised and augmented ed. by William F. Arndt and F. Wilbur Gingrich (1957). 2d ed. rev. and augmented by F. Wilbur Gingrich and Frederick W. Danker from Bauer's 5th ed. (Chicago: University of Chicago Press, 1979).

Benefactor

Frederick W. Danker. *Benefactor: Epigraphic Study of a Graeco-Roman Semantic Field.* (St. Louis: Clayton Publishing House. 1982). The commentary includes some revision of the translations in this work.

IG

Inscriptiones Graecae (1873–   )

JANA

Jesus and the New Age

LXX

The Septuagint, the ancient Greek version of the Old Testament. For translations of the apocrypha and pseudepigrapha, see *APOT*. For details on the Septuagint, see Frederick W. Danker, *Multipurpose Tools for Bible Study,* 3d rev. ed. (St. Louis: Concordia, 1970), 63–79; on the apocrypha and pseudepigrapha, 204–8.

NEB

The New English Bible

NT

New Testament

OGI

W. Dittenberger, ed. *Orientis Graeci Inscriptiones Selectae,* 2 vols. (Leipzig, 1903–1905).

OT

Old Testament

Preisigke

Friedrich Preisigke, ed. *Berichtigungsliste der Griechischen Papyrusurkunden aus Agypten* (Berlin and Leipzig: Walter de Gruyter, 1922).

SB

Hermann L. Strack and Paul Billerbeck. *Kommentar zum Neuen Testament aus Talmud und Midrasch,* 5 vols. (Munich: Beck, 1922–28; 2d ed. 4 vols. in 5, 1954–61).

Seferis

George Seferis. *On the Greek Style: Selected Essays in Poetry and Hellenism,* transl. by Rex Warner and Th. D. Frangopoulos (London: Bodley Head, 1967).

SIG (= *SIG*[3])

W. Dittenberger, ed. *Sylloge Inscriptionum Graecarum;* 3d ed., 4 vols. (Leipzig, 1915–24).

INTRODUCTION TO THE
COMMENTARY

The Gospel according to St. Luke is part of a two-volume publication that includes the Book of Acts. These two parts are usually separated by the Gospel according to St. John, with the result that many readers fail to appreciate the continuity of the author's story line and the coherence of his thought.

The user of this commentary may therefore choose first to read all of Luke's work and then to use both this commentary on the Gospel and a commentary on Acts as aids to understanding. Besides its value as a reference tool, the present work is designed to help the modern reader enter into the story lines of Luke's work and thus appreciate some of the dramatic impact that Luke's Gospel made on first-century auditors. It can therefore be read as a self-sustained narrative in several sittings, in the course of which the reader can bypass the parenthetical references.

THE AUTHOR

A Christian named Luke is mentioned three times in the NT. At Col. 4:14 he is identified as a physician especially dear to Paul. According to Philemon, he was a colleague of the apostle, and 2 Tim. 4:11 indicates that he was loyal and dependable, not hesitating to run the risk of associating with the apostle during his imprisonment. From distinctions made in Col. 4:10–14 it can be inferred that this Luke was a gentile. A Lucius receives recognition in Acts 13:1 and Rom. 16:21, but since Paul calls him a relative—that is, a Jew—identification with the physician is questionable. Moreover, Lucius was a common Roman name.

Whether Luke the physician and companion of Paul actually wrote the Third Gospel is heavily debated. Because of the tendency on the part of early tradition to ascribe NT writings to apostles, association of the Third Gospel with one who was not an apostle in the narrow definition of the term is not to be lightly dismissed.

It was once thought that the language of the Gospel clearly pointed to a physician as the writer. At best, such a demonstration would merely indicate that the tradition is not to be slighted in the absence of other evidence to the contrary. On the other hand, ancient medicine was not nearly so technical as it is today, and numerous writers outside the medical profession used expressions similar to those found in the Third Gospel. The fact that the author revises at Luke 8:43 what appears to be a harsh indictment of physicians in Mark 5:26 is no conclusive indication that he here defends the medical profession, for he frequently abbreviates Mark and softens some of Mark's judgments. In this particular case he emphasizes the woman's desperate situation. No one was able to heal her.

Since tradition is not an infallible source of historical veracity, and since the identification of the author with Paul's "beloved physician" rests on a number of inferences, the anonymity of the two-volume work must be respected. For easy reference, though, the name Luke will be used throughout this commentary.

Although the author's professional identity is in a twilight zone, the same may not be said of his literary credentials. He does not take second rank among Hellenistic writers. Like the ancient historian Polybios, who was impressed by the phenomenon of the rise of the city of Rome to worldwide dominion, Luke recognized that in the life and fortunes of Jesus of Nazareth, history had taken an unprecedented turn. But unlike Polybios—whom Basil Gildersleeve described as scrupulous in the avoidance of every hiatus, except one, "the yawn in the face of his reader"—Luke maintains a grip on the attention of his public. His linguistic versatility and compositional technique combine with keen perception of the substantive issues of history to produce a unique work permeated with dramatic sensitivity. One can only marvel at the structural strength of many of his sparsely worded narratives that bear such awesome weight of "things fulfilled among us" (1:1★). To record the birth of Jesus, for example, Luke uses only 104 words (2:1–7), and to this day they appear annually on the front page of newspapers, some with a circulation of a million or more. An intriguing variety of rhetorical devices give the plot arresting expression. Much of Luke's story suggests a journey in which his auditors are frequently invited to look backward as well as beyond the horizon, so as to grasp the whole at each stage of the presentation of the parts. Especially elegant is his use of terms, *à double sens,* that is, the use of diction that in certain contexts admits of more than one interpretation. For Luke's auditors soon learn to know that with the arrival of Jesus, the One Name (Acts 4:12), there is always more than immediately meets eye or ear.

In the iconographic tradition the ox became Luke's symbol. During the thirteenth century, painters derived many of their themes from the Third Gospel and counted its author as their patron saint. About the sixth century, a notion surfaced that Luke had done a portrait of the Virgin Mary, but there is no evidence that he was a master of the brush.

LUKE AS CULTURAL BRIDGEBUILDER

Luke's primary claim to greatness as a writer is his ability to engage the attention of his auditors across a variety of cultural fronts.

It is reported that at the age of twelve the modern Greek poet Konstantine Kavafy set himself the task of composing a historical dictionary. He soon abandoned it after he had written down what was for him the fateful word—Alexander. If Luke ever had such ideas, he certainly abandoned them when he came to the One Name. For his two-volume work expresses in its own way what Paul stated:

> I am a debtor to those who know Greek and to those who don't know Greek, to the educated and to the uneducated. . . . I am not ashamed of the gospel, for it functions as God's instrument to rescue anyone who is committed to it—Jews first, then gentiles. (Rom. 1:14–16★)

Challenged by the mystique of divine action in connection with Jesus Christ, Luke proposed for himself the task of writing a coherent account of **the things which have been accomplished among us** (Luke 1:1). A crafter of the first order, he destroyed himself, as every great artist does, for the sake of his work. Intent on bridging Jewish and gentile religious-cultural experience, after the fourth verse of his first chapter he abandons the lofty flight and adopts a style of writing, a biblical Greek, that itself suggests the ancient roots of all that he relates. At the same time, he formulates his narrative in such a way that Greco-Roman audiences could make contact with material that would otherwise have been dismissed as tales recited in an unknown tongue. In this way Luke reaches out to Jew and gentile, and his very mode of communication discloses the message in his story line. In brief, Luke takes account of the evocative power possessed by a literary work and shows awareness of the cultural models that various publics might bring as instruments for interpreting such a work.

Supreme Excellence

In search of a model that would aid him in his projection of the significance of Jesus outside a purely Jewish frame of reference, Luke opted for the Greco-Roman ideal of superior excellence *(aretē)*. Basic to such perception is the role played by deities in the welfare of their devotees and by public-spirited citizens who put the welfare of their city and citizenry above personal considerations.

Since the Greek term *aretē* was frequently used in reference to "superior excellence," recitals of extraordinary performance are sometimes called aretalogies in modern discussions of the subject, but the term "aretalogy" is not a technical one in ancient usage and it lacks the modern scientific value of a specific signifier. It is more accurate to state that documents that are exclusively concerned with recitals of a specific person's or deity's exceptional performance or characteristics might well be classed as "aretalogies." For example, a decree published between 55 and 59 C.E. by the inhabitants of Busiris, Egypt, praises the prefect Tiberius Claudius Balbillus for his distinguished service and at the same time recognizes the *aretē* of Nero and of the god of the Nile:

With Good Fortune. Whereas Nero Claudius Caesar Augustus Germanicus Imperator, the Good Divinity of the world, in addition to all the good benefits that he conferred in the past on Egypt has (once again) exercised his most brilliant foresight and sent to us Tiberius Claudius Balbillus as governor; and, owing to the latter's favors and benefactions, Egypt is teeming with all good things and sees the gifts of the Nile increasing annually and now all the more enjoys the equity with which the Nile-God floods the lands; (in view thereof) it was *resolved* by the inhabitants of Busiris... to erect a stone stele... [which is to reveal] by its inscribed list of benefits the philanthropy they have enjoyed; and from this recital everyone [will know] what wonderful service (Balbillus) has rendered [to all] of Egypt. Therefore it is appropriate that his godlike favors be inscribed in sacred letters for all time to remember.

(Adapted from *Benefactor*, No. 35)

Most literary works, though, contain a variety of contents, among which may be narratives of an aretalogical type. Luke's two-volume work is a mixed genre, exhibiting historical and biographical interests, with a strong aretalogical ingredient. Luke, of course, does not use the term *aretē,* because he prefers synonyms and specific expressions that make concrete some of the features that come to expression when *aretē* is otherwise used in Greco-Roman writings. On the other hand, there are long stretches of Greek poetry and prose in which the term *aretē* is lacking but not the features ordinarily associated with subjects that evoke admiration for their *aretē.*

Among the numerous terms and themes that found a place in public and private accolades in praise of deities or people, or both, are the following: fine and good; savior; liberator; helpful; displays good will; pious and upright; liturgist (i.e., one who defrays expenses for public events or structures); spares no expense (in behalf of the city, club, etc.); effective in word and deed; worthy of imitation; endures hazard (in behalf of others); friend of humanity (philanthropist); conferrer of benefits. Any one of these, or two or more in concert, whether expressed in verbs or nouns, would signal or suggest to an auditor familiar with Greek customs some aspect of the cultural ideal of an exceptional being.

In Homeric times, warriors were recognized along with deities as the chief exponents of superior excellence, or *aretē,* and bards sang their achievements in the halls of the mighty. Ultimately, the specific terms or thematic constructions associated with the ideal of *aretē* display a complete democratization. Stoicism played a major role in this development, and in the Hellenistic period the category of exceptional identity came to include individuals and corporate entities at a variety of levels.

Besides deities—including especially Isis and Sarapis—and immortalized heroes, honorands would be made up of heads of state, followed by bureaucrats, philosophers, physicians, athletes, artists, and a host of public-spirited citizens.

In this commentary "Benefactor" is therefore used as an umbrella term and is applied to someone who qualifies for one or more of the characterizations noted above. The word itself does not render any specific Greek term, except when used in reference to such expressions as *chrēstos* (5:39, in reference to God); *agathopoiein* (6:9, in a question by Jesus); *agathos kai dikaios* (23:50, of Joseph of Arimathea); *euergetēs* (22:15, of secular rulers; cf. the participle *euergetōn,* of Jesus, Acts 10:38); *dynatos en ergō kai logō* (24:19, of Jesus).

GOD AND JESUS

Because deities in the Greco-Roman world were evaluated in terms of their beneficence, Luke stresses that the God of Israel is the ultimate in philanthropic excellence, the Supreme Benefactor (cf. Luke 1:32). Since uprightness and a sense of justice are among the primary attributes celebrated in many Greco-Roman honorary documents, Luke exhibits these explicitly and implicitly as the dominating features of the God and Parent of Jesus Christ. For such understanding within Jewish circles Philo had set the pattern.

Since Jesus functions in the interest of his Parent, Luke displays him as the Great Benefactor (cf. Luke 1:32), whose beneficence is crowned with resurrection and ascension (Acts 1:11; 2:33–34; 10:37–40). As the unique Son of God, Jesus naturally manifests the primary characteristics of his heavenly Parent, and the centurion so affirms it with his verdict that no one is more entitled to be called "upright" than is Jesus (Luke 23:47). The Book of Acts echoes that assessment (Acts 3:14; 7:52; 22:14): Jesus is indeed upright, righteous, just *(dikaios).*

To emphasize the preeminence of Jesus as benefactor and yet distinguish him from his divine Parent, Luke shows him sitting at the right hand of God (Acts 1:11; 2:33–34) as the One Name "under heaven" (Acts 4:12). Similar glorification was interpreted in Greco-Roman circles as entry into the select circle of immortals, such as Romulus, Herakles, Dionysios, Asklepios, Alexander the Great, Julius Caesar, Caesar Augustus, and others. All of these earned their place in the select circle because of the benefits they conferred. Hence Jesus is, first—from Greco-Roman perspective—a benefactor and then an immortal. My term "Great Benefactor" distinguishes him from his heavenly Parent and at the same time from all other benefactors.

To flesh out the fact that Jesus is a benefactor and the One Name, Luke punctuates Jesus' career with types of recitals and phenomena that the evangelist's auditors would connect with their recollection of accounts concerning Greco-Roman deities and superstars. Portents, miracles, prophecies—these are part of the scenario that alerts Luke's publics to the extraordinary identity of Jesus. Jews with long roots in OT tradition, as well as gentiles who eavesdropped on Israel's experiences, would of course understand such materials also in terms of Israel's ancestral heroes. And those who were acquainted with the Book of Isaiah would be alert to the relationship between Jesus and the Servant of the Lord (see Isaiah 42, 49, 53: they would note Luke's apparent association of Isaiah 61 with the "servant songs").

Jesus as Savior

A key term in the identification of Jesus is the word "savior" and its cognates. God is, of course, Savior Supreme (Luke 1:47), and Luke spells out details in 1:69, 71, 77. But since Jesus is God's primary instrument for effecting salvation, "savior" is also appropriate in reference to him (Luke 2:11; Acts 5:31; 13:23), and salvation is repeatedly associated with his person and action (Luke 6:9; 7:50; 8:36, 48, 50; 9:56; 17:19; 18:42; 19:9, 10; Acts 2:1, 40, 47; 4:9, 12; 11:14; 14:9; 15:11; 16:31).

The Greek Bible (Septuagint) is replete with references to God's role as rescuer of Israel. But those among Luke's Greco-Roman auditors who were unfamiliar with this Jewish Bible would understand the terminology in the light of its applications within their culture, without necessarily bringing the entire baggage of such association to Luke's distinctive usage.

Since heads of state were frequently identified as "saviors" because of their expected or real benefactions, Luke's references to Jesus as a person with royal credentials (Luke 1:33; 19:38; 22:29, 30; 23:42; indirectly, 19:14, 27; 23:2, 3, 37, 38; Acts 17:7) form part of the unified picture of the Man from Nazareth as the Great Benefactor. But it is to be observed in this connection that Luke's more frequent use of royal terminology in connection with God than with Jesus is also consistent with the evangelist's perception that Jesus is the instrument of the Supreme Benefactor's purpose and mission to effect salvation for all humanity.

Jesus' Death and Resurrection

Luke's understanding of the manner in which Jesus effects salvation for Israel and all humanity is different from Paul's interpretation. In some of Paul's writings the suffering and death of Jesus are interpreted in terms of OT views of sacrifice, in which blood plays a dominant role. It is true that Luke also emphasizes the death of Jesus, but he does not view it as a sacrifice or as an expiation for sin. Instead, the evangelist focuses attention on God as the Supreme Benefactor, who offers Jesus as the ultimate benefaction to humanity. Coincident with this theme is an emphasis on "necessity" that pervades Luke's two-volume work, beginning with Luke 2:49 and terminating at Acts 27:24, 26. This theme would convey to Greco-Romans a modification of the Greek term for foresight (*pronoia*) which appears in numerous inscriptions to denote the prescient concern of a beneficent deity or a public-spirited benefactor. Through this theme Luke helps his publics perceive that the life of Jesus was one of uninterrupted obedience and dedication to divine purpose.

Despite all this beneficent activity, Jerusalem was instrumental in secur-
ing the crucifixion of Jesus. But like many public-spirited people of distinction who endured unusual hazards in behalf of their constituency, Jesus
perseveres in his commitment through any and every peril. He is the
endangered benefactor par excellence, whose devotion in behalf of his
associates is signally displayed in the eucharistic recital (Luke 22:14–20).

No plots of Satan or human beings can interfere with or disrupt God's
beneficent intention. Hence the death of Jesus also falls into the category of
"necessity" (Luke 9:22; 13:33; 17:25; 22:37; 24:7, 26, 44; Acts 17:3). Through
the resurrection of Jesus, God demonstrates the farthest reaches of beneficence. Greco-Roman auditors would be familiar with declarations of amnesty, such as the one granted by Caesar Augustus to his adversaries in the
civil rebellion that he quenched. At Pentecost and thereafter, Peter and his
associates proclaim that God raised up Jesus and reversed the verdict of
those who crucified him. Despite such rebellion against the divine purpose,
God has shown that Jesus remains heaven's choice for the fulfillment of the
promises made to Israel. That is to say, his credentials as Christ and Lord did
not lose their validity because of the crucifixion (Acts 2:36). "No one can
avert what God has decreed," wrote Herodotos (9.16) five centuries earlier.
Luke gave the doctrine a more tender tone.

Jesus as Healer

In addition to exhibiting God as a benefactor in connection with the death
of Jesus, Luke interprets that death as the outcome of Jesus' own beneficence. Acts 10:38 declares that God gave Jesus a messianic status by anointing him with "the Holy Spirit and with power." In this messianic capacity
Jesus "went about doing good" (the Greek *evergetōn*: "went about as a
benefactor"), and specifically by "healing all who were tyrannized by the
devil."*

To appreciate further the implications of Luke's statement in Acts 10:38, it
is necessary to recall that the Mediterranean deity Isis received numerous
acknowledgments for her beneficent care as a healing god. And Asklepios,
who according to tradition had been exalted to full divinity, was recognized
especially at Epidauros and at Kos for his miraculous cures and restorations
to life. Numerous stone inscriptions also attest the remarkable skill of
physicians, some of whom restored patients who were afflicted with terminal illnesses.

In keeping with the expectations of his auditors, for whom healings were
a mark of special beneficence, Luke emphasizes such activity of Jesus and
from time to time puts it under the rubric of salvation (see, e.g., Luke 6:9;
8:36, 48, 50; 18:42). This latter practice is in harmony with Greco-Roman
documents in which the verb cognate of "savior" is applied to acts of
healing.

Many of the inscriptions that record the cures effected by physicians include the observation that the physician in question reached out to *all* who needed help. Similarly, Luke calls attention to Jesus' broad outreach by editing Mark so as to include a larger circle of beneficiaries (against parallels in Mark: cf. Luke 4:40–41; 6:19; 9:6; and note the additional recitals of healing and resuscitation: 7:12–17; 13:10–17; 14:1–6; 17:12–19).

Because it was considered the height of poor public manners to permit a public-spirited deed to go without appropriate accolades, the character and performance of Greco-Roman honorands were recited in detail on stone for every passer-by to read. Should the imperial administration object to expenditures connected with such recognition, the honoring committee would "witness to" or "attest to" the prospective honorand's performance. In Jesus' case, the primary attestant of his beneficence is God (Acts 2:22; 3:13; 10:40–41). The secondary attestants are the disciples (Luke 24:48; Acts 1:8; 10:42), who witness to the mighty performance of Jesus (Acts 2:22; 4:10; 10:38–39).

In view of such significance attached in Greco-Roman society to recognition and attestation of a benefactor's performance, it is only natural that Luke should have emphasized the importance of gratitude and testimony in his two-volume work. The story of the One Grateful Leper (Luke 17:12–19) and the early sermons in Acts (chaps. 2—4) offer eloquent exposition of the gratitude-ingratitude theme. A succinct thematic summary of the divine generosity and the strange fortunes it encountered, climaxing with an unprecedented display of beneficence, is given in Acts 10:34–43.

Outreach to All

As noted above, the evangelist's recital of the miracles of Jesus included the pandemic theme—universal outreach—that is found in numerous Greco-Roman honorary documents. But it is clear from Acts 10:38 that Luke intends this feature to be understood as part of a coherent account of God's beneficent intentions for outsiders as well as insiders relative to the divine promises made to Israel. The Gospel begins with much of the literary focus on Jerusalem, and Acts ends with Paul in Rome. Between these two locales Luke stages the divine outreach.

Israel is the privileged benefactor of the world, for the Light to the gentiles comes forth from it (Luke 2:32). The drama of Luke-Acts has to do with the question whether God will be successful. Israel seems to destroy her own destiny through the crucifixion of the very instrument of her prestige. But God raises Jesus from the dead and gives Israel a second chance.

Israel's leadership again unwittingly frustrates the divine purpose by attempting to silence chosen witnesses of Jesus, who are also from the family of Israel. But the word of the Lord grows (Acts 6:7; 12:24). Saul of Tarsus, also an Israelite, shows himself hostile, but after his conversion he becomes the chief instrument for carrying out the mission of Israel to the nations. The divine success is celebrated in Acts 28:28. In this passage the stress is on the fact that God has overcome many odds in delivering the promised salvation to the nations. To level a charge of anti-Semitism against Luke is patently libelous. Even if he does appear to heighten the guilt of Jews in connection with the crucifixion, the observation would relate to a literary-structural datum and not to insensitivity. By emphasizing the guilt, Luke brings into sharper focus the divine amnesty. If anything, Luke is the one evangelist who redeems Israel from failure. Through Paul, one of Israel's superstars, God's chosen people achieve their destiny.

Associated with this theme of universal outreach is Luke's inclusiveness in respect to various societal strata. If Greco-Roman physicians are to be praised for their beneficence to *all* who come within the reach of their curative powers, it is to be expected that Luke would portray Jesus through a variety of examples, many of which are not found in the other Gospels. The treatment of women as inferiors is declared obsolete by Luke's Jesus, who appears aware of their uphill struggle in a society where males determine their destiny. The Third Evangelist gives center stage to Elizabeth; Mary the mother of Jesus; Anna (1:36–38); a widow at Nain (7:1–10); an unnamed benefactor who anointed his feet (7:36–50); two sisters, Mary and Martha (10:38–42); a woman who lost a coin (15:8–10); a widow who wanted justice (18:1–8); and others (see, e.g., 8:2–3; 23:55–56; 24:1–11).

Primary factors in God's salvation are assurance of forgiveness and familial acceptance. Therefore Luke shows Jesus searching for people on a broad front that avoids all partisan bias. This commitment on his part engages him in a conflict in which insiders and outsiders are the protagonists. In the front ranks of concern to Jesus are the victims of religious snobbery who cannot find comfort in the society of God as portrayed by the prevailing cultic establishment. Included in this category are the so-called sinners, that is, outsiders relative to traditional religious values as sustained, for example, by some of the Pharisees.

A large proportion of the population whose economic and political power was severely limited is known as "the poor." They receive consolation that goes beyond wealth-in-the-sky rhetoric, for Luke's two-volume work (Luke-Acts) includes recitals that invite the exploration of innovative ways in which individual and societal resources may be mobilized to relieve the miseries of the poor. In such ways both the poor and the rich can experience salvation in more than one dimension.

Included among the outsiders who are given an opportunity to join the insiders are collectors of tolls (publicans), in whose number are Levi and Zacchaeus. Nor does Jesus hesitate to draw the circle around representatives of the military as well as of the religious establishment that at times opposes him. And at the very end of his life, Jesus grants executive pardon to a repentant criminal. Of such is the constituency of the New Age.

To dramatize God's familial interest in both outsiders and self-styled insiders, Luke repeatedly shows Jesus participating with them at mealtime. Both Jews and Greco-Romans would be impressed by the Lord's creative use of this profoundly meaningful social convention. Correspondingly, Luke emphasizes repentance, which means that one commits what is in essence a personal revolution. In practice this means that one faces up to anything that obstructs God's efforts to achieve the familial program of the New Age.

Among the refuse of the Old Age that must be jettisoned are selfish regard for money and material things, misused personal qualities, prejudice, inflexibility in approach to social and religious conventions, envy, jealousy, status search, sacrifice of human concern to maintenance of traditional structures, and insensitivity to the rights of others. These are but a few of the characteristics and practices that interfere with God's intentions for the well-being of all humanity. They are the antithesis of the two basic qualities featured in Jewish and Greco-Roman thinking: righteousness in human affairs and reverence in relation to God. By emphasizing Jesus' intimate encounter with publicans and sinners, as well as with sponsors of more highly perched morality, Luke shows that the debris and litter of the Old Age can be disposed of in the presence of Jesus without fear of reprisal.

PROBLEMS

Because of Luke's dedication to clarification (Luke 1:1–4), the main lines of his work are readily discernible, but some attention must be paid to special problems that he encountered in the course of his endeavor to bring order out of a medley of reports concerning words and events associated with Jesus and his followers.

Although it is impossible, given the meager data we have at the present time, to identify the Theophilos mentioned in Luke 1:1–4, it is indisputable that whatever in Luke's narrative helped this Theophilos gain a clearer conception of Christianity would also have helped others. In any case, Luke's work does not appear to have been designed for a bureaucratic archive.

Messianic Identity and the Last Things

Fundamental to at least some expression of the early Christian message was the belief that Jesus qualified as a ruler. But the precise relationship between Jesus and messianic expectation among Jews was a subject of constant debate, and Roman officials could readily be excused for being confused. Luke does not hesitate to affirm that Jesus is a king, but by clarifying Jesus' identity as the Messiah of Israel—who is in Greek terms "the Anointed One" (the Christ)—he is able to inform Theophilos that Jesus did not run for Caesar's office and therefore did not head a partisan coalition. On the contrary, as Acts attests, Jesus Christ as resurrected Lord directs the mission of Israel in her assigned task to bring the knowledge of God to the world. Such being the case, the Christian sect, many of whose members were Jews, is entitled, Luke argues, to the special privileges that Jews enjoy throughout the Roman Empire.

One of the chief areas of disagreement among early Christians was the subject of *eschatology* (instruction respecting the last things). Closely related to the term "eschatology" is the word *apocalyptic* (derived from a Greek word meaning "disclosure" and specifically used in reference to descriptions of events at the end of the normal course of history). Examples of apocalyptic writing in the canonical OT include Isaiah 24—27; Ezekiel 37; Daniel; Joel; and Zechariah 12—14. A number of writings not included in the canon of Sacred Scripture are also devoted to this theme. Especially significant are the books ascribed to *Enoch, Assumption of Moses,* and *Fourth Ezra.* Their themes and descriptions fired the popular imagination of people who thought the use of a word spelled the thing itself and therefore anticipated spectacular developments on earth and in the heavens that would be in precise accord with the written descriptions.

Apocalyptic thought, kaleidoscopic in its variety as well as in its descriptions, saw the world as a battleground for the forces of God and Evil. At some time God would inactivate the opposition, either by setting up a new reign on earth or by completely destroying the old order and ushering in a new creation. Resurrection of the righteous became a central feature in scenarios of the latter expectation. In either case, those on God's side would be privileged participants in the new regime, the Kingdom of God.

In dealing with such expectation, a writer who wished to vindicate Christian faith in the ultimate triumph of God could not evade resolution of several pressing problems: (1) If Jesus is the deliverer at the end time, then the power of Satan ought to be destroyed. Yet Jesus died an ignominious death, and demonic forces still appear to be in control. (2) If Jesus is the anticipated deliverer, then the close of history ought to be taking place and one should be able to identify clear signs that the end is in fact near. In their absence, unfortunately, false prophets find the early believers easy pickings. (3) If Jesus is the deliverer, then certainly his own nation ought to respond to his coming. Yet his own religious and theological establishment rejected him.

Demonic Power

In answer to the first question, Luke shows that Jesus not only overcame the temptations but made a frontal attack on demonic forces by curing the demon-possessed. His death came about through alliance of established religious power, secular strength, and demonic forces (Luke 22). Making use of a dominant motif in such works of wisdom literature as Proverbs, Wisdom of Solomon, and Sirach, that the wise and upright person is ultimately triumphant, Luke shows that Jesus is vindicated by none other than God through the resurrection. Suffering and death are necessary factors in the ascent of Jesus to glory. Demonic forces still attempt to reclaim their power, but Jesus' victory over demons, demonstrated both in his healings and in his faithful surrender to God's purpose that climaxed at the crucifixion, assures Christians that they will not fall victim to demonic devices. In demonstration of the victory, the Book of Acts presents a number of recitals of apostolic success over the forces of evil.

Signs of the End Time

Connected with questions concerning the moment when the normal course of history would come to an end was misunderstanding concerning the relationship of Jesus to the end-time events. Was Jesus but one of a series of end-time figures or is he the last and definitive One? Luke's answer takes a two-stage form. Jesus is a genuine human being. He is the Son of humanity (RSV and others: "Son of man"), that is, one who identifies totally with our human lot in all its fragility. On the other hand, he has come to usher in the new era of the Reign of God (Luke 22:29).

The Reign of God comes to climactic expression at the cross. Death is the pathway to Jesus' enthronement. No special apocalyptic effects are necessary to validate that kingship. The end time has in fact begun, and God's people live in the entire period of the end time. At what is ordinarily termed judgment day, but in Luke's thought "the end of the end time," Jesus will reappear and carry out in full all God's promises to the elect. Between these two stages the believers carry out their assigned mission task.

Associated with questions about the end time was the expectation of a reappearance of Elijah. His coming was to signal the end time and the windup of history (cf. Mal. 4:5). Some Christians viewed John the Baptist as fulfillment of this expectation but were distressed that the end of the end time was not actually taking place. Since according to some popular notions the Deliverer of Israel was to make a glorious appearance when Elijah returned, the question was naturally asked: Is Jesus really the Messiah? Conversely, since Jesus, although acknowledged as Messiah, did not in fact usher in the apocalyptic era as conceived in some circles, was it not a mistake to identify John as Elijah? Luke answers: John is not Elijah (see my commentary on Luke 7:27), but he did function as a prophet calling the nation to repentance before Jesus arrived on the scene (Acts 13:24). Jesus himself is in certain respects an Elijah figure (cf. Luke 3:16; 4:25–27; 7:16, 19; 9:8, 19) and therefore needs no Elijah forerunner to verify his credentials as authentic deliverer of the windup announced in Malachi 3—4. Absence of scheduled apocalyptic "signs" is therefore due to the fact that the Kingdom comes in the two stages defined by Luke.

For the benefit of those who anticipated a prophet like Moses, Luke shows that Jesus is more than Moses and replaces Moses as the official teacher in the Israel of the end time. Another deliverance takes place under him, and the twelve apostles form the core of a latter-day Israel that is in continuity with the twelve tribes of days of yore (Luke 22:30).

Once Luke's basic orientation in apocalyptic is grasped, the modern reader will not be surprised at the evangelist's apparently conflicting use of apocalyptic terminology, motifs, and scenery. Luke is opposed not to apocalyptic language or apocalyptic hope as such but to the mistaken notion that divine fulfillment must precisely match prior prophetic descriptions. Traditional apocalyptic is not to be read as a specific blueprint for God's action. Rather, Jesus is the blueprint for understanding apocalyptic hope. What happens in the life and time of Jesus is not to be checked for validation against traditional apocalyptic description. Jesus in his person is the apocalypse (the revelation). Therefore such normal ingredients of apocalyptic writing as angels and references to responses of fear or astonishment, and even the recital of the transfiguration of Jesus (Luke 9:28–36), are included to inform auditors that they must revise their thinking about the end of history and associate apocalyptic hope especially with God's present communication focused on Jesus as the center of the New Age. In other words, Luke provides a christological focus for apocalyptic and gives it an historical dimension. Instead of putting the emphasis on salvation at the end of history, Luke shows that much of what was ordinarily connected with history's termination takes place in the life and work of Jesus, who is Christ and Lord, and in the ongoing experience of the post-Pentecost believers.

In brief, Luke's use of some apocalyptic terminology and motifs in connection with events that would not be considered apocalyptic from the standpoint of his opponents is one of the many strokes of literary genius that permeate his work. But the literary genius is at one with the theological perspective. Such a shift in apocalyptic thinking requires faith. By eliminating the weird and bizarre as a rallying point for Christian identity, Luke disencumbered the People of God of the necessity of determining Jesus' messianic credentials through proofs supplied by "signs." Thereby Luke paved the way for an ecumenical awareness that transcended parochial interests based on rival interpretations of apocalyptic tradition. At the same time he helped God's people understand how they might live in constant expectation of the end of the world and yet function creatively during each period of time that remained.

A Nation's Rejection

Not only did the repudiation of Jesus by the religious leadership bear on the matter of Jesus' messianic credentials but it raised the further question of Christianity's validity as a legitimate participant in the promises to which Israel claimed to be heir. Luke therefore stresses the criteria of the New Age. The high and mighty, including especially those who might be classified as the religious establishment, have no assured automatic claim to the Kingdom. Those who rely on traditional associations are warned not even to begin to say, "We have Abraham as our Father" (Luke 3:8). Simeon's warning about the rise and fall of many (2:34) is the thematic statement of what becomes in Luke's narrative a major literary structural feature: the theme of reversal. Those who think that they have an inside track with God may find themselves excluded from the blessings of the New Age, whereas those considered least likely to succeed will have choice seats at the heavenly banquet (11:23–30). "Don't even begin to say to yourselves, 'Our father is Abraham,' " warned John the Baptist. "I tell you, out of these stones God can raise up children for Abraham" (3:8). A certain rich man ignored the warning and found torment in Hades, whereas the poor beggar at his door became Abraham's honored guest (16:19–31). According to Jesus' inaugural address, the poor, the captives, the blind, and the bruised can look forward to a new day, but the elite must ponder the fact that no leper except an outsider named Naaman was cleansed in ancient Israel, and the only widow to whom Elijah was sent came from beyond Israel's borders (4:16–30). Some will see and hear, others will be blind and deaf in response to the message of the New Age (8:9–10). Those who celebrate God's gift of Jesus will have status in the heavenly court; those who deny him will lose it (12:8–9). Many will be scratched from the guest list, and invitations will go out to society's misfits (14:16–24). A young man will go from rags to riches, whereas his older brother refuses to join the party (15:11–32). A rich man declined to join the ranks of the poor and lost the prize (18:18–23); another named Zacchaeus gave up his old sense of values and found salvation (19:1–10). And so it goes throughout Luke-Acts.

Much of the opposition to Jesus was a reaction to the inclusive social register popularized by Jesus: peasants, religious outsiders, women of low as well as of high status, toll collectors, and persons with various social diseases. Salvation, Jesus taught, is freedom for access to God; release from stifling religious partisanship; and liberation from conventional standards of behavior that do not meet the requirements of avowed claims to interest in God. Reports by Luke of such uncompromising rejection of the status quo would naturally invite the criticism that Luke engages in the popular game of assaulting "the establishment," thereby negating his stress on the importance of love. But Luke follows his Master and plays no games.

Anti-Semitism?

Love and truthful confrontation are not mutually exclusive. Some discount may be made for early partisan interpretation of the ongoing battle of Jesus and the early Christian communities with forces of reaction, exploitative interests, and powers that were allergic to proposals from the future, but no responsible commentator can whitewash history. Therefore, if the terms "system," "partisan politics," and "establishment" occur quite often in the commentary, this is not to be construed as a reading of the present into the past but as a means of conveying Luke's appreciation of the issues that surface in his Gospel.

Nor is such procedure to be interpreted as a device for using ancient Jews as "whipping boys for Christian sins," as one critic put it. On the contrary, it is precisely to preserve Christians of a latter day from anti-Semitism that Luke's plain talk about religious and secular partisan politics is spelled out in equally plain terms.

It was therefore ungallant of E. P. Sanders to state on the basis of someone else's review that in a previous edition of this commentary I was guilty of "denigrating" Judaism *(Paul and Palestinian Judaism* [1977], p. 55 n. 76). Had he bothered to read the commentary in the edition under critique he could have seen, among other explicit disavowals of such procedure, the following: "Especially Luke is concerned to point out that it was not the Jewish people but their leaders who brought ruin to Jerusalem. . . . Anti-Semitism does display its ugly head when especially the Christian reader of the gospel thinks that 'the Jews,' not he, are under the evangelist's scrutiny. Seven million Jews have known the pain of such evil application of the text" (introduction to comment on Luke 22:54–71). On Luke 5:18 I made the following observation concerning Pharisees: "Because of their notoriety in the New Testament they have as a class received a bad press, but their contribution to the continuity of the moral and religious life of Israel was enormous. Without them Israel might well have been assimilated beyond recall." The term "Pharisee," I stated, "need not carry an unsavory connotation. Rather, their zeal to observe the precepts of holiness prompted them to isolate themselves from all ritual and moral contamination. Like the Puritans and many Victorians, who have also been maligned, they tried to stem what they considered a secularistic tide."

With interpretations such as the following, on Luke 23:14, I endeavored to protect Jews against generalized charges: "It is clear that not all the individual people within the larger group known as the people of Israel were responsible for handing Jesus over to Pilate." Again, on 23:25: "From Luke's account it might be inferred that the Jews were responsible for carrying out the execution they had demanded. But the impression is a result of Luke's theological interpretation. Pilate would, of course, be in charge of the actual execution."

To discourage any further generalized statements about Jews, I had repeatedly emphasized that Luke places upon the hierarchy the onus for hostility against Jesus. It is naive to think that Caiaphas and company would not have been upset by someone who spoke so radically as did Jesus and who was so deliberate in his challenging of recognized protocol. Or are we to imagine that, out of a desire to pillory Caiaphas, skin-saving disciples invented the brave new words that are attributed to Jesus? Finally, there is a vast difference between Jews in general and some of the Pharisees and leaders of the time of Jesus. Jews-in-general did not crucify Jesus. For example, Luke does not implicate the Pharisees in the crucifixion proceedings. In his view of the matter, a shortsighted religious leader and those immediately associated with his misunderstanding of the intentions of Jesus formed a temporary alliance with a Roman administrator and, according to the testimony of all the Gospels, perpetrated with him a gross travesty of justice.

Luke's book contains a broad range of sandal sizes to fit any foot. The reason he sounds so contemporary is due to his broad grasp of humanity in its universal aspects.

SOURCES

Luke was not the first to write a gospel. His preface (1:1–4) clearly indicates that he possessed a knowledge of other documents. A comparison of his account with the accounts composed by Mark and Matthew reveals that he was in large debt to Mark, either as we have Mark in its present form or in a recital so similar that for all practical purposes we may assume use of Mark substantially as we know it.

In addition to Mark, Luke relied on a source that was used also by Matthew. This source is ordinarily designated Q, a symbol whose origin is debated. Whether Q was a written account or an oral tradition with variations cannot be determined, but I share the view that the evidence points to a written source. The designation Q is, in any case, helpful as an instrument of reference to identify the material common to Matthew and Luke but not found in Mark. Some allowance, though, must be made for overlapping in the sources. That is, some Q material may also have contained recitals that are now found in Mark and some of Mark's material may have had parallels in Q.

If construed as a document, Q included most or all of the following material in Luke's Gospel: 3:7–9, 16–22; 4:1–13; most of 6:20–49; some of 7:1–10 and most of 18–35; 9:57–60; 10:2–16, 21–24; perhaps 11:2–4 and most of 9–51; 12:2–12 and most of 22–34, 39–46, 51–59; 13:18–29, 34–35; 14:11 (?), 16–24, 26–27, 34–35; 15:4–7; 16:13, 16–18; 17:1–6, 23–24, 26–27, 33–35, 37; 19:11–27; 22:28–30.

That Luke used Matthew as a source has not met with any widespread support from scholars. From the parallel passages listed under each reference in the commentary, readers will be able to determine the extent and identity of the probable sources, Mark and Q, that were used by Luke. If only parallels from Matthew are cited, readers may assume that at that point in the narrative Luke draws on Q material, for, by the general rule, Q is material common to Matthew and Luke but not found in Mark.

In a number of places the reader will note that no parallels from Mark or Matthew are listed. Such passages suggest that Luke drew on a special source, usually labeled L. Much of this source is represented especially in 9:51—18:15. The infancy narratives (chaps. 1—2) are perhaps drawn from still another source. Besides these resources, Luke ranges freely in the Greek bible (Septuagint), with special interest in the prophet Isaiah, and appears to have more than passing acquaintance with wisdom literary tradition, including the Wisdom of Sirach (Ecclesiasticus) and the Wisdom of Solomon.

Luke's heavy dependence on the Bible of Israel in its Greek form poses a special problem, for inclusion of the supporting biblical data in the commentary risks marring the continuity and disrupting the train of thought. On the other hand, students who wish to explore in greater depth the history of Luke's form of the text might be unnecessarily frustrated through omission of the citations and might also find some of the conclusions, apart from the supporting evidence, inexplicable or arbitrary. Therefore I have made liberal use of parentheses. Those who wish merely to follow a story that is good in its own right and are willing to postpone their exploration of the details may want to skip over the parentheses and stay on the main line. Others may welcome the bountiful supply of resource material for further study.

Neither Matthew nor Luke is a slave to sources, nor do they engage in mechanistic compilation of materials. Luke's theological and apologetic interests prompt him to modify and rearrange in accordance with his avowed aim to present **an orderly account** (Luke 1:3). Readers are therefore not to be dismayed by variations in the recitals when compared with those in the other Gospels. Words of Jesus (dominical words) and stories about him were used by the earliest Christians in sermons and other types of instruction. Their meaning was constantly subject to fresh inquiry and application, and the form in which they are cast is the result of much lively usage. The process of application continues in the use to which they were put in development of the presentations made in the individual Gospels. It is clear that the Gospel writers are not mere compilers but authors and editors. Like artful preachers who expand on a text of Scripture, they are theologians in their own right.

As Director of the People of God, Jesus speaks to each succeeding generation. Therefore it is impossible to recover without argument the very words of Jesus spoken on a given historical occasion. Early Christians possessed a lively awareness of the power of the Spirit of God in their midst, and the Spirit stimulated Christians to ponder the significance of Jesus and his words and actions for their time. Even new sayings would be uttered, for the Lord had not ceased to speak. Hence the Gospels are not less authoritative or less true than would be a strictly biographical record. None of the evangelists, and least of all Luke, is interested in writing biography for biography's sake. Indeed, such a work would lack the distinguishing feature of our Gospels, namely, the manner in which the convictions, problems, and interests of Christian communities at the time of writing blend with the words and deeds of Jesus as he responds to various situations and interacts with the personalities that parade across the Gospel pages. One of the harmful effects of red-letter editions of the NT and some research relative to the "historical Jesus" has been the intimation that Jesus' words are somewhat more authoritative than other words in the NT, and that any attribution of sayings to Jesus that emanate from a later period would a priori put them and his authority into question. Proponents of such views are obligated not only to consider the implications in advocacy of a canon within the biblical canon but also to clarify what they mean by inspiration.

DATE

Luke appears to have written after the destruction of Jerusalem in the year 70 C.E. It has been argued that the absence of any specific reference to the fall of the city and the fact that Luke concludes Acts without any reference to Paul's death prove that Luke-Acts was completed in the decade preceding the destruction. The argument relating to Paul's death rests on the assumption that historians would necessarily include events that transpired up to the time when they put their data into final literary form. But the literary probability is that Luke has achieved his purpose with the present ending of Acts. Jesus is the Messiah, God's gift to the world. It is Israel's mission to proclaim him as such. Despite the fact that her leadership exempts itself from the privilege, God's purpose remains on course, and Paul is the principal instrument for carrying out the responsibility of Israel. Acts 28 therefore concludes with a summary statement: The credentials of Jesus are not invalidated by the rejection he experiences from leaders of the Jews, and their refusal to participate in the divine program will not stop God's salvation from being proclaimed to the nations. And an Israelite does it under the very nose of the emperor.

As for the fall of Jerusalem, no specific reference to the fulfillment of Jesus' prophecy (Luke 21:20–24) is required, for the horrible catastrophe was well known, and Luke's literary tact ought to elicit admiration. In the light of that catastrophe Luke interprets numerous dominical sayings and actions.

In view of the evangelist's use of Mark's Gospel, which was written either shortly before or shortly after the destruction of Jerusalem, it is probable that Luke's two-volume work was published in the late seventies or early eighties of the first century.

The Strategy of This Commentary

This exposition of Luke's Gospel uses as the basic point of reference for the Greekless reader the *Revised Standard Version of the New Testament*. In a Scripture passage under discussion, the following style is used for Scripture quotations: Exact RSV phrases from that passage are set in boldface; single words from the RSV, and rephrased wording from the immediate passage, are in quotation marks; and Scripture quotations cited from parts of Luke other than the immediate passage under comment or from other books of the Bible are also in quotation marks. Any Scripture verse or verses that are my own translation are indicated by an asterisk (*).

In the instances of rephrased wording of the RSV, readers can readily infer the word or phrase in the RSV—that is, the referent for the interpretation given in the text. Thus the Greekless reader can know what the original in my judgment expresses, and students with Greek can readily check against the original and other discussions of the text.

Unless otherwise specified, translations of Latin and Greek authors and others, ancient or modern, are my own. Names and places associated with the Greek world are ordinarily spelled in the form adopted by most classicists: for example, Theophilos (RSV: Theophilus), Sophokles, Theokritos, Thoukydides.

The translation of the Revised Standard Version is based on a reconstructed text, derived from consideration of the best evidence available to the revisers. Because it has no corresponding existence in any single manuscript, such a text is called eclectic. Scholarly judgment differs on the probable originality of certain readings. My reasons for preferring in certain instances an alternate text are given at appropriate points in the commentary.

A translator's task differs from that of the commentator. The former ordinarily endeavors to render the original without interpretive comment into contemporary idiom. All translation necessarily involves paraphrase, for resources differ from language to language. Hence a word that is used to convey a number of ideas in the original language may be variously rendered in a translation. For example, the Greek term *kyrios* may, among other possibilities and depending on the context, be rendered "Lord," "Master" (as owner of a slave), or "Sir" (as mark of respect or in address to a superior). Translators must make judgment calls. Commentators will review the call, for they are obliged to display as much as possible the verbal phenomena of the original, so that especially the Greekless reader may capture some of the tonality that is frequently lost in translation.

Moreover, a translator may omit, for example, particles used by the original writer. One of Luke's favorite introductory phrases is: "And behold!" Often the producers of the RSV paraphrase or simply ignore this expression, but awareness of its existence may contribute to the reader's understanding of Luke's methods of argumentation. This must be said lest a reader assume that the RSV is unreliable. That would be an erroneous assessment. Yet it is true that in some cases the revisers may have totally missed the point of the original. The same, of course, is true in the case of jokes: risibility depends on the manner in which they are retold.

Persons familiar with specialized studies of the Gospels will readily recognize results that are the distinctive contributions of other scholars as well as those that are the necessary and universal product of application of generally accepted methodology. To burden this commentary with references to the large number of articles that have appeared in technical journals in the past few decades would therefore duplicate for a few what is for the most part already accessible in Joseph Fitzmyer's and I. H. Marshall's commentaries (see Selected Bibliography). It would also defeat one of the major purposes in producing this commentary, namely, to offer a format in which readers of Luke's Gospel can appreciate a trip through Luke's beautiful forest as a whole without compounding the distraction occasioned by a mass of bibliographical references. My own lexical and epigraphic researches have suggested to me a number of new insights and levels of understandings. (See especially my Proclamation Commentary on *Luke,* and *Benefactor.*)

It should be readily apparent, then, that I am not interested in creating what the modern Greek poet George Sepheris in another context called "a state of personal litigation between the public and the work of art" (*On the Greek Style* [1966], p. 77). Rather, in the spirit of Luke 18:17, I provide an enclosure in which Luke's literary masterpiece can be appreciated as a totality. Yet even though the commentary can be read as a self-contained unit, it will undoubtedly serve as a reference tool. Scholars will also find interpretations advanced that will, I hope, contribute to solution of other problems connected with Luke's work.

Luke's books are classic literary productions. This commentary strives to convey that fact not only through affirmation about their excellence at many points but through the manner in which Luke's story line is reported in the commentary. Although his publics are to some extent omniscient with respect to the main lines of his story, Luke manages by virtue of his literary wizardry to maintain suspense. This commentary therefore endeavors to capture in the telling some of the dramatic values of Luke's work. If this approach contributes to what one critic termed "a peculiar flatness," it is the inevitable price to be paid for gains that can be purchased in no other way.

I must confess that Luke's Jesus is far more interesting than any Jesus who is the subject of questionable historical reconstruction. Therefore, when the commentary states that "Jesus said" this or that, the reader will know that it is Luke's Jesus who speaks. This does not mean that Luke invents dominical words. On the contrary, Joachim Jeremias has shown that Luke does less editing on Jesus' words than he does on other traditional material. But the contextual and thematic positioning of the dominical words attributes to them a special nuance.

A word remains to be said about certain formal features of this commentary. Since ancient writings were designed to be read aloud, I refer throughout this commentary to "auditors" rather than to "readers" of Luke's Gospel. Moreover, in view of Luke's broad outreach, as well as scholars' uncertainty about publication details relative to Luke-Acts, one lacks scientific sanction to speak of "Luke's community." It is therefore more accurate to think of Luke's total audience as comprised of people with a variety of religious, political, economic, and social experiences, and not necessarily located in one geographical area. From this perspective I earlier used the plural term "publics" (p. 20), which is so employed in the commentary when the context calls for such qualification. I use the singular form "public" in reference to a specific cultural orientation, such as Jewish or Greco-Roman, or as a generalizing synonym for Luke's auditors. At all times it must be kept in mind that Jewishness does not mean ignorance of Greco-Roman cultural tradition, and being Greco-Roman (i.e., of non-

Jewish ancestry) does not imply ignorance of Jewish tradition. Thus, on the one hand, the evangelist's Greco-Roman auditors would grasp meaning in terms of continuity of Luke's text with their own cultural context. Conversely, they would find themselves encouraged, because of Luke's specific story line, to transpose their encounter with his text into a Christian key. In other words, Luke counts on parallel story lines in Greco-Roman cultural experience—whether literary, political, or social—to provide the medium for interpretive access to his own story line. In this respect he shares a modern perception that authors are not in charge of their work once it has left their hands. Those of Luke's auditors who had deep roots in Jewish experience would, of course, have an advantage in understanding what he was up to.

To help the modern reader develop some of the sensitivity that many of Luke's auditors had for his Hellenically flavored document, I have incorporated in the commentary numerous references to the literature and customs of ancient Greece, with emphasis on the Hellenistic age, the period that begins with the conquests of Alexander. Besides these cultural antennae, the commentary includes a multitude of references to the OT, for auditors steeped in Jewish tradition would reflect on the significance of Luke's recitals in the light of their ancestral experience. The evocative power of Luke's work in this respect is blatantly apparent in his ability to write what can be called biblical Greek.

The twofold tonality in Luke's work is coherent with his basic message of divine outreach through Jesus Christ to humanity through representatives of Israel. But a caution must be registered. The citation of parallels does not necessarily indicate identity of thought patterns. Parallel lines never meet. Nor do such citations imply that Luke or his auditors made conscious association with the item cited. On the other hand, parallels do suggest the existence of avenues of consideration that made it possible for unique perspectives of Christianity to be explored without impatient dismissal. Similarly, contemporary applications suggest the immediacy that Luke's work had for its first auditors.

Since this work is designed also to help the nonprofessional student of the Bible share in the results of scholarly research, technical jargon is held to a minimum. Frequent recapitulations will assist students in following Luke's argument, and cross-references to later and earlier parts of Luke's work will alert them to its conceptual unity.

The line between literary criticism and homiletical application may not always appear clearly marked, but engagement with contemporary problems often turns the key to an understanding of the ancient political, theological, social, and moral issues. Such is the lingusitic reality, and this commentary is a product of modern developments in linguistics. Of course, an approach of this type brings the ministry of Jesus and the message of the earliest Christians threateningly close to cherished idols and to the point at which hostility may be involved. But a commentator who takes seriously Luke's emphasis on the presence of the future cannot opt for a safe archaeological or antiquarian haven. For such practical encounter, then, I do not apologize.

Luke belongs to those writers who take their readers into the mainstream of humanity. The meanness and the pettiness, envy's reprisal, the shallowness of capricious loyalty—all this and more unites us in a macabre approach to life's enterprise. What George Seferis said of the well-nigh illiterate General Makryannis, who wrote largely in cipher a major contribution to the knowledge of Greek history, can be said of Luke: "He can tell us what we are and how we are in our deepest selves. . . . He comes to whisper to us that our beauties and ornaments and riches, which we thought so valuable, are clean gone, worn out and turned to corruption; they can serve no purpose but to burden us and weigh us down, as in the case of the tragic Phaedra in her despair" (*On the Greek Style,* p. 63). But Luke does more. At the same time that he tells us the darker truth about ourselves, he awakens our wonder before the brilliance of God's gift that is the light for all who sit in darkness and in the shadow of death. For Luke shows us Jesus Christ, the glory of God's ancient people Israel, who dispels despair, creates enthusiasm for present opportunity, and lifts the veil before God's future that opens up for each person a singular identity.

THE HISTORIAN'S PREFACE

The very form of Luke's preface expresses the focus of his two-volume work: Jesus Christ, Son of God, Most Distinguished Israelite, and Light for the World.

Luke manifests the kind of grasp that the Greek historians Herodotos, Thoukydides, and Polybios had of the significance of events that ought to be recorded for abiding memory.

1:1–2. The preface is a model of precisely crafted prose that would make a favorable impression on Greco-Romans across a broad cultural front. It is formulated very much like a public decree in the traditional Greek style, with preamble introduced by "whereas" (*epeidēper:* **inasmuch as**) and followed by a resolution prefaced by "I resolved" (*edoxe emoi:* **it seemed good to me**). This formulation suggests that what is here recorded is intended for the Greco-Roman public square.

Few of Luke's auditors could fail to note that such formulation was most frequently used in honor of benefactors or public-spirited persons. This preface therefore images a larger reality than a historian's resolution. It is an indirect forecast of Luke's narrative concerning One who emerges as the brightest star in the Greco-Roman and world firmament.

Following literary convention of his time, Luke apologizes for adding yet another work to a long list of publications on the same subject. Scholars are almost unanimous in their agreement that Mark and some form of a document consisting especially of sayings, known as Q, were among the sources used by Luke in the composition of his Gospel. The subject is more narrowly defined as **things which have been accomplished among us.** These "things" would include events in the life of Jesus as well as his resurrection.

Since there are so many items in Luke's Gospel that anticipate recitals and themes in Acts, it is probable that this preface has in mind the second volume, the Book of Acts (see Acts 1:1). If such is indeed the case, then the "things" include development of the apostolic outreach in mission. The words "among us" emphasize the writer's conviction that his community is the center for the understanding of these events.

Many historians of antiquity failed to encourage confidence in the citation of their data. So frequent was the gap between truth and fiction that an ancient master of the Greek language, Lucian of Samosata, introduced his tongue-in-cheek *True History* with the reminder: "MY lying is far more honest than theirs [other historians]; for though I tell the truth in nothing else, I shall at least be truthful in saying that I am a liar." Luke refrains from such harsh negative judgment of colleagues in his craft.

Others **have undertaken** (*epicheireō;* i.e., they had as their objective) to report what **eyewitnesses and ministers** (*hypēretai:* literally, "helpers") **of the word** delivered to the community. That they were not completely successful is apparent from Luke's own decision to take pen in hand. Some of them may even have been heretics (cf. Acts 20:29–30) who used traditional material in the interest of their own perverse propaganda.

A form of the verb "delivered" *(paradidōmi)* is elsewhere rendered "tradition" (1 Cor. 11:2). The expression "the word" *(ho logos)* refers to the story of the events spoken of in Luke 1:1. It is the normal term in historical writings for "history" and is so used in Acts 1:1. Even in the more common rendering "word of God" (as in Acts 6:4, 7) the connotation "story" is still dominant, for the content of the "word" is the major events in the life of Jesus (see Acts 10:37–44). The singular form (see Acts 10:44) is used to comprise the various events recorded by various writers.

The "eyewitnesses" were active also as participants ("helpers") in the promotion of the story (see Acts 26:16; 6:4). They had observed things **from the beginning,** that is, from the time that Jesus began to carry out his mission and to teach (see Acts 1:1–2; 10:37).

1:3–4. Luke contrasts his own work with the work of the "many" and submits his own qualifications. He has **followed all things closely for some time past.** Since Luke includes infancy narratives and numerous events in which he was not personally involved, the word "followed" *(parakoloutheō)* must refer to his investigation of, not merely involvement in, these events. "All things" refers to the matters discussed by his predecessors as well as items that came to his attention independently of their inquiry. Hence the scope of his work ought to commend it to his publics.

"Closely" *(akribōs)* emphasizes the care that has gone into his research. "For some time past" *(anōthen)* is better rendered "from the beginning." Luke has made every effort to trace events to their origins. Hence he includes infancy narratives. Possessed of all these qualifications, he aims to write an **orderly account** for Theophilos. "Orderly" *(kathexēs)* does not here primarily mean chronological sequence but arrangement of material, so as to leave the auditor with clear impressions. His purpose is spelled out in the concluding verse of the preface: **that you may know the truth concerning the things of which you have been informed.** This is not an annalistic type of recital, consisting of memoirs or collections of sayings, but a persuasive presentation is Luke's objective. Similarly, the Roman poet Ovid assured his readers that he would not ramble but would present things in their order (*Metamorphoses* 7.520).

The word for "things" *(logōn)* is the plural of the term rendered "the word" at v. 2 *(tou logou)*. There is one story, but many accounts of that story. Since some of these accounts have come to the attention of Theophilos and may have caused him some confusion, Luke wants him to have one systematic presentation that will give him a broader understanding and appreciation and the opportunity to form a more proper judgment.

Actions or sayings taken out of context, even though compilers claim that they are guaranteed by eyewitnesses, may at a later time convey a false impression. For example, in his second volume (Acts 21:34) Luke relates that a Roman officer heard some in a crowd shouting one thing, some another. Since he could not learn the "facts" (a form of the word rendered "truth" [*asphaleia*] in Luke 1:4), he ordered Paul back to the barracks, evidently for further examination. Again, in Acts 25:26 Festus says that he has nothing definite to write to Caesar about Paul. Luke hopes that his story will clarify much for Theophilos and his own auditors.

To judge from the honorific **most excellent** *(kratiste)*, Theophilos (Latin, Theophilus) appears to be a Roman official with a Greek name who might do much to clear the Christians of charges of anti-Roman activity. We do not know whether he himself was a Christian. Through him as patron Luke's work goes out to the People of God for their instruction and admonition and to all others who might want to know why Christians believe what they profess. Hence much that Theophilos might not grasp would nevertheless communicate to knowledgeable Christians as well as to others who had expressed curiosity about the new sect.

Luke's preface helps us also to understand the frequent departures he makes from Mark's Gospel and the portions in Matthew known as Q. A modern historian would cite the data and then evaluate it. Luke is sparing in overt interpretive comment, relying in the main on arrangement of traditional material, with modification of phrasing, with paraphrase, or with deletion of matter that is irrelevant to his purpose.

From the manner in which Luke relates himself to the general craft of historical writing, it is evident that he considers his work to fall into that category. That his work is not to be judged by the canons of modern scientific historical or biographical writing is a cliché, pompous, and irrelevant, for no such works from antiquity can stand that type of scrutiny. It is more accurate to state that he does not aspire to production of the same types of historical works that we have from the pens of Herodotos, Thoukydides, Polybios, Livy, and Tacitus, all of whom contain passages that can be ascribed to all other muses except Klio. The fact that words and deeds of Jesus dominate the first volume of Luke's work does not mean that he endeavors to write a so-called Life of Jesus. Rather, we have biographical considerations intertwined with historical interests in a unique production, which is penetrated by theological awareness.

None of the historians mentioned above, not even Herodotos, went to such lengths as does Luke in exploring human destiny and divine purpose. Polybios found the focus for his history in Rome's will to govern the world. Luke was fascinated by God's resolve to carry out the salvation of humanity and saw in Jesus Christ the key to the fulfillment of that purpose. Luke's historical interests therefore led him to adapt a traditional gospel form, of the kind found in Mark, to the presentation of a more complex type of work, whose subject is "The Things Fulfilled Among Us" (1:1*).

The archives of Caesar's official library or Pilate's personal memoirs would, even if they were to be discovered, contribute little or nothing to Luke's main theme. Luke is a disciple, and for this he makes no apology.

PART ONE: BEGINNINGS

After his carefully worded preface, written in the finest Greek, Luke begins his account. In a style reminiscent of the Septuagint he drowns much of his literary skill and adapts himself to the language of his sources. The effect is something like that of a contemporary sermon delivered in the style of the King James Version. The result is a recital that bears the marks of continuity with God's action as recorded in the OT. Coupled with Luke's emphasis on prophecy in the first chapter, this antique flavor is evidently an appeal to Roman respect for Jews because of their ancient traditions, some of which antedated even the founding of Rome, which the Roman scholar Marcus Varro fixed at 753 B.C.E..

Samuel Coleridge was so impressed by Luke's entire infancy narrative that in a comparative assessment he denigrated Matthew's account. The recital in Matthew, he wrote, "is like a rude tale in an old chronicle compared with the same taken up by a Southey or Scott & worked up into a splendid Poem" (*The Notebooks* 3:4402.22.78 [March–April 1818]).

ANNOUNCEMENT OF THE CONCEPTION
OF JOHN
Luke 1:5–25

1:5. The RSV does not render the initial Greek word, *egeneto*, "It came to pass," a verb that is used in a related formal structure at 2:1. Two sets of data are to be distinguished. Luke 1 introduced John and Jesus to the auditors. Since Jesus is, from Luke's perspective, greater than Rome's greatest emperors, it is important that a lesser figure serve as an advance party. At the same time, Luke is able to help Christian communities sort out the relative functions of John and Jesus. John is not a competitor but an instrument of God's climactic purpose, which finds its highest expression in Jesus, whose name is above all other names (Acts 4:12). Luke 2 focuses attention on the person and mission of Jesus, apart from any reference to John. Luke 3 again introduces John and Jesus, this time as grown men, but John disappears from the scene completely, except for allusions to his previous activity. The recital in Luke 1 begins with a reference to Herod the Great, who reigned over Palestine from 37 to 4 B.C.E. Luke 2 introduces the gentile ruler Caesar Augustus.

Zechariah, a common name in the OT, means "the Lord remembers." He was **of the division of Abijah.** David had organized the Levites into divisions or courses (1 Chron. 23:6; 2 Chron. 8:14). Each division contributed in sequence a week's service at the temple. Thus each division would serve twice a year. The Levites were to assist the priests, the descendants of Aaron, who were also organized into divisions (1 Chron. 24:1–19). The division of Abijah was the eighth (1 Chron. 24:10). **Elizabeth** was of the tribe of Aaron and therefore shared the priestly ancestry of Zechariah as well as the name of Aaron's wife (Elisheba, Exod. 6:23).

Some rabbis expressed the thought that God's presence would rest only on pedigreed families in Israel (see G. F. Moore, *Judaism* [1954] 2:359). Zechariah and Elizabeth qualify genealogically for the parentage of John the Baptist, who is to function before Israel as a unique high priest, and Israel ought to listen to him (Luke 7:24–35). To Greco-Roman auditors the credentials would be impressive. By virtue of his association with Jesus, John exceeds in dignity the chief priests at Rome's imperial cult centers, especially in the eastern Mediterranean.

1:6. Zechariah and Elizabeth also qualify morally: **they were both righteous before God, walking . . . blameless.** That Luke endeavors to secure the attention of the Greek-speaking world seems clear from his choice of the terms "righteous" *(dikaios)* and "blameless" *(amemptos)*, which, besides expressing OT piety, are used in praise of priests in the Greco-Roman world. The second of the two terms appears only here in Luke's work. Unlike Samuel's sons (1 Sam. 8:3), John's parents are as impeccable in their conduct as was ancestor Abraham (see Gen. 26:5). Their childlessness (see Luke 1:25), like that of Abraham and Sarah, could not therefore be charged to God's displeasure.

1:7. Luke expressly notes that **Elizabeth was barren** (sterile) and adds the comment about their advanced years in order to emphasize that hope for a child had long faded away. Thus this pair resembles Abraham and Sarah (Genesis 17—18); Isaac and Rebekah (Gen. 25:21); Jacob and Rachel (Gen. 30:1); Manoah and his wife, the parents of Samson (Judges 13); and Elkanah and Hannah, parents of Samuel (1 Samuel 1). Luke's auditors who know the fortunes of Israel could readily anticipate the divine solution. God always comes through!

1:8–10. Since there were large numbers of Levites (estimates run as high as eighteen thousand priests and Levites in Palestine at the time of Jesus), lots (cf. Acts 1:26) were cast to determine who would have the opportunity to serve at a particular time. To burn incense in the holy place (emblematic of prayers ascending to God; see Rev. 5:8; Ps. 141:2) was a great privilege, for God drew near to his people (cf. Exod. 30:1–9). Luke's reference to the crowd of people outside (cf. Luke 6:17; 23:27) anticipates their presence at v. 21.

According to rabbinic tradition they said: "May the God of all mercy come to his temple and graciously accept the offering of his people" (SB 2:79). Luke frequently associates prayer with special moments in his narrative (see Luke 5:16; 6:12; 9:18, 28; 22:41). The auditor is never to forget the divine dimension. Like Daniel (see Dan. 9:20–24), Zechariah finds himself at the center of apocalyptic action.

1:11–13. Like the high priest John Hyrcanus (Josephus *Antiquities* 13.282–83), Zechariah receives a heavenly message while burning incense alone in the temple. Outside Jewish and Christian communities there were traditions of heavenly visitations: a certain Demetrios, to cite but one, founded a shrine to the Egyptian deity Sarapis after receiving instructions in a nocturnal visitation from Sarapis (see *Benefactor*, No. 27). It is not necessary to assume acquaintance on the part of Luke with these specific narratives, but the significance of Luke's account would be readily understood on cultural fronts where heavenly visitations were an accepted feature in reports about exceptional personalities. In addition to related recitals in 1:26–38 and 2:8–10, Luke makes periodic use of the motif in Acts (Acts 5:19; 8:26; 12:7; cf. Acts 9:1–19; 10:1–23, 30–33; 11:1–15; 16:6–12; 18:9–11; 22:6–11, 17–21; 23:11; 26:12–18; 27:23–26).

In the OT it was customary to call attention to God's presence by describing the reaction of the human participants. To be troubled and filled with fear, as Zechariah was, is a characteristic response to divine manifestation or apocalyptic moment. Daniel 7:28 records that the prophet's thoughts alarmed him so greatly that his color changed. And the Roman historian Livy (*History* 1.16) relates that Julius Proculus was frightened when Romulus appeared.

The **right side** of the altar signifies divine authority (cf. Luke 22:69), without excluding a suggestion of beneficence. The phrase **Do not be afraid** is, in its Greek form, common in the OT (e.g., Gen. 15:1; 21:17; Isa. 7:4; 35:4; Dan. 10:7, 12; Tob. 12:17). Related expressions are also used in the Hellenic world as early as Homer (cf. *Iliad* 24.171). It appears with some frequency in Luke's Gospel (see Luke 1:30; 2:10; 5:10; 8:50; 12:32) and in Acts (Acts 18:9; 27:24). Its usage here signals the fact that the time of God's intervention for his people has arrived. God comes not to destroy but to help. Zechariah has prayed for a son—this is the dramatic assumption—and his petition is now to be granted. The promise addressed to Zechariah is similar to the words spoken to Abraham: "Sarah your wife shall bear you a son, and you shall call his name Isaac" (Gen. 17:19). The name John ("God is gracious") is explicitly mentioned in order to emphasize that God himself distinguished the mission of this son from that of the son of Mary. John is not the Messiah (cf. Luke 3:15).

1:14. "Joy" was the keynote that marked the beginning of Roman imperial reigns. With the birth of the one who is to proclaim the New Age that is to be ushered in by God through Jesus, there will be no end of rejoicing (see Luke 2:10; 15:6–10; 24:52; Acts 8:8; 13:52). This joy is marked by "gladness," that is, exultant shrieking, like that of jubilant contestants. Such joy will not be confined to Zechariah but to "many" in Israel. "Many" is probably a Semitic expression for the totality of the people. There is no discriminatory clause in the invitation to God's banquet. In harmony with this pronouncement, Luke later says that John proclaimed good news to the people (3:18).

1:15. To be **great before the Lord** means that God will use John for his own good purpose (cf. 7:26–28). He is to **drink no wine nor strong drink.** "Strong drink" probably refers to beer made from barley (Num. 6:3; Judg. 13:4). This prohibition was imposed on priests before entry into the tabernacle (Lev. 10:9). John, who is to call the nation to repentance, is a priestly figure, the son of a priestly family. Nazirites, according to Numbers 6, took special vows, including abstinence from wine and beer, for an extended period or for an entire life. Samson was declared a Nazirite "from [his] mother's womb" (Judg. 16:17; cf. 13:5–7; Isa. 44:2; 49:1). From Luke 1:41 it can be inferred that Luke thinks of prenatal identity. Although John is not specifically defined as a Nazirite, there is no question concerning his devotion to an ascetic life, with a prophet's assignment given to him "while still in the womb."

In some quarters of the Greco-Roman world wine was viewed as a barrier to revelation (cf. the comic poet Aristophon 10.3 [Edmonds 2.524]). Instead of being under the influence of strong drink, John will be "intoxicated" with the Holy Spirit (cf. Acts 2:13–21). Luke repeatedly mentions the Spirit in the first two chapters: Luke 1:35, 41, 67; 2:25, 26, 27. To be **filled with the Holy Spirit,** a favorite expression of Luke's (see Luke 1:41, 67; Acts 2:4; 4:8, 31; 9:17; 13:9), means to have one's life totally under the direction of God. People like that are marked for death.

1:16. John's task will be to **turn many . . . of Israel to the Lord their God.** From similar phrasing in Sir. 48:10 and Mal. 4:5 it is apparent that the tradition used by Luke associates John with the prophet Elijah. As a priestly and prophetic figure (cf. Malachi 2—3) he will effect a reconciliation between God and his people by calling the nation to repentance.

1:17. This verse explicitly associates John with Elijah, but nowhere does Luke associate John so closely with Elijah as Matthew (Matt. 11:14) and

Mark (Mark 9:13) had done. According to John 1:21, the son of Zechariah denies that he is Elijah. Luke shares this viewpoint and in fact shows that Jesus, far more than John, is to be associated with Elijah (see below on 4:25–27; 7:16; 9:18–19), especially by virtue of the miracles that he performs. Jesus' superiority is evident, for Luke assigns no miracles to John.

By including the two traditions, which variously associate John and Jesus with Elijah, Luke reinforces his main point, that God in connection with Jesus Christ has ushered in Malachi's anticipated Day of the Lord. At the same time, he eliminates the conception of an actual reappearance of Elijah. The credentials of Jesus are not to be determined by a spectacular apocalyptic sign, such as the reappearance of Elijah in the role of a predecessor. Hence Luke omits in his third chapter Mark's description of John, who appears there in the same type of garb worn by the Tishbite (Mark 1:6; cf. 2 Kings 1:8).

Mark 1:2 interprets Mal. 3:1 as a prophecy about John, who makes his appearance as the promised latter-day Elijah. Luke omits this portion of the quotation at 3:4 and confines his citation of the OT to Isa. 40:3–5. At 7:27 Luke introduces a composite quotation from Exod. 23:20 and Mal. 3:1 but indicates that the messenger goes before the face of *Israel* to prepare her way, which is to be one of obedience (cf. Exod. 23:21). Here at 1:17 Luke says that John **will go before him.** "Him" could refer to Jesus as the Anointed One (cf. Luke 2:11), but the entire phrase is more probably to be understood in reference to "Lord God" of the previous verse (see also Mal. 3:1). When God's way is prepared through repentance, the rescuing action in Jesus, the Lord of the community, will be readily appreciated. Hence there is no inconsistency between this statement and that of 7:27, for the preparation of Israel's way is equivalent to preparing the way for the Lord.

John does his work **in the spirit and power of Elijah.** "Spirit" and "power" are frequently associated (Luke 1:35; 4:14; Acts 1:8; 10:38; cf. Luke 24:49). Elijah was zealous for the rights of the Lord, and divine authority supported his effort (see 1 Kings 17—21; Sirach 48). This also will be John's mission, minus the type of miracles performed by Elijah. His task will be **to turn the hearts of the fathers to the children.** These words are very similar to the phrasing in Sir. 48:10 (cf. Mal. 4:6) and mean that the fathers would recognize their children as God's righteous people and would rejoice that they were following in the ways of the Lord.

A cultured Greek might well have recalled the lament of the Greek poet Hesiod about the Age of Iron, that parent was unlike children and children unlike parent (*Works and Days* 182). Former worshipers of Isis would note that the recipient of their pre-Christian devotions was similarly concerned about familial relations (see *Benefactor,* Nos. 26 and 29).

The second phrase, **and the disobedient to the wisdom of the just**, in typical Semitic fashion restates the previous thought and with emphasis on moral change (cf. Dan. 12:3). In this way the people of Israel would be made "ready and prepared for the Lord" (cf. 1:76; 3:4; 7:27). Accordingly, John is not an apocalyptic judge but a priestly prophetic figure who is to prepare the people for God's rescuing action. There is pathos in this description of John. The anticipation of Israel's renewal is in contrast to the picture of a house divided against itself as portrayed in 7:29–30.

1:18. How shall I know this? asks Zechariah. The RSV blurs the distinction between his question and Mary's query (v. 34). Zechariah asks, "On what basis shall I be sure of this?" Abraham made a similar inquiry (Gen. 15:8; cf. Judg. 6:26–40), yet he suffered no penalty. But to Luke, who abhors demands for signs, Zechariah's request was reprehensible. Sign seekers are typical of the unbelieving response to the ministry of Jesus (cf. Luke 11:16, 29–30; Matt. 16:1; Mark 8:11; John 4:48; 1 Cor. 1:22). Hence Zechariah is, despite his righteousness, in his own person an ominous forecast. Yet his very appeal to physical impossibilities brings the divine deed into sharper prominence. Without Zechariah's query the scenario respecting the naming of his son could not have been written.

1:19. The angel now announces his name: **I am Gabriel** (cf. Tob. 12:15: "I am Raphael"). He is one out of the select groups that stand in the presence of God. Speculation about angels became popular in the intertestamental period, and names were assigned to numerous messengers (angels) of God. According to *Enoch* 40:9, Gabriel (probably meaning "God is my Hero," or "God is my Warrior") is one of the four angels who are under special orders in the presence of God. Since he is an important figure in apocalyptic literature (see Dan. 8:16; 9:21), his presence is appropriate in this narrative, which describes the beginning of the end-time fulfillment.

Zechariah is now in double jeopardy. Not only does he encounter one of God's highest officers but Gabriel speaks for God himself and has "proclaimed these things." The RSV's **to bring you this good news** suggests that "good news" is a definable object. But this rendering obscures the fact that apart from Acts 15:7 and 20:24 Luke never uses the Greek noun *(euanggelion)*, which is ordinarily rendered "good news." Instead, he uses the cognate verb, with emphasis on the act of proclamation, thus calling further attention to the authority with which Gabriel speaks. There is a majestic seriousness about God's intentions in the New Age that is dawning. "This," or "these things," refers not only to the promise of a son but to all that the son is expected to do. To ignore the knell of judgment is disastrous, but to question the divine procedure, as Zechariah does, is to invite the tolling of the bell.

1:20. And behold, you will be silent and unable to speak. Zechariah is fortunate that a worse fate than muteness does not befall him. This is itself a sign of God's beneficence. But his muteness was also a prophetic sign, associated with rebellion (cf. Ezek. 3:26–27; and see related miracles in Acts 5:1–10; 13:6–12) and indicative of judgment (2 Macc. 3:29; cf. Mic. 7:16). Here Zechariah, not the people, is the rebellious one, as the phrase **because you did not believe my words** clearly attests. But these words are of a sort that **will be fulfilled in their time.** Time and fulfillment of promise are two of Luke's favorite themes. Greco-Roman auditors were accustomed to bureaucrats who were slow and sometimes remiss in fulfilling their promises. The Supreme Benefactor can be relied on for performance. Luke here anticipates similar phrasing in 4:21 and 24:44.

The term "time" is not simply a chronological moment but the "proper time," or "the time determined by God" (*kairos,* cf. 19:44). The phrase **these things** does not refer to everything in v. 17 but is a general statement referring mainly to John's birth (see 21:31 for similar usage).

1:21. Since Zechariah lingered longer than was customary, the people **wondered at his delay in the temple.** According to the *Mishnah* (Yoma 5:1), a high priest ought not to "put Israel in terror" by prolonging his prayer in the temple. Zechariah is not a high priest, but the anxiety factor is nevertheless present. Had God found some impurity in Zechariah and punished him? Because he was unable to speak the Aaronic blessing (Num. 6:24–26), the people concluded that he had seen a vision, for muteness is an aftermath of apocalyptic experience (cf. Dan. 10:15–17). Thus the reaction of the people contributes a second dimension for understanding the choice of sign in this narrative.

From Luke's perspective, popular apocalyptic expectations lead to a distortion of the messianic hope. God, implies the evangelist, does not mark the advent of the messianic age with spectacular signs, such as cosmic disturbances, but with the announcement of good news. This good news is the apocalypse, or revelation. Hence Luke uses the apocalyptic terminology that he does incorporate so as to impress on his publics that the absence of traditional apocalyptic signs in the ministry of Jesus is no proof that Jesus is deficient in messianic credentials. Experience of God's delivering hand, the basic theme of apocalyptic, is to be had in the least expected places and at the most unexpected times. Luke will expand on this thought through repeated reminders to watchfulness (see esp. 21:34–36).

1:22–23. Not being able to speak, Zechariah contented himself with signing the anticipated benediction. Nor does he recover his speech within a few moments. Luke's form of the verb "remained" (imperfect tense) indicates that he is not to be cured for some time, about nine months in fact. After completing his period of service in the temple, the priest went **to his home.**

1:24. The identification of Elizabeth as Zechariah's wife is not superfluous. Gabriel had specifically said that she would bear Zechariah a son (v. 13).

Once Abraham had tried to circumvent the Lord's promise by accepting Sarai's offer of Hagar (Genesis 16). Zechariah, on the other hand, keeps faith with the angel's word. There is in Luke's mode of narration a suggestion of an echo generated by 1 Sam. 1:19–20: Hannah conceives a son after her return from the temple; here Elizabeth conceives after her husband's return from the temple. After Elizabeth conceived, **for five months she hid herself.** Luke thus prepares the way for his subsequent recital of the encounter between Mary and Elizabeth (see v. 36). There was, he hints, no prior conversation between the two.

1:25. Elizabeth's explanation for her seclusion may suggest a motif of judgment (cf. Isa. 26:20). In the face of the extraordinary circumstances surrounding her conception she does not wish to incur further divine displeasure, such as was signaled by her husband's muteness. In effect she is presented as saying: "The Lord has intervened to take away from me the stigma of childlessness [cf. Gen. 30:23; Isa. 4:1], but the way he has chosen to do it is indeed most frightening! What has he done to me?" Peter will similarly display anxiety in the face of divine beneficence (Luke 5:8–10). Luke's scenario of course requires a delay in the announcement. When Mary comes Elizabeth will receive enlightenment through the Holy Spirit (v. 41).

ANNOUNCEMENT OF THE CONCEPTION
OF JESUS
Luke 1:26–38

In his story of the announcement of the conception of Jesus, Luke includes themes and expressions used by OT writers in such type of narrative (cf. Genesis 16—17, Ishmael and Isaac; Judges 13, Samson; 1 Samuel 1, Samuel). As in his recital of the announcements about John, Luke presents the story about Jesus in five stages: (1) appearance of the divine messenger; (2) perplexity of the recipient of the message; (3) the message; (4) query by the recipient; (5) confirmation of the message. This announcement and vv. 39–56 bridge the two parts of the narrative about Zechariah and his son. By bringing the two women together, Luke is able to amplify the unique distinctiveness of Jesus through the prophetic portent and pronouncements made in vv. 39–55. That the details of the story were derived from Mary herself is pure speculation; that they were invented by Luke is sheer conjecture. In all probability, various traditions have finally undergone compositional reorganization by Luke, whose theological interests have left a firm impress on this and other narrations in Luke 1—2.

1:26–27. These verses set the stage for the dramatic dialogue that follows. The first hint of a contrast between Jerusalem and Galilee is given at v. 26.

Events begin and end at Jerusalem, but Galilee is the major scene of Jesus' ministry and the place where witnesses will be gathered (cf. Luke 23:5; Acts 10:37; 13:31). Nazareth was a little village, despised by some Jews (cf. John 1:46). Details on this little village are provided by Jack Finegan (*The Archaeology of the New Testament* [1964], pp. 27–33).

Since the parental home of Jesus was messianically unprepossessing, Luke emphasizes that **Joseph** (meaning, "May [God] add [posterity]"), the legal father, was of Davidic ancestry. **Mary,** or Miriam (the meaning of the name is uncertain), was a "virgin" *(parthenos)* at the time of Gabriel's visit, and Luke wants it understood that she has had no intimate relations with a man (cf. vv. 34–35; 2:7). That Luke had Isa. 7:14 in mind is impossible to determine.

Mary was "betrothed" to Joseph. To all intents and purposes she was his wife, awaiting only the climactic wedding ceremony and the consummation of their vows. Women in the East were ordinarily married between the ages of twelve and eighteen. There is no reliable evidence to suggest that Joseph was far older than Mary. At the time of the death of Jesus both of them would be considered old according to ancient calculation. John 19:26–27, which may suggest that Mary was then a widow, tells us nothing about the age of Joseph. The observation that Joseph was **of the house of David,** that is, a "descendant of David," prepares the auditor for vv. 31–32. God is about to restore the fortunes of the house of David (cf. Acts 15:16–17). There is no indication that Mary was of Davidic descent.

That Gabriel, one of the eminent members of the heavenly council, should come to insignificant Nazareth and present himself before this undistinguished villager is a miracle of the New Age. This event presages the announcement of the Magnificat, that the mighty are brought low and the humble exalted (v. 52).

1:28. "Hail!" *(chaire)*, the first word of Gabriel's greeting, was a standard mode of bidding someone good day in the Greco-Roman world. In similar fashion the prophet Zephaniah addressed the women of Jerusalem (Zeph. 3:14; see also Zech. 9:9; Joel 2:21; Lam. 4:21; and, by way of contrast, Hos. 9:1), but it is highly speculative to conclude that Luke is making an implicit association. Rather, the point is that a heavenly messenger adopts a familiar mode of greeting in relating to a mere earthling and especially, from the standpoint of Mediterranean society, to a lowly woman.

In keeping with his eschatological instruction, Luke suggests that the Messiah does not come in a spectacular demonstration of force in behalf of Israel but begins his reign among her in most unprepossessing fashion. Like the shepherds (Luke 2:8), Mary is typical of candidates for the Kingdom in the New Age about to dawn.

In the Greek, the phrase **O favored one** is a single word (verb: *charizomai*) related to the noun "grace" and rhymes in part with "Hail" *(chaire).*

It means: "You, the recipient of a gift" or "privileged one." Bestowal of benefactions was a common theme in the Mediterranean world. Deities are the supreme benefactors, and Luke's choice of the term "favored" introduces the main line of thought that runs through the succeeding narrative. The angel explains the expression, with the additional phrase, **The Lord is with you**. In Ruth 2:4 this phrase is part of a normal social exchange, equivalent to the response, "The Lord bless you." Precisely the same words were once spoken to Gideon (Judg. 6:12; cf. Zeph. 3:17) and meant that God was about to intervene with a remarkable demonstration of beneficence and power (cf. Luke 1:25, 49). Such is the case here. Designed or not, the context would also suggest to some auditors that there is more than meets the ear in the term "Lord" *(kyrios)*. From the OT point of view, one understands Yahweh. From the post-Easter community point of view, one understands Jesus Christ.

1:29. Mary is agitated **(greatly troubled),** and even more so than was Zechariah (v. 12). The diction is that of apocalyptic narrative. But in her case it is not the vision but **the saying** that disturbs her. She asked herself **what sort of greeting this might be,** that is, what the salutation might mean.

1:30. As did Zechariah, Mary hears the consoling word: **Do not be afraid** (a related expression appears in Zeph. 3:16 LXX). The pronouncement of her name (cf. Luke 1:13) emphasizes the personal concern of the Lord, before whom the humblest has identity. **You have found favor with God** is a Semitic expression used also of Noah at Gen. 6:8 and of Gideon at Judg. 6:17. This phrase includes the noun *charis* resembling the verb *charizomai* used in the angel's greeting (Luke 1: 28). The meaning again is that God is about to shower on her a special benefit, but not in answer to a prayer, as was the case with Zechariah (v. 13).

Greco-Roman auditors were accustomed to associating the term "favor" *(charis)* with a variety of benefactions bestowed by administrators. Through this and other politically and culturally significant terms, Luke makes contact not only with Jewish auditors but with a Mediterranean public beyond the boundaries of the Semitic world.

1:31. And behold introduces the extraordinary gift that God brings her (cf. Gen. 16:11; Judg. 13:5). She is to have a son, whom she must call **Jesus.** The form of statement closely resembles that of Luke 1:13 (see also Gen. 16:11, concerning Ishmael; and Isa. 7:14). In the light of Isa. 49:1 it is probable that, rather than emphasizing the meaning of the name itself, Luke puts emphasis on the fact that God has ordered a special destiny for this child.

That Luke attaches primary significance to the assignment of the name is apparent from Luke 2:21; 3:23; Acts 4:12. "Jesus" is another form of the name of Joshua, which means "God saves" (cf. Luke 2:11). The name Joshua was a common name, but as given to Jesus the common becomes uncommon, and that portion of Luke's public which was familiar with the exploits of Joshua would add a dimension of understanding to Luke's account. For some the name might even have been reminiscent of the promise in Zeph. 3:17 LXX. Mary, it appears, will have other children (cf. Luke 8:20), but her firstborn (2:7) is God's unique donation to the world.

1:32. Like John (see v. 15), he is to be **"great"** *(megas)*, but there the similarity ends, for Jesus will be great in the sense of prestige enjoyed by a world figure such as Alexander the Great. He **will be called the Son of the Most High.** "To be called" means not only to have a name attached but to be what the term signifies. "Most High" (cf. vv. 35, 76; 8:22; Acts 7:48; 16:17) is used often of Yahweh in the OT and of Zeus in the Greco-Roman world. Again Luke demonstrates his ability to communicate Semitic tradition in a manner that would be understood transculturally.

Jesus promised his disciples that they would be recognized as "sons of the Highest" (6:35*), assuming of course that they do not void the possibility by electing their own route to greatness (22:24); but Jesus, as the angel's succeeding words attest, enjoys a special status. On the other hand, the expression "Son of the Most High," along with other phraseology in this verse which is attested at Qumran (Cave 4), does not here connote what later credal statements mean by "Son of God." Rather, it is a firm messianic statement in continuity with 2 Sam. 7:13–16; Ps. 89:26–29. These passages speak of a deliverer who is to come from David's line, whose fortunes were to be restored according to Amos 9:11 (cf. Psalm 45). To people steeped in Greco-Roman culture the declaration would mean that in connection with Jesus all the character and the beneficence of God comes to expression.

1:33. Through Jesus, God will in effect reign over Israel (cf. Zeph. 3:15; Mic. 4:7; 5:2). And **there will be no end** to this reign (cf. 2 Sam. 7:13; see also Psalm 2 and Dan. 7:14). Luke appears to be citing from Mic. 4:7 LXX but omits the prophet's reference to Mount Zion and instead of the words "over them" has **over the house of Jacob** (cf. Isa. 9:7). The reign of Jesus does not begin after the resurrection; the resurrection, rather, confirms the validity of the first stage of Jesus' reign and introduces him to the second phase (cf. Acts 2:22–36; 13:22–37). The expression "house of Jacob" anticipates Acts 7:46. Nothing is said about abstinence from strong drink (cf. Luke 1:15), for Jesus will in fact attend many parties and drink the wine that is offered. But he will be unjustly charged with being a drunkard (7:34).

Through this description of Jesus' messianic credentials Luke affirms that Jesus qualifies in every way for Israel's highest office. The opposition identifies him correctly, albeit out of animosity, at 23:2. His crucifixion at the instigation of his own nation will not discredit him. The tragedy will be that Israel did not know the things that made for her peace (19:41–44). Thus Luke's work aims to give the lie to those who claim that Jesus could not be the Christ or Messiah because he failed to restore the ancient fortunes of Israel. If Israel's leadership fails as an instrument of divine design, Jesus will nevertheless be successful in gathering the Israel of the end time. The cross will be the place for public affirmation of his royal credentials (23:37–43), and his chosen disciples will sit on thrones judging the twelve tribes of Israel (22:30). Subsequent recitals in Luke's Gospel, together with the culminating question in Acts 1:6, offer necessary corrective to the misunderstanding that some readers might have found in Luke 1:32–33.

1:34. Through Mary's query Luke displays a contrast between the young woman and Zechariah. The latter had asked for a sign; Mary merely asks for further information. In such stance she is a model of the "poor" *(anawim)* who are proper candidates for the Kingdom promised in the words of vv. 32–33 (cf. 6:20). The rendering **since I have no husband** is delicate but obscures a Semitic idiom meaning, "I know no man intimately" (cf. Gen. 19:8; Judg. 11:39; 21:12).

Strictly speaking, the question would have been irrelevant, for Mary was betrothed *(mnēsteuō)* and could look forward to a normal marriage. Luke evidently does not lay stress on the biological aspects of the query and does not anticipate that his readers should ask intrusive questions and miss the main point of his narrative.

Psychologizing of ancient personalities is best left to writers of romances. Primarily, the question that Luke assigns to Mary gives him opportunity to relate the singular circumstances surrounding the conception of Jesus.

1:35. Holy Spirit and **power of the Most High** are parallel expressions (for similar association of spirit with power, see Luke 1:17; 4:14; Acts 1:8; 10:38; Eph. 3:16), as are also the verbs "come upon" and "overshadow." **Come upon** is frequently used by Luke of God's intervention in humanity's affairs (cf. Luke 21:26; Acts 1:8; 8:24; 13:40), and in Acts 1:8 this verb is associated with "the Holy Spirit" to describe a phenomenon parallel to the conception of Jesus, namely, the creation of the post-Easter apostolic mission.

"Overshadow" *(episkiazō)* is used elsewhere in the Gospels only of the cloud at the transfiguration (Luke 9:34; Mark 9:7; Matt. 17:5). The single other occurrence is Acts 5:15. The expression indicates the presence of God's mighty power (cf. Exod. 40:35). John was to be filled with the Holy Spirit after Elizabeth's conception (Luke 1:15), but Jesus is the product of a unique demonstration of God's power.

The evangelist emphasizes "virginal conception," not "virgin birth." Some overcurious theologians have suggested, in contradiction of Luke 2:23, that Jesus was born with a "closed womb." Luke's principal aim, though, is to prepare the reader for the emphasis made in 3:23–38, that Jesus is to be identified with all humanity (strongly affirmed in Gal. 4:4), yet as unique Son of God. The Holy Spirit is the Father of Jesus.

Because of such action of the Holy Spirit this particular child **will be called holy,** and this in the face of the misunderstanding he must endure because of the popular uncertainty concerning his paternity (cf. Luke 7:34; John 8:41). "Holy" means "set apart for God's service." Every firstborn in Israel theoretically belonged to the priesthood, but after the establishment of the Levitical priesthood a mother could release her child from such service by paying five shekels (Num. 18:15–16; cf. Exod. 13:12; Luke 2:23).

Jesus will be "holy" in a special sense. He will indeed be Mary's firstborn (Luke 2:7), but first of all he will be **the Son of God.** Similar terms are used to describe God's people (cf. Exod. 4:22; Jer. 31:9) or the king of Israel (Ps. 2:7), but the evangelist, as is apparent from vv. 36–37, uses the expression here in a unique sense. The Holy Spirit is to be the Father of Jesus. A demon will attest the link between holiness and an intimate relationship to God in the phrase "I know who you are, the Holy One of God" (4:34). The Sanhedrin will condemn Jesus for presumption (22:70–71). But a centurion will attest his uprightness (23:47), one of the principal characteristics of a beneficent political figure in Jewish (see 1 Kings 3:6; Isa. 32:1) and Greco-Roman cultures (see *Benefactor*, pp. 345–48).

The association of the divine spirit with a woman in the generative process was not unknown to the Greco-Roman world (see Plutarch *Numa* 4). Ancient Greek tradition is replete with stories of deities who generated notable offspring through such women as Danae, mother of Perseus by Zeus; Antiope, whose sons Amphion and Zethos were fathered by the same deity; and Kalliope, who bore Orpheus to Apollo. But Luke does not borrow from Mediterranean myths to convey the significance of Jesus. Non-Jewish auditors, though, would bring to his recital their acquaintance with Greco-Roman culture and would readily recognize that the singular parentage of Jesus provides him with a claim to excellence that was accorded in that world to such figures as Herakles, Asklepios, Pythagoras, Plato, Alexander the Great, Scipio Africanus, Julius Caesar, and Augustus.

1:36. Like Miriam and Elisheba (Exod. 6:23; 15:20), Mary and Elizabeth are relatives, but the degree of kinship cannot be determined. That John and Jesus were cousins is sheer conjecture. Because of the Fourth Evangelist's frequent use of words in a transferred sense, it is not possible to determine from his Gospel (see John 1:33) how well John and Jesus might have known each other. In any event, suggests Luke, besides his royal credentials Jesus can boast Aaronic lineage. Although Mary requested no sign, the angel encourages her faith with the example of Elizabeth's experience. Not only has Elizabeth conceived, she is now in her **sixth month** (see v. 24).

1:37–38. Since Elizabeth appears to image Sarah, the evangelist includes a paraphrase of Gen. 18:14: **For with God nothing will be impossible** (cf. Job 42:2; Jer. 32:27; Zech. 8:6). In contrast to Zechariah (v. 20), Mary believes the word of the angel: **Let it be to me according to your word.** The phrasing is Semitic in its declaration of compliance (cf. Josh. 2:21; Judg. 11:10; 2 Kings 14:25). Like Hannah of old (1 Sam. 1:11), Mary identifies herself as a slave girl (*doulē*; RSV: **handmaid**) of the **Lord** (*kyrios,* the term for "master"). According to Isa. 65:8, 13–15, Israelites are slaves (RSV: "servants") of God. Malachi 3:18 states that in the end time people will be able to distinguish between those who slave (RSV: "serve") for God and those who do not. Mary is therefore a model of what Israel ought to be, and her self-description is a mark of identity for the new community (Acts 2:18; 4:29; 1 Cor. 7:22; 1 Pet. 2:16).

PROPHETIC WORDS OF ELIZABETH
Luke 1:39–55

Encounter with Mary
Luke 1:39–45

This is the third episode in Luke's account of his two "great" stars, who as embryos now encounter each other, with one of them identifying the other as the Superstar.

1:39. A divine sign is not to be taken for granted, and Mary hastens to see her relative (cf. 2:15), who is in **a city of Judah** (cf. 2 Sam. 2:1).

1:40–41. In response to **the greeting of Mary**, the embryo in Elizabeth's womb makes a quick movement (**the babe leaped** [*skirtaō*] **in her womb**). Another woman, Rebekah, wife of Isaac, who was also barren for a long time, had a similar experience, when Jacob and Esau struggled in her womb (Gen. 25:22), indicating that the elder child would serve the younger. For the suggestion of joy in the child's activity, cf. Ps. 114:4, "skipped"; Mal. 4:2, "leaping"; *Pss. of Sol.* 28:3).

The movement in the womb is not to be interpreted as the product of emotional factors; it is one of the portents Luke reports so as to maintain his public's attention on the divine purpose that pervades the entire recital, and Elizabeth's words express the import of John's activity. John relates to Jesus. Elizabeth is **filled with the Holy Spirit.** Her son has already displayed the truth of Gabriel's words (v. 15), and she now speaks as a prophetess.

A prophet was able to deduce from ordinary circumstances what was the mind and intention of God (cf. Isa. 7:14–17). Frequently women were gifted with prophetic powers (Deborah, Judg. 4:4; four daughters of Philip, Acts

21.9; women in general, 1 Cor. 11:5). Elizabeth's response forecasts the recognition of women at Pentecost (Acts 2:17).

1:42. The formulation of a two-phase blessing is found also in Gen. 14:19–20. In diction reminiscent of Judith 13:18–19 (cf. Judg. 5:24, of Jael), Elizabeth cries out her response to God's activity in connection with Mary and pronounces Mary a unique object of praise. No woman is as privileged as she. But the main focus is not on Mary. It is customary in the East to praise remarkable offspring by praising the parents (cf. Luke 11:27–28). Luke points this out through the parallel phrase **blessed is the fruit of your womb** (cf. Gen. 30:2, 13). The conception of Jesus has already taken place. "Blessed" (perfect participle of *eulogeō*) here means that Mary's child is to be the recipient of such honors and favors from God that people will adore and praise God for the lavish display (cf. Luke 19:38).

1:43. The Semitic form of the question here in v. 43 parallels the query with which Araunah disclaims his worthiness to receive King David (2 Sam. 24:21). Elizabeth recognizes Mary's child as her **Lord** *(kyrios),* the title applied to Jesus by the Christian community. The term was used variously of God, kings, distinguished persons, or owners of slaves. In this passage Elizabeth recognizes Mary's child as her "Master." Before him she is like a slave and unworthy to receive so distinguished a person as Mary. Her words are important, for they set before the reader a clear distinction between John and Jesus (cf. Luke 3:15–16).

1:44. Even Elizabeth, John's own mother, recognized the superiority of Jesus, and she was merely echoing John's own understanding while he was yet unborn. At Mary's greeting he jumped in ecstatic joy (see on v. 41).

1:45. A final verdict is pronounced on Mary, who serves as a model of faith for Israel. Here the word for "blessed" *(makaria)* is different from the term at v. 42 and does not reappear until 6:20. *Makaria* means "fortunate" or "happy," in the sense of being in good grace with God, often despite appearances. Mary can count herself fortunate that unlike Zechariah (v. 20) she responded in faith. She will not be disappointed, for what the Lord God has said through Gabriel will come to pass. I therefore translate the verse, "And fortunate is she who believed, for she will find the Lord's words fulfilled."

The Magnificat

Luke 1:46–55

Elizabeth now summarizes in prophetic utterance the meaning of the New Age that is dawning. (Greek manuscripts favor Mary as the subject, but the witness of Old Latin texts may take us closer to the original text.)

Although ascription of the Magnificat to Mary enjoys broad scholarly support, the following considerations point to Elizabeth as the speaker of the psalm: (1) The pronoun in the phrase **Mary remained with her** (v. 56) suggests that Elizabeth is the speaker. If Mary had been the speaker, we would expect to read "She remained with Elizabeth." (2) Expressions such as **the low estate of his handmaiden** (v. 48) and **his mercy is on those who fear him** (v. 50) more naturally describe Elizabeth's situation. Her childlessness brought her into reproach (v. 25), and her neighbors remark that the Lord had shown mercy to her (v. 58). (3) The song is partly modeled after the song of Hannah (1 Sam. 2:1–10), a childless woman who became the mother of Samuel. In an earlier description of herself (1 Sam. 1:11) Hannah uses precisely the words cited at Luke 1:48a. (4) A twofold attestation from the aged parents of John (the Magnificat by Elizabeth and the Benedictus by Zechariah, vv. 68–79) would be in harmony with Luke's view of the superior position enjoyed by Jesus. Both of John's parents praise the Lord for the arrival of salvation that centers in Jesus. (5) Elizabeth is described as "filled with the Holy Spirit" (v. 41). A prophetic message like the Magnificat is therefore appropriately associated with her name. Since v. 25 expresses Elizabeth's desire for seclusion, the psalm would have been inappropriate at that point.

It has been argued that the assignment of the Magnificat to Elizabeth is improbable because it gives her two speeches. But Luke would find ample precedent in the OT for such a sequence: in Genesis 48—49; Num. 24:12–24; Deut. 31:26—32:43 the sequence of two speeches is also from one speaker. Moreover, the very same chapters in 1 Samuel to which Luke makes frequent allusion (1 Samuel 1—2) contain in succession two speeches by Hannah, and these are connected in the OT Greek text, the Septuagint (LXX), by precisely the same phrase that Luke uses at the beginning of v. 46. These data are not ordinarily dealt with by sponsors of the Marian ascription.

The psalm is a literary mosaic, drawn from various parts of the OT, with frequent dependence on the Septuagint, and it celebrates the character of God in two major divisions. Verses 46–50 express Elizabeth's personal experience, and vv. 51–55 describe God as Savior of Israel. Verses 46–47 lead naturally to the affirmation of v. 48. Verse 49 finds parallel expression in v. 50. Verses 51–53 present three pairs of contrasts. Verses 54–55 summarize God's total activity in behalf of Israel.

1:46–50. Verses 46–47 contain several phrases that echo verbatim the Greek text of 1 Sam. 2:1. **My soul magnifies the Lord.** In most instances where the RSV renders "soul" (*psychē*) the reader can mentally substitute "self" or "I." The Hebrew word (*nephesh*) underlying the term *psychē* means the totality of one's being.

1:47. The word "spirit" *(pneuma)* refers to that which enlivens the individual. When people die, not their "soul," in the Platonic sense of the term, but their breath or life leaves them (cf. 23:46). "Magnifies" *(megalynō)* means that Elizabeth celebrates the "greatness" of the Lord God and is filled with praise for God's beneficent and liberating deeds. Verse 47 is almost totally a reproduction of Hab. 3:18. For a description of God as Savior, see also Pss. 24:5; 35:9; Sir. 51:1; *Pss. of Sol.* 3:6; 17:3. Saviorhood was also a dominant feature in Greco-Roman views of deity.

1:48. This verse reproduces Hannah's words (1 Sam. 1:11). God saves by helping those who either are the victims of oppression or are scoffed at by their enemies. **Low estate** (better, "humiliation") applies most naturally to Elizabeth, who has spoken of her reproach (v. 25; cf. Gen. 29:32, spoken by Leah, who was loved less than Rachel; Psalm 31, esp. vv. 7–11). The echo of Gen. 30:13 at Luke 1:48b further points to the association of humiliation with infertility. If the psalm is to be attributed to Mary, then the term connotes inferiority of social position. In any event, the primary theme of the program for the New Age is here announced.

For behold, henceforth all generations will call me blessed *(makarizō)*. According to Mark 14:9, an unnamed woman will be remembered for all time because of her generous deed toward Jesus. Here Elizabeth claims the attention of the ages, not because of any quality in herself, but because of John, whose greatness lies in the prestige that will be his as the prophet who announces the arrival of the New Age in the mission and ministry of Jesus. Such praise by indirection is echoed at Luke 11:27. The view that this self-ascription is more appropriate on Mary's than on Elizabeth's lips suffers from subjective considerations that are stimulated by centuries of association.

1:49–50. Psalm 111:2, 9 may have encouraged much of the wording of this verse, but Deut. 10:21 closely parallels the first line. Verse 50 is an amplification of the thought in v. 49. God's mercy (expressed in rescuing action) corresponds to the "great things," and **those who fear** God (Ps. 103:11, 13, 17) are those who recognize that the divine name is "holy" (as described in Ps. 111:9). This means that proper recognition of God's majesty, coupled with appropriate moral response and life style, befits the worshiper (cf. Josh. 24:19–24). One does not take lightly a God who can perform mighty wonders. Pride and arrogance are typical of those who do not recognize the holiness of God, and to these the prophet now turns her attention.

1:51–53. Typical of prophetic language is the use of the past tense to describe the certainty of fulfillment for God's promises. Verse 51 combines expressions from Pss. 118:15 and 89:10 (cf. 147:6). The thought is: "God displays power and nullifies the plans of those who are arrogant in thought and mind." There is a simplicity in the basic structure of power. Viewed from divine perspective and exercise, it is primarily designed to secure the interests of the powerless, but the same power that protects the weak recoils on those who abuse the powerless through misuse of the instruments of power. Luke 11:17 and 23 define the awesome obligation.

The understanding of God that is here exhibited to some extent reflects Greco-Roman views of deities and public figures as arbiters of justice and deliverers of the oppressed (see *Benefactor,* Nos. 26, 30, and 43). But quite often reference is made to caprice rather than justice (e.g., Horace *Odes* 1.34.12–16). No people were more acquainted with the dynamics of reversal than were the Greeks, who found the theme at its loftiest expression in the Homeric epics and in the tragedies of Aischylos and Euripides. The poet Archilochos (*Fragments* 58; cf. Pindar *Olympian Odes* 12.10–12) expressed a consensus:

> The deities are ever just. Full oft they raise
> those who lie prostrate on the darkened earth.
> Full oft the prosperous are tripped, their bellies
> to the sky; and miseries untold attend them.
> Mindless, in aimless poverty they wander.

It is typical of some religious structures to view with alarm the application of words like those in the Magnificat to everyday social, political, and economic conditions. But God's immediate concern for the oppressed, repressed, and depressed will not be spiritualized into impotence. From Acts 4:19–20 it is clear that Luke envisages the occasional necessity of ecclesiastical and civil disobedience.

1:52. Underlying the thought expressed in v. 52 is 1 Sam. 2:7, but the language is closer to that of Sir. 10:14 and Ezek. 21:26 (v. 31 LXX). The sentiment is proverbial. When asked what God was doing, Chilon, the Lacedaemonian poet, replied: "Humbling the lofty and exalting the humble" (Diogenes Laertius 1.69). The "mighty" contrast with those in the despised lower classes, who were also frequently victims of oppression.

1:53. The text for v. 53 appears to be 1 Sam. 2:5, but the language is derived from various sources, including Pss. 107:9 and 146:7. Taken together, vv. 51–53 express the revolutionary character of the New Age. These lines could be understood in an anti-Roman sense, and to some it would appear that Jesus has failed to meet the specifications spelled out in this poem, so expressive of the traditional hope.

Luke does not here refute naive popular expectation. History demonstrates that political liberation of the poor frequently has as its outcome the rise of a new aristocracy that is expert in tyranny. The fact is that conquerors are alert to local tentacles of oppression, which have far more crushing capacity than the mere exercise of a foreign political presence. Lust for preferential treatment, encouragement of venality for self-interest, guardianship of traditional prerogatives against participation by outsiders, silence in the face of outrage, irresponsibility in social relationships, lack of commitment to spouse, the use of religion as a refuge from responsibility—these are but samples of the potential for tyranny that lies beneath the facade of any state or institution.

In his subsequent record of the activity of Jesus, Luke shows that traditional hope must undergo modification if the messianic mission of Jesus is to be understood. At Nazareth (4:18–19) and later near a mountain (6:20–26) these words of the Magnificat will find fulfillment (see also 16:19–31). And ultimately Luke will show that there are those within the nation who are more dangerous to God's interests than is the Roman power.

1:54. Verse 54 echoes Isa. 41:8–9 and Ps. 98:3. Israel is God's "servant" *(pais)*. By sending the Messiah into her midst, God celebrates the distinctive privilege of the Chosen People. As the Servant of Yahweh, Israel is of course expected to be a light to the gentiles (Isa. 49:3–6), but this thought will be made more explicit at Luke 2:3.

1:55. Elizabeth appropriately concludes with a reference to **Abraham,** to whom Isaac was given in his old age, born of a woman who had long been barren. The language of v. 55 is closely akin to that of Mic. 7:20 and Gen. 17:7–8.

RETURN OF MARY

Luke 1:56

1:56. And Mary remained with her [Elizabeth] **about three months.** The initial phrasing is a further indication that Elizabeth is the reciter of the foregoing psalm. "Three months" would approximate the time of Elizabeth's parturition. The fact that Luke does not have Mary take part in the next developments is not at all strange. John and Jesus are indeed contemporaneous, but Luke is at pains to keep the two separated, with the exception of the encounter described in vv. 41–44 (but this is prior to the birth of either one) and at 3:31 (and here Luke does not explicitly mention John). Jesus, not John, is the Christ. Moreover, the credentials of Jesus are validated not by John but by God.

THE BIRTH OF JOHN

Luke 1:57–80

Birth and Circumcision

Luke 1:57–66

1:57–58. Elizabeth evidently remained in retirement (cf. v. 24) until the time she was to give birth (similar phrasing in Gen. 25:24), for her neighbors and relatives now hear the news. What they hear corresponds in phrasing to vv. 46 and 50. Elizabeth had "magnified" the Lord, and now the Lord "magnifies" (to make great; cf. Gen. 19:19) mercy to Elizabeth. The joint rejoicing of the women echoes Luke 1:14 and in both Jewish and Greco-Roman culture is a proper response to divine action (cf. 15:6, 9 and see *Benefactor*, No. 28).

1:59. According to instructions cited at Gen. 17:9–14, the child is circumcised on the eighth day. Jewish children were ordinarily given a name at the time of birth. Association of the naming with the rite of circumcision is exceptional (see also Luke 2:21) and may reflect influence of Hellenistic practice. For evidence from the OT of mothers naming their children, see Gen. 19:37–38 and 29:32–35 (Tob. 1:9 cites an exception). A child frequently would be named after a grandfather (1 Macc. 2:1–2), but in view of the extraordinary circumstances attention is here focused on the father.

1:60–61. In response to the clamor for the paternal name—Luke's grammar suggests that they were already referring to the infant by the name Zechariah—Elizabeth insists that he is to be called John.

It is contrary to the formal requirements of such narrative to inquire whether Zechariah had or had not earlier communicated this detail to his wife.

1:62. Although there is no suggestion in v. 22 that Zechariah had also been afflicted with deafness, in the popular mind muteness and deafness would be inseparably connected, just as inability to understand another's language is accompanied by a heightening of voice level and use of body language. Luke registers normal cultural reactions and he records that the relatives made signs to the father. Thereby the miracle of restoration of speech is all the more apparent.

1:63. With the aid of **a writing tablet** (wood coated with wax), Zechariah informs them emphatically: "John *is* his name." Elizabeth had used the future tense. Zechariah's statement in the present tense takes auditors back to the pronouncement at v. 13. The name has already been fixed by divine decree. **And they all marveled.** These words suggest that Luke wants his publics to understand that Elizabeth's insistence on the name John was the result of her prophetic inspiration (v. 41) and found a remarkable endorsement in Zechariah's verdict.

1:64. Gabriel had spoken of "the day that these things come to pass" (v. 20). The moment has arrived and is marked by one of Luke's favorite words: "immediately" *(parachrēma)*. This word will be attached to numerous recitals of miracles in Luke-Acts: Luke 4:39; 5:25; 8:44, 47, 55; 13:13; 18:43;

Acts 3:7; 16:26 (the Greek word is used only once elsewhere in the NT: Matt. 21:19). The New Age does not creep in.

Zechariah had been struck with muteness for his unbelief. Now he displays faith in God's purpose and the sign is removed. He then proceeds to praise God. The content of that praise is given in vv. 68–79, but the evangelist first records the reaction of the people.

1:65–66. Fear had fallen on Zechariah at the announcement of John's birth (v. 12); now fear comes over all the neighbors, as it does in response to other miracles (Luke 5:26; 8:25, 37; Acts 5:11). There is an apocalyptic tone in the narrative, and all who hear the wonderful things that were being recited **laid them up in their hearts** (cf. 1 Sam. 21:12; Dan. 7:28; Luke 2:19).

Comments followed two lines of expression. Some asked, **What then will this child be?** Others said, "The hand of the Lord is with him," that is, he will be a mighty instrument of the Lord. (The RSV, following other manuscript traditions, reads the last part of v. 66 as an explanation by the evangelist.) **The hand of the Lord** refers to divine power (cf. Isa. 41:20) and anticipates its opposition at v. 71.

The Benedictus

Luke 1:67–79

Filled with the Holy Spirit (cf. v. 41), Zechariah now interprets the will of God for his child within a laudatory poem. As Elizabeth had done (vv. 46–55), Zechariah gives expression to Luke's main theme: salvation. Elizabeth began with personal references (vv. 46–50); Zechariah begins with the people of God (vv. 68–75). The verbs are again, for the most part, in the past tense, for God majors in certain success.

1:68–75. The first part of v. 68, **Blessed be the Lord God of Israel,** reproduces words found at Pss. 41:13; 72:18. **He has visited** means that God intervened when the fortunes of the Chosen People were at low ebb. Luke will make a point of this at 19:44, for Israel failed to realize that God's visitation was indeed taking place. The alternative is a visitation of judgment. In harmony with the theme of visitation Luke displays Jesus as a guest in various places (cf. 7:36–50; 10:38–42; 19:1–10). The phrasing **redeemed his people** is similar to that of Ps. 111:9. The Messiah was to release God's people from the yoke of their oppressors (cf. Luke 2:38; 21:28; 24:21).

1:69. Psalms 18:2; 132 (esp. v. 17); and perhaps 1 Sam. 2:10 appear to underlie the thought and wording in this verse. A "horn" is an emblem of power. God's power is to display itself in an offshoot from David (see 2 Sam. 7:12–13). David is called God's "servant" *(pais)* also in Acts 4:25. Zechariah gives expression to the conviction that the messianic era dawns with the arrival of John, but John is subordinate to the Davidic Messiah. Thus Zechariah's statement echoes that of Elizabeth at v. 43 and parallels the fifteenth benediction of the Jewish prayer *Shemoneh Esre* (SB 4:213).

1:70–71. Verse 70 is similar in form to v. 55. Zechariah, himself a prophet, brings to summation what the ancient prophets declared and promised. Verse 71 continues the theme of salvation taken up at v. 69, but this time in language reminiscent of the exodus (cf. Ps. 106:10 and see Ps. 18:17; Zeph. 3:15). Zechariah's words here are not to be taken in a strictly nonsecular sense. He utters traditional national hope, as expressed throughout Israel's history when confronted with oppression. Luke's task will be to explain how Jesus can be the Messiah despite the fact that deliverance did not come as anticipated by many in Israel (note the disappointment expressed at 24:21). On the other hand, Christian auditors who were acquainted with the numerous experiences of deliverance recited in Acts would recognize a variety of "enemies." For the theme, see also 1QM 10.

1:72–73. These verses have much in common with Ps. 105:8–9, 42 and Mic. 7:20 and emphasize that God keeps faith with Israel's ancestors, especially Abraham (cf. Gen. 22:16–18). The "covenant" described here is an agreement initiated alone by God. As the supreme politician, sovereign of the universe, God promises to protect those who come under the jurisdiction of this covenant. Hence the history of Israel is a continuing story of rescue out of disaster (see Exod. 2:24). God keeps covenant even though the people fail to fulfill their responsibilities. And the divine responsibility extends to all nations (Acts 3:25).

The phrase **oath which he swore** echoes Gen. 26:3 and Jer. 11:5 and refers to the promise that is outlined in Gen. 22:16–17. To Greco-Roman auditors the formulation would sound a bureaucratic tone that is in keeping with the political flavor of the entire poem.

1:74–75. Deliverance from the hands of the enemy (see v. 71; cf. Pss. 17:1 and 106:2 LXX) means that one can live **without fear.** Public stability was a dominant theme in official Greco-Roman documents. The personal dimension will be dramatically demonstrated when Jesus commits himself out of the hands of his enemies into the hands of God (Luke 23:46).

Zechariah's poem views deliverance as an opportunity for Israel to "serve" *(latreuō)* God, that is, to carry out her religious obligations, understood here from a moral perspective as a life in conformity with the divine will and purpose (cf. Jer. 30:8–9). The logic is that of Ps. 105:44–45.

In the phrase service **in holiness and righteousness,** "holiness" *(hosiotēs)* describes the proper attitude in respect to God; "righteousness" *(dikaiosynē)* is conformity with God's precepts, especially as they involve one in relation to others (cf. Wisd. of Sol. 9:3; Eph. 4:24). To a Greco-Roman, these two qualities suggest people of the highest excellence. In Plato's *Protagoras* (329c) these two words are used to define the acme of good citizenship, and the two terms or their cognates appear on various monuments erected in honor of outstanding contributors to the public welfare. The Supreme Benefactor's action begets the qualities that promote the general welfare.

1:76–79. Zechariah now addresses his own child in terms that anticipate 7:26. The phrase **prophet of the Most High** appears as a messianic title in *Testament of Levi* 8:15. The question will be asked of John whether he is the Messiah (Luke 3:15). Since the messianic hope took various directions during the lifetime of John and Jesus, Luke does not hesitate to permit messianic notions associated with John to stand at this point. But he has given priority to the "horn of salvation" in the house of David (v. 69). Through the recital at 2:1–14 (note esp. v. 11) he will correct any erroneous deductions that might have been prompted by traditional messianic expectations. At the same time, this personal address to the child modifies nationalistic messianic hopes by making forgiveness of sins the dominant feature (cf. 7:47).

As a prophet, John is to **go before the Lord to prepare his ways.** These words appear to be a combination of thoughts expressed in Mal. 3:1 and Isa. 40:3. In both of these OT passages the way is prepared before God (cf. Luke 1:17). The words in Luke are not strictly parallel to Mark 1:2, where the initial phrasing is taken from Exod. 23:20. In other words, Zechariah does not say that John in his person as an apocalyptic figure validates the credentials of the messiah, a role never performed by John in Luke's narrative.

By including these words, Luke prepares the way for a correct understanding of John's function as one whose proclamation does not usher in the end of the end time but sounds the note of repentance (see on 1:17, and cf. Acts 13:23–24), without which God's salvation, present in Jesus' person, will be lost in misunderstanding.

To dissipate such misunderstanding based on traditional apocalyptic expectations and to discourage what he considers crass interpretations of Malachi, Luke presents the origins of Jesus and John in parallel accounts. John has no relative temporal advantage over Jesus. His ministry ends almost as soon as it begins (cf. 3:18–19), and Jesus comes on the scene to announce good news to the people. Accordingly, John is the one anticipated by Malachi, but his message, not his person, prepared the way of the Lord spelled out in Jesus the Messiah.

1:77. John will prepare the way of the Lord God by announcing "salvation" *(sōtēria).* The politics of the Reign of God deals with two major concerns: external conditions and the internal or relation of the individual to God. The first part of Zechariah's poem discussed the external factor (vv. 68–75). Verse 75 offers a transition to the second aspect.

Through **forgiveness of their sins** (cf. Mark 1:4), God solves the problem of people's relationship to their Deity. By stressing forgiveness of sins, a familiar feature in the Hebrew Scriptures, Luke is able to secure a universal applicability for Israel's hope (see also *Testament of Levi* 4:4). Because of the mission beyond the borders of Israel, God's people will include immigrants from the broadest reaches of the Greco-Roman world. Peoplehood will not be determined by ethnic credentials as understood in the past, and the moral product will be a sharpened understanding of personal responsibility within the extended family of humanity (see, e.g., Luke 7:36–50; 10:30–36).

1:78. Forgiveness is the result of God's **tender mercy** *(splagchna eleous).* Luke nowhere spells out an intricate process whereby God removes sin. God simply displays willingness to share with people (cf. Jer. 31:34) and demonstrates goodwill (Luke 2:14) by sending the Messiah. After the gift of Jesus is rejected, God extends Israel a renewed opportunity for a personal relationship (cf. Luke 24:47; Acts 5:31). Not even the crucifixion can nullify God's profound love. Jesus in his person remains God's gift to the world. As one who associates also with the lowly, the outcasts, the publicans and sinners, he is the living demonstration of God's forgiving intent. John will parallel this activity of Jesus by his proclamation of "a baptism of repentance for the forgiveness of sins" (Luke 3:3).

The second line of v. 78 may be translated "in which the light-filled branch from on high shall visit us." God's mercy (= "in which"; cf. *Testament of Levi* 4:4) is the point of origin or the source for the visitation (the word for "visit" *[episkeptomai]* echoes the word in v. 68 and anticipates the usage in 7:16).

God's visitation takes place in forgiveness. The word *anatolē* (RSV margin: "dayspring") is used in Jer. 23:5 LXX in the sense of "shoot" or "branch" (cf. Jer. 33:15; Zech. 3:8; 6:12). This association may have combined in the tradition with the thought of Isa. 9:1 and 42:7 (cf. Num. 24:17 and Luke 1:79) and prompted the use of a term that ordinarily refers to the rising of heavenly bodies. In any event, "dayspring" may be a case of double sense, but the expression clearly refers to the Messiah (cf. Matt. 2:2).

Greco-Roman auditors would have had no problem with the imagery. Association of the sun with emperors was a commonplace, and Caesar Augustus is termed in one inscription "the risen star of all Hellas" (*Benefactor,* p. 285). To Christians with roots in the Greco-Roman world, Jesus is the Great Benefactor. As in Luke 24:49, the phrase **from on high** *(ex hypsous)* refers to God as the point of origin.

1:79. Isaiah 9:1 and 42:7 (cf. Ps. 107:10) are the probable sources for the first part of this verse. "Darkness" and "death" were frequently linked in lamentations about the hazards and brevity of life. The grave would offer no further opportunity for the association with God once enjoyed on earth (cf.

Ps. 6:5). The New Age will be marked by the dispelling of darkness, symbolized especially by blindness (cf. Isa. 59:10). Fear of death, marked by frantic love for gain, will dissolve in the presence of One who will point his disciples to the true riches (cf. Luke 9:24; 12:4–7, 32–34). Thus the "light" aims to guide those who are sitting in darkness but dare not move because they will stumble (cf. Isa. 59:10, Mic. 7:8).

According to Isa. 59:10, **the way of peace** is associated with justice. To Greco-Romans, as to Israelites, peace went hand in hand with stability as the choicest benefaction that a head of state could render. When justice is perverted and the rights of the neighbor are violated, there is no peace and people's sins cry out against them (Isa. 59:12–15). Only those who turn from transgression will experience God as a redeemer (Isa. 59:20; cf. Luke 1:74). Luke's auditors will recall this passage when they hear his later recital of Jerusalem's failure to recognize the things that make for her peace (Luke 19:42). Instead of being rescued out of the hands of the enemy (1:74), Jerusalem will be utterly destroyed by her enemies (19:43–44).

The fulfillment of some of Israel's material hopes (1:68–74) is clearly conditioned by Luke on the acceptance of the guidance that the Messiah gives to God's people. Messianic credentials are independent of the fate of Israel as a nation. Not apocalyptic speculation that is nationally oriented, but searching of the deepest motive for living is to mark the congregation of the end time. Such is the dialectic that comes to expression in Luke's masterful juxtaposition of apparently divergent traditions.

John's Retirement to the Wilderness

Luke 1:80

1:80. This verse concludes the first of Luke's two major recitals dealing with the infancies of John and Jesus. It is parallel in form to 2:40, which concludes the second installment. Like Samson (Judg. 13:24–25), John grows physically and spiritually. To become **strong in spirit** means to develop inner resources for the understanding and performance of God's will (cf. Eph. 3:16–19). According to v. 15, John was to be filled with the Holy Spirit.

Because of the phrase **in the wilderness,** it has been suggested that John the Baptist was associated with communities that settled near the Dead Sea. But there are a number of differences between John and the Essenes and members of the community at Qumran. For example, his proclamation does not consist of legal prescriptions, and it is addressed to all who come and not merely to a closed fellowship. One can only speculate whether John had a youthful encounter with Qumran and then struck out on paths of his own. Demonstrable is Luke's emphasis, that John and Jesus are to be kept separate for a time, for Luke says of Jesus that he was brought up in Nazareth (2:50; 4:16).

The words **till the day of his manifestation** *(heōs hēmeras anadeixeōs* *autou)* refer to the beginning of John's public ministry. The expression has a bureaucratic connotation, being used in the Greco-Roman world of administrative assignment. In Luke's work, only Jesus (Luke 10:1) or God (Acts 1:24) is the agent of such demonstration. Hence John does not appear until the word of the Lord comes to him (Luke 3:2).

Throughout his recital of the content of chap. 1, Luke makes a number of points, chief of which are the following:

1. The messianic era dawns with the announcement of the births of John and Jesus.

2. John shares in the power and spirit of Elijah, but Jesus is the heir to David's throne. Thus John is subordinate to Jesus, and his ministry does not validate that of Jesus.

3. The messianic era is to be introduced not by special apocalyptic effects but by a preparation of the people for the performance of God's will.

4. Faith, accompanied by piety and uprightness, is the criterion of a people prepared for the Lord. Zechariah's sign-seeking is repudiated. Mary anticipates the disciple who will hear the word of God and keep it.

5. The New Age is a time of revolution, but not along traditional partisan lines. God raises the lowly and depresses the mighty.

6. The national hope of Israel is dependent on her recognition of the things that pertain to her peace. Moral earnestness is the primary mark of the New Age, and a new understanding of redemption and salvation, independent of the national fortunes of Israel, is now possible.

7. The New Age is in continuity with the promises made to Abraham and the fathers. God is determined to carry out the divine purpose over all opposition.

8. The Holy Spirit is the documentation for God's action in the New Age.

THE BIRTH AND CHILDHOOD OF JESUS
Luke 2:1–52

Luke described a number of features of the messianic age in his first chapter. John and Jesus were introduced in parallel recitals, but the superiority of Jesus was clearly indicated. Now Luke proceeds to show that in Jesus the main outlines of the New Age begin to take shape. Many of the themes accented in Luke 1 are repeated in Luke 2, itself a masterpiece of literary economy.

The Birth of Jesus
Luke 2:1–7

2:1. The very vagueness of the phrase **in those days** hints at the historical problems associated with the narrative. During his reign from 27 B.C.E. to

14 C.E., Caesar Augustus made a number of administrative reforms. Military and fiscal concerns encouraged him to undertake various types of census in the course of his control of the empire that numbered from seventy million to a hundred million inhabitants. In his *Res Gestae,* Augustus refers to three enrollments of Roman citizenry (28 B.C.E., 10 to 8 B.C.E., and 14 C.E.). Census-taking of provincial inhabitants for purposes of taxation was done in various localities, but there is no evidence of one edict covering all of the empire.

2:2. Luke (Acts 5:37) knows of an "enrollment" *(apographē)* for taxation which, according to Josephus, took place in Palestine, when Syria was annexed as a province in 6 C.E. *(Antiquities* 17.13.5; 18.3; *War* 7.253). But there is no evidence for a census in Palestine for the years immediately preceding the death of Herod. Yet Luke appears to identify the census of Acts 5:37 ("in the days of the census") with the census cited in Luke 2:1, which he calls **the first enrollment.** The key to the identification and at the same time the principal agent of confusion for historians is the reference to Publius Sulpicius **Quirinius,** who was well known for his extraordinary administrative ability (cf. Josephus *Antiquities* 18.1.1) and is certainly to be associated with the census of 6 C.E. but probably not with one in "the days of Herod." Luke's inexactitude is nevertheless forgivable. How many Roman officials could even have called the roll of Rome's consuls and their years of service, not to mention her provincial governors? Luke is far more precise when he writes about events closer to his own generation.

Aware of the problem, Tertullian, a church father of the second century C.E., did not hesitate to correct Luke and offers in place of Quirinius the name of Saturninus *(Against Marcion* 4.19). But this view is attended with too many difficulties to be taken seriously.

Until new evidence is submitted, the problem of Luke's mode of dating the birth of Jesus will invite what a classicist said in another context, "endless and unprofitable discussion." Of more immediate interest is Luke's line of thought. Writing seventy to eighty years after the event, Luke aims at fidelity to his sources. At the same time, he wants his auditors to appreciate the worldwide importance of Jesus, whose birth takes place at a critical moment in Jewish history and in the history of the entire world. The phrase "in those days" is undeniably vague. But in the vagueness lies the truth, and one is not to lose the thread out of fondness either for archaeological debate or for a twentieth-century type of precision to which the writers of Scripture lay no claim. To establish the contours of Luke's main conception, there is no need of further evidence. In the days of King Herod the Great, and of Caesar Augustus, whom all the world would call "divine" *(divus),* there was born "the king of the Jews" (23:38), who bears the One Name (Acts 4:12) and pronounces futile all routes to greatness other than his own (22:27).

2:3. The use of the word "all" *(pas, pasa, pan)* is one of Luke's Hellenistic mannerisms (cf. v. 1). Luke relates that **all went to be enrolled, each to his own city,** probably on the assumption that the practice of returning to one's current home city for enrollment—for which there is support in papyri from Egypt—also applied to Palestine. His phrasing can only mean that he understands the directive in reference to "ancestral" abode, but the evidence from Egypt does not point to such a requirement. It is therefore further probable that Luke romanticizes to some extent in order to connect the birth of Jesus at Bethlehem in the context of imperial policy. A mighty empire in commotion, and all, as a Scottish divine wrote, for "a certain baby's birth in a certain little town in a wee part of the world."

2:4. The name Augustus would have reminded some readers of the glorious expectations associated with that emperor's reign. In 27 B.C.E. the Senate urged him to head the state and voted him the title "Augustus," meaning "one who is worthy of great honor," approved by gods and people. In various parts of the empire he was acclaimed as "God" *(divus)* and "Savior" *(sōtēr),* and recognized as the world's great architect of peace. It was Rome's custom to keep the doors of the portal of Janus Quirinus open when her soldiers were engaged in battle. In his *Res Gestae,* a résumé of his reign, Augustus reports the following for posterity: "Only twice before my birth does history record that the gates were closed, but three times during my principate the Senate decreed that they be shut" (Tablet 1, chap. 13, 40–45; see *Benefactor,* p. 262). An inscription found at Priene, celebrating his birthday in 9 B.C.E., commemorates the birth of Augustus as the "beginning of the good news [gospel]," perhaps in reference to celebrations held in his honor. The inscription reads in part:

> Providence, that orders everything in our lives, has displayed extraordinary concern and compassion and crowned our life with perfection itself. She has brought into the world Augustus and filled him with distinguished goodness for the benefit of humanity. In her beneficence she has granted us and those who will come after us [a Savior] who has made war to cease and who shall order all things well. The [epiphany] of Caesar transcends the expectations of [all who anticipated the good news]. Not only has he outstripped all benefactors who have gone before him, but he will leave posterity no hope of surpassing him. The birth date of our God has signaled the beginning of good news for the world. (*Benefactor,* p. 217)

(For details on this inscription, see *Benefactor,* pp. 215–22.)

About the time that this inscription was made, Jesus was born at **Bethlehem.** The contrast between two emperors and benefactors is masterfully expressed. What Luke does not say about Augustus gives profounder meaning first to what he has said earlier in Luke 1 about the messianic age and, second, to the restrained recital he is about to make of the birth of Israel's king. The Davidic credentials of Joseph were spelled out also at 1:27; of the Messiah, at 1:32–33, 69. Jesus is to be born not in Galilee but in Judea; for neither the Messiah nor even any prophet of note comes from Galilee (cf. John 7:41, 52). Bethlehem is David's town (1 Sam. 16:1; cf. Mic. 5:2).

2:5–6. On the assumption that a betrothed couple would not ordinarily travel together as is stated in these verses, some readers have wondered whether Mary and Joseph were now legally married. Others have marveled over Mary's journey under the prevailing conditions. Luke does not bother to answer the overly curious. The reference to Mary being "betrothed" recalls 1:27 and reminds the reader that Mary stands in the same relationship to Joseph. The mention of her pregnancy simply accounts for the fact that while they were in Bethlehem she gave birth (cf. 1:57). One can in fact ascribe much of Luke's literary art to his economy of narrative and his resistance to pedantic adornment.

2:7. In the light of 1:32, **first-born** *(prōtotokos)* **son** emphasizes that this son has the right of inheritance to the throne of David (cf. 2 Chron. 21:3). With the same stroke of the pen Luke's public is prepared for 2:22–24, which treats the dedication of Jesus in accordance with Mosaic ordinance. Secondarily, some auditors would conclude that Jesus is here distinguished from other children of Mary and Joseph who might lay claim to special privilege (cf. 8:19–21). Like any infant, this baby requires normal attention and is wrapped in **swaddling cloths,** the normal attire of any newly born infant in Palestine. The mightiest begin their career in no other way, affirms King Solomon of himself in Wisd. of Sol. 7:4–5 (see below on v. 12). His crib is **a manger,** that is, a feeding trough (not a wooden crate on legs). Because of him, others will recline in the Kingdom of God (13:29); but, in extraordinary contrast to expectations raised by 1:32–33, his head rests where the cattle have fed. Luke explains the strange phenomenon with his observation that **there was no place for them in the inn**. But he who found no customary lodgings at his birth will make arrangements for such personally a few hours before his death (22:11).

The rendering "inn" *(katalyma)* at v. 7 invites misunderstanding. Luke would know that inns of that time were the haunts of ill-bred people and often poorly kept. But despite his emphasis on Jesus' association with publicans and sinners, it is questionable whether he would go to such a length to make a point. In 10:34 he uses another term for "inn" *(pandocheion)*, but at 22:11 he uses the same Greek word that is found here at 2:7, and there is no question that in 22:11 a room in a house is meant (cf. 22:12). Luke evidently concludes that Bethlehem would have a number of visitors, and a crowded room would be no place for a couple in these straits.

Animals were often kept near the family quarters, as they are to this day even in some European villages. But pictures that have cows and asses looking into the crib are patent invention. This does not mean that some of Luke's public would not have made association with Isa. 1:3: "The ox knows its owner, and the ass its master's crib; but Israel does not know, my people does not understand."

The inference that the birth took place in a cave (see *Apocryphal Book of James,* or *Protevangelium,* 18.1) can be traced to local legend associated with Greco-Roman cult. Caves were favored haunts for divine activity. Suggestions of a gruff and inhospitable innkeeper are of course part of later legend and, like most of the post-canonical imaginary additions of folk piety, are out of harmony with the integrity and sobriety of the narrative, which is as far from sentimentality as it is sublime in simplicity. Luke's point is that Jesus does not come with the splendor that one might associate with the world deliverer. To ally oneself with the fortunes of a messiah who lacks all recognized status will call for a counting of the cost (14:25–35). For the Son of humanity has no place to lay his head (9:58). George MacDonald summed it:

> They all were looking for a king
>   To slay their foes and lift them high:
> Thou cam'st, a little baby thing
>   That made a woman cry.

The Shepherds

Luke 2:8–20

2:8. The Magnificat announced the revolutionary character of the New Age (1:51–53). Luke now shows how that passage is to be understood. He introduces his readers to shepherds, who are the first to receive the announcement of the birth. Bethlehem, as a locale of shepherds, is mentioned at Gen. 35:19–21; 1 Sam. 17:12; Mic. 5:2–4. Servius, a commentator on the Roman poet Vergil (*Eclogues* 10.26), notes that "divinities are especially in the habit of revealing themselves to rural people." These shepherds share a profession with the most blue-blooded in Israel—namely, Abraham, Moses, and David—and are emblematic of those who will share the Kingdom with the patriarchs (cf. Luke 13:28–29).

The phrase **keeping watch over their flock by night** is equivalent to "keeping night watch over their flock." The point is not that they received the news during the night, but that they were ready for it when it came, apparently at daybreak. Thus is anticipated the thematic note expressed in 12:16–21, 35–40; 17:26–37; 21:34–36; 22:39–46. Since the apocalyptic finale cannot be determined by the usual signs, readiness at all times is required lest the revelation of God go unnoticed, as it did for almost everyone but the shepherds on the day that God's Son came to birth. Much ingenuity has gone to waste in attempts to date the birth of Jesus on the basis of this passage.

2:9. An angel of the Lord appeared. Jacob Wettstein calls attention to a number of instances in Greek literature in which the verb "appeared" *(ephistēmi)* is used of communication between deities and people with the help of dreams and visions; and Alfred Plummer (p. 55) cites *Iliad* 10.496; 23.106; Herodotos 1.34.2; 7.14.1. For other instances of Luke's use of the term to express heavenly visitation, see Luke 21:34; 24:4; Acts 12:7; 23:11.

The **glory of the Lord** (cf. Isa. 40:5; 60:1–2; Ezek. 8:4; 9:3; 10:19) is the brilliant effulgence marking the presence of God. "Glory" *(doxa)* also means true worth or dignity. A king, for example, may be despised by his enemies, but in victory he will be seen for what he really is, a powerful potentate who gives orders to his new slaves. Glory stands in contrast to the night, for this is the time of the "dayspring" (Luke 1:78). Glory is mentioned here and omitted at 3:5, for the glory is not seen by all flesh, whereas God's salvation is to be made known to all the nations. In Isa. 40:5 LXX, glory and salvation are brought into close association. The profoundest demonstration of God's being is in an act of rescue. The announcement that a "Savior" *(sōtēr,* Luke 2:11) has been born therefore accords well with the "glory of the Lord." Such glory is not to be seen again until the transfiguration (9:31), and it anticipates the final success of Jesus (24:26). The reaction of the shepherds is similar to the response recorded at 1:12.

2:10. As in 1:19, the phrase **I bring you good news** is one word in Greek *(euanggelizō)* and means "announce." Then follows the content of the announcement. The birth date of Augustus was celebrated as a day prophetic of joy for the entire world. But his edict, with its statement of fiscal policy, was probably received as bad news. The divine messenger's proclamation pronounces "joy" with every word. It is a theme that dominates Luke-Acts (see Luke 6:23; 8:8, 13; 10:17, 20; 13:17; 15:5, 9, 32; 19:6, 37; 24:41, 52; Acts 5:41; 8:39; 11:23; 13:48, 52; 15:31) and repeatedly signals to Luke's auditors the preeminent majesty of Jesus Christ as the great benefactor. This declaration concerning joy assures the shepherds that they need not fear (v. 9) some negative action by their God.

The theme of divine communication is one that Luke will not dismiss (see, e.g., 3:18; 4:18). Like Zechariah, they are sharers in a joy (1:14) that is here described as **great joy** and of a sort that applies to **all the people.** Luke means the entire nation of *Israel* (cf. 1:16–17, 68, 77; 2:32b; 24:19), which in turn is to be a source of blessing to all the world (2:32a; cf. Gen. 12:3). All ceremonial requirement is shattered with this one piece of good news, for even unclean shepherds are welcome in God's presence.

2:11. The word "for" *(hoti)* is important. It introduces a phrase that explains why the joy is great for all the people. **To you**—namely, the shepherds—a Savior has been born. No good news was ever more personalized. Mangy, stinking, bathless shepherds are, in their ritual uncleanness, an encouragement for all who lack religious status. All chief seats are melted down in the white heat of this glory.

"Today" *(sēmeron)* is one of Luke's favorite words (cf. 3:22; 4:21; 5:26; 13:32–33; 19:5, 9; 23:43). Not in some future apocalyptic hour, but at that very moment a Savior makes his appearance. The term "today" need not exclude a portion of the night, but the popular conception that the birth took place at night is Christmas legend, perhaps traceable to Wisd. of Sol. 18:14–15.

"Savior" *(sōtēr)* echoes the double theme of the Benedictus. The term appears in the Greek Bible of the OT in reference both to God (see, e.g., Deut. 32:15; 1 Sam. 10:19; 1 Chron. 16:35; Pss. 24:5; 27:1) and to human beings as deliverers of the nation (Judg. 3:9, 15; Neh. 9:27). It is Jesus who is now to spell fresh hope for the nation as a whole (Luke 1:69, 71) and for the individual in particular (1:77; 19:9). God carries on the work of salvation (cf. 1:47) through Jesus (cf. Acts 4:12; Luke 7:50; 8:48; 9:24; 13:23; 17:19; 18:42; 19:9–10).

The Hellenistic world had numerous gods and rulers called "Savior" (see the comment above on vv. 2–4 respecting Augustus). The term is a synonym for "benefactor" in Demosthenes' *On the Crown* (43). Speaking of King Philip of Macedon, he declares that the Thessalians and Thebans considered him "their friend, benefactor, and savior." It must have seemed ludicrous to some that this child born at Bethlehem could qualify as a savior or liberator. Luke does not apologize. This is part of the revolutionary character of the New Age—the unexpected becomes an invitation to faith.

This Savior is both **Christ** and **Lord** ("Christ the Lord"; cf. Acts 2:36, and see Luke 1:43). The term "Lord" *(kyrios),* here used in the sense that it ordinarily carried when applied to a head of state, interprets "Christ" *(christos)* for the Greek world. **In the city of David** specifies again that Jesus the Messiah is of Davidic descent (cf. Luke 1:69). At Luke 20:41–43 the terms "Christ," "Lord," and "David" are again linked. Acts 2—4 shows the importance of such Davidic association.

2:12. The shepherds do not ask for a "sign" *(sēmeion),* but the angel gives them one (cf. 1:18–20, Zechariah; and 1:36, Mary). Such confirmation of divine intervention was common in Israel's history (e.g., Exod. 3:12; 1 Sam. 2:34; Isa. 37:30). It almost sounds like a joke: **You will find a babe wrapped in swaddling cloths and lying in a manger.** Yet it is a sign. The shepherds are not to be disappointed after their vision.

The very humble circumstances of this Savior's birth (cf. v. 7) are his choicest credentials. He identified with peasant people at his birth. At his crucifixion he will identify with a criminal (23:43). Such identification will exact a price from anyone who would understand God's work in and through him—that price is faith (cf. 7:9)! To Solomon, the personification of wisdom, was attributed the confession that, like all others, he was nursed in **swaddling cloths** (Wisd. of Sol. 7:4). A greater than Solomon is here (Luke 11:31), but in addition to wearing swaddling cloths he must lie in a

manger. Like wisdom itself, he is a stranger to the world (cf. *Enoch* 42:1–2);
and the Son of humanity has no place to lay his head (Luke 9:58). Isaiah
complains: "The ox knows its owner, and the ass its master's crib; but Israel
does not know, my people does not understand" (Isa. 1:3). This passage may
well have been a stimulant in the recitation of the tradition from which Luke
drew. If so, the sign is indeed prophetic.

2:13. The word "suddenly" *(exaiphnēs)* marks either an end-time occurrence (eschatological) or a supramundane occurrence (cf. Luke 9:39; Acts
9:3; 22:6; see also Acts 2:2; 16:26; 28:6, where a related term is used). Luke
surrounds the announcement of the humble birth with two declarations of
glory, themselves a cradle of consummate literary artistry. The second of
these speaks of **a multitude of the heavenly host.** Daniel 7:10 indicates
what is meant by "multitudes" *(plēthos).* (See also Ps. 68:17; *Enoch* 40:1;
71:7–11.)

To highlight his own prestige, Caesar Augustus wrote in his *Res Gestae*
(10) that Rome had never seen so great a multitude as the one that gathered
from every part of Italy for his election. In Luke's narrative Jesus eclipses
Augustus. The phrase **heavenly host** (cf. Acts 7:42) is similar to formulations used in the OT both of heavenly bodies (Jer. 8:2; 19:13) and of God's
attendants (1 Kings 22:19). In intertestamental times, angels are associated
with stars (cf. *Enoch* 43). Some of the angels disobeyed God's orders and
raised up a race of giants (cf. *Enoch* 10; Jude 6–7; and see Gen. 6:2). They are
called "wandering [i.e., erring] stars" at Jude 13, in a metaphor describing
false teachers.

2:14. Psalms 147—150 are the best commentary on v. 14, which is composed of two separate statements connected by the conjunction "and" (the
RSV interprets this conjunction as a part of the acclamation):

> "Glory to God in the highest"
> and
> "On earth peace among people with whom God is pleased."

These words are in form an encomium, with phraseology similar to that
incised in honor of Augustus (see on v. 4). "Glory" *(doxa)* refers to the
recognition taken of God's mighty action in humanity's behalf. Jesus is the
instrument of that action. Thus this passage anticipates the amplification of
the theme of glory and glorification expressed in 4:15; 5:25–26; 7:16; 13:13;
17:15, 18; 18:43; 19:38; 21:27; 23:47; 24:26.

Since the angels are associated with the heavenly bodies, they speak of
God's glory **in the highest,** that is, among the hosts of heaven (cf. Ps.
148:1, "in the heights"). First the majesty of God is given expression. The
question is, Will human beings be able to stand in the presence of such
glory? This tension is resolved by the second statement. **On earth** forms a

contrast to **in the highest.** Luke will make a big point of this in a subsequent narrative (cf. 5:24). The majesty of God does not preclude the possibility of an encounter favorable to people. "Peace" *(eirēnē)* is the assurance that God does not seek to crush people but to establish a relationship with them (see on 1:79). "Among people" does not refer to international or interpersonal relationships but to human beings as the recipients of God's benefits. This thought is amplified by the concluding phrase, "with whom God is pleased" (cf. Ps. 149:4).

There is general agreement that the meaning of this last phrase is now beyond all controversy. The words in Luke 2:14b do not mean that God is pleased with people because of their status as respected members of a religious community. Not national origin, nor descent from Abraham, nor conformity to ceremony determines their acceptance by God. For God takes "no delight [pleasure] in sacrifice" (Ps. 51:16), but in those who fear God (Ps. 147:10–11; cf. 34:18, and note the emphasis on salvation; 51:17; Isa. 66:2). The oppressed and the needy will see God's salvation (Ps. 69:29–32), and they are heard in the acceptable time (i.e., the time of God's good pleasure, Ps. 69:13).

The angels' message reiterates the theme of the Magnificat. The mighty are brought low and the lowly exalted, and the shepherds are among the latter. Related thoughts on God's "good pleasure" were expressed at Qumran (cf. 1QH 4:32–33; 11:9), but the perspective differs somewhat from Luke's theology (see Luke 10:21). A similar juxtaposition of the majesty of God and favor displayed to the humble is found in Isa. 57:15 (cf. 66:2):

> I dwell in the high and holy place,
> and also with one who is of a contrite and humble
> spirit.★

In sum, to have the assurance of God's favorable intention is equivalent to experiencing the peace of God (cf. Isa. 57:17–21), and the messiah is the point of demonstration for that peace (cf. Isa. 9:6; 62:4). The angels' declaration echoes the promise of Luke 1:79 and anticipates the acclamation recorded at 19:38.

2:15–17. The faith of the shepherds is revealed by their decision to proceed to Bethlehem to **see this thing** (cf. Acts 10:37).

2:16. As did Mary in an earlier recital (Luke 1:39), the shepherds **went with haste.** Their speed is in response to the heavenly timetable: "Today." What they found at Bethlehem is spelled out in detail in order to emphasize the nature of the response that follows. Depth of spiritual commitment is determined by the quality of one's fidelity after the majestic voice is no longer heard.

2:17. The shepherds find an ordinary Jewish couple and the child who lies in the manger, but instead of being disappointed they published the angelic interpretation of the child Jesus (cf. 1:65). Thus they are the first evangelists. Characteristic of the literary restraint in this recital is the absence of a reference to an act of worship by the shepherds.

2:18. Their listeners "wondered" *(thaumazō)*, a normal response to description of divine actions (cf. Luke 1:21, 63) but not necessarily indicative of faith (cf. Acts 3:12). Wonderment can even be associated with unbelief (Luke 24:41). The contrast with Mary's response (v. 19) suggests that the person of Jesus will be subject to misunderstanding (cf. 4:22–24; 8:25; 9:43–45; 11:14–16).

2:19. Since angelic manifestations are a characteristic of apocalyptic, although of course not limited to such writing, Luke describes Mary's reaction in language very close to that used in a description of Daniel (Dan. 7:28 and cf. Luke 1:66). Similarly, Jacob pondered the significance of Joseph's dreams (Gen. 37:11; cf. *Testament of Levi* 6:2). The Greek term for "pondering" *(symballō)* suggests that Mary was "trying to get it all together." How God's purpose will develop is not yet apparent. To receive a vision is one thing. To understand its meaning in the concrete circumstances of life is another matter (cf. "kept all these things," Luke 2:51). But Mary is a model for the community (cf. 1:45), and thoughtful hearing of the word of God is a major theme in Luke's Gospel (see 8:15, 19–21; 10:39; 11:28).

2:20. The shepherds return without depreciation of enthusiasm and add their praises to those of the angels (see v. 13). Luke has a high regard for these shepherds. They do not ask for signs, and they believe what they have been told by their heavenly visitor. The disciples will display far less faith and understanding when they hear the predictions of the suffering and death of this same one who was acclaimed by shepherds (cf. 9:45; 24:25–26). Glorification or praise of God (cf. Dan. 3:26, 55 LXX) is one of Luke's favorite themes in description of responses to divine action (Luke 5:25–26; 7:16; 13:13; 17:15; 18:43; 23:41; Acts 4:21; 11:18; 21:20).

The Naming of the Infant

Luke 2:21

2:21. As in the case of John (Luke 1:59), the evangelist attaches greater significance to the naming of Jesus than to the circumcision. Lest there be any doubt about the divine purpose behind this child, Luke reminds his auditors that this was the name decreed by the angel (1:31). All the deeper, therefore, is the mystery of his person. This one, heralded by angels, enters into the mainstream of Israel's history through the normal route taken by every male Israelite. But his life-and-death style will put every norm under investigation.

The Presentation

Luke 2:22–24

2:22–24. The RSV obscures the fact that the initial clauses of vv. 21 and 22 consist of eight words and are structurally parallel, with the first three words in each reading: *kai hote eplēsthesan* ("when the days were fulfilled," i.e., "when the time came"). Through the parallel structures Luke calls attention to the importance of the two procedures that are described in vv. 21–24.

In the announcement to Mary, the child is also to be called "holy" (1:35). Thus 2:21 corresponds to 1:31, and 2:22–24 corresponds to 1:35. Luke's use of the pronoun "their" is typical of colloquial imprecision that is found in the best classical writings. It is not their collective purification that is required, but engagement by the parents in the purification process for the mother. Levitical ordinance did not require purification for the husband, nor is anything said about purification of a firstborn son.

Combination of two different legal prescriptions complicates this paragraph for the modern reader. In accordance with the Law of Moses, Mary had to complete a period of "purification" *(katharismos)* that continued thirty-three days after the circumcision (Lev. 12:2–4). During this period the mother was not allowed to come near the temple. Thus Luke confronts his publics with the astounding circumstance that Jesus, who came to restore relationships between people and God, now involves his mother in ritual impurity. Paul did not overstate the case: "born under the law" (Gal. 4:4).

At the end of the period the mother was to present to "the priest at the door of the tent of meeting" a year-old lamb as a burnt offering and a young pigeon or a turtledove for a sin offering (Lev. 12:6). If she could not afford a lamb, she could bring **a pair of turtledoves** or **two young pigeons,** one for each of the offerings. Mary. is one of the "poor" in the land (cf. Luke 6:20) and offers two birds. The second prescription (**Every male that opens the womb shall be called holy to the Lord;** cf. Exod. 13:2, 12, 15) concerned the presentation of the firstborn (cf. Luke 2:7 and see the comment on 1:35). Luke does not mention the customary fee of five sanctuary shekels for redemption of the child (cf. Num. 3:47; 18:16) but uses the occasion of Mary's offering for her purification as an opportunity to introduce Simeon's encounter with Jesus at the temple.

The Law of Moses did not prescribe appearance at the temple, but the presentation at that sacred place is itself especially meaningful, since Jesus, the Son of God, is presented to his Parent, as Samuel was once dedicated to God (1 Sam. 1:11–28). Thus the declaration of the angel (see Luke 1:35) is profoundly fulfilled. Acquitted of responsibility for the normal priesthood in Israel, Jesus will nevertheless be the one who marks the place of meeting between God and the People of God.

Dogmaticians have argued at length whether Jesus was born with Mary's womb remaining closed. A glance at Luke 2:22–24 should have spared them much useless speculation. Luke is more interested in the impact he can make through his account on Greco-Roman auditors. Having heard of the alleged lack of traditional religious credentials in Christian communities, they would be impressed by this record of painstaking devotion to hallowed Jewish institutions. Piety and uprightness, the two basic virtues for Greco-Romans and Jews, pervade the infancy narrative.

Simeon and Hannah (Anna)

Luke 2:25–38

Greco-Romans were accustomed to attestations of excellence, especially with reference to the honorand's contributions to the welfare of the community or the state. Similarly, the public addressed by Jesus son of Sirach heard about the piety and performance of the most famed in Israel (Sirach 44—50). In Luke 2:25–38 Jesus of Nazareth receives endorsement from two superb examples of Jewish piety.

Simeon   Luke 2:25–35

2:25. Luke marks the entry of Simeon (meaning "[God] has heard") on the scene with the words "And behold" (RSV: **now**). Resembling Job of old (Job 1:1) and Zechariah (Luke 1:6), Simeon is **righteous and devout** (dikaios kai eulabēs). That is, he was anxious to conform to God's will and showed himself conscientious in his religious obligations (cf. Acts 2:5; 8:2; 22:12). By describing Simeon in terms that suggest to both Jews and Greco-Romans an ideal member of the community (on the Greek side, see Plato Politikos 311B), Luke opens a literary path for the inference that Jesus, who is about to be extolled by Simeon, is the very definition of excellence.

There is no proof that Simeon was a very old man, but the association of one who is about to die with one who has just been given life dramatically highlights the problem that is about to be exposed: the tug of the past and the thrust of the future. And joy does not come without tears. It is questionable whether any passage in literature contains more compression of the basic structures of human existence. Despite his age, Simeon is already enrolled among those who "shall dream dreams" (Acts 2:17).

Simeon was **looking for the consolation of Israel.** This appears to echo Isa. 40:1–2. People in the ancient world ordinarily conceived of deliverance in terms of divine manifestation, or human instrumentality, or both. Simeon's expectation (cf. Luke 2:38; 12:36; 23:51) is of a similar order and is emphasized so as to focus on the fulfillment at hand in the person and work of Jesus (for such association, see also 24:21). At the same time, Luke confronts his readers with the fact that an amateur or a layperson, not a scribe or a chief priest, interprets the real significance of this child (cf. 10:21–24). At 6:24 Luke will show how pitiful is the shortsightedness that identifies the divine consolation with financial success. Later it will be said of the post-Easter Christians that they were filled with the "consolation" (RSV: "comfort") of the Holy Spirit (Acts 9:31; cf. 13:15). Similarly, Luke here links "consolation" *(paraklēsis)* and the Holy Spirit. **The Holy Spirit was upon him** means that he was empowered by God to understand what God was doing at this hour in Israel's history.

2:26. Simeon has no independent knowledge of the peculiar circumstances surrounding the birth of the infant Jesus, but the same Holy Spirit who was responsible for the entry of Jesus into the world had communicated to Simeon in some way that he **should not see death before he had seen the Lord's Christ.** According to biblical and rabbinic tradition, the Holy Spirit would make his presence known especially in the messianic age (cf. Isa. 40:1; Joel 2:28–29; SB 2:126–27).

Luke's heavy stress on the Holy Spirit in these initial chapters is in accord with such understanding and emphasizes that it is God who gives this child all the credentials he needs. Greco-Roman auditors, familiar with the important role played by oracles in Mediterranean culture, would see in the emphasis on Simeon's encounter with the divine a further indication of the exceptional status of the child whose destiny he is about to interpret.

The fulfillment of Simeon's expectation carries out the theme announced at 1:1 and is the answer to a poignant question once asked by an ancient poet (Ps. 89:48). At the same time, it is the realization of the prophecy made by Zechariah (Luke 1:79). The phrase **the Lord's Christ** (similar in form to "the Christ of God" in 9:20) assures auditors that the "consolation" of v. 25 is the Messiah.

2:27. The Spirit had given Simeon hope and now leads him to its realization, for he comes to the temple **inspired by the Spirit.** Again it is clear that what Simeon is about to say in the temple is of prophetic inspiration, without prior acquaintance with this child or his parents. Luke sharpens the auditor's appreciation of this fact with the observation that Simeon came in at the time they were acting **according to the custom of the law.** To all appearances, this was an ordinary Jewish child, but Simeon will interpret along different lines. Jesus will one day welcome children into his presence (18:15–17); now Simeon takes Jesus into his arms.

2:28. Simeon **blessed God.** This means that he recognizes Jesus as a remarkable demonstration of God's goodness. Then he gives utterance to the poem known as the Nunc Dimittis. As an expression of hope that finds fulfillment, it rivals the words spoken by the watchman in Aischylos's

Agamemnon (lines 20–24). Long he had waited for the signal fire that would announce the fall of Troy:

> Now would this sentry find release from toil,
> and see the murky-nighted beacon fire
> beam with good news. O hail, bright light!
> that makes the night as day and brings to Argos
> joy of dance and song in Fortune's hour.

2:29. "Now" *(nyn)* is the first word in the Greek phrasing of Simeon's poem and emphasizes that the present moment is the hour of salvation. Greco-Roman auditors were accustomed to finding this particle used as introduction to a statement of reversal in fortune, ordinarily from prosperity to disaster. To those of his public who were steeped in Jewish tradition, Simeon's statement of reversal would be heard as a refutation of popular apocalyptic doctrine.

Despota, the Greek word for **Lord,** occurs only here and at Acts 4:24 in Luke's two-volume work and means "Master" (see also Dan. 3:37 LXX; 9:8, 16, 17, 19; Rev. 6:10). In Greek literature it is used in reference to deities and heads of state as well as to those of lesser status. The term is appropriate as a foil for Simeon's own self-designation as "slave" (RSV less accurately: **servant**). As a faithful Israelite, Simeon acknowledges himself as one who is exclusively dedicated to the service of God (see on 1:38, and cf. Rev. 1:1; 2:20; 7:3; 15:3; 19:2).

The words **now lettest ... depart in peace** are better rendered: "Now you are permitting me to depart in peace." The word for "depart" *(apoluō)* is thematic (cf. Luke 8:33; 13:12; 14:4) and is here a euphemism for death (cf. Gen. 15:2; Num. 20:29 LXX; Tob. 3:6). Similarly, a gentile philosopher wrote: "When God gives the signal and *releases* you from this service, then you shall go to God" (Epiktetos 1.9.16). There is some measure of dignity in meeting the inevitability of death with a sense of reservation for the future.

"In peace" is reminiscent of Luke 1:79; 2:14. Simeon had been assured that he would not die before he had seen the Christ. Now he expresses his confidence that the promise has found fulfillment **(according to thy word).** In similar vein Jacob expresses his willingness to die, now that he has seen Joseph (Gen. 46:30). The only alternative to this interpretation is to suppose that Simeon sees in this hour a release from his "slavery." But this is improbable, since he loves God his Master and would not seek manumission on any terms, for even in heaven the redeemed are called slaves (Rev. 19:5; 22:3: RSV: "servants"). Luke might have had in mind the oppression experienced by the "poor" in the land *(anawim;* see on 6:20), but this thought does not accord with the context. Simeon is able to "depart in peace," for the time of the Messiah is the age of fresh assurance of God's concern for his people. Thus Simeon's words begin where the Benedictus had left off (Luke 1:79). Such expressions of hope are in brilliant contrast to the despair expressed on countless headstones of antiquity. This epitaph commemorating an unwedded woman exemplifies many:

> Leonto is my name, a virgin when I died
> like a new flower, first blossom of the timely
> blooming hour. About to wed, at fifteen years
> I join the dead in this long sleep.
>   (*Inscriptiones Graecae* 9.2.649.)

2:30. Simeon now gives the reason for his statement on peace. Once salvation was a matter of promise, but according to Isa. 40:5 (quoted at Luke 3:6) it would one day be seen. Simeon's function in the narrative is to establish the fact that Jesus is in his person the embodiment of the salvation spoken of in the Benedictus (1:69–71, 77). The contrast between what is here seen and the moment of "death" that is viewed at 2:26 conveys a suggestion of life in the use of the term "salvation" *(sōtēria)*. The combination sets up a further contrast to the gloom-filled moment recited in 2:35, and the effect is painfully poignant. No one escapes the sight of death. The Roman poet Horace shattered such euphemism and wrote: "One night awaits us all" (*Odes* 1.18.15). But, says the poet-historian of the New Age, life in its fullest phase can be seen and it triumphs over the night. This was Zechariah's anticipation (Luke 1:79). Yet there will be those who experience the ultimate reverse—a fall from the light that has drawn so close. All humanity meets at the threshold of this text.

2:31. This salvation God has **prepared in the presence of all peoples,** a thought expressed in Isa. 52:10 and Ps. 98:2. But the wording of the Greek version of Isaiah and the psalm (LXX: *ethnos*) is ordinarily rendered "gentiles," not "peoples" (but see Ps. 97:9 LXX). The alteration here is in line with one of the main themes in the Gospel, that the good news comes to all nations by way of Israel and that no one nation, not even Israel, has a monopoly on salvation. Gentiles can also lay claim to peoplehood under God; and Israel, albeit a nation of special privilege as light-bearer, is only one people out of many peoples.

2:32. The term "all peoples" in v. 31 is divided here in v. 32 into two separate groups: gentiles and Israel. God's salvation is to be **a light for revelation to the Gentiles** (cf. Acts 13:47; 18:6). Psalm 97:2 LXX (98:2 RSV), in combination with Isa. 40:5 and 49:6 (cf. 42:6), suggests how the passage is to be understood.

In the Magnificat (Luke 1:54), reference was made to Ps. 98:3, and the promise of mercy was limited to Israel. Luke 2:32 adds the thought expressed at Ps. 98:2 and includes the gentiles as beneficiaries of the light that Zechariah had anticipated for Israel (Luke 1:78). This light brings revelation (the Greek word [*apokalypsis*] is the term for "apocalypse") or salvation to the gentiles. Auditors with roots in Greco-Roman traditions would readily grasp the imagery: Achilles, sang Homer, was a "light to the Greeks" (*Iliad* 16.39). A rhetorician named Menander echoed entrenched tradition when he counselled budding orators to reinforce the narrative of a king's birth by likening him to a shining star already from his mother's womb (cf. Luke 1:41).

And for glory to thy people Israel. Instead of **for glory,** it is best to render "as glory," making glory stand with light in apposition to salvation (v. 30). Simeon sees Jesus as the light *(phōs)* and the glory *(doxa)*. Isaiah 46:13 (cf. 9:2) seems to be the source for the closing phrase. Jesus is the climax of God's revelations to Israel (cf. Luke 20:9–18; Acts 7:52; 13:23). Therefore Jesus is Israel's glory and the means whereby she can achieve her ultimate purpose as God's people. The Benedictus expressed hope for rescue from those who oppressed her (Luke 1:71–73). Psalm 91:15 declares that those who are in trouble will be rescued by the Lord, who will honor (or, glorify) them. This thought is expressed at greater length in Isaiah 60 (see esp. 60:19).

Once it was said of Moses that he was unable to enter the tent of meeting, lest he die, for the glory of the Lord filled the tabernacle (Exod. 40:35). Simeon now beholds the glory of the Lord and is prepared to make his departure, for he has found peace and has seen the light in the shadow of death (cf. Luke 1:79). But there are others who will deny themselves such experience, and of them Simeon shortly will speak.

2:33. And his father and his mother marveled at what was said about him. The colloquial style of the Greek with which this verse opens (a singular verb with two nouns and a plural participle) helps to set off the carefully balanced phrasing of the blessing in vv. 29–32 and the somberly toned address to Mary in vv. 34–35.

Despite the angel's revelation to Mary (1:31–35) and the news brought by the shepherds (2:17), the parents of Jesus respond with astonishment and perplexity (cf. 1:29; 2:18) at Simeon's prophecy. It is difficult for them to connect his words with their child. But if his own parents do not grasp the miracle of divine purpose, what is to be expected of Israel as a whole? This question is the theme of Simeon's concluding prophecy, and the dramatic tension that will finally break at a cross-crowned hill begins to tighten. Luke's reference to the father and mother of Jesus is a hint of the mystery that will confound many, and the high court of Israel will condemn Jesus for claiming to be the Son of God (22:70–71). Mary herself will soon have more to ponder (see 2:49–51).

2:34. Before announcing the coming of the gloom that is to put the light into question, **Simeon blessed** the parents. What is to come will be under divine direction and they are especially privileged participants in God's purposes. Then he addresses Mary personally, for this child is not Joseph's but hers. Thus Luke stresses the prophetic power of Simeon and thereby sharpens the focus on the extraordinary person in Simeon's arms. The word "behold" *(idou)* calls Mary to attention:

> **Behold, this child is set for the fall and rising of many in Israel,**
> **and for a sign that is spoken against**
> **(and a sword will pierce through your own soul also),**
> **that thoughts out of many hearts may be revealed.** (vv. 34–35)

To be "set for the fall and rising" means that Jesus is the point of decision for Israel. The words reflect the thought expressed in Elizabeth's Magnificat that the mighty are to be brought low and the humble exalted (1:52–53; cf. 6:20–26; 16:25). Those who consider themselves "arrived" (cf. 3:8; 13:28) in the Kingdom of God will fall, that is, find themselves outside; those whom the elite consider least likely to succeed will rise, that is, be welcomed into fellowship with God (cf. 13:29; 18:13–14). The Book of Acts will dramatize the truth of Simeon's warning. Three thousand persons, according to Acts 2:41, received the apostolic message, and Acts 4:4 refers to five thousand believers in a context of opposition. Receptive and unreceptive Jews are contrasted in Acts 13:42–45, which includes the very expression "speak against" that appears here in Luke 2:34 (see also Acts 17:1–9; 18:1–8, 19–22). And Acts ends with an exhibit of division at Rome (Acts 28:25).

By placing Simeon's prediction about steady resistance against the backdrop of his positive declarations concerning God's firm desire to reach out in saving love (Luke 2:30–32), Luke achieves a contrapuntal effect that is dynamically exhibited in the concluding measures of Paul D. Weber's musical rendition, *Song of Simeon* (1986).

The language of Isa. 8:14–15 applies to the first of the two groups identified in the "fall-rise" theme. According to the prophet, God is "a rock of stumbling . . . and many shall stumble thereon; they shall fall and be broken." Luke 20:18 applies a similar thought to those who are hostile to the "stone which . . . has become the head of the corner" (Luke 20:17, quoting Ps. 118:22; cf. Acts 4:11). Micah 7:8 indeed speaks of the rising of those who have fallen and are ridiculed by their enemies, but the passage is no argument for viewing Luke 2:34 as a description of one class of people, who fall and then rise. At Luke 2:34 the falling lies in the future. Micah 7:8 pictures it as a present reality for the oppressed. Lowly people like that, says Simeon, are certain to have a rising, that is, a vindication from God. People who think of themselves as insiders will be told that the Ninevites are to have such privileged status (Luke 11:32).

Luke's infancy narratives convey a hard reality, of which T. S. Eliot shows such firm grasp in the "Interlude" of his *Murder in the Cathedral*. Within a few months the high anticipation of restored relationships (see 1:17) turns into realization that humanity's routine patterns of dissension are not easily exorcised. And at 12:51–53 Jesus himself will repitch the language of peace that was pronounced at 2:14. The fact that the credentials of Jesus do not seem to measure up to messianic specifications will prompt many to ask for a sign (cf. 11:29–32). Already the angel had declared a manger the sign of the messianic presence (2:12). No other sign would be given. Jesus' message, his proclamation, would be his badge of authority (11:29). Another Herod will find that he cannot budge Jesus from that decision (23:8–9).

Jesus himself being a sign will find himself **spoken against.** In Luke this expression occurs always in contexts expressing hostility from religious elements (Luke 20:27; Acts 13:45; 28:19, 22). It was and remains the fate of Jesus that much of the opposition to him or to his principles comes from the ranks of those who claim allegiance to God. But those who do the opposing also do the falling (cf. Luke 20:18). And the fact that the division does take place is proof of the credentials of Jesus. He knew it well and sold nothing at bargain prices (cf. 12:51–53; 15:25–33).

2:35. It is certainly a mistake to put within parentheses the climactic words of Simeon's description (as in the RSV). In form the prophecy preceding the statement of purpose resembles the more elaborate predictions by Jesus of his own death (9:22; 18:32). This veiled reference to the outcome of the call to decision in Israel makes more credible the introduction of the hostility at Nazareth (4:29) early in Luke's narrative. Luke's conception here is of a piece with his sensitivity to women and their experiences and is not to be associated with a Johannine view of Mary at the foot of the cross.

The sword that pierces through Mary will inch its way into her heart as the months of Jesus' public ministry record a series of rejections that culminate at Calvary. Moreover, it is typically oriental to describe the fate of a child through the sorrow of the mother. The figure of the "sword" echoes Ezek. 14:17 (see also *Sibylline Oracles* 3:316), and the phrase **pierce through your own soul** is similar to formulation in Ps. 36:15. The Greek word for the type of sword *(rhomphaia)* mentioned by Simeon refers to a very heavy weapon, signaling terrible destruction.

This final statement, **that thoughts out of many hearts may be revealed,** expresses the divine objective in all that Simeon has said about the child. The apparent failure of Jesus is no sign of divine displeasure. On the contrary, through him God strips people of all disguise. The Greek word for "thoughts" *(dialogismoi)* appears frequently in Luke-Acts in the sense of hostile attitudes, ordinarily resident in the religious leaders (cf. 5:22; 6:8; 20:14, but as a verb). Since the scribes and the Pharisees, the core of the religious establishment, claim devotion to God, the genuineness of their claim will be tested in their response to Jesus. This is what it means to have the thoughts **revealed** (cf. 12:1–3; 16:14; 20:19; and see 1 Cor. 14:25). The verb for "revealed" *(apokalyptō)* makes an ironic contrast to the noun "revelation" in v. 32. Outsiders will benefit from the light; insiders will be exposed by the light.

Simeon began with a vision of large vistas for Israel (vv. 29–32). He closes with compelling demand for a decision that no one can evade. At this text, horizons are bridged, and antiquarian preference cannot silence the demand. The high spiritual moment, the crescendo of full-throated choirs—all this may give a feeling of walking in the presence of God. But the critical hour is the moment when one encounters the needs of the poor, the outcast, the forgotten ones; when the course lies to the right or to the left, to the safe and easy haven or to the dangerous, the creative, and the imagined possibility. Then the integrity of the heart's devotion will be known. The sword that has gone through the land; the chasms in the social structure—these have also at the beginning of the twenty-first century laid bare the emptiness of much that lays claim to God and have annulled much of the vision of what might have been. Whatever failure there is, Luke is adamant—it cannot be charged to the account of Jesus.

Hannah (Anna)   Luke 2:36–38

2:36–37. The second witness in the temple precincts is Hannah (meaning "grace"). In Greek her name is spelled the same as Hannah's in 1 Samuel. It is unfortunate that the RSV obscured Luke's evident effort to signal the intimate connection of his total infancy narrative with the early chapters of 1 Samuel. Hannah is one of a number of female prophets who appear on the pages of Scripture: Miriam (Exod. 15:20), Deborah (Judg. 4:4), Huldah (2 Kings 22:14), Noadiah (Neh. 6:14), the wife of Isaiah (Isa. 8:3), and Jezebel (Rev. 2:20). To a large extent, prophesying found continuance in the proclamation of the later regularized public ministry.

Like Simeon, this aged woman is a model of the type of person who is open to the vision of the New Age (Acts 2:18). Until ecclesiastical regulations foreclosed on the right of women to use such gifts as hers within the perimeters of a sanctuary, the People of God found enrichment through the preaching of such as Hannah. In the pre-Luke cycle of the infancy narratives her father's name, **Phanuel,** may have suggested associations with a place-name in Gen. 32:30–31. In this Genesis passage the variant form Penuel means "face of God." Phanuel is a transliteration of the Hebrew place-name. Hannah, one would then infer, has a face-to-face encounter with God in this messianic gift to Israel. But Luke could not have intended his public to grasp such complicated etymological associations. If the meaning of a Hebrew name is important, he translates it (cf. Acts 1:19) or replaces it with a Greek equivalent (Luke 23:33).

Hannah is **of the tribe of Asher,** a tribe in northern Palestine. Asher (meaning "happy") was eighth in line of birth (Gen. 30:12–13), is mentioned last in the list of Jacob's sons (Gen. 35:26), and appears in ninth place in Jacob's blessing (Gen. 49:20). The political history of the tribe was insignificant, and the name is omitted from the list of rulers at 1 Chron. 27:16–22. As were Zechariah and Elizabeth, Hannah is described as **of a great age** (the Greek verb used in Luke 1:7 is identical with the one in 2:36: *probainō*).

Hannah had been married for seven years and remained a widow for eighty-four years (not the RSV's **till she was eighty-four**; see comment below). To emphasize the integrity of her character, Luke records that she had never remarried. Gravestones of antiquity praise spouses for renouncing a second marriage. This act of self-denial was considered a mark of special piety, and the writer of 1 Timothy cites it as a requirement for church administrators and for widows who are to be enrolled on an official list (1 Tim. 3:2, 12; 5:9).

Having lost her principal means of support, Hannah cast herself completely on the mercy of God (cf. Luke 21:1–4) and spent her time continually in the temple precincts. There she worshiped God with **fasting and prayer night and day** (cf. Luke 24:53; Acts 26:7; cf. Judith 11:17). This appraisal bears the marks of what is called hyperbole, or literary exaggeration, designed to accent her profound piety. A similar sketch of the model widow is set forth in 1 Tim. 5:5.

Luke's description on the whole bears a remarkable resemblance to an earlier portrayal of Judith, a heroine of Jewish history. Judith also was a widow, and she fasted all the days of her widowhood, except on festivals (Judith 8:4–8). She refused offers of a second marriage and died at the age of 105 (Judith 16:22–23). The high age attributed by Luke to Hannah parallels that of Judith. Given fourteen years as the age of marriage, seven additional years plus eighty-four would add up to 105 years. Luke's ambivalent syntax not only permits this view of a very advanced age but even seems to demand it.

Luke, who otherwise displays some familiarity with intertestamental writings, may well have thought of the parallel with Judith, and in any event some of his auditors who were familiar with the more ancient story would have made the connection. Whatever the possibilities, the verdict on Judith applies to Hannah: "There was none who spoke an evil word against her; for she feared God exceedingly" (Judith 8:8*).

Luke's interest in Hannah's genealogy is now apparent. It is of importance to him that this aged woman is an Israelite born and bred. Others will boast of Abraham as their father (cf. Luke 3:8; 16:19–31). Not only does Hannah have the lineage but she is an Israelite good and true. Her tribe may be insignificant, but God raises the lowly, and the mighty fall. Jesus receives the attestation of prophets who have the finest credentials. Zechariah, Elizabeth, Simeon, and now Hannah—all these are Israel as Israel ought to be, and the reader will soon see that these contrast with some among the scribes and Pharisees and chief religious administrators. Among the last was Hannas (RSV: "Annas," 3:2), who bears the masculine form of Hannah's name. Simeon's presence in the temple was motivated by a special revelation. Hannah requires no previous notice, for she is in constant attendance in the temple area.

Hannah's piety finds itself matched in the plaintive words engraved by a devotee of Asklepios:

> These are the words of your loving servant, O Asklepios. . . . O blessed one, joy of my desire, my Divine Head, how can I come to your golden dwelling while I lack the strength in my limbs that once brought me to your shrine, unless your heart is inclined to me and you are willing to heal and permit me once again to enter your abode, that I might behold you, my God, more resplendent than earth in the spring tide. (*Benefactor*, p. 193)

2:38. She gave thanks to God. The Greek word *anthomologeomai* ("to thank") occurs only here in the NT, but it is used in the Greek version of Ps. 79:13 in a context that speaks of God's salvation for Jerusalem and deliverance of prisoners (cf. Luke 1:68–75). Simeon had been looking for the consolation of Israel (2:25) and associated his expectation with the infant in his arms. Echoing Simeon, Hannah spoke to those who were looking for the **redemption of Jerusalem** (cf. Isa. 52:9; Luke 23:51) and said, "It is here in the person of this child" (cf. Luke 2:17). Isaiah 8:17 contrasts those who wait for the Lord with those who stumble (Isa. 8:15).

Hannah came at the **very hour** (see BAGD on the Greek phrasing) that Simeon had recited his prophecy of stumbling. Yet her faith remains firm. Two men on the road to Emmaus (Luke 24:21) will display less understanding than does Hannah.

The place of Jesus in the family of Israel has now been firmly nailed down. Jerusalem has heard the testimony out of two witnesses (cf. Deut. 19:15). It remains to be seen how those who found refuge in tradition will respond to that testimony.

Return to Nazareth

Luke 2:39–40

2:39. Jesus' parents **performed everything according to the law of the Lord.** Although Jesus was brought up in Galilee and in a village despised by religious circles, he shares in the traditions of his ancestors. And he has familial roots. This factor would be important for Greco-Roman auditors, but it forms a contrast to the apparent rootlessness of Jesus' adult life. John had gone into the wilderness (1:80). Jesus remains with his parents. But he will have his days in the desert (4:1–13).

2:40. Under the God-fearing tutelage of his parents **the child grew** physically and inwardly. The description in this verse is similar to that of Luke 1:66 and 80 (cf. Gen. 21:8, 20; Judg. 13:24; 1 Sam. 3:19), for Luke has now concluded his story of the parallel infancies of John and Jesus and established for his readers basic differences between the two. At the same time, Luke prepares his public for the growth of the post-Easter community, which is, as was Jesus, the product of the Holy Spirit's activity (cf. Acts 2:41, 47; 6:7; 12:24; 19:20).

John was empowered by the Spirit, as prophets normally were, for his prophetic task. Jesus is fathered by the Spirit and will receive the credentials of the Spirit for his messianic assignment—but after his baptism (3:21–22)—and will finally superintend the mission that was entrusted to Israel. At this point, therefore, Luke notes that he was **filled with wisdom** (cf. Wisd. of Sol. 7:7). "Wisdom" *(sophia)* is understanding of the will and purpose of God, reflected in performance according to the law of God (cf. Proverbs 1). Thus Luke sets the stage for his recital of the trip to Jerusalem, where Jesus will display not only exceptional intelligence but understanding of God's "favor" *(charis)* (Luke 1:28, 30). That same favor rests on the child. And with this note the aura of the annunciation blends into the routine of a Jewish child's upbringing.

Luke's restraint in describing the personal appearance of Jesus contrasts with the recommendation that the rhetorician Menander gave biographers of imperial personages three centuries later: "After the ancestral recital you must describe them along the following lines, that they were so brilliantly handsome from the moment of their birth that they rivalled the fairest star in the heavens" *(On Declamations* 613).

Jesus at the Age of Twelve

Luke 2:41–52

Luke did not set out to write edifying legends or a detailed biography of Jesus. He aims, rather, at establishing certainty concerning things "accomplished among us" (1:1–4) and selects such episodes and dialogue as will advance his avowed objective. Since the ultimate destiny of Jesus and his followers involves confrontation with Israel's cultic and theological establishment, as signaled by 2:34–35, it is literarily appropriate that Luke's public hear of the promise that Jesus showed already at the age of twelve as agent for the destined fulfillment.

Knowing how the story ends, Luke's auditors would note the contrast between the response at this time to Jesus' display of wisdom and the hostility that built up in official circles as time went on. Idyllic features in the infancy narrative cycle, punctuated at intervals by ominous notes, will soon give way to *Realpolitik.*

At the end of his thirteenth year a boy was obligated to observe all the commandments, including ritual regulations. The fact that Jesus is taken to the temple at his twelfth year indicates that his parents are concerned that in addition to his previous training he be introduced to other responsibilities that await him as a fully grown Israelite (cf. SB 2:144–47). Luke locates this fact within a larger perspective. Jerusalem is the locale where God begins and brings to a climax his redemptive purpose. Jesus goes to Jerusalem in complete harmony with the traditional law of Israel, yet more profoundly implicated than any Israelite in his obligation to One whom he recognizes as his Father, for he is the Son of God, declared so by an angel (1:35).

2:41–42. Whether women and children (with the exception of boys who had reached the age of thirteen) were to be excused from attending the three great feasts prescribed by Moses was a matter of debate among rabbis of a later time. The three feasts were Unleavened Bread (or Passover); Weeks, marking the end of the grain harvest; and Booths, commemorating the wandering in the wilderness (see Exodus 12 and 23; Leviticus 23; Numbers 28—29; Deuteronomy 16).

The piety of Jesus' parents is expressed by the observation that they went **every year at the feast of the Passover.** This feast is particularly noted, since the visit by Jesus anticipates one other trip that Jesus will make to Jerusalem, beginning at Luke 9:51 (the visit described at 4:9 is of a different order) and climaxing at the time of Passover. Auditors who caught the echoes of 1 Samuel in the earlier recitals might well recall that "Elkanah and all his house" were to be found annually at Shiloh (1 Sam. 1:21; cf. 2:19).

2:43–45. Despite their poverty (see on Luke 2:24), the family stay for the entire period of seven to eight days. They cut no corners. But Jesus stayed even longer. For the first time he is identified as **the boy** *(pais)*. Since Jesus is about to become a full-fledged Israelite, the term "child" (v. 40) no longer properly applies to him. But Luke appears to be sensitive to other implications in the term. Earlier he had used it in description of Israel (1:54) and of David (1:69). Isaiah 41:8 and 42:1 apply the term to Jacob (= Israel) in the sense of "servant." The second of these passages is especially significant, for it speaks of Israel's receipt of the Spirit.

According to Luke, Jesus is "the boy" or Servant of the Lord in a sense that transcends Israel's mission. Luke's story therefore suggests that Jesus comprehends in his person the identity of Israel, and this is demonstrated by his subsequent declaration of identity to his parents (2:49). Luke's usage in the Book of Acts confirms this line of interpretation (cf. Acts 3:13, 26; 4:27, 30). It is probable, therefore, that "boy" is to be understood in a double sense.

His parents did not know it. Inferences concerning possible neglect by the parents or thoughtlessness on the part of Jesus are irrelevant, and they obscure the literary function of Luke's reference to the parents' ignorance. Not only are the parents unaware of Jesus' whereabouts but they do not understand the situation. In the Greek there is no subject to the verb "know" (v. 43). They took it for granted that he would be **in the company,** that is, a caravan, with **kinsfolk and acquaintances.** But he, from whom acquaintances would one day remain at a distance (23:49), stands in a much closer relationship to Another, as he will be quick to inform his parents (2:49).

2:46. Like the Marys who failed to find the body of the Lord Jesus in the tomb (24:3), the parents looked for their son in the wrong place. **After three days they found him in the temple.** The phrase "after three days" has suggested to some interpreters Luke's use of "the third day" in reference to the resurrection of Jesus, but the references in the Gospel (9:22; 18:33; 24:7, 46) specifically note "on the third day," and the phrase "after three days" is used in other contexts in Acts 25:1; 28:17. On the other hand, Luke's auditors, who know how the story finally ends but do not know in advance Luke's variety in phrasing, would catch a hint of that lifting of the sword that was one day to pierce Mary's heart (Luke 2:35). Their world of community experience meets at the borders of the world of Luke's narrative.

They found him ... sitting among the teachers (cf. Wisd. of Sol. 8:10), even as he would on the third day be "among" the disciples (Luke 24:36). On this occasion, and on this occasion only, is Jesus described as being in the presence of teachers. Hereafter in the Gospel, Jesus will be the teacher (the one exception is John the Baptist, 3:12). Here Jesus is not a teacher but a pupil, for he was **listening to them and asking them questions.** One day his questions will pierce to the very core of the religious establishment, and he will give answers to his own questions (see, e.g., 11:19–20; 13:2–5).

2:47. All who heard him were amazed at his understanding and his answers. This is not the first time that amazement will be registered in connection with Jesus or events involving him (see the same verb [*existēmi*] used at Luke 8:56; 24:22; Acts 2:7, 12; and often).

Commentators have drawn attention to the parallel between this recital and other accounts of children who displayed extraordinary talent or ability. Plutarch relates the following about Alexander:

> Once, during King Philip's absence, legates from the king of Persia came to the court, and Alexander charmed them with his gracious hospitality and his inquiring manner. He put no puerile or trivial questions, but asked about distances and means of access to the interior and about the king and his military prowess. He made inquiry about the Persians, their courage in battle, and the strength of their forces. The envoys were impressed and concluded that Philip's reputed shrewdness was nothing compared to the young lad's aspiration for greatness. (*Alexander* 5)

Similarly, Josephus wrote of himself:

> When I was a child, about fourteen years of age, I was commended by all for my interest in learning. For this reason high priests and leading men of

the city came frequently to me in a body, to determine my view about
precise interpretations of the law. (*Life* 2)

The point of such evidence of promise in early youth was not to draw
attention to precocity as such. Indeed, the very word "precocity" is mislead-
ing, for a child of twelve in ancient times is the equivalent of a young person
of seventeen or eighteen in the United States. Rather, stories such as these
demonstrate that the later adult performance of the person in question was
no product of the moment but was part of a long-standing pattern of
commitment to excellence.

Greco-Roman society valued ancestral features, and an early display of
talent suggested innate rather than affected interest in the community.
Lucian's description of Demonax, a philosopher of the second century,
reflects a long tradition: "Already from boyhood he was moved by a resident
impulse toward nobility and by an innate love for philosophy" (*Demonax* 3).
Luke's incorporation of such type of encomium or eulogy therefore advances his thematic stress on Jesus as an Israelite of exceptional merit.
Begotten through the Holy Spirit, he is totally dedicated to his heavenly
Parent's purpose. Jesus demonstrates that fact by his intense desire to learn
what he can from Israel's experts in matters that have to do with his Parent.
Here at Jerusalem the genes show.

Luke had written at v. 40 that Jesus was filled with wisdom. The composer of the Wisdom of Solomon observed: Because of wisdom "I shall have
glory among multitudes, and honor in the sight of elders, though I be
young" (Wisd. of Sol. 8:10*; see also Sir. 47:14). Luke will point out that a
greater one than Solomon is here (Luke 11:31), and the residents of Capernaum will be astounded at the instruction of Jesus (4:32). But wisdom is not
a goal in itself. For an Israelite the summation of wisdom is to know and
love God and to do the divine will (cf. Prov. 28:7). Luke makes it abundantly
clear that what the centurion observed one dark hour (Luke 23:47) was true
of Jesus from the very beginning.

2:48. The syntax of the Greek bears the marks of colloquial recital. The
parents of Jesus on this occasion display a reaction similar to that of the
residents at Capernaum (4:32) and demonstrate that they do not com-
prehend the destiny of this child. But the focus is on Mary and her relationship to Jesus. Therefore she is the one who enters first into the dialogue.

It was natural for Mary to address her child as "Son" (the Greek word
teknon normally means "child"; at Luke 1:32, 35 the customary term for
"son" [*hyios*] is used). But Luke suggests that in a sense it was a misunderstanding on her part, intensified by her further words: **Behold, your
father and I have been looking for you anxiously.**

The rendering "anxiously" does not bring out the force of the Greek verb
(*odynaomai*), which speaks of pain, such as that experienced by those who
are faced with the prospect of never again seeing their loved one (Acts

20:38). Luke is the only writer in the NT to use the expression, and the two other instances occur at Luke 16:24 and 25, in the story of the tormented rich man. In the context of his total work the term is well chosen, for Simeon had predicted that a sword would pierce Mary's heart (2:35), and the three-day interval would one day be repeated. But the major literary impact results from collision of the universal motif of parental concern with an extraordinary commitment that involves denial of the customary parental claim. In competition with high destiny Mary must be the loser, but she will ultimately be with the winners (see Acts 1:14).

2:49. At the grave two men asked some women who were visiting the tomb of Jesus: "Why do you seek the living among the dead?" (Luke 24:5). Jesus asks his parents: **How is it that you sought me?** The words echo the language about the search at 2:44. There is good reason for addressing this and the next question to both parents. They must learn to live with the fact that he, their son, is a stranger and a guest in their house, for he is under orders from Another.

I must be in my Father's house. The Greek syntax is ambiguous, and Luke may have intended a double sense: "in my Father's house" or "with my Father." But the RSV renders correctly a common Greek idiom, and there is no doubt where the emphasis lies. Jesus is totally committed to God, his Father (1:35; cf. Ps. 27:4). Greco-Romans would think of a phrase such as the one found in an inscription in honor of a certain Aristagoras: "He walked in the footsteps of his ancestors" (*SIG* 708.6), that is, the genes show.

Unlike John, who comes on the scene at a later time, Jesus "knows" at the age of twelve, if not the content, the large dimension of his task. The word "must" (impersonal *dei*) characterizes his entire life (cf. 4:43; 9:22; 13:33; 17:25; 19:5; 22:37; 24:7, 26, 44). Only the Son knows the Father, and only the Father really knows the Son (10:21–22). And into the Father's hands he will one day commit his spirit (23:46). Greco-Roman auditors who recalled how tragedians explored the theme of conflict between obligation to traditional mores and the claims of a head of state or a superior (see, e.g., Aischylos *Prometheus Bound*; Sophokles *Antigone*) would subtract factors of stubbornness and ill will in the Greek productions and capture some of the breadth of meaning in Luke's masterful recital.

2:50. Jesus showed profound understanding (2:47) in the temple. His parents, on the other hand, **did not understand** what he had just told them. The future disciples of Jesus will not have less difficulty (18:34). But Jesus will finally expound all (24:45), for he is the Teacher of the community of Israel. It is probable that Mary, who was present with the Eleven in the "upper room" after Jesus' resurrection (Acts 1:12–14), was also among those gathered together at Pentecost (Acts 2:1). If such was the case, she again became the beneficiary of the Holy Spirit (Acts 2:4), but in a different manner from the event recorded in Luke 1:34.

2:51. Once again Luke draws the veil. Jesus, who was soon to reveal an extraordinarily free and creative spirit that would shock all Israel, returns to Nazareth: he **was obedient** to parents who did not understand the fire that burned within him. This return to Nazareth may appear to be in contradiction with Jesus' interest in staying at the temple. But Luke's technique of anticipating future developments must be kept in mind. Jerusalem is the ultimate goal, and one of Jesus' first acts on his arrival at the city will be the cleansing of the temple (19:45–46). There he will spend his time teaching (cf. 19:47; 20:1; 21:37). Again religious leaders will ask him questions, and he in turn will question them (20:1–8; cf. 22:53).

The experience at Jerusalem had a revelatory tone to it. Mary's response is appropriate. **And his mother kept all these things in her heart** (cf. Dan. 7:28, and see on Luke 2:19). The shepherd's recital, and now this! But why does Luke stress the fact that Mary, of all people, lacks fuller understanding? Modern attempts at psychologizing will not touch the meaning of Luke's narrative. The answer to the question is suggested by Luke's critique of popular apocalyptic. The credentials of Jesus are not to be determined by spectacular signs or special apocalyptic effects. The word of God, spoken also through the mouth of Jesus and of his chosen apostles, is the vehicle for the communication of God's purpose.

Despite the unusual experience of a visit from Gabriel himself, Mary is faced, says Luke, with the same problem that confronts all who hear the word of God. Ultimately faith, independent of signs, is the single port of entry into the mystery of Jesus' person. Mary is not relieved of that responsibility. Hence Jesus has no special comfort for those, including Mary, who claim a close physical kinship with him (8:19–21; 11:27–28). Except for these last passages and a brief mention at Acts 1:14, Mary disappears from the pages of Luke-Acts.

If, as some hold, Mary is representative of Israel, her disappearance in the succeeding narrative is all the more comprehensible. Now Israel must do like Mary and ponder the word that Jesus will bring. A story about another Mary will reinforce the point (10:38–42).

2:52. This verse demonstrates Luke's ability to relate both to a Semitic and to a Greco-Roman oriented public. Greco-Roman honorary documents frequently call attention to an honorand's superior excellence by stating that it was already manifest "from youth on." For example, a decree that was proclaimed at the ancient city of Priene praises a certain Herakleitos for offering his own way of life as a model for citizenship from "his earliest childhood" (*Benefactor*, p. 349).

The description here in v. 52 bears a resemblance, especially in the concluding words **with God and man,** to the thought expressed in 1 Sam. 2:21, 26 (cf. Prov. 3:4; Sir. 51:17). The phrase **increased in wisdom and in stature** is better rendered "advanced in wisdom and maturity." The formulation, apart from the word for "wisdom," follows the stereotyped wording found, for example, in the inscription cited in connection with v. 49. It is said of an official named Aristagoras that in the course of his duties "he advanced in maturity" (*SIG* 708.17); public servant that he was, he became even more effective in innovative approach to problems as time went on. Luke's emphasis, relative to the passage in 1 Samuel, on the word "wisdom," exemplifies his careful editorial technique. Jesus is a prophet in the tradition of Samuel, but he will be charged with breaking the Law of Moses. The Hellenistic cast of the verse would signify to a Greco-Roman public that Jesus is to be understood as a person of exceptional merit, deserving of public recognition. His Excellency Theophilos would appreciate the dash of bureaucratese.

The words **in favor with God and man** echo similar phrasing in 1 Sam. 2:26 (cf. Prov. 3:4; Sir. 45:1). They are a signal that the cycle of parallel accounts for the "infancy" of John and Jesus, with the first chapters of Samuel constantly in the background, is at an end. Reference to the progress made by Jesus reduces some of the surprise generated by the long gap from twelve years of age to the time when Jesus began his ministry "about thirty years of age" (3:23). "Favor" *(charis)* is God's gift to the humble (cf. Sir. 3:18). Jesus displayed humility in his self-subjection to his parents (Luke 2:51), and the Lord would exalt him. Greco-Roman auditors would be alert to the fact that the closing phrase expresses a fundamental cultural perspective: people of excellence can count on the response of heaven because of their piety, and humanity will praise them for their goodness and uprightness. Of Aristagoras (see on 2:49) it was said in the same breath with affirmation of his maturation that he "forged ahead in piety" (*SIG* 708.17).

Through this summation Luke reminds his public that it is not Jesus but elements in the prevailing religious establishment who are to be put into question. Neither from the side of people nor from the side of God was any fault to be found with this young man. Pilate will be puzzled that Jerusalem should think otherwise. A centurion will say the same thing in his own way (23:47). And Acts 2:47 will record that "all the people" similarly affirmed the credentials of the Christian community.

PART TWO: JOHN THE BAPTIST
AND JESUS

MINISTRY OF JOHN THE BAPTIST
Luke 3:1–20
(Mark 1:2–8; Matthew 3:1–12)

At Luke 1:76 John was called "the prophet of the Most High." As in Hosea 1 and Jeremiah 1, the date of the prophet's public introduction is solemnly recited, with emphasis on the contemporary rulers. As Luke indicates at Acts 26:26, the revolution of the Kingdom of God will not be buried in a corner of history. Yet even while he invites the attention of those who know the Greek Scriptures of the Prophets, Luke appeals to the ears of a broader Greco-Roman public.

The Ruling Powers
Luke 3:1–2

Luke highlighted the moment of Jesus' birth with reference to a decree of enrollment published by Caesar Augustus. Now, in accordance with his avowed intent, expressed at Acts 10:37–38 to focus special attention on the beginning of Jesus' career as the Great Benefactor of humanity and the arch-foe of the devil, Luke follows the practice of some Greco-Roman historians and provides his public with an even more elaborate chronological formulation than the type used by Hosea and Jeremiah.

To mark the beginning of the Peloponnesian War, Thoukydides (2.1) wrote as follows:

> In the fifteenth year [of the armistice concluded after the conquest of Euboea], when Chrysis of Argos was in her forty-eighth year of service as priest, when Ainesias was ephor at Sparta, and Pythodoros was archon at Athens, in the sixth month after the battle at Potidaia, at the beginning of spring, men came from Thebes.

Luke imitates this type of formulation but preserves the Semitic flavor of his book by concluding in v. 2 with typical OT phraseology.

3:1. Tiberius Caesar, successor to Augustus, began his reign in the year 14 C.E. He combined rigorous fiscal policy with a personal austerity that did not endear him to the Roman populace. But allegations of addiction to vice that were made about him in connection with his self-imposed exile at Capreae are to be discounted as irresponsible gossip. His **fifteenth year** would date the beginning of John's ministry in 28–29 C.E. (On problems connected with the date, see Jack Finegan, *Handbook of Biblical Chronology* [1964].)

Pontius Pilate . . . governor of Judea was prefect from the year 26 to 36 C.E. (On Pilate's official title, see A. N. Sherwin-White, *Roman Society and Roman Law in the New Testament* [1963], p. 6.) His reputation for repressive measures is unmistakably signaled at 13:1 and in his delivery of Jesus to ignominious death by crucifixion (23:24–25). On complaint of the Samaritans, some of whom Pilate had attacked in the year 36 C.E. at Mt. Gerizim, Tiberius summoned him to Rome to answer charges. Pilate arrived after the emperor's death, and after disappearing from history entered into the world of ecclesiastical legend.

Herod . . . tetrarch of Galilee was Herod Antipas, the younger son of Malthace and Herod the Great; he governed Galilee and Perea as tetrarch from 4 B.C.E. until 39 C.E. Originally "tetrarch" meant "ruler over a fourth part of a region," but in time the term was loosely applied to petty, dependent princes, whose authority was lower than that of a king. Incited by Herodias, the niece whom he married, Herod petitioned Emperor Gaius for the official title of king, but his ambition challenged the bounds of the emperor's beneficence and he was deposed in 39 C.E. on trumped-up charges of treason by his nephew Agrippa I.

Philip tetrarch of the region of Ituraea and Trachonitis, northeast of Galilee, ruled from 4 B.C.E. to 33 or 34 C.E. He was the brother of Herod Antipas and the son of Herod the Great and Cleopatra of Jerusalem.

Lysanias (otherwise known only from inscriptions) was **tetrarch of Abilene,** a region around the town of Abila, northwest of Damascus. His insignificance was such that his presence in the list of political figures has puzzled interpreters. But the sequence from the most powerful head of state to a petty officeholder provides an eloquent context for what is to follow. The essence of history is politics, and Luke will shortly present the greatest political figure the world would ever know. And it is precisely in the kind of political world that Luke has suggested by his list of names that Jesus and his followers will carry out their destiny.

3:2. After a brief look at the secular realm, Luke turns to the religious scene, the flipside of political reality. Besides Roman power, religious forces will play a major role in the story that is about to unfold. Aware of how power is brokered, Luke first mentions **the high-priesthood of Annas;** he was appointed in the year 6 C.E. by the Roman governor Publius Sulpicius Quirinius (cf. 2:2) and deposed in the year 15 C.E. A successor, **Caiaphas,** his son-in-law, held the post for the years 18 to 36 C.E. The term "high priest" appears to be applied honorifically to Annas. It was not necessary to

specify that Caiaphas was actually the officeholder. In other passages the
term "chief priests" also includes the presidium of the Sanhedrin (cf. 9:22;
20:19; 23:13; 24:20).

Of the persons mentioned in vv. 1–2, all except Lysanias play some role in
the succeeding narrative: Tiberius Caesar—20:20–26; Pontius Pilate—13:1;
chap. 23; Antipas—3:19; 8:3; 9:7, 9; 13:31; 23:7–15; Acts 4:27; 13:1; Philip—
3:19; the chief priest(s)—9:22; 19:47; 20:1, 19; 22:2, 4, 50, 52, 54, 66; 23:4,
10, 13; 24:20.

Following the style of OT writings (e.g., Jer. 1:1–4; Hos. 1:1; Joel 1:1),
Luke says that **the word of God came to John.** The phraseology is
derived from the Septuagint version of Jer. 1:1 and is a solemn way of
asserting that God signally intervenes at this moment in history, so carefully
defined against the background of imperial and ecclesiastical systems. Reference to the locale **(in the wilderness)** anticipates the use of Isa. 40:3 at v. 4
(see also 1:80).

Prophetic Fulfillment

Luke 3:3–6
(Mark 1:2–6; Matthew 3:1–6)

John's mission is not limited to a narrow area: **he went into all the
region about the Jordan,** apparently west of the river. Rich with meaning
for Israelites, the name "Jordan" reminded them of their exodus traditions
and the story of a Syrian named Naaman, who was cured of leprosy in the
river Jordan after accepting direction from Elisha. John does not invite his
hearers to an isolated life, such as that at Qumran. Verse 3 does not
emphasize that he baptized but that he proclaimed a **baptism of repentance for the forgiveness of sins.** Without repentance a washing would
only spell disaster for those who used it as another ritualistic device to
manipulate God.

The word "baptism" is a transliteration of the Greek word *baptisma*,
meaning a "washing" or "cleansing." "Wash" is used by Luke also of
experience of death (12:50) and of receipt of the Holy Spirit (3:16). Here it is
applied, also without primary stress on water, to the experience of "repentance" (*metanoia*), that is, an alteration of mind and attitude, a willingness to
entertain the changes that a future endowed with surprises must inevitably
bring. Those who received John's baptism would thereby give visible expression to the revolution within themselves. The prophets repeatedly assert
that Israel's sins have separated them from God and that a right about-face is
required (Isa. 46:8–9; Jer. 8:6), usually described as a turning back to the
Lord. Such earnestness was also proclaimed at Qumran (1QS 3:3–12;
5:13–14). Without repentance, the coming of Jesus as the end-time bearer of
salvation will be of no benefit, for without repentance there can be no
receipt of "forgiveness" (or "removal"—*aphesis*). Forgiveness, the primary
feature of the New Age that has dawned (Luke 1:77), is the opportunity for

the new start that is necessary for enjoyment of its benefits. In subsequent narratives Luke will describe the Savior as one who offers forgiveness (5:23; 7:47–49; cf. 17:3–4; 23:34). For those who are repentant, the baptism, being God's own action, is the seal of that forgiveness (see also Acts 2:38, and cf. Acts 3:19; 13:38–39).

To those of Greco-Roman background Luke's account would be especially striking, for popular gentile piety required strict adherence to ritual procedure, and violations thereof constituted sin *(hamartia)*—the "missing of the mark." John's message would be viewed as a release from anxiety concerning the attitudes of any one of a number of deities whose rites were either improperly performed or in some way neglected. At the same time, Luke's Greco-Roman publics would be impressed by John's moral earnestness, which compared favorably with positions taken, for example, by Stoic preachers.

Questions about the relationship of John's baptism to what is known as Christian baptism receive a partial answer at 3:16 and a fuller one at Acts 19:1–7.

3:4–5. Luke's quotation from Isa. 40:3–5, which is also used by the writer of 1QS 8:12–15, recapitulates the meaning in v. 3. There is no mention of ritual cleansing, for baptisms were common in the Jewish community (cf. Luke 11:38; Mark 7:4). Rather, the emphasis is on moral alteration.

The words describing the preparation of **the way of the Lord** typify pains that were taken to smooth the path for an Eastern potentate. In their context in Isaiah they refer to Israel's deliverance from captivity under the imagery of a second exodus. Luke applies them to the intellectual and moral change that Israel must undergo for reception of God's new action in connection with Jesus. Traditional patterns will be inadequate for accommodation of the future. At Acts 8:21 and 13:10 Luke himself illustrates what is meant by **the crooked shall be made straight.** Repeatedly in the Book of Acts, Luke refers to Christians as travelers of "the Way" (Acts 9:2; 19:9, 23; 22:4, 24:14, 22).

Lord *(kyrios)* is used of God or Jesus Christ in the NT. At v. 4 God, as understood in the OT, is meant (cf. 1:17, 76). A reference to Jesus first appears in the concluding clause: and all flesh (including the gentiles) shall see (i.e., be invited to share) **the salvation of God** (cf. 1:69, 71, 77; 2:11, 30–32). Jesus, as the content of God's rescuing action, is that salvation *(sōtēria).*

Important for the understanding of Luke's presentation is the manner in which he departs from Mark's use of the OT in this account about John. Mark begins with a citation from Exod. 23:20, a reference to God's special messenger sent to guide the Israelites on their journey. As the messenger went before Israel, so John goes before Jesus Christ, to prepare his way. Luke deletes the words "Behold, I send my messenger before thy face, who shall prepare thy way" (Mark 1:2), reserving them for a later stage in his narrative (Luke 7:27).

Association of the deleted words (Mark 1:2) with Mal. 3:1–4 apparently gave rise to the speculation that John's task was that of a second Elijah, to announce as imminent the great Day of the Lord, the end of the normal course of history. As the Messiah, Jesus was to usher this in immediately. Mark himself attempted through his secrecy motif to explain the puzzling delay and at the same time discourage speculative apocalyptic: only after Jesus' death and resurrection and extensive publication of the good news would the spectacular appearance take place. But how long must the People of God wait? Mark explained that the destruction of Jerusalem would spell the birth pangs of the end of the end time (Mark 13). After Mark had written, Christians remained perplexed by continuing delay in the windup of history. Luke's answer to this problem is that the figure of Elijah does not center in John, and the Baptist's appearance was certainly not meant to be construed as the first of two end-time installments.

3:6. John's task is not to prepare the nation for the sudden advent in power of the messianic deliverer. He prepares the way for God so that God may announce salvation for **all flesh.** That salvation is Jesus, in whose person and activity the forgiveness of sins, the display of God's good pleasure, becomes reality for all humanity (cf. Simeon's vision of the future at 2:30, and see 24:47; Acts 1:8). Since Jesus does not measure up to popular messianic expectation, repentance is all the more required. Only a major revision of national and religious thought will make possible proper appreciation of God's program in connection with Jesus.

Luke's omission of the phrase "and the glory of the Lord shall be revealed" (Isa. 40:5) reinforces this interpretation of his thought. Inclusion of the phrase at this point might have suggested that an apocalyptic demonstration of a spectacular sort is about to take place. Luke had earlier transposed the phrase to his account of the shepherds: "and the glory of the Lord shone around them" (2:9). Jesus, in the humble circumstances of his birth (2:12) and as a sign to be spoken against (2:34), *is* the apocalyptic event. The child in the manger, the child in Simeon's arms—this is the Savior, this is the scandal of the New Age.

By dissociating John from Malachi 3 and therefore from traditional speculations about the return of Elijah, Luke intends to eliminate doubts concerning Jesus' messianic credentials. Even though the apocalyptic timetable, as popularly understood, was not followed, Jesus is nevertheless the fulfillment of Israel's and the world's hope. John comes in the spirit of Elijah (1:17; cf. Mal. 4:5), but Jesus is the real second Elijah, that is, if one is to speak at all of a latter-day Elijah. No signs as traditionally understood are needed to document his credentials, and the refining function described in Mal. 3:2–4; 4:1–2 is reserved for Jesus, not for John (cf. Luke 3:16–17).

Call to Repentance

Luke 3:7–14
(Matthew 3:7–10)

Luke omits Mark's description of John as a second Elijah wearing camel's hair and a belt of leather (cf. 2 Kings 1:8). In Mark, the association has point, but in Luke's time, because of popular misunderstanding, a fresh approach must be taken. The statement in Zech. 13:4, that in the latter day a true prophet would not put on a hairy garment, may also have influenced the evangelist.

3:7–8. Since Luke is not yet ready to introduce indictments of specific religious groups, he does not spell out, as does Matthew, that Pharisees and Sadducees come under critique. Instead, he simply uses the word "multi-tudes." This general term for "crowds" *(ochlos)* replaces Mark's references to "all the country of Judea, and all the people of Jerusalem" (Mark 1:5). Encounter with Jerusalem is preserved for Jesus, and at a later time. The news of John's baptism had spread. The implication is that the crowds understood this as another ritual cleansing.

Isaiah had addressed the people as a "sinful nation, a people laden with iniquity, offspring of evildoers, sons who deal corruptly!" (Isa. 1:4). John uses similar uncomplimentary language. **Brood of vipers,** he calls them, a description for which there is precedent in Isa. 59:5 (see also Jer. 46:22–23). People in the Near East were accustomed to exposure to an incredible variety of unflattering appellations involving references, if not to vipers, to camels. John's term was urbane by comparison. But he got the attention of his audience. Vipers move fast amid the hazards of their environment.

John's question is satirical and means: "From whom, in the world, are you getting your directions to escape the impending wrath? You want another wash? Then do it right. Bring out fruits that really show repentance." Isaiah 1:16–18 says, "Wash yourselves; make yourselves clean; remove the evil of your doings from before my eyes. . . . Though your sins are like scarlet, they shall be as white as snow." These admonitions are preceded by the Lord's request: "Bring no more vain offerings. . . . Your new moons and your appointed feasts my soul hates" (Isa. 1:13–14).

Ritual is meaningless without repentance, that is, a turning from wicked-ness or from attempts to manipulate or patronize God. Therefore John is critical of a populace that misinterprets his proclamation of a washing of repentance as an invitation to another bit of ritual. At Luke 7:30 a devastat-ing verdict will be pronounced on those who refused to heed John's warning and invitation. "Your iniquities have made a separation between you and your God, and your sins have hid his face from you," said Isaiah (59:2), and the chapter from which his words are taken is the best commentary on Luke's meaning. Paul took Isaiah seriously, and his rehearsal at Acts 26:20 of his own style of ministry, according to Luke, echoes John's program.

In keeping with his theme of the New Age, one of Luke's favorite words is the verb "begin" *(archomai:* see, e.g., Luke 3:23; 4:23; 12:1; 23:5; Acts 1:1, 22; 10:37). But there is a proper way and a wrong way to begin. "Do not even *begin* to say to yourselves: But *our* father is Abraham!" That slogan plunged one rich man into flames (Luke 16:24). Traditional securities are of no avail in the New Age that now dawns. It is not enough to recite the proper religious words. One must deal with God in depth. For God is able **to raise up children to Abraham** out of the very **stones** (cf. Rom. 4:17). This is John's word to those whose hands, as a Greek poet of a later time expressed it, are "full of jars, heavy with the ashes of their ancestors." In brief, criteria of birth, national identity, class, or status mean nothing to God. Attitude and disposition of mind and life are central. And God will improvise as need requires. This is radical apocalyptic, in a truly theological and moral dimension.

3:9. The axe is laid to the root of the trees. Hosea 10:1–2 describes Israel as "a luxuriant vine," but headed for destruction. Jeremiah 2:21–22 states that Israel is "a choice vine," but though she "wash [herself] with lye and use much soap," she could not remove the stain of her guilt. No mere ritual washing will save these crowds. The ax is heading not only toward the base of the tree but toward the very roots—total destruction. Such was the word of Amos concerning the Amorites (Amos 2:9). And the ax is in its downward stroke for all humanity. No wonder John asked, "Who was it who misguided you?" Trees without good fruit on them are headed for the flames. Luke will have more to say on that subject (Luke 6:43–49). God is patient, but time can run out (13:6–9).

As for inanimate objects being the source of human creatures, some Greco-Romans would readily recall the field that brought up a crop of warriors out of the dragon's teeth that Medea's husband Jason had sowed in it at the bidding of his wicked adversary King Aietes. But these warriors were hostile and meant to destroy the hero. It was different in the case of Kadmos son of the Tyrian king Agenor. After a crop of warriors had come up out of a set of dragon's teeth, most of them destroyed one another, but five put down their arms and pledged to serve Kadmos.

3:10–11. In response to the anxious question, "What are we to do?" John answers simply, "One who has two undergarments (RSV: *coats)* is to share with one who has none. Do the same with your food" (cf. Job 31:16–20). In the wake of the overpowering apocalyptic and prophetic rhetoric that precedes in vv. 7–9, these words appear colorless. No unusual activities are required. No recital of religious obligation is made. It is merely a call to unselfishness.

At Luke 10:25 an expert in the Mosaic code put the question to Jesus, only to discover that the world was his neighborhood. At 18:18 a man of some station repeated the question and was shocked by the lesson he received in redistribution of wealth. At Acts 2:37 a crowd echoes the question addressed to John, and Acts 2:44–45 and 4:32–36 further exemplify what is meant by his reply. A prison guard finds life totally revised after he has put the question to Paul and Silas (Acts 16:30–34). Paul knew the answer, for he himself had learned how to be under orders of the New Age (Acts 22:10).

The Greek term for coats *(chitōn)* refers to the undergarment that was worn next to the skin. Two of these might be worn for protection against the cold. Despite their apparent innocuous tone, the directives as given in Luke's context are revolutionary. Nothing less is called for than a critical examination of all systems whereby humanity lays claim to civilized accomplishment. The haves are to share with the have-nots, for God exalts the poor and elevates the rich (Luke 1:52–53). Those who refuse such direction will, like the rich man, see Lazarus at Abraham's side and themselves— while calling on their national, ecclesiastical, or cultural paternity—forever removed from the presence of God (16:26; cf. 13:28).

The ax is heading downstroke in any society that thinks these words are an invitation merely to distribute Christmas food baskets, handouts of castoff clothes, or money. Anyone who is insensitive to the broadening gulf between the prosperous and the economically disadvantaged deserves to know that prophets did not risk their necks for petty moralizing of that sort. A call to repentance, an across-the-board review of respectable resources for injustice, prejudice, and indifference to the needs of human beings, this is what set apart true prophets from the bogus.

3:12. Tax collectors also came to be baptized. Since one of Luke's main themes is the place of religious outcasts in the program of the New Age, he skillfully separates their arrival from that of the "crowds." Besides, it would have been inappropriate to suggest that these people, who, despite their Jewish ancestry, were considered outside the religious establishment, would complacently claim Abraham as their father. By introducing them at this point, Luke is able to contrast them with those who were in fact the complacent ones.

"Toll collectors" is a more accurate rendering of the officials *(telōnai)* here described. Their function was to collect not the land tax and the poll tax but indirect taxes such as tolls, customs, imposts, and tariffs. A chief tax collector, like Zacchaeus (Luke 19:2), would purchase the franchise and let out the collection process to subordinates. Costs would be passed on to the public. In the absence of compliance with imperial administrative controls, there was obviously extensive opportunity for extortion (cf. *OGI* 519.21–22). "The sheep are to be shorn, not fleeced," warned Emperor Tiberius (Dio Cassius *Roman History* 57.10.5; Suetonius *Tiberius* 52).

Some assessment of the emotional impact that Luke's reference to these representatives of Roman fiscal policy had on his public can be made at the hand of other documents. Lucian of Samosata, a gentile writer in the second century, summed the sentiment of both Jew and Greek when he lumped "adulterers, pimps, tax collectors, yes-men and informers" as part of a vast "crowd of people who only stir up huge confusion" (*Descent into Hades* 2). Paul, in 1 Cor. 6:9–10, submits much the same list as he looks back on his first recruits at Corinth, but omits reference to tax collectors, who are mentioned in the NT only in the first three Gospels.

Such, then, are the candidates for participation in the program of the New Age. But unlike the fate of many who have lost much sense of worth as persons and fall easy victims to entrepreneurs in personality cult under the guise of idealistic goals, these people are not exploited in the interest of promoting John's ego. They get no patronizing sympathy but hear a challenging invitation to become persons in their own right, with identity, and to become new as the age that is dawning. They come indeed to be washed, but not merely to get a feel of the water. Their first question is: **Teacher, what shall we do?** The complacent claimed Moses as their teacher. These people listen to one who has interrupted business as usual.

3:13. Once again the directions are simple. Nothing is said about dropping their profession. But the ax comes down on the system. **Collect no more than is appointed you.** The words are much like those in an inscription from the year 137, found at Palmyra, and cited by Creed (*OGI* 629.14–15). John's simple phrasing cuts through roots of graft, cost overruns, the payoff, the kickback, the torn-up ticket—all the tentacles that reach out to destroy the health and substance, the moral fiber, and the ethical backbone of individuals and their nation. No cynical acceptance of realities here! Fair and just dealing, without attempts to aggrandize oneself at the expense of another—this is the expectation of the Kingdom. Not many moons later a short man will climb a tree and volunteer such deeds without command (Luke 19:8).

3:14. Soldiers also asked him, "And we, what shall we do?" They are given similar direction. These are probably Jews in the service of Herod Antipas who function as agents of law enforcement. Their entry on the scene is not ususual in a narrative that deals with a revolutionary figure. Herod, who ruled by grace of Rome, would want to know what was afoot. Besides, Luke must give some account of Christian attitudes toward imperial policy. Does Christianity spell the end of military establishments or of forces limited to internal security? The answer: soldiery or activity in law enforcement agencies can be honorable professions, but force and false accusation must not be used to shake down the weak. The appearance of soldiers in the narrative next to tax collectors suggests that security forces are to be brought under prophetic indictment when associated with oppressive systems. Especially insightful is Luke's apparent awareness that

systems of taxation are often intimately linked with vast budgetary alloca-
tions for arms. Rome was to pay dearly for such investment at the expense
of human needs.

Luke's Jesus is no threat to imperial authority that lives up to avowed
claims of espousing justice. But it or any other authority that does not
recognize the validity of his stance ultimately signs its own expiration
warrant, for the mighty will be brought low. Luke permits no skepticism
about that! Justice is the bond of security for the people and the state. As
Hannibal and all great generals have recognized, the principal objective of an
armed force is to achieve and maintain a lasting peace.

The final word to the soldiers, "Be satisfied with your wages," would be
especially noted in a period when soldiers were notoriously disgruntled
about their daily stipend of money and grain and strongly tempted to pad it
out of the meager provisions of the poor. Theophilos can inform his
superiors that Christians are no troublemakers, but let Caesar know there
are limits! Paul's record of imprisonment is testimony that Christians will
neither tolerate infringement of their allegiance to Jesus as Lord nor capitu-
late to establishments that claim more than their dues.

After reading John's speech, Theophilos might have asked: "Is this what
all the fuss is about? Some revolution, this!" But he would have missed the
point. John's preaching emphasized the importance of individual decision in
place of dependence on the rules of noninnovative scribes or the stuffy
moralizing of certain Pharisees, who considered some jobs to be degrading.
John upgraded jobs to the level of human responsibility. That tack could be
dangerous once moved to a high pitch of authority by the One who waits in
the wings, a threat to those who resist change with automatic reflex. On the
other hand, those who expected the Messiah to produce spectacular signs
must be disabused of their misconceptions. Jesus will give no signs, and he
will repeat in various ways much of what John said. Yet there is hard-hitting
radicality in Jesus' words, as reported by Luke, that pales John's expression
into comparative insignificance. By underplaying John, Luke prepares the
way for Jesus' ministry.

The Stronger One

Luke 3:15–17

(Mark 1:7–8; Matthew 3:11–12)

Since debates on the mission field and also within the longer established
churches (cf. Acts 18:24—19:7) included the question of the relationship of
John and Jesus to the end-time program of God, Luke moves into the
messianic issue. Since Jesus was an apparent failure, rejected by the top
religious leadership, some claimed that he could not be the Messiah. Others
said that John was a kind of messiah but perhaps someone else would
follow. In any case, some argued, Jesus might be merely another teacher or
prophet. Especially potent was the opinion that John was a second Elijah.

When the second Elijah came, the Messiah was shortly to appear. Jesus, perhaps some arguments ran, was clearly not the Messiah. Some other figure who would introduce the scenes described in John's preaching—the cleansing of the threshing floor, the burning of the chaff with fire—would come over the horizon.

As pointed out earlier, one of Luke's main objectives is to quash the idea that Elijah reappears in some way in the person of John, so that only the final stage in the apocalyptic timetable is left—the spectacular demonstration from heaven of the Deliverer, whose arrival is to be preceded by catastrophic events in nature. Luke therefore has been at pains to dissociate Jesus' mission from too great dependence on John's appearance. The infancy narrative aimed to do justice to the importance of John, but it left no doubt that he is definitely subordinate (see also Acts 1:5; 11:16; 18:25). Luke's inclusion of 3:15–16, not found in Mark, reinforces this interpretation of his intention. In any case, there emerges a picture of intense theological vitality out of Luke's endeavor to aid the Christian community in discovery of truth. The church can move to other levels of understanding without disintegrating under the heat of controversy.

3:15. The initial words, **as the people were in expectation**, have a messianic orientation (cf. 7:19–20, where the word "expectation" [*prosdokaō*] recurs). Of special interest is the shift from the word "crowd" or "multitudes" (*ochlos,* v. 10) to "the people" (the Greek *laos* is the source of the word "laity"). "The people" in Luke's Gospel are usually presented as favorable to Jesus. Here they are viewed as expecting **the Christ.** The term "Christ" transliterates a Greek word *(christos)* meaning "anointed one," which in turn translates the Hebrew term *(māšiaḥ)* from which "Messiah" is derived.

David is called God's "anointed" (the term for "Christ" in the Greek OT) in 2 Sam. 22:21 and 23:1. Since expectations for redress of fortunes in the future are customarily expressed in terms of outstanding features in the past, David, who symbolizes the high point of Israel's national success, becomes the model for a future royal figure (see Jer. 33:13–15; Ezek. 37:24). But the term "anointed" is not applied to such a royal figure before the writing of Dan. 9:25.

The people debate within themselves about the role of John, but conclude: "This man isn't the Messiah, is he?" The negative form of the question is Luke's way of disqualifying John for the office. By stressing that the question was in the minds (RSV: **hearts**) of the people and not overtly expressed, Luke is able to secure a double rejection of the hypothesis, for John replies of his own accord to their unworded question, thereby eliminating all doubt about the matter.

3:16. The Stronger One **(mightier)** is on the way, and John is not worthy even to perform a slave's deed for him—to untie his sandals. (Matthew 3:11 highlights the slave's action with the word "carry.") The distance between John and Jesus is strikingly affirmed in Luke's account by what he does not include, namely, Mark's phrase "after me" (Mark 1:7). As in the infancy narrative, John and Jesus appear at approximately the same time. John has only a minor chronological priority (cf. Acts 13:25).

According to Jer. 50:34, God is the "Strong One" who ransoms his people (see also Isa. 11:2), and Isa. 40:10 declares that God is on the way to intervene in behalf of Israel. Luke clearly wants the words of John about the Stronger One to be understood in reference to Jesus. John washes with water only. The Stronger One will wash them **with the Holy Spirit** (cf. Acts 1:5; 11:16) **and with fire** (understood here as in Acts 2:1–3; cf. Isa. 4:4; Ezek. 36:25–27; Ps. 51:9–11; 1QS 4:20–26). Elijah was noted for a performance with fire (1 Kings 18), and Luke later associates some features of Jesus' ministry with that of Ahab's nemesis, but through the linkage of "Holy Spirit" and "fire" Luke aims to correct misinterpretations of the Messiah's mission as one of special apocalyptic effects. Emphasis on the Spirit dominates his two-volume work (cf. Acts 1:8 and esp. 2:1–3).

In Acts 2:16–21, Luke applies Joel 3:1–5 (an apocalyptic text that promises an outpouring of the Spirit) to the event of Pentecost that had been recited a few verses earlier. Luke's inclusion in 3:16 of a traditional association of the Spirit with fire (see the Q passage in Matt. 3:11) forms an integral element in Luke's plot, for v. 16 anticipates the moment of Pentecost, which is already part of Christian history at the time he was writing. Thus the evangelist is consistent in his approach to apocalyptic as he shows that apocalyptic terminology can be used to express not only future hope but events that lie in the past, for Pentecost spelled not the conclusion of history but the acceleration of God's ongoing mission. To state it theologically, Luke gave apocalyptic an ecclesiological dimension.

3:17. This verse is to be understood in the light of 3:16. Luke offers a corrective to those who used John's words as an endorsement for their own traditional apocalyptic viewpoints. Instead of sending fire immediately to demolish the opposition (a course rejected by Jesus at Luke 9:54), Jesus will accomplish the separation in Israel through bestowal of the Spirit. The criterion will be sincerity of claim in recognizing Jesus as Lord (cf. 6:46–49), resulting in abundant fruit (8:15). The "chaff," that is, those who rest on the pillow of meaningless liturgy, theological jargon, and religious ease, will be cast off as refuse (cf. 16:19–31; 17:25–37) in the apocalyptic moment that puts the possibility of present choice beyond recall.

Such passages as Isa. 5:24; 10:17; 47:14; Mal. 4:1, with their language about weeds and stubble that are consumed by fire, provide the background for the imagery. According to Isa. 41:15–16, Israel, the servant of the Lord, will do God's winnowing; here Jesus is to do it. In brief, despite his apparent lack of credentials, Jesus is the Messiah, and words once spoken by John are to be understood in the light of God's subsequent mission carried out through Jesus and the apostolic community. But the words of Simeon at Luke 2:34 will remain a valid description of the response that will be made wherever the gospel is proclaimed.

Exit of John
Luke 3:18–20
(Mark 6:17–18; Matthew 14:3–4)

3:18–20. The preceding analysis of Luke's interpretation of John's ministry and preaching is confirmed by the summary in 3:18. The key word is in the phrase **preached good news.** In the Greek this entire phrase is one verb (*euanggelizomai;* see 1:19; 2:10; 4:18, 43; 7:22; 8:1; 9:6; 16:16; 20:1; and often in Acts), from which the term "evangelize" is derived. Luke uses the noun only at Acts 15:7; 20:24, for from his perspective the Christian message is not a static statement of belief that people can control, as in clever theological debate; rather, it breaks out in various patterns of expression as human beings are confronted with God's rescuing action. The central meaning of *euanggelizomai* is not "preach good news" but "make a proclamation." If the context indicates that God's saving action is involved, the term connotes "proclaim good news." In Acts 20:24, Luke adds a specific qualifier, "grace of God."

Since John shows the people how to avoid the divine wrath, his message is good news, despite the fact that some of his words sound like the thunder of judgment. A similar conjunction of thought occurs in Isaiah 40. One person's lightning is another's anticipation of life-giving rain, and what John spoke of as future became reality in Jesus' presence and at Pentecost.

Even more remarkable at first exposure is the statement that his exhortation (or "encouragement"; *parakaleō*), which consisted also of moral precepts, was good news. But Greco-Roman auditors, who would note that "evangelize" was here used in a narrative about the superstar Jesus, in all probability instantly understood it in the sense of "proclaim a new age," for John's words are an expression of the new era.

That publicans and soldiers could be included in God's purposes without the detours of fussy scribal guidelines—this was a revolutionary idea for the time. That oppressors must ultimately render account is good news to the disadvantaged. The "multitudes" (*ochlos,* v. 7) heard bad news; **the people** (*laos,* v. 18; cf. 1:77) heard good news. A similar contrast appears at Acts 8:14–25. It is the way in which one hears the voice of God that spells the difference. Of interest also is the fact that Luke does not ascribe proclamation of the Kingdom of God to John. That is reserved for Jesus (Luke 4:43).

John was impartial. To soldiers he said, "Do your duty honorably." To Herod Antipas, high representative of an ego-centered establishment, he cried aloud and spared not: "You did wrong to marry your brother's wife."

But that was only one item on the list, and Herod could not stand the light. On top of everything else (for *touto epi pasin,* cf. Col. 3:14), he clapped John in jail. It was the finishing touch. With this brief sketch of John's last days in public life Luke succeeds in clearing Christians of any charge that their involvement with John the Baptist was subversive. John was not anti-Rome. He was a preacher of righteousness.

Herod **shut up John in prison.** John dared to speak words of power to moral weakness that was masked by an offensive and irresponsible display of power. The tetrarch deposed his first wife, daughter of the Arabian king Aretas, and in violation of Lev. 20:21 married his niece Herodias, formerly married to his half brother Herod. Luke, keenly aware of political dimensions, places this notice in the context of world judgment. Josephus (*Antiquities* 18.5.2) spells out details. At the same time, the announcement is dramatically integral to Luke's plotting of the narrative.

Christians acquainted with Isa. 61:1 apparently concluded that Jesus is the Servant of the Lord who ought to liberate the captives (Luke 4:18). It is part of the expectation, and expectation is a major theme in Luke's story. How Jesus meets such expectation is an integral factor in evaluation of his role as Savior or Deliverer. And John not long hence will interrogate Jesus about his credentials and in his own way learn the meaning of Simeon's words (2:34–35).

Many months elapsed between John's first public appearance and his arrest (cf. Matt. 14:3–4 and Mark 6:17–18, where the arrest is noted as taking place during the course of Jesus' ministry). But Luke, with the exception of the longer glance (Luke 7:18–30) noted above and a number of brief restrospective references (9:7, 9, 19; 11:1; 16:16; 20:4, 6; Acts 1:5, 22; 10:37; 11:16; 13:24–25; 18:25; 19:3–4), is done with John. Like the Greek actor who concealed his own power as he played a role subordinate to that of the star in the performance, John gives way to the Main Player.

JESUS INTRODUCED
Luke 3:21–38

The Washing of Jesus
Luke 3:21–22
(Mark 1:9–11; Matthew 3:13–17)

3:21-22. This episode is so important that it is introduced by the words "and it came to pass" (*egeneto;* RSV: **now**). In view of Luke 16:16; Acts 1:22; and 10:37, it is impossible to evade the importance Luke attaches to this moment. The rest of the syntax of Luke 3:21 is tense with especially careful statement. Luke wishes to emphasize the close association of Jesus with **all the people,** a characteristic expression, which is in accordance with the angel's declaration (Luke 2:11), anticipates Jesus' genealogy, and forecasts the style of his entire life as one in intimate contact with publicans and sinners.

On the other hand, Luke is at pains to separate the washing undergone by Jesus from the one received by the people. Repentance was required of the latter, and Luke wishes to avoid the suggestion that Jesus was included in this exhortation. In the people's case, receipt of John's washing meant that they acknowledged the supremacy of God in their lives; in Jesus' case, it spelled his total dedication to the Father's purpose.

Jesus' close relationship to his Parent is stressed through the observation that while he was praying, the heaven was opened. Luke's accounts of Jesus at prayer (5:16; 6:12; 9:18, 28–29; 11:1; 22:41; see also 10:21–22; 22:32; 23:34, 46) usually indicate a crucial moment, and his language is emphatic on this point—the revelation that follows did *not* take place *during* the washing. Attestation of the Messiah is made independently of John; in a way it comes in answer to Jesus' prayer.

When **the heaven was opened, . . . the Holy Spirit descended** on Jesus. The people would see nothing unusual, for it ("spirit" in Greek [*pneuma*] is neuter) makes its presence known through some bodily form, something that looked like (RSV: **as**) a "pigeon" (*peristera,* the word used at 2:24). **And a voice came from heaven,** but again there is no suggestion that the people were aware of it, for the words are addressed to Jesus personally (in Matt. 3:17 indirectly, "this one"). Luke will explain later what is the purpose of the Spirit's descent (Luke 4:18–19) but, as often in Jewish literature, the Spirit's presence here signifies divine activity.

According to Isa. 42:1, Jacob is God's chosen servant, and God gives the Spirit to him. In Ps. 2:7 the Lord says to the king: "You are my son, today I have begotten you." The words addressed to Jesus—**Thou art my beloved Son; with thee I am well pleased**—are probably a composite of these and related statements, with the word "beloved" *(agapētos)* doing duty for "chosen" (cf. Isa. 44:2 LXX, and see Gen. 22:2). The first pronoun is emphatic. Jesus and no other is, from Christian perspectives that Luke shares, the end-time Israel of God, God's Servant, God's Chosen One. Nor is the present tense in the phrase "thou art" without significance. Not John's baptism, but the Spirit itself has given Jesus his unique role. Once more Luke expects his readers to recall a part of the infancy narrative: "Therefore the child . . . will be called holy, the Son of God" (Luke 1:35). When Jesus was an infant, the grace of God was with him (2:40). At the age of twelve he recognized his obligation to his Parent. After his visit to the temple, he advanced in wisdom and stature and favor before God and people (2:52).

Humanity is God's business (cf. 2:14), and in Jesus, God is "well pleased." Whether Luke had before him a Greek version of Isa. 42:1 in a form different from the Septuagint cannot be determined. But the expression "well pleased" *(eudokeō)* means that Jesus is at the service of the Parent, who places special claims on him. The Spirit will soon demonstrate that the claim is not misplaced (4:1–13), and at the cross Jesus will terminate the first stage of his mission with the surrender of his spirit (23:46).

Without any special apocalyptic effects Jesus has arrived on the scene, but his credentials are all in order. As Acts 10:38 affirms, the Spirit is the one whereby he is anointed (the verb in Greek [*chriō*] is similar to the word "Christ" [*christos*], which means anointed one, and this in turn corresponds to the Hebrew term [*māšiaḥ*] that is rendered "Messiah").

Although the narrative itself does not originate in Hellenistic circles, it is necessary always to ask how a biblical account might be understood in such a cultural environment. From a Greco-Roman perspective the narrative would exhibit Jesus as a distinguished person of superior excellence, with the pigeon especially emblematic of beneficence (see E. Goodenough, *Jewish Symbols in the Greco-Roman Period* [Princeton, 1953–68] 8:404). The presence of the Spirit in bodily form speaks to the Greco-Roman interest in substantive demonstration of power. But Jesus is neither adopted nor equipped for his task at the baptism. He has come of age to assume his destined burden as the One Name that surpasses all others (see Acts 4:12).

Genealogy of the Son of God

Luke 3:23–38
(Matthew 1:1–16)

3:23–38. Through his separation of John from the subsequent narrative in vv. 21–22, Luke focused all attention on Jesus. Now, to remove any doubt whether Jesus or John is the Messiah, he follows up the announcement of Jesus' divine sonship with a genealogy. In his infancy narratives (chaps. 1–2) he had adopted a system of parallel presentations. By reserving Jesus' genealogy for the position it has in chap. 3, Luke is able to highlight further the essential difference between John and Jesus, for John does not merit a genealogy.

Through such organization, Luke is also able to impress his Greco-Roman public that Christians have a leader who can trace—as did heads of state and other notable figures in history—his ancestry to God. Moreover, secular authorities are to be impressed with the ancient heritage claimed by Christians, who were frequently accused of sponsoring a new "superstition" (fanaticism or *superstitio* versus religious expression or *religio*).

The translation **Jesus, when he began his ministry** is not accurate. Luke says, "And he was Jesus" (*kai autos ēn Iēsous;* cf. 19:2, "and he was a chief tax collector"). With these words he emphasizes that the voice from heaven was a personal address to Jesus, not to John, and at the same time he prepares his readers for the genealogical verification of Jesus as Son of God through David's line (1:31–32). The identification is amplified with a phrase that reads verbatim in Greek "beginning about thirty years."

The word "beginning" *(archomai)* is important, for Luke stresses at Acts

1:22 that a replacement for Judas must be found from among those who were associated with Jesus from the time he began to go in and out among them, namely, from the time of his baptism. Similarly at Acts 10:37–38, the "beginning" of Jesus' activity in Galilee is closely associated with the anointing by the Spirit which he received after his baptism. Not without design, therefore, Luke will introduce his readers to Galilean soil (Luke 4:14) immediately after Jesus' temptation (4:1–13), and the first witnesses will be gathered in Galilee (4:38; 5:1–11).

Jesus now begins the career that was defined immediately before and after his birth. The choice of the word "beginning" may also indicate a desire on Luke's part to modify slightly Mark's opening words—"Beginning *(archē)* of the good news of Jesus Christ."* Luke could not borrow such a statement, for his prologue (1:19 and 2:10) already contained announcements of good news, and John had preached good news (3:18). Luke therefore suggests that the question of "beginnings" can be viewed from another angle.

The words **about thirty years of age** reflect theological appreciation of Jesus' distinctive mission. Some early Christians appear to have viewed Jesus as a messianic high priest. According to Num. 4:3, men from thirty years of age up to fifty are to be canvassed for service in the tabernacle. But it cannot be demonstrated that Luke made such a connection.

According to Gen. 41:46, Joseph was thirty years old when he entered the service of Pharaoh; David was thirty years old when he began his reign (2 Sam. 5:4); and Ezekiel received a vision at the age of thirty (Ezek. 1:1). Joseph plays a large part in the recital of Stephen's speech (Acts 7), and 2 Sam. 5:2 contains a personal address by God to David, Jesus' ancestor, along the lines of Luke 3:22. It is probable that Luke, who knew that Jesus was in his thirties when he made his appearance, uses the typical age to invite readers to assess the stature of Jesus at the hand of notable figures in the Old Testament. As did Joseph and David, Jesus comes into Israel's history at a crucial moment, and with even greater credentials: if also as a prophet, then certainly greater than Ezekiel, even as he is greater than Jonah (Luke 11:32).

Matthew placed Jesus' genealogy at the beginning of his Gospel and traced his descent from Abraham, thereby placing Jesus squarely in the mainstream of Israel's history. Luke begins his genealogy with Jesus and traces him all the way back to Adam, and through Adam to God. The names in Luke's and Matthew's genealogies do not all coincide, and it has been suggested that Luke gives the descent through Mary, and Matthew through Joseph. But such interpretation of Luke's list is based on slender patristic evidence. The fact is that no satisfactory solution has yet been found, and some of the differences probably have their origin in early christological discussion (see also on 11:31–32). The absence of any reference to Tamar (cf. Matt. 1:3) has suggested to some interpreters that Luke aims at elimination of any embarrassing ancestors, but Luke has no hesitation in documenting Jesus' association with people of unsavory reputation.

David had his moment as a Peeping Tom (2 Sam. 11:2), yet his importance as a principal royal ancestor earns him inclusion in the genealogy.

The genealogy as a whole is important for at least two reasons: (1) Merely on strict grounds of legal descent, Jesus can join Adam in claiming affinity with God in terms of sonship. In addition, the voice from heaven has recognized him for his specific mission. Through association with Jesus, *all* people can find the way of return to the Parent, for Jesus' mission is *humanity.* (2) The parenthetical words **as was supposed** (v. 23) represent clearly Luke's understanding that the mystery of Jesus' person is not solved by taking into account mere natural processes. Jesus enjoys a special relationship with God, but without having his identification with the human race thereby vitiated. John's mother bore him in her old age, and that was most unusual, but Zechariah was his father. Jesus was born of a virgin, fathered by the Spirit. The presence of the Holy Spirit at his baptism pointed backward to the conception of Jesus but forward to his inaugural address at Nazareth. The word of the Lord came to John, but Jesus heard the voice from heaven—"You are my son." John spoke accurately—here comes the Stronger One.

PART THREE: OUTREACH TO ISRAEL

ENGAGEMENT IN THE TASK
Luke 4:1—5:11

The Temptation of Jesus
Luke 4:1–13
(Mark 1:12–13; Matthew 4:1–11)

The Spirit that came down on Jesus at the baptism remains with him, so that Jesus is fully under the direction of God (see Luke 1:15, 41, 67; Acts 6:3, 5; 7:55; 11:24). Thus he is marked as a wise man (cf. Wisd. of Sol. 1:4–5; 7:7; Sir. 39:6).

In view of the disappointing outcome of Jesus' life, looked at from the perspective of nationalistic hopes, it is important that Luke establish divine sanction for all that is to follow. This is all the more necessary since Jesus' apparent failure to carry out the messianic assignment, as popularly understood, is presented as the consequence of diabolic opposition. The tradition of the conflict would probably be further illuminated for those who brought to their auditing of the Lukan account concepts of the messianic high priest engaged in combat with the arch-adversary, the devil (see *Testament of Levi* 18; *Testament of Dan* 5:10). In any event, hostility against Jesus is not to be viewed as a proof of Jesus' lack of divine credentials but rather as a testimony to the thoroughgoing nature of his program.

To the more Hellenistically oriented, Luke's account marks a dramatic moment of encounter between superstars. Publius Sulpicius Scipio played for high stakes when he met Hannibal at Zama in the decisive battle of the Punic Wars. Octavian and Antony altered Rome's course when they defeated Brutus and Cassius, assassins of Julius Caesar, at Philippi. All fought for control of a few hundred thousand square miles. Jesus the Son of God meets Diabolos, self-styled broker of all the world's kingdoms.

Because the devil *(diabolos)* belongs to the spirit world, it is important that Jesus be **full of the Holy Spirit** (see 3:22). Like Jesus, a number of Luke's heroes are full of the Spirit (Acts 2:4; 4:8, 31; 6:3, 5; 7:55; 9:17, 31; 11:24;

13:9, 52; for the opposite, see Acts 13:10 and 19:28). Luke is aware that evil finds its most powerful threat in the presence of the holy.

To argue that Jesus disclaims a political style of messiahship is to miss the point. According to Luke, Jesus is the Great Politician. The question addressed by the temptation narrative is this: How will Jesus carry on his politics? Will it be as one obedient to God the Supreme Head of the Universe or as one who is self-serving?

Jesus was baptized for a specific apostolate, to short-circuit forces that shatter community (cf. Luke 4:18; Acts 13:8–12) and to withdraw human beings from the grip of a darkness that isolates them from the light of the New Age inaugurated through Jesus Christ (see Acts 26:18, and cf. Luke 1:78–79). That God had assigned him the task is specified by the information that he **was led by the Spirit** (v. 2). According to Rom. 8:14, those who are led by the Spirit are the children of God. This means that they are the righteous ones, and according to rabbinic thought (SB 1:135–36) as well as biblical thought, the just can anticipate temptation or a time of testing. The centurion (Luke 23:47–48) will pronounce the verdict after the final temptation: "No doubt about it, this man was upright."

4:2. In the reference to **for forty days,** Luke may have had in mind the forty days and forty nights (Exod. 34:28; cf. Matt. 4:2) that Moses spent on Mt. Sinai. This possibility is supported by the fact that both Exod. 34:28 and Luke 4:2 (cf. Matt. 4:2) observe that time was spent in fasting (in Moses' case also no drinking of water). But Luke presents Jesus also as an Elijah figure, and one might with probability conclude that these words are an echo of 1 Kings 19:8, where Elijah's fasting for forty days and forty nights is mentioned. Israel's wandering of forty years in the wilderness (Deut. 8:2) is a third option. There Israel was tested to determine whether she would observe God's commandments. Since Deut. 8:3 is cited by Luke, it may well have been his intention to contrast Jesus' obedience with Israel's failure. According to Mark 1:13, Jesus was tempted *during* the forty days. Matthew and Luke indicate that the recorded temptations occurred at the end of the period of fasting, although Luke does not use the technical ritual word for fasting. Through emphasis on the weakness of Jesus the magnitude of his victory is enhanced.

4:3. "The devil" (derived from the Greek *diabolos,* which underlies the adjective "diabolic") means slanderer or adversary. The corresponding Hebrew term is "the satan" *(hâ sâtân).* The term is descriptive rather than nominal, but in the course of usage it has been understood to refer to a specific being as the focal point of evil and is therefore frequently capitalized in English.

In the OT the satan is presented variously as an inquisitor (cf. Job 1:6–7); as one who accuses (cf. Zech. 3:1); and ultimately as a tempter (1 Chron.

21:1); and during the intertestamental period as one who aims to disrupt relationships between God and people, that is, he stirs up business for himself. In the NT he appears variously as the accuser (Rev. 12:10), the power of darkness (Col. 1:13), or the ruler of this world (John 12:31). To this last claim Jesus addresses his counterclaim of the Kingdom, and in the passion account the issues will be clearly defined (Luke 22:3, 31, 53).

The first temptation begins with a reference to the words addressed to Jesus after his baptism (3:22). The phrase **if you are the Son of God** (cf. 23:35–39) is not to be construed as a hypothetical assertion that awaits demonstration to validate it. Rather, the status of Jesus is made the starting point of the temptation. Granted that Jesus is the Son of God, as such he ought to exercise his powers and miraculously satisfy himself with food by turning stones into bread (*artos* = "a loaf"). Just one loaf would turn the trick. Even Israel was given manna during the wandering of forty years in the wilderness (Deut. 8:2–3). Surely God's own Son, the epitome of Israel, is entitled to similar preservation. The force of the temptation, then, is to use power for selfish ends and independently of divine intent.

4:4. As the obedient Son of God, Jesus heeds the words of the law in Deut. 8:3, and answers the devil: "People do not live by bread alone" (cf. Wisd. of Sol. 16:26). The thought is thematic in Luke, and the Lord who renounced the tempter on this issue will repeatedly warn his followers not to give in to similar temptation (see, e.g., Luke 16). No onlookers are present in the scene, but to Greco-Roman auditors, accustomed to the use of donations of grain ("bread and circuses") for political advantage, the implications were obvious. What Jesus is tempted to do for himself he could do for others. The question is: To what end? Some exploration of that will be made at 9:12–17. In societies where bread and money form an equation, the meaning of this temptation is inescapable.

4:5–7. In the second temptation the Kingdom of God and the kingdom of Satan are set side by side. The simple statement, that **the devil took him up** (in v. 1, Luke uses the same verb [*agō*] minus the preposition [*ana*]; the tempter reproduces action of the Holy Spirit), omits any reference to a high place (Matt. 4:8 reads: "to a very high mountain"). Luke may suggest thereby that mountains are to be reserved for revelations from God. On the other hand, he may be well aware that no mountain in Palestine would offer a high enough pinnacle for review of the empire.

In **a moment of time,** that is, in a split second, the devil shows Jesus all the pomp and circumstance of the world. God, of course, is the landlord of the earth and allots part of it at various times to someone like Nebuchadnezzar (see Jer. 27:5; cf. Ps. 2:8). As "the god of this world" (2 Cor. 4:4), the devil claims brokerage rights over all its kingdoms and promises them to

Jesus on one condition: "Recognize my supremacy." In similar words spoke Lucan's Caesar before the battle of Pharsalia (*Civil War* 299–300):

> When Mars has done his work, I am the one with
> power to give what kings and nations now possess.

And Nero said to Tiridates, "I have power to take away kingdoms and to bestow them" (Dio Cassius *Roman History* 62.5.3).

Before Israel entered the promised land, Moses described the goodness of the land, its cities and fertile fields, but reminded them that they were not to forget God (Deut. 6:10–12). The warning was not heeded, and now Jesus as God's end-time Israel, the chosen Son, is confronted with a similar temptation.

In the world of politics all normally have their price, so thinks the cynic. Will Jesus opt for standard success criteria or will he choose God's directions? Will he question the promise of Ps. 2:8 and attempt to realize at a discount the donation guaranteed in Dan. 7:14 to the "son of humanity"? Will his career be a mere review of power struggles of the Pharaohs, the Nebuchadnezzars, and the Caesars? Or will he play for the highest stakes and be able to say, "All things have been delivered to me by my Father" (Luke 10:22), and "As my Father appointed a kingdom for me, so do I appoint for you that you may eat and drink at my table in my kingdom" (22:29)? "We can have the coronation right now," says the tempter.

If Jesus renounces the offer, he must feel the full destructive weight of the system. Caiaphas and Pilate, connivers in distribution of power, will crush him, for there will be other takers (on false Christs, see 21:8; cf. Rev. 13:2). And the long history of the institutionalized church will reveal how difficult it is to keep distorted political ambition from contaminating the mission of the People of God. Not government or administration as such is here challenged by the evangelist, but any attempt to reduce God's revolutionary action in Jesus Christ to power grabs in the name of religion is here given its proper ancestry. As Luke 22:24–27 and Acts 1:6 attest, the disciples of Jesus set the pace for slow learning on this topic.

4:8. The die is cast in terms of Deut. 6:13 when Jesus answers the devil: **You shall worship the Lord your God, and him only shall you serve.** He who astounded his teachers at the age of twelve and reminded his parents about the identity of his Parent now gives lessons in statecraft! His is a decisive vote for the Kingdom of God but also a certified invitation to the cross.

Lucian, in his *Dialogues of the Dead* (14), reports the following conversation between Philip of Macedon and his son Alexander, who had been assured by Egyptian priests that he could not fail to be victorious since he was the offspring of Zeus-Ammon.

PHILIP: Surely you can't deny that you are my son, can you, Alexander? If you had been Ammon's son, you would not have died.

ALEXANDER: There was never a doubt in my mind that you were my father. I accepted the word of the oracle only because I thought it was good policy. . . . I had no trouble defeating the barbarians once they thought they were engaged in conflict with a god.

No contrast could be greater than the decision of Alexander and that of Jesus. Alexander was a king but identified himself as a deity with a view to domination over many nations. Jesus was the Son of God but established his identity as king by refusing the standard well-marked routes to political success. Alexander glorified himself. Jesus sought the prestige of his heavenly Parent. Thus Jesus once and for all declared exploitation obsolete and offered a fresh definition of power as opportunity to rescue those who appear beyond hope (see Luke 19:10). Alexander tried on the mantle of deity and lay naked in death at the age of thirty-three. Jesus renounced the way of self-aggrandizement and invited death, but within three days he reversed the verdict of Alexander's cheap imitators.

Ironically it was the Father, not Satan, who delivered "all things" to Jesus (Luke 10:22), and Jesus in turn gave his disciples "authority" over the demons (9:1; 10:19), one of whom pleaded with Jesus not to torture him (8:28–29). In his attempt to switch loyalty from God to himself, Satan underestimated the Stronger One.

4:9–13. For the third and final temptation Jesus is "led" (*ēgagen,* rendered **took,** but the same verb [*agō*] appears in the phrase "led by the Spirit," 4:1) to Jerusalem, to take his stand on a pinnacle of the temple, that is, the complex of buildings that comprised Jerusalem's central place of liturgy. The scene is in keeping with the expectation of Mal. 3:1. Matthew terminates his record of the temptation with the vision of the kingdoms. For him this was the climax, since Jesus renounced Satan's offer and through his obedience inherited all power in heaven and on earth (Matt. 28:18). Luke prefers to end the series with Jerusalem, for his Gospel begins and ends with events taking place in the capital, and the third temptation raises the main question: Will Jesus accept the cross or will he avoid it? The first two temptations coax Jesus to defy God; the third invites him to show complete trust in God.

Expectations of a spectacular messianic demonstration from the temple are described in rabbinic sources (see SB 1:151), but it is debatable whether Luke had this in mind. Once more it is a question of sonship, and this is the prime concern of Luke. Perhaps the fact that the second temptation did not and could not begin with the words "If you are the Son of God" was an additional factor in assigning the third position to this temptation. The basic question is: In view of the outcome of events, will Jesus appear to be the

Son of God? If all goes well with him, God is on his side. If disaster overtakes him, it will be quite clear that he was in the wrong.

"Cast yourself down! You have nothing to worry about, for you are God's Son. The Scripture says that God will direct angels to protect you and that they will lift you up and keep you from stubbing your toes against a rock" (see Ps. 91:11–12). This temptation will be rephrased at Calvary (Luke 23:35, 37, 39). There Jesus will appear to be rejected by the Father. There his enemies will expose his blasphemy in calling himself "the Son of God" (22:70).

In the devil's citation of Scripture the words "in all your ways" are omitted. Some interpreters have seen in this omission an insidious trick. But such interpretation is irrelevant. Biblical citations in the NT are frequently contracted. At v. 18 Jesus himself omits the phrase "day of vengeance" in a quotation from Isa. 61:2. The point is that Jesus is tempted to determine the outcome of his mission in terms of the world's criteria for success, and a cross is scarcely a success symbol.

Jesus retorts a third time (v. 12) with words from Deut. 6:16: "You shall not put the Lord your God to the test." If Jesus suffers, he will suffer as a righteous one (Luke 23:47). Israel suffered much, but the Lord's anger was kindled against her because of her disobedience (cf. Deut. 6:15). But there is no single rule of cause and effect. The righteous can suffer, because God has a purpose to fulfill, and Jesus will be obedient to the rigors of sonship. Thus all three temptations suggest that Jesus avoid the path of suffering and take the easy road to success as determined by the standard criteria. For Luke's auditors these temptations are a reminder not to be misled by the ignominy of Jesus' death. It was all in obedience to his task.

How might some of Luke's Greco-Roman auditors have heard the rest of the story? Not since Homer's depiction of Achilles had auditors of literature heard the hard choice of destiny put more dramatically. What does one put into the scales against the fulfillment of a life with integrity? Achilles's mother, Thetis, told Achilles that two paths were open to him: to die with glory in the prime of life at Troy or to return home without further combat and live a long life without glory. In a world that saw nothing but gloom in the realm beyond the light, life was everything, but Achilles finally chose the short term and opted for glory in a combat that would lead to certain death. On the mount of temptation Jesus was offered the kind of glory that has excited the imagination of countless Alexanders and Caesars. But he had his eyes on a more real glory—a reputation for loyalty to his heavenly Parent's purpose. Unlike Achilles, Jesus showed no hesitation in making his choice. But like Achilles, he must pay the awful fee.

Luke declares that the devil **departed from him.** The devil has made a most reasonable offer—at least it had worked for centuries with others. Jesus will have to learn what the real world of politics is like. He has had his chance. If the devil cannot buy him, he will take an approved political route, and at a far cheaper price. He will discredit Jesus. And the **opportune time** *(kairos)* will not be far off (cf. 22:3–6). The evangelist's auditors, who know how the story ends, hear in these last words the driving of the nails by the hammer at the Hill of the Skull. Not only has Jesus turned his back on glory but he invites himself to the worst of possible ignominies. His is the strangest of all routes to glory.

Jesus had been handed the world and he knows what to do! In the not-too-distant future one of the devil's devotees will discover that the opportune time can be most inopportune (Acts 13:11) for the presumptuous.

Jesus Returns to Galilee
Luke 4:14–15
(Mark 1:14–15; Matthew 4:12–17)

4:14–15. These two verses are programmatic, announcing the first phase of Jesus' ministry. In keeping with the renunciation expressed in the temptation episode, Jesus returns to Galilee, not to Jerusalem, the seat of Israel's traditional power. That city will become the objective, beginning at 9:51.

Galilee signals the worldwide mission of the church (cf. Acts 10:35–37). Despite the fact that Jesus follows unconventional methods to achieve success, he will be victorious, for he accepts the guidance of God (**in the power of the Spirit**). The word "power" *(dynamis)* refers to beneficent function rather than imperious dominion and finds further definition at Luke 4:36; 6:19; 8:46.

Luke's summary recital suggests that Jesus is to be understood as one "mighty in deed and word" (24:19), the twin mark, in the Greco-Roman world, of a person of superior excellence. As recipient of the Spirit (4:18), Jesus is able to transmit the power he possesses to the twelve disciples (9:1; cf. Acts 1:8). The "report" *(phēmē)* concerning him is evidently due to mighty works that are not specified here, for the audience knows the miracle repertoire of Jesus. And beginning as a loyal son of Israel, Jesus teaches in the synagogues. This pattern will be followed also by the apostle Paul, for the promise is first to Israel.

Primarily because of his instruction, Jesus is **glorified by all** *(doxazomenos hypo pantōn)*. In the traditional account there was apparently no reference to human observers of the temptation. This circumstance provides Luke with the literary opportunity to permit his Mediterranean public to realize for themselves the impact of Jesus' victory. Jesus is acclaimed as though he were a victorious head of state. Having renounced the "glory" *(doxa)* of the kingdoms (v. 6), he now begins to gain what Simeon prophesied (2:32; see also 2:14, 20) and is ready to announce the program of the New Age.

Temptation at Nazareth
Luke 4:16–30
(Mark 6:1–6a; Matthew 13:53–58)

Luke 4:14–15 had suggested success. The episode at Nazareth now puts into bold and dramatic relief the meaning of the temptations. Success alternating with rejection (cf. 2:34–35)—that will be the story of Jesus' life, and it will be relived in Christian communities, with change of names and places in the Book of Acts (see, e.g., Acts 3—5; 13; 18). To highlight Jesus' ultimate fate, Luke here uses what appears to be a variant version of what is recited in Mark 6:1–5. Luke's omission of the account at 8:56 confirms this interpretation of his editorial tactic.

4:16. In keeping with a basic theme in Luke's two-volume work, Jesus is portrayed as one who is loyal to ancestral tradition, a person of commendable piety, who spends the sabbath studying Jewish law and custom (cf. Josephus *Antiquities* 61.2.4.43). His followers will similarly be found with regularity in the temple (Acts 2:46; 3:1; 5:42). The mission to the world begins within Israel.

4:17–19. In accordance with synagogal practice, Jesus is given the opportunity to read a passage of Scripture. To judge from Acts 13:15, it was customary in some localities to have a reading from both the Law and the Prophets. The same passage indicates that it was the practice of the president of the synagogue to invite someone to offer an exposition of a portion of Scripture that had been read during the service. In Luke's narrative, Jesus appears to make an independent selection. He **opened the book,** that is, he unrolled the scroll. Whether the passage chosen by Jesus was a fixed lesson for the day cannot be determined. Nor can the exact words read on the occasion be recovered, for Luke's rendering of the text from Isaiah is a composite of Isa. 61:1; 58:6; 61:2. As an "anointed" prophet, Isaiah spoke with authority. But Luke's auditors are prepared for the blending of the past into the future. The Holy Spirit had come upon Jesus at his baptism (Luke 3:22; cf. Acts 10:38), and Jesus had overcome Satan at the site of temptation.

The inclusion of the words from Isa. 58:6 (**to set at liberty** [*aposteilai*] **those who are oppressed**) is prompted by Luke's connection of the episode with the preceding account of Jesus' fasting and temptation. Isaiah 58 raised a question about fasting. The prophet's complaint is that Israel fasts but does not understand that fasting is to be accompanied with justice. The fast that God prefers is the loosing of "the bonds of wickedness, to undo the thongs of the yoke, to let the oppressed go free" (Isa. 58:6). Jesus fasted, but now we see his purpose. Satan suggested a selfish course. Jesus aims to carry out with precision the Isaianic program of righteousness. He does what Israel was criticized for not doing. And for this, as the sequel shows, he is to incur rejection (Luke 4:28–29). The words taken from Isaiah will be expanded in the beatitudes (6:20–23).

Jesus' primary function as liberator is to proclaim the **good news to the poor.** The poor are, according to traditional expression, the politically powerless, those who therefore must look to God for help. Unlike the rich, those who are at ease in Zion, the poor observe God's precepts. But they are despised by the bluebloods of Israel. These words about the poor and the sight given to the blind will be recalled on a subsequent occasion (7:22–23). In summary, it is the prophet's obligation to proclaim **the acceptable year of the Lord.** This is a symbolic reference to the year of Jubilee (Lev. 25:10), when debts were canceled. Jesus' ministry (distinct from that of John's, cf. Luke 16:16) is its practical expression, for it is a ministry of liberation to the poor and the oppressed. The theme of forgiveness is constant in Luke's work and climaxes at 24:47. In line with this emphasis Luke omits the apocalyptic phrase "the day of vengeance of our God" (Isa. 61:2), for it will be taken up at 21:22.

The political language of the text is unmistakable. Greco-Roman auditors would associate with these prophetic words the kinds of expectations that were pronounced at the beginning of an imperial reign. But inhabitants of the Mediterranean had also become accustomed to the routine of recycled bureaucratic failure. Standard processes of political action are therefore put on notice in Jesus' reading of the future; for as someone has said, "God makes no little plans that have no magic to stir the people's blood."

Jesus' interaction with his own townsfolk suggests that there will be no accommodation with political procedures that purchase peace at the price of any sacrifice of hope. The politics of the New Age versus the politics of the Old Age. And the great temptation confronting the People of God is the use of political action for preservation of inherited turf. What happens in the sequel at Nazareth will be symptomatic of the difficulties that God faces in any attempt to sharpen perspectives for the enrichment of humanity.

4:20–21. With words such as these Jesus rolled up the scroll and gave **it back to the attendant.** He then **sat down,** a teacher's customary posture (cf. Luke 5:3; Matt. 5:1; 23:2). With all eyes fixed on him, a gesture that is duplicated in the reaction to Stephen (Acts 6:15), **he began** (once again the thematic *archomai;* see Luke 3:23; Acts 10:37) to deliver an informal homily, introduced with the statement: **Today this scripture has been fulfilled in your hearing.**

"Today" *(sēmeron)* is an important word in Luke's Gospel, stressing the immediate action of the Kingdom in contrast to future apocalyptic fireworks (2:11; 5:26; 19:5, 9: 23:43). Similar to the response described in v. 15 is the reaction at Nazareth. "In your hearing" focuses attention on the authoritative call for immediate response to the royal proclamation. Jesus did not come to establish rabbinic or ecclesiastical debating societies. Nor did he come to arouse the populace to effect a mere change in bureaucratic systems. Within the Roman system a tiny locale such as Nazareth is an empire that awaits renewal. And Everyplace is Nazareth.

4:22. All . . . wondered at the gracious words which proceeded out of his mouth. The word "gracious" *(charis)* would suggest to an OT-oriented public that the words they have heard are those of a wise person (Sir. 21:16; cf. Acts 14:3; 20:24, 32), and the wise person according to Jewish thought is one who observes God's will. Deuteronomy 8:3 says that a person shall live by "everything that proceeds out of the mouth of the Lord." Luke had omitted these words from his citation of the passage in 4:4 (Matthew includes them, 4:4) and reserved the thought for this occasion. Jesus' ministry is the commentary on the words proceeding from the mouth of God and is a strong refutation of all devilish attempts under religious guise to manipulate people in the interests of egocentric objectives.

Unlike Kypselos, who also claimed for himself the fulfillment of an oracle and in the seventh century B.C.E. became the harsh tyrant of Corinth (Herodotos 5.92), Jesus is a beneficent person and is immediately recognized as such. To Greco-Roman auditors the emphasis on words of grace would suggest one of two major characteristics that marked a person of exceptional merit, and the phrase **spoke well of him** refers to the attestation that such merit would elicit (see *Benefactor*, pp. 442–47, and cf. Acts 14:3).

The words of Jesus find living expression in his total dedication. But the observation, **Is not this Joseph's Son?** (cf. Luke 3:23), evokes a warning from Jesus. The misunderstanding of his parents (2:48) is repeated in his hometown, and Luke's public know that they should have exclaimed, "This is God's Son!" It is apparent that Luke aims at expressing both the positive impression that Jesus gives of his real person and the rejection he is to endure, but the rejections must follow Jesus' own prophetic pronouncement. Some of Luke's Greco-Roman public might have recalled Herodotos's account of Maiandrios (3.142), who was to be the successor of Polykrates, the sovereign of Samos. When he approached the Samians in a democratic spirit and offered them the opportunity to share his power, one of the assembly rose up and said: "You are not worthy to reign over us. You're a nobody and a rascal."

Any attempt to analyze the thinking of the crowd at Nazareth is bound to fail. Luke's recital of events at Nazareth is a neural center that sensitizes his entire two-volume work.

4:23. Luke plays with dramatic effect on his auditors' expectations for expression of the second major component of exceptional merit—namely, performance. Near the end of Luke's first stage of the story, one of the two men on the road to Emmaus will describe Jesus as "a prophet mighty in deed and word" (24:19). A civic-minded person who hopes to be recognized as a person of exceptional merit ought to perform especially in his or her hometown. Here at 4:23 Luke highlights hostility toward Jesus, a response that is thematic throughout his two-volume work and that serves here as an impediment to any constructive demonstration by Jesus. The "proverb" (*parabolē*) echoes transcultural wit. Some Greco-Romans would recall Aischylos, who has a chorus make reference to Prometheus as "a quack who has no drugs to prescribe for himself when he is sick" (*Prometheus Bound* 473–75); or Cicero, who writes, "Do not imitate quacks, who claim to have credentials when others are sick but cannot cure themselves" (*Epistles* 4.5.5.; both cited by Wettstein).

Jesus will indeed do deeds in Capernaum (cf. Luke 4:31) that he will later refuse to do in Nazareth because of her unbelief. Gentiles and strangers will receive him, but not his own family circle (cf. 8:19–21). But even Capernaum will be caught in the rise-and-fall syndrome (see 10:15). Through use of the future tense in the phrase **you will quote**, Luke overcomes the difficulty posed by not yet having spoken of Jesus' activity at Capernaum.

The demand by the townspeople (**what we have heard ... country**) would be readily appreciated by Luke's Greco-Roman auditors. Dio Chrysostom (1.48.10) summarized ancient expectations when he observed that one ought to help first one's own city *(patris)*. The words also clarify the use of the proverb, which in its context is not strictly to the point, for it is the townspeople who claim a need. On the other hand, as the sequel shows in an unusual twist of the story, Jesus will display an uncanny ability to heal himself (v. 30).

4:24–27. The modern Greek poet George Seferis relates the story of a painter named Theophilos who was brutally teased by townsfolk who ridiculed his "canvasses" made of cardboard or cheap sailcloth. But after his death a traveler from Paris took about fifty examples of his work and showed them to "the illustrious critics of the Seine. And the illustrious critics gave this verdict: 'Theophilos is a great painter,' and we in Athens could hear our jaws drop" (*On the Greek Style,* 36–37). Someone said of Homer: "Seven cities claimed great Homer dead, through which the living Homer begged his bread." Irony of ironies! Jesus proclaims the "acceptable" year of the Lord (v. 19) but finds no acceptance of himself (v. 24).

Rejection of Jesus by his own people will ultimately encourage distribution of the message elsewhere, even as **Elijah** and **Elisha** performed their miracles outside the boundaries of the Chosen People. There were **many widows** who might have been helped by Elijah, but a foreigner (at Zarephath) benefited from his services (1 Kings 17:9; cf. Luke 7:11–17). There were also **many lepers in Israel**, but only **Naaman the Syrian** was cured (2 Kings 5:14). The theme of selectivity will be taken up again (see Luke 11:29–32; 17:34–35), and 7:1–10; 17:11–19; Acts 8:26–40; 10:1–48 are but a few of Luke's passages that call attention to specific outsiders who benefit from the promises made to Israel.

4:28–30. Through his association of Jesus' ministry with that of Elijah (1 Kings 17) and Elisha (2 Kings 5), Luke once more emphasizes that Jesus' credentials are not validated by the appearance of some other Elijah figure anticipated at the closing of history. Some in Luke's publics would hear a connotation of apocalyptic in the recitation of the tradition ("three years and six months," see Dan. 7:25; 12:7; Rev. 11:2; 13:5; "famine," see Luke 21:11) and infer that the end time is here in the presence of Jesus. Such is indeed Luke's perspective, but with the understanding that Jesus' presence does not mark the end of the end time. No extraordinary signs generally associated with apocalyptic are given at Nazareth. Jesus' own share in the lot of the prophets is validation of his claim to fulfill the Isaianic program here and now.

Simeon had talked about the sign to be spoken against, so that the thoughts of many hearts might be revealed (Luke 2:34–35). Nazareth is a commentary on that prophecy. Satan had suggested that Jesus should test God's intention to preserve him. Jesus chose the way of obedience. At the same time, Jesus will be, as was Elijah, the object of official hatred. According to Deut. 13:1–5, a false prophet was to be put to death. The citizens of Nazareth thought they had their man and were ready to carry out a threat once made against Jeremiah (Jer. 11:21). But the Father has arranged the schedule for Jesus, and the time will come when there will be no escape (cf. Luke 20:15; 23:33); for Jesus committed the ultimate political gaffe of finding fault with his own people.

Jerusalem, headquarters of established religion, will not find challenged her monopoly on elimination of nonconforming prophets (Luke 13:33). Caiaphas will let Judas "finger" Jesus, and Pilate will make the "hit." The words **when they heard** will be echoed at Acts 7:54 after a loyal follower of Jesus has engaged in a more extensive rehearsal of Israel's history. To be "put out" because of association with Jesus will become a passport to fame for such as Stephen (Acts 7:58) and Paul and Barnabas (Acts 13:50; cf. 16:37). And Paul will be left to his fate on the outskirts of Lystra (Acts 14:19). As of now, Jesus evades the murderous intent of the angry crowd. And, suggests Luke, the devil was correct when he spoke about stubbing one's toe (see Luke 4:10–11). Attempts to account for the departure on psychological grounds, such as "the majesty of Jesus' bearing," fail to do justice to the theological perspective. For the present, at least, the Great Physician had healed himself.

Activity in Capernaum
Luke 4:31–44
(Mark 1:21–39; Matthew 8:14–17)

A Demoniac Healed
Luke 4:31–37
(Mark 1:21–28)

4:31–32. As stated in 4:23, Jesus proceeds to carry out part of his ministry in Capernaum, specifically noted as a city in Galilee (see on 4:14). As at Nazareth, he teaches **on the sabbath**, for his mission is first to Israel. His word elicits "astonishment" *(ekplēssō),* for he speaks with authority, that is, as one who has firsthand knowledge of God. He has not learned his theology by rote. Through him fresh waters flowed into the stagnant reservoirs of standard phrase and predictable opinion.

For his word was with authority. "Word" *(logos),* for Luke, is more than instruction *(didachē).* One can be an eyewitness of this word (1:2), for it is attended with powerful action (4:36; 5:1; 7:7; 22:61; 24:19; and often in Acts). According to Isa. 11:4, the root out of Jesse will destroy the impious with the breath of his mouth. Capernaum will shortly see the deeds that back the words of Jesus. And a few years later a proconsul on Cyprus will be "astonished at the teaching of the Lord" when a magician named Bar-Jesus (Elymas) becomes blind for a time under the indictment of Saul, "also called Paul" (Acts 13:4–12).

4:33. He who turned back the tempter now encounters one of his minions. That Luke associates demons with Satan is clear from 10:17–18. To differentiate it from other psychic influences recognized in the Hellenistic world, the demon is described as "unclean" *(akathartos).* But it is important to observe that nowhere in the Gospels is a demon-possessed person charged with moral defects. Stress is placed on the oppressed, depressed, or otherwise debilitated condition of the victim. It is characteristic of Mark to describe demons as shouting **with a loud voice**, and Luke retains this expression.

4:34. Like the widow who asked Elijah whether he had come to cause death in her family (1 Kings 17:18), the demoniac asks, **What have you to do with us?**—that is, "Why this interference?" With the citation of the final words uttered by the demon, Luke tells his public explicitly what Jesus' ultimate objective is—the destruction of Satan (cf. 10:18–19). Instead of "Son of God," the demon says **Holy One of God**, a phrase similar to the one used by the widow in her description of Elisha (2 Kings 4:9, cf. Ps. 106:16; also Judg. 13:7 LXX, ms. Vaticanus; Luke 1:35). The word "holy" *(hagios)* contrasts with "unclean" in v. 33 and highlights the conflict.

Luke's intention in his sketch of the proceedings in vv. 33–34 is now clear. The demonized man is so controlled by the demon that he has lost his individuality. The demon confuses the issue by suggesting that the only way to get rid of him is to destroy the man in the process, hence the plural in the question **Have you come to destroy** *us*? As the Holy One of God, as one obedient to the Law (see his responses in 4:4, 8, 12), Jesus should not tolerate the presence of an unclean person. In short, Jesus is put to the test. How will he preserve the integrity of his own person and yet carry out the program of deliverance announced at Nazareth (4:18)? He must either deliver on the apocalyptic dream and shut down the normal course of history or abandon the program announced in his hometown. In either case, the poor sufferer would be the loser. But Jesus, master of the innovative move, has resources for another option.

4:35. The Greek verb *(epitimaō)* underlying the rendering "rebuked" is used by Luke in the technical sense of "exorcise" (see also 4:39, 41; 8:24; 9:42). Jesus deals summarily with the demon. As one who makes a noisy cur slink away, he says: "Quit your barking and get out of the man." Thus Jesus distinguishes between the man and the demon that possessed him. The demon's destructive power is engaged in a last effort to overpower the man, but out he must come, and Luke notes that the man was not harmed. Luke omits "with a great cry" (see Mark 1:26), so as to make more prominent the complete mastery that Jesus has over the demon.

Through his record of the proceedings Luke shows that delay in the arrival of the end time is not incompatible with the claims made for Jesus as "the Holy One of God." The "acceptable year of the Lord" (4:19) is not one of special apocalyptic effects but the ongoing period in which God shows his deliverance through Jesus. Let Satan know that his days are numbered.

4:36–37. In contrast to the citizens of Nazareth who looked at his person and low position, the people at Capernaum concentrated on the word he speaks: **What is this word?** It is viewed **with authority and power** (*dynamis* recalls 4:14). Satan had tried to detour Jesus, and he had good reason for doing so, but Jesus made no deal with the powers of darkness, and he will be determined to see the battle through to the finish (cf. 10:18–19; 22:28). For the benefit of Theophilos, who may have heard this story (the word for "reports" [*ēchos*] is related to the word "informed" [*katēchēthēs*] in 1:4), Luke has reinforced the depth of the truth contained in the report.

Simon's Mother-in-Law   Luke 4:38–39
(Mark 1:29–31; Matthew 8:14–15)

4:38–39. We are now introduced to the first of the witnesses who are to be gathered in Galilee. As in 5:3, it is suggested that Jesus' movements are by design. Simon's mother-in-law was afflicted with **a high fever.** Simon's married status is mentioned also in 1 Cor. 9:5.

Jesus' fame has gone before him, and the family pleads with him to heal her. Whereas Mark and Matthew say that she was healed at the touch of his hand, without a word being spoken, Luke brings the account in close connection with Jesus' mastery over the demon. Just as he had rebuked the demon (v. 35), so he **rebuked the fever.** In view of the earlier usage of "rebuke" *(epitimaō),* Luke's public probably understood the fever as a demonic effect. Fever-ridden patients are frequently delirious, a physical symptom that was associated in antiquity with demonic influence. Whether such perspective played a part in the choice of diction cannot be determined with certainty. In any event, Luke once more stresses the authority behind Jesus' word.

The cure is instantaneous, for not only does the woman immediately rise up (in Matthew, Mark, and Luke there is a suggestion of resurrection power) but she also proceeded to wait on Jesus and the household (cf. 8:3). According to Deut. 28:22, fever is one of the curses Israel can anticipate for breaking God's covenant. Jesus has come to proclaim the good news and deliverance for the captives. Through him the curse is removed, even as the chasm between clean and unclean was bridged in the case of the demoniac.

Miscellaneous Activity   Luke 4:40–44
(Mark 1:32–39; Matthew 8:16–17)

4:40. The healing of both the demoniac and Simon's mother-in-law had taken place on the sabbath day. But it would not be long before the religious leaders got wind of it (6:7). Up to this moment there is no hint of opposition to Jesus for healing on the sabbath. Yet awareness of the problem is evident in Luke's observation that at sundown, that is, when the sabbath was past, the townspeople brought their sick to him. Jesus, suggests Luke, is careful not to arouse hostility unnecessarily. At the same time, the promise of 1:78–79 may be said to find fulfillment, but that Luke designed a connection between the passages is not certain. Luke's observation that Jesus put his hands on each of the sick persons points to the personal interest Jesus took in the sufferers as well as to his lack of fear of contracting ritual defilement. (Acts 28:8–10 parallels the recitals of Luke 4:38–41.)

4:41. Once more "demons" *(daimonia)* are specifically mentioned (cf. Acts 19:12). Luke's addition to Mark's account, that the demons identified him as the Son of God, gives him an opportunity to equate this name with Jesus' role as the "Christ" (see on 2:11, and cf. 22:67–70). Thus Luke suggests that the healings enumerated are in keeping with the program announced at Nazareth, where Jesus said that the Spirit of the Lord had anointed (= *"christed"*) him (4:18).

In keeping with Mark's account, Luke observes that Jesus imposed silence (**he rebuked them,** as in vv. 35, 39) on the demons. Jesus refuses to receive any help from that source (cf. 11:14–20). Such advertisement could only lead to misunderstanding, and Jesus does not sponsor a personality cult. Moreover, Jesus as the Christ must suffer and die and rise again (9:22). Satan had suggested that Jesus bypass the cross. Jesus' refusal to permit the demons to identify him is a restatement of his resolution to resist the tempter. For this reason even the disciples were later forbidden to proclaim that he was the Christ (9:21).

Jesus has no intention of making a spectacular apocalyptic demonstration. His real identity rests on the claims he will make before the chief priests (22:69–70) and on the cross (23:35–46). Apart from these considerations, some in Luke's publics would have been impressed by the ability of Jesus to overcome the malevolent intention that lay behind the effort to expose the identity of Jesus. To silence the demonic opposition, as Jesus did, was a demonstration of extraordinary competence.

4:43. In keeping with his practice of avoiding any partisan messianic movement, Jesus resists the temptation to solidify his popularity in Capernaum. In his reply to the crowds, the words **I must preach the good news** and **I was sent for this purpose** reproduce the program announced at Nazareth, for the same terms *(euanggelizō, apostellō)* are used in v. 18 (plus Luke's own "must" [*dei*]). The expression **the kingdom of God** occurs for the first time in Luke. God's political action is to be seen in a remarkably dramatic manner. Some hint of it appeared in 1:33, but now, in the light of Jesus' encounter with demonic forces and in view of his program announced at Nazareth, it is clear that the Kingdom of God is a major assault on the forces of evil and a realization of Isaianic expectation. In practical terms this means that the People of God are to implement justice, which is the foundation of God's throne (Ps. 97:2).

So intimately is the Reign of God *(basileia tou theou)* connected with the person of Jesus Christ that Acts 8:12 describes Philip as making a proclamation "about the kingdom of God and the name of Jesus Christ." Let Theophilos know that this King is no tool to be manipulated by nationalistic interests! A divine necessity rests on him: He "must" (on *dei*, see also Luke 9:22; 13:33; 17:25; 19:5; 22:37; 24:7, 26, 44) preach the good news of this reign.

4:44. The concluding geographical reference to **Judea** is a remarkable departure from Mark's Galilee (Mark 1:39). Galilee is important to Mark as a locality, but not to Luke. In Luke, Galilee is significant primarily because of the witnesses who are gathered from that region, whereas Jerusalem is the central locale for much of the decisive action described in Luke's twin work. Reference to Judea suggests activity that takes in all of Israel (cf. Luke 1:5; 6:17; 7:17). "Other ancient authorities read Galilee," says the margin of the RSV, but the reading "Galilee" is apparently an attempt to bring Luke into harmony with Mark.

Acts 10:37 echoes Luke 23:5 in the stress laid on Judea as a totality. Israel cannot claim lack of opportunity. It is also probable that Luke aims in v. 44 to exonerate Jesus of subversive charges. Galilee was the hotbed of the Zealots' liberation movement. Jesus, suggests Luke, did not limit his ministry to that area and, what is more, he disclaimed partisan misconceptions of his mission.

The Kingdom of God is not a demonstration of patronizing power. Jesus renounced that in his rebuff of Satan (4:8). The reign proclaimed by Jesus is God in outreach to claim what is properly God's: the poor, the estranged, the outcast—all who by established religious or social custom have been excluded from association with God. This is the radical politics of the New Age. Jesus, the obedient Son of God, has come to lead people to the understanding that God is a Parent who cares for them and invites them to obedient recognition of the divine reign. There will be trouble only if those with too great a vested interest in the past resist the validity of that claim.

The First Disciples

Luke 5:1–11
(Mark 1:16–20; Matthew 4:18–22)

The Kingdom of God is defined more explicitly in this chapter as one of renewed relationships between God and people. Prophets viewed the basic problem of Israel as one of elimination of the sin that separated them from God. In contrast to Jesus' experience of rejection at Nazareth is his own reception of outcasts. The acceptable year of the Lord (Luke 4:19) has indeed arrived!

Mark's recital (Mark 1:16–20) of the call of the first disciples is expanded by Luke, who makes use of a tradition that was apparently known in a different form to the Fourth Evangelist (see John 21:1–11). Luke gives greater prominence to Peter than does Mark. He appears to be aware of special problems raised in the early community by those who questioned Peter's apostolic credentials, for Peter had denied the Lord and had also embarrassed the mission to the gentiles (cf. Gal. 2:11–14). Luke's account of his call therefore underwrites the legitimacy of his apostolic office.

Peter qualifies as one of the witnesses required for the proclamation of God's action in Jesus Christ, and Luke suggests that he has known Jesus for some time (5:3; cf. 4:38). Since Peter was prominent in the church, it is probable that he might have been suspected of subversive activity. If such had been the case, Luke's account clarifies for Theophilos the nature of Peter's interest in One who was accused of insurrection.

5:1. At Luke 4:40 the crowds came for healing. Now the crowds *(ochlos)* **pressed upon him to hear the word of God.** "Word of God" is equivalent to the good news of the Kingdom of God (4:43). The phrase "word of God" is more common in the Book of Acts than in the Gospel, which provides the background for the usage in Acts. Luke will soon offer a sample of the content of Jesus' preaching (6:20–49). The press of the crowd forces Jesus to adopt the stratagem of delivering his message from a boat. (Once again the RSV overlooks the first Greek word of the verse: *egeneto*.)

5:2. Luke's chief interest is in Jesus' encounter with Simon. This is apparent from Luke's emphasis on the **two boats** and the fact that the fishers (for the names of others, see Mark 1:16) were washing their nets. The night's work was over. Luke uses the correct term "lake" *(limnē)* for the body of water popularly known as the Sea of Galilee and identified in v. 1 in terms of the district, Gennesaret, near which it was located.

5:3. Luke suggests that Jesus chose **Simon's** boat by design. From this boat he kept on delivering his message to the crowds (the posture of sitting is borrowed from Mark 4:1, as is indicated by the omission at Luke 8:4 of any reference to Jesus' presence in a boat). This instruction is now the setting for the episode that follows.

5:4. The dialogue is compressed. Jesus tells Simon: **Put out into the deep.** Simon, it is to be inferred, does so. At the deep point Jesus gives a second order: **Let down your nets for a catch.** (The plural in the Greek verb [*chalasate*] is not translated by the RSV.)

5:5–6. The picture up to this point is that of one in command of the situation. *Epistatēs,* the Greek word for **Master**, is used only by Luke (5:5; 8:24, 45; 9:33, 49; 17:13), and with the exception of 17:13 it is found only on the lips of disciples ("teacher" [*didaskale*] is the usual expression employed by those outside the immediate circle; see, e.g., 7:40; 8:49; 9:38). *Epistatēs* was applied in the Roman Empire to holders of various types of administrative posts. In keeping with the point made in 4:43, Luke uses "kingdom" diction. Jesus is a politician in his own right. His word, Luke implies, is one of authority. But now Simon the professional informs an amateur that the fishing is simply no good. His remarks about the long night's fruitless labor are of course a literary foil for the description of the great catch soon to follow. The dialogue attests the authority of Jesus. Simon orders the nets dropped. "Blessed are those who hear the word of God and keep it" is one of Luke's repeated themes. And the fishers have their reward, but it is more than they can handle.

5:7–8. The crew make frantic motions to their companions, who are still apparently on shore (v. 2). Now both boats are so full with fish that the water laps at the gunwales. Luke's economy of description focuses all attention on the immensity of the catch in order to explain why Simon Peter reacts as he does. A normal professional experience can be taken in stride. But this Amateur finding fish in this quantity at a most unlikely hour! It can mean only one thing. He must have a firsthand contact with God—and Simon wants no trouble from that source. Simon is not a bad man, but certainly not a model of piety, and he confesses, "I am a sinner" (cf. 1 Sam. 6:20). The term "sinful person" *(hamartōlos)* denotes one of a mass of people classified by the Pharisees as outcasts, not entitled to God's favor (see above on 3:12).

Instead of "Master" (v. 5), Simon terminates his request (which will be echoed at 8:37) with "Lord" *(kyrios),* a clear link of the confession of the Christian community with the history of Jesus.

5:9. But the main point is missed if Simon's confession is traced to awareness of the sinlessness of Jesus. Luke plainly says that the confession was prompted by astonishment over the catch of fish. According to Acts 17:25–28 and Rom. 2:4, the "goodness" of God, the Supreme Benefactor, aims to bring people to repentance. Simon's confession is one of unworthiness of such signal demonstration of God's beneficence. But the proclamation of the Kingdom declares that such favor is not extended on the basis of worth and that the distance between the unclean and the holy is bridged in the person of Jesus, the Lord of the community (see on 4:33–34).

Greco-Romans recognize the effect that manifestations of divine power can have. For example, after receiving a visitation from the deity Sarapis, a devotee named Maiestas got over his astonishment and proceeded to carry out the instructions of his divine visitor (see *Benefactor,* No. 27, lines 60–65).

5:10. Luke mentions those **partners with Simon** (i.e., business partners) who were also impressed by the catch, but Simon is singled out for a specific consolation. The words **Do not be afraid** appear frequently in Isaiah. Instead of encouraging Simon's departure, Jesus takes him into his own profession—"catching people alive" (this contrast to the threat expressed in Jer. 16:16 is striking). The roles are now reversed. Simon has become the amateur! By commissioning him for his own program, Jesus pronounces an absolution that would never be superseded. Not a word is spoken about assurance of forgiveness. Such words would be superfluous after an invitation like this.

The mode of absolution pronounced by Jesus is a reminder that the gospel is more than words and syllables. When the church, because of inadequate attitudes and status patterns, fails to communicate the forgiving presence of Christ, it is questionable whether liturgical pronouncement will convince the sinner that God has better intentions.

Simon, who became an instrument of prosperity to his few colleagues, will be a source of blessing to many of God's people inside and outside Israel. On this occasion Luke introduced the name Peter (*Petros,* "Rockman," v. 8) into the narrative. Matthew (16:13–20) views the confession of Simon at Caesarea Philippi as the crucial moment to display the contrast between the inadequate religious establishment and the informed apostolic communities. Luke sees this incident on the Lake of Galilee as the moment in which the far-flung mission of the church begins to crystallize. The Kingdom of God is in action. The Christian missionary movement is seen rooted in this kind of invitation to join what will soon be the apostolic circle.

5:11. It is remarkable that these fishers, who are savoring their most striking professional success, leave all to follow Jesus (see also 5:28; 14:33; 18:28). Luke could not write more forcefully that he spoke with authority and with power (cf. 4:36). The call of Jesus is the authentic way into the presence of God, who has given Jesus the authentic authority that Satan could not deliver (cf. 4:6). But Nazareth relied on traditional rights (4:16–30)!

COLLISION COURSE

Luke 5:12—6:16

A Leper Healed

Luke 5:12–16
(Mark 1:40–45; Matthew 8:1–4)

5:12. At this point Luke returns to Mark's narrative order of events for his second outcast, a leper. Just as Simon Peter had confessed himself outside the normal religious patterns of Israel, so this man is unable to participate in the liturgy of his people. A counterpart to Israel's experience with Naaman (see 4:27) is about to be recited.

The generic term "leprosy" *(lepros)* is recognizable especially in translations of Leviticus 13, which contains the specific order that the leper is to cry out in warning: "Unclean, unclean" (Lev. 13:45). Unfortunately many readers of the Bible conclude that the term "leprosy," which is found in most translations, refers to very specific types of a disease that is associated with *Hansen's bacillus* and identified clinically as *Bacillus leprae*. The latter, known as "true leprosy," is characterized either by the formation of nodules that ultimately lead to degeneration especially of the extremities or by loss of sensation in the nerves serving such parts of the body, or by a mixture of both.

It is questionable whether Leviticus 13 and the story of Naaman the Syrian in 2 Kings 5 refer to this specific disease, but sufferers from *Bacillus leprae* have during much of the history of the disease borne the brunt of the social and religious ostracism practiced in the name of fidelity to Moses. As if this were not enough, popular insensitivity has also associated leprosy with sinfulness, but the Bible nowhere states that leprosy is a type of sin. The closest present-day phenomenon in terms of societal attitude is acquired immunodeficiency syndrome (AIDS).

Peter had grasped the knees of Jesus as a suppliant. This man **fell on his face** in most humble petition and, as did Peter, uses the term **Lord** *(Kyrios),* the form of address used by the early community in its liturgy. He asks for cleansing, a request that goes beyond a mere cure. Once more the emphasis is on Jesus' power to restore interrupted relationships, whether with God or with man. The statement **if you will** prepares the reader for Jesus' response

I will (v. 13), with stress placed on Jesus' initiative. Luke omits Mark's reference to the anger of Jesus. In the context of Luke's recital it would be meaningless. It is frequently stated that Luke downplays the emotions of Jesus, but this is not observable in some narratives that are even peculiar to his Gospel (see, e.g., 7:13; 19:41).

5:13. The fact that Jesus reaches his hand out to touch the leper is another reminder that Jesus does not contract defilement but removes it. Officialdom of course would expect "the Holy One of God" to uphold Moses and warn the man to keep his distance. But Jesus approaches no one gingerly, and tradition, no matter how rock-ribbed, must make way for the compassion of the New Age. Since Jesus' word is one of power, the leper is cured in the instant. But Jesus does not seek notoriety for cures. His healings are but one facet of a total ministry that seeks return of the person to the Father (see Luke 15).

5:14. Whenever possible, if it does not jeopardize that overriding concern, Jesus observes traditional ordinances. It is a theme in keeping with Luke's interest in displaying the continuity of the Christian proclamation with Israel's tradition. Jesus therefore tells the man to show himself to the priest and perform the required ritual described in Leviticus 13—14.

The phrase **for a proof to the people** has generated a variety of interpretations. Literally the Greek reads: "as a testimony to them" *(eis martyrion autois).* Similar expressions occur in 9:5; 21:13. Since the words that precede this phrase emphasize legal performance, Luke evidently understood the plural form "them" in Mark 1:44 as a colloquial and general reference to the religious authorities. And since the very next episode raises the question of Jesus' sense of legal responsibility, it is probable that Luke understood the phrase to say that Jesus' fidelity to the Law is beyond criticism: "Let headquarters know that we do not undermine Moses" (cf. 16:31). Expressed another way, if adherence to Moses is to be the criterion whereby Jesus' activity is to be judged, let them cope with Moses in the light of this extraordinary development. In any event, Luke has again fulfilled his promise to give an orderly account (1:4).

Through this incident, coupled with the story of Simon's call and the cure of the demoniac, Luke has sketched the basic outlines of Jesus' ministry. He could not postpone indefinitely encounter with the religious establishment. But Jesus has been guilty of no overt criticism of the priests. Even John's remarks (Luke 3:7) were addressed to the crowds, without singling out the religious leaders as is done in Matthew's account (Matt. 3:7). Moreover, the ministry of Jesus and that of John have been scrupulously kept separate. Any hostility that emerges must be the result of Jesus' own peculiar activity, that of one who bridges the chasm between God and the outcast. Only in

that sense can Jesus be called subversive, but responsibility for misunderstanding will rest with Israel's religious leadership.

5:15. Whereas Jesus has been proclaiming "the word of God" (5:1), now
the "word" (RSV: **report** for *logos*) about Jesus goes out everywhere. **So
much the more** suggests that a high point relative to 4:14 and 37 has been
reached. The Kingdom of God and the name of Jesus are synonymous (Acts
8:12). Word and action, to Greco-Roman auditors the major components of
superior excellence, surface thematically in Luke's rephrasing of Mark 1:45,
for many are **gathered to hear and to be healed.** Acts 5:16 echoes the
summary and shows that the experience of Jesus continues in the course of
apostolic ministry (cf. Acts 10:38).

5:16. In Luke's Gospel, Jesus prays at crucial moments. With his final
sentence concerning Jesus at prayer in the wilderness (a note absent in Mark
1:45) Luke alerts his public to a fresh phase in the ministry of Jesus. He had
heard the voice from heaven in answer to his prayers. Before the series of
temptations he had fasted. Now, before encountering the Pharisees and the
teachers of the Law, he communes with heaven. All his work is to be
understood in terms of performance of the Father's will.

A Paralytic Healed

Luke 5:17–26
(Mark 2:1–12; Matthew 9:1–8)

Although this episode initiates a new phase, the words "and it came to
pass" (*kai egeneto,* omitted by the RSV also in vv. 1 and 12) link the narrative
to the two preceding accounts. Simon Peter, the unnamed leper, and the
paralytic all have the same basic problem. From a restrictive religious
standpoint they are outsiders.

5:17. In anticipation of the unusual scene described in vv. 24–25, the
narrative begins with emphasis on Jesus' teaching and with a reference to
"God's power" *(dynamis kyriou)* that was at his disposal—**the power . . . to
heal.** Greco-Roman auditors would gather from Luke's editing of Mark
that Jesus continues to be presented as the supreme manifestation of divine
beneficence. That this Hellenistic perspective is indeed a part of Luke's
conception is clear from 24:19, and especially from Acts 10:38. In this latter
passage Luke reminds his public of the anointing of Jesus "with the Holy
Spirit and with power," and then summarizes Jesus' healing activity as that
of a benefactor (the Greek verb for "doing good," *evergetō,* is the standard
term for the performance of a civic-minded person in the Greco-Roman
world. "Benefactor" is a Latin loanword).

In the story about the paralytic, word and action again join in the person
of Jesus, and the miracle is not so much a revelation of Jesus' ability to heal

as an interpretation of his total instruction. God demonstrates through this contact with sinners that the forgiveness of sins spoken of in 1:77 is divine reality. It is evident that Luke attaches great importance to this incident, for Mark's "many" (2:2) is expanded by Luke into an impressive group of personages—**from every village of Galilee and Judea and from Jerusalem.** To focus attention on the issues raised by Jesus' activity, Luke specifically mentions **Pharisees and teachers of the law.** In this recital we are to see matched one lone scribe against the nation's best legal experts.

The teachers of the Law are also called "scribes" and "lawyers" in this Gospel. During the exile, the Law (Torah) became the center of attention for Israel. Gradually a special class of interpreters or scholars gained prestige and became the recognized experts. Their task was to determine practical applications of the written law, teach in the temple precincts or synagogues, and serve as judges in courts of law. Writing of laws was limited to copying of the OT. Attracted to their ranks were many nonspecialists in legal matters who dedicated themselves to practical observance of the law. Because of their notoriety in the NT they have as a class received a bad press, but their contribution to the continuity of the moral and religious life of Israel was enormous. Without them Israel might well have been assimilated beyond recall.

These nonspecialists were called "Pharisees," a term variously explained as "interpreters" (of the Scriptures) or "separated ones." The latter term need not carry an unsavory connotation. Rather, their zeal to observe the precepts of holiness prompted them to isolate themselves from all ritual and moral contamination. Like the Puritans and many Victorians, who have also been maligned, they tried to stem what they considered a secularistic tide. Some went further in their zeal than did others, and, as frequently happens, the overzealous put the reputation of the more moderate into disrepute.

Similarly, rigorous people today resist the avalanche of dirty books or obscenity in other visual media in an attempt to hold the line for well-established social, political, or religious tradition. As in ancient times, the zeal of some is displayed in censoriousness, invasion of personal liberties, or refusal to recognize legitimate differences in point of view. Such extremists in turn register resentment toward those who question such rigorous application of inherited precept or moral theory. The hostility toward Jesus described in the subsequent recital is therefore understandable. Moral arrogance is a perennial disease. And no one who interferes with the system goes unscathed.

The phrase **and the power of the Lord was with him to heal** is unparalleled in Luke (4:14, 36; 6:19; 8:46 display a modified form). "Lord" *(kyrios)* is ambiguous. It could refer either to Jesus or to God, but the context, which raises the issue whether man or God has the right to forgive sins, suggests that God is in mind here. God is behind the healing that is to take place, and this will mean that the forgiveness pronounced by Jesus is validated from the same source. There is the further suggestion that Jesus is conscious of the power available to him. He does not proceed on his own initiative, and the bold step he is about to take has the Father's sanction.

5:18. The solemnity of the hour is further highlighted with the words **And behold** *(kai idou),* old English for "Now note!" The popularity of Jesus is suggested not only by Luke's repeated reference to crowds but by the fearlessness of the four men who ignore the presence of the dignitaries and let their sick friend down toward the Center of attraction (v. 18).

5:19. In place of Mark's description of a thatched roof (Mark 2:4, "made an opening" = "dug through"), Luke, apparently portraying an architectural style more familiar to some of his Mediterranean public, observes that part of the roof consisted of tiles.

5:20. Jesus **saw their faith**, which contrasted with the unbending legalism of the religious leaders. The pronoun "their" certainly includes the paralytic. The point is that the man and his friends are linked in a relationship of trust and commitment that ought to characterize Israel (cf. 7:9; 17:18–19).

Jesus responds to their faith with the words **Man, your sins are forgiven you.** The reader must infer that the sick man is here addressed. In the popular mind, sickness and sin were intimately associated (cf. John 9:2; and see the modification of Isa. 53:4 in Matt. 8:17), but there is no hint in the text that the man had been guilty of some great sin or that he is overwhelmed with a feeling of intense guilt. It should be noted, furthermore, that Jesus does not explicitly say: "I forgive you your sin." The Greek words are to be rendered: "Your sins have been forgiven you." This could be understood as an objective declaration of God's absolution. Had not Isaiah (33:24) said of things in later time: "No inhabitant will say, 'I am sick'; the people who dwell there will be forgiven their iniquity"? The line of thought is in line with Jesus' prayer at 23:34: "Father, forgive them."

5:21. Certain scribes (experts in the Law of Moses) and Pharisees are quick to make assumptions. Their legal minds told them, suggests Luke, that this man could not be pronounced forgiven, for he still remains paralyzed. Forgiveness must mean the removal of sickness (see, e.g., the Qumran scroll 4QNahum 4). In any case, the pronounced forgiveness remains in question, and Jesus, they conclude, takes too much on himself. He must be guilty of "blasphemies," for only God can forgive sin; that is, only God can determine whether a person is forgiven.

5:22. All this is going on in the minds of the Pharisees, so Luke points out with Jesus' question: **Why do you question** *(dialogizesthe)* **in your hearts?**

that is, "within yourselves." That Jesus understands what is going on within them is quite a blow to their reasoning, for they question the ability of Jesus to deal with an unknown quantity. But they fail to realize that he had already seen another unknown quantity, the faith of the other men, and faith is a prerequisite for forgiveness.

Some of Luke's public with knowledge of the Jewish Scriptures would view Jesus as an insightful person. Samuel, for example, knows what is on Saul's mind (1 Sam. 9:19), and Daniel can interpret dreams whose details Nebuchadnezzar forgot upon awakening (Daniel 2). To Greco-Roman auditors, the fact that Jesus knows what is on the minds and in the hearts of others would suggest that he was endowed with divine powers (see also Luke 6:8; 9:47; 24:38). For example, the emperor Tiberius retained the services of Thrasyllus, an astrologer, because of his apparent prescience (Dio Cassius *Roman History* 55.11.1–2).

5:23. Since the Pharisees have questioned the power of Jesus' words to effect a change that could not be perceived by man, Jesus asks, **Which is easier, to say, "Your sins are forgiven you," or to say, "Rise and walk"?** The point is that the one statement appears easy, for who can prove it? The second is subject to observation. Yet in either case an inference must be made. Thus all is resolved into one question: Does the word of Jesus have God's power behind it or not? By omitting Mark's reference to the paralytic (Mark 2:9), Luke turns the recital concerning relative ease into a more generalized inquiry concerning word and performance.

5:24. Jesus addresses his questioners with the words: **But that you may know that the Son of man has authority on earth to forgive sins.** Apart from what Mark might have thought about the source of these words, Luke appears to consider them a continuation of the dialogue ascribed to Jesus. The form of statement seems to contradict the previous interpretation that Jesus himself does not forgive sins. But in this statement Jesus declares that he has the right to make such a pronouncement because his credentials are from God (cf. 2:14). His words are ratified by God's own decision *now* **on earth.** (On Son of humanity, see comment on 6:5.)

Now for the second time Jesus addresses the paralytic, directing him to rise and take up his bed. The command to return home is a further touch to emphasize his restoration to community. Jesus said not one word about healing. He gave the man an order such as one might give to someone in good health. As in the case of the pronouncement of forgiveness, an inference must be made. In and through Jesus' very presence and action God expresses love for the individual.

5:25. The man must have been made well, for on the spot he rose, took his belongings, and went home. The Pharisees must grant that the same inference is valid concerning Jesus' word of forgiveness. As one would say, it must have taken effect. And all the more since it is a rabbinic axiom that God does not listen to sinners. But those who revere God and do the divine will have assurance that God listens to them (cf. John 9:31). In an observation peculiar to Luke, the healed man glorifies God, even as the shepherds did on their return from the manger (Luke 2:20).

5:26. And amazement *(ekstasis)* **seized them all**, including the Pharisees and legal experts, and they gave praise to God. Thus Luke points out that even those who later were hostile had to confess that Jesus possessed the authority he claimed. And this took place "today" (on *sēmeron*, see on 4:21).

Luke's editorial modifications of Mark 2:12 suggest that Luke incorporates the story of the paralytic as a primary exhibit for the program of the New Age. Especially significant are the following alterations: (1) The addition of the paralytic's response to the healing; he went home "glorifying God" *(doxazōn ton theon)*. (2) Use of the noun "amazement" in place of the cognate verb. (3) Complete revision of Mark's concluding phrases, with emphasis on "fear" (RSV: *awe*) and the **strange things** *(paradoxa)* the people had seen. Such stress on response is found at Acts 3:8–10, in the conclusion to Luke's flagship recital of the healing of a lame man. As Luke reports it, the healed man exuberantly praises God, and the people are filled with "wonder and amazement." Almost an entire chapter (Acts 4) is then spent on the relation of the response of the religious hierarchy to the participation of Peter and John in the event.

A key verse (4:9–10) sets forth the fundamental theological perspective: God's beneficence is signally demonstrated in both word and deed through Jesus Christ of Nazareth. The program of "forgiveness," announced at Nazareth (4:18) is a fundamental feature of the divine benefaction. It is therefore proclaimed at Acts 3:19, and the apostolic experience is dramatically foreshadowed at Luke 5:23. In Mark's narrative, the opponents ask, "Why does this man speak thus?" (Mark 2:7). Appropriate to the movement of Luke's total literary work, they ask, "Who is this . . .?" (Luke 5:21). The query will be repeated at 7:49.

Banquet at the House of Levi
Luke 5:27–39
(Mark 2:13–22; Matthew 9:9–17)

Another Disciple
Luke 5:27–32
(Mark 2:13–17; Matthew 9:9–13)

Two stories of people in need of healing have been recited back to back. Luke now provides them with literary boundaries through recording of a counterpart to his story about Simon (5:1–11). Thus two narratives of healing are embraced by accounts concerning two professionals whose lives undergo strange redirection, and the common thread of restoration or forgiveness binds them all. The threat to propitiatory cultic systems and social boundaryizing requires no elaboration. Apartheid in all its various destructive forms falls under the downward thrust of the New Age ax.

5:27–28. The story of the call of **a tax collector named Levi** continues the account of Jesus' outreach to the outcasts. Jesus deliberately selects such a person for his fellowship (on tax collectors, see comment on 3:12), with no special consideration for the sentiments of Pharisees. The Pharisees, using the same type of generalizing yardstick that has put them under opprobrium, considered toll collectors as extortioners and in the main dishonest. Some Pharisees who were merchants might also be hostile in principle to people who collected tolls on goods that entered Herod Antipas's domain. For such antipathy based on economic considerations there is ample evidence in antiquity.

At Jesus' command, Levi **left everything, and rose and followed** Jesus (cf. 5:11). There is no indication that Jesus has known him before. Once again the focus is on the power of Jesus' word to command response.

The identity of Levi has long been in dispute. Mark and Luke do not mention him in their list of apostles (Mark 3:16–19; Luke 6:14–16). In Matt. 9:9 he is identified with the apostle Matthew.

5:29. Levi proceeds to hold a farewell party. Jesus has second thoughts about delays of this kind (Luke 9:61), but apparently in this case Levi is not presumed to be guilty of temporizing, and in any case a banquet scene is desirable for the holding of such dialogue as Luke presents in vv. 30–39 (for similar "banquet discourses," see 7:36–50; 10:38–42; 14:1–24; 19:1–10, and perhaps through v. 27). Like Abraham's celebration at the time Isaac was weaned (Gen. 21:8), this was **a great feast.** Mediterranean wit might well have theorized that the cost ensured Levi's abandonment of everything (5:28).

Luke notes that many tax collectors were present. But in place of Mark's "sinners," Luke simply records that "others" were with them. He lets the term "sinners," a contemptuous classification, come on the lips of the Pharisees at v. 30. Luke evidently realizes the improbability of Pharisees dining with tax collectors and does not include them in the guest list. That they are in the vicinity is clear from his narrative.

5:30. The Pharisees are irked by the young upstart from Nazareth, and their annoyance finds circuitous expression. Instead of criticizing Jesus directly (as they do in Mark 2:16: "Why does he eat . . .?"), these particular experts in legalized exclusion murmured against the disciples' participation: **Why do you eat and drink with tax collectors and sinners?** The word "murmured" *(goggyzō)* echoes Israel's flagrant violation of their covenant with God (see, e.g., Num. 14:26–35).

Modern readers find it tempting to condemn the scribal reaction without taking inventory of their own community standards. In St. Louis, Missouri, a victim of AIDS was forced off the stage moments before a live television talk show was to begin; fearful television technicians refused to hook a microphone on the guest, who then participated offstage by telephone. In Indiana a group of parents for a time set up an alternate school rather than permit their children to attend classes with a young victim of AIDS.

5:31–32. Jesus takes the heat off his disciples with a proverb known in many ages of antiquity: "The sick, not the well, require the services of a physician." The proverb would remind Luke's public of an earlier one about physicians (4:23). Jesus explains it in terms of his own policy and practice: **I have not come to call** *(kalesai,* "invite") **the righteous, but sinners to repentance.** Rabbinic classification of sinners included thieves, cutthroats, liars, cheats, and fornicators as well as a long list of ordinary occupations. In fairness to Judaism it should be noted that rabbis did not discourage fellowship with repentant sinners, but it is clear that Jesus' liberality went beyond the bounds of Pharisaic practice. Philosophers were frequently charged with similar breaches of polite morality. In defense of his association with undesirable elements, Antisthenes acidly commented: "Doctors associate with the sick but do not contract fevers" (Diogenes Laertius 6.6).

What is especially remarkable about Jesus' reply is the shift in initiative. He speaks as one who does the calling or inviting. He is the host (see 14:16, where the same Greek verb *(kaleō)* is rendered "invited," and cf. 19:5) even though he appears to be the guest. He chooses whom he wishes for his company, and the outcasts are especially welcome. He does not, as suggested by the Pharisees, thereby make light of or condone sin. He invites the sinners, not their sin; for he makes his invitation with a view to the guest's "repentance" *(metanoia;* a note missing in Mark 2:17; see on Luke 3:3, 8). One cannot accomplish that objective by refusing to associate with those in need of it (cf. 1 Cor. 5:9–13). On the other hand, there is no need to urge repentance on **the righteous** *(dikaious),* that is, those who are already (from the standpoint of accepted standards) conforming to God's will. God, of course, searches the inner being (Luke 16:15). Jesus did not encourage a phony radicalism that bought its own prestige at the cheap price of downgrading virtue.

Up to this point Pharisees have not been a special object of attack and Luke depicts Jesus as still avoiding any ground for hostility. Pharisees, if they are genuinely concerned about God's will, are entitled to the Kingdom, but they ought to congratulate Jesus instead of criticizing him for his outreach to those whom they classify as "tax collectors and sinners."

Luke speaks to his contemporary Christian communities through this account. Where the congregation complains that the minister spends too much time on reaching those outside the respected borders of the church, there the word is being misunderstood. Both Pharisee and church are therefore warned against developing into a society of self-congratulators. And unless there is a sympathy with Jesus' stance, self-styled insiders will find themselves requiring repentance.

Misunderstanding: New versus Old   Luke 5:33–39

The Bridegroom   Luke 5:33–35
(Mark 2:18–20; Matthew 9:14–15)

Jesus is now addressed directly. It is a matter of instruction, say the opposition, presumably those of 5:30. Other religious parties require frequent fasting and prayers, but Jesus' disciples always seem to be partying. (Despite their leader's arrest, John's disciples carried on; cf. 7:18; 11:1; and Acts 18:25—19:5.) In other words, Jesus violates the system. The fact is, Moses prescribed only one fast day, the tenth of Tishri (Lev. 16:29–34; 23:26–32; Num. 29:7–11), but guardians of tradition increased the dosage and, as in every age, found threatening any challenge to rule-oriented custom by a nonconformist such as Jesus.

From Luke's perspective, in support of Jesus' action one ought to observe that fasting was ordinarily thought of as a means of improving relationships with the Deity. But Jesus himself is the expression of God's goodwill; therefore banqueting rather than fasting is appropriate to the New Age that has dawned. This does not mean that fasting is to be discouraged. Jesus himself fasted before his encounter with Satan (4:2). At Acts 13:2 fasting is associated with the presence of the Holy Spirit (see also Acts 14:23). The error lies in the assumption that fasting is a matter of rule and regulation. In later times the same type of debate to which Jesus was subject would take place over the introduction of inclusive-language lectionaries, the use of Latin versus the vernacular, and informal versus prescribed liturgy.

5:33. At oriental weddings the bridegroom and his relatives are the chief participants. Hence there is no mention of the bride in this account (nor in John 2:1–10).

5:34. Jesus likens himself to a "bridegroom," for the messianic age is a time of happiness, and a wedding is the supreme example of joy. Hosea had described Israel as a faithless wife (Hos. 2:5) and pronounced dire judgment (Hos. 2:10–13). But there was to be a fresh betrothal in time to come (Hos. 2:14–23). John had called for repentance in order to make that betrothal possible. Now it is bridal and festival time, and since Jews did not fast on sabbaths and festival days, it would be inappropriate for the disciples to fast in the time of fulfillment for Israel's marriage to God (cf. Eph. 5:25–27).

Jesus does not here enter into the question of prayers. Prayer and fasting are closely joined in Jewish thought, and the purpose of the fasting is to improve the praying. Jesus will later instruct his disciples how to pray (Luke 11:1–13). Whether the community will preserve habits of fasting is to be subject to local decision and not to the dictatorship of custom. By his juxtaposition of John's and Jesus' practice, Luke suggests in 5:33–35 that John's views on fasting are not authoritative, since Jesus disclaimed it for his own followers.

Through his recital Luke aims to remove one other obstacle barring harmony in the church. To many, the new order would at first prove confusing, for the average person finds it difficult to distinguish between the transient and the permanently valid in religious and theological matters. But responsible confusion is a small price to pay for growth in appreciation of the values of unity in creative diversity. To encourage such innovative enterprise is the privilege and responsibility of ecclesiastical administration.

5:35. The statement about removal of the bridgegroom, followed by fasting **in those days**, is not introduced by Luke to support fasting practice in his time by appeal to Jesus' words. Rather, this is the first preview during Jesus' public ministry of events that will culminate at Jerusalem. It is ironical that the hostility against Jesus will generate the opposite of the celebration that apocalyptic hope anticipated for God's people. As in 2:35, we have an oblique reference to Jesus' death (see also 4:29). Fasting here means that there will be great sorrow when he is taken away. The language is typically oriental in its symbolism. Luke is soon to write the words in 6:11. The gulf between Jesus and the religious leadership is widening. The latter are determined to save their pride by sacrificing the living to the dead. But beyond Jesus' own death lies the judgment on Jerusalem (cf. 17:22; 19:43–44; 21:6; 23:29). The fasting of her inbabitants will be longer than that of the disciples (cf. 21:20–24).

Incompatibility   Luke 5:36–39
                                                          (Mark 2:21–22; Matthew 9:16–17)

5:36–39. Two proverb-like illustrations point up the contrast between the New Age and the old legal system. According to Mark's wording of this saying (Mark 2:21), no one puts a patch of unshrunk cloth on an old garment, because it will pull away from the old fibers and make the hole larger. Coupled with the saying about the wineskins, this means that the old cannot be patched up with the new, lest the old be in worse shape than before. On the other hand, the old is not to be preserved at the expense of the new. The new must be made available, but in new forms. (On the figure of the garment, see Isa. 61:10; Matt. 22:11–12; Rev. 19:8.)

According to Luke's interpretation of the saying, both the old and the new are in danger of being harmed if old and new are mixed. Therefore he writes not merely about a patch but about a piece taken from a new garment. Not only does the removal of the patch spoil the new garment but it does not fit in with the old. Fresh wine put into old wineskins will ferment and break the old wineskins, and both the wineskin and the new wine are lost. Thus two points emerge: lack of harmony and the loss of both. Then Luke adds a saying not found in Mark, to the effect that tastes are difficult to change. One prefers that to which one has become accustomed.

The point of all this is that those Pharisees who object to Jesus' conduct and directions taken in the community of the New Age should be content with their adherence to tradition. If they wish to fast, well and good. But they must recognize the need for a fresh approach for those who cannot share their inherited customs. From Luke's perspective, too many Pharisees unfortunately thought their way was the only path to serve God. Their position is, of course, understandable.

In the early church, composed also of converted Pharisees and people who had been brought up under their tutelage, the insouciance of Jesus relative to much tradition would be threatening to some. But an imposition of Pharisaic regulations and customs on gentiles would spell destruction of the exciting view of the gospel that made possible a broader outreach to "tax collectors and sinners," who by circumstance were excluded from any hope of conformity to the many neat distinctions of scribal law. Luke's record of Paul's approach to the question of circumcision is an example of the application of this principle. Let Jews within the Christian community—such as Timothy, whose mother was Jewish, Acts 16:3—be circumcised. No harm done. But gentiles must be permitted to retain their freedom in the gospel. Thus both could worship together without disharmony or loss to either (cf. Gal. 2:1–5; Acts 15). Compromise is the essence of politics, and this approach possessed the merit of eminent reasonableness without sacrifice of principle.

Similarly in the church today established congregations are accustomed to certain modes or types of formulation of the truth and to traditional forms of polity. Debate on the last ordinarily flares into a blaze at mention of the word "ordination," for maintenance of rank is the last bastion of dedication to religious tradition (cf. Luke 22:24–27). Yet all such formulations or concern may be meaningless to the unconverted on the many and varied social, economic, and intellectual fronts where the gospel must make its outreach.

Provision is to be made for those who have opted for the past, but the old dare not be permitted to halt the progress of the new; for truth must never be frozen into form, proclaims Luke's Jesus. Modern means of rapid communication complicate the problem, but exploration of the principles expressed in the gospel will, under the Spirit's direction, guide the People of God to appropriate solutions. In place of the refuge ordinarily taken within denominational walls under the protection of sectarian policies, the unity of the Spirit is to be sought in terms of the creative possibilities described, for example, in the Book of Acts (see also Eph. 4:12–16). Denominational structures need not be demolished, but bridge-building and free exchange of gifts and functions, counsels Luke, ought to mark the People of God in the New Age.

Further Misunderstanding: Controversy
Concerning the Sabbath

Luke 6:1–11

Threshing of Grain

Luke 6:1–5
(Mark 2:23–28; Matthew 12:1–8)

At Capernaum, Jesus demonstrated his ultimate objective—triumph of the Reign of God especially over demonic forces (4:31–44). In Luke 5 the stress was on the reception of outcasts and the questions this would raise for traditional scribal thought. Luke 6:1–11 deals specifically with legal issues concerning the sabbath and illustrates the kind of freedom practiced by Jesus and the early Christians. Thus the way is prepared for the description of the break that eventually developed and that is highlighted by Luke in the selection of the twelve apostles (6:12–16).

6:1. Luke's use of the term **sabbath** at this juncture in the narrative has all the force of a buzzword. Tension builds for the auditor. Is this sacred cow also to fall?

A marginal note in the RSV calls attention to the phrase **on the second first sabbath,** which is quite meaningless to a modern reader but may originally have been a reference to specifications in Lev. 23:15–16. In any case, the action of the disciples, which is otherwise sanctioned by Deut. 23:25, takes place on the **sabbath.** Their rubbing of the beards of wheat would therefore be tantamount to threshing and come under indictment of the sabbatical antiwork regulation, as refined by the legal experts. Once again the liberalizing interpretations of Jesus threaten the security of the system.

6:2–3. Instead of approaching Jesus directly (as they do at Mark 2:24) for what appears to be a flaunting of tradition, the Pharisees in Luke's account address their rebuke, as at 5:30, to the disciples. In the early Christian community there would be disputes between Jewish Christians (including converted Pharisees) and gentile Christians on prescriptive legislation. Appeal to the Scriptures (in this case 1 Sam. 21:1–6) for adjudication of practice would be popular. Such reference to Scripture would involve some torturing of the texts, as witnessed by the admission in the *Mishnah:* "The rules about the Sabbath . . . are as mountains hanging by a hair, for [teaching of] Scripture [thereon] is scanty and the rules many" (*Hagigah* 1.8).

Nothing is said in 1 Sam. 21:1–9 about the sabbath. Jesus simply counters a charge of illegality with a story of illegal activity by one of the most respected ancestors in Israel's history. David himself ate the bread that had been laid out on the table of showbread facing the lampstand in the holy place of the tabernacle (Exod. 40:22; cf. Lev. 24:5–9). The loaves were prepared overnight by the Levites (1 Chron. 9:32) and were replaced with fresh loaves each sabbath (1 Sam. 21:6).

In his reply to the Pharisees, Jesus calls their attention to the fact that not only David ate but **those who were with him.** Jesus, as noted above, was not personally charged with violation of the Law, and Luke may be suggesting that Jesus was often more permissive about the actions of others than of his own. This, then, is the substance of the Pharisees' complaint: Jesus ought to observe tradition and instruct his disciples properly. Thus Luke's recital of the Pharisees' indirect attack through their rebuke of the disciples has the added advantage (as at 5:31) of permitting Jesus to take the initiative.

6:4. Jesus goes on to point out that David and his associates ate the bread in **the house of God.** According to regulation, the bread was to be eaten only in the sanctuary. And it was to be eaten only by the priests (Lev. 24:9). This rule is reinforced by Jesus with the words **not lawful for any but the priests.** David's action was definitely illegal. The Pharisees in their rebuke had asked, "Why are you doing what is not lawful?" (6:2). Jesus echoes their question and compels them to place David under their own indictment. *Bien touché!*

6:5. Then Jesus concludes his refutation: **The Son of man is lord of the sabbath**, with "lord" in the emphatic primary position in Greek. Luke is fond of the term "Son of humanity," for it gives him opportunity to define Jesus as one who identifies wholeheartedly with the human race (cf. 3:23–38) and with all the fragility that such identification implies. At the same time, Jesus is recognized by Luke's auditors as the exalted Son of humanity, and they know that he has every right to refer to himself as "lord of the sabbath." The saying in connection with David's prerogative in the matter of the showbread would be especially appropriate, since Luke has shown that Jesus is a Davidian (cf. 1:32). According to Ezek. 34:20–24, a latter-day David is to feed his flock and be their shepherd. God's sanctuary is to be set up in the midst of Israel, with David as her prince (Ezek. 37:24–28).

Luke's genealogy of Jesus, with David as a pivotal ancestor (Luke 3:31), had identified Jesus as truly one with humankind and therefore the Son of humanity par excellence. With such credentials Jesus is indeed Lord of the sabbath; and the church, guided through him to fresh interpretation of the Scriptures, finds his authority sufficient to break with any tradition that impedes the forward movement of the gospel. Ecclesiastical disobedience is the correlative of civil disobedience as a means of appeal to loftier concern for humanity—and Jesus implements both with his authority (see Acts 5:29). Luke 20:41–44 will carry the discussion a step farther.

Healing of the Man with a Withered Hand   Luke 6:6–11
(Mark 3:1–6: Matthew 12:9–14)

6:6. Luke modifies Mark 3:1 such a way that the introductory words to this episode, "And it came to pass" *(egeneto de)* **on another sabbath**, conform to the wording of Luke 6:1. Thus the story recited in 6:6–11 is to be viewed as an extension of the issue raised at vv. 1–5. Debate about the sabbath is not merely academic, argues Luke. Involved ultimately is the question whether human beings are more important than the security of any establishment where interest in rules and regulations in a situation takes precedence over the importance of meeting needs.

Once again Jesus is presented as a teacher. As in other passages, the observation is not trivial. The basic question is about to be raised: Since Jesus breaks with tradition, can his instruction be trusted? Once before, he had healed a man on the sabbath (4:31–35). But the present case is different. In cases of emergency it is probable that tradition, even before rabbinic statements on the matter, granted exemption from the general prohibition against medical work on the sabbath. This man's life, though, was not in such danger that Jesus could not have waited until sundown (see on 4:40). Instead, he makes waves by taking the initiative, without so much as a whispered plea from the sick man.

The data submitted by Luke make useless any speculation as to the precise nature of the man's ailment. Whatever the circumstances, Jesus' motto is: Whatever is beneficial tomorrow is best done today. It is best left unsaid what he thinks about standard contemporary policy of deferring action on sensitive problems that involve immediate needs of people, while exploration is made of "where the people are."

6:7. For the first time Luke explicitly draws attention to hostility from the ranks of scribes and Pharisees. They **watched** this well-intentioned but wrongheaded prophet in the hope of finding some facts on which they might ground an accusation.

6:8–9. But he knew their thoughts *(dialogismous)*. Simeon had spoken of "thoughts" that were to be revealed (2:35). As at 5:22, Jesus uncovers their unspoken plot. He is a prophet, yet more than a prophet. Then he carries the battle to the opposition by ordering the man to stand as the center of attraction and asks the experts what **is . . . lawful** (the same Greek word *[exestin]* as in 6:2, 4; see also 14:3). His either-or inquiry focuses attention on the main purpose of the sabbath—to preserve human beings from harm and exploitation.

The first part of the question (v. 9) deals with morality, the second part with the physical well-being of another. According to Isa. 1:11–17, ritual observance, including observance of the sabbath, means nothing unless attended by change of conduct and performance of justice. Isaiah 56:2 pronounces a blessing on those who observe the sabbath with hands that refrain from evil. These prophetic statements are in harmony with Deut. 5:12–15. The spirit of the sabbath ordinance is that people should be preserved from exploitation by others and have the opportunity to ponder the goodness of God. Since the sabbath is the day on which God's goodness is especially to be noted, there is no better occasion for Jesus to display that goodness.

Ritual and tradition are not in themselves unsalutary. On the contrary, they have great potential as spiritual, moral, and civilizing forces, but they are never to take precedence over the meeting of human need. To the average Greco-Roman ear the phrase **to do good** *(agathopoiēsai)* would also connote good citizenship. Well-motivated piety promotes the general welfare. The People of God, Luke suggests, cannot afford to debate ways and means to preserve traditional protocol while others suffer for want of a spokesperson. Is it right **to save life or to destroy it?** The church cannot avoid the summons to hear and then respond promptly to the groans of humanity.

6:10. In the absence of any instruction from the experts, Jesus looked at all of them, evidently waiting for a response. Finally he said to the man, **Stretch out your hand.** It was a bold directive. As in the desert of temptation, Jesus moved in a direction from which there was no return. To have capitulated at this moment would have meant resignation to the system. Yet in the command there is no violation of traditional rules. Jesus did not say, "Be well." On the other hand, his word is a word of power and the man obeys. But it is not an automatic reflex under the power of suggestion. Such an interpretation is typical of rationalistic solutions proposed in the nineteenth century. **His hand was restored.**

6:11. Now the Pharisees were in a dilemma. God does not hear sinners, yet this man reached out his hand simply at Jesus' command. According to their own principles, God must have been at work on this sabbath day. In any case, Jesus had not broken their rules, at least not technically. And technicalities were their specialty. Faced with the stubborn facts, with their own system called into question, they can respond only with the rage of frustration (RSV: *fury*). No match for Jesus' amplitude of mind, they discuss, as also chief priests and scribes will do later (19:48), **what they might do to** him.

The Russian poet Yevgeny Yevtushenko, after an attack on his person on a field house stage in St. Paul, Minnesota, complained bitterly: "When I begin to recite a love poem I feel hate." He was making reference to the weird combination of allegiance to the high ideals expressed in the Bill of Rights with denial of freedom of expression to those who are connected in some way and perhaps involuntarily with different points of view.

An official in the Second World War complained about bureaucratic hacks who impeded the war effort by their lack of initiative and inability to improvise.

Similarly the opposition to Jesus interpret their chief task to be the mounting of obstacles for one who knows what the hour demands and endeavors to do something about it. Some Greco-Roman auditors would catch the implicit wordplay in the use of the Greek word for "fury" *(anoia)*. From their acquaintance with bureaucratic prose they would note that the opposition should have responded in a positive way that could have been described by a different and rhyming word meaning "good will" *(ennoia)* as opposed to "bad will."

Jesus did not interpret Moses as a hindrance to love. Entrenched interests saw it differently. Mark concludes: "And the Pharisees immediately counseled with the Herodians how they might kill him" (Mark 3:6★). Piety was on their lips, murder on their hearts. Luke prefers to emphasize Jesus' initiative in the progress toward his death (see Luke 4:30; 9:22, 51), and Herod's involvement will be demonstrated in due course. Besides, to judge from Acts 15:5, there were some among the Pharisees who repented after Pentecost. In any case, Luke refrains from implicating Pharisees in a plot against Jesus' life and in fact shows at Luke 13:31 that some Pharisees warned Jesus about Herod's evil intentions. According to Mark 3:5, Jesus labeled those who were present as hard of heart. Luke does not here pick up this pejorative note.

Call of the Apostles

Luke 6:12–16
(Mark 3:13–19; Matthew 5:1; 10:1–4)

It is apparent that Jesus must now make preparations for the survival of his mission. There is no real hope from traditional sources. To emphasize this point Luke shifts the content of Mark 3:13–19 ahead of the recital in Mark 3:7–12 (Luke 6:17–19). Connection with the two preceding accounts is indicated by the phrase "and it came to pass" *(egeneto de* omitted by the RSV; cf. 6:1,6) and the words **in these days.** In view of the development noted at v. 11, Jesus goes to a mountain to pray (see also 9:28; 22:39–46). Thereby Luke emphasizes that what follows has divine sanction, for, with the exception of 8:32, mountains in Luke's work are places of revelation. The succeeding phrase in 6:12b sounds superfluous, but since it is an amplification of Mark 3:13, Luke, we are to infer, would have his readers note the solemnity and urgency of the recital about to take place (cf. Acts 1:24–26).

6:13. The events recorded in this and succeeding recitals bear resemblance to the account in Exodus 24 concerning Moses and the seventy elders who went up a mountain to receive God's revelation of the Law. Luke thus again displays the continuity of Jesus' activity with the history of Israel, yet without equating Moses with Jesus, for Jesus is not a carbon copy of Moses.

Jesus called **his disciples and chose from them twelve, whom he named apostles.** In Luke's time, "disciples" *(mathētai)* would connote the members of the Christian communities, and "apostles" *(apostoloi)* the principal sponsors of the Lord's mission. Mark refers to the chosen ones simply as the "twelve" but indicates with the verb *(apostellō,* rendered "sent"), from which "apostle" is derived, that they have apostolic authority (Mark 3:14). Luke says that Jesus expressively named them "apostles," evidently to emphasize for the Christians of his day that Jesus is the source of their authority and that they have their roots in his ministry. As the center and supreme head of the Kingdom operation, Jesus selects people who are to have plenipotentiary power in his name (see also 22:30). Whether Luke was acquainted with the rabbinic term *shaliach*—that is, the one who is sent as the sender himself—is questionable. But his view of the apostolate is substantially similar, and in Greco-Roman circles the cognate verb also expressed delegated authority.

Luke omits at this point Mark's (3:15) reference to the assignment to proclaim and exorcise demons, deferring such information for recitation at 9:1 (parallel Mark 6:7). Through this arrangement Luke is able to give top billing to the Sermon on the Plain as the platform for the apostolic mission.

6:14–16. Luke's list (like that of Acts 1:13) differs in some details from Mark's (Mark 3:17–19), perhaps because of Luke's special researches (cf. Luke 1:1–4). At the time he was writing, not a little of the history of the early Christian communities had become obscure, and the term "apostle" had undergone some fluidity. Not infrequently people went by two names (e.g., Saul-Paul and Simon-Peter), and this may account for some of the differences.

At 10:1 delegates are sent out two by two. Also here at 6:14–16 the apostles appear in pairs. Remarkable is the inclusion of **Simon who was called the Zealot.** The Zealots were a revolutionary element from Galilee. Mark (3:18) prefers the Aramaic transliteration "Cananaean," perhaps to avoid any suggestion of subversive activity within Jesus' band. But Luke exposes the problem and through his presentation of Jesus' message shows that also a Zealot could be used constructively by Jesus.

The fact that Judas had been chosen by Jesus caused perplexity in the church. To eliminate any confusion with others bearing the same name, he is identified as the one **who became a traitor.** This identification serves also to contribute a dramatic dimension to the episode at hand—it forecasts the climactic event of 22:3. At the same time, the mention of his deed completes the theological focus of v. 12. Jesus is under final orders from God. He had renounced the easy way out in the desert of temptation. Now he is led by his Father to select the one who would destroy him. Christians are thus consoled with the thought of God's providential direction. Jesus did not make a mistake. Judas was part of his destiny (cf. Acts 1:16–26). Yet this does not mean that Judas was victim of a plot over which he had no control. God's people are interested in the consolation, not in the ultimate question of theodicy, that is, the justifying of the ways of God with men. There is in all of this the dramatic ingredient of a Greek tragedy. But Jesus' death is not viewed as a tragedy.

The innovativeness of Jesus in choosing a cast of totally nonclerical people for his mission puts heavily bureaucratized forms of institutional Christianity under scrutiny. Blunt is Luke's message: when holders of traditional offices obstruct paths to the future, the Lord of the churches directs his people to carry on through other channels.

KINGDOM CANDIDATES AND REQUIREMENTS
Luke 6:17–49

Before the Sermon
Luke 6:17–19
(Mark 3:7–12; Matthew 4:23—5:1)

As noted above (see on 6:12), Luke shifted Mark's account of the selection of the apostles in order to bring to a climax the issues raised in 6:1–11. But he also requires a place in the narrative for a sermon that will outline the type of instruction that Jesus' apostles would present. Patterning the fate of Jesus, the early community underwent harassment from the hierarchy and required authoritative guidance.

6:17. Since mountains are reserved in Luke for special communication with the upper world, Luke has the sermon delivered on a level plain, after Jesus' descent from the mountain. Similarly, Moses came down from Sinai (Exod. 34:29) and addressed Israel. Mark 3:7–8 offered the appropriate context for such a presentation. And Luke adds the thought that they **came to hear him and to be healed.** The **great crowd of his disciples** anticipates expansion of the church (cf. Acts 6:1).

The recital of healings just before the sermon appropriately continues Luke's thematic demonstration of Jesus' authority in deed and word. The geographical names in 6:17 echo the list in 5:17 and emphasize the point that this is a message for Israel as a people (the *am ha eretz;* cf. 2:10).

Galilee is not mentioned, perhaps for the reason that Mark 3:9 implies the Lake of Galilee, whereas Luke shows Jesus on a level plain near a mountainside (**he came down . . . and stood on a level place**). The mention of Tyre and Sidon (see Mark 3:8 and cf. Luke 10:13–14) may be Luke's way of hinting at the implications in the selection of an apostolic delegation. From Jerusalem to the gentiles is a main theme of Luke's two-volume work, and Tyre and Sidon suggest a broad outreach. Both at 5:17 and here at 6:17 the geographical lists add weight to what follows and emphasize the stature Jesus enjoyed as a teacher and healer. At the same time, they preview the worldwide mission envisaged at 2:32 and described in detail in Acts.

As in other references to Jesus' healing power that are borrowed from Mark, Luke edits Mark so as to accent in Jesus' case the twofold distinction of the Greco-Roman superstar: expertness in word and deed. The people come **to hear him and to be healed.**

6:18. As often, stress is laid on exorcisms. Luke's publics are not to forget that Jesus' battle is ultimately with Satan.

6:19. "Power" went out from Jesus (on *dynamis,* see on 5:17), that is, it was clear that despite the criticism of the Pharisees, God was with him. (A related scene will be repeated at Acts 5:16.) It was a crowded "caravan of pain," but he **healed them all**, without distinction—and, Luke may imply, without hope of personal profit. Luke is fond of highlighting Jesus' pandemic outreach and frequently edits Mark so as to bring out the theme. Greco-Roman auditors, accustomed to adulation of public benefactors, especially physicians who embraced the general public with their generosity, would be impressed. One of the inscriptions reads:

> Whereas [Hippokrates] . . . constantly renders all [aid] and assistance to the people as a whole and privately to citizens who request his services, be it resolved by the People to commend Hippokrates, citizen of Kos, for his policy of goodwill to the people, and to crown him in the theater . . . with a golden crown in recognition of his exceptional concern and goodwill. (*Benefactor,* p. 61)

The Sermon on the Plain
Luke 6:20–49

Luke's carefully structured presentation of a major discourse delivered by Jesus is Q material and is largely paralleled in Matthew's Sermon on the Mount (Matthew 5—7). But much of Matthew's sermon is not to be found in Luke 6. It is scattered here and there in Luke's Gospel (on the question of sources, see my Introduction).

The evangelist has now programmed his record to the stage where Jesus has come under searching critique. The issue of Jesus' authority and the validity of his teaching has been raised. His authority has been demonstrated in deeds. At this point Luke presents his auditors with a sample of Jesus' words, which amount to an exhalation of the future and conclude with the strongest possible claim to authority. In contrast to Matthew's more Semitically oriented rendering, Luke's version of the sermon, with its emphasis on contrasting fortunes and divine beneficence as a model for believers, appeals especially to a Greco-Roman public.

A major theme of Luke's Gospel is here presented: the rich and the mighty are brought low and the humble are exalted. But exaltation of the lowly does not mean apocalyptic victory, with enemies crushed in a nationalistic Armageddon. The humble can expect trouble and even persecution. Thus the apostolic community is encouraged to abide by Jesus' instruction to love the enemy and at the same time is reminded not to commit the mistake of Israel by confusing formal liturgy with the performance of the divine will. A prophetic tone pervades the whole, revealing Jesus in continuity with the best in Israel's tradition, yet with the added conviction that in his person a greater one than any prophet has appeared. Luke's historical sensitivity is once again displayed. What the religious opposition objects to is clearly revealed, and thereby the failure of that system is exposed. Thus the persecution suffered by Christians is of a piece with the attack on Jesus.

Interpreters are not in agreement on the progression of thought in the sermon. The following breakdown suggests the main lines of movement: (1) Vv. 20–26: Words of promise and of woe. (2) Vv. 27–38: Reciprocity. (3) Vv. 39–49: Self-Search.

Words of Promise and of Woe   Luke 6:20–26

Words of Promise   Luke 6:20–23
(Matthew 5:3, 4, 6, 11–12)

6:20. He lifted up his eyes on his disciples. Luke moves from the apostles (vv. 12–16) to the crowds (vv. 17–19) and finally to the disciples. These disciples, to be distinguished from the apostles, are of the same order as the disciples in the early community. The instruction they receive here is a pattern of the kind of instruction the apostles had given to the church. The Epistle of James is an excellent example of a parallel type of exhortation, and the inclusion of the rich in that homily (James 4:13—5:6) suggests that the beatitudes are not meant exclusively for the disciples, with the rest of the sermon intended for the people, as might be erroneously inferred from Luke 7:1.

The beatitudes expand the message delivered at Nazareth. Isaiah 61 is the best commentary on these words. The word "blessed" (Greek: *makarios*) in the context means more than happy. It suggests people who are the privileged recipients of God's special gifts. God is for them, not against them.

Especially favored are "the poor" *(hoi ptochoi)*. In the light of OT usage, this term has both an economic and a religious connotation. It contrasts, first of all, the economically disadvantaged in Israel *(anawim)* with the more privileged members of the higher social strata located especially in Jerusalem. Most of the poor were tillers of the soil or small tradespeople. Generally speaking, they observed the spirit of Israel's religion more faithfully than did the elite in the cities. Hence they became models of the faithful worshiper, the second connotation in the term. They are frequently linked with "the meek" in the OT (see, e.g., Isa. 29:18–19). This does not mean they are doormats but that they submit themselves to God for the purpose of carrying out his will. Unlike many in the privileged classes, they resist the temptation to win riches through sin (cf. Luke 20:45—21:4).

The nature of their work would prevent many of them from carrying out the minutiae stressed by the Pharisees, who were not infrequently men of wealth and had greater leisure for religious duties. This circumstance, coupled with the fact that the poor were often victims of oppression and had only God to turn to for hope of rescue (see, e.g., Pss. 9:17–20; 70), made them special objects of compassion. Thus the term "poor" in this passage is in effect a double sense, meaning both the economically poor and those who recognize their dependence on God. Matthew's "poor in spirit" (Matt. 5:3) emphasizes the latter.

Luke uses the more general expression because of the contrast expressed in v. 24. See also 14:13, 21; 18:22; 19:8; 21:3, all defining the poor in terms of the contrasting rich. Matthew's "in spirit" may well be an interpretive addition. And the thrust of the dominical promise is caught with a dash of wry humor in an epitaph at Ashburton Church, in England, which commemorates a certain Elizabeth Ireland:

> Here I lie at the chancel door,
> Here I lie because I'm poor
> The farther in, the more you pay;
> Here I lie as warm as they.

In Matthew's Gospel most of the beatitudes are expressed in the third person; Luke's beatitudes are addressed in the second, hence **you . . . yours.** It was understood in the ancient world that a head of state was responsible for administration of justice, with stress on consideration for the poor and the oppressed. Not counted religiously successful by the Pharisees, the poor are here pronounced the favored recipients of the new reign ushered in by Jesus. His frequent association with publicans and sinners is a practical demonstration of this beatitude. Thus the direct address is extraordinarily authoritative. These disciples belong to Jesus. Precisely because they are his disciples, the Kingdom is theirs. The present tense emphasizes the presence of the Kingdom in the presence of Jesus. By separating the disciples from the crowds, Luke has also made it clear that the Kingdom as an expression of divine politics is not a "crowd" movement with competitive secular overtones.

6:21. A primary exhibition of royal beneficence in the Mediterranean world was assurance of a regular food supply. Emperors vied with one another in maintaining the grain supply for Rome's teeming citizenry.

The thought in the second beatitude (cf. Luke 1:53) bears close resemblance to themes in Psalms 37 (see esp. v. 19); 107:9; 132 (esp. v. 15); 146:7; Isa. 25:6; 49:10; 55:1–2; 65:13; Ezek. 34:29. The third echoes Psalm 126 and Isa. 25:8; 40:1–2. In both beatitudes the present misery of the poor is contrasted with a future reversal of their lot.

According to some versions of Jewish apocalyptic scenario, the fortunes of the poor were to be redressed in a radical transformation initiated by God in an end-time cataclysm that was to spell the downfall of the mighty. In the popular mind this would inaugurate the long-awaited Kingdom. Luke teaches that the Kingdom is present reality, being here in the activity of Jesus' deed and word, which anticipates that those who wield the instruments of power will use them in the interests of the powerless. Future benefits await the faithful but only as the climax of God's ongoing Kingdom demonstration.

Of primary theological importance in these beatitudes is the assurance given to the disciples that God's favor does not depend on external fortunes. The theory that the quality of people's morality could be determined by looking at their fortunes here and now ("You must be living right," goes the phrase) was a cliché among writers of wisdom literature but was questioned also by Jesus (see Luke 13:1–9 for the sterner moral perspective, and cf. John 9:1–3).

Obviously the beatitudes in Luke 6:21–22 are not an endorsement for social or political inaction. The beatitudes rather stress that Jesus' presence is the realization of what the psalmists and prophets in Israel had proclaimed. Jesus was not of that breed of shallow idealists who with eyes fixed on tomorrow stumble over present reality. The liberation proclaimed by Jesus would indeed be hollow if it had no bearing on the depressing conditions of those who are victimized by the powerful and exploited by vested interests. Jesus is unjustly attacked by the system for his association with publicans and sinners and for what traditionalists considered his unorthodox disinterest in their fasting regulations and sabbatical ordinances. Yet his companions, the "poor" in the land, are the very ones to whom the dream for ultimate victory expressed in popular apocalyptic applies. As the balance of the sermon will display, Jesus does not call them to lawlessness but to rigorous moral response.

From another perspective the presence of the poor is an invitation to self-inventory by those who enjoy relatively greater benefits. The latter cannot take refuge in an interpretation that gives the poor assurance only of a future recompense for present misery. Spiritualizing promises to the poor is a luxury that the rich can love too much. The promise to the poor is at the same time an invitation to the more prosperous to engage now in the process of redistribution and help God do the "filling." Lest there be any

doubt about the interpretation, at 16:19–31 Luke includes Jesus' own explanation of the passage, and at Acts 2:44–45 and 4:32–37 he shows how the
early Christian community put the proclamation into practice.

As for those who weep, in addition to what is said in vv. 22–23 Luke has a
number of reminders of Jesus' power to dry up tears: the widow of Nain
(7:13); the woman with ointment (7:38, 50); Jairus's daughter (8:52, 56);
Peter (22:62; 24:34, 41); and the friends of Tabitha (Acts 9:36–42). But, as
23:28 will point out, there are others who would do well to weep.

6:22. The prosaic and extended form of vv. 22–23 contrasts with the crisp
brevity of the blessings that precede, and the content suggests amplification
of Jesus' words at a later stage in the tradition. Persecutions endured in the
apostolic period at the hands of Jewish opposition prompt inclusion of the
fourth beatitude. Compared with Matthew's account (Matt. 5:11), two
notable additions appear. The first is the word "people" (RSV: **men**) and
the second, "the Son of humanity." At 5:20 Luke had changed Mark's "son"
to "man" in order to make the term "the Son of humanity" (5:24) more
comprehensible. Here Luke plays on the term "human beings" *(anthrōpoi;
hyios tou anthrōpou)* in his identification of Jesus as "the Son of humanity."
"Human beings" will excommunicate (RSV: **exclude**) Jesus' followers from
the synagogue (John 9:22; 12:42; 16:1; note also the fate of Stephen, Acts
6—7).

The reference to the Son of humanity may well be meant to qualify the
phrase **cast out your name as evil.** In such a case, the latter words
probably mean that the followers of Jesus will be met with hostility simply
because they are associated with him, the Son of humanity, the one who has
identified with them in their situation and has preceded them in similar
experience by being pronounced worthy of the most shameful death. For a
similar view, see James 2:7; 1 Pet. 4:14.

6:23. Despite the negative experiences of some of their associates, Luke's
public knows that the fragile Jesus emerged victoriously from the grave and
sits at the right hand of God. He may not come to their immediate rescue in
an apocalyptic demonstration, but his followers are to know that their
opponents do not have the last word. Therefore they must remain patient
(cf. 8:15) and rejoice when such things happen. Indeed, they are to leap, or
dance, for joy (the same word used of John in 1:41). Acts 4:23–41 records an
incident in which followers of Jesus did just that (cf. Jer. 31:12–14).

The phrase **your reward is great** (cf. Jer. 31:16) does not intend to
motivate their conduct through expectation of a reward. Rather, the words
are consolatory. Their experience will be a sign that they are on the right
road and that they have God's endorsement (see again Acts 4:23–31). Reward as motivation is condemned in Luke 17:7–10. In any event, the

Kingdom of God in all its fullness is theirs. As added encouragement they have the example of the prophets, such as Jeremiah, Ezekiel, and Amos.

The example of the prophets is important, for Jesus' followers might ask themselves whether their sufferings are not in fact the consequence, as some Pharisees would be quick to point out, of breaking faith with Israel's traditions. Jesus assures them that they are in good company. What they will experience is, from Luke's perspective, merely the result of a habit in Israel, to persecute the righteous (see Stephen's speech, Acts 7). Along such lines Jesus constantly overturned standard criteria for success. He was not a sponsor of the current rate of exchange.

Words of Woe   Luke 6:24–26

Corresponding to the four blessings are four woes that echo Luke 1:42–53 and parallel Isa. 65:13–15 and James 4—5. These pronouncements are intimately linked with the blessings that precede, for those who have the woes pronounced on them are the ones who must share a large portion of the blame for the negative conditions described in 6:20–23. In their present literary context they explain why the immediate enjoyment of blessings that were promised for the New Age (see 1:46–55 and 68–70) has not been realized in anticipated measure.

6:24–25. But woe to you that are rich. The word "woe" *(ouai)* expresses a sense of dreadful doom approaching. Among notable OT passages that incorporate this interjection in social evaluations are Amos 6 and Isaiah 5. In the present context it is a watchman's warning, appealing to hearers not to ignore the inevitable summons to the bar of justice.

The rich are not attacked because they are rich, and Jesus' sermon does not pit poor against rich; for according to Lev. 19:15 one is not to be partial to the poor or defer to the great. But in contrast to the poor, who must rely on God, the rich can be misled by their prosperity into a false sense of security (see Luke 12:13–21; 16:19–31) that makes entry into the Kingdom difficult (18:25). In their eyes the moral guidelines that follow would appear ridiculous. They could not sponsor the going rate with such precepts any more than those who think that the church's business is to "preach the gospel" while refraining from criticism and redress of society's oppressions. Zacchaeus (19:1–10) remains the model for the miracle of grace (see 18:27) that can save even those who have forgotten the principal purpose for having things.

The rich **have received** their consolation. Like a buyer who gets a receipt for money delivered on goods, they are in receipt of their consolation now. The present tense of the original corresponds to the tense in "yours is the kingdom of God" (v. 20). The promise of plenty for the hungry (1:53) produces an ironic echo here. And it is not the "consolation" *(paraklesis)* of Luke 2:25. They live in the illusion that they are the privileged recipients of the benefits of the New Age. But all they can await is lamentation (cf. 16:25). A society that lives at the expense of the future sows the wind and reaps the whirlwind. Apparent escape in the immediate moment is no warrant for immunity to judgment (cf. 13:1–9).

6:26. Parallel to the words about persecution addressed to the poor is the warning that congratulations may be endorsement for disaster. **False prophets** as described here are not people who teach wrong doctrine but are, rather, those who make hypocritical claim to being God's mouthpieces. They operate under the guise of established tradition and are highly respected in their religious communities for maintaining the status quo. They make no waves and rock no boats. Nevertheless, they are religious quacks, unable to offer a real remedy, while they exploit people for their own ends.

Bogus prophets have always enjoyed popular acclaim, for they promise peace when there is no peace. "What you want to hear is what's right" is their slogan. But ruin and confusion is their chief legacy to those who fawn them into deceit. Jesus does not speak like the bogus prophets. He turns the people from their evil ways (cf. Jer. 23:21–32).

Reciprocity   Luke 6:27–38

In continuity with vv. 20–26, Luke here explores the theme of reciprocity, a basic factor in human relationships and integral to the politics of the New Age. Greco-Roman auditors would readily interpret Luke's recital via their benefactor-beneficiary model: goodness is to be reciprocated by recognition, and ingratitude is despicable.

In many respects the injunctions of this part of the sermon are in harmony with the theme of Jubilee expressed in 4:18–19.

Generosity in Love   Luke 6:27–35
(Matthew 5:44, 39–42; 7:12; 5:46, 45)

6:27. I say to you that hear. Two classes of hearers have been sketched— the poor and the rich. The poor are receptive to God; the rich, self-sufficient. A spirit of receptivity is important, for without it there will be no response to the moral directions that Jesus is about to give. Thus "hearing" is more than catching syllables. It is openness to the Kingdom communication. It is not a wait-see attitude but a conviction that the Kingdom makes claims that supersede all others.

Once the stance of hearing is taken, then the doing follows. Thus the evangelist separates the demands of the Kingdom, expressed in vv. 27–30, from the grace or beneficence pronounced in vv. 20–23, but in his subsequent recital, climaxed by vv. 46–49, he demonstrates how interlocked are the hearing and the doing (see also 8:15, 21).

"Love," as understood in Luke's cultural world, is not first of all an expression of emotion but a willingness to accept responsibility to meet an evident need. The verb is used also by secular administrators who assure their populace of their personal goodwill, manifested in a variety of benefits. The nominal Greek cognate, *agapē,* appears to be a colloquial or street formation that did not find ready acceptance in formal writing.

The OT contains much expression of retaliation against enemies, but love and kindness are enjoined, for example, in Exod. 23:4–5 and Prov. 25:21–22. Love in the abstract without performance is self-delusion. Romans 12:16–21 expands on the principle. The missionaries who returned to the Auca Indians after some of their band had been murdered required no extraordinary logic to persuade their hearers of the authenticity of their message.

As in the case of Jews, Luke's Greco-Roman public would come to the audition of the verse with conflicting traditions. Symptomatic of the hard line is the satirical comment about an alleged impious Athenian by an imitator of Lysias: "He possessed the skill of harming his friends and rewarding his enemies" (*Andokides* 7). Diogenes Laertius (1.91) reports that a philosopher named Kleoboulos recommended showing beneficence to friends for closer bonding and to enemies in the hope of forming a friendship. A soft turn found expression especially among Stoics and Pythagoreans and in the foreign and domestic policy of Caesar Augustus (*Res Gestae* 1.3; 4.24; cited in *Benefactor,* pp. 259–60).

6:28. In contrast, for example, to the spirit of Deuteronomy 27—28, of the Psalms (e.g., Pss. 58 and 137), and of 1QS 2:1–17, followers of Jesus are to ask God to show favor to their enemies. Jesus' own rebuke of his disciples when they wished to rain fire down on the Samaritans (Luke 9:51–55); his concern for Jerusalem (13:34; 19:41); his prayer for his enemies (see on 23:34); Stephen's petition (Acts 7:60); and Paul's wish in behalf of fellow Jews (Rom. 9:3) illustrate the meaning.

In summary, vv. 27–28 express a principle of non-retaliation, not non-violence. It must be kept in mind that the directions apply to communities that find themselves subject to social and religious persecution. Followers of Jesus ought to know before they take to the road of discipleship what the cost will be (Luke 14:25–35). Having opted for the consequences, they must be prepared to accept them. Retaliation would defeat their profession of faith. Jesus' own attitude toward his persecutors at his trial was a standard example for the early community (cf. 1 Pet. 2:21–25).

These verses say nothing about self-defense unrelated to religious persecution, nor do they speak to the question of the use of legal resources when these are available. A sample of Luke's own thinking on the latter topic is offered at Acts 16:35–40. The Christian, in other words, is not to be a simpleton but must judge circumstances in the light of the principle that vengeance belongs to the Lord (Rom. 12:19) and that one is called not to curse but to bless.

6:29–30. The thought in these verses contradicts the legislation of Lev. 24:20 and Deut. 19:21. There is a striking shift from the plural form of address to the singular in these verses, another indication perhaps that some of the sayings in this sermon derive from exhortations modeled after popular types of discourse or preaching, sometimes referred to as *diatribe*. (A similar shift occurs at James 4:11–12.) Greek has separate forms for the singular and plural in personal address. "You" does duty in English for both.

Disciples have been called not to fasting but to righteousness, and it may well be that the thought of Isa. 58:4–7, even more so than that of 50:6, lies behind Luke 6:29. The prophet complains that those who claim to seek God daily (Isa. 58:2) "fast only to quarrel and to fight and to hit with wicked fist" (Isa. 58:4). After suffering an insulting blow, disciples are not to perpetuate quarrels by retaliation; much less are they to initiate them. Instead, they are urged to break cycles of violence by sharing bread with the hungry and covering the naked (Isa. 58:7). The thought of sharing is reproduced in Luke 6:30.

Behind the words "from one who takes away your cloak do not withhold your coat as well" Jewish auditors might well have construed the figure of the stern creditor who has taken the debtor's outer garment *(himation)* as pledge (cf. Deut. 24:10–13) but has not returned it, and now comes back for the undergarment *(chitōn)* as well. The undergarment would be the last resource for the poor against exposure. But they are told to give it up, an action suggesting total reliance on God; for God is compassionate to debtors who cry to the Lord in their helplessness (see Exod. 22:25–27 and Amos 2:7–8. The creditor in turn would stand out as a totally shameless person. A less Jewishly oriented public would find themselves compelled to recognize that there are values in life that far outweigh material considerations. All would understand that these words of Jesus are an expansion of the beatitudes, for they describe the plight of the righteous, with God as their only recourse.

The Stoic philosopher Epiktetos (1.18.8) offered advice along related lines:

> It is people's own perceptions that harass them. For when a tyrant says to this or that person, "I will fetter your leg," those who value their legs will say, "No, have mercy." But those who value their own moral resolution will say to the tyrant, "If you think it is to your advantage, bring on the chains."

6:30. **Give to every one who begs from you.** "Every one" is more properly to be rendered "any one." This verse anticipates the discussion on motivation for lending (vv. 34–35). The term "every one" *(panti)* is non-restrictive. Jesus says that disciples are not to make distinctions between friends and enemies, fellow believers and unbelievers, or between those who have a good credit rating and those who are poor risks, perhaps because they are very poor. "Begs" is, therefore, too limited in meaning. Luke uses a more general term: "asks" *(aiteō),* as one would do in petitioning a loan. **Of him who takes away your goods do not ask them again.** The phrase "takes away" *(haireō)* does not necessarily refer to use of force. In view of the succeeding remarks (vv. 32–35) that express the principle behind these statements in vv. 27–30 and include words about lending, it is probable that Luke had borrowing in mind (so also Matt. 5:42). Luke 6:29, then, describes disciples as debtors, and v. 30 views them as creditors.

The Greek term behind the phrase "Do not ask them again" is a commercial expression applied to one who makes demand for payment and should be rendered: "Don't press continually for payment" *(mē apaitei).* That is, the disciple is not to dun the poor debtor in the manner of the creditors described in Sir. 20:15: "Today they lend and tomorrow they ask it back."*

If it is assumed that the average auditor would not catch all the nuances suggested above, it is nevertheless true that all of Luke's public would grasp the central range of meaning: What others consider an imposition or experience of duress, you yourself are to value as an opportunity for generosity.

After the generation of such thought, Luke can assist his Greco-Roman public to understand the apparently absurd ethics of Jesus in the light of a broader Mediterranean cultural appreciation.

6:31. Luke mediates his expansion of the thought of Jesus through recital of the so-called Golden Rule. Ironically, what appears to be a brilliant ethical maxim is shown to be in need of reconsideration, from the perspective of both Hellenistic culture and basic theology.

The Golden Rule is not original with Jesus. Kalypso tells Odysseus that she has the same plans for him that she would have for herself were she in his place (Homer *Odyssey* 5.188–89); and Seneca, Nero's chaplain, puts it in equally positive form in a treatise entitled *On Benefits* (2.1.1): "Let us show our generosity in the same manner that we would wish to have it bestowed on us." Maiandrios, vice-regent of Polykrates, declared in related vein before the assembly of his townspeople: "I shall do all in my power not to do the things that I find offensive in my neighbor" (Herodotos 3.142; cf. Isokrates *Nikokles* 61–62 [39c–e]). Leviticus 19:18, "You shall love your neighbor as yourself," is akin to it. Tobit 4:15 put it in a negative form, and so did Rabbi Hillel: "That which you hate do not do to your neighbor; this is the whole law, and all the rest is commentary" (*Sabbat* 31a).

The negative form permitted the priest and the Levite to pass by the wounded man (Luke 10:25–37). The rich man did not harm Lazarus, but neither did he show him any special consideration (16:19–31). On the other hand, even the positive form does not compass the possibilities of creative moral action. For I may do to another what I would wish for myself, but my need may not be the other's need, nor my interest the other's interest.

Most people do in fact live by the Golden Rule: "I want to be left alone, so I leave others alone." Or, "I like to make my own way, and I'd like to see others make their own way." Therefore, unless one has the motivation of the "poor" (6:20), even the Golden Rule can become an instrument of self-congratulation and selfish morality.

In any case, the Golden Rule is not a fundamental principle in Jesus' thought but a slide rule "for the purpose of guiding those who already accept the fundamental principles of love to God and love to neighbor when they are puzzled about what to do for the best in particular cases" (T. W. Manson, *The Sayings of Jesus* [1954], p. 52). What Jesus himself understands by the rule is shockingly radical, and vv. 32–35 cancel out most of those who crowd in to espouse it on a shallow prudential level.

6:32–34a. In these verses Luke explores the heart of the Greco-Roman reciprocity system. To **do good** *(agathopoieō)* referred in ancient society primarily to conferral of some private or public benefit. In Greco-Roman circles, good citizenship and good statecraft meant acceptance of responsibility for a broad range of philanthropic endeavor, including, among other things, construction of temples, theaters, and baths; underwriting of theatrical productions and of supplies for gymnastic activities; and distributions of grain. Within smaller groups of a more private nature, such as clubs and associations, an officer might be recognized for contributions of oil and wine. Basic to the system was the understanding that a grateful public would answer beneficence with bestowal of appropriate honors. For example, in response to the services of a priest and envoy named Akornion, the people of Dionysopolis (modern Baltschik near Sofia) passed a decree that concludes with the following words:

> Therefore, in order that all might know that the People (of Dionysopolis) honor such wonderful human beings who prove to be their benefactors, be it resolved by the Council and the Assembly, that Akornion, son of Dionysios, be commended for all these things (here enumerated) and that he be awarded a golden crown and a bronze likeness at the Dionysia, and that he be crowned annually at the Dionysia with a golden crown, and that the most advantageous place in the agora be allotted him for the erection of his statue. (*Benefactor*, p. 78)

This political, economic, and cultural phenomenon was only the most visible aspect of the larger network of reciprocity whereby human relations are fostered. The remarkable feature in Luke's account is Jesus' acute exposure of the broad application of the system in its crasser forms, especially in the private sector.

6:32–33. Fundamental to public-service awareness is the axiom expressed by Aristotle: "To be on the giving end rather than on the receiving end is the mark of excellence" (*Nikomachean Ethics* 4.1.7). Verses 32–34a cut through the bargaining system that characterizes much of substandard ethics: Do good to those who can return the favor. "He never did anything for me" is a complaint often heard. To be seen "in the right crowd" may be the main social objective. "But remember, I'm running a business, not a charity." Jesus replies in withering words: **Even sinners do the same**.

"Sinners," as usual in Luke, are those who from the standpoint of the Pharisees have no capacity for religion. Luke prefers the term to "tax collector" and "gentiles" (Matt. 5:46–47). Even at the bottom of the scale, in the underworld, the firmest ethic is to be found. There is no stricter code, and violators may end up on the missing persons list or eventually be found in a concrete coffin. "Grease my palm, and I'll grease yours." The graft changes hands, the bribes are taken, the votes are delivered, and the disciple who prides himself on what is merely the going ethical rate hears the indictment: **What credit is that to you?**

"Charity" is derived from the Greek word underlying the term "credit" *(charis)*. When used of something bestowed, as is often the case in ancient documents drafted in honor of philanthropists, the noun *charis* means "gift," "benefit," or "favor." When used of a response to something bestowed, it means "thanks," or in this passage "reason for thanks." That is: "Why should you expect to be congratulated for that? It's only normal, accepted practice" (cf. 1 Pet. 2:20). Such words run counter to the sentiment expressed by Jesus son of Sirach: Help a good person, not a sinner (Sir. 12:1–6).

6:34. Just as vv. 32–33 account for the manner of statement in vv. 27–28, so v. 34 argues the case for liberal lending expressed in v. 30. Sirach 29 discusses the virtues and hazards of lending. There is no special virtue in making a risk-free loan, says Jesus. Mosaic Law forbade the taking of interest from a fellow Israelite (Deut. 23:19–20). The aim of the legislation was to protect the poor from exploitation. The godly person is one who observes this law (Ps.15:5; Prov. 28:8). It is clear, then, that Jesus has in mind the problem of permitting the use of money to people who because of their poverty may not be able to return it. Prudence dictates that one make a "safe" loan that will be returned in full. But the disciple is expected to rise above the requirements of a sound banking system. According to Deut. 15:1–11, debts were to be remitted at the end of every seven years. According to Jesus, every encounter is an opportunity to put into effect such a year of liberation.

Herodes Atticus, whose theater in Athens remains a monument to his generosity, went beyond the lending. Endorsing Aristotle, who said that the liberal person is "one who esteems wealth not for itself but as a means of giving," Herodes proclaimed that "right use of wealth means giving to the needy so that their need might end; and to those who need not, so that they might have no acquaintance with need" (Philostratos *Lives of the Sophists* 2.1 [547]).

6:35. This verse summarizes the preceding discussion. Aristotle said that the proper use of wealth relates to spending and giving, not to getting and keeping it (*Nikomachean Ethics* 4.1.7). Emperor Marcus Aurelius said of philanthropy in general: "We are constituted by nature to be benefactors to others" (*Meditations* 9.42.13). Having done one good deed, he exhorted, we ought not look for a return but bestow another (*Meditations* 5.6.1–4; cf. 7.73). Decades earlier, Jesus had given philanthropy a theological dimension. To **do good** means to "render service" to others.

Loving the enemy, nonpartisan goodness, and willingness to **lend, expecting nothing in return**—there is here a play on the word for "hope" in v. 34, "hoping it back" *(apelpizō)* whether of the loan itself or of a favor in kind or in general—are to be among the characteristics of the poor, who rest their case with God (cf. Sir. 29:1–2). That such counsel should be given to the "poor" by Jesus is itself an indication of the radical character of Jesus' preaching. He does not aim to have the poor repeat what they themselves criticize about the rich. All this is a blow at a reciprocity system under which favors received are a kind of IOU held for payment. Much social, political, and economic injustice can be traced to the selective-favor and patronage system, with penalties for favors not delivered. Jesus disclaims the "scratch my back and I'll scratch yours" or the "now we owe them" arrangement.

The city of Chicago, with its long history of aldermanic turf protection, has long been a major exhibit of the folly in ignoring Jesus' counsel. Clearly Jesus' pronouncements are radical, running counter to many standard and accepted rules for so-called civilized existence. Yet they are largely repetition of Mosaic and prophetic pronouncement. The difference between Jesus and the prophets, though, is that Jesus in his person is the living embodiment of the validity of these sayings and expects his followers to be guided by them, for the Kingdom is here. You will be **sons of the Most High**, he says. Jesus son of Sirach also referred to "the Most High" to motivate his public (see Sir. 12:6), but, as indicated above (see on v. 33), Luke shows Jesus son of Mary in contradiction to that sage.

In Jewish eschatological and apocalyptic writing (cf. *Pss. of Sol.* 17:27; *Enoch* 62:1), kinship with God is a privilege conferred in the New Age (see Rom. 8:23; Gal. 4:5). The term "Most High" (Luke 1:32, 35, 76; Acts 7:48) expresses the majesty and sovereignty of God. Remarkable is the fact that Jesus identifies his disciples with a relationship attributed to himself by the angel at the annunciation (Luke 1:35). This promise does not await the future for validation but is a description of the authentic follower here and now.

The Kingdom of God is God's lavish self-expression, and Jesus is the proof of that generosity. The term for "kind" *(chrēstos)* is standard in Greco-Roman documents relating to philanthropy. God is kind to **the ungrateful and the selfish.** The word "selfish" *(ponēros)* is the antonym of *chrēstos* (cf. Dio Chrysostom 1.48.2, in criticism of those who chose to be generous to the mean-spirited [*ponēroi*] rather than to the public-spirited [*chrēstoi*] citizenry).

In his *Satyricon* (100), Petronius includes the following tribute: "Are not the finest things in nature the property of all? The sun shines on every one. And the moon, escorted by stars without number, leads even wild beasts to their food." Seneca (*Epistles* 73.6) writes in similar vein: "Although they do not rise for me alone, I am in heavy debt to the sun and the moon. I am under obligation to the seasons and to the deity who administrates them, even though they are not appointed for me personally."

The "ungrateful" are boors who do not know enough to express appreciation for benefits received. Numerous decrees in honor of benefactors carry a statement like the following expressed by the League of Artists of Dionysos in honor of a flutist named Kraton, to whom a crown and three icons were awarded, that there might be remembrance "of the appreciation . . . by the Guild because it honored its benefactor, Kraton, by rendering right and just requital in gratitude for all his benefactions" (*Benefactor* p. 168).

Encouragement of generosity by others was one of the objectives of some ancient philanthropists. Menas, of Sestos, administrator of a gymnasium, received the compliment that "through his personal dedication he impressed on the young men the importance of cultivating discipline and tolerance of hardship, with the result that, being engaged in competition for manliness, the personalities of the younger men are directed in the development of their character toward the goal of arete or exceptional distinction (*Benefactor*, p. 94). In other words, the honored benefactor helps make benefactors out of others.

Greco-Roman auditors of Luke would readily grasp the evangelist's point: those who enjoy the benefits conferred by the Parent of Jesus are obligated to reflect the character of the Supreme Benefactor and be benefactors in their own right. In so doing, they have the distinction of being "sons and daughters of the Most High." Epiktetos (2:12–13) summarizes deeply entrenched tradition:

> It is of prime importance for those who would please and obey the deities to be as much like them as lies within their power. If fidelity is a divine characteristic, then they are to be faithful; if generous, they are to be generous; if beneficent, they are to be beneficent; if magnanimous, they are to be magnanimous. In brief, they are to do and say everything in emulation of God.

Just as benefactors in the world about them receive awards for their beneficence, so the followers of Jesus will find that their **reward will be great**. These words are an echo of the phrase in v. 23. The text does not spell out details of the reward *(misthos)*, and the silence is powerfully suggestive. Luke's auditors bring to the text their understanding that the Supreme Benefactor's award, a further benefit, will certainly outweigh anything that an earthly head of state might be able to offer. Nero thought he had outstripped all others when he liberated Greece from tribute. "Other commanders have liberated cities," he proclaimed, "[but Nero] an entire province" *(Benefactor,* p. 284). It was a boast constructed on a narrow data base.

Freely the disciples have received, and freely they must give. Experience of the Father's kindness is the source of their motivation (cf. 1 John 4:19). And the promise and reward are really an invitation to personal identity. Thus through use of Greco-Roman cultural models Luke clarifies the tradition of Jesus' teaching about eschatological awards, and Luke 12:12–14 will offer further commentary on the theme.

On Judging Others
Luke 6:36–38
(Matthew 5:48; 7:1–2)

Verse 36 nuances the theme of beneficence through reference to mercy and introduces a directive on faultfinding, which in turn is followed by a concluding observation on beneficence. Faultfinding is a mark of the mean-spirited person and ill befits a person who aspires to the extraordinary excellence portrayed in the Sermon on the Plain. Aristotle similarly associates discussion of ill-tempered people with philanthropy *(Nikomachean Ethics* 4.5). In keeping with such association, but from a different perspective, Jesus son of Sirach warns against giving aid or comfort to "sinners" (Sirach 12). Luke continues to discard that sage's advice in favor of magnanimity, for mercy is a primary feature of uprightness.

6:36. To **be merciful** means that one is not quick to pounce on the evildoer or to demand the last ounce of flesh, even if one has a legal right to it. Matthew 5:48 is a variant form of this saying. As in v. 35, the character of God as gracious and beneficent Parent, without regard to recompense, provides the pattern for imitation.

6:37. Judge not does not mean that one glosses over sin or ignores it. Nor are these words to be used by one who is caught in some wrongdoing and then says to the admonisher, "Remember, 'Judge not'!" Jesus means that one is not to assume the role of keeper of other people's consciences. One is not to be a faultfinder, a nitpicker, creating the impression that one shares none of the flaws of humanity. This idea will be expanded in succeeding verses. A self-righteous approach, therefore, is here condemned.

The positive motivation lies in the knowledge of God's own attitude (cf.

Ps. 103:13), **and you will not be judged**. God does not hunt people down but is forgiving. Thus these last words are parallel to those in v. 36. On the other hand, the words "you will not be judged" suggest that persons who prefer to apply an inexorable standard to others do in fact invite God to treat them in the same fashion—and from that judgment there is no escape! In other words, one's attitude toward a brother or a sister does not itself evoke God's mercy, for Jesus plainly says, "Be merciful, even as your Father is merciful" (v. 36), but to misunderstand God's forgiveness is to invoke divine judgment.

To **condemn not** means that one does not pronounce a verdict on others as though they were morally or spiritually hopeless and therefore ineligible for one's beneficence. Expectations of better things from the other is to characterize the disciples' approach, for God mercifully gives sinners an opportunity to repent.

On the positive side, **forgive, and you will be forgiven**. In legal usage the Greek word rendered "forgive" *(apoluō)* means to "dismiss a charge." In the light of the economic overtones of the context, these words appear to have as their primary referent for the forgiveness of monetary debts (cf. 11:4), which in turn suggests a broader exercise of forgiveness that invites divine dismissal of charges. God's forgiveness is not the result of a human being's forgiveness of others, but those who are unforgiving show that they do not understand forgiveness from God as an invitation to understand themselves anew in relation to others.

6:38. This verse summarizes the preceding remarks. The imagery relates to oriental grain market practice. Grain is measured out to overflowing in order to ensure the purchaser a full measure. An example of imagistic reference to a garment as a receptacle for abstractions is exhibited in Livy's *History* (21.18). After the fall of Saguntum to Hannibal, a Roman envoy met with the Carthaginian Council and listened patiently to their lecture on words about covenants. When his turn came to respond, he made a fold in his toga and said: "Look, I hold here in my robe both war and peace. The choice is yours" (see also Polybios 3.33.2).

The phrase rendered **will be put** reads literally, "They will give" *(dōsousin)*. In the light of the context, God is the subject. A similar use of this colloquialism appears in Luke 12:20, 48. Our measure will become God's measure. That is, if we deny mercy to the other, we short-circuit God's mercy toward us. A similar principle is expressed in the Lord's Prayer (11:4). A different application of the proverb is made in Mark 4:24. In Isa. 65:7 the figure is used of God's adverse judgment (cf. Ps. 79:12). Josh Billings summed it all up in his homespun way. "Generosity," said the humorist, "iz diffrent from justiss—justiss iz 16 ounces tew the pound, and no more."

Self-Search   Luke 6:39–49
Verses 39–49 form the third part of the Sermon on the Plain.

Luke explores further the theme of self-centered moral exclusiveness that was suggested in vv. 31–35 and maintains connection with the central thought of vv. 20–26, which stressed the ultimate vindication of the poor through God's intervention. Verses 39–40 introduce the illustration of mote and beam found in vv. 41–42 and anticipate the expanded exposition of the pupil-teacher relationship in vv. 46–49. The imagery of the good tree and the bad tree of vv. 43–45 balances the imagery of the mote and beam of vv. 43–45, which in their turn formulate an answer to the verdict pronounced by the enemies in v. 22. The conclusion of the sermon, vv. 46–49, reaffirms the presentation in vv. 39–40 about the mutual responsibility of teacher and learner. There can be no question concerning the credentials of Jesus. It is the pupils who bear the principal responsibility—careful audition of the Lord's words. The entire unit, vv. 39–49, is constructed chiastically. Verses 39–40 have as their correspondent vv. 46–49, and these two portions embrace the thematically related illustrations in vv. 41–42 and 43–45.

Blind Leading the Blind   Luke 6:39–42
(Matthew 15:14; 10:24–25; 7:3–5)

6:39–40. This series of proverbs describes the false teachers and prepares the way for the understanding of the succeeding illustration in vv. 41–42. The picture of self-righteous or amateur pedagogues who try to improve others while ignoring their own weaknesses appears, as can be gathered from Jakob Wettstein's collection, with many variations in the world's literature. Sextus Empiricus (*Against the Professors* 1.31) declares that an amateur cannot teach an amateur anymore than the blind can lead the blind. And Horace (*Epistles* 1.17.4) jocosely writes to a patron named Scaeva: "I have still much to learn, but listen to me anyway, even if I appear to be a blind man giving directions."

Proverbs naturally do not take in the exceptions but sum up the general experience of the race. Teachers who use incorrect grammar can scarcely expect their pupils to become masters of rhetoric. In Matt. 10:24–25 the proverb of pupil and teacher is applied to experience of persecution, but here it refers to efforts at moral improvement. "What you are speaks louder than what you say" sums up the matter.

6:41–42. Jesus' proverbial speech was stocked with humorous contrasts. The picture is purposely overdrawn in order to make the point that any effort at the moral improvement of others without taking stock of oneself is utterly ridiculous. His words do not mean that since the disciple is also a sinner he should live and let live and be blind to moral imperfections about him. Such a stance would give the green light to evil and spell the end of mutual admonition in the community. What is criticized by Jesus is the moralist's patronizing attitude, which receives censure also from numerous Greco-Roman authors.

Already in the fifth century B.C.E. Demokritos had written, "Better it is to correct one's own faults than those of others" (*Fragments* 60). When Thales was asked what was easy, he answered, "Counseling of others." At another time, someone inquired how one might conduct oneself "in the best and most upright manner." He replied, "Avoid doing what you find blameworthy in others" (Diogenes Laertius 1.36). "Before you charge your neighbor with a flaw," wrote Menander, "ponder well what deep within yourself you saw" (*Fragment* 710, J. M. Edmonds). "You manage to see the tiny louse on your neighbor but not the large tick on yourself," wrote Petronius (*Satyricon* 57). And Persius of Rome complained in different imagery about a lack in soul-searching. "All are on the march," he wrote, "and eye the burden on the other's back" (*Satires* 4.23–24).

6:42. Jesus sketches the approach: "Friend, just let me get that splinter out of your eye." But all the while this self-styled ophthalmologist ignores the beam that blocks a self-assumed penetrating gaze. Followers of Christ who aim to improve others must make a frontal attack on their own moral problems, their foibles, their weaknesses, their sins. Again, this does not mean that they must first succeed in eradicating all that is substandard in their own lives before confronting others. Rather, they must approach their own weaknesses in a manner suggesting that they are taking seriously God's call to repentance for themselves also. Then what they say will be more convincing to others and not a matter of the pot calling the kettle black.

"Hypocrite" is a transliteration of a Greek term *(hypokritēs)* that is frequently associated with play-acting and here connotes one who plays a role that does not bear up under scrutiny in real life. In its anglicized usage the term bears a stronger negative tone than the Greek term probably conveyed. Posturing or dissembling is here indicated. "Reynard is still Reynard, though he put on a cowl." Dissembling is the "homage that vice pays to virtue." The proverbs are legion. Disciples of Jesus are not to pose as judges when in fact they are themselves liable to judgment. Self-righteous people buy their own righteousness at the expense of denying it to others. Only the poor person in Jesus' sense of the term will be convincing to others. Seeing "clearly," such a person will be able to say to others, "Imitate me, as I imitate Christ" (1 Cor. 11:1; see also 2 Thess. 3:9; 1 Pet. 5:3; 1 Tim. 4:11–12). "He preaches well that lives well. That's all the divinity I understand," said Sancho in response to Don Quixote's commendation of his discourse on death. The Don replied, "You have divinity enough."

Known by the Fruit   Luke 6:43–45
                                                    (Matthew 7:16–21: cf. 12:33–35)

6:43–45. These verses amplify the thought in the illustrations embodied in vv. 41–42. Good trees bear good fruit, bad trees bad fruit. "Tree" in Greek applies to a number of growing things, including what we would call plants or shrubs. A **bad tree** is therefore a plant that produces inedible or useless fruit. Bushes bearing beautiful berries but bitter to the taste would fall into this classification. Luke includes thorns and bramble bushes. The false teacher invites censoriousness, legalistic bootstrap lifting, judgmental and patronizing criticism (cf. James 3:10–12; Mark 7:21–22).

The "good," or poor, person, dependent on the resources of a God whom he or she experiences to be merciful, **produces good** (cf. Prov. 11:30), such as blessing instead of cursing, thanksgiving instead of complaint, commendation and encouragement of the other, and honest expression of concern. The "heart" *(kardia)*, the real spiritual mind-set of the individual, this is what determines goodness. Unless the heart is reconstructed, law remains unproductive (cf. Luke 18:9–14).

It has been suggested that Jesus showed himself loveless by engaging in what appears to be abrasive critique of lovelessness. But it must be remembered that he did not discourage correction of others in the community. Rather, he attacked the spirit of isolationism that subverts, in the name of religion, the outreaching love of God. Also, it may seem odd that Luke, who desired to bring together diverse parties in the church, should repeat such abrasive sentences. But forthrightness is no crime. To conceal one's own potential for evil is. Besides, no surgeon ever healed without a cut. But shun that one who enjoys the cutting more than the healing.

Conclusion   Luke 6:46–49
                                                                     (Matthew 7:21, 24–27)

6:46. This verse climaxes the preceding exhortation and serves as a transition to the concluding paragraph (vv. 47–49). The words **Lord, Lord** are an echo of liturgical practice. Christians are reminded that they must take seriously the Lord's words. To go through the ritual without bringing forth the fruits expected from a supposedly good tree is phony religion (cf. Isa. 5:4). If Jesus is Lord, he is the controller of the disciple's life. And if he is the Lord of the disciple, then the disciple is not lord over others. These words, then, are the climax of all that precedes. The poor are those who are prepared to make of their lives a constant and real liturgy. Jesus puts the dynamism of religion within the reach of the proletariat.

6:47–49. At v. 27 Jesus said, "I say to you that hear." Now he couples doing with hearing of his words (cf. 8:21, 15; 10:37). His words are not theoretical statement. They are not presented as discussion themes, as theses for ecclesiastical committee work designed to make the church think it is doing God's will because it spends so much time talking about it. He expects his words to be carried out. To build on rock means to hear and do. The builder on sand hears but does not act. False prophets cause a wall to fall under a deluge (Ezek. 13:8–16). Jesus is God's true prophet, but more than a prophet, for no prophet ever said, "The one who comes to me is like a house built on rock" (see also Matt. 16:13–20). His words have authority because he is God's own Kingdom expression.

The words of Jesus address themselves to the depths of existence. They are not an invitation to an ethical salad bar. Cross-bearers are not given the option of moral electives, and Luke will have more to relate on the subject of builders' fiascoes (see 14:26–30). Jesus' words are not interesting religious or humanitarian specimens, designed to entertain and arouse sentiment over "such idealistic thought." They do not permit business as usual. No one can remain a disciple who prefers to have morality determined by institutional patterns that admit of no critique.

JESUS' CREDENTIALS
Luke 7:1—8:3

The Sermon on the Plain offered commentary on Jesus' earlier proclamation at Nazareth, where he propounded ideas that put under review the dominant hypotheses and class and social structures of his time. Reflective of his experience at Nazareth was Jesus' reference to the prospect of persecution. But his stress was on God's beneficence, which is to serve as a model for those committed to the New Age. In closing remarks (6:46–49), Jesus called attention to the importance of his words. In 7:1—8:3 Luke shows how the performance of Jesus brings the divine beneficence to powerful expression. The Sermon on the Plain had spoken about attitudes toward outsiders. Luke now shows through the story about a centurion (7:1–10) how "enemies" can treat one another without acrimony.

The New Age spells the end of weeping (6:21), and Jesus demonstrates the fact at Nain (7:11–17). What does it mean, not to judge (6:37)? Jesus offers an indelible answer in 7:36–50. Verses 8:1–3 then terminate the series of benefactions with a summary statement on beneficence and reciprocity. Embedded between the story of the widow at Nain and the recital about the generous woman is the account concerning John the Baptist's quandary (7:18–28). But his experience is dramatic exposition of 6:22–23, and John qualifies as one of the blessed (v. 23). As for Jesus, his broad sympathies for outsiders necessarily brought him into conflict with strict interpretations of standing rules and regulations, and 7:29–35 presents the sponsors of legal concern in striking contrast to the response of the general public.

Recognition
Luke 7:1–17

Remarkable Faith
Luke 7:1–10
(Matthew 8:5–10, 13)

Once more the words spoken at Nazareth (Luke 4:23) find fulfillment. And once again Luke underlines the authority of Jesus' word with authoritative deed. Zechariah was chastised for his lack of faith (1:20) and

Mary was commended (1:45). The five men cited in 5:17–26 gained their objective because of their faith (v. 20). Now a centurion becomes a model for the proper response to Jesus' authority, so eloquently asserted in 6:47–49. Matthew prefers at this point to emphasize Jesus' contact with outcasts, of whom a leper is exhibit A. Unlike Moses, who ascended a mountain surrounded by barriers to keep the Israelites from approaching too closely to God, Jesus encourages such encounter. Luke, on the other hand, had discussed Jesus' treatment of outcasts, including the leper, in a series of recitals placed *before* the sermon. Here he sees the issue as one of faith, and the centurion is his prize example.

Luke's recital is closer to that of Matt. 8:5–13 than that of John 4:46–54, except that in Matthew the centurion encounters Jesus personally (in line with the motif expressed in Matthew's account of the leper), whereas in Luke the centurion sends word through intermediaries. Through this shape of the story Luke is able to show that even Jewish leaders recognize Jesus' power and urge him to use it for the benefit of a gentile. The gesture fits Luke's Jew-to-gentile theme and his concern to establish continuity between Israel and the gentiles (cf. Acts 10:35). Not all in Israel, he suggests, shared Jerusalem's attitude toward mission to gentiles. Matthew is concerned to show that the apostles replace Jerusalem's hierarchy as teaching authority; therefore he naturally omits reference to any Jewish delegation.

After exposure to the theme of reciprocity as expressed in the Sermon on the Plain, Luke's Greco-Roman public would find the text additionally meaningful because of its power to evoke awareness of their cultural context in which philanthropy played such a significant role. The same Jesus who called on his disciples to "do good," even to outsiders, puts his own word into practice.

Writing about a decade after the fall of Jerusalem, Luke was probably not in a position to be precise about the military connection of the centurion in this account. That he was a gentile is clear from the narrative. Since Galilee was not a part of a Roman province until the death of Agrippa I in the year 44 c.e., the centurion was probably not on direct assignment from Rome but may have been a veteran who assisted Herod Antipas in his police force, which was modeled along Roman lines. In any event, the word "centurion" would automatically evoke in Luke's public the image of Roman majesty and power. And such would be the case even if the centurion had historically never been a Roman officer, for Antipas ruled by grace of Rome. It is from such perspective of Roman ascendancy and the probable perception of it by Luke and his public that the commentary concerning this centurion is here developed.

7:1. Verse 1 stresses the verbal power of Jesus. But the reference to **Capernaum** prepares Luke's public for a recital of equally powerful deeds (cf. 4:23).

7:2. The recital is marked with pathos. Centurions were officers in charge nominally of a hundred men, although the number varied. Persius, the Roman satirist, thought of them as uneducated, uncultured blobs of humanity, totally unequipped for philosophy (*Satires* 3.77–85; 5.189–191), but some deduction must be made in view of the genre in which he writes; in any case, generalizations made by ancient Roman moralists are notoriously untrustworthy.

Now a centurion had a slave who was dear to him. Luke's refined sympathies seize on the man's appreciation of his slave. Given the condition of slaves in the ancient world, it is questionable whether he would have been "dear" *(entimos)* to the centurion had he not been a capable worker. Of any special intimacy there is no suggestion in the text. The fact that he has a terminal illness serves to heighten the anticipated demonstration of healing power.

7:3–7. The dominant structuring feature of the narrative is a series of embassies that engage a number of dignitaries. Luke's Mediterranean public, familiar with such bureaucratic procedures, would sense the author's effort to highlight the prestige of Jesus. The drama lies in the focus on two powerful political figures: Jesus, representative of the Kingdom of God, and a centurion, representative of Eternal Rome.

The first embassy consists of **elders of the Jews,** sent by the centurion to request Jesus to come down and heal his slave. The reciprocity system is on go. These Jews, on their own admission, "owe him one," as politicians phrase it, and they carry out their mission with an earnestness that echoes typical praise in ancient documents concerning envoys. The centurion is a benefactor, who has respect and affection for Israel, even to the extent of assuming the costs of a synagogue for Capernaum. The story suggests that, despite occasional arrogant displays of authority, as for example by Pontius Pilate, Rome endeavored to maintain good relationships with her subjects.

Luke's centurion is not the only gentile honored by Jews. An inscription from Berenike in Cyrenaica, dated near the turn of the current era, records a decree, passed unanimously on the Feast of Tabernacles by an assembly of the Jewish community, in commendation of a Roman procurator for his many displays of beneficence:

> Whereas Marcus Titius of Sestos, son of Aimilia and a man of exceptional merit, after his assumption of office as procurator carried out his public responsibilities in a generous and distinguished manner and in all his conduct continues to display such a conciliatory attitude that his presence is no burden either to the people in general or to anyone in particular; and whereas, in the course of his administration that affects our Jewish community he has sought our best interests both publicly and privately, and does many things for us that are worthy of his reputation for exceptional nobility, be it resolved by the archons and the community of the Jews who are in Berenike to commend him and to recognize him by name at each

> assembly and observance of the new moon and to award him an olive
> wreath fastened with a woolen fillet; and be it further resolved that our
> archons have this decree inscribed on a pillar of Parian marble, which is to
> be placed in the most noticeable part of the amphitheater. (*CIG* 3.5361)

Some measure of their affection can be gauged from their use of a marble
that was ordinarily reserved for the sculpting of statues for the imperial
establishment.

Jesus is anxious to do both the Jews and the Roman a courtesy. But just as
he, in company with the Jewish elders, draws near the centurion's residence,
the officer sends his second delegation, this time his personal friends. The
elders had said the centurion was "worthy" *(axios)* (v. 4). The centurion uses
a synonym in v. 6 *(hikanos;* RSV: **worthy**) that suggests he is outranked by
Jesus. Then, in v. 7, the centurion uses a verb *(axioō;* RSV: **I did not
presume**) that is cognate with the term for "worthy" *(axios)* in v. 4.

The dialogue captures much in few words. Jesus does not fear to contract
defilement by entry into a gentile's home (see on 5:13). On the other hand,
the centurion, who would not hesitate to offend religious scruples by
entering a Jewish house if he suspected trouble, does not wish to expose an
eminent person like Jesus to undue criticism. But Luke's chief interest in the
reticence of the centurion is to highlight the fact that Jesus heals the slave
without a personal contact and that the centurion requires no sign but
simply recognizes the authority of Jesus' word.

7:8. The dialogue in this verse points to a perception of the kind of
military discipline for which Rome was highly regarded (but see also 1 Esd.
4:1–12 on the oriental despot). In Pompeii the body of a soldier was
discovered in the ashes, still at his post. Machine-like discipline was demanded by Rome. Through his simile, then, the centurion was not equating
himself with Jesus as an authority figure. On the contrary, his point is that if
the orders of a man of such comparatively low rank are obeyed, how much
more Jesus' command (see Epiktetos 1.25.10 for a Greek philosopher's
viewpoint). A slave is told, "Go" *(poreuthēti),* and he goes; in 5:24 Jesus had
used a modified form of that imperative *(poreuou),* with extraordinary effect
on a crowd. And experts at fishing had learned that Jesus was no amateur
(5:1–11). But this centurion's statement is among the finest tributes ever
paid by one human being to another. It was the acme of professional
courtesy.

7:9. Even Jesus marveled (the only instance in the Gospels) at this miracle
of faith and repays the courtesy with the finest compliment a Jew could give
to a gentile: "I have not found faith like this in all Israel." At the same time,
Luke's public knows that many in Israel had in fact not responded to God's
action in Jesus as did the centurion.

7:10. On their return, the messengers found the slave doing well. Yet no specific command of healing is recorded. Not even a word was necessary. The centurion did not require it. His faith secured the benefit. Such people would be among the "poor" and they would be living commentaries on the meaning of Jesus' words, "Why do you call me 'Lord, Lord,' and not do what I say?" (6:46*). It is true that the Greek term *kyrios,* rendered "Lord," is a standard expression, equaling "Sir." But the structure of the text creates a bureaucratic or chancery atmosphere. Caesar was accustomed to being addressed as "Lord." In Luke's account, the centurion accords this honor to Jesus (7:6). Luke 23:47 will echo this recital, and Acts 10 is its epilogue. There is no marveling over the miracle of healing, for Luke wishes to focus on the greater miracle—the faith of the centurion.

It is a fascinating account, an account in which the two principals never meet and the anticipated word of power is never pronounced. Politics of an unusual order. At the same time, it is a lesson in cross-cultural relations. The representative of world power comes with a request for aid to one who belongs to a troublesome minority. It is a lesson learned with difficulty by imperialists in secular and ecclesiastical structures.

Resurrection at Nain   Luke 7:11–17

Numerous physicians receive praises in antiquity for successfully treating people who were considered terminally ill (see *Benefactor,* pp. 59–60). Luke's story of a resurrection at Nain reveals Jesus at a further level of beneficent competence, at the very borders of the "lone dominions of the silent dead."

Commentators from Jakob Wettstein on have called attention to parallels from ancient literature (e.g., Artemidoros 4.82; Pliny *Natural History* 26.15, concerning Asklepiades; Apuleius *Florida* 19; and Philostratos *Life of Apollonios of Tyana* 4.45). Such information, in concert with parallel material cited from the OT, contributes to one's understanding of the meaning of Luke's account by disclosing the fact that ability to raise the dead was considered in antiquity the mark of an exceptionally endowed person. By repeating a related account from Jesus' ministry, Luke shows that the miracle is not itself unique but is part of a total pattern that contributes to the ultimate uniqueness of Jesus.

The recital is peculiar to Luke and is introduced here to prepare the way for the answer to John's question at 7:19 and to anticipate accounts in 8:40–56 and Acts 9:36–43. At the same time, this story reinforces Jesus' call to faith in his word that once more finds expression in a merciful deed. Since 7:18–35 deals with the problem of Jesus' credentials, Luke emphasizes here that Jesus himself is an Elijah figure, not to prove that Jesus is therefore the Messiah but to take the wind out of the sails of the grossly apocalyptic-minded members of the Christian community. No whirlwind type of apocalyptic sign is required to signal the Messiah's arrival. Jesus in his person renders superfluous the end-time return of Elijah. Elijah had raised the son of the widow at Zarephath, which is located near Sidon (1 Kings

17:9–10, 17–24), and Elisha performed a similar miracle at Shunem (2 Kings 4:32–39).

7:11. Nain lies between Endor and Shunem. Since Sidon lay outside Jesus' normal itinerary, tradition prior to Luke appears to have fixed on Nain as the locale for the miracle. But Luke's narrative is patterned in its wording more after the account in 1 Kings than in 2 Kings. Yet some of his public would sense no problem, for Elijah and Elisha traditionally constituted two facets of a composite prophetic mission. As in 6:19–20, the disciples are distinguished from the crowd, perhaps to set up a contrast with John's disciples (7:18). (The verse opens with Luke's stock phrase "And it came to pass" [*kai egeneto*]).

7:12. Luke calls attention to the **gate of the city**, for the dead were buried outside the city. The word "behold" (*idou,* cf. 1 Kings 17:10) calls attention to an extraordinary circumstance. The centurion's slave had been on the point of death (Luke 7:2), but this young man was already dead, and his mother's plight is poignantly described. He was her sole mainstay (cf. 8:42; 9:38; the expression **only son** [*monogenēs*] is applied to Jesus in John 1:18). In a time when there was no social security, this was an especially grievous calamity. One is to understand that the funeral was, according to Eastern custom, taking place on the day of the young man's death, and probably toward evening.

7:13. The compassion of the crowd is superseded only by the concern of Jesus, who "shares the sorrow woven into the very fabric of life." His "compassion" *(splagchnizomai)* evokes recollection of 1:78–79. In the preceding narrative a group of village elders had taken the initiative, and the faith of the centurion was emphasized; here Jesus moves unasked, and nothing is said about the spiritual condition of others in the story. That Luke writes **the Lord** *(ho kyrios)* is not accidental. "Lord" means master. In the presence of death, he who was recognized by the community as Lord by virtue of his own resurrection is about to display his mastery. His command that she stop her flow of tears is remarkable in an oriental setting where profuse lamentation with hired mourners was customary. On his lips it is a command with promise, a call to faith.

7:14. Even more remarkable is the fact that Jesus, a noted teacher in Israel, **touched the bier,** for contact with the dead defiles (cf. Num. 19:11, 16; Sir. 34:25–26). But the Lord, who had previously invited himself to the centurion's house, does not contract defilement; he removes it. Great physician that he is, he encounters disaster at its depth, and his own body which will soon itself lie still in death is the instrument of life. The "bier" is a litter on which the dead man, probably concealed only with cloth, was being transported. As in other recitals of resurrection (cf. Luke 8:54; John 11:43), Jesus addresses the dead man personally. The dead man is not merely a corpse, or a soul, but a person, and the pronoun "you" is in an emphatic position in the Greek text *(soi legō)*.

7:15. Elijah prayed three times to the Lord. Jesus speaks on his own authority, and the response is immediate. There is no delay in the restoration of the young man's powers. He sat up (as Tabitha will also do, Acts 9:40) and began to speak. As Elijah had done, Jesus gives him back to his mother (1 Kings 17:23; cf. Acts 9:41). Death destroys relationships; Jesus restores them.

7:16. The crowd recognizes the power of God displayed in its midst (cf. Luke 2:20), for resurrection of the dead is God's prerogative. The word "arise" *(egerthēti),* which Jesus had addressed to the young man, is now referred to Jesus: **A great prophet has arisen among us**, perhaps a reference to the popular expectation of Elijah's return. Others say, **God has visited his people** (see on 1:68, 78). The story circulates in all Judea, thus setting the eventual rejection of Jesus against a background of witness to his person as the instrument of God.

As noted above, a parallel to this healing is frequently cited from Philostratos's *Life of Apollonius of Tyana* (4.45), an account about a charismatic first-century Neopythagorean sage.

> A girl had died just before she was to be married and the bridegroom was following her bier, lamenting naturally his unfulfilled marriage. Since the girl belonged to a prominent family, the whole of Rome joined in his mourning. Apollonius, who happened to come by, witnessed their grief and said: "Put down the bier, for I shall put away the tears you shed for her." The crowd thought he would deliver a eulogy . . . but he did nothing of the sort. Instead he merely touched the girl, said something inaudible over her, and without delay awakened her. The girl spoke out loud and returned to her own home.

The biographer is skeptical and suggests that there may have been a spark of life in the girl. Luke entertains no doubt that the young man was dead.

Perplexity
Luke 7:18–50

John's Question
Luke 7:18–23
(Matthew 11:2–6)

How the functions of John the Baptist and Jesus related to one another was a heated subject of debate in the early church. From Luke's manner of presentation it appears that some Christians connected Elijah's anticipated reappearance at the end time with John's ministry and viewed him as a forerunner of the Messiah, who, they thought, was to make his appearance with extraordinary signs and wonders. Jesus was being proclaimed as the Messiah, but he had apparently failed to fulfill the apocalyptic expectation. John had said that One who was stronger than he would come and bring the refining fire (3:16–17). Luke does not indicate that when John spoke those words he had any idea that Jesus was indeed the Stronger One, for the voice from heaven had spoken to Jesus, not to the people (23:22).

While he was in prison, John heard about Jesus, who had a large following and performed mighty deeds. But Jesus preached mercy, not judgment, and associated with publicans and sinners. Could Jesus therefore qualify as the Coming One? Luke now uses the occasion of John's perplexity to show that Jesus is indeed the Coming One. To do this, he reinforces his teaching that John is not Elijah (cf. the explicit denial, John 1:21). On the contrary, Jesus is the one who carries out the functions of Elijah; and his ministry, as sketched in the preceding portion of the Gospel, is the badge of his credentials as the Great Reformer of the end time.

In effect, Luke eliminates John as an apocalyptic sign in the popular sense of the term and shows that apocalyptic demonstration of the spectacular kind envisaged for the windup of history is not a necessary feature of the Messiah's (see 3:15) ministry. As the Coming One, Jesus will enter Jerusalem (19:38). There he will be questioned about his role as Messiah (22:67), and at the crucifixion he will be publicly identified as Israel's King (23:38), a title that will be defined in 24:26 as the equivalent of Messiah. In due course he will also come with apocalyptic splendor (21:27). John's mistake, like that of many Christians in Luke's time, was to concentrate on the apocalyptic aspect. Luke corrects the error by focusing attention on the less spectacular coming. The Kingdom of God, as Jesus will point out later, is not subject to human verification (17:20), and it comes in two stages. Even slight acquaintance with Luke's Gospel could spare the pains of many a calculator of the time of the second coming of Jesus.

7:18–20. Luke had recorded at 3:20 the imprisonment of John, thus making possible an interval in which Jesus preaches and performs acts of mercy. Now John's disciples inform their teacher about these words and deeds (**all these things**). John then sends **two of his disciples** to secure an explanation from **the Lord** (see v. 13) concerning his mission. Two is the customary number of witnesses required by Mosaic Law (cf. Deut. 19:15). But Luke's Greco-Roman public would note that embassies of two were common in bureaucratic circles. As at Luke 7:1–10, Luke modifies his source from the perspective taken in Acts 4:12 so as to project the importance of Jesus as the great agent of divine favor (see Luke 7:21).

There is no hint in the text that the disciples had raised the question. John wants to know whether Jesus is the one **who is to come** (*ho erchomenos;* cf. Hab. 2:3; Luke 3:16; the term is used of God, Rev. 1:4, 8; 4:8; the imperative "come" [*erchou*] is addressed to Jesus in Rev. 22:20). It is important again to make a distinction. On the one side is John's perspective—a historical question that cannot be resolved with certainty—respecting Jesus' relation to Jewish expectations. On the other side is Luke's perspective, which is explicitly messianic (cf. 2:11, 26; 3:15; 24:26, 46; Acts 2:31, 36; 3:18, 20; 4:26; 9:22; 17:3; 18:5, 28; 26:23) and which colors the dialogue in a story like that of John's perplexity, which is in effect the kind of perplexity expressed by some of Luke's public. Is Jesus, then, the Messiah in the sense John spelled it out during his ministry at the Jordan?

7:21. Jesus gives John's emissaries a demonstration before their very eyes. It is now even clearer why Luke recorded a series of sayings and healings before introducing this account concerning John. But Jesus offers no spectacular signs, such as fire from heaven. The miracles recorded here are similar to those presented prior to this recital, and they echo the program announced at Nazareth (4:18). They are rather routine for Jesus, but not earth-rocking or heaven-shaking enough for those who looked for special apocalyptic effects. In other words, nothing is said or done beyond "all these things" (v. 18).

On many that were blind he bestowed sight. Of special significance is the expression "bestowed." The Greek verb *(charizomai)* is the cognate of the noun from which the word *charis* is derived and it denotes "bestowal of a favor." The fact that Luke is the only evangelist to use the verb (Luke 7:42, 43, of forgiveness; Acts 3:14, of a political favor; 25:16, in a political context; 27:24, of divine beneficence) is of a piece with his interest in Jesus as the ultimate expression of divine generosity. In Greco-Roman literary, bureaucratic, and sacral documents it is a standard term to express bestowal of benefits by a deity or a head of state.

7:22. Since it is John who has the problem, the disciples are sent back to report to him what they have **seen and heard.** Once again the stress is on both deed and word, the twin mark of exceptional merit (cf. 24:19); but the most important feature, namely, that the poor hear the good news, climaxes the list. That Jesus performed deeds that transcend normal explanation is beyond question. That God was revealing his saving intentions through those extraordinary deeds is an affirmation of faith. Keeping these two basic propositions separate is important for resolution of debate concerning the relation of scientific and biblical truth.

Christians who tend to use Jesus' miracles as props for their faith in his person need to heed the reminder that his proclamation to the poor is the primary badge of his messianic office. The authority of Jesus' word is independent of the ability of historians to establish whether an alleged miracle took place or not. God's activity is not subject to the limitations of human knowledge, and any attempt to prove miracles through scientific demonstration is itself a denial of belief in God's miraculous dealings. Geologists can hazard educated guesses about the age of the earth. They can neither prove nor disprove God's relation to observable phenomena. Precisely in an age that senses both the power and the futility of purely rational processes, Luke's interpretation of reality is particularly helpful. And this is especially so if the church recognizes that it loses all credibility if it loses sight of the central concern of Jesus: good news for the powerless.

Expressions and thoughts from Isa. 26:19; 29:18–19; 35:5; and 61:1 form the background for much of the recital here in v. 22, except that the cure of lepers is not mentioned in these passages. But the last type of miracle does fit, along with resuscitation of the dead, into the Elijah-Elisha tradition (cf. Luke 4:25–27). Thus Jesus stands clearly in the prophetic-apocalyptic anticipation, but with modifications. John is not to be "offended" (v. 23: *skandalizō*, to be caught in a trap). That is, he is not to be distressed over the absence of special apocalyptic effects. Everything happens in its due course, but for the present, and that means also for the age of the church, the main evidence of Jesus' authority and messianic credentials is that the poor hear the good news.

Those who were apocalyptically conditioned naturally expected the good news to be a promise of deliverance of oppressed Israel from her Roman enemy (cf. 1:68–74); instead, Jerusalem was crushed in the revolt of 70 C.E. Luke corrects such misinterpretation by pointing out that the good news is a message of assurance to the "poor" (see on 6:20) and that they have as much title to a relationship with God as do the scribes and the Pharisees. What, then, is the role of John? Luke answers this question in vv. 24–28.

7:23. The Sermon on the Plain had opened with a message of blessing for the poor. The first phase of the story about John terminates with a statement of blessing *after* a reference to the poor. The ambiguity of blessedness accompanied by persecution found expression in 6:22, and John's experience is a ratification of the bewildering Kingdom process. But the future tenses of promise that are found in the beatitudes are to be taken seriously. Hence the admonition not to take offense at Jesus is an invitation not only to John but to all who audit Luke's Gospel, to share in the larger hope.

The fact that John is warned not to take offense means that there are those who will, and their role will be taken up in vv. 29–35. John had asked whether it might be appropriate to "look for another" (v. 20). Acts 4:12 provides the definitive answer: "There is no other name under heaven."

Answers of Jesus to John and the Crowds   Luke 7:24–35
                                                              (Matthew 11:7–19)

John's problem is a problem in Christian communities, and the answer relayed by Jesus to John is in reality an answer to Luke's public. Luke 7:24–35 is a further expression of that literary tactic.

7:24–27. The questions addressed by Jesus **to the crowds** are quasi-satirical. Surely they did not go into the wilderness (see 3:7) merely to see reeds blowing in the wilderness. Nor did they expect to audition a prince who was dressed in fine robes (cf. Esth. 6:7–9). At Acts 17:21 Luke will make a related social comment about the shallow who treat history in the making as a sideshow. Some of Luke's auditors may have pondered a contrast between Ahijah's picture of Israel, unstable "as a reed shaken in the water" (1 Kings 14:15) and Jesus' portrait of John, which suggested steadiness in the fiercest sirocco of political intimidation. And certainly they did not expect to audition a man who was attired in garments with which rulers signalled special status (cf. 1 Kings 10:5). What Haman anticipated for himself (Esth. 6:9) and what was ultimately assigned to Mordecai (8:15) was a nonexistent possibility for John, who, as Paul would do later in the presence of Governor Felix (Acts 24:25), reminded Herod Antipas that kings were not exempt from morality (cf. Luke 3:19). No, they went to see **a prophet** (cf. 1:76). Yes, **more than a prophet.** John was a prophet's prophet. No ancient prophet's coming had been so foretold as was John's arrival. This is the one who shares the credentials of the messenger who went before the children of Israel in their wanderings (Exod. 23:20).

Failure to note the citation from Exodus has led many readers to think that Jesus is referring to himself in the pronouns. But it is Israel's way that the messenger is "to prepare" (v. 27; cf. 1:17, the only other occurrence of *kataskeuazō* in Luke, and in specific reference to preparation of the people). The voice cries out in Luke 3:4: "Make ready the way of the Lord."* Israel was to "make ready" *(hetoimazō)* for the arrival of the Lord God by heeding John's call to repentance (cf. Exod. 23:21). And John's task was "to prepare" the way before Israel, so that Israel might be readied for God. In this sense he was indeed a forerunner.

By shifting Mark's citation (Mark 1:2) of the OT quotation (note its absence at Luke 3:4), Luke is able to give fresh significance to the pronoun "you." The second line of the quotation is usually traced to Mal. 3:1, but it is doubtful whether Luke so understood it; for this prophetic passage was popularly applied to Elijah, and Luke prefers to associate, at least for a time, Elijah's activity with that of Jesus. The sequence of wording, in any event, does not match any passage in the OT.

In a striking illumination of the use made of the quotation in v. 27, Acts 13:8–10 shows that God uses Barnabas and Paul as messengers to help direct Sergius Paulus along the way to Christian understanding, but Elymas the magician makes "crooked the straight paths of the Lord."

7:28. Since John's task is to prepare the people for God's demonstration of salvation (cf. 1:76–77), revealed with finality in Jesus, Jesus can say in affirmation of 1:15 that John is the greatest mortal ever born. Yet the person **who is least in the kingdom of God is greater than he.** This does not mean that John is excluded from the Kingdom but that fulfillment is relatively better than anticipation, and the poor in Jesus' fellowship are the beneficiaries of John's proclamation to Israel. The logic is not Western but Eastern in its assertion that the Kingdom is here.

7:29–30. This paragraph is found in a related form at Matt. 21:32. In Luke's recital the words are to be understood as a continuation of Jesus' remarks. Had Luke meant the words to be parenthetical he would very probably have introduced v. 31 with a phrase such as, "Then he said" (cf. 19:12, following a comment by the evangelist). If Luke construes the words as part of Jesus' conversation, then the word "this" in the phrase **when they heard this** is to be dropped. In any case, the word "this" has no counterpart in the Greek text.

The word "least" (v. 28: *mikroteros*) prepared the way for the statement about the tax collectors. John may be dismayed that the religious leaders do not recognize Jesus, but their refusal does not affect the validity of Jesus' own credentials. **All the people** (cf. 2:10; 3:21) **and the tax collectors justified God** (cf. *Pss. of Sol.* 2:15), that is, affirmed God to be in the right (cf. Rom. 3:4) and accepted John's baptism. But **the Pharisees and the lawyers** (experts in the Law of Moses), secure in their legal performance (cf. Luke 3:8), **rejected** God's demand for a change of heart. They refused to admit that they could be in the wrong and declined to be baptized (cf. 20:1–8). The word rendered "purpose" has in this context the bureaucratic connotation of "deliberate plan, decision" (on *boulē,* cf. Acts 2:23; 4:28; 13:36; 19:1; 27:12). God has deliberated on a course of action, namely, to exalt the lowly and bring low the mighty (1:52). Hence the least becomes great (v. 28; cf. 22:24–27).

7:31. Jesus now characterizes the people **of this generation.** "Generation" *(genea)* may be used simply to call attention to a particular period in a nation's history, or it may be used in connection with a moral judgment. Thus "this generation" in Gen. 7:1 means "these wicked people." Psalm 78:8 looks back on the ancestors in the wilderness as a "stubborn" generation. Similarly, Ps. 95:10 speaks of them as "that generation," loathed by God. Their unfaithful character becomes a yardstick against which one's contemporaries may be measured. In Ps. 24:6 the term is applied in a positive sense, and without reference to any historical moment, to "those who seek" the Lord, that is, the righteous (see also Isa. 61:3 LXX).

In Luke's context the words "this generation" are used in a negative sense, and 9:41 gives Luke's own definition: it is an unbelieving and perverse kind of people. But not everyone alive belongs to it (cf. Acts 2:40). The language is, of course, no more anti-Semitic than similar statements by the prophets in the OT. Jesus himself is a Jew, proclaimed to Jew and gentile alike, and the revolutionary call to participate in God's salvation beyond caste of nationality or birth is the point at which every person is called to decision.

7:32. For his characterization Jesus draws on children at play who cannot agree on the game. Some want to play wedding, others funeral. One misses the point if the couplet is pressed and the identity of the "we" is sought in John or Jesus, or both. This would be Western logic. The illustration focuses attention on the inability of the participants to decide on what they want. But on one thing they are agreed—both John and Jesus betrayed the system. All levels of Greco-Roman society, from the refined Athenians described by Bdelykion in Aristophanes's *Wasps* (1174–1263) to schoolchildren whose morality was directed by Aisop and other masters of the storyteller's art, would appreciate the wit of Jesus.

7:33. John's asceticism outdoes the claim of the Pharisee in 18:12 and yet provokes the charge that he is possessed by a demon *(daimonion).*

7:34. The Son of humanity **has come eating and drinking.** Some of Luke's auditors would probably have caught a play on the word "come." John had asked, "Are you he who is to come?" (v. 20). Both John and Jesus "have come." But Luke's auditors are in on the secret, and they know that Jesus is the Coming One in a special sense that the contemporaries of Jesus failed to grasp, for he comes at the end of time as the glorified Son of humanity.

True to his identity as the Son of humanity, Jesus joins humanity in normal patterns of life. He enjoys the company of ordinary people and loves a party. Result? His detractors charge him with gross self-indulgence and with moving in the wrong crowd. Thus they endeavor to contradict the verdict expressed at 2:47. Jesus appears to shame his father (cf. Prov. 28:7). In their eyes he is the type of rebellious son featured in the indictment made in Deut. 21:20. The fact is, they felt comfortable in their snobbery, and in the presence of Jesus saw some slippage in their own prestige and influence. Or, to use Luke's words, they "rejected the purpose of God for themselves" (v. 30). But Jesus holds steadfast course and will one day make an astounding display of affection for his heavenly Parent (23:46).

7:35. The term "all" in the final saying, **Yet wisdom is justified by all her children** (cf. Sir. 26:29 for the syntax; and for the offspring of wisdom, see Prov. 8:32), is one of Luke's favorite words. Its presence in this revised form of Q (see Matt. 11:19) suggests that Luke understands Jesus to say that wisdom shows her true potential when a broad range of humanity is enclosed in her family. By concentrating on insiders, the opposition narrows the possibilities for wisdom's nurture; Jesus, through his outreach to publicans and sinners, brings many outsiders under her tutelage. The repentant woman described in Luke 7:36–50 is a prime exhibit for the truth of the saying.

If Luke meant the verse to be understood as a continuation of the criticism leveled by his opponents, the statement suggests that they claim to stand on the side of wisdom and declare that they will be vindicated. In that case they would be inferring that Jesus sponsors the way of the fool (cf. Prov. 23:20–21; Sir. 15:1–8), and Luke 7:36–50 would then contradict their self-appraisal.

Either interpretation points to the main issue: The alternatives are wisdom or folly. Where do Jesus and the representatives of the religious establishment stand?

Reply of Jesus to a Pharisee   Luke 7:36–50

The conflict outlined in vv. 33–35 now breaks into the open. Jesus appears to be a fool, in the sense conveyed by writers of wisdom literature, for he seems to endorse sinful behavior. The Pharisee appears to be devoted to wisdom, with chapter and verse in his favor (cf. Proverbs 2). The fact that a Pharisee invites Jesus to dine with him indicates that Jesus does not, as charged at v. 34, limit his association to the worst. Jesus is no respecter of persons, not even of tax collectors and sinners. Thus this story is at the same time an exhibition of the theme of divine beneficence that Jesus had announced at Nazareth and reinforced in the Sermon on the Plain. As can be seen in Jesus' actions, God embraces all levels and circumstances of humanity.

7:36. Jesus earlier (5:27) had accepted Levi's invitation. Now he dines with a Pharisee.

7:37. The word "behold" *(idou)* calls the reader's attention to an unusual development and alerts him to the point to be made by the writer. The woman had a bad reputation in the town. "Sinner" is the usual equivalent for one who breaks the Law of Moses. "Where is Jesus?" she asked. "Over there, in Simon's house," came the reply. The fact that she dares to enter the house of a Pharisee not only suggests her courage and determination but is in harmony with the esteem in which Jesus was held by "sinners." His very presence proclaimed, "Here you will find a friend." And he was not one to let highly perched piety divert his customary sympathy.

7:38. Jesus, following the practice of the time, reclined while he was dining, and the woman stood behind him at his extended feet—feet that had walked many miles to preach good news to people like her (cf. Isa. 52:7). After showering his feet with tears, she dried them with her hair, and the very looseness of it was certain to provide gossip about her character.

Commentators have spent more space on probing the reason for the woman's tears than for Simon's rudeness. But there are moments of truth that only an artist or a poet of consummate tact can capture. And Luke is the gallant master of the reticent touch that defies banal comment on this moment of sacred affection. The RSV obscures the sensitivity in Luke's choice of tenses (note his use of the imperfect tense). She did not kiss his feet once only (*katephilei:* "she kept on kissing"; cf. v. 45), and her use of the perfume was lavish. Gaius Petronius, Rome's arbiter of taste, was taken aback by a related type of gesture (*Satyricon* 70.8–9). Ordinarily Pharisees were concerned about observing laws of cleanliness. Here it is the woman who, as the sequel shows, displays even more concern than the Pharisee. Luke's Greco-Roman public would grasp the point: this unnamed woman's generosity qualifies her for the status of a person of exceptional merit. But the Pharisee has problems relating to status, and now the text explodes into a conflict of competing claims to status.

7:39. Luke's qualifying remark, the one **who had invited him,** indicates that there are other Pharisees at this dinner (see vs. 49). The Pharisee's inward thought betrays his misunderstanding. One who claims to be God's spokesperson ought to know what sort of woman this is and not permit such shameless display, for to be on the side of God means that sins of her kind are not to be tolerated (cf. Deut. 23:18). Beyond question, the host had the constitution of Sinai on his side. But it did not occur to him to ask what could be done about men who were responsible for lack of quality in women's lives.

7:40. Jesus' reply to the Pharisee's standardized line of thought is a further piece of irony in the account. He who challenged Jesus' credentials as a prophet now is about to have his own inner mind exposed (cf. 2:35; 5:22). Jesus' urbane manner is demonstrated in his gentle treatment of the Pharisee, one of the few occasions in which a partner in dialogue is addressed by name. Simon's self-assured address to Jesus as a revered "teacher" *(didaskalos)* momentarily masks his real thought and his basic discourtesy.

7:41–42. Picking up on a theme that was expressed in the Sermon on the Plain, Jesus relates a story about two debtors who were blessed with a beneficent creditor: the term rendered "forgave" is the same Greek verb *(charizomai)* that underlies the rendering "bestowed" in v. 21. It would have taken a day laborer about a year and a half to earn **five hundred denarii.** The question about "love" puts deed and response in perspective and anticipates the verdict pronounced in v. 47. "Love" here means "to demonstrate affection" *(agapaō)*. Only one who has spent some time in the East can know what an outpouring of gratitude such beneficence would elicit.

7:43. The Pharisee's response to Jesus' illustration is a grudging admission, but at least it is a response (for the silence of Jesus' opponents see 6:9). The

identities of the big and the little debtor remain to be determined as Jesus
sets the "Sokratic trap" (**You have judged rightly**; cf. 10:28) so familar to
students of Plato's dialogues in the form *panu orthos (Protagoras* 359e; *Phaido*
67b).

7:44–46. One Greek verb form *(eisēlthon)* underlies the phrases **I entered**
(v. 44) and **I came in** (v. 45) thereby structuring the dramatic contrast
between the stinting Pharisee and the generous woman. The content of his
reply and Jesus' verdict on it are crucial for the understanding of the sequel.
Forgiveness begets love. Simon does not understand love in depth. Had he
appreciated Jesus as an unusual gift of God, he would have gone beyond
normal social protocol and displayed all the courtesies that are ascribed to
the woman. (On the usc of oil—far cheaper than perfume—for a guest at a
banquet, see Ps. 23:5 and Amos 6:6; on the kiss, Luke 15:20; Acts 20:37;
Rom. 16:16; and 1 Cor. 16:20; on the foot washing, John 13:4 and 1 Tim.
5:10.)

7:47–48. Jesus informs Simon, expert in legalized exclusion, not to judge
in terms of traditional slots for people. People are to be judged not by
generic labels but in terms of themselves as individuals in their own right. It
is evident, says Jesus, that the woman must have already received forgiveness, for it would be impossible to assign any other reason for such
great love. And Jesus adds the phrase "her many sins," not to embarrass the
woman, but to make her deed of love stand out in bolder relief. The
addition also indicates that Jesus does not, as some of his critics have
complained, take sin lightly.

Jesus concludes his remarks to Simon with the converse of Simon's
verdict at v. 43: The one who has experienced but little forgiveness **loves
little.** Simon stands convicted out of his own mouth, but the rebuke is
tenderly sparing in the presence of the other guests. It was, indeed, a most
gracious invitation to the Kingdom, as gracious as the absolution pronounced on the woman: **Your sins are forgiven** (literally, "Your sins have
been forgiven"). The year of Jubilee had begun for her (cf. 4:18). In the
presence of Jesus this woman, who was classified by sponsors of dull
respectability as a person of no account, becomes a celebrity.

7:49–50. The other guests now dialogue within themselves, as Simon had
done earlier. Their problem is the same as that expressed in 5:21. Jesus'
answer to them is a further word of benediction to the woman: **Your faith
has saved you; go in peace.** At 12:8 Jesus will have something to say about
the importance of acknowledging him in public. This woman's conduct is
the clearest exposition of that verse. Her faith in God's demonstration of his
love through the ministry of Jesus brings her the salvation promised in 1:71,
77; 2:11. The specifications for the New Age were clearly announced in the

prologue. Jesus must meet them if he is indeed the Messiah. The words **Go in peace** echo 1 Sam. 1:17 and Luke 2:14. God's peace is the pronouncement of reconciliation, of a mending of the breach between the Deity and the sinner (cf. Is. 59:2).

The Pharisees were correct—only God can forgive sins. But Jesus embodies in his person the divine intention, which not only prevails over sin but endeavors to overcome all devices whereby one human being seeks isolation from the other. Who was the woman? Simon's name made Luke's history book. But ecclesiastical gossips have ignored Luke's genteel sensitivity in burying the woman's identity, which remains unknown. In St. Louis, Missouri, a house for "sinners" was named Magdala House. But there is no reliable foundation for identifying the woman with Mary the Magdalene (see 8:2).

In some respects the story parallels the account in John 12:1–8, and there are affinities with Mark 14:3–9 (cf. Matt. 26:6–13), especially in the choice of the name Simon. It is certain that accounts of incidents from Jesus' life would in the course of their retelling undergo variation and even contamination from recitals of related incidents. But beyond this generalization are the boundless steppes of exegetical fancy that characterizes so many attempts to trace the history of specific traditions.

Women Disciples

Luke 8:1–3

8:1–3. It is clear from the preceding account what Luke means by the comment that Jesus was spreading **the good news of the kingdom of God.** The Kingdom is God in action claiming people for the New Age and breaking down the barriers of separation, whether those are sin or legalistic walls that divide the righteous from the sinner. Luke's introductory phrase, *kai egeneto* ("and it came to pass"; RSV: **soon afterward**), signals a fresh development, reinforced by the express mention of **the twelve.** They, together with the women in Jesus' company, are the witnesses to his ministry which climaxes with his death and resurrection.

The reference to the Twelve and to the women again would suggest to Theophilos that Christianity is scarcely a subversive movement. To the more discerning reader it would also be apparent that Jesus' choice of women for his company was highly unusual for an esteemed teacher. From John 4:27 one can gather how highly women's brains and personal social initiative were valued in some religious circles.

Nonconformist that he was, Jesus refused to permit tradition to endorse second-class status for women. Unlike church officials of all ages who conveniently say when confronted with controversial issues, "Not in my time," Jesus accepted responsibility and said, "The time is now." Prophetic ministry does not permanently, if indeed ever, enjoy institutional support, and Jesus' enemies would counter, as at Luke 23:5, that it was poor judgment to flaunt custom in this way. Jesus' view is that those who hear and observe God's words belong to his family (8:21).

Among the women was **Mary, called Magdalene.** Magdala was a little fishing village off the shore of Lake Galilee. **Seven demons** had been driven out of her, but there is no hint here, nor in any other portion of the Gospels, that she was the sinful woman mentioned in the preceding narrative. This piece of gossip was first circulated by Tertullian. Moreover, demon possession was not construed as a sinful condition. The reference to **Joanna, the wife of Chuza, Herod's steward,** indicates that Jesus has penetrated Herod's own establishment.

Theophilos is also to note that Christian communities can boast a broad range of social status. Mary and Joanna will reappear at 24:10. Of **Susanna** we know nothing further. Luke mentions "many other women" *(heterai pollai),* which contributes further to our understanding of Jesus' proclamation. It was a word that reached beyond normal and accepted social restrictions. What people might think of his conduct was outweighed by his own forethought in the interests of people. Like the unnamed woman in 7:36–50, these women are generous. Voluntarily they provide for Jesus' company, not limiting their largesse to the leader (cf. 4:39, a passage which must be taken into account when evaluating the marginal reading cited by the RSV at 8:3), and their beneficence is of the same order as that recorded in Acts 4:32–37. But we are not to imagine that they were in constant attendance during the Lord's many travels. By suggesting that they are to be included within the class of benefactors that was so esteemed in Mediterranean society, Luke invites attention to the intrinsic quality of Christian communities.

How important the role of women is in the program of the New Age is apparent from Luke's stress on the presence of women at the post-Easter gathering mentioned in Acts 1:14. And the recitation from Joel at Acts 2:17–21 reinforces the point.

The implications of this passage are far-reaching. Ecclesiastical leaders who search the Gospels for data that will justify their own traditional views and practices are challenged to recognize that Jesus' departures from tradition are a model for their own responsibility to face the future in a creative and innovative manner.

EXPANSION ON THE THEME OF FAITH
Luke 8:4–56

After his interpolation, beginning at 6:20, Luke picks up at 8:4 the thread of Mark's account. Since so much of Luke's two-volume work has to do with the proclamation of the word or story concerning God's action in Jesus Christ, Luke selects Mark's account about a farmer who broadcast seed with varying results.

Right Hearing

Luke 8:4–21

Parable of the Sower   Luke 8:4–15
(Mark 4:1–20; Matthew 13:1–13, 18–23)

8:4. Luke's mention of the crowd *(ochlos)* helps prepare the reader for the significance of the recital that follows. Jesus does not accept a following in terms of sheer numbers. His Kingdom call is not propaganda for the rabble but an invitation to accept the rigors of discipleship. Political innovators do not ordinarily approach their followers in such fashion. As for "most moralists, ancient and modern," G. K. Chesterton charged that they can "be trusted to make a rush for the obvious." Not so Jesus, he said, and submitted the Lord's parables as partial testimony to the accuracy of such judgment.

The word "parable" was used in 4:23; 5:36; 6:39. In those passages the RSV merely transliterates the Greek *parabolē,* and the reference is to proverb rather than story. Unfortunately, much unnecessary confusion has been generated in biblical study circles by persons who approach the biblical data with ready-made definitions of "parable." The result is endless discussion concerning the kinds of stories told by Jesus, with, for example, specification of similitudes and illustrations in addition to alleged pure parables.

In a very general and nontechnical sense the term "parable" can be applied to any story told by Jesus in which he probes people's behavior or attitudes, especially as these involve others, or God, or both. The point is to expose the auditors to some feature of life in the world around them in such a way that they find themselves and their destiny scrutinized in a shockingly arresting manner. In some of these stories the metaphorical feature will be stronger than in others, but in every case the hearers are expected to abstract from the illustration to their own situation vis-à-vis their responsibilities toward God or the neighbor.

When a story is told in such a way that various details require decoding, it is termed an allegory. John Bunyan's *The Pilgrim's Progress* is a modern expression of this type. Narrow definitions of allegory frequently begin with Greek forms and scholarly methods developed at Alexandria. But OT examples of allegory in the sense cited above include Ezek. 17:1–11 and 24:3–5. Details in the two stories are respectively explained in Ezek. 17:12–24 and 24:6–14. The explanations, which appear to come from the same source as the stories themselves, are therefore not allegorizations but expositions of allegories.

In the interest of clarity, the term "allegorization" is best applied to interpretation of stories that were probably not originally conceived as allegories. Ancient Alexandrine scholars of Greek literature used allegory to develop edifying discourse about deities and heroes. Similarly, in the course of biblical exposition all of Jesus' stories and miracles were put through an elaborate decoding process. For example, in his interpretation of the story of the Good Samaritan (Luke 10:30–37), Chrysostom interprets the wine as the blood of the Lord's suffering and the oil as the anointing of the Holy Spirit. Nor, says Archbishop Trench, "is it far-fetched to see in the inn the figure of the Church, the place of spiritual reflection, in which the healing of souls is ever going forward."

To explain parables allegorically is not in itself wrong, provided that the interpreter declares what is being done. But the history of interpretation reveals that interpreters who take that route frequently read their own dogmatic and ecclesiastical concerns into the text and isolate themselves from the very critique to which the text exposes their vested interest. Biblical allegorization avoids such protection of vested interest. And a commentator has the obligation to liberate the text as much as possible from later patented appropriation.

Luke follows Mark in recording both the story of the sower (Luke 8:4–8) and its explanation (vv. 11–15). If these two components are to be considered authentic statements by Jesus, one could with a high degree of probability conclude that Jesus followed the coupling of story and exposition expressed in Ezekiel 17 and 24. If, on the other hand, Jesus told only the story (Luke 8:4–8), his alleged explanation (vv. 11–15) must be attributed to someone in the post-Pentecost community. In that event, the explanation would be an allegorizing exposition, probably in imitation of Ezek. 17:12–24 or 24:6–14, and the original recital (Luke 8:4–8) could have been a story that required no decoding of its parts. In either case, Jesus emerges as a prophetic figure whose proclamation encounters some of the rejection experienced in the course of Ezekiel's proclamation (Ezek. 3:4–11).

In favor of allegorizing exposition of Jesus' story of the sower by early Christians are the indications of variable fortunes experienced in the course of apostolic outreach. This suggestion of later origin is already apparent in Mark's record. Luke's use of the paired narrative would also reflect his interest in Jesus as the Son of humanity, a term that may well also echo the form of address with which God frequently approaches Ezekiel (see esp. Ezek. 17:2). Whatever the probabilities may be concerning the relation of the exposition (Luke 8:11–15) to the story (vv. 4–8), it is important that rigid notions as to what constitutes allegory are resisted when interpretation of an ancient text is undertaken. Above all, allegorical story is to be distinguished from allegorization of a story. And allegorical features in Gospel narratives are no necessary indication of Hellenistic origin. Yet they may suggest an interest in communicating beyond the boundaries of an in-group.

Most of the stories attributed to Jesus make a single point, and the original auditors required no special education or inside information to understand them, for the story itself was the meaning. If such is the case with the story in Luke 8:4–8, it is to be interpreted without assumption of encoded details.

8:5–8. Jesus' parable of the sower should not have been difficult to understand. In ancient Palestine the field appears to have been plowed *after* the seed had been broadcast by hand. Because of paths worn through the field, rocky surfaces hidden by the remaining stubble, or patches of weed, the sower of the seed does not have equal success. Only that which fell on **good soil** amounted to anything. Jesus' concluding words, "Those who have ears to hear let them hear" (cf. Rev. 2:7), bid the hearer at the very least to draw the conclusion that one must take Jesus' message seriously. It is not enough to say, "Lord, Lord" while neglecting to heed his teaching (cf. Luke 6:46). Anyone who heard Jesus would know what was meant, and those who did not like the admonition would indict themselves. Thus parables are, in effect, invitations to self-disclosure.

8:9. The request of the disciples for an interpretation of the parable appears rather remarkable at first sight, in view of the simplicity of the simile. But the reader of Luke's Gospel must not forget that Luke is writing for the benefit of his contemporaries.

In Mark 4:10 the disciples ask Jesus about his parables in general. Luke alters their question into a request for the meaning of the parable, because he wishes to clarify further for the church Jesus' use of parables. In the process he eliminates the uncomplimentary remark addressed by Jesus to the disciples (Mark 4:13). Since Jesus' parables had been misused by gnostics, who claimed special insight into God's mysteries and looked with disdain on the untutored and less spiritual members in the church, Luke aims to show that the parables were not given to conceal but to reveal the truth to all the disciples. Hence in Luke many of the parables are accompanied with some word of explanation so that the hearer might not be left in doubt about their intention.

8:10. In keeping with the motif pronounced at Luke 2:34 concerning *the fall and rising of many in Israel,* Luke carries the reply of Jesus that there are two major classes of hearers: those who have been given the privilege of knowing the "mysteries" (*mystēria;* RSV: **secrets**) and those who see but do not in reality see. The mysteries are not secret things but the wisdom (cf. Wisd. of Sol. 6:22) and purpose of God now ripening in the work of Jesus and the mission of the church (cf. Rev. 10:7; 17:7). Those who have been given the privilege to know them are the believers (cf. Luke 6:20–23; 10:23–24; 1 Cor. 2:12–15; Rev. 3:18). Those who see and yet do not see are the unbelievers (cf. Acts 28:23–28). The disciples therefore have the greater responsibility. Jesus' statement then means: "You ought to know the meaning, because you are the ones who have received the privilege of knowing the mysteries of the Kingdom of God. The rest also hear them, as you do, in parables, but in their case a judgment takes place." The latter think they are secure in their relationship with God and require no further enlightenment; therefore they cannot really see or hear. In other words, the message goes past them.

The fact that many in Israel had rejected the apostolic message required some explanation. Luke's wording of Jesus' reply is one form of the answer to this perplexing development. Thus the words "in order that" (*hina*; RSV: **so that**) do not express purpose but tragic realization (see v. 18). Luke does not include Mark's phrase "lest they should turn again, and be forgiven" (Mark 4:12), for the post-Easter proclamation to Israel begins with the assumption that they will repent (Acts 2—3).

8:11–15. Since application of Jesus' instruction was made by teachers in the church in accordance with the mind of Christ, under the guidance of the one Spirit, Luke does not hesitate to follow Mark in attributing the explanation to Jesus, for he is the authoritative Teacher (cf. Luke 24:32). As for Mark, he probably found precedent in Ezekiel 17 for the association of illustration and explanation that he found in the tradition of the recital.

The four classes of hearers suggest types of response encountered by the apostolic proclamation. The word "patience" in v. 15 especially points in that direction. "Patience" (*hypomenē*) means endurance or perseverance and describes disciples who hold out in the face of opposition (cf. 21:19), not succumbing like the shallow-rooted people of v. 13, who fall away in time of temptation. The fact that the word "patience" does not appear in Mark's recital points to Luke's editorial activity or familiarity with a variant version of sermonic material.

Certainly the parable and its explanation are thoroughly in concert with Luke's thematic emphases, including faith (cf. 7:9), perseverance in time of temptation (cf. 22:28), resistance to consumerism (cf. chap. 12), and especially an undivided heart dedicated to the performance of the word that has been heard (cf. 13:22–30).

Undeniably a part of Luke's Hellenistic perspective is the phrase **an honest and good heart** (*en kardia kalē kai agathē*). The terms for "honest" and "good" (cf. Tob. 5:14 and 2 Macc. 15:12) are commonly combined by Greek writers into one expression, denoting a person of exceptional merit (see *Benefactor* pp. 319–20, and cf. the variant reading for the term "suffering" in James 5:10). By embedding the message of Jesus in diction that takes account of broad Mediterranean culture, Luke aids materially in the bridging of class distinctions.

"Take Heed How You Hear"   Luke 8:16–18
                                                                (Mark 4:21–25)

8:16. Little oil-burning lamps, notorious for their wretched light, here serve as a lively point of departure for the subsequent description of the revelation that takes place through Jesus.

8:17. The words in v. 17 further explain the point made in v. 10. It may be Luke's intention to stress that Jesus has no secret communication (cf. 22:53). He has taught openly, and there is nothing subversive in his activity. But it is more probable that the words originally echoed Deut. 29:29: "The secret things belong to the Lord our God; but things that are revealed belong to us and to our children for ever, that we may do all the words of this law." With the advent of the Messiah, God reveals the mysteries, that is, the plans for the end time, expressed without reservation in Jesus (cf. 1:78–79). Wisdom of Solomon 6:22, though, may have been in Luke's mind as he read Mark's version: "But what wisdom is, and how she came into being, I will declare, and I will not hide mysteries from you; but I will trace her out from the beginning of creation, and bring the knowledge of her into the clear light and I will not pass by the truth."* This passage comes from a book ascribed in ancient times to Solomon (see also Sir. 39:1–3). In 11:31, Luke reports that the queen of Sheba came to hear Solomon's wisdom but that a greater than Solomon is now here. Jesus, as the supreme Wisdom figure, reveals God's will also to the most untutored in his following (cf. 10:21).

8:18. Since the revelation is so open, hearers have all the more responsibility to take heed how they hear. Wisdom multiplies to the one who comes for instruction, not confutation (cf. Prov. 1:2–6; 9:9), and this is the meaning of the phrase, to one **who has will more be given.** The mysteries of the Kingdom have been given to the disciples. These mysteries become even more meaningful to them as they ponder their responsibility in the light of the message.

The words in v. 18b express the opposite experience and restate the thought of v. 10b. Mark's rendering: "And from him who has not, even what he has will be taken away" is rephrased by Luke to read: "Even what they think that they have will be taken away." The sentence means: People who are complacent, resist further instruction, and do not review themselves in the light of Jesus' message will experience collapse of the foundations on which they built their false lives. Thus Jesus says (Luke 19:41–44) that the fall of Jerusalem was hidden from Israel's eyes. They thought they possessed knowledge, but he was the instrument of the peace and security they thought they had in their temple. They rejected him and lost the temple and their city. Now, in the apostolic age, Luke recites Jesus' warning to his first disciples. The church's disciples are not to make the same mistake that Jerusalem's inhabitants once made.

The word of Jesus calls for responsive and responsible hearing, of the type commended by Elizabeth (1:45). In addition to this note of admonition, the proverb conveys a forceful consolation for the Christian community. The fact that much of Israel's religious leadership rejected the apostolic proclamation led to profound heart-searching. Had the church perhaps made a mistake? Luke answers: If some do not respond, it is not because they lacked the light. They did see, but they did not like what they saw. Instead, they preferred their own vision and brought their city down in ruins.

Jesus' True Family   Luke 8:19–21
                                                    (Mark 3:31–35; Matthew 12:46–50)

8:19–21. Luke returns to Mark 3:31–35 for this account about the family of Jesus. He omits entirely one of Mark's parables (Mark 4:26–29) and postpones another (Mark 4:30–32; see Luke 13:18–19). Nothing is permitted at this point to detract from the main theme: Responsive Hearing. There is no reason to understand "brothers" *(adelphoi)* in any other than the usual sense. A basic rule of interpretation requires that unless there is evidence in the text for a less customary understanding of a term (see, e.g., John 20:17, where the disciples are meant), the central meaning or ordinary sense of the term is to be accepted. Passages that are frequently cited from nonbiblical literature in favor of the extended meaning "relatives" contain contextual information that clarifies the broader sense and are therefore not strictly pertinent. That Mary should not have had other children stems from a gnostic line of thought, according to which sexual relations are inferior to ascetic discipline. James was one of the brothers and became leader of the church in Jerusalem (see Acts 12:17 and chap. 15). John 7:3–5 relates the earlier hostility of the brothers toward Jesus.

The fact that in 11:28 Luke reproduces the thought of 8:21, followed by an indictment of sign seekers in 11:29, suggests that the phrase **desiring to see you** is perhaps to be understood from the same perspective. Like Herod, Jesus' own family demands signs. Luke's inclusion of the criticism would be in harmony with his earlier treatment of Mary at 2:48–51. Moreover, the passage endorses the knowledge of his divine sonship possessed by Jesus at his visit to the temple (2:49). He had heeded his Father's word (4:1–13), and all those who through him hear and do God's word are his family. Together with him they share the Father (6:36). Thus the passage does not record a rejection of his own family by Jesus but corrects a basic misunderstanding.

At Acts 1:14, Mary and the siblings of Jesus meet with a number of women and the eleven disciples. Whether the problem of factions in the church, with some rallying around members of Jesus' immediate family, lies behind Luke's record cannot be determined with certainty. The thought of the passage in the Gospel is in harmony with Luke's frequent emphasis on the precedence of the Kingdom of God over tribal loyalties (cf. 9:59–62; 12:51–53; 14:25–26). One must be able to break out of the constricting cocoon. Jesus' own practice serves as an example to the community to be open to new relationships.

To "hear the word of God" is a recurring phrase in Luke-Acts (Luke 11:28; Acts 13:7, 44; 19:10).

Word of Power

Luke 8:22–56

Just as the Sermon on the Plain was followed with a record of Jesus' supporting actions, so the section on "the word" is followed in 8:22–56 with a series of powerful deeds that demonstrate Jesus as savior in desperate situations.

Power over the Storm

Luke 8:22–25
(Mark 4:35–41; Matthew 8:18, 23–27)

This account continues the theme of responsive hearing. The followers of Jesus (Luke does not say how many) were warned through the parable of the sower about falling away in time of temptation (v. 13). Now in a moment of trial they betray the lack of faith described in the parable. That is, they do not apply to the present situation what they have heard from Jesus' lips.

As for the choice of story, Luke is familiar with his public's expectations. Greco-Roman deities and heads of state from time to time displayed or attempted to display mastery over the elements (cf. Homer *Odyssey* 10. 21–22, of Aiolos, lord of the winds). Isis not only "invented maritime commerce," but boasts, "I calm or enrage the sea at will" (*Benefactor*, p. 198). Antiochos IV Epiphanes is alleged in 2 Macc. 9:8 to have thought that he could "command the waves of the sea." Luke therefore takes advantage of Mark's tradition to set forth in even greater detail his portrait of Jesus as Man of Exceptional Excellence, "mighty in deed and word" (Luke 24:19).

8:23. Jesus **fell asleep.** He seems unconcerned about their peril. And he is! For even in sleep he is in command. It is quite possible that the recitation of this story was designed to console the church in its conflicts and sufferings at the hand of the opposition. At times it would appear that the Lord was not in charge.

8:24. Not realizing that Jesus is in their presence and that with him they are safe, the disciples cry out, **We are perishing.** Instead of Mark's "Teacher, do you not care if we perish?" Luke allows the twice-repeated "Master" (*epistata,* the same Greek word in 5:5) to express the disciples' agitation as well as their dissatisfaction with Jesus. There is no hint that they expect unusual help from him. **He awoke and rebuked the wind.** The Greek word for "rebuked" *(epitimaō)* was used earlier in the recital of the demoniac (4:35) and of Peter's mother-in-law (4:39). Here it is used in his command to the wind and wave. The response is immediate. He who tells the storm to be still is the one who urges the disciples to hear the word of God and keep it.

8:25. Mark reads: "Why are you afraid? Have you no faith?" Luke omits the suggestion of cowardice (Mark 4:40); and, while granting that the disciples do have faith, Jesus asks, **Where is your faith?** They ought to be watchful in the time of temptation (Luke 8:13). Their concluding question, **Who then is this?** betrays the misunderstanding that prompted Jesus earlier to say of the centurion, "I have not found such great faith in Israel" (7:9★). If the winds and water "obey" *(hypakouō)* him, how much more ought the diciples to obey him! The question also prepares the reader for the messianic inquiry at 9:20.

In the Psalter, God is frequently pictured as having mastery of the waters (cf. Pss. 29:3–4; 65:7; 89:9), and Luke's account is practically an exposition of Ps. 107:23–29. Luke also may have had Psalm 78 in mind, which begins with a statement about parabolic instruction and then goes on to describe rebellious Israel. Yet God showed his mighty deliverance, overwhelming their enemies in the sea (Ps. 78:53). Again, when they were suffering under their chastisements, "the Lord awoke as from sleep" (Ps. 78:65; cf. Luke 8:24). The disciples are not to be like that part of Israel which thinks it sees but does not see (Luke 8:10).

Power over a Demon

Luke 8:26–39
(Mark 5:1–20; Matthew 8:28–34)

The story of the Gerasene demoniac is a thematic complement to the preceding account. According to Luke 8:22–25, Jesus has total mastery over the raging waters. In this recital Jesus succeeds in terminating the power of a host of demons who, bereft of their prey, end up in the lake over which Jesus has demonstrated his mastery. Jesus has power over deep water and demons, that is, over all that is hostile to people.

Moreover, Jesus' new relationships are to be found also in an area heavily populated by gentiles. As an anticipation of outreach through the apostolic mission which Luke records in Acts this account would be especially meaningful. Hence, despite unusual accretions that the story experienced in the course of tradition, Luke takes over its main lines from Mark.

8:26. Since the city of Gerasa is located more than thirty miles inland from Lake Gennesaret, the textual tradition relating to the place-name for location of the story next to the lake is confusing. Luke knows that he is dealing with a locale **opposite Galilee** and is conveniently vague with the phrase **the country of the Gerasenes.**

8:27. The symptoms of the man relate to those of a manic depressive, but such disorders are declared a part of the demonic usurpation now being halted through the action of the Kingdom of God. As of Acts 19:16, nakedness is one of the conditions into which people are forced by demons (cf. Luke 23:34). Also, he apparently has not been permitted to live at home. This in itself marked him as an alienated person, and Luke's public awaits the solution to this man's social as well as personal problem.

Luke prepares his public for the entry of a legion of demons at v. 30 by changing Mark's single demon (Mark 5:2) to a plurality; but because of the demands of the dialogue, borrowed from Mark, Luke retains the singular in v. 29.

8:28. The wretched man is as one among the dead, for he inhabits the tombs, a favorite haunt of demons (cf. SB 1:491–92, with references to Deut. 18:11 and Isa. 65:4). The desperate conflict within the man is described in terms of the great cry he emitted and his falling at Jesus' feet. So totally has the demonic taken control of this person that identities are blurred. As at Luke 5:35, the demon seeks to gain the mastery of Jesus by unveiling his identity. He knows that Jesus has come to consign him to the apocalyptic pangs. Therefore he says, "Do not torture me."

There is also a suggestion of pathos in the man's encounter with Jesus. Will Jesus' mastery over the demon spell the destruction of the individual who is possessed? Again, as in 1 Kings 17:18, the question **What have you to do with me?** expresses the anxiety of one who encounters the holy. But Jesus, like his prototype, comes not to destroy. In keeping with this assumption of eagerness on the part of Jesus to be of help, Luke omits Mark's observation that the man had come running from a distance (Mark 5:6). There is no distance to cross! Society knows how to maintain distances between the stable and the unstable. Jesus is on the scene. Alert auditors would have noted that the demon assumes a posture of abject deference, so out of character with the approach proposed by the devil at 4:7.

8:29. Luke accounts for the cry (v. 28) with the words **for he had commanded the unclean spirit to come out of the man.** Mark states, "for he *had* said to him" (Mark 5:8). Luke uses the imperfect tense of the verb *paranggelō:* "he *was about to command* the unclean spirit," wishing to avoid the implication that Jesus' word could be ineffectual. By shifting Mark's description of the unsuccessful efforts to bind the man (Mark 5:4; see Luke 8:29), Luke is able through this literary cutaway, to account for the delay in the demon's departure and prepare the ground for the subsequent dialogue.

The drama has reached a point of high tension. Demons in departure can leave in their wake a scene of desolation. Should they leave, what will happen to this man? The demon speaks through the man, but the demon's problem could make things worse for the man. And one thing he does not need is more upsetting of the demons. The very confusion in identity contributes to the drama.

8:30. In turn, Jesus asks the man, **What is your name?** Luke's public knows that Jesus would not really have to ask, but the query parallels the demons' attempt (v. 28) to expose Jesus to vulnerability. The demons endeavor to assert their authority over the man and say **Legion.** This is not a name, it is a statistic. It is the Roman military term for a regiment and expresses the man's total bondage. Modern views of disintegration of the man's personality are not interpretations of the text but homiletical applications. Luke's point is that the demons have met their match and are now suppliants. The net effect is one of satirical demolition of the emphasis placed on names in ancient magical formulation. Jesus will have control over the demons even without knowing their name or names. And in the post-Pentecost mission the emissaries of Jesus will outmagic all magicians.

8:31. Demons spend their times wandering around in desert places, haunting tombs, and disorienting people (cf. Luke 11:24–26). They do not wish to be sent to the "abyss," a word for the depths or pit to which the dead (Rom. 10:7) or evil spirits (Rev. 9:1–21) are consigned. In apocalyptic writing this fate of the demons at the end of all things finds repeated expression (cf. 2 Pet. 2:4; Jude 6; Rev. 20:1–3). Luke shows that the end of the end time will be but the consummation of what has already been experienced.

8:32. Demons are not content to wander about without inhabiting something (cf. Luke 11:24). Since the demon spoken of in 8:29 was "unclean," it is appropriate that the demons request to enter the herd of swine.

8:33. Deprived of their victim, the once-united legionary force breaks up, and the swine leap into the sea. Mark says there were about two thousand (Mark 5:13), undoubtedly one for each of the demons. Some readers have been disturbed by the fact that Jesus' miracle caused such wholesale destruction to helpless animals. But observations of the Society for the Prevention of Cruelty to Animals are irrelevant and contribute little to the understanding of Luke's account. The text does not say that Jesus commanded the herd to plunge into the sea. Both Mark and Luke clearly establish the fact that demons can only destroy, but Jesus brings salvation (see 8:36). And, as is stated elsewhere, a person is worth more than "many sparrows" (12:6–7).

Throughout the story there runs a strain of macabre Kingdom humor. The demons end up in the deep waters, which are emblematic of the abyss that awaits them. Ironically, Jesus had just demonstrated his power over that sector of the creation. According to Job 5:13, "the schemes of the wily are brought to a quick end." Jesus proved it to be true also in Satan's case. In the presence of the Stronger One the demons determined their own fate.

8:34–37. Through the succeeding description of the reaction of the swineherds and the citizenry, the miracle gains in power. The cured man, now clothed, is the center of attention. Luke modifies Mark's phrasing to get in one of his favorite words, "saved" (RSV: **healed,** v. 36; the Greek verb is *sōzō*). Jesus has come on the scene as the Great Benefactor. Because of the power of Jesus, the departure of the demons caused damage to the swine and not to the man. For what could have happened, see v. 29.

That the citizens of the Gerasene area cared more for their swine than for the cure of a townsperson is not stated. But it is certain that elimination of demonic features in the twentieth century is frequently considered a display of cost ineffectiveness, and as a corporation executive put it during a strike, "Our business is profits, not sociology." Luke says that **great fear** lay behind their request for Jesus' departure. They are alarmed at the evidence of powers beyond their comprehension (cf. 5:8). In a text full of comings and goings and strange denouements this desire for Jesus' departure is dramatically important. As Luke will shortly demonstrate, their request will be honored only temporarily.

8:38–39. At this point in the narrative Mark suggests that the man makes his request to **be with** Jesus *while* Jesus is taking leave (Mark 5:18). Luke in effect separates Jesus' departure (Luke 8:40) from the dialogue in vv. 38–39. Luke's concern is with the departure of the healed man. Apparently he is suggesting to his auditors that the man who had experienced so much separation from society thinks that a permanent solution lies in being "with" Jesus. Instead, Jesus "dismissed him," that is, told him to leave (the same Greek word [*apoluō*] used in 2:29; 9:12; 14:4). Thereby Jesus releases him from any dependence, even on his own presence. The man is now free to make his own departures.

Return to your home, and declare how much God has done for you. The word "return" is the clue to what at first seems an unusual move away from Luke's normal practice of smoothing Mark stylistically. This is gentile area. Jesus returns to his own sphere, Israel, but the man, who for some time had no home except the tombs (v. 27), is to return to his own "home" (*oikos,* "house"). In modern terms, that will "complete his cure." But there is more. In his own house he is to "declare" (or narrate; cf. 1:1) what God has done for him. Luke's alteration of Mark's "the Lord" (Mark 5:19) is not accidental. The man "proclaims" (*kēryssō,* the standard verb for apostolic preaching) what **Jesus** had done for him. Luke emphasizes through his change of wording that God is at work in Jesus (cf. Luke 17:18).

As did Israel, the Gerasenes misunderstood Jesus. But the gospel comes back both to Israel and to the gentiles through the apostolic proclamation. God is determined to crash into human stupidity with forgiving beneficence. The Gerasenes had asked Jesus to depart (v. 37), which he does (v. 44). But the man who had requested to be "with" Jesus (v. 38) now becomes the instrument to communicate what the Gerasenes denied themselves through the departure of Jesus, who nevertheless is determined to have the last word. So it will be, according to Acts 2—3, after the resurrection of Jesus. An alternate expression for being "with" Jesus is to "follow." Following Jesus means to hear and do his word. This can be done outside physical association with him. For the apostolic mission, this understanding was important. Preachers of the gospel were not to be limited to the disciples or their circle (cf. 9:49–50). Moreover, in the Mediterranean world it is understood that any recipient of extraordinary blessing ought to acknowledge publicly the source of such a benefit. Luke will add more on that subject at 17:12–19.

Many are the enemies, said John the Baptist's father (1:71). In this, a story replete with surprises, Jesus directs the routing of enemies on many fronts.

Power over Sickness and Death   Luke 8:40–56
                                                    (Mark 5:21–43; Matthew 9:18–26)

Luke adheres to Mark's narrative and retains his device of intercalating a story within a story, or "the cutaway effect": Luke 8:40–42a [Luke 8:42b–48], Luke 8:49–56.

According to Luke 7:2, a centurion's slave was terminally ill but did not die. The youth at Nain had died before Jesus came to the city (7:12). In the present account the request for Jesus' benevolence is made before death occurs, but the patient will be dead when Jesus arrives.

8:40. At 7:19–20 the question was asked, "Are you the coming one, or are we to expect another?"* The word "waiting" (8:40) is the same word *(prosdokaō)* rendered "expect" in the earlier passage, and the succeeding series of miracles is a further answer to the question.

8:41. The story of Jairus's daughter commences. The RSV omits Luke's initial phrase, "And behold!" In addition to its presence in striking sayings of Jesus and a few other passages, Luke uses this septuagintalism with the force of italics to introduce a number of stories in which Jesus performs a miracle or otherwise acts in an extraordinary manner (5:12; 7:37; 9:30, 38; 10:25; 13:11; 14:2; 19:2; 24:4, 49).

Evidently not all the religious leaders reject Jesus, for this president of a synagogue pleads for Jesus' help.

8:42. At this point Luke picks up Mark's later observation that the young woman was "twelve years of age" (Mark 5:42), with the slight modification "about." Thus he anticipates the woman's malady of twelve years' standing (Luke 8:43) as well as suggesting perhaps that the young woman was ready for marriage. The father's request is for healing; the young woman, his only daughter (cf. 7:12; 9:38), is not yet dead. A centurion had similarly pleaded for Jesus' help but changed his mind about the need for Jesus' presence in his home (7:3, 6). Now the cutaway episode.

8:43. Unless the longer version of the text is to be preferred (see the margin of the RSV), one must assume that Luke condenses Mark's discussion of the woman's problem with the medical profession. But since Luke abbreviates elsewhere in the story, it cannot be ascertained whether he does so out of professional courtesy, especially since he declares the woman's case medically hopeless (compare his language in 8:27). More probably, his stress on the seriousness of the malady focuses attention on the greater power of Jesus (see on 7:2). Similarly, the philosopher Empedokles, who enjoyed extraordinary prestige in antiquity, is said to have healed a woman of Agrigentum who had been given up by her physicians (Diogenes Laertius 8.69).

Physician were easy prey for the type of humor that seeps through this verse and in Mark's account (Mark 5:26). Pliny (*Natural History* 29.11) knew of an inscription that read, "I perished through a multitude of doctors." And Plutarch (*Moralia* 231A) records the following indictment of ancient malpractice:

> PHYSICIAN: Sir, you're an old man.
> PATIENT: Well, you never were my doctor.

On the other hand, there are numerous inscriptions in praise of physicians who succeeded in healing even terminally ill patients (see *Benefactor*, p. 59).

8:44. According to Lev. 15:25–31, a woman with a chronic case of bloody discharge was ceremonially unclean, and strict separation from the body of Israel was required. The woman's approach to Jesus and her fear of discovery relate to this regulation. Superstition and belief in magic were especially common, and not only among the uneducated classes. The woman, therefore, thinks that she must touch something that belongs to Jesus in order that his power might reach out to her (cf. Luke 5:17 and Acts 19:12). Yet her confidence in Jesus' person is a tribute to her. She does not want to defile Jesus by touching him personally. Instead, she reaches for his garment.

Following the precept of Num. 15:37–41 and Deut. 22:12, pious Israelites wore tassels terminating in a cord of blue to remind them of God's commandments. Jesus, from the standpoint of the system, was a nonconformist, but as a true "child of the law" he does not protest in meaningless disregard of tradition. The woman's choice of **the fringe of his garment** is remarkable, but the formulators of the tradition behind Luke's account may have wished to emphasize that Jesus came not to judge but to save. To understand this would require great faith (see v. 48). In any event, at her touch her malady was cured.

8:45. In the dialogue that follows, **Peter** replaces "the disciples" mentioned in Mark 5:31, for he is an acknowledged spokesperson for the apostolic band.

8:46. As at 5:17 and 6:19, power (cf. Acts 8:10) is viewed as coming out of Jesus. According to Luke 4:14, Jesus functions through the Holy Spirit. That divine power is here involved in the healing process, even in the presence of ritual uncleanness. The woman's cure is not to be ascribed to fortuitous circumstances or to God in the abstract.

8:47–48. The woman's confession is made before all the people. But instead of a reprimand she hears an absolution, similar to the one pronounced on the sinful woman (7:50). Not confidence in magic but faith (cf. 8:12) had overcome ritual obstacles, for Jesus spells a New Age. "Daughter" is a reminder that she is to be accepted in the family of Israel. Like the demoniac, this woman is rehabilitated socially. A similar word will be spoken at 19:9 over Zacchaeus. After reading this story, a clinical scientist would think "placebo effect." Luke views her experience as part of the great display of divine beneficence in the New Age.

The Greek term (verb: *sōzō*) underlying the phrase **has made . . . well** also means "save," with "salvation" as nominal cognate. Salvation and peace are the twin benefits traditionally conferred by a head of state. Jesus bestows them, suggests Luke, to a degree unparalleled in history. End cutaway.

One problem of defilement has been overcome. What will Jesus do with the next case?

8:49. The story of Jairus's daughter resumes. Again, as in vv. 42–43, there is a link between one account and the second installment of the other. One daughter has been saved, now Jairus's daughter has her turn.

8:50. In words that echo Isa. 41:13, Jesus says, "Fear not." The program spoken of at Luke 7:22 is still in movement. The faith of Jairus is now required to secure his daughter's salvation. In the older woman's case, salvation focused on healing. Here salvation has to do with return from the dead. To the Great Benefactor, performance is merely one of degree. Faith applies to both. In the diction relating to "salvation" the community's faith in Jesus as the bringer of ultimate rescue through resurrection from the dead also finds utterance. Salvation for Luke is rescue from all that separates one human being from another, or humanity from God (cf. Luke 2:11; 8:12; 8:36; Acts 16:31). Greco-Roman physicians were praised for taking on even terminal cases. Jesus accepts the ultimate challenge!

8:51. Luke's reference to the three disciples, **Peter and John and James**, prepares for the account of the transfiguration (see 9:28) and for the association of Peter and John in Acts 3 and 4. Although Mark 5:40 records the expulsion of the mourners (usually hired), Luke omits this detail as well as some of the satirical humor in Jesus' rebuke as recorded by Mark (5:39): "Why are you causing such an uproar? You act as though she were dead. She's sleeping,"* with the implication, "Are you trying to wake her up?"

8:52. Through his briefer account Luke brings into sharper focus the picture of Jesus in full command of a most desperate situation. For him the girl is as one who sleeps—but too soundly, as the sequel shows, for those

about her. Throughout the Greco-Roman world, people consoled themselves with the euphemism of sleep in reference to death. On Jesus' lips the
words she **is not dead but sleeping** are not a self-deceptive euphemism but
a peremptory challenge.

8:53. The only laughter comes from those who ridicule Jesus for his
simile. They knew better. She was dead! But this mockery, itself short-
lived, will highlight the fact of Jesus' greater power.

8:54. Isaiah's God took Israel by the hand (Isa. 41:13; 42:6). Jesus takes the
young girl **by the hand** and, as in Luke 7:14, calls out in personal address,
Child, arise.

8:55. Not only did she rise (**she got up**, *anestē*, a verb used of Jesus'
resurrection) but her recovery was complete—at once *(parachrēma)*. They
were not "seeing ghosts" (cf. 24:36–43). The word **directed** *(diatassō)* is a
bureaucratic term (cf. 3:13; Acts 18:2; 23:31; 24:23). This is the emperor of
the universe speaking (cf. Acts 4:12).

8:56. In response to the astonishment, Jesus forbids the parents to recite
the miracle. The three disciples are apparently not put under restriction (see
below). The verb **charged** *(paranggelō)* is in the same class with "directed"
of v. 55. The miracle is but a small part of a much larger message—the
proclamation of the good news. His directive is not out of harmony with
the command given at v. 39. There the recovery of the demoniac had
become well known, and Jesus' encouragement of the demoniac to return
and relate what he had experienced was a sign that Jesus bore no resentment
to the citizens. They had yet another chance to understand God's message at
work among them.

More significant is the contrast between the directive of v. 56 and the
procedure cited in v. 48. In the case of the woman's healing, Jesus could well
have preserved anonymity. But he did not choose to do so. It was important
that she be restored to the larger family of Israel. In the second case, it was a
restoration to the immediate family. From such varied observations one
strong picture emerges—Jesus did not seek notoriety for himself. He was a
person on a mission, sent to do the Father's will. Resurrection is God's work
(cf. SB 1:523), and God will more fully reveal the divine counsel after raising
Jesus from the dead. Peter, John, and James are among those entrusted with
the full story. After Pentecost no power on earth will seal their mouths.
Because of such perception of the apostolic task, Luke is not concerned
about the fact that his preservation of Mark's interest in secrecy might at the
same time conserve the apparent absurdity of trying to conceal an event of
such magnitude.

PARTNERS IN THE KINGDOM
Luke 9:1–50

The death of Jesus, followed by his resurrection and ascension, will challenge the use to which the followers of Jesus will be put. This portion of Luke's Gospel therefore serves as a prelude to the criminal proceedings against Jesus and to the mission activity described in the Book of Acts.

Sharing the Mission
Luke 9:1–17

Mission of the Twelve   Luke 9:1–6
(Mark 6:7–16; Matthew 10:1, 7, 9–11, 14)

Endorsement of the apostolic mission is once more located in the ministry of Jesus. Since Luke had already at 4:16–30 recorded Mark's account of the rejection at Nazareth (Mark 6:1–6), he now picks up Mark's recital (Mark 6:6–13) of the sending of the Twelve.

9:1. Notice is here served to Satan (cf. Luke 10:18–19). Since Jesus is the bearer of the Spirit (4:18), which empowers him, he is able to give the Twelve "power" (*dynamis*; cf. 8:46) and the "authority" (*exousia;* cf. 5:24) to function accordingly through exorcisms and healings. Satan may think that his plan to discredit Jesus (see 4:13 and 22:3) will put an end to the Nazarene's disruption of his operation, but Jesus provides for all contingencies. Some of Luke's auditors might well have thought of the continuity of Elijah's and Elisha's prophetic ministries, a continuity that will clamor for even more attention at Acts 1.

9:2. Mark makes no mention of the proclamation of the Kingdom. Luke enlarges on this aspect. This verse is not a repetition of v. 1 but affirms that the authority given by Jesus coincides with God's interests. The Kingdom proclamation is Jesus' responsibility (4:18, 43; 8:1), and he administrates it through the Twelve. The Reign of God they are to proclaim is to be accompanied by the healing power they have just received from Jesus. Once again, word and deed are correlatives, and Jesus' ministry is viewed as God's action. But how is the reality of such power to be grasped in the light of the fate that will shortly befall Jesus? Acts 3—4 is Luke's commentary on the passage.

9:3. The standard equipment for the traveler is not for the apostles. They are to rely completely on the resources of the King. Mark's text permits them a staff (Mark 6:8; cf. 2 Kings 4:29).

Down to one tunic, they run the hazard of putting to a test their audition of the Sermon on the Plain (Luke 6:29). Whereas Mark has them sent out two by two, Luke reserves that detail for the mission of the Seventy (10:1).

9:4. Unlike itinerant philosophers who brought their philosophy into disrepute by begging from house to house (see the warning in 10:7), the church's missionaries are emissaries of the King and from their hospitable bases they are to carry out the Kingdom assignment. How the injunction was carried out may be learned from Acts 9:43; 16:15.

9:5. Wherever they are not favorably received, they are to make the gesture of prophets who declare themselves free of the judgment about to overtake those who reject God's message (cf. Luke 10:10–11). This is the meaning of the phrase **as a testimony against them** (see on 5:14). Paul and Barnabas followed the practice at Pisidian Antioch (Acts 13:51). For a similar gesture by Paul's enemies, see Acts 22:23.

9:6. The summary account prepares for the introduction of Herod. "Villages" (*kōmai*; compare "town" [*polis*], v. 5) suggests outreach to the "poor" in Israel. Luke himself defines the meaning of "proclaim the kingdom of God": it means **preaching the gospel** or evangelizing. The verse ends on a pandemic note: evangelizing and healing were done "everywhere."

Herod's Perplexity   Luke 9:7–9
(Mark 6:14–16; Matthew 14:1–2)

9:7–8. Luke generalizes Mark's more immediate reference to Jesus and writes: "all that was happening." Thus the activity of Jesus and that of the apostles are telescoped. This conjunction permits the discussion of Jesus' identity (vv. 7–9) as the generating force of all that lies behind the reports and at the same time prepares for the recital of apostolic success (vv. 10–11). Much of the succeeding narrative owes its dramatic quality to the interplay within this combination.

9:9. According to Mark, Herod Antipas thought that John was raised from the dead. Luke has him phrase the important question: Who *is* Jesus? The answer to it is the burden of the succeeding recitals, which make a synthetic impact through Luke's elimination of Mark's (6:21–29) detailed description of John's death (cf. Luke 3:19). Luke's revision of Mark's account about Herod's superstition relating to John is in harmony with the evangelist's own distinction between the ministry of John and the ministry of Jesus. Certainly Jesus is not a reincarnation or second edition of John. His function as an Elijah figure will be taken up in the subsequent narratives.

As did the family of Jesus (8:19–21), Herod seeks **to see him**, but his opportunity will not come until the week of Jesus' arrest (23:8). Herod's hostility toward Jesus is taken up at 13:31, but Luke points out that in the final encounter Herod exonerates Jesus (23:15). Thus the evangelist endeavors to guard the Christian movement against a charge of subversion.

Mark's narrative suggests that John is a latter-day Elijah, for he is the victim of a second Ahab and Jezebel (cf. 1 Kings 18). Luke, on the other hand, does not interpret John as a second Elijah. Instead, he parallels some of Jesus' activity with that of Ahab's enemy, and his omission of Mark's story of the beheading of John the Baptist (Mark 6:17–29) permits immediate presentation of the feeding narrative with its Elijah-Elisha associations.

The Return of the Twelve and the Feeding
of the Five Thousand
Luke 9:10–17
(Mark 6:30–44; Matthew 14:13–21)

9:10. Because the Twelve were "sent out" *(apostellō)* by Jesus, they are referred to as "apostles" *(apostoloi,* see Mark 6:30), that is, the "sent ones." In contrast to the focus on God in 8:39 and on Jesus in 9:7–9, the disciples recount what **they had done.** Whatever the historical apostles might have included in their report, the fact is that Luke has them say nothing explicit about their obligation to proclaim the kingdom of God (v. 2). They are thus deficient in the word side of the word-deed pair. Within a short time they will have opportunity to put things into better perspective, and their inadequacy in the face of new demands (vv. 12–13) will be in challenging contrast to their present self-congratulation.

9:11. Luke had stressed the preaching of the Kingdom and the healing of the sick in Jesus' injunction to the disciples (v. 2). Now Jesus preaches the Kingdom of God and cures the sick. Thus his own practice underwrites the activity of the church. But response will vary, and Jesus will have something to say later about the quality of faith at Bethsaida (see 10:13). Luke omits Mark's reference (Mark 6:34) to Jesus' compassion. But this datum is not to be used in support of an alleged downplaying of Jesus' emotions by Luke. Emperors did not make distributions of grain out of pity for the populace. In an expression of total liberality, and in concert with his heavenly Parent (see v. 16), Jesus feeds the multitude.

9:12. This verse begins with a phrase that will be echoed at 24:29 ("the day is now far spent" = RSV: **to wear away**). It is a way of saying, "It was mealtime." Luke abbreviates the preliminaries to Mark's account (Mark 6:30–31) of the feeding of the five thousand, perhaps with the intent of eliminating the suggestion that Jesus seeks to escape the crowds, for Luke emphasizes that Jesus "welcomed them" (v. 11). Luke omits Mark's observation that they were as sheep without a shepherd (Num. 27:17; Ezek. 34:5), for Jesus is the shepherd who has *welcomed* them. The reference to the "wilderness" (RSV: **lonely place**) makes the need all the more acute.

9:13. The Twelve, who are the basic resource for the Christian community (cf. Acts 2:42), are given instructions to feed the multitude, "all the people" (as in Luke 2:10). Similar instructions were given by Elijah to a man from

Baalshalishah (2 Kings 4:42). The reply is similar to the one in 2 Kings 4:43 (cf. Num. 11:22).

9:14–15. The command to distribute the guests in companies of fifty may be an echo of ancient practice in Israel (Exod. 18:21; Deut. 1:15). Jesus is the head of the latter-day Israel, and Acts 4:4 repeats the numeral 5,000.

9:16. The blessing and the breaking of the bread anticipate two significant narratives (22:19 and 24:30), and what the Lord did near Bethsaida is continued in the apostolic community: in shared meals (Acts 2:46) and in distribution to the needy (Acts 4:35). Specific associations with the Lord's Supper are not apparent to the degree found in the Fourth Gospel, where a parallel recital is used in place of an account of the Lord's Supper (John 6). The prayer of blessing suggests that the multiplication of the loaves is traceable to God's power invoked through the prayer. God's action is present in Jesus. The disciples, who are to nourish the Christian community, are the intermediaries for distribution.

9:17. In accordance with 6:21, "all" are satisfied. Luke's Greco-Roman public, well acquainted with distributions by generous patrons, would note this emphasis on the inclusiveness of the Great Benefactor's bounty. As in the case of Elisha's banquet (2 Kings 4:43–44), which itself mirrors the feeding recorded in Exodus 16, there was ample left over—twelve full baskets, one for each of the apostles. The Kingdom of God does not terminate with Jesus' activity. The apostles continue to answer in full measure the question once asked in a Hebrew poem: "Can God spread a table in the wilderness?" (Ps. 78:19).

Identity of the King
Luke 9:18–36

Who Am I? First Prediction of the Passion
Luke 9:18–22
(Mark 8:27–33; Matthew 16:13–23)

At this point Luke omits a large portion of Mark's narrative (Mark 6:45—8:26). Mark 6:45–52 could easily be construed as a doublet for Luke 8:22–25. Mark 6:53–56 contains accounts of miscellaneous healings. Mark 7:1–23 incorporates criticism of the Pharisees, which is taken up by Luke in 11:37–54. Mark 7:24–30 violates Luke's theme, to Jews first, then to gentiles (Luke 8:26–39, parallel in Mark 5:1–20, was a sufficient exception for Luke). Mark 8:1–10 is a doublet for the feeding of the five thousand. Mark 8:11–13 discusses the sign seekers. These are taken up by Luke in 11:16 and 29 and 12:54–56. Mark 8:14–21 raises the question of the leaven of the Pharisees, discussed in Luke 12:1. Mark 8:22–26 relates the story of a blind man, which Luke omits in favor of the narrative preceding the entry into

Jerusalem (Luke 18:35–43). Luke's primary reason, though, for omitting the section is prompted by his concern to bring the question of Jesus' messianic office into immediate relation with the feeding of the five thousand. In that narrative Jesus was clearly revealed as an Elijah figure. Now it is important to clarify Jesus' real identity.

9:18. Luke omits Mark's reference to a journey (Mark 8:27), for he will accord that theme special attention, beginning at 9:51. As in 3:21; 5:16; 6:12 (see also 22:41–43), the sight of Jesus at prayer introduces an exceptional communication. From vv. 9, 12, 14, 16 one may conclude that the Twelve are meant by the term "disciples."

9:19. As in 9:7–8, the suggestion is made that Jesus may be John the Baptist or Elijah, or one of the prophets now resurrected (cf. 9:8). The emphasis on their reappearance provides the background against which the fate of Jesus, so contradictory to the various popular assumptions, is to be pronounced. Instead of being a resurrected John the Baptist or a resurrected prophet or an Elijah making another appearance, Jesus will suffer and die and after that he will be resurrected. Such a sequence runs counter to the expectation.

To translate past greatness into present experience as an undergirding of hope appears to be a basic human tendency. Thus, for example, during the Second Punic War (221 B.C.E.), older veterans thought that in Hannibal they were seeing the return of his father, Hamilcar (Livy 21.4).

9:20. Peter's reply, that Jesus is **the Christ of God** (cf. 2:26) will be on the lips of the leaders of Israel at 23:35. With exquisite dramatic sensitivity Luke connects this specific identification with the passion prediction in 9:22. Peter will call both to Israel's attention at Acts 3:18. The identification aids in distinguishing Jesus from John the Baptist or from any other figures in Israel's past history. Luke's association of Elijah with Jesus has served its purpose. Now the evangelist is prepared to have Jesus examined in terms of his messianic credentials.

9:21. Most attempts to account for the command to silence are speculative, but consideration of Luke's literary perspective reveals the clarity of the text. Despite rejection by the authorities, Jesus' credentials as Master and Anointed One (Acts 2:36) are ratified by God through the resurrection on the third day. After Pentecost, the disciples will be free to make the full proclamation. Until that time, the disciples are instructed not to publish Jesus' identity. God's beneficent action in returning Jesus from the dead will offer them opportunity to proclaim a full gospel.

9:22. Luke omits Mark's criticism of Peter's confession (Mark 8:33), but in this first prediction of the Passion (see also 9:44; 12:50; 13:32–33; 17:25; 18:31–34) Luke shares with Mark the understanding that messiahship involves suffering, rejection, and death followed by victorious resurrection (9:22; cf. 24:7, 26). The word "must" (*dei,* v. 22) emphasizes that this is of God's design (cf. Acts 2:23–24), as indicated by its primary emphatic position in the Greek.

As the Son of humanity, Jesus identifies completely with human beings in all their fragility. Any conception of his messiahship must include that perspective. Therefore any announcement of Jesus' messiahship before the culmination would have been premature and might have been misunderstood in nationalistic or other terms. Stated in Luke's thought: Jesus' death, perpetrated by the cream of the system, does not invalidate his credentials as the Messiah. On the contrary, the path to apparent disaster is the upward road to victory. As Luke 24:21 will reveal, the evangelist has much invested in the phrase **on the third day.**

In subsequent chapters Luke will reinforce the point that Israel's leadership must accept primary responsibility for the death of Jesus (see Luke 19:47; 20:1, 19; 22:2, 4, 52, 54, 66; 23:4–5, 10, 13), and in Acts (Acts 4:1–4; 5:33; 6:12–15; 7:54–60) he will indict it for continuing to remain in opposition, especially after Peter proclaims a message of divine beneficence in proclaiming a second chance to all the people of Israel after Pentecost (Acts 2:37–41; 3:12–26, with John; 5:29–32).

Taking up the Cross   Luke 9:23–27
(Mark 8:34—9:1; Matthew 16:24–28)

9:23. The words **he said to all** suggest that Luke is alerting his community to the call of Jesus. The word "all" is equivalent to "everyone, without restriction" and is used by Luke to make a smooth transition from the account in vv. 18–22 that made reference to a smaller circle associated with Jesus; but Luke apparently failed to notice that he had made no literary provision for the appearance of a general audience.

In the evangelist's time it would be a matter of identifying with Jesus' fate. Hence the disciple must **take up his cross.** The use of this metaphor indicates that Christians must be willing to run the risk of being misunderstood as criminals and that Jesus himself is viewed by the state as an enemy.

That Greco-Roman auditors would have no difficulty grasping the thought is apparent, for example, from a glance at Plato's *Republic* (2.361e–362b). Glaukon, one of the dialoguers, puts the following words in the mouth of those who show a preference for injustice: "Given the disposition of the upright, they can expect to be scourged, to be put on the rack, to be chained, to have their eyes burned out, and finally, after all manner of suffering, to be impaled . . . ." In a similar discourse in the *Gorgias* (473b)

Plato used the common word for crucifixion in a description of a wicked person's fate.

The term "daily" *(kath' hēmeran)* suggests that occasional scintillating displays of courage or interest in notoriety are not under discussion here. For modern Christians this means accepting the call to practical discipleship and welcoming the conditions under which they may qualify with ongoing dedication as cross-bearers through proper challenge of their social and economic environment and their secular and ecclesiastical structures, as these conflict with responsible concern for others. Commitment to the policies of the Great Liberator will from time to time bring one in conflict with ecclesiastical and secular authorities. The words **come after me** *(akoloutheitō moi)* are more appropriate on the lips of Jesus than on John's; Luke therefore omitted at 3:16 Mark's use of the phrase (Mark 1:7).

9:24. Only with total commitment will the disciple be able to realize Jesus' promise, **whoever loses his life for my sake . . . will save it.** Evidently Jesus did not consider it too high a price to pay for bringing zest, vitality, and spontaneity back into style. He was indeed great master of the calculated risk. One day, Rome will be envious of Jesus' power to command such loyalty.

9:25–26. The words in v. 25 are a reminder of the second temptation (4:5–8). In his phrasing of v. 26 Luke eliminates Mark's reference to "this . . . generation" (Mark 8:38), perhaps to retain a more general application to the church of his time. At the same time, he avoids Mark's harsh description of Jesus' contemporaries: Luke takes no anti-Jewish stance.

Verse 26 affirms that Jesus' ministry and words will be ratified upon his return as the glorified Son of humanity. Luke prepared his public for proper understanding of this passage by including "Son of humanity" as a synonym for Jesus at v. 22. To avoid the suggestion that special apocalyptic effects are required to validate Jesus' messianic mission Luke omits in v. 27 Mark's words "with power" (Mark 9:1). Jesus is indeed the Son of humanity also in the triumphant phase that is associated with the term in Christian circles, but **his glory** at the end of the end time is of a piece with the glory into which Jesus enters at his resurrection (24:26).

Luke's apportionment of glory to Jesus, the Father, and the holy angels contrasts with Mark's focus on the Father (Mark 8:38). Jesus has his own "glory" because of his extraordinary distinction as the One Name "under heaven" (Acts 4:12), but it is in association with that of the Father and of the angels. The linkage of the term "Son of humanity" with "Father" suggests that Luke's public is to understand "Son of humanity" in ascription to Jesus, as a synonym for "Son of God." The emphasis on Jesus' "words" contrasts with the disciples' interest in their performance (Luke 9:10). Peter will later have good reason to ponder Jesus' words (see 22:56–60).

9:27. This verse echoes 2:27. It is important to keep in mind the perspective that derives from consideration of Luke's total work. The Kingdom of God, present now in Jesus' ministry (cf. 7:28; 17:21), will be especially manifest at the cross and recognized by the robber (23:42–43, with stress on "today"). After that comes the period of the post-Pentecost community, followed by the coming of the Son of humanity. Thus v. 26 is futuristic and v. 27 contemporary.

In Mark's context the statement in Luke 9:27 would suggest to Christians that the second coming of Jesus Christ could be expected at any moment. Its nonarrival was a source of embarrassment for them, and Luke resolves the problem with his perspective of a two-stage kingdom. His omission of Mark's phrase "with power" (see above on v. 26) is a sure indication of his intent. Mark's view is apocalyptic. Luke's is conditioned by emphasis on historical factors. Luke 21:31, which speaks of the second stage of the Kingdom's manifestation, corresponds to 9:26. It is therefore improbable that v. 27 has reference to the transfiguration scene, which took place only about eight days later. The oath-like formulation in v. 27 requires a more climactic occurrence: namely, 23:39–43. The transfiguration is but a preview, which puts into focus subsequent developments and explains the twofold sense in which Jesus' Kingdom is to be understood: (1) historical demonstration in suffering, death, and resurrection; and (2) apocalyptic fulfillment.

Others before Jesus have lived up to some of the challenge that is mirrored by these words. "When Sokrates had the opportunity to save himself," says Epiktetos (4.1.163–67), "Krito urged him, 'For the sake of your children, escape!' And what does Sokrates say? Does he consider it a lucky break? Hardly! He thinks only of what is seemly, and neither sees nor gives a thought to anything else. 'I do not wish to save this paltry hide of mine, but that part of me which develops and is preserved by uprightness and can only be diminished and destroyed by unrighteousness.' No, Sokrates does not betray his soul. . . . This man who scorned authoritarian rulers; this man who discoursed so eloquently about personal excellence and exceptional merits; this man no one will save by dishonor. Salvation is his by dying not by fleeing." Sokrates accepted his responsibility for the moral health of Athens. So also Queen Esther accepted hers in behalf of the security of the Jewish nation (Esth. 5:15–16).

Generals have for eons invited soldiers to embolden themselves in a crisis for honor and for country. Typical is Livy's account (21:40–44) of preparations for the Battle of Ticinus in the Second Punic War. The Roman historian records back to back the exhortations of Scipio and Hannibal to their troops. In his summation Scipio urged: "Let each soldier think not of protecting his own body, but through arms his wife and little children." And on the other front Hannibal declared: "No sharper weapon do the immortal deities give one for victory than contempt of death." But after all comparisons are made, a striking feature of Jesus' declamation is the estimate he places on the importance of his own person for the destiny of every human being.

"This Is My Beloved Son"   Luke 9:28–36
                                                    (Mark 9:2–8; Matthew 17:1–8)

At the beginning of Jesus' ministry, and just before his encounter with Satan, the heavenly voice affirmed Jesus as the Son of God. Now, before the journey to Jerusalem, which begins at 9:51, the voice sounds forth a modified version, with stress on divine choice. Luke is emphasizing that the crucifixion is an integral part of Jesus' career, whose beginning was cited at 3:21. This connection is further cadenced by Luke through an echo in 18:31a of the phraseology in 9:28 relating to apostolic companions and their ascent with Jesus.

Exploration of the question whether the disciples had any such experience as is attested by the synoptists and by the writer of 2 Pet. 1:16–18 has, because of the large speculative factor associated with the discussion, not resulted in any consensus.

Whether, after such exalted experience, Peter could have denied the Lord (see 22:54–62), with the other disciples forsaking Jesus, belongs in the realm of psychological inquiry, but lack of sufficient data about the historical apostles precludes serious investigation. Yet, to judge from the church's post-apostolic performance, one must grant the probability of their disappointing performance. For in a variety of ways, and over a period of two millennia, the church in its many and varied institutional phases has accumulated an astonishing record of infidelity to Jesus' instructions. And this despite the advantage of acquaintance with the message of Jesus' resurrection and the event of Pentecost. That the form of the tradition concerning the transfiguration has undergone considerable editing since the recital of its earliest kernel is undeniable, and the principal outlines of Luke's own literary use of the tradition can be determined with reasonable certainty.

9:28. Luke's manner of connecting the present episode with vv. 18–27 is more explicit than Mark's (Mark 9:1–2), for Luke adds: **after these sayings.** The phrase "and it came to pass" (*egeneto de;* RSV: **now**) introduces an important development in the narrative. Luke's alteration of Mark's "after six days" may be an attempt to avoid the suggestion that Jesus' experience is a repetition of Moses' interview with God (Exod. 24:15–18). In the latter account Moses hears the voice of the Lord on the seventh day and remains on the mount for forty days and forty nights. Luke's Jesus is not a second Moses.

It has been suggested that the six days in Mark may refer to the Feast of Tabernacles, originally a joyous harvest feast, described in Lev. 23:33–43. Israel was to live in temporary booths for seven days and observe a solemn convocation on the eighth day. Luke's awareness of ritual is evidenced elsewhere, and his phrase **about eight days** may point even more precisely to this festival. And since the story of the transfiguration does relate the suggestion of building temporary shelters ("booths"; *skenas,* the same term used in the Greek text of Leviticus 23), there is something to be said for the interpretation. Yet it is odd that the suggestion should come at the end of the period rather than at the beginning.

The most that can be said with certainty is that typological considerations involving the Feast of Tabernacles have entered into the tradition of the account of the transfiguration. At Jesus' time this feast was observed as a national recollection of ancient liberties, and messianic hopes might tend to rise to fever pitch. If the account of the transfiguration is to be connected with the feast, the synoptists may be considered unanimous in rejecting the false hopes generated during the festival. But the probability remains that Luke may simply be construing Mark's phrase as equivalent to "about a week." This commentator has heard citizens of Greece use the phrase "in eight days" in precisely that sense. Idiom of this type has a long life.

As at 8:51, Jesus takes **Peter and John and James** to witness his transfiguration. The mountain suggests a place of special revelation. Jesus at prayer is reminiscent of 3:21, and the answer out of the cloud (9:3) echoes 3:22. The demon described in 9:37–43 will discover, as did Satan, how invincible Jesus is after prayer.

9:29. Exodus 34:29–35 describes an extraordinary glowing of Moses' face (cf. 2 Cor. 3:7–18). Whether this passage entered into Luke's mind cannot be determined. But expectations of a prophet like Moses were stimulated by Deut. 18:15–18, and this latter passage is cited in Acts 3:22 and 7:37. Luke's account supports the view that Jesus is the fulfillment of the anticipation, but without endorsement of a second Moses typology that treats Jesus as a new lawgiver. The evangelist prefers to stress Moses' function as the leader of Israel's exodus (see on v. 31). Thus Jesus is a replacement for Moses, not a new Moses. Luke 9:19–20 clearly indicates that Jesus is more than a prophet; he is the Anointed One.

Since Mark's use of the Greek verb *metamorphoō* for "transfiguration" (Mark 9:2) might have suggested a metamorphosis of the kind attributed to Greco-Roman deities, Luke says of Jesus that **the appearance of his countenance was altered** *(heteron).* Coupled with the description of the shining garments (cf. Luke 24:4; Acts 1:10), Luke's phrasing, which echoes at Acts 6:15, suggests *not* a reincarnation of Moses but the righteous one who comes through apocalyptic tribulation (cf. Dan. 12:3; cited in Matt. 13:43; Rev. 3:5). A centurion will judge correctly (Luke 23:47). Whiteness is the standard color in apocalyptic description (Rev. 2:17; 6:2; 20:11). Thus Jesus' Kingdom is described as one transcending the standard suggested by Satan in the wilderness of temptation (Luke 4:6–8). Auditors familiar with Homer's *Iliad* (18.203–6) might well have attributed heroic dimensions to Jesus through recollection of the moment in which Athena covered the shoulders of Achilles with her fringed aegis, whereupon a golden cloud surrounded his head and from it Athena kindled a brilliant flame.

9:30–31. The word "behold" *(idou)* calls attention to an especially remarkable phenomenon. **Moses and Elijah** now appear and speak, not to the disciples, but with Jesus. These two prophets are often interpreted as emblematic of, respectively, the Law and the Prophets. But Elijah was not, in Jewish thought, a representative of the prophets, in the sense of a part for the whole. Rather, he was recognized as the one who would return and restore all things (cf. Mark 9:12). Luke retains Mark's mention of Elijah to endorse his own view that John the Baptist is not a second Elijah. Jesus, more so than John, takes over Elijah's functions. Yet Jesus is more than Elijah, and there are aspects in Elijah's ministry that cannot be applied to Jesus (see on Luke 9:54). Elijah therefore disappears, along with Moses, in the sequel. Moreover, according to popular thinking, Elijah comes to the rescue of the sufferer (cf. Mark 15:36). Jesus, though, must endure the last frontiers of disaster. Luke therefore eliminates Elijah from consideration as one who is to validate the appearance of the Messiah through apocalyptic revelation. Instead, both Moses and Elijah speak of Jesus' "departure" *(exodus,* an item not found in the account of Matthew or Mark).

"Departure" *(exodus)* contrasts with Luke's reference to Jesus' "coming" *(eisodus,* Acts 13:24). There is a double sense to "departure." It suggests not only the exodus led by Moses but also physical death, which is followed by his resurrection and ascension. Luke therefore will omit in his Passion account Mark's (Mark 15:33–37) reference to Elijah; it would be superfluous as well as inappropriate. Jerusalem is emphasized in accordance with Luke's perspective, "beginning at Jerusalem" (Luke 1—2; 24:47). But the reader is not to infer that Jesus is dependent on Moses and Elijah for information concerning his suffering.

At 9:22 Jesus himself had informed his disciples about his fate, and at 9:51 he is to "set his face to go to Jerusalem." The heavenly visitants merely ratify what has already been determined as the Father's will, and Jesus goes the route foretold by Moses and the prophets (cf. 16:31; 24:25). Apocalyptic, says Luke, is to be interpreted in terms of Jesus' own message, not Jesus from the standpoint of traditional apocalyptic. Thus his inclusion of apocalyptic narrative and phraseology does not contradict his repeated rejection of apocalyptic as the structure for communicating the mission of Jesus.

The appearance of the two **in glory** forms a contrast to their conversation. According to Luke's view, Jesus' suffering is his way to glory (24:26).

Hence "two men" appear in shining garments at the grave (24:4) and reappear in Acts 1:10 for Jesus' ascension. Consistent with Luke's eschatological perspective, their presence in both instances is a way of introducing a terminal dimension to Jesus' action, while at the same time repudiating the doctrine that the Messiah must make himself known in accordance with popular apocalyptic hope. It cannot be asserted definitely that in the last two passages Luke has in mind Moses and Elijah, but the account of the transfiguration might well have been recollected by some of Luke's public.

9:32–33. The motif of sleep (here *hypnos;* cf. Mark 14:40) is a feature of apocalyptic narrative (cf. Dan. 10:9). The disciples are warned against sleep in the face of the undetermined end (Luke 21:34). In the Garden of Gethsemane they are overpowered with drowsiness (22:45). It is to be inferred that they were unaware of the conversation between Jesus and his heavenly visitants. They are pictured as ignorant of the urgency of the hour, failing to note the intimate connection between suffering and glory.

The disciples awaken and take note only of the glory and are distressed as they see Moses and Elijah slipping away (Luke's own feature) from Jesus. Had they remained awake, they would have been informed about Jesus' exodus. Peter was a young man with old ideas and did not see that the time was past for setting up booths. Out of ignorance he suggests that the disciples be permitted to make **three booths**, one for each of the dignitaries.

The painstaking description vividly illustrates Peter's misunderstanding. Jesus is not merely one alongside two prophets, nor do the disciples require the continuing presence of these heavenly visitors to assure themselves of Jesus' authority. Besides, Jesus is the living manifestation of God's presence amid people (see Ezek. 37:27; 43:7, 9; Zech. 2:10; Luke 19:6–10; Rev. 21:3). The disciples require no apocalyptic camp-out. Still another aspect of Peter's misunderstanding is suggested by Luke's multi-faceted interest in the theme of hospitality. Of special interest is the fact that Jesus on occasion emerges as the host instead of the guest. At 5:27–32 his participation at a banquet in Levi's home concludes with his own self-description as one who in such a situation is inviting sinners to repentance. At 10:38–42 Jesus reveals his desire to serve Martha and Mary. At 19:1–10 Zacchaeus finds himself on the receiving end in his own house. And two disciples watch him play the host in their home at Emmaus (24:30). Peter is slow to understand that Jesus will count no home except his Father's "house" (2:49) as his own.

9:34–35. At this point **a cloud came and overshadowed them** (cf. Exod. 40:35 LXX; Acts 1:9). This cloud is no ordinary cloud but the traditional indication of God's presence. In Exod. 13:21 a "cloud" guided the Israelites; in Exod. 24:15 a "cloud" covered Mt. Sinai; and in 1 Kings 8:10–11 a "cloud" filled Solomon's new house for the Lord. According to

2 Macc. 2:8 the "cloud" is to return to signal God's presence among the people.

It is God who now pronounces the correct interpretation of all that has transpired: **This is my Son, my Chosen; listen to him!** The disciples' fear, **as they entered the cloud**, expresses the normal reaction to divine intervention (cf. Dan. 10:7; Luke 5:8–10) and lends to these words an additional solemnity. At his baptism Jesus heard a portion of these words addressed to him personally (Luke 3:22). Now the words are directed to the disciples, and through the disciples to the Christian communities.

Of special interest is the alteration of "beloved" (*agapētos* in Luke 3:22 and in Mark 9:7) to "chosen" *(eklelegmenos)*. "Choice" in this context is used in reference to function and connotes appointment to specific obligations. Luke appears to draw on Isa. 42:1, which describes Jacob as God's chosen or elect one. The context of the Isaiah passage speaks of the light to the gentiles (Isa. 42:6; cf. v. 4 and Luke 2:32) and echoes the program outlined in Luke 1:79; 4:18; 7:22. At 23:35 the role of Jesus as Chosen One will be called into question by Israel's own hierarchy. Since Jesus speaks with authority that far exceeds even that of Moses, the disciples must **listen to him** (cf. Deut. 18:15; Acts 3:22–23). The pronoun is emphatic in Luke's text *(autou akouete)*. God's way of bringing plans to completion for the chosen does not include a spectacular apocalyptic demonstration but the continuing presence of Jesus in the Christian communities.

9:36. Jesus, the light of the gentiles, has been separated from Moses and Elijah. This is stressed by the fact that Jesus is found alone, after the voice has spoken. The community is not to limit its thinking exclusively to traditional molds. It is to heed the word of Jesus, now authoritatively communicated through the apostolic mission. Above all, the disciple must hear Jesus' word about his approaching death (9:22).

The revelatory nature of the account is once more stressed through the observation that the disciples were silent (cf. Dan. 10:15). So overcome were they with the vision that they **told no one . . . anything of what they had seen.** But the significant words **in those days** are added. After the resurrection of Jesus the truth concerning Jesus' person would be better understood (cf. Luke 24:9). Mark's wording (Mark 9:9), that they should not relate what they had seen until the Son of humanity had risen from the dead, is eliminated. Luke 9:21 took care of this detail, and Luke's omission here indicates that the recital of the transfiguration sums up his christological instruction (cf. 9:20).

Summary: The transfiguration reveals the following: (1) God's tenting among people does not take place through the observance of the ritual of booths or the maintenance of other OT ritual. God's promise to tent among people is fulfilled in Jesus' presence. (2) Traditional patterns of apocalyptic thinking are not applicable to Jesus. Jesus' ministry is not validated by apocalyptic demonstration. His Kingdom is a present reality, awaiting its consummation. Apocalyptic in the strict sense of the term applies to the latter. (3) Jesus' suffering and death are God's design for the Son. Jesus' credentials are in no way invalidated by the verdict pronounced in Jerusalem. Rather, his glory begins at the cross. (4) Jesus' Kingdom is not of this world. That is, it is not to be defined in terms of standard human criteria or prevailing systems.

A final word needs to be said about the connection of this account with the account of the resurrected Lord. It has been suggested that a resurrection story has been retrojected into the narrative. Against this view are the following: (1) In resurrection accounts Jesus does not appear in white, nor is his glory observed. Luke, in any case, does not promote the idea of a retrojection, for the two men on the road to Emmaus are convinced through Jesus' word and action (24:30–32), having been ignorant beforehand of his identity. (2) Moses and Elijah do not appear in the resurrection stories. If they are to be inferred in 24:4, it is the result of projection from the transfiguration account, not vice versa. (3) The number six or "about eight days" does not fit a resurrection account, at least not Luke's. All of the events recorded in Luke 24 take place on Easter Day. If the retrojection did indeed occur, it must have taken place at a very early stage in the tradition, for Luke displays no awareness of it. But in that event the living witnesses were a strong control for the recital of experiences in the life of Jesus and the disciples.

Misunderstanding

Luke 9:37–50

Healing of a Demoniac

Luke 9:37–43a
(Mark 9:14–29; Matthew 17:14–21)

Between the story of the transfiguration and the healing of the demoniac, Mark (9:9–13) had introduced a discussion about Elijah and John the Baptist's identification with Elijah. In Luke's time, such association of John with Elijah could be used to cast doubt on Jesus' messianic credentials, for the conclusion could be drawn that since the expected special apocalyptic effects had not taken place Jesus could not be the anticipated deliverer. Luke therefore eliminates the recital. Whatever John was or did, Jesus can be fully understood apart from him.

9:37–40. Mark's account of the healing suggests that the incident took place on the same day as the transfiguration, but it may have been his intention to suggest a night scene. To make the incident stand out in bolder relief against the command given in the account of the transfiguration (see Luke 9:43–45), Luke is very definite in his chronology: **on the next day** (the RSV does not translate *egeneto de,* "And it came to pass"). Thus the pattern of mountain scene followed by encounter with demons (cf. 6:12–18) is maintained.

By eliminating the scene of disputation between the disciples (whom Jesus had left behind) and the scribes, Luke is able to focus attention on the basic problem: the disciples are not heeding Jesus' word. Hence they could not **cast . . . out** the demon (v. 40). It is not a matter of legal technicalities. The man pleads with Jesus **to look upon** (the Greek verb *epiblepō* is rendered "has regarded" in 1:48) his child. Luke adds in v. 38 the words **only child** *(monogenēs)* to emphasize the father's plight (cf. 7:12; 8:42). The symptoms are those of epilepsy. Luke emphasizes the weakness of a human being exploited by demonic forces. Thus the unfortunate sufferer is not to be classed as a sinner but deserves all the compassion that can be mustered in his behalf. In view of the hostility, the prediction concerning Jesus' own suffering is a natural development.

9:41. Jesus' reply is not, as in Mark 9:19, directed specifically to the disciples but is a general statement on the type of response his message encounters (see on Luke 7:31). The word "perverse" *(diestrammenos,* "crooked") is an addition to Mark's text and recalls Deut. 32:5; Prov. 6:14; Isa. 59:8. It reappears in Acts 13:8, 10 (cf. Phil. 2:15). In the words **bear with you**, Luke's Jesus echoes the diction of God in Isa. 46:4 LXX. Luke evidently intends to spare the disciples some embarrassment, but there is no doubt that the community is warned not to make the mistake of this "generation."

9:42. In the description that follows, Luke omits Mark's recital about the father's faith (Mark 9:21–24). Luke apparently considers it irrelevant, for the problem is the disciples' inability to carry out the injunctions given them by Jesus not long before the transfiguration (Luke 9:1–2). It was their task to proclaim the Kingdom of God and to heal, yet on the mountain they wanted to prepare tents for Jesus, Moses, and Elijah! They wished to retain Elijah, but like Gehazi, the servant of Elijah's successor Elisha (see 2 Kings 4:29–31), they could not carry out instructions.

Through his casting out of the demon, Jesus once more reinforces his purpose—to demolish the works of Satan. Luke relates that Jesus **healed the boy.** "Heal" *(iaomai)* echoes the command in 9:2. Jesus does what he had given his disciples instructions to do. Once more an Elijah motif enters Luke's recital. Jesus **gave him back to his father** (see on Luke 7:15). Jesus does not require the presence of Elijah for validation. He in his own person initiates the end time. Or, to express it theologically, apocalyptic is christologized.

9:43. The concluding words, **And all were astonished at the majesty of God,** clearly indicate that God is at work in Jesus' action (cf. Acts 10:38).

In like manner, the voice from heaven (Luke 9:35) endorsed his total ministry. Mark 9:15 refers to astonishment of the crowds at the time of Jesus' descent from the mountain; Luke speaks of astonishment at the later moment spelled out in v. 37. The word "majesty" *(megaleiotēs)* is used in only one other passage in the NT (2 Pet. 1:16), and there in the context of a reference to the transfiguration.

Luke affirms that Jesus' daily round of activity is his own authentication and a continuing transfiguration. There in the routine performance of his task is *the* sign, *the* proof that God is at work in Jesus. Such mode of revelation was too tame for those who had made up their minds that God's hand would be seen in more spectacular fashion. Luke omits Mark 9:28–29, which includes a query by the disciples concerning their inability to exorcise (cf. Luke 9:40 and 9:1) as well as Jesus' reference to the importance of fasting and prayer. The praying has already been done at 9:28.

At 19:37 recognition is made of Jesus' powerful deeds that take place just before the events of Holy Week gain momentum. Here at 9:43a a related response is followed by a prediction of the betrayal. Through the omission of Mark 9:28–29, Luke is able to maintain an intimate connection between Jesus' demonstrated power over the demonic and the affirmation of his credentials by the heavenly voice. Despite all efforts of Satan to discredit him, especially in Holy Week (see 22:3), Jesus will win. The exorcism functions as a forecast of victory. As vv. 44–50 indicate, the disciples' problem relates to their failure to grasp the reality of the fate that awaits Jesus as one who is on assignment from his Parent.

Second Prediction of the Passion   Luke 9:43b–45
                                                      (Mark 9:30–32; Matthew 17:22–23)

9:44. The first and second predictions of the Passion serve as framework for the account of the transfiguration and accompanying recital of exorcism. In view of Luke's economy of statement elsewhere, his repetition of the motif of the astonishment of the crowd is noteworthy. He is affirming that the majesty of God is indeed being revealed but that the climactic demonstration is yet to come—when the Son of humanity is handed over **into the hands** of human beings (see also 9:22; 12:50; 13:32–33; 17:25; 18:31–34). This is the ultimate in divine mystery, and the verbal assonance is striking. He who identified with the human situation is to be rejected by human beings.

The phrase **Let these words sink into your ears** parallels the expression in Exod. 17:14. Luke's frequent references to "delivered" *(paradidomi)* in connection with Jesus' arrest and death (see Luke 18:32; 20:20; 22:4, 6, 21, 22, 48; 23:25; 24:7, 20; Acts 3:13) are prompted by his sources and by his interest in identifying the fate of Jesus with that of the sufferer described by this term in the Greek version of Isa. 53:6, 12. Since a victorious return in glory was associated with Jesus as the Son of humanity, Luke's auditors would catch an additional dramatic note. To mistreat in such manner the one who ultimately sits at the right hand of God is to invite certain disaster.

9:45. Luke adds to Mark's account (Mark 9:32) that the disciples' ignorance (cf. Acts 13:27; 17:23) is traceable to divine intervention—**it was concealed** *(parakalyptō)* **from them.** They could have asked Jesus for details, but they feared to make the inquiry. Such reference to impact made on others is a powerful rhetorical device for registering the uniqueness of the principal character in the story. Jesus himself later removes the misunderstanding of two disciples on the road to Emmaus (24:16–32). Thus it is affirmed that Jesus' ministry transcends all normal patterns of human expectation, and it will take divine power, expressed through Jesus and the Holy Spirit, to open the minds of people for faith (cf. 10:21–22). The fact that Jesus was rejected is no proof that he was not what he or the apostolic mission claims him to be.

Argument about Greatness   Luke 9:46–50
                                              (Mark 9:33–41; Matthew 18:1–5)

9:46. Mark (9:33) disconnects this account from the preceding prediction by introducing a fresh development at Capernaum. Luke preserves the association by eliminating that visit. In his recital the dispute over prestige is a misunderstanding of the Kingdom, about to be climaxed by Jesus' own rejection of standard greatness through acceptance of the cross. The lowly are to be exalted, and the mighty are to be brought low (Luke 1:52). Luke does not limit the discussion to the circle of the Twelve (Mark 9:35). The entire church is to learn this lesson.

9:47. Jesus perceives **the thought** *(dialogismos)* **of their hearts.** The Greek philosopher Thales was asked whether one could hide an evil deed from God. "No," he answered, "not even the thought" (Diogenes Laertius 1.36). A child is an excellent illustration to use in teaching the lesson of humility. It can do nothing for the disciple and cannot satisfy the one who asks, "What's in it for me?" All hollow status-seeking is here brought under indictment. The disciple is not to share the criteria of the old age.

9:48. Jesus identifies so closely with the child that reception of the child is a reception of Jesus himself. And he who receives Jesus receives the Sender—namely, the Father. Luke here omits Mark's wording "receives not me but," for Luke emphasizes that Jesus is intimately linked with the Father (cf. Luke 10:22).

One who learns leastness learns greatness. The word "least" *(mikroteros)* is a reminder of the words in 7:28. Since Jesus is the one who "shall be called great" (1:32*), all claims to greatness are to be measured in terms of the route he takes to establish his identity.

9:49. It is indeed remarkable how Jesus could talk past his disciples—"in one ear and out the other." Now it is a question of union rights. Do others, besides the apostles, have the privilege of exorcising? The story echoes Num. 11:26–30.

The question would be asked for centuries to come, with established churches zealously guarding their prerogatives and traditions against the encroachments of spiritual gifts that could not be subject to firm institutional control. Luke, who is the spokesperson for division of labor in the apostolic community (cf. Acts 6:1–6), lays his finger on a primary cause of the malady—status-seeking. But Jesus' proclamation is not limited to one magisterial center. God's Spirit, to the dismay of many an ecclesiastical administrator, does not always go through channels.

John's question may also reflect the early church's problem of recognizing the ministry of people not associated with the mainstream of Christianity as it emanated from Jerusalem. Apollos was one of these nonconformist preachers, being acquainted only with the baptism of John the Baptist (Acts 18:24–26). But he was graciously treated, and notably by Priscilla and Aquila (Acts 18:26).

9:50. John had said to Jesus, "We tried to prevent him" (imperfect tense; not as the RSV renders: "we forbade him"). Jesus answers: "Stop preventing him!" (better than RSV: **Do not forbid him**). The reasoning of Jesus does not at first sight strike a Western reader as particularly sound: **He that is not against you is for you.** It seems to encourage spineless neutrality and appears to be in contradiction to 11:23. But from the Eastern point of view it means: "Those who are not associated with you are not necessarily opposed to you. Let them carry on their activity."

In related vein Cicero pleaded with Caesar in behalf of a client: "We have frequently heard you say that, while *we* considered all who were not on our side to be our opponents, *you* held all those who were not against you to be your adherents" (*In Behalf of Ligarius* 33). The church does well to recognize the value also of humanitarian effort that lacks a professed Christian base. The church's long sad tale of persecution of dissenters is only a reminder that the thickheadedness of the earliest disciples did not go out of style after Pentecost. One need only think of the renowned philosopher Hypatia, master of Neoplatonic thought, and highly esteemed by bishop Synesios. It was probably during the season of Lent in 415 C.E. that she was torn from her chariot by adherents of Cyril of Alexandria, divested on the church steps of the Caesarion, and there murdered with oyster shells. The distinguished classical scholar Ernest Sihler wrote concerning similar persecutions of non-Christians: "Strong were the imperial decrees against heretics and for the Nicene Creed."

Luke's story is naturally not included in Matthew's Gospel.

PART FOUR: WE GO UP TO JERUSALEM

From 8:4—9:50, Luke has been following Mark's sequence (Mark 4:1—9:40). Omitting Mark 9:41—10:12, Luke strikes out on his own at 9:51 and, except for variations of Mark 9:42–50 in 17:1–2 and 14:34–35, he will not pick up Mark's thread until 18:15.

FIRST PHASE

Luke 9:51—13:21

Hazards of Discipleship

Luke 9:51–62

In Samaria

Luke 9:51–56

9:51. Marked by the words "And it came to pass" *(egeneto de,* omitted in the RSV), this verse begins a major section, in which Luke collects miscellaneous sayings and deeds of Jesus, which are for the most part peculiar to his Gospel or drawn from Q. The picture of Jesus that emerges provides more of the background for the verdict in 24:19 and Acts 10:38. Because of Luke's ostensible interest in showing Jesus on the move toward Jerusalem, 9:51—19:27 is frequently referred to as Luke's Travel Account (cf. 9:57; 10:1, 38; 13:22, 33; 17:11; 18:31, 35; 19:1).

Since thematic considerations dictate the structure, this "journey" becomes one of the most leisurely literary trips ever made. The Gospel began in Jerusalem and it will terminate there, but only to mark a fresh beginning (24:47). The "exodus" of Jesus (9:31) is a journey toward death and out of death to exaltation. His deeds and sayings on the way are a manifesto for the church. And his followers are called people of "the Way" at Acts 9:2.

The experience of rejection by the Samaritans (v. 52) parallels the rejection at Nazareth (4:16–30). Once more the figure of Elijah haunts the narrative. The same expression that appears as a verb *(analambanō)* in Sir. 48:9 and 1 Macc. 2:58 in reference to Elijah's departure for heaven is here used in its nominal form *(analēmpsis),* which the RSV accurately renders with the dynamic equivalent: **to be received up.** Philo uses the cognate verb in a recital of Moses' ascent to heaven (*Moses* 2.291). This reception actually takes place at the end of the Gospel (*anapherō* at Luke 24:50–51; cf. Acts 1:1–2, where the verb *analambanō* is used), but Luke's mode of presentation shows that the fate Jesus suffers in Jerusalem is the main stage toward his enthronement as the son of David (cf. 1:32–33) and exaltation as the dedicated Son of God.

Jesus has "his face set." The expression "his face" is a Semitic formulation meaning "himself." Luke's phrase is remarkably similar to one in Ezek. 6:2 and 13:17, and especially striking is the fact that the term "son of humanity" (son of man) in these OT passages describes the prophet. In formal-equivalence translation the phrase "the son of the human being" (= the son of the man) discloses a structure that is linguistically equal to the plural form, "the sons of the human beings" (= the sons of men) as it appears frequently in Ecclesiastes (Eccl. 1:13, to cite but one). It is not improbable that Luke, unencumbered with Aramaic, saw in the modified expression "the Son of humanity" (see Luke 9:44) a term that expressed the uniqueness of Jesus relative to a prophetic figure like Ezekiel, yet without disclaiming a strain of tradition that ran alongside the apocalyptic view. Luke had no problem with such hospitality for a variety of views relating to a single term. His magnanimous theology and the One Name theme took care of that.

The total phrase, **he set his face,** expresses Jesus' fixed purpose (cf. Isa. 50:7; Jer. 44:11). What is to befall him is no tragic set of circumstances from which there was to be no escape. Satan had offered a way out (4:6–8). But Jesus is obedient to the Father's will (2:49). Just as Ezekiel's face was directed *(sterizō)* toward **Jerusalem** (Ezek. 21:7 [= RSV 21:2]), so Jesus earnestly heads for his city. The Book of Acts (19:21, 22; 21:12–15) will display Paul similarly intent on journeying to the Holy City, despite warnings of mounting hostility. Ezekiel's message was one of judgment. Jesus goes to seek her peace (Luke 19:42), but also must pronounce prophetic judgment on her.

9:52. John went before God in the spirit and power of Elijah (1:17), and he was sent as a messenger "before the face" of Israel (7:27). Jesus sends his own advance people "before *his* [own] face" **(ahead of him).** Since Jesus is himself an Elijah figure, he requires no Elijah to precede him. John goes in the *spirit* of Elijah, but Jesus himself gives content to the role of Elijah, and according to Luke's thought divests the people of erroneous apocalyptic associations concerning Elijah.

Luke has a special interest in **Samaritans,** whose capital, Samaria, nearly seventy kilometers north of Jerusalem, was founded by King Omri about the year 870 B.C.E. The Assyrians conquered the city in 772 B.C.E., deported a number of the inhabitants, and introduced non-Jewish colonists. The Samaritans who had been left in the land were faced by their Judean neighbors with charges of infidelity to Jewish tradition, but they and their descendants insisted on their national integrity and doctrinal purity, especially with reference to emphasis on the Pentateuch and maintenance of worship at Mt. Gerizim.

Verse 52 records Luke's only reference to the hostility of Samaritans toward Judeans, and John 4:9 indicates that the feeling was mutual. At Luke 10:33 and 17:16 Luke will record his own attitude toward them. The directive to the disciples to prepare the Samaritans for his visit echoes earlier notices of preparation (1:17, 76; 3:4) and is a sign of things to come. The totality of Israel, north and south, is to be reclaimed for God.

9:53. The Samaritans **would not receive** him, for he was headed toward Jerusalem. They would have preferred that he recognize Mt. Gerizim as the holy locale (see John 4:19–20). At Acts 7, Stephen will show that God does not locate in a specific spot, and the mission of Jesus will be liberated for worldwide outreach. But history records that the New Age conception of a church not bound to property and dispensable tradition meets with as little understanding from those intent on guarding turf as does Jesus' mission from the disciples.

Acts 8:14 will reverse what is said in Luke 9:53 of the Samaritans. Using the same verb *(dechomai)*, Luke records that they "received" God's message.

9:54. James and John once again display their misunderstanding and are prepared to exceed earlier directions about shaking the dust off their feet (9:5), whereas Jesus exemplifies the directive in 6:29. At 9:48 Jesus spoke of those who "receive" him, yet said nothing about those who rejected him. But James and John want to see apocalyptic fire rain down on the Samaritans. They share only too plainly the hostility of their compatriots. At the same time, there is a suggestion that Jesus demonstrate that he is a "man of God." The RSV marginal reading, "as Elijah did," calls to mind 2 Kings 1:9–12. Elijah said, "If I am a man of God, let fire come down from heaven" (2 Kings 1:12).

9:55–56. Jesus rebukes *(epitimaō)* the disciples, even as he had to rebuke demons. Jesus is an Elijah figure, but his pattern is not of destructive stripe (see 19:10), and he is under no compulsion to prove his intimate relationship with God. His fire is of a different order (see 12:49), but beneficence spurned will elicit destruction (cf. 21:20; Rev. 11:5). Luke's recital anticipates his record of the proclamation of the good news in Samaria (see Acts 1:8; 8:1–25; 9:31; 13:15). As were those responsible for Jesus' death (see Acts 3:12–26), so the Samaritans are entitled to another chance.

The RSV translators are on sound textual ground in relegating to the margin the addition to 9:55 that is found in some manuscripts (for the thought, cf. Luke 19:10).

On Rash Discipleship
Luke 9:57–62
(Matthew 8:19–22)

The previous rebuke to the disciples discouraged the thought that the Kingdom is a demonstration of force. Association with Jesus is not entry into a popularity contest. The three sayings that follow amplify the rigors imposed on the follower of Jesus. In ascending order they link the Son of humanity with the Elijah cycle, climaxing with a statement on the Kingdom.

9:57. The words **as they were going along** are Luke's editorial addition and are in keeping with his travel motif. The involvement of the disciples in the journey of Jesus anticipates Luke's frequent reference to the "way" in Acts.

9:58. Tiberius Gracchus once said of the poor: "The wild beasts roam over Italy and each one has his own hole and lair, but those who fight and die for Italy have only the light and the air as their portion" (Plutarch *Lives* 828c). Tiberius's imagery evokes pathos. In Luke's recital the hazard of association with Jesus is stressed, more along the lines of Sir. 36:26: "Who will trust a nimble robber that skips from city to city? Even so who shall trust a man who has no nest, and lodges wherever he finds himself at nightfall?"★

As the Son of humanity, Jesus is one who appears to offer nothing and is even a source of risk to his followers. In Luke's work, Jesus is never found "at home," as in Mark (2:1; 3:20; 7:17; 9:28). His Kingdom is not offered to the lowest bidder. He does not appeal to the baser motives of those who seek gain and advancement. And his own life style is the paradigm for those who will be made homeless because of the allegiance that he elicits. But Luke's auditors know how the story ends. This same homeless Son of humanity is the one who will one day be standing at the right hand of God to receive one of his courageous followers (see Acts 7:56).

9:59–60. The second reply runs counter to the prudential ethic espoused in Sir. 38:16–17. The saying is not to be softened by the suggestion that the man's father was either elderly or on the point of death. Jesus' Kingdom program permits no delays. One is not to imagine that Jesus precludes provision for support systems. The dead—that is, those who have no interests beyond their daily routines and will not risk a resurrection into creative enterprise—can take care of the deceased.

Like the Nazirite (Num. 6:6–8), disciples are to live in total commitment. Mark was one who had to learn the lesson (see Acts 13:13; 15:36–40). Many a would-be follower of Jesus has pleaded the requirements of social obligation or prior business demands as an excuse for not meeting the imperative of obedience. On the other hand, this saying offers no comfort to those who fail to take their familial obligations seriously and use devotion to church activities as an escape hatch.

9:61. The third request echoes the plea of Elisha, who requested permission from Elijah to bid farewell to his parents (1 Kings 19:19–21). Elijah gave him permission. Jesus tolerates no such temporizing. His authority is greater than Elijah's and the requirements of the Kingdom more rigorous.

9:62. The proverb about the distracted plower, who appears also in Greek literature (cf. Hesiod *Works and Days* 442–43) may have been stimulated by the observation in 1 Kings 19:19 that Elisha was plowing when Elijah cast his mantle on him. It is impossible to plow straight furrows while looking backward. Paul knew well the meaning of such words (Phil. 3:13), which appear to express a wisdom motif (cf. Sir. 38:25). Taken together, the stern words of Jesus are also a reminder to the church to be wary of the volunteer. The policy in Acts is to choose people "full of the Spirit" (Acts 6:3).

Mission of the Seventy
Luke 10:1–20
(Matthew 9:37–38; 10:7–16; 11:20–23)

Now that the requirements for disciples have been defined, the stage is set for the massive propaganda offensive described in Luke 10. Some of the details in the recital echo instructions given to the Twelve (9:1–6). Luke, who frequently avoids recitation of Mark's doublets, appears to have developed one of his own out of variant forms of a tradition. So complex is the history of the traditions that at 22:35 the dispatch of the Twelve is recollected in diction that recalls 10:4.

Luke's record of two groups engaged in proclamation meshes with his perception of bureaucratic flexibility as a basic ingredient of the New Age. Authorization for the mission is by no means limited to the Twelve.

10:1. Luke's choice of the numeral "seventy" (RSV margin: "seventy-two") and his bureaucratic terminology transmit much of the meaning of the entire passage. The Greek verb for "appointed" *(anadeiknymi)* is common in diplomatic contexts. Luke reserves the term for action by Jesus, as here, and by God at Acts 1:24. The cognate noun *(anadeixis)* appears in Luke 1:80, and the context requires God as the agent. These are the only occurrences in the NT. The implication is clear: Jesus functions as a head of state.

The fact that seventy envoys are involved suggests not only the authority of the Sender but the magnitude and urgency of his program. The term for "sent" is *apostellō,* a standard word in the Greco-Roman world for dispatch of messengers or envoys. Since Greco-Roman envoys were frequently sent out in pairs, Luke either himself conjectures that they were sent out **two by**

two or pounces on the datum found in his source. Those with an ear for Moses might have thought that Luke was emphasizing the envoys' responsibility as witnesses (cf. Deut. 19:15). But Luke's Greco-Roman public would hear in this a further accent on the magisterial action of Jesus. And after hearing of the pairings in Acts 8:14 (Peter and John); 13:2 (Barnabas and Saul); 15:39 (Barnabas and Mark); 15:40 (Paul and Silas), they would be reinforced in their understanding.

No end of speculation has surrounded the use of the term "seventy." In view of the Septuagintal aura surrounding much of Luke's structuring of the story of Jesus, it is not improbable that his predecessors or he, or both, when writing about Jesus' mission tactics, had recollections of Moses' appointment of seventy men of the elders of Israel to assist him in his work (Num. 11:16–17). Some of Luke's public might have recollected the numbers of the nations cited in Genesis 10 and thought in terms of Jesus' worldwide mission as developed in the Book of Acts. If this association with Genesis 10 was Luke's own view of the matter, one must assume that he wrote "seventy-two," which is the count of nations in the Septuagint version of Genesis 10 and is at the same time a reading that enjoys respected manuscript support. The fact is that we do not know what data were circulating in Luke's head when he formulated 10:1. Yet his text sends out clear signals.

In the light of all that has been recited earlier, climaxing in the transfiguration and subsequent events recited in Luke 9, the bureaucratese of 10:1 announces that here is one who transcends all leaders of nations, including Moses. Luke's public would therefore conclude from Luke's recital of the mission of the Seventy (Seventy-two) that the success of the empirewide apostolic mission had its basis in Jesus' vision of Israel saturated with proclamation of the Kingdom of God. "Seventy" signaled completeness, and the term would stimulate varieties of ways in which such completeness would find expression.

"Every," like the word "all," is one of Luke's favorite terms (both from *pas, pasa, pan*). Did Jesus actually intend to visit each of the cities to which his envoys went? To ask the question is to miss the point. Luke's public, accustomed to announcements of visits by imperial dignitaries, would note again the prestige of Jesus. His advance corps prepares for his arrival. And he is on the way to Jerusalem, the place from which the gospel goes out to the world. Luke 10 is the preview (see also 2:30–32; 3:6).

The word "others" (**seventy others**) is important. Luke is at pains to emphasize that the proclamation of the Kingdom is not limited to the efforts of the Twelve. As Elisha did with Gehazi (2 Kings 4:29–31), Jesus sends his disciples **on ahead** (see the same Greek expression in Luke 9:52: "And he sent messengers ahead of him" = "before his face," RSV).

10:2. Imagery relating to "harvest" *(therismos)* is used in Isa. 27:12–13, with reference to God's separation of the chaff from the grain in Israel. In Joel 3 the nations surrounding Israel are shown to be ripe for judgment. The motif of decisive moment is certainly present in Luke 10:1–16, but the stress is on God's claim to Israel. This is not an outreach to those who are so often pejoratively termed "heathen" or "pagan." From Luke's perspective, once Israel knows her destiny, she can fulfill the expectation expressed by Simeon (Luke 2:30–32). If the nation fails, workers will be found—among them, Paul (Acts 26:17–18). The truth of the text begins to be grasped when the contemporary church ponders the need for undergoing a harvesting process so that its sense of mission to the world may be refined.

The fruit to be harvested is bountiful, but the workers are "few." Yet Jesus did not lower the requirements for messengers (cf. 9:57–62). Success of the Kingdom is not to be bought at the price of mediocrity. The saying also reminds the church that her orders for messengers of the gospel are not limited to the patterns set by Jesus, whether those be the Twelve or the Seventy. That the institutional church should ever speak of overproduction of ministerial personnel is odd in the light of this text. That the church's approaches to ministerial functions and offices require constant reexamination is quite apparent. Yet it is not to be forgotten that the harvest belongs to God and not to the church (see the warning in Acts 20:28).

10:3. According to rabbinic tradition, a Roman emperor Hadrian once remarked to a rabbi that Israel was like a sheep among the seventy wolves (i.e., the nations of the world). Jesus' disciples are not invited to beds of ease. In advance they are warned of the perils. And one's own kin and institutional relatives can generate the most hazards. Christian proclamation worthy of its name is bound at some point to confront auditors with the challenges of the New Age. Nor is "prophetic ministry" something that can be consigned by ecclesiastical bureaus to a few nonconformists. These envoys described in Luke 10 are Jesus' total crew. It is truly anti-Semitic thinking which suggests that Israel required such call to decision, but not the church of latter days.

10:4. If they are concerned about their possessions, they have not read the job specifications. The variations in wording from Matthew's parallels (Matt. 10:9–10) reflect the homiletical application of Jesus' words in the preaching of Luke's day. Naturally the details would differ according to the situation. But the picture emerging is clearly that of a disciple who lives and works in total dependence on the Lord of the harvest (cf. Luke 22:35). Gehazi (2 Kings 4:29) was reminded by Elisha not to greet anyone along the way.

Oriental formalities can be time-consuming. Jesus, who transcends the ministry of Elijah and Elisha, sends out his messengers with no less urgency. This is the point of the saying, not that the disciple should pass up even a casual opportunity to share the good news. Since they have the power to walk on scorpions without hazard (see 10:19), they require no sandals. As 22:35 indicates, the absence of standard traveling equipment is to indicate their total dependence on the Sender. If the text reaches back into the very history of Jesus, it is not absurd to suggest that the meaning of the disciples' message was already conveyed by their very attire and total abandonment to divine beneficence. How the contemporary church may find such para-linguistic power of communication deserves careful consideration.

10:5. Jesus also tells his disciples what they are to say. The message of the good news should be their first word. There is no mention of a call to repentance, for the message is first of all good news of God's reign for Israel. In place of the ceremonial greetings, the messengers are to say, **Peace be to this house.** These were the instructions given by David to part of his band who were sent to Nabal (1 Sam. 25:6). The word "house" includes all the residents (cf. Acts 10:2; 16:15).

10:6. "Child of peace" is a Semitic expression meaning one who is not wickedly inclined but concerned about righteousness (cf. Isaiah 59), as would be displayed in willingness to receive the messenger. Nabal showed himself not a child of peace but a child of folly (1 Sam. 25:25), for he assaulted the messengers who were sent to him. Greco-Roman auditors would find the expression interestingly quaint, but its type not unparalleled in Hellenistic literature. For them the expression would signal one of the most precious bounties that could be bestowed by a head of state.

Jesus is at work wherever his disciples are. His efforts will bring out the secrets of people's hearts, and they will no longer be able to sit on the fence. For or against God? The reaction to Jesus' message will reflect where people really stand beneath their facade of religious ritual (cf. 2:35). The disciple's pronouncement of peace does not work magically. Only if there is a receptive mind will that peace be valid. If the mind-set is wrong, the peace that is pronounced will return to the disciple. That is, the intended recipient will lose the benefit.

10:7. Unlike itinerant philosophers who are alleged to have begged their way across the country, the disciples are to accept, as did Elijah (1 Kings 17:15) and Elisha (2 Kings 4:8), the hospitality of *one* house. They are not to create the impression of peddling God's wares for personal gain. On the other hand, they can hold their heads high as emissaries of the King. They need not be apologetic about accepting food and lodgings. Thus Luke clarifies for his own time the problem of the "paid worker."

10:8–9. Since Jewish dietary regulations would raise a problem for the church's missionaries (see Acts 15; cf. 1 Cor. 10:27), Luke points out that

Jesus' words envisioned removal of such scruples. Missionaries are to eat whatever is set before them, for their journeys will take them to homes of Pharisees as well as to those of the "poor." They are also to **heal the sick** (as did Elijah, 1 Kings 17:17–24) and to accompany their deeds of mercy with the pronouncement that the Kingdom of God has **come near** *(enggiken)* the recipients of their message, that is, has made its presence known in their midst (cf. Luke 11:20). The perfect tense of the Greek verb for "come near" means that the *process* of drawing near has now come to an end (compare the statements in Isa. 51:5 LXX, the present tense; and Ezek. 12:23 LXX, perfect tense). Thus Luke again affirms that the Kingdom is not to be defined in popular apocalyptic terms but can make its appearance even in the act of human proclamation.

10:10–11. Because the disciples displayed misunderstanding in the case of the Samaritan's rejection of Jesus, they require instruction on how to handle similar situations. Instead of calling down fire from heaven, they are to use a prophet's symbolic gesture and shake the dust off their feet (cf. 9:5; Acts 13:51). To some auditors this might have suggested that the city was viewed as a ritually unclean place. For those whose confidence was placed in Moses, this gesture would be most meaningful. The gesture is to be accompanied with the solemn announcement that their hearers have had encounter with the Kingdom.

10:12. To reject engagement with the New Age is a tragic invitation to judgment. **Sodom**, a paradigm for injustice, oppression, and exploitation (cf. Ezek. 16:49), would have an easier time than some of Israel's cities in the day of judgment. Israel's responsibility is all the greater, for her opportunities were unparalleled. Luke is not anti-Semitic, but later interpretation that remains at the surface level of his geographical references cannot escape censure. It is vital that today's readers of his Gospel grasp the meaning by reading their own city's name in place of Jerusalem.

10:13–14. Chorazin and Bethsaida, probably cities of some prosperity in the land of Israel, would be called to sterner account than *Tyre* and *Sidon,* for the former cities had received in vain the witness of Jesus' mighty deeds. "Sackcloth" is a reminder of judgment (Isa. 50:3). "Ashes" symbolize repentance (Job 42:6; Isa. 58:5). From the topics developed in OT prophetic declarations it can be inferred that the cities in question were not interested in conforming to the radical changes in thinking and life style proclaimed by Jesus. And, as Acts 19:38–44 will declare, divine offer of peace has disaster as its counterpart.

It does not appear that the statements in these verses comprise part of the proclamatory portfolio of the Seventy. Rather, they are drawn by Luke from Q and displayed here to illustrate the magnitude of responsibility that accompanies privileged receipt of the divine message. Luke's Greco-Roman public would note the outrageousness of such response to God's beneficence.

10:15. Capernaum, privileged recipient of Jesus' beneficence (see Luke 4:23), will suffer the fate of Babylon (cf. Isa. 14:13–15). These woes are a striking reminder of Luke 6:24–26. That they come from a Jewish tradition within the land of Israel indicates that the proclamation of the gospel is to take no account of national identity, rank, or status. It is not a placebo.

Those who thought, in erroneous perception of the kinds of thoughts that found expression in the Magnificat (1:51–53), that humiliation applied to outsiders and exaltation to insiders will receive a lesson in New Age protocol.

10:16. The disciples are not to take the rejection personally. Jesus accepts full responsibility for their mission, and it is he and his Parent who are ultimately rejected (see also John 5:23; 15:23). Thus the apostolic mission is clearly viewed as God's own effort.

Semitic ears would understand the principle that the one sent is to be treated as one would treat the sender. And Luke's Greco-Roman auditors would have no difficulty identifying with the sender whose envoys were mistreated. Julius Caesar noted that "all nations hold the name of envoy sacred and inviolate" (*Gallic War* 3.9). A nation that failed to make reparation after injury or insult had been sustained by an envoy from Rome could expect severe retaliation, including declaration of war (cf. Cicero *Against Verres* 2.1.79). The leading men of Illyria paid with their lives for Queen Teuta's assassination of one of Rome's legates who had rebuked her for her cavalier approach to piratical attacks on Rome's merchant marine (Polybios *History* 2.8.12). For a similar viewpoint on reprisal, see Acts 3:22–23.

Luke's perception of the two-stage demonstration of the Kingdom comes out clearly in Luke 10:9–16. The Kingdom of God can be present without apocalyptic fanfare. After the departure of Jesus, the People of God remain entrusted with the message of the Kingdom, and where that message goes the Kingdom comes. The destiny of human beings is ultimately decided in terms of their response to the message. But Luke's primary interest is to explain Israel's rejection of the apostolic proclamation. Jesus himself anticipated it, he says, and his followers are not to be disheartened. The apocalyptic moment will come—but not until the harvest has been garnered.

10:17. The seventy returned with joy. How thirty-five pairs of disciples happened to arrive with the same message and receive the same reply is not explained. As is frequently the case, Luke subordinates an accounting for details to exhibition of the dynamic kernel of the recital. Their address of Jesus as "Lord" *(kyrios)* is appropriate to the dignity of their mission. And they are delighted with their power over the demons. Unlike the experience of the Twelve (9:40), in their case it worked! "Joy" marks the New Age (see 1:14; 2:10; 6:3; Acts 8:8; 13:52; 15:3).

10:18. Luke's record of Jesus' answer is not only integral to the line of thought in vv. 17–20 but is a masterpiece of style: "Yes, I was watching Satan falling like lightning from heaven." In other words, "You were really in good form. Satan toppled over before your advances" (cf. Isa. 14:12; Rev. 12:9). But they say nothing about the proclamation of the Kingdom of God!

10:19. The devil's boast at 4:6 is once more exposed for all its hollowness. Jesus' own authority and power have been placed in his envoys' hands. But ability to exorcise is not to be a disciple's major ambition. It is possible for an emissary of the Lord to do mighty works in his name and yet lose the Kingdom (see Matt. 7:22, and cf. Luke 13:26).

Popular association of **serpents and scorpions** with sinister forces (cf. Ps. 91:13, and see also Gen. 3:15; Rev. 12:9) may account for Luke's reference to them in this verse. According to *Test. Levi* 18:12, the messianic high priest will bind Belial (Satan) and give his children power to tread on evil spirits. Acts 28:3–6 is perhaps the best clue to Luke's own understanding of Luke 10:19a.

10:20. Possession of spiritual powers is no guarantee of salvation. Even though they are given specialized authority, followers of Jesus are to reflect on the importance of having their names inscribed in the book of life (see, e.g., Exod. 32:32; Isa. 4:3; *Enoch* 47:3; Dan. 12:1; Rev. 3:5). The imagery is drawn from the ancient bureaucratic practice of maintaining lists of citizens. Jesus means that one must stand in a proper relationship to God, and that means in Luke's language to hear and keep Jesus' word (Luke 8:21).

Jesus Rejoices
Luke 10:21–24
(Matthew 11:25–27; 13:16–17)

Luke again marks a notable moment in Jesus' career by providing his public not only with a brief reference to Jesus at prayer but with the content of his devotion. Also distinctive is the fact that, unlike 3:21–22 and 9:29–35, where Jesus' sonship is affirmed by a heavenly voice in a context of prayer by Jesus, here in 10:21–22 Jesus himself affirms the fact and uses the occasion to extol his Parent's beneficence.

The saying in vv. 21–22 is paralleled in Matt. 11:25–27, but Luke omits from the common source Q the words of comfort for the heavily burdened (Matt. 11:28–30). In Luke's context they would be inappropriate, since his stress is on the disciples, whose names are written in God's book, in contrast to representatives of Israel's religious leadership who do not grasp the message. The succeeding narrative about the lawyer exhibits their blindness, and 10:38–42 reinforces Luke's conviction that Jesus is the source of true wisdom. See also 11:29–32, which is followed by a saying on light (vv. 33–36) and indictment of the Pharisees and the scribes (vv. 37–54).

Matthew's form of the saying (Matt. 11:25–30) follows Sirach 51 in its pattern of thought: (1) thanksgiving (Sir. 51:1); (2) God the source of wisdom (v. 17); (3) invitation (v. 23). An even closer parallel, but about a half century later than either Matthew's or Luke's Gospel, is to be found in a gnostic Hermetic tract, which reads:

> I believe and bear witness. Praise to you, O Father. You have delivered to me, your Son, the fullness of your power. For you have permitted yourself to be known, and through your revelation you have become known. This knowledge I share with people of worth, in accordance with your commandment. The unworthy close their minds to it. (See E. Norden, *Agnostos Theos* [1913], p. 293)

The anti-exclusive reformulation in Q of what appears to have been a widespread type of utterance was to Luke's liking. God reveals his mysteries (cf. 8:10) through Jesus. And he reveals them not to sophisticated initiates but to the unlearned. See also Psalm 111; 1 Cor. 1:21; and 1QH 7:26–27: "I [praise you, Lord], for you have given me understanding through your truth, and you have given me knowledge through your wonderful mysteries."

10:21. In that same hour he rejoiced in the Holy Spirit. The word "rejoiced" *(agalliaomai)* is typical of the New Age (see the cognate noun [agalliasis] in 1:14). Luke is frequently alleged to tone down Jesus' emotional life. Such is certainly not the case here. "Holy Spirit" is in contrast to the hostile spirits referred to in vv. 17–20. The Spirit is to be given in the messianic age to God's servant (Isa. 42:1).

One way to assert the truth of something is to express thanks for it (cf. Ps. 118:19–21 and, from a false perspective, the Pharisee's prayer in Luke 18:11). From the standpoint of Hebrew thought, God is the ultimate source of good and evil. If the wise and prudent (i.e., the learned theologians among the Jews; cf. 1QH 1:35), and the sophisticated of this world (cf. 1 Cor. 1:18–25; 2:1–16), do not accept the message, the disciple is assured that it is God's doing, not a deficiency in the message or in the disciple. The wordplay of the original might be rendered: "You have *concealed (apokryptō)* these things from the wise and prudent and *revealed (apokalyptō)* them to children." Simeon's words here find one of their numerous fulfillments.

The phrase "these things" (**that thou hast hidden these things from the wise**) includes the understanding that it is more important to have one's name in the book of life than to perform dazzling miracles (Luke 10:20). A sign-seeking generation would need to learn the lesson (11:29). Stoics, who claimed that only a wise man could be godly, would find it even more difficult. Christianity does not invite renunciation of the intellect, but participation in the Kingdom does not depend on intellectual resources. Jesus laid the ax on snob appeal. "Good pleasure" (*eudokia:* **gracious will**), as God's outreaching love, was used at 2:14. The cosmic perspective in the phrase **Lord of heaven and earth** (cf. Acts 4:24; 14:15; 17:24) finds here its saving counterpart.

10:22. The referent for **all things** is not defined by Luke, but some of his public must certainly have noticed an echo of 4:6 (cf. Dan. 7:13–14), and 9:22 affirms that Jesus' devotion expressed at 4:8 is not misplaced. Whereas those responsible for instruction in Israel would emphasize the role of tradition in their teaching, Jesus receives whatever wisdom he possesses and whatever authority he exercises in deed from the one Parent in heaven.

Since God's will comes to expression in Jesus, the Son of God, only the Parent knows the fullness of the divine intent in Jesus. Therefore the Parent must reveal it. Conversely, since Jesus is the chosen instrument to reveal the Parent, only the Son knows the scope of the Parent's will (cf. 2:49). The first of these propositions was supported after the baptism. At 3:22 Luke records God's own understanding of Jesus. The second proposition found endorsement at the transfiguration. Jesus was pronounced the sole revealer of the Parent, and the disciples are to listen to this Parent (9:35), for those to whom the Son wishes to reveal the Parent are the believers. In association with Jesus they become children of the heavenly Parent (cf. 6:36; Rom. 8:15–26; Gal. 4:5–7).

God's loving concern and willingness to bestow forgiveness is not an intellectual datum but a reality in Jesus Christ. Hence Paul puts being known by God ahead of his own knowledge (1 Cor. 8:3; 13:12; Gal. 4:9).

10:23. The words **Then turning to the disciples, he said privately** are added to a Q passage (see Matt. 13:16–17). This addition suggests that Luke understands the prayer in vv. 21–22 as an unspoken kind of meditation, permitting at this point easy introduction of a related thought from another portion of his source. That Luke has shifted attention here from the Seventy to the Twelve is by no means certain. Luke's point is that the disciples—and from his post-Pentecost perspective, this would mean the Christian believers—are the recipients of the revelation discussed in v. 22. The formulation of the beatitude is similar to those in 6:20–22.

10:24. The reference to the **many prophets** (e.g., Isa. 9:1–7) **and kings** (cf. Isa. 60:3) focuses attention on the magnitude of the blessing enjoyed. There is no esoteric knowledge yet to be revealed, no "secrets of the pyramids." Those who are associated with Jesus and hear his word have the knowledge that counts in the New Age. The subsequent account portrays a priest and a Levite immobilized by untimely concern for traditional rules and regulations. Jesus' disciples, on the other hand, experience the blessing of liberation in the New Age. To Luke's Greco-Roman public the words "see" and "hear" would suggest deed and word, the word pair that signals the manifestation of excellence.

Misunderstanding

Luke 10:25–42

Despite their lack of status in learned circles, the disciples possess knowledge that was beyond the reach of ancient prophets. Luke now goes on to show how Jesus endeavors to provide remedial instruction for a legal expert who instead of listening carefully to Jesus tries to justify himself. The story about a Samaritan who went to the aid of an injured traveler is Jesus' answer to the lawyer's question about action. A recital about two women named Martha and Mary reinforces the importance of attention to Jesus' message.

A Lawyer

Luke 10:25–37

A Lawyer's Question

Luke 10:25–29
(Mark 12:28–34; Matthew 22:35–40)

10:25. Luke's omission of Mark 12:28–34, with the exception of a portion of v. 34, at 20:40 of his Gospel, permits him at that point in his recital to show Jesus on the offensive. By positioning here in his tenth chapter an account similar to Mark's story Luke is able to exhibit an example of the kind of lack of understanding displayed by those who are ordinarily considered to be among the "wise" (*sophoi*, v. 21). So remarkable is the contrast that Luke introduces the story with the phrase **And behold.** "Lawyer" (*nomikos*) is Luke's alternate term for scribe. It denotes an expert in the law of Moses. The phrase **put him to the test** ("tempting him"; *ekpeirazō*, used elsewhere by Luke only in 4:12) is not found in Mark 12:28. It augments the contrast between him and the disciples, with a suggestion of hostility. He would have done better had he formulated his question along the lines of John's inquirers (Luke 3:10–14) and simply asked, "What shall I do?" Instead, he attaches a rider about inheriting **eternal life** through a program, as he shortly indicates, of selective virtue (cf. 18:18).

10:26–27. In Matt. 22:36 and Mark 12:29 Jesus answers a question about the chief commandment. Here the lawyer asks about inheriting eternal life and is in turn queried by Jesus in typical rabbinic debate. Jesus in effect asks, "What does the constitution say?" The lawyer quite appropriately derives his answer from Deut. 6:5 and Lev. 19:18. The double command is also found in *Test. Issachar* 5:2 and *Test. Dan* 5:3, but problems connected with the textual history of these documents preclude determination of the direction of influence.

Reference to the various parts of a human being does not depend for its meaning on detailed diagnosis. Verse 27 is thoroughly Semitic in its expression of the totality of one's being. God is to absorb all our resources, and the neighbor is to be entrusted with the love we have for ourselves. Self-love is not to be denied or disparaged. On the other hand, the rule "Love your neighbor as yourself" can easily lead to casuistry. One can say, "I do not wish my neighbors to interfere in my life, and I will not interfere in theirs." Or one may, as the lawyer does, first try to secure a definition of "neighbor." Prolonged debate and routine routing to committee are the time-honored methods of shunning collective and individual responsibility. To Luke's Greco-Roman public the Semitic formulation would clearly signal the basic characteristics of virtuous people: piety (in relation to God) and uprightness (in relation to others).

10:28–29. Jesus now challenges the lawyer to action (cf. 7:43): **Do this, and you will live.** These words are in accordance with Jesus' repeated admonition: "Hear the word and keep it." The lawyer, though, needs to learn that to observe the will of God he must transcend the thinking of his own rule-oriented establishment. Otherwise he will remain on the level of self-justification (cf. 16:15; 18:19–21). Objective yardsticks for behavior, with the rules closely defined, make it possible for any person to be a paragon of virtue. But on the basis of love, God alone is in a position to judge. The lawyer therefore seeks a more definable criterion.

Once determined, the neighbor and a thousand other intrusions on one's privacy can be eliminated. All the bother of independent decision can be cleared out. Time-honored cultural patterns can be maintained. For stability is dependent on definition. Hence scribes have a socially significant assignment. But if one follows Jesus' line of thinking, what future is there for the scribal profession? That was the lawyer's problem. The Christian minister usually hears it this way: "Be concerned about social issues, but not too close to home. It might affect the church's income. Preach the gospel." In brief: "I am willing to love my neighbor as myself, but don't get me involved with the wrong neighbors." Divestment programs relating to a far-off place are far more popular for people of the United States than is invitation to engagement in processes for local justice.

Story of the Good Samaritan   Luke 10:30–37

One might have expected Jesus to make a Samaritan the object of a Jew's concern but not the principal actor in the story. For according to much popular Jewish tradition a non-Israelite was not thought of in the same neighborly terms as one who shared Jewishness. But it is possible to transcend national preference and yet not have real neighborly concern. A respectable Samaritan might even merit a scribe's help (cf. Rom. 5:7). The problem of the lawyer requires a deeper probe. He needs to see the phoniness of cult without love, of legal adherence without awareness of the spirit.

Eyes that were opened to the New Age would have no difficulty in seeing that the narrow definition of neighbor as a consociate Jew is old wine (cf. Luke 5:37, and see on 9:52–53). Hence the answer is confined to a problem within the lawyer's own peer group, priests and Levites. But the story does not permit one to take sides. Up to the end of v. 32, auditors of the parable, as Luke relates it, might have thought to themselves: "That's the way religious leaders are. Don't want to get involved. Give it to 'em, Jesus." But with the introduction of the Samaritan even those who side with the wounded man, ignored as he is by the religious system, are compelled to look at themselves afresh. The Samaritan is the outsider, and the sympathizers of the wounded man are now the insiders along with the priest and the Levite.

If a modern audience is to grasp the impact of the story with some of the force it had in Luke's time, one must provide it with a change in cast: for example, a bishop and a professor, a citizen who is robbed while on business and a communist. Neither Jesus nor Luke permits cheap identification with the Samaritan.

10:30. The road from **Jerusalem to Jericho** ran for about thirty kilometers and was notorious for its hazards. Attacks by punks were frequent. Gnaeus Pompeius (Pompey), enemy of crime, organized or private, made war on them (Strabo 16.2.41). From the fact that Jesus makes much of the help of the Samaritan, it is probable that auditors of the story are to view the victim as a Jew, but in the network of the story he becomes in effect Anyperson.

10:31–32. The term **by chance** (the first Greek words of v. 31) opens possibilities of understanding for the auditors of the story. For one of life's privileges is the exercise of choice. Both priest and Levite were traveling from Jerusalem. Hence they were not on the way to discharge heavy religious obligations. Whether they nevertheless feared contamination from a person who might be dead (cf. Leviticus 19 and Numbers 19) the text does not say. Nor is it suggested that they themselves were concerned that they might be robbed. Any speculation about their reasons is irrelevant. This is a story, and the story focuses attention on their basic malady—a lovelessness that finds comfort in distance. Luke may at the same time be pointing out that popular theories of retribution lead to callousness toward one who in the judgment of religious experts must be a *sinner* (cf. Luke 13:1–5). The man's fate was proof of that! Independently of each other—so pandemic is the malady—both priest and Levite pass on the other side to avoid encounter. And the text carefully notes that both men **saw him.** Someone has facetiously suggested that they were in a rush to attend a meeting on making Jericho Road safe for travelers.

Arthur Hugh Clough, who resigned his post at Oxford rather than subscribe to the Thirty-nine Articles of the Church of England, captured the thought in a poem titled "The Latest Decalogue":

Thou shalt not kill; but need'st not strive
Officiously to keep alive.

10:33. The first word in Luke's Greek sentence identifies the third traveler with explosive force: Samaritan. The evangelist's clipped grammar embosses the scene. Of the Levite it was said that he came, he saw, he passed by. Of the Samaritan it was said that he came, he saw, he pitied. The verse can be rendered: "Then a certain Samaritan who was traveling came upon the man. When he saw him, he felt pity."

10:34–35. The Samaritan (see on 9:53) had good reason to keep moving. He had an ass (RSV: **beast**) and money (RSV: **denarii**) and was therefore a man of means and a target for robbers. It may be presumed that he too was acquainted with the Mosaic provisions concerning contraction of impurity. But as a story figure he knows more. Despite the fact that he sees what the others had seen, he responds with compassion, as did his ancestors centuries earlier (2 Chron. 28:8–15) and as God did to Jerusalem when the city weltered in her own blood (Ezek. 16:5–14).

He poured on **oil and wine.** Oil would serve as a salve and wine as a disinfectant. At the hotel (*pandocheion;* see 2:7, where *katalyma* is used) he remains with the man. Inns of that time were worse than five-dollar-a-night hotels in the United States. And innkeepers were not generally noted for their humanitarian sentiments. Therefore the Samaritan makes a generous down payment of what amounts to two days' normal wages, with the assurance that he will pay the balance on his return. The pronoun "I" is emphatic: "I, not the man, will pay." He takes all precautions to ensure good service for the wounded man and at the same time preserves him from indebtedness.

Of Jesus it was said that he loved his own to the end (John 13:2). Like the Good Samaritan, he qualified for Aristotle's definition of the truly great and distinguished person—"An artist in generosity" (*Nikomachean Ethics* 4.2.5). "Petty calculation is dowdy," commented the same philosopher (4.2.8). A casual Good Samaritan will do the spectacular emergency deed as a kind of sentimental reaction, but when the needy one becomes a burden or makes demands on time, a quick exit is sought. Public officials know the do-gooder, the self-serving humanitarian, who will not follow through, the "baskets at Thanksgiving" type, the enthusiasm that falters when political patterns change and benevolences begin to shrink with loss of pew patronage. But this Samaritan kept a vigil through the night and did not leave his "neighbor" to chance assistance. He acted as God did toward Jerusalem, and his action is the commentary on Hos. 6:6: divine compassion is the model for neighborly love (see Luke 1:50, 54, 58, 72, 78; cf. 7:13).

10:36. Jesus goes beyond the biblical definition of Leviticus 19 in his correction of the initial question: "Who was neighbor to that man?" The lawyer's question had been wrongly phrased. Not, Who is qualified for my help? But, What need can I meet? Love, not law or social strata, determines the choice of neighbor. Love finds a way out of cozy refuge in rules and regulations into a life of imaginative and innovative enterprise. Ministers have been known to be informed by the ruling body in their congregations that certain types of "converts" are not their kind of people. This text provides the chance for a better way.

10:37. The lawyer had asked what he might do to inherit eternal life. Jesus answers: "Do this and you will live." Verse 37 provides the commentary: "Go, and see that you make a habit of doing likewise." In Greek the present tense of the imperative *(poreuo)* and the emphatic "you" *(su poiei)* are of the essence, and both are obscured by the RSV. Adopt this Samaritan's way of thinking! It is a reminder of Luke 6:31–36. Divine mercy does not ask the worth of the recipient. It only sees the need. Herein lies the creative possibility for action not measured by rules for neighborly behavior. The lawyer broke his own law through his casuistry. The Samaritan kept it. Those who hear and do Jesus' word are like a person who builds on rock (6:47–49).

Martha: One Thing Needful   Luke 10:38–42

Just as the story about the ill-mannered Simon (7:36–50) was followed by a vignette about women who ministered to Jesus and his followers (8:1–3), and then by a parable on the proper hearing of the word (8:4–15). Similarly the story of the unsympathetic priest and Levite is followed by a recital that blends the theme of service with interest in Jesus' word, which is registered by Luke on an equal plane with the OT quoted by the lawyer (cf. 10:24; 11:28).

10:38. Since the home of Martha and Mary, friends of Jesus, was located at Bethany (John 11:1; 12:1–8), and since Luke is not yet prepared to announce Jesus' arrival at this village located so close to Jerusalem, in harmony with his journey theme announced in 9:51, he speaks vaguely of "a certain village." Here Martha "welcomed" Jesus *(hypodechomai;* RSV: **received**, as in Luke 19:6; Acts 17:7). This stress on hospitality is in keeping with the thematic tone of chapter 10.

10:39. In Acts 22:3, Paul is said to have sat at the feet of Gamaliel. Here Mary sits at the feet of Jesus **and listened to his teaching** *(ton logon autou).*

The lawyer learned his lesson from Jesus, and this account underlines the fact that Jesus is the authoritative Teacher for Israel. The title **Lord** *(kyrios)* would remind the community of the resurrected Lord. Of extraordinary significance, and in keeping with the spirit of the New Age, is the recognition—in contrast to later rabbinic and ecclesiastical attitudes—that a woman is as much entitled as a man to receive instruction from an eminent teacher of divinity. Martha, in turn, is offered liberation from dependency on household routines as a prime instrument for evaluating female identity.

In general, the text puts under scrutiny any and all prejudice and practice that stereotypes women into a second-class role in religious circles or in society in general. Certainly the paucity of references to female scholars in the history of biblical research and pedagogy is an abiding source of scandal: such accomplished scholars as Anna Maria von Schurman (17th century) and Helen Spurrell (19th century), to cite but two, go unnoticed in many discussions of the history of interpretation or Bible translations.

10:40. Martha appears to be acting in harmony with the picture of the women sketched in 8:1–3 (cf. 7:44–45), but she is in effect embarrassing her distinguished guest by an obvious demonstration of the trouble to which his visit had put her. Besides, she upbraids him for his lack of consideration and implies that Jesus ought to have reminded Mary to help her. At 18:9–14 Luke will unveil another instance of self-justification at the expense of another. Had Martha given more thought to what it means to love the Lord, she would have considered it a privilege to do all the serving herself. Unfortunately she measures her own performance, as does the Pharisee in 18:9–14, against lack of performance in others.

10:41–42. Martha would have to learn the lesson set down in the Sermon on the Plain (6:41–42). Paul had a similar reminder for the Christians at Corinth (1 Cor. 7:34). The double mention of Martha's name reflects the sensitivity of the narrator (cf. 22:31; Acts 9:4). All this hubbub needs to be toned down. The wit in Jesus' dialogue is a choice bit of stylistic relief of the tension built up in the narrative: **One thing is needful.** And Jesus has provided it. If the marginal reading of the RSV ("few things are needful, or only one") is adopted, the point would be: An olive or two will now suffice, for the main course has already been served. In contrast to Martha's involvement in many things, Mary has had the "best course" (RSV: **good portion**), and it cannot be taken away from her. Jesus has beneficently dispensed the banquet of life, for Mary has been treated to his word (v. 39). And blessed are those who hear the word of God and keep it (8:21). In the end it is Mary who, as J. Duncan Derrett observed (p. 170) renders Jesus the type of service that was denied him by Martha.

Martha made the mistake of thinking that she was the host and Jesus the guest. It was the other way around (see 5:32; 12:37); and both Zacchaeus

(19:1–10) and two men from Emmaus (24:13–32) will find their role as hosts preempted. As 22:27 notes, the Son of humanity came not to be served but to serve.

The lawyer had come to find the answer to his legal problem. Jesus' word to Mary and Martha is an answer also to the scribe and a constant source of life for the church. With this understanding, the church can avoid the impasse of activism without love. At the same time, those who are alert to the sounds of this text will not immobilize Mary in a role of passivity. The word of Jesus is designed to prepare one for responsible action. In the last analysis, Luke's recital declares that the fruits of salvation, as is apparent, for example, in Zacchaeus's case (19:8–9), grow out of salvation that is received in and through the Word (cf. 8:4–8, 11–15). Thus Luke's association of the story of Mary and Martha with that of the Good Samaritan illustrates well his grasp of the challenge of Jesus' address to any process of dehumanization under the guise of religion. And those among Luke's auditors who were familiar with tales of notoriously sumptuous banquets would catch a note of satire in Luke's sketch of Jesus' invitation to simplicity. For the church of Luke's time the hospitality accorded Jesus as an itinerant proclaimer served as a model for the treatment of missionaries and suggests the important role that house churches played in the spread of Christianity.

Of Good and Evil Spirits

Luke 11:1–28

On Prayer and the Holy Spirit

Luke 11:1–13

The Lord's Prayer

Luke 11:1–4
(Matthew 6:9–13)

The story of Mary and Martha focused attention on Jesus as teacher. Luke continues this theme, and prayer is the first topic (11:1–13). Jesus' own communication with his Parent (10:21–22; 11:1) eminently displays his credentials for instructing others on the subject.

11:1. The words *kai egeneto* ("and it came to pass"; omitted by the RSV) and the fact that Jesus is at prayer alert the reader to a fresh development in the narrative. Legal casuistry and Jesus' authoritative word were contrasted in 10:25–42. Now dependence on God, with receipt of the Spirit, is contrasted with a charge that Jesus is in league with an evil demon (11:14–23). At 5:33 the Pharisees had said that John taught his disciples to pray. Luke takes the present occasion in his travel document to point out that Jesus also instructed his own disciples on this matter. The *Psalms of Thanksgiving (Hodayot)* and 1QS 10—11 provide samples of the type of prayers used in some Jewish sectors about the time of Jesus. Luke himself exhibits improvisations modeled after the Hebrew psalms (see Luke 1).

Romans 8:15 and Gal. 4:6 may indicate that the Lord's Prayer early in apostolic times became a liturgical formulation, but the evidence is inconclusive. Many of the variations, as attested by a comparison of Luke's version with that in Matthew and by the different readings of the manuscripts, are the result of liturgical adaptation. In the case of Luke's version, concern for comprehension by a non-Jewish public probably accounts for some of the variations. Which are prior to Luke and which are the result of Luke's editorial work cannot be determined with certainty.

11:2. Formulations of personalized address of God as **Father** are used in Hellenistic circles (cf. Sir. 23:1, 4; Wisd. of Sol. 14:3; 3 Macc. 6:3, 8) but appear to lack the intimate tone of Luke 11:2. The older literature also speaks of God as Father, but descriptively as guardian of the entire people or of groups within the nation (Deut. 32:6; Ps. 68:5; Isa. 63:16; 64:8; Jer. 3:4; Mal. 1:6; 2:10). Neither the writings of Qumran nor those of the OT contain examples of the type of personal address found in Luke 11:2.

In Aramaic the word here rendered "Father" is *abba*. The preservation of the word *abba* in Rom. 8:15 and Gal. 4:6 suggests that this expression was used by Jesus himself (see also Mark 14:36). Luke naturally avoids an Aramaic word in a document designed for Greek-speaking publics, some of whom would be familiar with the term "father" in reference to Zeus. But apart from the recognition that God is responsible for the well-being of humanity, all other features in the prayer would remain singularly Jewish in their outlook.

Through the term "Father" *(patēr)*, Jesus encouraged his disciples to understand God, not as one far removed from their existence but as one who could be known intimately as their own fathers (see on 10:22). It is a term in keeping with his stress on the faith of the child (18:15–17). In its simplicity it contrasts with the more fulsome formulations used in some Jewish and Greco-Roman prayers. To Greco-Romans who recalled Plato's views in the *Timaios* (28c), the invitation to intimacy would be arresting. For the revered philosopher had declared that the Maker and Father of all creation's fabric is difficult to find and that, once found, it is impossible to speak of this deity to all the people.

The fact that Jesus encourages the disciples to use the same term that he himself used in address of God is in keeping with his general resistance to religious cant. On the other hand, familiarity does not spell contempt, for the disciple is to pray that God's name be holy (RSV: **hallowed**).

A name in antiquity meant more than mere identification. The totality of the person was understood in a formulation of this type. The nature of God's being is revealed through God's association with people and through their response to divine direction. When God's people violate divine ordinances, they bring God's name or person into disrepute (see Rom. 2:24; Isa. 52:5; Ezek. 36:20). At Isa. 52:5 a word transliterated "blaspheme" is used in the Greek version *(blasphēmeō)*. Blasphemy is the opposite of treating God's name as holy, a subject to be taken up in Luke 11:14–20. But Isa. 52:6 goes on to state that God's name will be known "in that day."

Luke's emphasis on Jesus' directions for prayer is a part of his instruction that Jesus is the one who introduces the New Age, a distinctive mark of that age being a fresh understanding of God as Parent. He, the Son of God, is especially equipped to reveal the Parent's purpose for them (cf. 19:21–22). **Hallowed be thy name**, then, is another aspect of Jesus' constant reminder: "Blessed are those who hear the word of God and keep it" (cf. Lev. 11:45). Not to hallow God's name is to repeat the mistake of those in Israel who were unfaithful to the One who wanted to be called Father (Jer. 3:19–20). The genes are to show. The death of God takes place when Christian profession is not matched by performance, when the children of God give no indication of the style of their parentage.

"Let your kingdom come" is another way of realizing the holiness of God's name. God's kingdom, the divine mode of politics, destroys the work of Satan (see Luke 11:17–20). God's political presence is experienced in the person of Jesus and the proclamation of the good news, the constitution for the New Age. But the disciples are to pray for its expression especially in their own existence, and for its full implementation at the end of the end time.

The petition is not out of harmony with Luke's two-stage view of the Kingdom. Some manuscripts have in place of this petition the words "Let your Holy Spirit come on us and cleanse us" (see also 1QH 3:21). The thought is in harmony with Luke's subsequent stress on the donation of the Spirit, but the change may well represent post-Luke clarification that gained liturgical status and displaced the petition for the Kingdom. More important, though, is the witness of this variation to the church's liturgical freedom of its boldness in revising even the words of Jesus.

The Lord's Prayer was not meant to be a rigid formulation but a guide for the petitioner. The church today is also at liberty to modify, revise, and restate the Lord's Prayer in terms that will not require such elaborate clarification as these comments aim to accomplish. Yet liturgical commissions know how strongly people can feel and react to any tampering with time-hallowed phrases. In this respect some Christians are much like the sponsors of official ancient Roman religion, who placed much emphasis on syllable-for-syllable recitation of traditional prayers, some of whose words were no longer intelligible to any but the most learned votaries. They also fall under the same type of judgment that they inflict on alleged tradition-bound Jews of Jesus' day.

The petition "Your will be done" (in Matt. 6:10) may not have formed part of the original prayer. But Luke knows it as a firm element in the tradition concerning Jesus' prayer life (see Luke 22:42 and cf. Acts 21:14).

11:3. In the petition concerning "daily bread" Jesus exhorts his disciples to live in complete trust and dependence on their heavenly Parent. The Kingdom of God takes precedence over the claims made by any institutions, and anxiety over things (10:38–42) will frustrate its objectives. Jesus himself had given the disciples a demonstration of God's concern for them when he sent them out without extra provisions (see 10:4, and cf. 22:35). Now he tells them to pray for the bread they need "for the day," and no more. Today is the day! Having rebuffed the devil in connection with this subject on an earlier occasion (4:3–4), Jesus speaks magisterially.

What does the petition mean today? Churches saddled with heavy debts find themselves unable to carry out more needed missions of compassion. Involvement in commitment to high-risk ventures in social justice goes under review. Potential income determines choice of vocation for young men and women. The temptations are many. The wonder is that anyone today dares pray this petition! In subsequent chapters Luke presents the commentary on the petition (see, e.g., 12:16–21; 21:1–4).

11:4. The words of the petition on forgiveness for **every one who is indebted** are an echo of the themes expressed in 6:31–38. The thought is not that God should be as compassionate as the disciples are in their relationships to their associates. On the contrary, disciples can pray for forgiveness from God only if they understand that such forgiveness binds them to every human being in similar obligation. The word "every one" (*panti*) is emphatic. Luke sounds the Greco-Roman pandemic, or universal, note. God makes no distinctions; neither can the disciple. No one is to be excluded, and no score is to be kept (cf. 17:1–4). The petition is therefore a promise to God to take care of unfinished business. The mercy of God creates the climate for the disciple's growth in socially responsible behavior.

The concluding petition is a reminder to the disciples that they have good reason to ask for forgiveness instead of keeping score of wrongs done to them. Background for association of temptation with the petition for daily bread is found in Exod. 16:4: "Behold, I will rain bread from heaven for you; and the people shall go out and gather a day's portion every day, that I may prove them, whether they will walk in my law or not." Disciples who pray for bread only sufficient for the day are in reality affirming their commitment to the divine purpose.

Luke himself explains in 22:40 and 46 what is meant by the phrase **lead us not into temptation**: we are to pray that we may not enter into temptation. The best intention may fail of fulfillment. Peter, like a piece of wood snatched from the burning, found this out to his sorrow (see 22:31–32; 22:61–62, and cf. 22:46). Humility is therefore becoming to disciples as they ask their heavenly Parent to preserve them from the consequences of their own self-confidence. The words are a reminder of what was said at 8:13; and the fact that the demonic world has been vanquished (see 11:20) ought to sharpen the disciples' sense of responsibility.

Through this prayer recorded in vv. 2–4 Jesus again signals the advance of a New Age. Litany, he demonstrates, need not be sepulchral. And to our own age, which *communicates* less even while it *talks* more, the brevity is refreshing.

The Friend at Midnight   Luke 11:5–8

11:5. The Lord's Prayer lists a series of requests that might appear impossible to meet. Something more than human power is needed. Luke assures the church that superhuman resources are indeed available—the Holy Spirit (v. 13). The rhetorical question in vv. 5–7 advances an extreme situation in order to make that assurance stand out more strongly. The **three loaves** requested may be a normal ration. Jesus' sense of humor is reflected in the hilarious description that follows.

11:6–7. Palestinian homes were not large, and a single bedroom would suffice for the family. After stumbling over his children, the host would have to remove the huge timber that locked the door, but not without considerable effort and noise. The prospect is unbearable, and the friend shouts out that he cannot come.

11:8. But the man persists with his request. Soon the whole town will be up. Not friendship, but desperation to secure at least some night's rest prompts the donation. The man has won his plea because of his refusal to take no for an answer. The translation calls it **importunity,** but the Greek means "shamelessness." Luke does not, of course, suggest that God is as hard to move with a request as was this groggy friend. On the contrary, as the following series of sayings is quick to point out, God is anxious to give. Jesus' auditors enjoyed the humor. On the lookout for a syllogism, some dour commentators have not been able to risk a smile. To the biblically informed, the parable was in effect a commentary on Psalm 44.

Answer to Prayer   Luke 11:9–13
                                                                 (Matthew 7:7–11)

Luke continues the theme of persistence in prayer, but the purpose in such emphasis is to establish the main point, that God is fantastically beneficent.

11:9. The three imperatives (**ask, seek, knock**) in this verse emphasize the urgency to ask now for God's gifts and thereby gain what is expressed in the Lord's Prayer.

11:10. The pandemic aspect (**for every one who asks receives**) of divine beneficence would impress Luke's Greco-Roman public. In Acts 10, Luke will expand on this theme in connection with a centurion and his petitions.

Should the disciples fail to ask for and use the Father's gifts, they will find themselves as beggars without recourse (see the warning, with similar terminology, in 13:25–30).

11:11–13. *Patēr* ("father") in v. 11 echoes the directive to address God as Father (v. 2). The variant about the stone listed in the margin of the RSV comes from the parallel account in Matt. 7:9. For the snake and scorpion pair, see Deut. 8:15. Occasionally a fisher will catch a snake; and a scorpion, when rolled up, may look like an egg. God, says Jesus, is not less fatherly than are the disciples; and the heavenly Parent does not play practical jokes. The argument is typical of rabbinic reasoning. One argues from the lesser to the greater in the formula "If this, how much more this." In fact, though, there is no comparison between God and the disciple. Even the non-Christian Juvenal (10.350) said, "Dearer is a man to the gods than to himself."

Disciples are **evil** or second class (*ponēroi;* cf. 6:35). That is, in comparison to God they must say, as did Peter, "I am a sinful person" (5:8★). On the other hand, disciples know how to give good gifts. The Father in heaven, then, will most certainly give the best of all—the **Holy Spirit**! But one must want that gift. The word "Holy" before "Spirit" is not a mere formality. The disciples have been declared "evil." The Holy Spirit comes to make the changes described in the Lord's Prayer. The Spirit is available not only to theological bluebloods but also to the "poor" in the land (see on 6:20). Ultimately, not ritualistic observance but obedience from one who is a hearer and a keeper of Jesus' word is among the primary criteria of the New Age. And those who receive the gift of the Spirit must know that it is given to carry out the mission of Israel (cf. 24:44–48; Acts 1:8).

On Evil Spirits   Luke 11:14–28

Controversy on Exorcism   Luke 11:14–20
(Mark 3:20–26; Matthew 12:24–28)

11:14. Appropriate to the theme of petition is the introduction of a man who suffers from a demon, curiously described as mute (*kōphon;* the RSV's "dumb" displays insensitivity to those who suffer from deafness and associated disabilities). The demon is characterized by the effects it has on the man. In Luke 7:22 the cure of mutes is a sign of the New Age. This is in fulfillment of Isa. 35:6. The mute man had been kept from sharing Israel's liturgical life. Now he is able to speak. Matthew underlines the interruption in communication with the observation that he was also blind.

11:15. Despite his close relationship with the Father and his attack on the demonic world, Jesus is charged by some in the "crowds" *(ochloi)* with being in league with **Beelzebul, the prince of demons** *(tō archonti tōn daimoniōn)* and probably to be identified with Satan. Whereas Matthew defines the opposition as Pharisees, Luke, who is more kindly disposed to them but inclines to show them hung up on legal niceties, suggests that such a challenge may come from any quarter.

11:16. Others . . . sought from him a sign from heaven. They want a special demonstration—such as Gideon asked of the Lord (Judg. 6:36–40)—to establish Jesus' credentials. A parallel in modern times is the criticism that the Christian message is invalidated by the fact that the church has been unable to eradicate war and injustice. The principal flaw in the criticism is a confusion of the message with institutional forms that have at times distorted the message. Luke observes that the request was in the nature of a temptation (**to test him**). Ironically, while Jesus casts out a demon, this portion of the crowd takes over Beelzebul's or Satan's specialty (cf. Luke 4:2).

11:17–19. Jesus uses three arguments to refute the complaint concerning alleged alliance with Beelzebul. The first appears in vv. 17–19. **Satan** (apparently Luke's own definition of the name Beelzebul) would not permit rebellion in his own ranks. That would spell the dissolution of his regime. By ascribing a kingdom to Satan, Jesus asserts his own superior political claims. Verse 19 presents the second argument. Other Jewish exorcists are at work (cf. Josephus *Antiquities* 8.2.5; and in general, SB 4.1:501–35).

The opposition has taken God out of the picture. Very well, asks Jesus, "If I [*ei de ego;* the pronoun is emphatic] am using Beelzebul as an ally, whom do your sons employ?" The succeeding verse suggests that the Lord has in mind the magicians summoned by Pharaoh to duplicate the feats of Moses and Aaron (Exod. 7:11). The sons of the opposition would not want to be placed in that category. **Therefore**, says Jesus, **they shall be your judges.** That is, they will instruct you properly. (On the judge as a possessor of wisdom, see Sir. 10:1.)

The use of the present tense of *ekballō* (**I cast out**) may refer to the frustrated attempts of the exorcists, who would use much mumbo jumbo. Jesus effected his cures with a single command. Hence other exorcists would readily recognize his superior power. If, then, devils were to be expelled with the help of Satan, why do they come out with such reluctance when other exorcists are at work (cf. 9:40)? Furthermore, why was it Jesus who had to expel the demon from the mute man? Why did they not do it? The argument of the opposition, suggests Luke, is patently ridiculous on any estimate of the circumstances.

11:20. The third argument is to the effect that God's reign is in process.

Jesus replaces Moses. Pharaoh's magicians could duplicate only the first two plagues of blood and frogs (Exod. 7:14—8:7), but they would have been better advised to eliminate the amphibians. The production of gnats stumped them (Exod. 8:18), and they were forced to confess, "This is the finger of God" (Exod. 8:19). Apparently they were making reference to Aaron's staff. In Luke 11:20, as in Exod. 31:18 and Deut. 9:10, the **finger of God** refers to divine power. Jesus was to accomplish an exodus at Jerusalem (Luke 9:31). His exorcisms are among the signs that anticipate that climactic event. They are evidence that the Kingdom of God has made its appearance. In the context these words suggest that divine politics can spell either success or disaster for human beings. Those who oppose Jesus are moving on a collision course.

The Strong and the Stronger   Luke 11:21–26
(Mark 3:27; Matthew 12:29–30, 43–45)

11:21–22. In Mark's version (3:27) and in Matthew's version (12:29–30) of the first part of this series of sayings, Jesus is viewed as the one who enters the house of the strong one—that is, Satan—the thought being originally derived from Isa. 49:24–25. Luke not only expands the saying but understands it differently and makes a fresh application of Isaiah 49. The strong one in his recital of the saying is first of all those in the Israel of Jesus' time who resist the arrival of the New Age, and then by extension—as is always the case in Luke's rendition of monitory sayings—alleged Christians in the evangelist's time. If God's people guard their inheritance, all is well and their goods are **in peace** (en eirēnē). But if they permit themselves to become weak, a stronger one, comparatively speaking, can come and conquer them, take all the armor in which they put their trust, and divide the spoil (an express allusion here to Isa. 53:12 cannot be proved).

Luke 19:41–44 pictures the tragic fate of Jerusalem, whose leaders had a short attention span. They failed to take note of her source of peace and instead took refuge in their traditions, which ultimately locked them in conflict. The "stronger one" (ischyroteros), Satan, had blinded Jerusalem's eyes (cf. 8:12). Her leaders, who attributed Jesus' works to Satan, could have no other expectation (see also 14:29–32), argues Luke. And what happened to some in Israel can happen to those who claim to share in her receipt of divine grace.

11:23. This second saying endorses the previous interpretation. The word "gather" (synagō) is the theme of Isaiah 49, an indication that this saying was associated in Q with the preceding saying. Jesus is the one who gathers Israel. The hope of Isa. 49:24–25 is that God will send help to the captives and deliver them from their strong oppressor. Jesus says in Luke's account that the reverse of this expectation can happen if one does not gather with him. In such case a scattering—that is, destruction—takes place (cf. Luke

1:51). And, as the preceding verses state, those who thought themselves strong will be overcome.

The interpretation advanced here appears to ignore the usage of "stronger" (RSV: "mightier") in Luke 3:16, but context takes precedence over verbal correspondence. On the other hand, if Jesus is understood as the "stronger one," the "strong man, fully armed" is Satan, and the story means that Jesus ultimately will be victorious, whereas those who are opposed to him will be the losers.

11:24–26. A comparison of the third saying with its placement in Matthew further confirms the interpretation given to the preceding sayings. Matthew has these words after the recital of the sign of Jonah (Matt. 12:39–42, 43–45). Luke appears to have shifted them from the position they held in the Q source in order to climax his description of what he considers Israel's basic problem, her failure to see that some in her midst could come under demonic control. Thus the three sayings (11:21–22, 23, 24–26) parallel the three "if" clauses in vv. 18–20.

11:24–25. A deserted area, and especially a place with ruins, is the standard locale for demons (cf. Isa. 13:21; 34:14), but they long to take up residence in human beings. Few descriptions of self-righteous security can match this proverb-like statement. Israel was a chosen instrument of God. She was like a person from whom a demon had been expelled. But now some of her religious leadership reject him who is Satan's most potent enemy (v. 20) and they become easy pickings for demonic forces. In Acts 5, Luke will describe the tragedy of a false sense of security within the earliest Christian community.

11:26. Seven other spirits return, a number expressing total annexation (cf. *Testament of Reuben* 2—3). Thus the final condition is **worse than the first** (see John 5:14). Rejection of the Holy Spirit (Luke 11:13) invites invasion of the evil spirit (cf. 1QS 3:18–25). In Luke's total account, the text also explains why demonic power was so apparent during the apostolic ministry. It is due to failure to heed the word. Satan has been defeated, but he still is operative in those who do not accept his defeat as real.

Flattery Rebuked   Luke 11:27–28

The story of Mary and Martha (10:38–42) had accented the importance of hearing Jesus' word as answer to loveless casuistry. Now a saying on hearing the word terminates the indictment of those who charged Jesus with being in league with Satan. It was customary to praise the offspring through congratulation of the mother (cf. 1:28, 42, 48). Thus Petronius writes in his *Satyricon* (94.1): "How blessed is the mother who bore such an one as you." And Ovid (*Metamorphoses* 4.320–24) sings:

> O Youth, most worthy
> to be named among the gods. If god
> you be, then Cupid is your name.
> And if a mortal, blessed are those
> who call you son. Blessed is the one
> who boasts you brother, and she who calls
> herself a sister. Blessed is the nurse
> who tendered you her breasts.

11:27. The "womb" is mentioned as the source of life, and the "breasts" as the source of nourishment. In Mary's case, the mention of the womb would be especially significant for Luke's auditors, since her offspring was the result of the Spirit's descent (1:35). As at 8:19–21, Jesus disavows an advantage based merely on natural association (see also 13:26). Luke implies that distorted pride in religious traditions, ancestry, and institutional forms are under indictment, without respect to national origin.

11:28. Jesus does not disclaim the woman's remarks, but through his emphasis on the word of God draws attention to the importance of hearing such words as have just been spoken, for example, in vv. 23–26 (cf. 8:21). "Word" *(logos)* echoes "while he was speaking" *en tō legein auton tauta* (RSV: **as he said this,** v. 27). Jesus' words are the authoritative message of God's Kingdom. Only those who renounce the reign of Satan will receive the Spirit of God, the one effective antidote to the powers of evil.

Some of Luke's Greco-Roman public would probably have noted that Jesus displays an appropriate regal bearing in his diversion of this flattery. "What delight," asks the poet Simonides in a conversation with Hieron of Sicily, "can a prince take in those who praise him, if he suspects that they do it out of flattery?" (Xenophon *Hieron* 1.15). In his exhortation to Nikokles, Isokrates notes that "most people do not come into contact with kings, and those who do tend to curry their favor" (*Nikokles* 4).

On Response to the Word
Luke 11:29–54

Sign Seekers
Luke 11:29–36

Sign of Jonah
Luke 11:29–32
(Matthew 12:38–42)

11:29. Luke now introduces Jesus' answer to the sign seekers of 11:16. On **this generation**, see the comment on 7:31; on sign seeking, see 11:16. Matthew (12:39) adds, or retains from his Q source, the expression "adulterous," a term readily understandable from the OT (see, e.g., Hosea). Some of Luke's Greco-Roman auditors, though, might have found the term puzzling. **This generation is an evil generation,** for it seeks a sign of ratification instead of heeding the message presented by Jesus.

Since Jesus, in accordance with the prophetic program, invited Israel to share the benefits of the New Age, there is nothing in his presentation that should arouse opposition, unless it be that the avowals of those who claim an interest in honoring God are not really genuine. In line with Simeon's prophecy (2:34–35), Jesus refuses to offer any other sign but his own person and message. In this respect he is like **Jonah.** Jonah was God's instrument of salvation for Nineveh. Had they not listened to Jonah's preaching, the Ninevites would have been destroyed. But they heeded it and were saved.

11:30. The Son of humanity—that is, Jesus in all his fragility, but nevertheless God's prophetic envoy—is likewise a sign to this generation. He can be God's instrument for the rising of many in Israel, but rejection will bring disaster and the falling of many in its wake—unless the nation repents. The Book of Acts will deal with that possibility, but Luke's auditors know that Jerusalem lies in ruins. Thus the sign is in the authority with which both Jonah and Jesus preached, backed by the decisive action of God. In Nineveh's case, it is a stay of execution; in the other, disaster.

11:31–32. Israel's response to Jesus is even more critical because he, the Davidian (1:32) and Son of God (1:35), the center of the end-time revelation, is "greater" than either Solomon or Jonah. The queen of Sheba (1 Kings 10:1–13) came to listen to Solomon (cf. Mary, Luke 10:42). Similarly the Ninevites, gentiles, heeded the message of Jonah. "This generation" therefore has two examples in past history that ought to shame it in the present hour. They will rise up in "judgment" *(en tē krisei)* against "this generation." Thus the ultimate disaster that befell many of Jesus' contemporaries is here reviewed, and the ready response to the good news by gentiles highlights Israel's reluctance to carry out her Isaianic mission assignment. God accomplishes the task (cf. Acts 28:28, "good news gets sent"★) without her general participation, and so the loss is theirs who do not ultimately identify with Paul in discharging the responsibility.

Solomon, the epitome of wisdom, may be included in the narrative also because of the reference to the Son of humanity, who is described in *Enoch* 49:1–3 as filled with the spirit of wisdom (see also Luke 2:47, 52; 10:21–22). Moreover, it is quite probable that Luke was familiar with the tradition that Solomon was deprived of the privilege of perpetuating the Davidic dynasty through his descendants. The writer of 1 Chron. 28:6–7 conditions the perpetuity of Solomon's house on his obedience, and 1 Kings 11:9–13 describes the disaster that befell him. Jeremiah 22:30 declares that no descendant of Jeconiah's (the last ruler in Solomon's line) would sit on the throne of David.

In his genealogy of Jesus, Luke bypassed a long line of kings and traced the Lord's descent through the obscure line of Nathan (Luke 3:31), another son of David (1 Chron. 3:5). Thereby he avoided any mention of Jeconiah

(Matt. 1:11) and also discouraged suggestion that Jesus' title to the throne of David was suspect in view of Jeremiah's pronouncement. Jesus is greater than Solomon also by virtue of his superior title to the Davidic throne. As Acts 4:12 will put it, "There is no other name."

The pandemic note in the recital is unmistakable. God's saving purpose in connection with Jesus extends to all between the farthest reaches of east and west. But "this generation" that seeks a sign is perennial. It is not the Jewish people as such. Church history demonstrates the numerous ways in which ecclesiastical powers and local congregations have sought and even yet seek to establish their own signs for discerning the validity and authority of the gospel. The sad truth is that ecclesiastical institutions have great difficulty in initiating any critique of their own policies and practices and are usually on the defensive when it is offered. Not so the early church. The Gospels and the epistles are saturated with institutional self-inventory.

Two Sayings on Light

Luke 11:33–36
(Matthew 5:15; 6:22–23)

In Matthew the first of these sayings appears at 5:15, the second at 6:22–23. Luke used the illustration of the light and the lampstand in Luke 8:16. He reproduces it here almost verbatim but in the interests of a different application. This procedure is a reminder of the extent to which traditional material was shifted about in the recital of Jesus' life and freely modified in public preaching and written records. Similarly in contemporary preaching the same text will be handled differently by various preachers.

11:33. This verse is not to be allegorized. It is true that in the OT both God and the Law are described as "light." (On God as light, see Isa. 60:19; on the Law as light, Ps. 119:105; Isa. 51:4.) But the purpose of the illustration is to emphasize that the function of a lamp is to give light.

11:34. In Luke 8:17 the illustration was applied to God's unveiling of mysteries. Here it introduces a pointed critique of the religious person who frustrates the purpose of the light through insincerity. The eye is here viewed as the light-bearing organ, flooding a person with light, as through a funnel. **When your eye is sound**, you are in good health. If the eye is **not sound** (*poneros* = bad or evil—the same word used to describe this generation, v. 29), one will be in the dark, that is, will lack perception and steer a course outside God's purposes (cf. Prov. 4:19).

11:35. Luke now applies this experience of the physical faculty to people's spiritual apprehension. Philo wrote along the same lines in his treatise *On the Creation* (53). But instead of directing his hearers to check their eyes, Jesus says that they must check what is within themselves—it may be darkness instead of light. In that case, they have serious eye trouble.

The word "sound" (v. 34) is the key to the meaning. The Greek word (*haplous*) is also used in moral discourse in the sense of pure, unalloyed, sincere, single-minded. To be single-minded means that what appears on the surface is matched by what is being actually thought (see *Testament of Issachar* 4—5). For example, a single-minded person does a kindness without privately wishing that he had not been obligated to do it. The elder brother, who said to his father, "All these years I have been slaving for you" (Luke 15:29★), was double-minded. His father thought he was obedient out of love. But the son soon showed his true colors. It was the same in the case of Jesus' opposition. They go through the rituals of their religious tradition, and it would appear that they are devoted to God. But then they charge Jesus—who gives countless demonstrations of divine goodness—with a demon and request a sign. They claim to see but do not see (cf. Luke 8:10; Acts 28:26–27), and their vaunted boast in the Torah is proved to be phony. The Semitic mind deals with concrete realities. Hence Jesus' final statement speaks of the light that floods the entire body.

11:36. If the body is filled with light, then the eye must be sound. The body, in view of the context, is the total personality. A peson who hears the word of God and keeps it qualifies as one who is sound or sincere. Jesus' opponents are in danger of blindness (despite their confidence in the Law as light; cf. Ps. 43:3; Prov. 6:23), for they attribute Jesus' works of light to the prince of darkness. With these sayings the thought in Luke 10:21–24 is seen in bold relief.

While drawing up material for the Book of Acts, Luke observed the accuracy of these sayings in connection with Saul of Tarsus, for whom the light that was associated with Jesus became darkness for a time. Such is the case whenever the demands of the future challenge a mind that is too firmly dedicated to the past or to its own concerns.

Luke's inclusion of so much material relative to the light and darkness theme must certainly have impressed his Greco-Roman auditors. Pindar (*Nemean Odes* 7.22–30) declares that "the vaster part of humanity is blind in heart" and offers as proof the stupidity of the Homeric Greeks in bypassing Ajax when they awarded Odysseus the prize for valor. The blind seer Tiresias at first "sees" far more than does Oidipous, until the latter's blindness, in Sophokles's tragedy. And one does not require long exposure to the philosophers Parmenides and Plato to learn how readily truth and God can be shrouded.

Indictment of the Pharisees   Luke 11:37–44
                                                  (Matthew 23:25–26, 6–7, 27).

11:37. The preceding discourses (11:5–36) spoke of true spirituality, climaxing with inward light versus inward darkness. A banquet scene continues this thought with a discussion of external rites and inner goodness. Jesus' failure to follow the ritual practices of certain Pharisees sets the stage for the dialogue. It is not to be thought that Luke's Jesus attacks all Pharisees indiscriminately. Many of those favorable to the program of the New Age (see Acts 15:5) might well have agreed that the indictments offered by Jesus applied in varying degrees.

Groups dedicated to the preservation of valued traditions run the hazard of appearing to promote a stuffy overzealousness, with a strong ingredient of isolationism. No religious group is free of the virus. Historically, the crime of Christians has been the tendency to justify themselves while reciting Jewish sins and to exculpate themselves from indictments cited against the Pharisees. Jesus saw no limits to God's outreach, and he expects those in charge of religious traditions to explore possibilities for renewal in the direction of more spacious hospitality.

11:38. The word for "wash" is the same word used in 3:21 *(baptizō),* where it is ordinarily rendered "baptized." Handwashing before meals was a religious ceremony, not an antimicrobe action. Jesus scandalized many of his contemporaries by not following certain recognized religious practices, and his encouragement of his followers in such independent attitudes infuriated others (see 6:1–11).

11:39. As the lamp can be a vehicle for expressing spiritual receptivity, so **the cup and ... dish** become a symbol of spiritual content (cf. Jer. 51:7; Rev. 17:4). Jesus lightens his heavy saying with a touch of humor. To wash the outside of something, without concern for the inside, is stupid, because what one eats or drinks comes from the inside. Some Pharisees were evidently more concerned with outward appearances than with their inward condition.

In the *Assumption of Moses* (chap. 7), impious men are described as "self-pleasers, dissemblers in all their own affairs and lovers of banquets at every hour of the day, gluttons, gourmands, ... devourers of the goods of the poor. ... And though their hands and their minds touch unclean things, yet their mouth shall speak great things, and they shall say furthermore: 'Do not touch me lest thou shouldst pollute me in the place (where I stand)' " (trans. R. H. Charles *APOT,* pp. 419–20). Jesus' words are therefore a strong rebuke, tantamount to classifying some Pharisees with the very publicans and sinners they despised. As defenders of the Law, they considered themselves among the wise, described in such literature as the Book of Proverbs (see, e.g., Proverbs 4). At Luke 18:11 a Pharisee will disclaim association with extortioners.

11:40. Jesus addresses his critics with the opposite term: **You fools,** *(aphrones).* No description of Pharisees could be more provocative, and the diction projects the differences that surfaced within the Jewish community especially during the course of the apostolic mission. In the OT a fool is a

wicked person (cf. Prov. 6:12) and godless (cf. Ps. 14:1). Boasting a knowledge of God, the Pharisees under indictment here know little about God.
Otherwise they would know that the inside is more important than the
outside. Luke does not include any statement resembling Matt. 5:22, and his
use of the term "fool" in personal address (here and in 12:20) is unique in the
Gospels.

11:41. According to Prov. 20:27, a person's spirit is "the lamp of the Lord,"
followed by these words: "Mercy and truth are the bulwark of the king"
(20:28 LXX). The word for "mercy" *(eleēmosynē)* used in Prov. 20:28 LXX
is the word rendered "alms" here. Almsgiving is the practical expression of
mercy (see Luke 12:33, and cf. Hos. 6:6). Mercy, then, is a characteristic of
the person who is full of light.

Whether this association of light with mercy prompted Luke to see a
connection between this section from Q and the earlier Logion (Luke
11:34–36) is impossible to determine with complete certainty. If the passages were already connected in Q, then Matthew has scattered them in his
Gospel, and there is a strong probability that Luke sensed the connection.
But there is a stronger probability for influence of Isa. 1:10–31 (esp. vv.
16–17) on the development of this passage. In Isaiah 1, Israel is indicted for
emphasizing cult to the exclusion of justice and is invited to "wash" herself
(Isa. 1:16) by removing wickedness (cf. Luke 11:39) and by practicing
"justice" (Isa. 1:17; cf. Luke 11:42). If Israel repents along these lines, she
will be pure (Isa. 1:16). This also is Luke's meaning in 11:41. If the Pharisees
practice mercy, they need not worry about contracting impurity from
external things (cf. Titus 1:15).

11:42. Deuteronomy 14:22–29 lays down the rules for tithing, but with
strong emphasis on meeting the needs of the poor through a portion of the
tithe. Certain Pharisees are at pains to carry out the provisions that deal with
produce, even to the extent of tithing the smallest herbs, but they bypass the
more important part of the legislation. **Justice and the love of God** echo
the two tables of the Law (cf. Luke 10:27).

To say that a Pharisee, who boasted of his delight in the Law of the Lord,
did not love God, would be enough to shock him into apoplexy. Yet this is
the trap into which fussy ritualism can lead anyone. Jesus does not suggest
that Pharisees should turn their backs on tradition, but they ought to make
their ritual a vehicle for reminder of the weightier requirements, and without making others feel less upright for not adopting their practices. Luke's
retention of the saying reflects debate in the church between Jerusalem and
the gentile mission. It was generally agreed that Jewish Christians should
practice their ancestral customs, but that gentiles be permitted to develop in
freedom (see Acts 15). Galatians 2:10 mirrors the general concern—ritual or
not, the poor are the responsibility of all.

11:43. The pitiful name-dropping and scrambling for recognition by being seen in the right places and in the most advantageous company are under indictment in the second woe. Some Pharisees evidently enjoyed the gaping esteem of portions of the populace that marveled at such last outposts of truth and righteousness. Yet it is they who are the great hazard. Petronius gave Roman social climbers their quietus in his *Satyricon,* and Desiderius Erasmus updated the theme in his spoof entitled *The Praise of Folly,* in which he took ecclesiastics to task for seeking security and prestige under a variety of titles. What areas of ecclesiastical service are to be recognized in rosters of clergy is a major question for some church bodies.

11:44. Concerned about ritual purity, the religious people under review are like unmarked tombs over which the wayfarer walks in ignorance. Far from being clean, they make others unclean through their presence (cf. Num. 19:16). In Matt. 23:27 the contrast is between a whitewashed exterior and decay within, thus displaying the Pharisees' fine outward show of piety against inner rottenness. Luke, on the other hand, writes for Greco-Roman publics who would be familiar with landscape dotted by tombs. Therefore he emphasizes the thought that the average person is unaware of the deep-seated inadequacy of such religious practitioners. In other words, they are deceiving people, not God.

Jesus' sayings have the effect of a cartoon. They pierce the posturing of overlarded egos and invite the sponsors of religious institutions to find enjoyment in the lighter touch. Jesus let fresh air into the first century. Pope John XXIII aired out Christendom. God does not delight in mustiness.

Indictment of the Lawyers   Luke 11:45–54
                                        (Matthew 23:4, 29–31, 34–36, 13)

11:45. The lawyers *(nomikoi)* correctly assess that they are also indicted in the Lord's pronouncement over the Pharisees, for they are the experts who interpret the constitution of Moses for their generation.

11:46. Luke's point is either that the lawyers place people under heavy burdens of obedience, but through their own casuistry excuse themselves from compliance (see, e.g., Mark 7:11–13); or, more probably, and as Acts 15:10 suggests, that they project an image of being more concerned about asserting their legal authority than exploring new ways and means of being helpful to the individual. Citing chapter and verse of canon law is far easier than finding a creative solution on the spot. Jesus casts out demons by "the finger of God" (Luke 11:20), but the lawyers do not not even use one of their fingers to assist the burdened—namely, by removing part of the load. Through his liberation of the people from guilt trips in connection with religious legal systems Jesus everywhere lightened burdens, and the church is to follow him in reassessment of tradition and polity.

11:47–48. At first sight, the criticism in vv. 47–48 appears irrelevant. Why should the lawyers be criticized for erecting tombs in honor of the prophets killed by their fathers? This would not necessarily mean that they endorse the murders done by their ancestors. It is prudent therefore to note that the saying in its present context carries with it the church's reflection on her contemporary experience. Not only was Jesus, prophet par excellence, executed (see a related critique in Acts 7:52) but Stephen, a man full of the Spirit (Acts 6:3), was stoned. Among those presiding over the verdict of execution were the legal experts (Acts 6:12).

On Jesus' lips the passage means: "You like only dead prophets, not living ones." Thus Jesus exposes the hypocrisy of religious people who invoke the authority of holy people of God from the past, while refusing to listen to similar contemporary voices. The ancient prophet, he says, is safe, for his words embalm situations that belong to a cadaverous age. But let those same prophets rise from the dead and pitch their message to a contemporary key, let them proclaim an end to protected seasons for self-privileging economics and theology, let them name names as in the time long gone, and they will soon find themselves charged with libel and remurdered by the very ones who boast that they have no equals as curators of tradition.

The Greek orator Demosthenes proclaimed in similar terms when he reminded the Athenians that living patriots who issue challenges are at a disadvantage when compared to dead ones. "Can anyone be found," he asks, "who does not know that the living are victims of various degrees of jealousy, whereas the dead experience no dislike even from their enemies?" (*On the Crown* 315).

11:49–51. Even while building memorials to the prophets they plot against Jesus (Luke 11:54). Their action is like that of the Egyptians, cited in Wisd. of Sol. 19:3, who interrupted their lamentations to pursue the Israelites. Wisdom of Solomon 19:4 goes on to say: "For fate rightly was bringing them to this end and made them forgetful of their past disasters, that they might fill up the full measure of their torment."[*] Similarly, Jesus says that God's emissaries are sent **that the blood of all the prophets, shed from the foundation of the world, may be required of this generation.** Thus in Wisd. of Sol. 19:4 and Luke 11:40 judgment ripens for the oppressor. Acts 7 recites some of the fortunes of God's representatives (cf. Jer. 7:25).

Luke refers Jesus' words in v. 49 to **the Wisdom of God.** The quotation is nowhere to be found in the wisdom literature; and it has been suggested that Jesus may here be identified as Wisdom, but the fact that Jesus speaks in the first person at the end of v. 51 suggests that Luke understands him to ratify what is said in the third person about the Wisdom of God. More light is to be derived from a consideration of 2 Chron. 24:19, which reads: "Yet he sent prophets among them to bring them back to the Lord."

Immediately following this verse from 2 Chronicles is the recital of the stoning of Zechariah, the son of Jehoiada the priest (vv. 20–22). Luke 11:51 would appear to have this **Zechariah** in mind. How are we to account for this striking combination of thought from 2 Chronicles 24 and Wisdom of Solomon 19? A common interpretive device used by rabbis was called *midrash pesher.* Through this method of interpretation a contemporary application was read into the ancient text, and the text would then be quoted in that updated form. At this point in his recital Luke appears to use a variant form of Q from Hellenistic Jewish-Christian circles. This version evidently included reflection based on a combination of the thoughts expressed in both Wisd. of Sol. 19:3–4 and 2 Chron. 24:19–22.

Such a view of Luke's text form would also account for the following facts: (1) the mention of **apostles** (v. 49), a term that reflects the church's apostolic mission, and (2) the phrase **the Wisdom of God** (v. 49). Instead of referring directly to the Wisdom of Solomon, this phrase takes it into account but speaks more broadly of God's providential wisdom in governing the affairs of the early community. Jerusalem had fallen, and this would be seen as divine wrath for the blood of the prophets (cf. Rev. 6:10) from Abel to Zechariah. God, who spoke in time past, now interprets the present in the light of the past. Hence **the Wisdom of God said.** An alternative to Zechariah the son of Jehoiada is Zechariah son of Bariscaeus, slain in 68 C.E. by two Zealots in the precincts of the temple (cf. Josephus *War* 4.5.4). But this view leaves largely unexplained Luke's peculiar handling of his Q source when compared with Matthew's treatment.

11:52. The Pharisees had three woes pronounced on them (vv. 42–43). A third is here pronounced on the lawyers. They claim possession of the **key of knowledge** to open the door but have no interest in going through the door, and they keep others from entering. A similar rebuke will be registered by Jesus against his own disciples (see 18:16). There seems to develop in religious circles a fatal attraction for restrictive association. One of the consequences is, as a critic complained about religious television programs, that such guardians of the past face issues "with all the force of a marshmallow bouncing off a pillow."

11:53. Encounter with institutionalized thinking has reached a point of no return. Jesus refuses to limit himself to work within the system. Both scribes and Pharisees now lie in wait for the maverick from Nazareth to utter some incriminating word.

On Careful Choice
Luke 12:1—13:9

Address to Disciples
Luke 12:1–53

Fearless Confession
Luke 12:1–12
(Matthew 10:26–33; 12:32; 10:19–20)

12:1. In the face of Jesus' encounter with the "multitude" *(ochlos),* which is said to number "tens of thousands" *(myriad),* the disciples are given special instruction on the hazards of association with their Lord and the need for single-minded devotion. Hence the stress on the word "first." The crowds have their turn at vv. 54–59 (see also Peter's question in v. 41). **Beware of the leaven of the Pharisees, which is hypocrisy.** Leaven is sour dough used as a yeast in the production of bread. Jews were well acquainted with its negative symbolic significance as a corrupting agent. Strict instructions on the removal of leaven during the Feast of Passover are given in Exod. 12:14–20. Jakob Wettstein's references to Plutarch and other writers in his comments on 1 Cor. 5:6–8 suggest that the symbolism was transcultural. Plutarch, for example, discusses why the priests of Jupiter were not permitted to touch either flour or yeast. His answers include the observation that yeast itself undergoes and incites corruption and may even spoil the flour (*Roman Questions* 109 [289e–f]).

Luke interprets Jesus' symbolic usage as an indictment of "hypocrisy" *(hypokrisis),* that is, the cultivation of a double standard or a fundamental lack of correspondence between what one is within and what one projects to others. Hypocrisy is the opposite of the soundness or single-mindedness described in 11:33–36. The details were described in 11:37–52, and 13:15 will offer a vivid example. Joseph Fitzmyer calls attention to "Essene opposition to the Pharisees," who are called "seekers after smooth things" (e.g., 1QH 2, 15, 32) and "seekers of deceit" (1QH 2:34), and proposes that "the reaction of the Lucan Jesus recorded" in Luke 12:1 "may well fit into a larger Palestinian background."

12:2–3. Verse 2 is commentary on v. 1 and related in thought to 11:33–35, while picking up the theme of 2:35. Matthew 10:26–27 applies the same illustration to Jesus' teaching, which is made available to the disciples and through them to the public. Luke, in turn, views the saying as a description of one whose interior character is brought to light (cf. 2:35; Rom. 2:16; 1 Cor. 4:5). Hypocrites will not be able to hide their true colors, and Jesus' disciples will have opportunity to display the genuineness of their profession. Disciples need the reminder, because discipleship involves persecution; and in the critical hour, described in Luke 12:4–12, it will soon be apparent of what stuff they are made. Will the profession of faith recited on beds of ease be maintained on the spikes?

12:4. The words **my friends** *(hoi philoi mou)* convey Jesus' confidence in his disciples as people whose words are backed by action (cf. John 15:14–16). Taken in association with the Christology fostered by Luke, the expression would connote for Greco-Roman auditors the tone of political intimacy suggested by the phrase *amici Caesaris,* friends of Caesar. Fear of what people may do is removed by emphasizing that once the body is destroyed, the enemies have done their worst.

In related vein the philosopher Epiktetos (1.19.8–9) draws up the following dialogue between a head of state and a subject who is threatened with imprisonment:

> Ruler: I will show you that I am your master. Subject: Impossible. God has set me free. You don't actually think, do you, that God would permit me, one of God's sons, to be enslaved? Of my dead body you are, of course, the master; so go ahead and take it.

12:5. With power over the totality of one's being, God not only can take life but can destroy a person in "hell" *(gehenna)*. This is the second death referred to in Rev. 20:14. Gehenna is a valley near Jerusalem, where children were once offered to Molech (see Jer. 7:31–32). Josiah's reform turned it into a garbage dump (see 2 Kings 23:10). Thus the locale became a symbol of punishment reserved for the rebellious (cf. Rev. 14:7–13).

The negative picture of God's ultimate authority derives from the discussion of fear. If one is to fear what another can do, it is wiser to fear God, who can do the greater damage. This means, of course, that God can also destroy those who persecute the friends of Jesus. In effect, then, vv. 4–5 say: "Do not fear what human beings may do. The enemy must ultimately reckon with One who can do far more." Thus these verses are a source of consolation as well as of admonition (cf. 1 Pet. 4:17–19).

12:6–7. These verses continue the description of God's concern for the disciples. Here is the perfect love that casts out fear. In typical rabbinic style Jesus argues from the lesser to the greater. **Five sparrows**, worth only a few cents, were apparently a source of protein for the poor (for their market value, consult the bibliography cited in BAGD, p. 771). Matthew 10:29 says that their death does not go unnoticed. Luke does not speak of their death, but of God's providential concern. Life, as well as death, is under divine direction. The illustration of the **hairs of your head**, like the reference to tens of thousands in v. 1, is a hyperbole. God does not spend time counting hairs. This is a Semitic way of saying that the disciple can rest assured that the God of the sparrows is not oblivious to the disciples' needs (cf. 1 Kings 1:52; Luke 21:18; Acts 27:34). Their names are recorded in heaven (Luke 10:20).

12:8–9. In Mark 8:38 the Son of humanity appears as a judge. Here he is first of all an advocate of the faithful and then judge of those whose profession of religion is hypocritical (cf. Luke 9:26). Luke emphasizes the continuity between Jesus' ministry and the onward course of history, culminating in the final judgment. Any claim to be made someday before Jesus—once the acme of fragility but at the end of time the glorified Son of humanity—is conditioned by response made now to Jesus' message (cf. Rev. 3:5) in the presence of human beings (RSV: **men**).

12:10. This verse is to be understood in the light of the apostolic missionary activity. After the resurrection of Jesus, the apostles would proclaim the significance of Jesus within God's redemptive plan for Israel. But could those who rejected Jesus receive assurance of forgiveness? The answer is positive: Anyone who speaks against Jesus, identified here as the Son of humanity, is eligible for forgiveness. But God will not tolerate the one **who blasphemes against the Holy Spirit.** To "blaspheme" in this context means to denigrate or depreciate the work of the Holy Spirit, whose chief function is to carry out the program of liberation and forgiveness announced at Luke 4:18–19. According to Acts 2:38, the Holy Spirit is God's gift, whose donation takes place in connection with repentance and attendant forgiveness of sins. This forgiveness is ratified by God's resurrection of Jesus (Acts 2:29–36). Through the apostolic proclamation the call to repentance was once again issued (cf. Acts 2:37–41; 3:26), thus in effect declaring that any words spoken against the Jesus Christ the Son of humanity could be forgiven. To denigrate the Holy Spirit means to repudiate this beneficent forgiving action of God as manifested through the Holy Spirit, who functions in accordance with the Scriptures, which are the Spirit's product. The charge of some that the disciples were inebriated at Pentecost came dangerously close to tightroping over a valley of disaster. Since repudiation of the Holy Spirit's activity in connection with Jesus Christ is a rejection of God's program of amnesty, Luke implies that there can be no forgiveness so long as an individual does not desire it. In keeping with his habit of clarifying difficult sayings through other type of narration, Luke records in Acts 7 that Stephen was compelled to acknowledge that his oppressors are among those who continue an ill-fated pattern set by some of their ancestors (7:51; cf. Acts 28:25–28) but that he interceded for his adversaries: "Lord, do not hold this sin against them" (v. 60). Christians are thereby reminded that instead of using Luke 12:10 as an instrument of foreclosure on others they are to pray for the repentance even of those whom they suspect of having discredited the Holy Spirit. In other words, the solemn declaration by Jesus is not designed to help the righteous draw up statistics, but to warn against trifling with divine beneficence. It is obvious that one who is concerned about having committed such a sin is an immediate candidate for forgiveness.

12:11. Experiences of the apostolic emissaries find expression in this verse. In Acts 7:51–52, Luke associates resistance to the Holy Spirit with persecution of God's prophets. A similar association appears here in Luke 12:10–11 (cf. Luke 21:12–15). Luke's point is that negative response to the apostolic message is no indication that the apostolic messengers are in default, either religiously or politically. Nor should they construe such experience as a sign that Jesus was not Israel's authentic Messiah.

12:12. Especially Israel's leadership must know that they are dealing not merely with human beings but with the Holy Spirit, who speaks through the disciples. Thus v. 12 parallels the thought of Mark 13:11. In the missionary situation the words find fulfillment in Peter's response to the charges of the leaders (Acts 4:5–22), and Acts 4:8 expressly states that Peter was filled with the Holy Spirit.

Worldly Cares   Luke 12:13–34

Since attachment to things may lead to a denial of Jesus in the face of various establishments, the evangelist supports the preceding consolation with sundry admonitions relating to possessions.

The Rich Fool   Luke 12:13–21

12:13. The fact that disputes concerning inheritance (cf. Num. 27:8–11; Deut. 21:17) would ordinarily be handled by a scribe (in Luke usually "lawyer") indicates that Jesus is viewed as one well trained in the Scriptures. Hence the address "teacher" *(didaskale)*. According to laws of inheritance, the eldest would receive more than the younger brothers. Perhaps the plaintiff is one of the latter and either feels himself cheated in the division of property or urges an immediate execution of the estate.

12:14. Jesus' reply is patterned after the words in Exod. 2:14 (cf. Acts 7:27), but in this case with a disclaimer of the role of Moses (see on Luke 9:28–36). The saying contrasts with Paul's admonition that disputes were to be settled within the fellowship, not in the secular courts (1 Cor. 6:1–6). Luke, who describes the voluntary sharing of possessions in the early community (see Acts 2:44–45), would find the words especially appropriate and in harmony with the appointment of almoners so that the apostles might concentrate on the proclamation of the word (Acts 6:1–4). The saying, then, does not provide excuse for Christians to ignore questions of social justice. This man's plea reflected private concern. It is another matter when the rights of others are involved. The fundamental priority of the good news over personal aggrandizement is at issue. Values are to be kept straight.

From another perspective, this text cautions against using even the counsels of Jesus as a legal code or set of sanctions. Disciples are not to abrogate their own responsibility for making decisions.

12:15. Covetousness *(pleonexia)*, or greed, can displace God, for it is the equivalent of idolatry (see Col. 3:5; Eph. 5:5). "How much is he worth?" This is the popular measurement of a person in terms of stocks and bonds. Jesus denies the validity of such equation. To a society that includes the deity Surplus in its pantheon, this counsel of Jesus will appear to be a further exhibition of disorientation to reality.

12:16–21. The word "soul" *(psychē,* v. 19) in the story of the wealthy farmer requires special attention. In 12:19–20 it specifies human beings in their totality, possessing life as that which animates them and having a personal identity that transcends and outlasts mere bodily existence. This farmer made the mistake of confusing his real self with his body. He is like a certain man who trained for the dental profession and at age thirty looked forward to retirement at age forty so that he might enjoy his country estate, ignoring the fact that his trained talents were needed by people. Luke's brief description applies to persons who forget God (Ps. 14:1) and refuse to use their bounty for the benefit of others (Prov. 11:26). Ephesians 4:28 offers a contrasting picture of people who do not think in terms of larger warehouses.

The man's action is typical of the "fool" (*aphrōn,* v. 20), as he is described in wisdom literature (see Sir. 11:18–19; cf. *Enoch* 97) and in the story of Nabal (the "foolish" one; 1 Samuel 25). He deserves the verdict (see on Luke 11:40), for he leaves God out of his reckoning (cf. James 4:13–15). The expression **is required** (*apaitousin,* v. 20) is a circumlocution for "God demands the return" (see on 6:38, and cf. Wisd. of Sol. 15:8).

That Jesus does not take a sectarian Semitic point of view can be appreciated from the Greek philosopher Empedokles' verdict on the Agrigentines of Sicily. "They live so luxuriously," he said, "one is inclined to think that they expect to die on the morrow; yet they design their houses as though they will live in them forever" (Diogenes Laertius 8.63).

Luke's Greco-Roman auditors also would readily recognize in the rich farmer the antithesis of a public-spirited citizen. Herodes Atticus is not a model for acquisition of wealth, but he had the correct perspective on its disposal. The main idea in having wealth, he said, was to engage in beneficent distribution. Illiberality is common, said Aristotle, and it takes two forms: stinginess and inordinate acquisitiveness (*Nikomachean Ethics* 4.1.38).

The supreme irony in Luke's story is the rich man's address to himself: **Take your ease, eat, drink, be merry** (v. 19). Some of Luke's auditors might have recalled phraseology in Isa. 22:13 (quoted by Paul in 1 Cor. 15:32) and Eccl. 8:15. Many of his Greco-Roman public would have been familiar with similar expressions on gravestones. In modern Timgad, Algeria, are the extensive ruins of Colonia Marciana, with this inscription on the forum: "Make love, bathe, play, and laugh. That's living!"

But "judge no one happy until death," Solon preached to Croesus, and drove home the lesson with these words: "One who dies well has lived well" (Herodotos 1.32.5). The *Oidipous Tyrannos* of Sophokles is in effect a commentary on the theme. By the time of Jesus son of Sirach, the advice had become a cliché (see Sir. 11:28). At Rome, Ovid turned the platitude into verse: "Prior to death and exequies/ no human being shall be called a blessed one" (*Metamorphoses* 3.135–37). "Look at life's last lap," counseled the Roman satirist Juvenal (10.274–75). Had the rich man taken to heart such maxims, he would not have pronounced his own epitaph! With almost brutal sarcasm comes the question about the things that were to spell his joy: **Whose will they be?** (v. 20; cf. Ps. 39:6).

The temporal phrase **this night** is part of Jesus' decisive vocabulary, and its counterpart is the word "today," which is heard affirmatively by another rich man (19:10) and by a malefactor (23:43). Some Greco-Romans could have quoted Homer in confirmation of the speed with which death overtakes one. Odysseus speeds the arrow to its mark against Antinoos, one of the suitors of Penelope. Even in the act of lifting the wine to his lips the young man dies. "And did he dream of death? How could he?" Homer asks.

Frequent is the lament in antiquity that a foolish heir may lay hands on the fruit of one's labors (see, e.g., Eccl. 2:18–19). This farmer dies in so unexpected a moment that the question comes with a shock. Quintus Dellius, friend of the Roman poet Horace, had a little more time: "You must leave the many groves you have purchased; you must leave your house and your Tiber-washed villa; and an heir will possess your highly piled riches" (*Odes* 2.3.17–20).

In the New Age there is no immunity for private wealth. Luke's Greco-Roman auditors were well acquainted with the awful syndrome known as satiety-insolence-infatuation *(koros-hybris-atē)*—that is, one who is unusually blessed can become a victim of arrogance or hybris and, deluded by a false sense of security, catapult to certain doom.

So it was for a group of the world's most successful men who met in 1923 at Chicago's Edgewater Beach hotel. Assembled were the president of the largest steel corporation; the greatest wheat speculator; a man who was to be president of the New York stock exchange; a member of the President's cabinet; the canniest investor on Wall Street; a future director of the World Bank for International Settlements; and the head of the world's largest monopoly. A few years later this was their fate: Charles Schwab died in debt; Arthur Cutten died abroad in obscurity; Richard Whitney became insolvent, did time in Sing Sing, and was blotted out of *Who's Who;* Albert Fall was pardoned from prison so that he might die at home; Jesse Livermore, Leon Fraser, and Ivar Kreuger, the match king, committed suicide. All learned how to make money. None of them learned how to live. All the bulls became lambs, and Schwab's bleating in 1930 was the most woeful of all: "I'm afraid; every man is afraid. I don't know, we don't know, whether the values we have are going to be real next month or not." So pitiful is the poverty of the rich.

Have No Cares   Luke 12:22—34
                                          (Matthew 6:25—33: 6:19—21)

12:22–23. The rich man's experience revealed that man receives his life temporarily on loan from God and that he cannot live only out of the resources that surround his bodily existence. The value of man's real being and body, says Jesus, is not to be measured by "food and clothing." These words are misunderstood if they are interpreted as an encouragement to idleness or improvidence. Nor do they sound an attack on any economic system, for Jesus said earlier, "The laborer is worthy of his pay" (10:7*). The key phrase is **Do not be anxious** *(mē merimnate).*

A deep-seated anxiety is reflected in the rich man's dialogue. But living is more than having. Seneca, Nero's chaplain, preached sternly on the hazards of wealth but from the vantage point of a personal fortune, and some of his critics have accused him of hypocrisy. In the case of Jesus, the poorest of the poor, there was no credibility gap, and he probed far more profoundly than did Seneca the theological issue.

12:24. Ravens, being birds of carrion, would be considered unclean. Yet God supplies them and their fledglings with food (Ps. 147:9; Job 38:41). Once again Jesus argues from the lesser to the greater. Unlike the rich farmer, the ravens have no barns.

12:25–26. The word rendered **span of life** *(hēlikia)* is used by Luke in 2:52 and 19:3 in the sense of "height." A number of ancient copyists understood the word in the latter sense, for they include in v. 27 the words "how they grow." Since the RSV also includes this addition in v. 27, it is inexplicable why the translators at v. 25 use "span of life" instead of "height" or "stature," which they relegate to the margin.

The conditional statement in v. 26 at first sight suggests that an addition to one's span of life would more easily qualify as a "small thing," relatively speaking, than would an addition of a cubit to one's height. Poetry is not to be interpreted by a slide rule, and Jesus' proverbial saying must be viewed from the Semitic point of view. Growth is dependent on the nourishment one receives. Disciples do not grow to their present heights through anxious thought. It is a natural process and a small thing (v. 26), because it is taken for granted in human experience. One might render: "Who grows by worrying about his or her height?" Such an interpretation clarifies the meaning of v. 26. A significant part of the disciples' growth, ironically called a small part, has been achieved without their own preoccupation. Need they be anxious about the maintenance from that point on?

12:27. The lilies mentioned in v. 27 probably refer to varieties of colorful flowers that dot the Galilean countryside in springtime. They grow in splendor out-rivaling Solomon's grandeur. Viewed from antiquity's perspective, man's work of sowing and reaping (v. 24) parallels woman's work of spinning and weaving (see the RSV margin).

12:28. Wild flowers, for which no one displays a moment of concern, blooming today and used for fuel on the morrow, are God's extravagant hobby. But God's chief business is humanity. The phrase "O people of little faith" *(oligopistoi)* calls the disciples to the realization of their true identity as God's major concern. "Little faith" means that one identifies security under God's providential hand in terms of material satisfaction. Grass appears frequently in the OT to express the transitoriness of life (cf. Job 8:12; Ps. 103:15; Isa. 37:27; 40:6–8).

12:29. This verse does not, as might appear at first sight, encourage irresponsibility, which is not a mark of piety or faith. The syntax of Luke's Greek suggests an agitated mind asking, "My goodness, what do I have to eat?" and "What in the world is there for me to drink?" The Greek word underlying **be of anxious mind** *(meteōrizomai)* is different from the one in vv. 22 and 26. It pictures a person suspended between sky and earth, that is, one who lacks security and a firm spot for the feet. Such attitudes are to be expected of people who lack the knowledge of God that is possessed by the disciples. Anxiety is a species of unbelief, for it suggests that God abandons people to their own resources. God is not stupid. God knows about the elementary necessities. But they are not the staple of life.

12:30. Instead of the RSV's **all the nations of the world seek these things**, the thought is: "The gentiles of the world are in search of all these things." Since Jewish or Christian communities would be in part composed of converted gentiles, Luke incorporates the qualifying phrase "of the world," that is, gentiles who are outsiders to the tradition of Israel. In contrast to the latter, the disciples are to show superior theological understanding. The hyperbole is typical of polemical rhetoric. Many gentiles outside the Jewish-Christian tradition did in fact express contempt for a materialistic approach to life.

12:31. In accordance with what was said at 11:2, they are to seek God's Kingdom. Then **these things** will become a plus in their life, not the main interest. Nonbelievers seek things, and that is all they have (cf. 6:24). The believer begins with God's reign, and the rest is extra. Hence, when the disciples' things are taken away, only the plus is lost, whereas nonbelievers end with nothing.

Clearly, then, possession of things is not in itself an evil. Unless their wealth is gained at the expense of the politics of the New Age (RSV: **kingdom**), prosperous people are not to feel guilty because of any economic advantage they may enjoy. Incalculable harm has been done by people whose guilt about possessions has prompted them to act thoughtlessly toward others. It is easy to dispense charity at the expense of the unlucky recipient of misdirected alms. It is far less threatening to put people on the dole than to make trade unions more generally accessible to development of skills among minorities.

12:32. This verse is not found in Matthew. The expression **good pleasure** (Greek verb: *eudokeō*) is typical of Luke (2:14; 10:21). Jesus is the head of a **little flock** (cf. Matt. 9:36; Mark 6:34; 14:27; Luke 15:3–6). There is a dash of paradoxical humor. Tacitus once said of Augustus that no one had such capacity as he for bearing the burden of the state. But according to Luke's record of the words of Jesus, history is to change course through developments connected with this "little flock," which is headed by the apostles (see Luke 22:29–30; 24:49; Acts 1:4–8).

Measured by human standards, Jesus' disciples are unsuccessful. And they are to avoid receipt of all accepted status symbols. Gentiles—that is, those who endorse the tyranny of things—seek control through wealth. The true power, or Kingdom, is God's to give, not one to gain through standard channels. This is a minority viewpoint. Sponsors of standard politics and economics pay homage only to what they call reality. But what seems folly to a society accustomed to domination by structures that are inimical to humane considerations is true wisdom. At some point a society that manages to pile up indebtedness in trillions of dollars, with much of it traceable to the manufacture of weaponry, might be well advised to give the words of Jesus a more careful hearing.

12:33. This verse is Luke's commentary on v. 21. To display their confidence in the heavenly Parent and in God's rejection of accepted criteria of human worth, Jesus' disciples are urged to sell their possessions and give alms. The words echo Tob. 4:7–11 rather than Matthew's version of Q, and they anticipate Acts 2:42–47.

Although he lived a number of decades after Luke had completed his literary work, Herodes Atticus, donor of the theater that bears his name in Athens, remains one of the primary models for ancient views on the proper use of wealth. In *Lives of the Sophists* (2.1. [547]), Philostratos writes:

> Of all men, [Atticus] knew the best use for wealth. And let no one think that this is easily managed. . . . They claim that Pluto is blind. That may hold true for other times, but in the case of Herodes he regained his sight. This man had eyes for his friends, eyes for cities, eyes for nations. Over all he maintained a careful watch and made a treasury out of the hearts of all who shared his wealth. Some of his words are indeed memorable. "Right use of wealth means giving to the needy so that their need might end; and to those who need not, so that they might have no acquaintance with need." Wealth that was kept close to home and knew no sharing he would call "dead riches." And the vaults in which some people put their money for safekeeping he called "detention centers for cash."

Luke's description of the treasure as one **that does not fail** anticipates 16:9. When material things are made the standard of success, then tyranny, oppression, and social injustice are the fruits. Concern about property values, for example, is a virus deeply embedded in racism. In ecclesiastical circles, considerations for economic survival surface whenever prophetic voices propose remedies or issue calls for repentance that challenge various supporting constituencies. Hierarchies have been known to submit to blackmail that is expressed in threats to withhold benevolences. Protests against apartheid in South Africa were for a long time far more popular than inventory taking of refined domestic oppression.

To ignore the directives of Jesus is to invite the destruction of society. Jesus' disciples are to set their sights on that which is permanent, and this is done through proper use of material things. Varying social situations will determine the wisest type of almsgiving. Certainly the Lord does not advocate scaling heaven by making poor people victims of selfishly motivated charity. In the United States, Christians need to face up to the need for a more equitable distribution of space and for a more creative use of political, cultural, and economic resources so that certain elements in the country do not remain rooted in a poverty-crime-poverty syndrome. Political action is necessary to achieve justice, and ecclesiastical institutions must accept their responsibility to secure that end.

12:34. If one's faith is first of all placed in God, the real choices of the person's life will be governed from that perspective. This is having one's heart where the treasure is. Not property values or political expedience, but concern for justice and the true well-being of people determines whether one has a vision of the Kingdom. Jesus said that if the Kingdom is first sought, all the things that assume so much importance in life will be added (v. 31). Once the Kingdom is a priority, the addition of things can become a trust fund to be administered for the benefit of the poor. The Good Samaritan saw his client through to the end (10:33–37). Stoicism endeavored to free people from anxiety but displayed little interest in the poor. Its self-discipline was in effect self-glorification. The Christian ideal is use of possessions, not ascetic rejection of things. Monasticism was the result of a misunderstanding. And while the monks were praying, Russia ripened for revolution. Luke 12:22–34 is authentic commentary on the meaning of the temptation of Jesus (4:1–13).

Watchfulness   Luke 12:35–48
                                                        (Matthew 24:43–51)

12:35–36. Because possessions and the power connected with them are such a hazard, Luke is emphatic about the Lord's directives on watchfulness. "Kingdom" *(basileia)* in vv. 31–32 suggests the second coming of Jesus. Since this may take place at any time, the disciple must be on the alert at all times. The "girded loins" picture a person with full outer garment taken up at the waist. This would be done either to expedite travel (as at Exod. 12:11; cf. Eph. 6:14) or to equip the wearer for the task at hand (see the figurative use in 1 Pet. 1:13). The latter interpretation is required by the context, which speaks of slaves being on the job.

The burning lights reminded Alfred Plummer of the parable of the ten virgins (Matt. 25:1–12), but Luke's imagery takes a different direction and is not dependent on Matthew's parable. The lamps would help the master enter his house at the late hour, and the slaves would be able to recognize him. That the disciple should be likened to a slave is not unusual (cf. Acts 4:29; Rom. 6:19). The term is descriptive of God's people in Isa. 65:8, 13–15; Ezek. 20:40; Mal. 3:18, and expresses the total devotion of disciples to the wishes of their Lord (i.e., their Master). The reference to knocking parallels imagery in Rev. 3:20.

12:37–38. The blessedness (cf. 6:20) of the slaves is mentioned twice, once at the beginning and again at the end of the saying. Much of the language parallels Mark 13:33–37. Jakob Wettstein calls attention to Horace's use of the image of the host as waiter (*Satires* 2.6.107–9; cf. 2.8.10). To remain awake (Greek verb: *grēgoreō*) means to remain in touch with the Lord. To sleep means to interrupt the fellowship (see on Luke 22:45–46).

So important is the theme of watchfulness that Jesus introduces his promise with *amēn* (Greek *amēn* = English "Amen"; RSV: **truly**). In contrast to the large number of amen sayings in Matthew and Mark, Luke has only six: Luke 4:24; 12:37; 18:17; 18:29; 21:32; 23:43. The saying reflects the confession of the church that Jesus is among them as one who serves (cf. Luke 22:27; Mark 10:45; John 13:1–11). Despite the late hour, the Master will treat his slaves to a banquet (cf. Luke 6:21; per contra 17:8). This description suggests the imagery of divine beneficence expressed in Psalm 23 and Psalm 78 (vv. 19–20) and anticipates the declaration by Jesus in 22:27. There is no conflict with the imagery in 17:8, which makes a different point. The uncertainty of the hour of arrival is repeatedly expressed (cf. Mark 13:35). He may come during the second watch (around midnight) or during the third one (in the early morning). In contrast to the rich man whose life terminated in Gehenna, the disciples will enjoy their returning Lord.

12:39–40. A second illustration picks up imagery from v. 33. Of course no one will stay awake all night on the chance that some prowler will make off with the silver. But the disciples must do just that. They do not know when Jesus, the glorified son of humanity, returns. Hence, continuous vigilance is needed. Overdrawn illustrations are characteristic of Eastern humor. The motif of the unexpected thief recurs in 1 Thess. 5:2; 2 Pet. 3:10; Rev. 3:3. The use of a morally reprehensible person or action for illustrative purposes occasions no surprise (see, e.g., the unjust steward, Luke 16:8; the inflexible judge, 18:1–6). J. Duncan Derrett notes that an allusion to Ezek. 12:1–16 may underlie the original utterance of these verses. If such is the case, Jesus addressed his warning to those in Israel who were oblivious to God's day of reckoning, and the break-in is analogous to the omen in Ezekiel's charade.

12:41. At 12:1 the disciples were addressed "first." Peter now asks whether the preceding parable was designed for a narrower or for a broader circle of auditors. The nature of Jesus' reply indicates that Luke intends to accentuate the responsibility of the ecclesiastical bureaucracy, somewhat in the manner of 9:46–48. The fact that Peter, a person of considerable importance in the community, is the questioner also points in this direction. Matthew follows Q without such editorial modification.

12:42. From Luke's vantage point the "household" *(therapeia)* is the serving staff in the church; and the "portion of food" *(sitometrion)*, that is, the daily rations, suggests the administrative authority that bureaucrats in the church are to exercise as stewards (cf. 1 Cor. 4:1).

12:43. The steward is also a slave *(doulos;* RSV: **servant**). The attribute of blessedness parallels 12:37. Those who discharge their responsibilities faithfully will be offered greater opportunities for service in the world to come. This saying by Jesus appears strange to ecclesiastical institutions that put leadership ahead of service in their instruments for determining ministerial capability.

12:45–46. The darker side of the church's life is depicted in these two verses. Roman emperors were on constant alert against autocratic administrators, and Domitian receives especially high marks from historians for his efforts to control abuses in the provinces. If Luke appears to come off hard against Jewish leaders, it must be granted that he also does not spare rebuke of Christian officials. In this respect he keeps company with the Greek historian Polybios.

In his own time Luke saw how easily personality cultists could exploit those entrusted to their care. He noted the jockeying for position and development of bureaucratic control mechanisms. Acts 20:26–35 is his commentary on the Lord's words, which in turn reflect the thought of Isaiah 5 (see also Amos 2). Included in Isaiah's indictment of the religious leadership is the charge of drunkenness (Isa. 5:11–12).

That the picture in Luke's account is not overdrawn appears clear from 1 Tim. 3:3. And the architecture of the Middle Ages replies "Amen." Cathedrals, strong and durable as fortresses, said to the surrounding inhabitants: The church is powerful and here to stay. Those who form a part of contemporary ecclesiastical establishments must let the light of this text shine on their own manner of functioning as caretakers of the Kingdom. Otherwise the end products of their institutional machinery can turn into powerful weapons against the claims of the future (see also 22:24–27).

12:47–48. In accordance with Jewish thought that distinguished unconscious sins and those based on better knowledge (see Lev. 5:14–19; 15:22–26; Ps. 19:12–13; cf. 2 Baruch 15:6), Jesus places leaders of the community under heavier culpability. According to Luke 8:10, they have been granted privileged knowledge of the mysteries of the Kingdom (see also 8:18). The thought parallels Wisd. of Sol. 6:6: "Persons of low estate may be pardoned in mercy, but the mighty shall be searched out mightily."* These verses do not pretend to offer detailed instruction on the afterlife, nor do they speak of degrees of punishment. Rather, they emphasize the importance of understanding the principle that responsibility is commensurate with endowment and opportunity. Those who possess the greater gifts are to use them not as devices to manipulate others but as instruments of service. The last words of v. 48 are an indirect reference to God, who demands an accounting for endowments that have been given. In brief, power-grabbing has no future. See 1 Cor. 3:10—4:5 for further commentary on the passage. On the theme of ignorance as a moral consideration in the Greek world, see Aristotle (*Nikomachean Ethics* 7.2–4) and Epiktetos (1.26.6–7).

Jesus, Source of Division: Third Prediction of the Passion

Luke 12:49–53
(Matthew 10:34–36)

The apocalyptic emphases in the preceding verses are brought to a conclusion in vv. 49–53, which depict Jesus as the focus of decision. The thought is in keeping with the theme of falling and rising that was enunciated by Simeon (2:34). Precisely because Jesus' first coming is a call to decision, the disciple must be on the alert for Jesus' second coming.

12:49. According to Luke 3:9, the advent of the Messiah is to usher in the great day of the Lord, with the fruitless trees cast into the fire. Luke's view is that the messianic fire burns now in the time of the apostolic proclamation. The disciples who requested fire for the destruction of the Samaritans (9:54) misunderstood their Lord's mission. Jesus does send down fire, but it is a fire that separates the false from the true. Malachi 3—4 is the background against which the Lord's words are to be understood. Jesus wishes to refine Israel so that she might present proper offerings to the Lord.

Symbolic of this refining fire are the firelike tongues that were distributed among the disciples at Pentecost (Acts 2:3). The Greek verb for "distributed" *(diamerizō)* in Acts 2:3 is the same word rendered "divided" in Luke 12:52 (cf. the noun, "division," v. 51). Evidently Luke views the fire as an expression of God's activity, resulting in changed attitudes on the part of some and hostility on the part of others. The popular apocalyptic program required a glorious demonstration of power that would advance in-group interests. Throughout his two-volume work Luke vehemently opposes such a concept and emphasizes Jesus' role as one obedient to his Father's will. Although Jesus is greater than all prophets, he must accept a prophet's fate (cf. Luke 11:47–54).

12:50. The price for refining Israel is death. Hence Jesus in this third prediction of his Passion (see 9:22, 44) speaks of the baptism that he must undergo. From Mark 10:38–39 it is clear that he means his crucifixion (on water as a symbol of great distress, see Pss. 42:7; 69:2). Thus Jesus' own experience is a foretaste of what will happen when the Holy Spirit comes with full force through the apostolic preaching. The consequences will be grave for many in Israel, yet God's will must be done. Therefore Jesus feels "constrained," that is, he cannot wait for his "baptism" to take place. Only after his death can the purifying action of the Spirit take place (see Acts 15:9). A philosopher once said, "We were not put on earth to be happy." Another said, "Therefore let us work hard." Jesus said, "Let us squander our lives in the opportunity of disaster."

12:51. Since Isaiah spoke of the messianic age as a time of peace (Isa. 65:25), the evangelist counters objections that Jesus failed to qualify as the great deliverer. Jesus was indeed the agent of peace (see Luke 2:14), but he does not offer it at a discount. His very interest in peace arouses hostility in those who refuse to accept his political platform as expressed at Nazareth (4:18–19). The question, **Do you think that I have come to give peace on earth?** has an ironical ring. Jesus' own answer is a declaration of the total conviction with which he carries out his mission. So radical is his commitment to peace that endorsement of it foments division. In response to him and his mode of ministering to humanity, people make responsible decision for or against God. The division is not his creation; others have made the choice (see Luke 2:34–35 and John 3:17–21). And upon his entry into Jerusalem, Jesus will shed tears when he repeats the lesson.

Jesus' opponents were of the opinion that the best way to ensure permanence for an institution was to proceed in an orderly and systematic way. Observance of time-honored rules and regulations effected such a process. But Jesus was unconventional and no team player. In the judgment of some of Jerusalem's hierarchy, his words and actions only helped to create chaotic conditions. In sum, he was not too helpful in maintaining either respect for ancestral traditions or stable relationships with the Roman imperial establishment.

12:52–53. The words "from now on" (*apo tou nyn*; RSV: **henceforth** at v. 52, but "from now on" at 22:69) are repeated in 22:69 and stress the climactic character of God's communication to Israel and humanity through the death and resurrection of Jesus Christ. It must not be forgotten that these words are spoken on the way to Jerusalem (see 9:51). The apostolic mission could take comfort from this saying. Apparent lack of success in converting their kinsmen was not to be construed as failure. Micah 7:6 used similar language to describe the division of God's people. Matthew 10:35–36 is closer to Micah's text, which speaks of the contempt of the younger generation for the older. Luke makes the responsibility mutual, but mentions the older generation first (see on Luke 6:36–39). The revolutionary character of the good news does not permit perpetuation of the status quo.

Luke's sense of tragedy is evident when these verses are heard as a reverse echo of 1:17, which reminds the auditors of what might have been.

Address to the Multitudes: On
Interpreting the Time

Luke 12:54–59
(Matthew 16:2–3; 5:25–26)

12:54–56. At 12:1–53 Jesus addressed himself to the disciples. Now he turns to the crowds. The introduction of these sayings at this point serves to underline the decisiveness of Jesus' mission described in 12:49–53. **The present time** (v. 56) is more than a chronological moment. It is the critical hour *(kairos)* in Israel's destiny—the opportune moment. Jesus' contemporaries are better at forecasting the weather than at noting the signs of God's activity among them. They must come to grips with the hazards of hypocrisy, or they will live to lament God's judgment on Jerusalem (see 19:41–44; especially worthy of note is the word "time" in v. 44). The sins of those in seats of power do not relieve the ordinary person of responsibility. Most tragic is the sight of communities whose members have placed their consciences in ecclesiastical safety vaults and who do not wish to have questions about their relationship with God reopened.

According to a Greco-Roman variation of the proverbial wisdom expressed by Jesus, an elderly woman took the Greek philosopher Thales out of doors to look at the stars. On the way he fell into a ditch and cried for help. The woman answered, "You want to know all about the heavens but can't see what's right at your feet" (Diogenes Laertius 1.34).

12:57–59. These verses are parabolic in form. Whatever the meaning may have been in other stages of tradition, Luke's organizational techniques suggest this as the point: God's people ought to use at least as much wisdom in facing God's judgment as they do in settling accounts with a bill collector. The truly wise are those who have an ear for the future. As in 11:4, God is viewed as a creditor. In the presence of such decisive call there is no room for business as usual. In Matt. 5:25–26 the saying is applied to personal relationships.

Some of Luke's public might have recalled that Jason spoke to his scheming uncle Pelias before heading the *Argo* in search of the Golden Fleece (cf. Pindar *Pythian Odes* 4.136–55). Others may have pondered in this connection the fate of Julius Caesar, who did not heed the prophetic voice. Alluding to that moment in Roman history, the modern Greek poet Konstantine Kavafy confronts Everyperson as he soliloquizes in a poem titled *The Ides of March* concerning a warning transmitted by a "certain Artemidoros," an ancient expert in the interpretation of dreams. Artemidoros speaks of things that cannot brook delay and urges a halt to all activity. "Forget," he counsels, "about acknowledging salutes of those who lie prostrate before you." Even the Senate, he says, can "wait the while you lose no time to know the urgent writings of Artemidoros."

Call to Repentance   Luke 13:1–9

13:1. The traditional chapter division obscures the intimate connection
between 13:1–9 and the preceding sayings on the urgency of awareness. The
first half of v. 1 is a rhetorical device to stress the subsequent lesson. On this
incident we have no further information, but Josephus records related
examples of Pilate's oppressive tactics (see, e.g., *Antiquities* 18.3.2; *War*
2.9.4). Luke's reference to the occasion as a time of sacrifice suggests a
conflict between religious profession and illicit practice.

13:2. It was an axiom among some Jewish teachers that God in this life
rewards the righteous and punishes the "wicked" (i.e., sinners; cf. the
arguments of Job's friends; Prov. 10:24–25). Using experience as a criterion,
one who experienced no reverses could easily conclude that he must be
righteous. As in John 9:1–3, Jesus rejects this popular theory and shows
awareness of the perplexing reality expressed in Ezek. 18:2 and throughout
the Book of Ecclesiastes. In the Greek world, Solon grappled with the
problem of suffering that befalls the righteous, Sophokles explored the
poignancy of piety and nobility crushed by forces beyond their control, and
Plato showed in his account of the death of Sokrates that suffering may
result from refusal to compromise one's profoundest commitments. From
many directions comes the verdict: Suffering is no sure determiner of guilt.

13:3. Repentance is required of all, without reference to accidents of life,
or they will themselves ultimately perish (cf. 12:58–59; 6:24–26).

13:4. Verse 4 suggests a case of pure accident, not mentioned by any other
historian. In place of the word "sinners" used in v. 2, Luke here employs the
term "debtors" (*opheiletai;* RSV: **offenders**). Sin is indebtedness to God (cf.
11:4). In the context of Luke's thematic structure, the reference to **Jerusalem** is especially significant. Galilee could conceivably be ripe for judgment, so the complacent would conclude. Not Jerusalem! Moscow, yes.
Not New York, Washington, St. Louis, Dallas, Philadelphia, Los Angeles,
or Minneapolis! The Kremlin. Not St. Peter's or First Lutheran! (For the
figure of falling towers, cf. Isa. 30:25.)

13:5. The Lord's answer to his own statement follows the formal pattern
in v. 3 but with one significant alteration, obscured in the RSV. In v. 3 the
translation "likewise" *(homoiōs)* is correct. In v. 5 a different word *(hōsautōs)*
is used meaning "in the same way" (RSV: **likewise**). The fall of the tower of
Siloam was a prelude to the fall of the towers of Jerusalem (see Luke 19:44).
Luke, writing after the fall of Jerusalem, impressed his readers with the
urgency of the call to repentance: unless they repent, they will all perish in
the same way. What was once spoken to Israel is now addressed to the

church. Christians are not to repeat the mistakes that led to Jerusalem's destruction. "All" refutes any thought about privileged exemption.

13:6–9. These verses explain the purpose in delayed judgment, which is erroneously construed by some as a sign of their own righteousness. If judgment does not immediately strike, this is indicative of God's mercy, not of his approval. To understand her relationship to God in any other way connotes Israel's failure to know the "time" (*kairos;* 12:56). According to prophetic teaching, Israel is God's "vineyard" (Isa. 5:1–7). Fig trees were frequently planted in vineyards. Micah 7:1 includes a lament over a fruitless fig tree, and the succeeding verse explains that the illustration points up the absence of righteousness in the land. Luke evidently had the prophetic passage in mind, for Mic. 7:6 is reproduced in Luke 12:53. If this interpretation is correct, we have a further indication that Luke 13:1–9 is an amplification of the argument in 12:49–59, and Luke's omission of Mark's narrative of the cursing of the fig tree (Mark 11:12–14) at the corresponding place in his own narrative (see Luke 19:44) finds cogent explanation.

13:7. The phrase **three years** is not a reference to the length of Jesus' ministry but rather a typical Semitic expression for completeness. The owner has extended the time to its limit, only to experience complete frustration. He gives the order: "Chop it down! It only takes up space."

13:8. The plea of the gardener further emphasizes the mercy of God. A parallel illustration is given by Lucilius, a Roman satirist. He describes how God was pondering what measures to take in order to preserve the city of Rome; so great was the wickedness of a certain Lupus and his followers. Finally five years was suggested as the limit for the testing of divine patience. In the case of Jerusalem, time was no ally. Judgment followed rejection of this earnest call to repentance. There can be no tampering with the grace of God. Luke's frequent reminder, "Blessed are those who hear the word of God and keep it," lurks in the shadow of this dramatic recital, which searches the nooks and crannies of all institutionalized religion.

Success in the Face of Misunderstanding

Luke 13:10–21

The nature of the problem discussed in 13:1–9 is further explained in 13:10–21, and the entire section permits an elegant transition to the discussion that begins at v. 22. The contrast between the flourishing tree of 13:18–19 and the worthless tree of 13:6–9 is evident, and the point of the whole is that Jesus is successful, but Israel left to her own resources is a failure. From the legal questions raised in the narrative it is apparent that Pharisaic casuistry is a primary issue. The lack of repentance discussed earlier came out into the open in the refusal of the religious leadership to grasp what Jesus is about as he relates his ministry to the problem of suffering.

A Crippled Woman Healed   Luke 13:10–17

13:10. The reference to Jesus' instruction in a synagogue is noteworthy. Luke records no other instance in his recital of the closing stage of Jesus' ministry. Evidently he meant the notation to be understood as an example of the mercy outlined in 13:6–9.

13:11. The RSV omits the words "And behold" *(kai idou)* at the beginning of v. 11. In Luke's recital they alert the reader to an extraordinary occurrence. The profounder aspect of Jesus' ministry, attack on Satan's empire, is stressed by the description of the woman's malady as a **spirit of infirmity** *(pneuma astheneias)*. Attempts to define her malady in precise medical terms remain speculative. The term **eighteen years** may serve as a rhetorical device to connect the recital with the previous discussion (see 13:4, and compare 13:21 with 13:7). A similar use of repeated numeral to link narratives was made in 8:42–43. In any event, this chronological note suggests that she was ill "for a long, long time." "Eight" appears frequently in the OT in combination with ten or a hundred or a thousand, without any suggestion of mathematical precision. In Judg. 3:14 and 10:8, "eighteen years" describes a long period of servitude or oppression. Conversely, *Test. Judah* 9:1 applies the term to a period of peace.

13:12. Since a woman would be suspected of being cultically unclean, Jesus' initiative in addressing her is remarkable.

13:13. His word, which pronounces thorough release from her disability, is reinforced by his action. The power resident in his own person reaches out to the woman. He, as the servant of the Lord, is the instrument of her healing. At his touch, immediately *(parachrēma)* she stands straight and begins to give all credit to God *(edoxazen ton theon)*, thereby affirming the credentials of Jesus as the Great Benefactor (cf. Acts 2:22–24; 10:38).

13:14. In protest, **the ruler of the synagogue** appeals to Deut. 5:13 and Exod. 20:9–10 but lacks the nerve to address Jesus directly.

13:15. Luke accentuates the authority of Jesus with his reference to **the Lord** *(ho kyrios)*, who has the last word on sabbath regulations (cf. 6:5). The plural form, *hypokritai*, displays profound awareness of political realities. Some in the crowd would be impressed by the line of argument of their local religious official. "Hypocrites" therefore applies both to the head of the synagogue and to those who share his view on the matter. In his reply Jesus appears as an authoritative expositor of the Law. He who had declared that the disciples were worth more than sparrows (12:6–7) now pronounces the woman worth more than an ox or an ass (cf. 1 Cor. 9:9). Jesus' warning about placing material things above the requirements of the Kingdom (see Luke 12:29–31) is seen here in its brilliant necessity. Religious leaders permitted watering of their animals (see SB 1:629–30; 2:199–200; cf. *Damascus Covenant Document* [CD] 11:5–6). To do this they would have to untie the halter.

13:16. Jesus plays on the verbs "to untie" (*luō*, v. 15) and "to bind" (*deō*, v. 16). The woman is entitled to more consideration than an animal. For **eighteen years** she has been, one might say, in Satan's stall. It is quite apparent that there is no real connection between the requirement of water for an animal and a woman's malady of eighteen years' standing. After all, she could have been healed on the next day.

The very playfulness of Jesus in the dialogue indicates that he takes no stock in casuistry. He could not care less about such picayunish reasoning. For him the **sabbath day** is an especially appropriate time to release this woman. Since she is a daughter of Abraham (see on 19:9), the oath sworn to Abraham (1:73) applies to her; for the sabbath is emblematic of God's outreach to his people. It is the climax of God's creative activity (Gen. 2:1–3) and a day of special blessing for the people (cf. Heb. 4:9–11; Matt. 11:29–30). The very purpose of the sabbath was to protect the interests of human beings from exploitation. Jesus' deed was in harmony with the spirit of the original ordinance. And Luke spotlights Jesus' act of benevolence with the word "ought" *(edei),* the evangelist's favorite term for urgency of commitment to divine purpose (cf. Luke 2:49).

Under indictment in this text are all attempts in religious circles to put rules and regulations ahead of demands for change in the interest of people and the forward motion of God's people in ministry. Administrators aspire to tidiness and view private initiative and creative cutting of ecclesiastical red tape as a threat to normalcy, and like the head of the synagogue they succeed in persuading their constituencies that time-honored procedures are tantamount to divine necessity. But Luke has canonized the dominical rage for blessed disorder, the politics of the New Age. Because of his propensity for quick solutions to problems that invite long debate by theologians, Jesus would pay a high price. On the other hand, total restoration would follow the temporary inconvenience he caused to overzealous guardians of the past (see Acts 3:21). It is no wonder that repentance is the basic requirement for travel in the New Age.

13:17. As Jesus predicted (Luke 12:51–53), there is divided response. His enemies are frustrated, but the crowd rejoiced (cf. Luke 9:43). Isaiah 45 is the best commentary on v. 17 (see esp. Isa. 45:16).

Two Parables on Growth   Luke 13:18–21
                                                   (Mark 4:30–32; Matthew 13:31–33)

13:18–19. The divided response leads naturally to the inclusion of the two parables that follow. Their common message is this: Jesus appears as one least likely to succeed. The leaders reject him, but God achieves his purposes through him. The presence of the Kingdom is made known through Jesus' deeds as well as through his words (cf. Luke 4:18–21; 7:22–23; 11:20). The disciples are entrusted with the mysteries of the Kingdom (cf. 8:10).

The tree begins as a small seed but develops into a refuge for the birds of heaven. This description is paralleled in Dan. 4:10–12, 18; Ezek. 17:23; 31:6. It speaks not of the growth of the institutionalized church but of the triumphant course of the good news (see Acts 6:7; 12:24; 19:20). The Kingdom is not the church, and the community of believers always remains relatively small, but God's Kingdom advances. Whatever may have been Jesus' intention in the reference to the "birds of heaven," Luke's auditors would certainly have interpreted the imagery in terms of their experience with gentiles who share in the promises made to Israel. But the tree that failed to produce fruit will perish (Luke 13:6–9; cf. 23:31). Jesus did not share the Kingdom thinking of his contemporaries, but his renunciation of the way of Satan (4:5–8) led to the enthronement envisaged in 13:19.

13:20–21. Leaven is ordinarily used in a pejorative sense (cf. 12:1), but in this second parable it is used in a good sense. Looking in from the outside, God appears to have made a mistake in connection with Jesus. But just as leaven works in unseen ways, so God ultimately succeeds through One rejected by Israel but exalted to God's right hand (cf. Acts 3:11).

SECOND PHASE OF THE JOURNEY
TO JERUSALEM
                                                    Luke 13:22—17:10

Are Few Saved?
                                                      Luke 13:22–30
                                          (Matthew 7:13–14; 25:10–12; 7:22–23;
                                                      8:11–12; 19:30; 20:16)

13:22. At this point Luke recalls his thematic note in 9:51: "Behold, we go up to Jerusalem." His publics are now prepared for another series of stories and sayings that will shed light on the meaning of Jesus' final action in Jerusalem. That Luke intends this section to be understood in the light of the foregoing sayings is clear from the parallel thoughts in 13:9 and 29–30. The stress on the Kingdom in 13:18–21 requires a further dismissal of apocalyptic misunderstanding.

13:23. As in 10:29; 11:45; 12:13, 41; and 13:1, questions are used to introduce authoritative replies of Jesus. According to 2 Esd. 8:3, "Many are created, but few are saved."* Some teachers, on the other hand, taught that only a few in Israel would immediately at death enjoy the blessings of heaven. The rest would wait in Gehenna. But all Israel would share in the blessing of the world to come, after the resurrection of the dead took place (see SB 1:883). Such types of speculation underlie the question: **Will those who are saved be few?** Jesus refuses to enter into such inquiries. Instead, he takes up the prophetic note of decisive commitment.

13:24. Since v. 24 speaks of the narrowness of the door, whereas v. 25 lays emphasis on the fact that it is shut, it is probable that Luke has brought together words of Jesus spoken on different occasions, with the word "door" as the linking factor. In Matthew 7 they are separated (Matt. 7:13–14, 22–23). The narrowness of the gate is stressed in order to express the fact that it is not made for crowds (see on 12:1). In 2 Esd. 7:3–7, the narrow way must be negotiated before entrance can be made to the broad ways that lie beyond the hazardous fire and water. There is no national or collective salvation. Each one is called to responsible decision, without reliance on inherited religious association. The thought is in accord with the theme of "rage for blessed disorder" (see on Luke 13:16).

13:25–27. The illustration of the locked door introduces a second motif—obedience divorced from empty liturgical confidence or institutional commitment. As in 6:46, those who are self-confident will use the proper address **Lord** (*kyrios;* cf. Matt. 25:11) and claim familiar association (see on Luke 8:19–21), but the Lord will reply: **I do not know where you come from.** That is, he will disclaim any relationship. The reason: they **all** are **workers of iniquity** (*pantes ergatai adikias*), a phrase taken from Ps. 6:8. It is not enough to hear Jesus' words with the ear, one must hear with integrity and perform accordingly (cf. Luke 6:47).

13:28–29. Not only will the hypocrites be locked out but they will catch a glimpse of their venerable ancestors and the prophets sharing the Kingdom. Yet they have no real complaint. They were warned not to say, "We have Abraham as our father" (3:8; see also on 16:19–31). As the climax of their total frustration, they will see the gentiles gathered in to share the blessings of the patriarchs and the prophets (cf. Isa. 2:2; 59:19; Mic. 4:1–2; Rev. 21:24). The end-time banquet of Isa. 25:6–8 is prepared for those who hear and do the Lord's word. The repetition of the phrase **kingdom of God** in Luke 13:28 and 29 draws attention to the inexorable triumph of God's purpose in Jesus (see 13:18–21).

13:30. And behold (*kai idou*) introduces the climactic summary. The

Kingdom does not follow traditional political patterns. As a word to Jesus' contemporaries, these sayings were an urgent call to repentance. Addressed to Christians through Luke's Gospel, they warn newcomers to the promises not to repeat the mistake of many in Israel. The principle is still valid: **Last** ones **first, first** ones **last**. Hence the previous warnings on watchfulness (12:35–59).

Misunderstanding in General
Luke 13:13–35

A Warning from the Pharisees: Fourth
Prediction of the Passion
Luke 13:31–33

The words **at that very hour** stress the connection of this account with the preceding sayings. The religious formalism described in the previous verses receives a climactic refutation in the indictment of Jerusalem (vv. 33–35). At the same time, the import of Jesus' words in 9:51 is caught in more ominous perspective.

13:31. Not all Pharisees are targets for negative criticism by Luke. A number of them helped shape directions in Christian communities (Acts 15:5). Therefore Luke (see on Luke 6:11) had completely altered Mark's description of Pharisaic animosity (Mark 3:6) and at this point in his narrative shows that certain Pharisees even tipped Jesus off about Herod's evil intentions.

The warning of the **Pharisees** points to the status quo that Jesus is disturbing. Herod liked things quiet (see Josephus *Antiquities* 18.7.2), a characteristic of petty men who are frightened by anyone who raises questions or rocks boats. In Palestine the fox is an insignificant predator next to the lion, the king of beasts. And in Rome the proverb went: "Today, when people are at home they tend to think of themselves as lions, but in public they're just foxes" (Petronius *Satyricon* 44). In Greco-Roman circles the fox was also recognized for its cunning (references in BAGD, p. 41). Jesus will be done in by greater powers than Herod. Some readers may have caught an allusion to Ezek. 13:4, which speaks of foxes among the ruins. Herod governs in a land that is soon to experience terrible disaster. Jesus' own political status will be defined at Acts 4:12.

13:32. Patience and a sense of irony, said a character in a French film, are marks of a true revolutionary. Jesus possessed both, and Luke's auditors well know that Jesus will be less safe in Jerusalem than in Herod's territory. The timetable in this verse does not refer to a three-day period. Like the numeral in 13:7, the three-day period connotes completeness. Jesus is on his way to Jerusalem, but not to escape from Herod, for his backbone was never curved through fear of anyone. He carries out his healing ministry as a part of his prophetic function (cf. 7:22; 24:19) and at the same time heads toward Jerusalem to endure the fate that Israel has in store for her prophets (cf. 4:24; 11:47–52).

Those among Luke's auditors who recalled that Satan would be waiting for an "opportune time" (*kairos,* 4:13) could not fail to catch the kind of confident resolution that Romans loved to recall as they reviewed their own history. Hannibal, head of the Carthaginian forces against Scipio's Roman army, had once sent three spies to reconnoiter the Roman camp. Arrested by the Romans, they were put under the guidance of a tribune, who showed them the layout of the camp. After their inspection, Scipio asked them whether the officer had given them a sufficiently thorough tour. They indicated their satisfaction, upon which Scipio sent them on their way, with orders to report on everything to Hannibal (Polybios *History* 15.5.4–7).

The reply made by Jesus is his fourth prediction (see 9:22, 44; 12:50), which firmly establishes him in the minds of Luke's auditors as one who enjoys an intimate relationship with God (see on 5:22). The fact that he forecasts details of his own death would be considered impressive proof of his prophetic credentials; so also, according to Philo, Moses just before his heavenly ascent had recited details concerning his own death (**Moses** 2.290–91). The suffering of Jesus will spell the end of his course (*teleioō;* cf. 12:50; 22:37). As at Nazareth (4:30), he remains, for the present, unharmed. At Acts 20:24, Paul will echo Jesus' statement about finishing one's course.

Address to Jerusalem

Luke 13:34–35
(Matthew 23:37–39)

13:34–35. The repetition of the name of the city accentuates the solemnity of the address (cf. 19:41). In Matthew these verses are recited after Jesus' entry into Jerusalem. Luke's omission of the words "from now on" found in Matt. 23:39 was necessary in order to facilitate the transfer, for in Luke's account Jesus is still on the way to Jerusalem. In their present position these verses explain the total absence in Luke's previous account of any ministry in Jerusalem. He, their Messiah, would have loved to offer them the protection of a mother hen (cf. Pss. 17:8; 57:1; 61:4), whom even Herod the fox could not intimidate. But their hostility has made this impossible (see Luke 13:4–5). The word "behold" *(idou)* in v. 35 echoes the word in v. 32. Despite his mighty and beneficent works, Jesus is rejected.

The phrase **your house is forsaken** has an ironic sound in conjunction with the words that follow it: **You will not see me until you say, Blessed is he who comes in the name of the Lord.** On the one hand, the first of these statements suggests that Jesus has not forced himself on the city, whose religious establishment wants no part of him. And the second, which takes on the solemnity of an oath (cf. Judith 6:5), hints that Jesus on his part does not reject Jerusalem but will give her another chance when he enters the city in Passover week (Luke 19:38). Thus Jerusalem's story could have a happy ending, and the forsakenness would be merely temporary. On the other hand, there is a tragic tonality in all these words. Luke's auditors know that the script of history took a turn away from the story line of things for which both Jerusalem and Jesus had hoped in their own ways. And as they hear the text, they know only too well what is meant by the words, "Your house is forsaken."

Those who knew their Jewish Scriptures would perhaps think of Jer. 22:5 and ponder the dissolution of Israel's hope for the restoration of the Davidic dynasty as a reigning power in the ancestral city. Others, with memory of Greco-Roman dramatic performances, might well recall the pity and fear that enveloped them when they watched Agamemnon, humbler of Troy, invite certain doom by treading on the carpet laid out for him by Klytemnestra; and they would say to themselves at this point in Luke's narrative: "Why, that's the week in which they killed their King!"

Through adroit use of his sources Luke penetrates his recital with profound pathos and prepares his auditors for the conjunction of acclamation and lament in 19:38–44. King of Israel he is, but Pilate will publish the fact (see 23:38). Jesus had warned his disciples. The things we love the most are at the mercy of the things we ought to love the least.

Specific Misunderstanding at a Dinner with a Pharisee

Luke 14:1–24

Luke 13 developed the thought that misunderstanding of Jesus' mission would ultimately bring disaster to those who relied on traditional religious association without real commitment. Luke 14 advances this theme to another plateau. As in 13:10–16, Luke introduces a chain of sayings and parables with a controversy concerning the sabbath (14:1–6). In 13:18–21 statements on the Kingdom precede the recital of the locked door at the messianic banquet (13:22–30). Similarly, 14:15 introduces the subject of the Kingdom, followed by a parable about the messianic banquet (vv. 16–24). The concluding series of sayings in vv. 25–35 sketches the total commitment of the disciple in contrast to Jerusalem's misplaced self-assurance (13:34–35). Like Jerusalem, false disciples may find themselves rejected (14:35).

Healing of a Man Ill with Dropsy   Luke 14:1–6

14:1–3. Jesus appears to have been at least an occasional guest in the homes of Pharisees (see 7:36; 11:37). In his reply to Herod, Jesus spoke of healings he had yet to perform (13:32). The saying offered an easy link for the healing narrative in 14:1–6. But Luke's choice of the particular type of healing, together with the specific reference to the "sabbath," was prompted by his apparent desire to establish a relationship between this stage of his narrative and the discussion begun in 13:10–17. It was customary to have a festive meal on the sabbath, for which the preparation would be made on Friday, with the food merely kept warm. In accordance with Jewish custom, distinguished religious leaders would be invited. The host in this case is himself a man of account in his community and quite possibly the leader of a group of Pharisees.

Earlier in 6:7 and 11:53–54 scribes and Pharisees were pictured as hostile. This appears to be Luke's intention also here in the phrase **they were watching him**, a standard procedure by religious authorities in the presence of one who has a reputation for deviation from the system. The plural "they" anticipates the reference in v. 3 to the Pharisees' colleagues. Further light is now shed on Luke's reference to the Pharisees at 13:31. That group was concerned about Jesus' safety. But the present company, suggests Luke, are among those who must share responsibility for Jerusalem's ultimate disaster. Their style of commitment to rules and regulations eats at the very vitals of Israel's religious life.

As at 13:11, **and behold** *(kai idou)* alerts the reader to a significant development. This time we have a man afflicted with dropsy *(hydrōpikos),* a disease caused by abnormal accumulation of serous fluid in the body. There is no indication in the text that the man, anymore than the woman at 7:37, was planted by the host or other guests. Jesus' question cuts through a tangled mass of casuistry on the question whether medicine could be practiced on the sabbath. In a later period, perhaps reflecting a long-established tradition, an exception was made in cases where life was at stake.

14:4. Like wily candidates for political office, these representatives of the religious establishment are not about to expose their system to attack. Instead, they retreat into the silence of the "no comment" tribe. Since they refuse to express themselves, Jesus proceeds on his own authority. True to his own counsel given earlier to the disciples (12:4), Jesus does not play it safe by telling the man to wait a day. That is the kind of prudence one might expect from a slave to the system. Jesus heals him and sends him off.

14:5–6. The question in 14:5 parallels 13:15 (cf. Matt. 12:11–12). It is another example of the formula "If that, how much more this." The word "immediately" *(eutheōs)* is the cue. While theologicians spend time in debate, urgent matters are tabled and needs left unfulfilled. Ecclesiastical officials sometimes talk as though they have forever. Jesus has only today, tomorrow, and the next day (13:33). In the face of his first query (14:3), the opposition retreated into silence (cf. 20:26). Now **they could not reply**, for they would have had to acknowledge their hypocrisy.

A Lesson on Kingdom Manners   Luke 14:7–11

14:7–11. Once more Luke gives evidence of his profound insight into human nature as he presents Jesus taking note of the complicated political and social algebra involving the seating of guests. A person given to casuistry may be signaling personal insecurity. Status-seeking is a badge of pettiness. The dinner party to which Jesus had been invited provides the framework for the parable about the first seats. Customarily the seating would consist of three couches, with three places on each couch. The place of honor would be at one end of the center couch. All guests would recline. The guest in the parable is advised to take a lower position, for more important guests, who often came later, would certainly displace and embarrass impertinent social climbers (cf. Prov. 25:6–7).

Petronius's *Satyricon* (70) shows the importance that Roman society attached to chief seats. The ancient Roman novelist has his mouthpiece complain that a cook who was reeking of pickles and sauces was seated above him at a banquet.

That Luke's story is illustrative, and not meant by Luke as a piece of social decorum, seems clear from v. 11, which is repeated at 18:14. The thought is in line with 1:46–53 and 2:34 (cf. 1 Pet. 5:5; James 4:6). Those who view the story as one would a paragraph from a book on etiquette forget that many serious economic and political problems take shape in accepted social routines. Law can enforce people's right to purchase property where they wish, but social patterns may still isolate the purchasers and encourage hostilities. The seeking of chief seats leads to graft and corruption, with further exploitation of the poor and the oppressed. That Luke makes the connection between self-advertisement and selfish disregard of the needy is clear from v. 13 (see also 10:25–37; 20:46–47).

On Planning the Guest List   Luke 14:12–14
                                                          (Matthew 22:1–10)

14:12 The first parable was addressed to the guests. Jesus now turns to the host. Accepted social practice is once more exposed in terms of its potential to exploit and isolate less fortunate members of society. Homer had given the theme poignant expression in the *Odyssey* (17.381–87). Inherited social patterns can become barriers to responsible encounter. It is easy to retreat into relationships that meet one's own needs and satisfy one's own interests. The "now we owe them" approach parallels the lending policies criticized in 6:34. Knowing the right people, cultivating those who may do one some good—these are the steppingstones to success but stumbling blocks for those who would enter the Kingdom. Everyday social habits have a way of rubbing off on one's religious thinking, but God makes no bargains.

14:13–14. The directive in v. 13 is in the spirit of Deut. 14:29 but is contrary to the policy expressed in 2 Sam. 5:8. As in Luke 6:23, the reward is delayed to a moment outside history—**the resurrection of the just** *(anastasis tōn dikaiōn)*. Thoughts on the subject of the resurrection of the dead began to surface especially during the intertestamental period and found strong support among the Pharisees. In Dan. 12:2 the resurrection of both righteous and unrighteous is anticipated, and so also by Paul (Acts 24:15). Luke 20:35 refers to those who are "accounted worthy" to attain the resurrection. In 14:14 these are the just, or the righteous.

The assurance of reward is not designed to redirect the disciple's thinking into commercial channels. Rather, by placing the reward outside the boundaries of present experience, the disciple is called to exercise faith. Faith, without evidence of return on the investment, is the way of the Kingdom. Since the way described is God's way, as reflected in Jesus' own reception of the poor, the disciple has no viable alternative. On the other hand, to use unfortunate people as a device to secure entry into paradise would be a misunderstanding of Jesus' words. The name for such self-servers is "do-gooders." Like many "do-gooders" in the public welfare system who lack creative understanding of the needs of people, they are more interested in projects than in persons. Those who prefer approved and sanctioned ways will undoubtedly find Jesus' advice flaky, out of tune with reality. And such it is, if politics as it is ordinarily played is humanity's ultimate instrument for survival.

The Rude Guests

Luke 14:15–24
(Matthew 22:1–10)

This parable about excuses enlarges on the theme of invitation and brings the preceding discussion into more immediate relation to Jesus' own ministry and revelation of the Kingdom. The recital parallels 13:22–30.

14:15. Silence is hard to bear at a dinner party. No matter how vapid the comment, the stillness must be broken. Perhaps the guest who pronounced the beatitude cited in 14:15 hoped to smooth an awkward moment. But the inane statement is useful only as a literary bridge from the one on candidates for the resurrection (v. 14) to their share in the messianic banquet (vv. 16–17). The guest's remark suggested smugness. Jesus therefore invites this person and others to more serious appraisal of their religious thinking.

14:16. The greatness of the feast emphasizes the generosity of the host. Since the story is, beyond question, a parable of divine Kingdom activity, the feast refers to God's feeding of the people, as in Isa. 25:6–8 (cf. Ps. 22:26).

14:17. In the Orient, as in the West, loose invitations are often given: "We must have you over sometime." Custom in some cases dictated that no one go to a feast without receiving two invitations, for the second would show that the first was meant seriously. Israel received her first invitation through the prophets. Now through Jesus and the apostolic proclamation she hears the final call to participate in the Kingdom.

14:18–20. As if in concert (for the Greek ellipse, see BAGD, p. 88), all excused themselves. Three samples are cited. The first two are at least politely stated; the third is curt. All three reveal disinterest in the feast and concentration on the material and physical aspects of life (see the warnings cited in Luke 12). In the third excuse, Jewish auditors would have noted a relationship to the directive in Deut. 24:5. A bridegroom was to be relieved of any communal responsibility for one year. There may be here a suggestion of legal correctness as a block to appreciation of the Kingdom. Luke 14:1–6 is the nearest illustration of this hazard. In any case, the Pharisees and other religious leaders are clearly envisaged as the recipients of the second invitation, for v. 21 mentions the same types of guests as those named in v. 13, and in precisely the same sequence.

14:21–22. The anger of the host suggests a strong note of judgment. He will have his feast, and his banquet hall must be filled. The double invitation stresses the liberality of the host. His guests come from the city and from the crossroads of commerce. Luke evidently understands these to include the poor in Israel and the gentiles, all outside the established religious grouping.

14:23. The command to compel them to come in was in time past taken literally by some church officials as a directive to use force on the mission field. We have here, of course, a bit of vivid oriental language. It is polite for the invited guest at first to refuse. This gives the host an opportunity to sound more generous and really in earnest as he repeats the invitation. As in Gen. 19:3, the thought is that those who are invited need to be urged. A Tamil proverb reads: "One who is anxious to give will strike people on the cheek" (i.e., compel them to receive).

14:24. This closing verdict would appropriately express the contempt of the host for those who had despised his invitation. But since this is a parable of the Kingdom, the words are to be understood as an expression of judgment. It is a strong way of asserting that those who claim an interest in God, yet are in fact no different from the first group of guests, will not share in the end-time blessings (cf. 13:28–29). The RSV obscures the direct address to the dramatic audience: "You" is plural. The guest described in v. 15 spoke about future blessedness. Jesus says that the future is determined by present response. The Great Party has begun!

Proper Response
Luke 14:25—15:32

Kingdom Cost Accounting
Luke 14:25–35
(Mark 9:50; Matthew 10:37–38; 5:13)

In 14:15–24 God's disappointing experience with Israel was depicted. The note of hostility is now extended to the experience of the disciples, who must count the cost of following One whose destiny was the cross. Unless radical decision is made, the disciple will repeat the mistake of those who rejected the invitation to the banquet.

14:25–27. The RSV obscures the fact that Luke continues his theme of the journey toward Jerusalem: the Greek reads literally, "as many crowds were journeying with him." Followers of Jesus in the New Age are people of "the Way," and they need to be warned of the price of association (see Acts 9:2). Verse 26 is to be understood from the Semitic perspective, which places more emphasis on the observable fact than on the emotion. Disciples must put Jesus so strongly in the center of their thinking that they will appear to others as despisers or haters of their closest relatives. That is, when confronted with a conflict of loyalty they will give priority to the requirements of the Kingdom, and even their own lives will be disposable (cf. Deut. 33:9; Luke 12:4; 16:13).

The stress on parents may suggest that proclamation of the good news had attracted many young people (cf. Acts 2:17). This means that the early community felt strongly the tension of the generation gap widened by the revolutionary nature of Jesus' preaching. Nothing short of opting for the cross will satisfy the totalitarian demand of the Kingdom. In time of persecution, family pressures would be brought to bear. Parents and siblings would urge the disciple not to endanger the family through stubborn allegiance to a suspected radical. Omission of any reference to husbands can be accounted for by the structure of the sentence: the singular subject cannot relate to both a husband and a wife. Clearly, the dangerous Christ of the first century is not the safe Jesus of established cultic patterns in the twentieth century. Matthew places the sayings in a mission directive (Matt. 10:37–38).

If there is any passage that illustrates Jesus' resistance to platitudinous expression, it is this one. And Luke's inclusion of it—with some editorial modification of the tradition—in the face of contrary Greco-Roman sentiments suggests that there is here a port of entry into the very sanctuary of Jesus' self-disclosure and the early believers' conviction of his ultimate claims on them.

This passage runs counter to the expectation pronounced at 1:17 (see on 12:49–53), and it challenges ideals that found expression across Mediterranean culture. The Greek dramatist Euripides writes (Nauck 852):

> Children who reverence their parents will,
> In life and death, have the Gods as friends.
> But I want no partnership at sacrifices,
> Nor will I share the peril at sea, with
> Any who dishonor the authors of their birth.

In related vein, the same dramatist has one of his characters declaim that "children ought to obey the command of their parents" (*Archelaos,* Nauck 234). A devotee of Isis proclaims: "You saw to it that parents were honored

by their children, and you thought of them not only as fathers but as gods"
(*Benefactor,* p. 181).

14:28–33. The two illustrations in these verses are found only in Luke. A
poor cost accountant must be prepared to hear the verdict of fool pronounced on his life. The prudential military counsel enunciated in v. 32 is
proverbial. On his march against Greece, the Persian general Mardonius
used it, albeit in a vain attempt, to win over the Athenians to his side
(Herodotos 8.140). Sempronius, a Roman general, would have done well to
heed it and thus avoid the consequences of his rash march against Hannibal
(Livy *History* 21.54). And Juvenal (1.169–70) warns that once the helmet is
on, it is too late to repent of the fight.

Following Jesus is no invitation to trivial adventure. A church that
encourages its followers to play it safe and to conform with the substandard
practices of surrounding society not only invites disaster but loses all claim
to association with the revolutionary cause of the Kingdom. The invitation
to commitment expressed in v. 33 echoes 6:46–49 and is as total as any
dictator could wish. Everything depends on the decision. A church that
does not spell this out clearly to prospective members or to its constituency
proves false to the good news. Indeed, failure to do so has led the institutionalized church to pussyfoot on a variety of issues.

Even gentile philosophers caught something of the vision expressed in
these sayings. Epiktetos writes:

> Do you imagine that you can keep on doing the things you are doing and
> still claim to be a philosopher? Do you actually think you can dine and
> drink as you do now, or continue to be given to anger and irritability? No,
> you must be alert, work hard, get the better of certain desires, leave those
> who are close to you, be despised by a mere slave, be ridiculed by all those
> who meet you, take second place in everything, including office, honor,
> and the courts. Consider these negatives carefully, and then decide whether
> you are willing to trade these for tranquillity, freedom, and repose. If not,
> don't bother, and don't act like a child—at one moment a philosopher, at
> another a toll collector, then an orator, and then one of Caesar's proc-
> urators. These are contradictory. You must be one person, either good or
> bad. That is to say, you must labor to develop your inner self or work on
> things outside it. Make up your mind. Do you want to be an expert or an
> amateur in matters philosophical?

14:34–35. Since the nature of the disciples' commitment will determine
whether they are good or bad persons, people of integrity or hypocrites (cf.
6:43–45), they may be likened to good or bad salt (see also Matt. 5:13; Mark
9:50). Salt that is hopelessly mixed with impurities is useless. It is good
neither as a condiment nor as a fertilizer (**for the land**). The disciple must
be totally dedicated. The closing words about hearing are not an invitation
to debate (cf. 8:18). To count the cost means to be prepared to risk all, even
life itself, in commitment to the Kingdom.

Finding the Lost   Luke 15:1–32

Luke joins three stories linked by a common theme: rejoicing over the lost. The entire chapter is an expansion of the banquet motif presented in Luke 14, for Jesus is shown to be feasting with **tax collectors and sinners** (v. 1). This is in accordance with his own advice to the Pharisees (14:12–14).

15:2. Unfortunately these particular Pharisees construe Jesus' action as a violation of the instruction laid down, for example, in the Book of Proverbs, that one is not to associate with evildoers (see also Psalm 1; Isa. 52:11; and 2 Cor. 6:14–18). If Jesus were a true prophet, they would argue, he ought to support holiness, and not appear to sanction sin (Luke 7:39). In view of his position as a distinguished teacher, the approach of Jesus is all the more reprehensible. In short, he gives them a bad image.

As some members of a congregation put it when faced with new arrivals: "They're not our kind of people." In everyday parlance such an attitude is called snobbery. Ignored is the fact that Jesus does not sink to the immoral level of sinners but meets them where they are in order to raise them. This grumbling *(diagoggyzō)* is therefore an ominous sign of misinterpretation of God's intentions at work in Jesus' ministry. Israel of old was punished severely for her grumbling in other circumstances (cf. Num. 11:1; 14:27, 29). Jesus would like to spare the Pharisees a repetition of disaster and, as he had done earlier (Luke 5:29–30; cf. Mark 2:15–16; Matt. 9:10–11), invites them to share his own interest in reclamation of the lost.

The Lost Sheep and the Lost Coin   Luke 15:3–10
                                                  (Luke 15:3–7 = Matthew 18:12–14)

15:3–10. Gently and winsomely Jesus tries to bring the Pharisees to God's point of view. The theme of the shepherd is common in the OT. Ezekiel 34:11–16 is programmatic of Jesus' activity as the shepherd of Israel (see also Jer. 31:10–14; Isa. 40:11; Mic. 5:1–4). What Jesus does in behalf of sinners is no different from God's concern for rebellious Israel in the period of the OT (cf. Isa. 65:1). Jesus appeals to common practice. The owner of **a hundred sheep** will **leave the ninety-nine** and restlessly search until he locates the one that is "lost" *(apolōlos,* v. 4). Thus the lost one is not treated as one outside the flock. Similarly, the woman who has lost a coin (v. 8) raises the dust in her earthen-floor home. There is no hint in the text that the coin is part of a necklace, or the like. It is simply one coin out of ten, and she will not rest until she finds it. Be the owner rich or poor, great energy is expended on one lost item. Can Jesus do less when human destiny is at stake?

Affluent Westerners smile at all this fuss, and the idea of a lost-and-found party over one mangy sheep or even a small coin seems utterly ridiculous. But that is just the point. Religious people expect God to be less concerned about lost sinners than they themselves are about some trivial possession. Values are completely perverted. God's most precious possession is humanity! God rejoices at the return of the lost (cf. 2:10) and cannot wait to put on a party.

Against so much that is drab in religion, Jesus depicts the gaiety of a Father who invites the angels to the homecoming festival. Heaven rings with the laughter of the feast (15:7 and 10). Somber, morbid religiosity has no place in the Kingdom. Dancing, the blowing of trumpets, the beating of drums is a legitimate part of the church's worship (cf. 2 Sam. 6:5). The cult of respectability must give way to the cultivation of the art of joy over God's delight in reclaiming the refuse of humanity. The church's first order of business is not to engage in strokes of the constituency. In worship the sheep congratulate the Shepherd, either for finding them or for finding others.

God does not commend the righteous for remaining righteous (15:7), and Jesus has not come to compliment them for what they ought to be in the first place. Nor has he criticized their standards. Their position is not made less secure by Jesus' outreach to publicans and sinners. All he expects of them is that they share his joy over the return of the lost. In the ministry of Jesus, they are to see the God of their ancestors at work. Jesus does not discredit God through his association with sinners. Scribes do it through their refusal to share in God's embrace of sinners.

Some commentators have looked for subtle differences between the two parables. The sheep, it has been suggested, was lost through its own stupidity; the coin, by the carelessness of its owner. The shepherd and the woman, it has been claimed, represent the church. This is all beside the point. The church comes under rebuke in these stories. It is precisely in the church that arrogant loveless attitudes toward the fallen and the disenfranchised display themselves.

The Parable of the Reluctant Brother   Luke 15:11–32

Among the papyri found in Egypt (Preisigke [1922], pp. 72–73) is a letter from Antonios Longus to his mother, Neilus:

> Greetings: I hope you are in good health; it is my constant prayer to Lord Sarapis. I did not expect you to come to Metropolis, therefore I did not go there myself. At the same time, I was ashamed to go to Kanaris, because I am so shabby. I am writing to tell you that I am naked. I plead with you, forgive me. I know well enough what I have done to myself. I have learned my lesson. I know I made a mistake. I have heard from Postumos, who met you in the area of Arsinoe. Unfortunately he told you everything. Don't you know that I would rather be a cripple than owe so much as a cent to anyone? I plead, I plead with you . . ." (Signed) Antonios Longus, your son.

The story that Jesus relates evidently recites a familiar tale of woe, but in Luke's form it goes far beyond any experience of a wayward son. For Jesus' story, as recorded in Luke, recites not so much the waywardness of a young man who fell on bad times as the vagrancy of a young man whose body stayed home but whose heart was lost in misunderstanding of a father's love. Like the parable of the lost coin, this story is found only in Luke. It is the tale of a would-be benefactor who has lost his way but in the end learns the meaning of true beneficence. For a detailed discussion of prodigality, see Aristotle *Nikomachean Ethics* 4.28–36.

15:12. According to laws of property, it was possible for children to receive a division of the father's capital during his lifetime (cf. Sir. 33:19–20). According to Deut. 21:17, the firstborn son is to receive twice the amount given to each of his brothers.

15:13–15. The young son was not going to put off living. He **gathered all he had**, that is, he turned his holdings, apparently a third of the estate, into cash. Yet in all this he did not stain the family name as did Ctesippos son of Chabrias, who sold the stones of his father's monument—which had cost the Athenians a thousand drachmas—to adopt a prodigal life style (Athenaeus *Deipnosophists* 4.165e). After he squandered his fortune and, to all intents and purposes, had thrown "the pearl of his soul into a cup of wine," he was reduced to feeding pigs, a degrading occupation for a Jew.

15:16. To say that he would have been happy to eat of the (carob) **pods that the swine ate** is a way of saying that he was in the most desperate circumstances. In the words of Petronius, a wastrel of literary fame, "Friendship endures only to the last coin" (*Satyricon* 80.9). Once himself a benefactor, the young man finds no benefactors in the far-off country.

15:17. Then he came to himself. He saw what a fool he was. His instinct for survival coincides with his memory of the parental hearth. Exploited by his boss, he thinks of his father's **hired servants**, who are paid enough to be able to keep themselves in food and other necessities, with money to spare. The contrast between his generous father and the tightfisted man for whom he works is sketched with pathetic economy.

15:18. His speech is prepared. The content is reminiscent of Isa. 63:16–19. Inclusion of "heaven," a roundabout expression for God, reemphasizes for the auditor that God is a forgiving father, acting through Jesus, who invites publicans and sinners to the banquet. In a less theological vein, Cicero put a similar plea to Caesar in behalf of a client: "He blundered, he behaved recklessly, he is sorry. I find refuge in your clemency, I plead indulgence for his fault, I implore that he be pardoned" (*Ligarius* 30).

15:19. The son does not expect to be received back as a member of the family. He does not even ask for the status of his father's household slaves, who enjoyed the constant companionship of a kind master. The hired servant, to be distinguished from a slave, did his work and went to his own quarters. But at least the young man would have some contact with his father.

15:20. The picture of the father waiting for his son is an echo of Jer. 31:18–20; God longs for the return of erring Israel.

15:21. The son is unable to complete his prepared speech, so great is the father's compassion (cf. Luke 1:78). There is not one word of recrimination. It is not a matter of worthiness but of the father's affection.

15:22. The father now gives orders to his "servants" (*douloi*, i.e., "slaves"). The robe is of the best quality. The ring, a symbol of authority (Wettstein cites 1 Macc. 1:15; Gen. 41:42; Esth. 3:10), confirms full sonship and right of inheritance. The shoes ("sandals") are a pathetic note, erasing the son's humiliation.

15:23. The **fatted calf** would be the animal saved for a special feast. And this is the moment!

15:24. Once Ezekiel asked whether the dry bones of Israel could throb again with life (Ezekiel 37). God's forgiving mercy assures the resurrection of one who is lost. The rich man had said to himself, "Enjoy life" (12:19), and ensured disaster. Yet there is a place for merriment—when one celebrates not oneself but the return of the lost.

15:25-26. The elder brother is an important feature of the story. His attitude reflects the grumbling of the Pharisees (v. 2), who could not bear to see certain social sanctions and status go by the board.

15:27. The reply of the slave is carefully worded. He reminds the elder brother that his **brother has come** home and that his **father has killed the fatted calf** because the young man returned **safe and sound** *(hygiainō)*. Emphasis is again placed on the feelings and attitudes of the father.

15:28. But the elder brother has no conception of what lies on his father's heart. His anger contrasts with the Father's repeated pleading.

15:29. When he says **I have served** (*douleuō*, i.e., "slaved"), the mask drops, revealing the frigidity of his soul. The father thought he had a son! But to the older son the father's house spelled slavery. And he was a good slave, never disobeying a "command" (*entolē*, usually used of God's commandments). Yet not so much as a little goat did his father give him for a barbecue party!

15:30. With contempt he says, **this son of yours.** He should have said "my brother," but he aims to cut a father's heart to shreds. How does he know that his brother spent his time with whores? Was his heart in the far country, while his body stayed home in obedience? But his estimate of his brother may not be fraternal overkill. Athenaeus makes reference in his discussion of prodigality to a number of instances in which females were partners in a prodigal's fling (*Deipnosophists* 4.165–69). As in the present day, many in the Mediterranean world would probably have shared the sentiments of the older brother. In a play of Menander's entitled *Ship's Captain,* one of the characters addresses Mother Earth and says: "It is only right that anyone who receives an estate and forthwith devours it should set sail, never to touch land again" (*Deipnosophists* 4.166b–c).

15:31. Few fathers could have appealed more tenderly to a wayward son. **Son, you are always with me.** *Teknon* (RSV: **son**) means "child." Thus the prophet spoke of Israel (Isa. 60:9). Was it not enough for the older brother that he was "with" the father? Another man would one day welcome such type of assurance (see Luke 23:42). The father thought he was loved for himself, not for the prospect of a kid. Besides, **all that is mine is yours.** There is no greater degree of beneficence. The elder son was free, not a slave. He had only to ask, and the father would have been more than glad to give (cf. 11:9). Moreover, he had received his part of the inheritance. What was his complaint? The younger son returned to be "with" the father. What more does the older brother want?

15:32. In his final word the father pleads necessity: **it was fitting** (*edei*, the Greek verb used frequently in Luke's gospel of salvation necessity (2:49; 4:43; 9:22; 13:16, 33; 17:25; 19:5; 22:37; 24:7, 26, 44). Joy is the only option if the sinner returns. Gently the older brother is reminded: not "this your son" (v. 30) but **this your brother.** The "far country" (v. 13) does not invalidate relationships. The older brother, like the righteous, needed no repentance as ordinarily understood (v. 7). Only one thing was lacking, willingness to share a father's joy. But like the instruction to the young man in 18:22, it was a call to decision.

A lost sinner is no less precious to God than a sheep is to a man or a coin to a woman. One's ability to rejoice with God over the return of the lost measures the validity of one's claim to understand and know God. The best commentary on the entire chapter is Eph. 2:1–19, but a paragraph in *The Christian Century* (July 17, 1968) illustrates well the point of Jesus' pronouncement. The writer had requested help from a pastor and his congregation for the rehabilitation of a parolee. After a series of disappointing attempts to interest Christians, he told his story to a friend who dealt professionally with troubled people. His friend reminded him that "the church is not for sinners." It "has become the place where people can come together once a week to reaffirm a sense of wellbeing and acceptance in society. They come not out of a sense of guilt or sinfulness, but to make overt manifestation of their righteousness and goodness. Most church goers," he said, "look on the fallen with scorn and distrust; they would find it practically impossible to speak to the needs of a recognized sinner." The fact that the church has turned much of its own work over to the YMCA, family service, and social welfare agencies, the writer went on, was proof that his friend was right.

Ultimately the elder brother was like the son in another parable (Matt. 21:28–32) who promised to work in the vineyard but never showed up. Another son disclaimed all interest in the vineyard but later on repented and began to work. Jesus concluded that parable with these words: "The tax collectors and the harlots go into the Kingdom of God before you."

Isokrates said in his *Panegyrikos* (46 [50]) that other localities held impressive festivals, yet only for a brief time, and at long intervals. But Athens, he boasted, was itself an ongoing festival for all who came to visit her. Jesus said something similar about the Kingdom of God. The partying never stops.

Urgent Appeal: Wisdom and Folly

Luke 16:1–31

The parables in Luke 15 were addressed to Pharisees. Luke 16 begins with address to the disciples and continues the theme of a proper sense of values. Possibly Luke also aims to correct a misunderstanding that might arise from the previous stress on forgiving mercy. The young son, in regard to the squandering of his possessions, is not a model for the community, and forgiveness is not an invitation to irresponsibility.

The Crooked Steward   Luke 16:1–9

The story of the crooked steward is simple enough, but one must be on guard not to concentrate on the character of the steward. His dishonesty is clear at the beginning, but gaps in our knowledge of ancient economic practice make it impossible to determine with certainty whether his terminal action was viewed on the same plane. Nor is it of major consequence. The point of the story is prudence. It is impossible to determine with certainty the traditional boundaries of the various sayings that Luke included in this chapter, but Greco-Roman auditors would be impressed by the common theme of proper use of money.

Ordered to surrender his books, the steward maintains a cool head in the crisis. Succinct phrases describe his predicament: "What shall I do?" "Digging's not for me!" "Begging's not my style." "Ah, I have it!" (**I have decided what to do**, v. 4) His mind pulls a fast trigger. Already he sees the welcome mats laid down.

16:5–7. The steward may have been in charge of the annual receipt of rental from tenant farmers who would pay in kind, or he may have kept accounts of his boss's dealings with merchants. In any case, he invites the debtors to alter with their own hand the figures on the contracts in his possession, thus clearing the debtors of any obligation beyond the stipulated amounts. Naturally their gratitude in response to such beneficence would be immense (see 6:32). Variation in the figures was part of the plot.

16:8. The owner is not deceived, but why his laudatory comment should have caused so much perplexity is one of the curiosities in the history of interpretation, for his reaction is not unique. Aristotle, in his *Politics* (1259a.7–8), recites the story of Dionysios, ruler of Syracuse, who ordered a competitive banker out of town but recognized the man's talent. In any event, numerous readers of Luke's story have boggled at the verdict and missed the main point.

Many a judge or warden has, in fact, scratched his head in amazement over the ingenuity of a client. West Germany's Judge Hans-Ulrich Schroeder told Konrad Kujau, forger of diaries ascribed to Adolf Hitler, that he had a rare gift for imitating handwriting and praised the quality of Kujau's work. Similarly, this master was forced to admit that his clerk was extraordinarily shrewd. And just as leaven could be used as an illustration of the Kingdom (13:20–21), or a dilatory judge in an encouragement to prayer (18:1–8), so this crook's cool thinking is used as a model for the disciple. Jesus did not launder truth relating to human nature. **The sons of this world** (a Semitism for "the people of this world") are more shrewd among their own kind (**own generation**) than are God's people, **the sons of light.** This last expression occurs in the scrolls of Qumran (1QS 1:9; 2:16; 3:13; see also Eph. 5:8) and may indicate a thrust at the Pharisees (Luke 16:14) who boasted in the Law as their light to life.

The story is an illustration of the principle expressed in Luke 6:30–35. In the everyday world of business, prudence is exercised to secure temporary advantage. God's people, who have higher goals and expectations, ought to display at least as much prudence in relation to God and their future hope. Yet when it comes to material possessions, they often forget that the proper use of those possessions is an integral part of their total religious experience.

16:9. As a result of his extraordinary benefactions the steward could face the future. By way of application, Jesus instructs his followers to be benefactors. "Mammon," an Aramaic term for wealth, is termed "unrighteous" *(adikia)* because it is often used as an instrument of injustice (cf. Mark 12:40, in an indictment of the scribes). The steward had demonstrated that fact in the behavior ascribed to him at v. 1. But as his subsequent action showed, it can be used constructively in behalf of others. Disciples of Jesus are to use it in the interests of justice.

It is improbable that with the words **make friends** Luke limits the application to poor people who will acknowledge their benefactors. Rather, the phrase is a reminder to the disciples that they must grasp the principle expressed in the illustration. A speaker, for example, may use an illustration drawn from athletics and point the moral: "Play a good game" (cf. 1 Cor. 9:24). As in v. 4, the verb "to receive" means "welcome" *(dechomai)*. Eternal habitations are the living quarters of the righteous (cf. *Enoch* 39:4). These are eternal as opposed to the temporary advantage on earth. Thus the fate of the disciple will not be that of the rich fool (Luke 12:21).

Instead of wealth being viewed as a criterion of success, its absence may be a stronger guarantee of a reception into heaven. In Menander's *Misanthrope*, Sostratos counsels his father, Kallipides, to stay in control of his wealth and not leave it to the whim of chance. One can do this, he says, by being kind and generous to others. And he concludes (lines 809–12):

> Then, should you slip on Fortune's path,
> you'll get your money back with interest.
> A friend whom you can see is better far
> than unspied money buried in the ground.

Mammon and the Kingdom   Luke 16:10–18
                                                    (Matthew 6:24; 11:12; 5:18, 32)

Other sayings of Jesus spoken on various occasions reinforce the message on proper use of wealth. Again there seems to be a thrust at Pharisees who claimed to be the guardians of God's interests. But the problem is perennial, and Pharisees had no monopoly on a common vice of religionists. See again the warning in 1 Tim. 3:3 and note the depreciation, since Vatican II, of emphasis on pomp and ecclesiastical extravagance in numerous Christian communities.

16:10–11. Lest auditors infer that the unjust steward is a model with respect to his misuse of his master's property, the disciples are reminded that they will be judged on the basis of faithful use. The word "little" *(elachistos)* is used to describe material possessions, thus making **the true riches** stand out in contrast. These true riches are of the same order as the treasure promised in 6:20–21, 38.

16:12. Should disciples conclude from the Lord's story that they have a right to dispose of other people's property, perhaps to make friends for themselves, they are reminded that faithless use of property belonging to another will jeopardize their own attainment of the promised hope.

16:13. This verse expresses the single-mindedness discussed in 11:34. Life is not to be lived in fragments. A disciple is to view the whole from the perspective of God's interests. The manner in which the material benefits are used will determine the integrity of one's religious claims. This saying is included in the Sermon on the Mount (Matt. 6:24).

16:14. In contrast to the spirit of generosity featured in the preceding verses, the Pharisees on Luke's dramatic stage are described as **lovers of money** *(philargyroi)*, a phrase that is probably to be construed as an indictment of illiberality.

16:15. This verse is a commentary on 11:42–44. The Pharisees justify *(dikaioō)* themselves before people, that is, they impress them with their religiosity; but God is the One with whom they have to do. The last part of v. 15 expands on this thought. Congratulations of their contemporaries only increase their guilt before God; for God, who searches the heart (cf. 2:35; 1 Sam. 16:7; Ps. 7:9; Prov. 17:3; 21:2; Jer. 11:20; Rev. 2:23), is not impressed by what people consider exalted (cf. Luke 1:52): **for what is exalted . . . is an abomination.**

16:16. This verse (cf. Matt. 11:12) appears to reflect a charge leveled against the church's proclamation of the Kingdom. Pharisees complain that the law and the prophets were in force until John the Baptist, but since his time the Kingdom of God is being proclaimed and all, with no distinction between good and bad, are taking it by storm (see the related criticism at 15:2). In short, from the perspective of some Pharisees the gospel lowers religious standards.

16:17. Jesus replies that the standards of the Kingdom are as high or higher than the Law. The single-minded devotion he urges does not detract from Moses but takes seriously every pronouncement of the Law. Matthew's version of this saying (Matt. 5:18) is put even more strongly. As Luke 16:18 will demonstrate, the point of Jesus' dictum is that rules and regulations are not to provide sanctions for one's own interests but to advance the well-being of others. The principal function of a constitution, ecclesiastical or civil, is to protect the rights of the powerless.

16:18. The Pharisees, not Jesus, are in question because of their undermining of the Law. Through their own casuistry in dealing with the problem of divorce, they accommodate the Law to their own interests. In Jewish law, only the husband had the right to secure a divorce (see Deut. 24:1–4), and an avaricious one might well find a woman who was more financially attractive than his wife. Divorce, says Jesus, is bad enough, but remarriage to another woman while the divorced party is living is adultery.

Jesus overcomes the disadvantages of a patriarchally devised legal system by proposing a standard that exceeds that of his contemporary legal experts. His word is also powerfully directed against what is, in effect, a pernicious repatriarchalization at the end of the twentieth century as increasing numbers of males exhibit lack of commitment to marriage responsibilities and enduring relationships. By implication, Jesus' instruction on the proper use of wealth is also in harmony with the strongest demand. Variations of this saying in Mark 10:12 and Matt. 5:32 reflect ecclesiastical debate because of special problems that developed as a result of the worldwide mission.

The Rich Man and Lazarus   Luke 16:19–31

Because of the shift back to the disciples in 17:1, the story of the rich man and Lazarus is probably to be viewed as addressed to the Pharisees (see 16:15). This is Luke's version of the life styles of the rich and the famous. The story carries out the theme of Luke's Gospel, namely, exaltation of the poor and humbling of the rich (1:51–53; 6:20–26), but with an additional warning to those who demand signs. According to Pharisaic viewpoint, riches would be a stamp of God's approval on a righteous life. Jesus' story overthrows this traditional view.

16:19–21. Unique in Jesus' parables is the use of a specific name for the poor man. Later tradition supplied one also for the rich man—*Neuēs,* read in a text of the second century. **Lazarus** means "God helps," and Jesus' intention may have been to emphasize by the use of only one name the contrast between the self-sufficient rich man and dependent Lazarus. But it is more certain that the name was included in order to expedite the succeeding dialogue. In any event, the rich man, despite his mastery of the good life, has no real identity; poor Lazarus enjoys personhood.

In a few bold strokes the ostentatious affluence of the rich man is contrasted with the degradation of Lazarus. The one is clothed in garments worthy of a king; he is a connoisseur of the finest cuisine. The other, too weak from hunger, cannot even ward off the pesky dogs that lick his sores. These unclean animals not only increase the distress of the poor man but sharpen the contrast between the rich man, who is secure in his ceremonial purity, and poor Lazarus, who can make no claim on God for ritual conformity.

Lest the point of the story be misunderstood, it is important to note that the rich man is not accused of refusing a minimum of alms to Lazarus. In contrast to what is stated in 15:16, there is no indication that he was denied the scraps. Lazarus lay in front of his door. Beggars are not directed to the homes of skinflints. And the Greek text says that "he was desirous of getting his fill of the scraps that were falling from the rich man's table." But the text does suggest that Lazarus never really got his fill. In accordance with the promise in 6:21, it was not long in coming, for the reversal is about to begin. (On the theme, cf. Juvenal 3.208–10.)

In fairness to this rich man, it must be pointed out that John Steinbruck, pastor of Luther Place Memorial Church, Washington, D.C., thought he found a paradigm of more lamentable insensitivity to the plight of the poor in the very capital of the United States. In response to one of his requests for leftovers from state banquets so that he might have additional distributions for the hungry, one spokesperson for the White House said to a reporter, "We think the idea is disgusting."

16:22–23. The text indicates that Lazarus was taken away bodily into the realm of the blessed to enjoy the intimate fellowship of Abraham, the hope of every pious Jew (see 1:73). The picture suggested may be that of a feast, where people recline at table. Lazarus has the place of honor and is able to lean closely toward Abraham, even as the beloved disciple did on the night of Jesus' betrayal (see John 13:23; cf. Matt. 8:11 and Luke 13:29–30). **The rich man also died**, but that was his only point of identity with Lazarus.

The simple statement, **and was buried**, does not suggest an elaborate funeral contrasting with that accorded to Lazarus. On the contrary, nothing is said of Lazarus's burial. In contrast to the rich man, who received the normal rites due a pious Israelite—and this he was, as the sequel shows—Lazarus was carried to **Abraham's bosom**. The subsequent narrative does not aim to give information on the furniture of heaven or the temperature of hell. Dialogue and description are all designed to sharpen the contrast in the conditions of the departed and to reinforce the perception that external circumstances on earth are no criterion of moral worth.

Greco-Roman auditors would be impressed by the reversal in fortunes. Only persons of exceptional excellence *(aretē)* gained entrance into what Greeks since Homer's time called the Elysian Isles of the Blest. Lazarus was one of the privileged number to enjoy blessedness in the afterlife. The rich man, on the other hand, having failed to grasp the point that was made in vv. 1–15, finds himself in the kind of torment described by Vergil in the *Aeneid* (6.540–43).

16:24. The rich man begins his plea with **Father Abraham,** and the words have the eerie force of a thunderclap of doom. They are precisely the words that John the Baptist had warned against (3:8). The phrase was a part of the rich man's liturgical pattern while he was in this world. His lips spoke to God, but his heart prayed to Mammon. Business was his religion.

Still arrogant, the rich man orders Abraham to send Lazarus on an errand. He knows the poor man's name; he does not know Lazarus. His alms were castoff clothing, toys that were no longer needed, time that satisfied a temporary curiosity, a ten-dollar bill to ease his conscience. But to become involved with one inadequate person, to really share problems and heartaches, and perhaps to endure the disappointment of failure—that was not to his liking. He had no comprehension of what really goes on in pockets of appalling hunger, malnutrition, and despair, and he had no grasp of the fact that poverty and sickness are alien to divine intention. The rich man was one of those ninety-nine righteous who needed no repentance (Luke 15:7). He made only one mistake. He was in violation of the instruction given in 14:13.

16:25. "And now" *(nyn de)* it is too late. To Abraham, the man remains a "child" *(teknon* as in 15:31), in response to the "Father." But the rich man has cut himself off from the fullness of the relationship. Luke 16:25 reproduces the thought of 6:21, 24. The rich man had thought along the lines of many a religious person who views wealth as a verdict of divine approval. But God's ways are not man's judgments. Riches per se are not condemmed, but misplaced confidence can keep one from having treasure in heaven (see 12:33–34; 18:22).

16:26. A great chasm has been fixed. Life on earth is the place for decision, but the rich man had created the chasm before his arrival; and even now he has not learned his lesson, for he views Lazarus as his personal lackey. There is no bridge! *Enoch* 102–3 is an eloquent commentary on the relative fates of the two men.

16:27–29. The rich man then takes a different tack, with a plea for his five brothers. In the economy of the story this figure suggests the large number of people in Israel who claim formal association with Abraham, but are in peril of suffering the same fate as the rich man. Wettstein cites Plato's *Republic* (10.614D) in illustration of messengers sent from the dead. In Lucian's *Demonax* (43) someone asks, "What are things like in Hades?" Comes the answer: "Wait, and I will see that you get information directly from the place."

Luke's auditors could not fail to note that the rich man's tedious orthodoxy greased his trip to the reversal pronounced at 6:24. John the Baptist had warned: "Do not begin to say to yourselves, 'We have Abraham as our father'" (3:8). But this man has now said it twice, and in a moment will confirm his inaccessibility to any challenging idea by saying it a third time.

16:30–31. The rich man's final request and the reply of Abraham are to be understood in the light of Jesus' and the church's mission experience. Jesus' contemporaries demanded signs as ratification of his credentials (see Luke 11:29). But the main sign is that the poor hear the good news (7:22; cf. 6:20). The apostles proclaimed the resurrection of Jesus, but there was no wholesale repentance on the part of Israel. Luke gives the reason in 16:29–31. Many in Israel claim allegiance to Moses and the prophets, but their ears are shut to the testimony of their Scriptures (see on 8:10). If they are not ready to hear them, no amount of signs will persuade them, not even the resurrection of Jesus. Thus 16:31 suggests an explanation for the fact that Jesus did not reveal himself as resurrected Lord to anyone but the disciples. The Scriptures are open to faith, and Jesus is the authentic teacher in Israel. Through the apostolic interpretation of the Scriptures, Jesus' death and resurrection are seen in proper perspective (cf. 24:25–27; Acts 2:37–42; 8:26–35).

Those who sense their need will understand. A Tamil proverb reads: "Though one pull out one's eyes and throw them before him, the other will only say, 'It is jugglery.'" There is none so blind as the one who *will* not see. The rich man felt no need, for he was secure in his wealth, and his religion was purely formal. About the worst that could be said of him is that he was engaged in no widespread plot to enhance the glory of God. Therefore his reservation in hell was assured.

Moral Responsibility and Faith
Luke 17:1–10

On Offenses
Luke 17:1–2
(Mark 9:42; Matthew 18:6–7)

17:1. The Lord now shifts his instruction to the disciples. Behind the phrase **temptations to sin** lies the word from which "scandal" is derived *(ta skandala)*. Traps or snares to sin rather than stumbling blocks are meant. A woe is pronounced (as in 6:24–26) on those who ought to know better, namely, Pharisees, and in Luke's time members of the Christian community.

17:2. Little ones *(mikroi)* are people of no account in the eyes of a public that subscribes to power and influence as determinants of identity. They lurk behind the figure of the lost sheep and the lost coin, the prodigal son, and poor Lazarus. The description in 7:28 applies to them. For such as these Jesus came, and those who are better informed have a larger responsibility. The severity of the punishment expresses Jesus' indignation.

On Forgiveness
Luke 17:3–4
(Matthew 18:15, 21–22)

17:3. Take heed to yourselves is not, as the semicolon in the RSV suggests, to be connected only with the subsequent saying. Rather, these words serve as a bridge between vv. 1–2 and 3–4. As at 12:1; 21:34; Acts 5:35; 20:28, this phrase reminds disciples to be conscious of the great peril confronting them. Not only may they expose others to entrapment, but, forgetting their own liability to sin, they may act arrogantly toward an erring brother or sister (cf. 6:37). If a believer misses the mark, one must rebuke *(epitimaō)* the person. The story of the prodigal son does not mean that sin is to be taken lightly, and an outlaw will reinforce the point at 23:40.

17:4. But (this is the force of the conjunction *kai* here) if he repents, he is to be forgiven. The prodigal returned submissive to his father. To berate him would have been unconscionable. The expression **seven times** is not to be taken statistically, nor does it encourage lighthearted repentance. Jesus confronts the disciple, not the erring brother. Luke's auditors would ask whether, for example, sins committed after baptism could be forgiven. The principle expressed in 6:37–38 and 11:4 is to be followed. No scores are to be kept; the door to the erring is always to be kept open. Thus 17:1–2 reminds disciples to maintain the highest standards for themselves, and vv. 3–4 discourage any pride or arrogance that might result from preoccupation with one's own piety.

Jewish literature is replete with admonitions about forgiveness (see, e.g., SB 1:424–26, 795–97). The boasts of clemency by certain Roman administrators toward their enemies are also well known (see, e.g., Augustus's self-adulation in the *Res Gestae* 1.3; cf. Horace *Secular Poem* 51–52). The growth of the Christian community after Pentecost was the direct result of proclamation of divine clemency at and after Pentecost (see, e.g., Acts 2:38; 3:17–20). In view of his denial of the Lord, Peter would have good cause to be grateful for this dominical saying (cf. 22:31–34).

On Total Commitment   Luke 17:5–10
(Mark 11:23; Matthew 17:20; 21:21)

At this point **the apostles** enter with dialogue. As role models for supervisory personnel, such as presbyters or bishops (cf. Acts 20), they must be exemplary in their attitudes and conduct. If they are to teach others how to handle grace in interpersonal relationships, they must be free of all arrogance and illusions of self-importance.

17:5. Most translations, including the RSV, obscure Luke's use of the "master-slave" word pair in vv. 5–10, with the result that his point is totally obscured.

The apostles address their "master" *(kyrios)*. The correlative in vv. 7–10 is "slave" *(doulos)*. Faith viewed as confidence is of course dependent on the reliability of the one in whom the confidence is placed. The concomitant of confidence is commitment. Masters answer to no one but themselves in respect to the assignments that they make, and slaves are to be totally committed to the execution of their master's instructions. Slaves do not second-guess their owner. The expression **Increase our faith!** is in effect a plea for further reassurance and at the same time a statement of commitment to the Master. In his two-volume work Luke presents both God and Jesus as recipients of total allegiance. Since Jesus Christ is the One Name (Acts 4:12), commitment to him is the equivalent of commitment to God. Apostleship begins with the Chief Apostle (see 4:18).

17:6. The illustration in this verse points out that what the church's officials and bureaucrats need is not additional faith but faith pure and simple, that is, with integrity. Both Matthew and Mark use a related form of this saying, except that in their versions a mountain (cf. Zech. 4:7), not a **sycamine tree**, is to be moved. Mark 11:23 and Matt. 21:21 are part of a story dealing with Jesus' cursing of a fig tree. Luke does not include this account in his book but uses in altered form the saying embedded in it. The simile **as a grain of mustard seed** is used in Matt. 17:20. A sycamine tree, or black mulberry, has an extensive root system. To tell a mulberry tree to be uprooted would therefore display confidence in the command of unique resources. Furthermore, trees are not usually planted in the sea. The point of the text is that faith, by drawing on unprecedented authority, accomplishes what is beyond the normal scope of humanity. Jesus majored in rhetoric of the bizarre, but far less so than did the philosopher Empedokles, who taught the use of drugs to assist in the control of nature (Diogenes Laertius 8.59). In related vein, Petronius has one of his characters speak of moving bushes from Mt. Ida to the sea (*Satyricon* 134).

At 9:37–43 Luke, perhaps in anticipation of the present account, omitted Mark's reference to a father's cry for help in his "unbelief" (Mark 9:24). In sum, Jesus, identified again as the Master, assures the apostles that he will back them in all their enterprises with his own apostolic authority, provided they never forget who they are in relation to him (vv. 7–10). Paul's self-identification as slave of Jesus Christ (Rom. 1:1; Gal. 1:10; Phil. 1:1; Tit. 1:10) is enlightening commentary on Luke's recital.

17:7–9. These verses describe the character of the faith required to bear the burdens of special ministries. Jesus' sense of humor once again finds expression. Any listener would at least smile at the thought of a master telling his slave: "See, I have supper ready for you. Sit down"; or a master saying to his slave, "It was very kind of you, sir, to plow up the fields today." Slaves did their assigned tasks and that was the end of it. Woe to the slave who disobeyed. This illustration would, of course, be misunderstood if one were to make negative inferences about the character of God, who is most frequently described as Father. As one can readily conclude from 12:37, Jesus can aim an illustration in more than one direction. Quite evidently the attitude of the disciple is the point of comparison. Just as the righteous of 15:7 were not to anticipate congratulations for remaining in the fold, so the disciple is not to expect a pat on the back for doing his assigned task. Paul once said that he awaited no laurels for preaching the gospel (1 Cor. 9:16).

A cavalryman once asked his commanding officer, Papirius Cursor, for some relief from a difficult campaign. "You are relieved from patting your horse," was the Roman officer's curt reply. A Tamil proverb asks: "Should one's stomach be honored for digesting food?" Were the church's officials to grasp this message with even greater sense of urgency, suggests Luke, the People of God would see less anxiety about personal popularity and institutional security and more vigorous interest in carrying out the mandates of Jesus Christ. There would be less concern to project the power of office, and more devotion to the creative enterprise of service. Jesus himself sets the standard (Luke 22:26–27).

17:10. This verse offers an effective antidote to burnout. To do **all that is commanded** is the assignment. Burnout partially results from an attempt to slave for two or more masters, including perhaps a congregation, the ecclesiastical system, and a family. The commands must be recognized from one direction only and all other obligations reviewed in the light of that commitment to God's action in Jesus Christ. As Acts 5:29 indicates, the apostles inwardly digested the message. They learned from Jesus the art of ecclesiastical disobedience and yet were totally committed to the ecclesiastical task.

A call to commitment is not an invitation to omnicompetence. Many so-called laypeople have gifts for ministry that their officials do not possess. Redistribution of tasks and revision of traditional views of ordination may be necessary to carry out more effectively God's program (see Acts 1:7–8). The church, its officials, its ministers, and all Christians who are engaged in special services are slaves of Jesus Christ, not of tradition.

Burnout is associated with feelings of indispensability. Periodic strokes make one feel needed, but they are irrelevant, suggests Jesus, in the kind of relationship that he envisages. Slaves who have done their duty are to say, **We are unworthy** slaves, that is, as the text goes on to explain, people who have merely done what they were obliged to do. This is the ultimate in faith. The Master could find others to do the job. His program is not dependent on the slaves in question. But service under him is a privilege. Moreover, one who works for reward will never get it, for the reward is a plus freely and lavishly given by a generous Father (see 6:23). Rabbi Johanan b. Zakkai underlined the words of Jesus: "Even though you have been faithful in carrying out the Law, claim no special merit; for to that end you were created" (SB 2:235).

Although vv. 7–10 appear primarily to address problems of internal governance, their message is pertinent for all Christians. But ministers engaged in proclamation will do well to let their hearers know that they themselves have made the primary application.

THIRD PHASE OF THE JOURNEY
TO JERUSALEM
Luke 17:11—18:30

A Grateful Samaritan
Luke 17:11–19

Reminders that Jesus is heading toward **Jerusalem** have appeared at intervals since 9:50, and always as a corrective of misunderstanding. In

9:51–56 the misunderstanding concerned Jesus' role as Elijah. The recital in 10:38–41 put into larger perspective the question of mercy discussed in the story of the Good Samaritan. The statement in 13:22 is followed by a question about salvation; 13:33 is embedded in a context describing Israel's hostility; and 14:25 introduces a series of sayings on decisive discipleship that are designed to cool rash enthusiasm.

Luke's introduction of the motif of the journey *(kai egeneto en tō poreuesthai)* in 17:11 indicates that he views the story of the lepers as an important illustration of basic misunderstanding in Israel. At 17:5 the apostles asked Jesus to increase their faith. The present story reveals that faith properly conceived is faith in Jesus. In 17:7–10 humble recognition of obligation, without sense of merit, was emphasized. The Samaritan who returned in gratitude contrasts with the nine Jews who accepted the messianic benefit as something owed them by God. Luke's geographical description at the end of v. 11 defies explanation.

17:12–13. Luke's grammar preserves the colloquial tone of his source. Since the lepers were not allowed to enter the village, they meet Jesus at the gate, yet maintaining the distance prescribed by Moses (Lev. 13:46).

17:14. Instead of speaking a word of healing (as in 5:13), Jesus tells them to show themselves to the priests (see on 5:14). The point is important for the understanding of the sequel, for the lepers are not yet healed. But when they do find themselves healed, will they attribute their good fortune to Jesus or go on their way without one word of recognition? The text does not specify the precise moment when the lepers were healed. But it was while they were on their "journey" *(poreuthentes* = **as they went**).

17:15–16. One of them, as soon as he **saw that he was healed**, returned. Faith makes him innovative in the instant. The need to thank his benefactor on the spot takes precedence over Mosaic regulations. His praise of God, like that of the shepherds (2:20), is accompanied by recognition of the instrument of his healing—Jesus. That the healed man should understand is all the more remarkable, at least from a Judean perspective, for he was a **Samaritan** (see on 10:33).

17:17–18. All the lepers had asked Jesus for mercy, and according to Ps. 30:10–12 thanksgiving is the proper response to mercy received. But nine of the lepers fail to understand the meaning of mercy and that God's most eloquent expression of it takes place in Jesus. Hence they are not criticized for failing to give thanks to Jesus but for failing to return and give God the glory, that is, the credit for disclosing the divine identity in and through Jesus, their Messiah. This is faith—to recognize the point at which God's glory is revealed, namely, in Jesus, who welcomes the lowly, the poor, the leper. This Jesus invites all to shed their legal self-confidence and their self-aggrandizement that is maintained at the expense of others.

17:19. The Samaritan is told: **Your faith has made you well.** The words "made you well" are used in a double sense, for the Greek word for "make well" *(sōzō)* is the word ordinarily rendered "save." The Samaritan now is confirmed in his faith. He came to the right place. Thus these words, **Your faith has made you well** (cf. 7:50; 8:48; 18:42), do not say that exertion of faith spells healing but that the one to whom the faith is directed has spelled the difference for this man. Faith without an agent who can respond to the faith is only a psychological phenomenon. Therefore the man's return to Jesus was of great importance. He saw the Giver in the gift. The nine also had faith that Jesus could heal them, but a plus accompanied the Samaritan's faith. He was made well in the profounder sense of the word (see 7:50; 8:12; 9:24, 56; 13:23; 19:10). And now, after his detour for gratitude's sake, he can presumably carry out the earlier injunction to "show" himself to the priests (v. 14).

Jesus is God's unique gift. Through him comes the assurance of God's love and desire to have people in communion with their Creator. Once the disciples wished to rain fire down on the Samaritans (9:51–56) because of their rejection of Jesus. But like the owner of the vineyard (13:6–9), the Lord was patient, and now a Samaritan becomes, like Naaman of old (2 Kings 5; cf. Luke 4:27), a model for Israel and a symbol of outreach to aliens (see Acts 8:14).

To Greco-Roman auditors, this story would be especially meaningful for its presentation of Jesus as a person of extraordinary distinction. Luke's triple reference (vv. 15, 16, 18) to the benefit conferred, with emphasis on the appropriate response of gratitude, unmistakably interprets Jesus as a benefactor (cf. Acts 4:9; 10:38; and see *Benefactor,* pp. 406–7). Luke's story therefore qualifies as an aretalogical account, that is, a recital about a person or deity whose performance is exceptional. The ingratitude of the nine is all the more blameworthy in the face of such beneficence. One of Menander's characters epitomized this aspect of human frailty *(Fragments* 595):

> 'Tis ever true; once saved, we show no gratitude.
> Once pity has been granted us, the thanks we swore
> Would be undying, with our need's end itself lies dead.

Coming of the Son of Humanity
Luke 17:20–37

The Kingdom of God Is Here
Luke 17:20–21

17:20–21. The attitude of the nine lepers is reflected in the misunderstanding that lies behind the question of certain Pharisees concerning the arrival of the **kingdom of God.** In Luke the Kingdom is viewed in two stages. It is now present in the word and work of Jesus *and* it will be realized in fullness when the Son of humanity comes. Thus no special apocalyptic effects are required to determine the validity of Jesus' credentials. Jesus therefore tells the Pharisees that the Kingdom does not come subject to human ratification through observance of signs (cf. 11:29).

The RSV has done well in adopting the rendering **in the midst of you** in preference to the marginal interpretation "within you." Luke never views the Kingdom of God as a psychological reality. It is always God's reigning action. The thought is related to that of Isa. 45:14 LXX: "God is in you" (i.e., present among you). In the same context Isaiah speaks of God's salvation (cf. Luke 17:18–19). Being "in the midst" of them, the Kingdom is something from which they can benefit; that is, it lies now within their grasp or power.

The Day of the Son of Humanity: Fifth Prediction of the Passion

Luke 17:22–37
(Matthew 24:26–28, 37–39; 10:39; 24:40, 28)

17:22–23. The disciples must be on their guard against false reports concerning the return of Jesus. Under pressure from hostile religious and social forces, Christians will long for (cf. Amos 5:18) **one of the days of the Son of man.** The plural "days" is a general term for the period in which the Son of humanity makes his appearance and for the New Age that follows this appearance. In the Prophets the plural term "in those days" is frequently associated with the singular "in that day" (cf. Amos 8:11, 13; Zech. 14:1, 4, 7). To long for "one" of these days means that the community will be in desperate straits and find little consolation in a vague and undetermined period of time. When they do not see their hope fulfilled, they will be tempted in their impatience to listen to those who fix on a particular time and say: **Lo, there!** or, **Lo, here!** But they are warned: **Do not follow** the false voice.

17:24. Jesus, the Son of humanity, does have one day, **his day**, but it comes with the dispatch of lightning.

17:25. The rejection of Jesus by many of his own people raised questions about the validity of his credentials. To reassure Christians of his own time, Luke reports that Jesus predicted not only his death but the very rejection that seemed to disqualify him as Israel's deliverer (see on 9:22; 11:29). In view of the perplexing experiences of Jesus, whose privileged status did not spare him from ignominy, his followers should not be dismayed if they are called upon to suffer. Rather, they must be prepared to take up the cross and follow Jesus (9:23; 14:27; cf. Acts 14:22). Even though all signs of deliverance for the communities of the New Age are lacking, the followers of Jesus are not to search for someone else (see 7:19). For Jesus and the Son of humanity are one and the same. (For other predictions of the Passion, see 9:22, 44; 12:50; 13:32–33.)

17:26–31. To discourage all sign-seeking, Jesus declares that **the days of the Son of humanity** (i.e., his appearance) will be preceded by completely unspectacular phenomena. There will be dining, marrying, trading, farming, building—all normal everyday activities. Nothing is said about religious functions, for the judgment is not based on the formula "Father Abraham' (see 3:8; 16:24). Only Noah's and some of Lot's family escaped the two catastrophes that presage **the day when** the Son of humanity **is revealed** (*apokalyptō,* the Greek from which "apocalyptic" is derived). Matthew 24:37–39 cites only the example of Noah.

Luke includes a reference to Sodom, notorious for its pride, its packed grocery shelves, its consumerism, and its lack of concern for the poor and needy (cf. Ezek. 16:49). His purpose is to paint as darkly as possible the fate that befalls those who defy God. If it will be "more tolerable on that day for Sodom than for that town" which rejects the emissaries of Jesus (see Luke 10:12), what a dreadful fate must be in store for the disciple who attempts to keep a foot in each of the two offered worlds. Precisely because everything goes on as usual, the disciple cannot carry on business as usual. Mark 13:15–16, which depicts the destruction of Jerusalem, is used in Luke 17:31 in reference to the last day. Since that event may take place at any time, and without advance signs beyond the customary phenomena in nature and society (see 21:15–16), the disciple must be prepared in every instant.

17:32. Lot's wife is mentioned because she looked back on the city of Sodom and became a pillar of salt (see Gen. 19:26). Jesus earlier had warned a would-be follower about laying hands on the plow and looking back (Luke 9:62). Preparation for the Kingdom to come is made in single-minded response to the Kingdom that is reality now. Such response, precisely because there are no special effects to document the validity of that to which one responds, is equivalent to faith.

17:33. This verse is paralleled by Matt. 10:39. There can be no divided allegiance, not even to the point of seeking **to gain** one's life (see 9:24; 12:4–7). Losing it will be the means to **preserve it** (*zōogoneō:* "make it live").

17:34–35. The decision is everything. Two people engaged in the same activity have totally different destinies (parallel in Matt. 24:40). Simeon had once spoken along similar lines (Luke 2:34). Like the house of Israel, deserted by God (13:35), one in each case is **left**, that is, abandoned, and one is **taken** *(paralambanō).* This latter word is used in 9:10, 28; 18:31 of one who takes another into close association (see also Col. 2:6, "received Christ"; 1 Thess. 2:13, "accepted").

The marginal reading, which is traditionally numbered v. 36, is not found in the best manuscripts; it may derive from reminiscence of Matt. 24:40.

17:37. The Pharisees had asked "When?" (v. 20). Now the disciples ask **Where, Lord?** The Kingdom comes neither "there" nor "then." Disciples must be so prepared that they are never like carrion waiting to be devoured by an eagle or a vulture. Throughout the hearing or reading of the entire paragraph, early Christians would think also of the fate of Jerusalem, and Luke's reference to the eagles may be a symbol for the Roman standards (cf. Josephus *War* 3.6.2). The disciples are not to repeat the mistake of Jerusalem's inhabitants or they will be as unprepared for the second coming of Jesus as Jerusalem was for the first.

Preparation for the Kingdom
Luke 18:1–30

The theme of salvation is continued in 18:1–30. The story of the unjust judge (vv. 1–8) is an expansion of the exhortation in 17:27–37, for 18:1 indicates that the disciples are still being addressed, and the reference to the Son of humanity in connection with the question of the vindication of God's elect (vv. 7–8) clearly echoes 17:22, 24, 26. The question of faith is raised in 18:8. Misplaced confidence in self (18:9–17) or in riches (18:18–27) can keep one from entry into the Kingdom. Those who are prepared to renounce everything for the sake of the Kingdom will have a share in the life to come (vv. 28–30).

Spirit of Acceptance   Luke 18:1–17

Persistence in Prayer   Luke 18:1–8

18:1. The parable of the reluctant judge is an answer to the problem of survival in the face of persecution (see 17:22). Hence the point of the parable is not that persistent prayer will guarantee the petitioners anything they want. Verse 1 unequivocally states that the disciples' prayers are to offset cowardly resignation in the face of the hazards they will run (cf. 11:4b and 22:46). One is not to grow weary because of apparent lack of interest on God's part. God will not fail the disciples. The woman did not receive immediate redress of wrong, but her persistence won a favorable verdict.

18:2–3. As Wettstein demonstrated, Luke's description of the judge is a piece of stock rhetoric. Plato depicts unscrupulous merchants who "show no respect for people and no piety for the gods" (*Laws* 11.917b). Similarly, Dionysios of Halikarnassos (10.10.7) writes about a conspiracy that was to be carried out by men who "neither feared divine wrath nor gave a second thought to human retribution." And Livy (*History* 22.3) calls attention to a Roman consul who was "fearful neither of the laws nor of the senatorial majesty, and not even of the gods."

The judge is not necessarily to be viewed as a crooked or irresponsible magistrate. Indeed, given the opportunity to tell his side of the story, he might well have pleaded total integrity: not even God could bribe him. His motto may well have been Exod. 23:1: total impartiality, and the widow must wait her turn and his careful sifting of the case. Yet, from the perspective of the underclass he is delinquent in office, and he is so characterized in v. 6.

18:4–5. The widow's persistence finally overcomes the judge. His dialogue is more vigorous than the translation in the RSV suggests. He says in effect: "I shall avenge her, or she will give me a black eye!" Jesus' verbal cartoon is a piece of masterful economy. This woman's theatrics suggest that she will not take no for an answer. The judge is more afraid of her than he is of God. The point is unmistakable: Justice delayed is justice denied. This widow wants it and she wants it now!

18:6. Townspeople would be on the side of the widow, and the judge would be viewed as an unfair and callous magistrate. From such perspective the switch he makes is all the more remarkable, and Jesus says: "Listen to what this unjust magistrate just said!"

18:7–8. Luke does not wish to suggest through his report of the dark portrait of the magistrate that God is like him (see comment on the unjust steward at 16:8). The point is, rather, that if even a judge like this finally grants a widow's petition, how much more will God, to whom widows are a primary concern (see Isa. 1:17 and Sir. 35:12–15), grant the petition of the disciples. This interpretation is borne out in the subsequent application of the story.

The syntax of v. 8 in Greek is compact and colloquial, but the sense of vv. 7–8 appears to be: "And will not God avenge the elect who cry to God night and day? Is God patient with them? I tell you, God will avenge them speedily. But the question is, Will the Son of humanity on his return find faith on the earth?" In this paraphase, the RSV's **delay long** (*makrothymei*) is replaced by the more usual rendering of the Greek term for "patient restraint" or "mercy" (see Sir. 18:11, and cf. Matt. 18:29).

The formal structure of the reply is a cue to the meaning. Verse 7 consists of two questions: One, "Will God avenge the elect?" (cf. Rev. 6:10). Two, "Is God patient with them?" This second question deals with the problem of divided allegiance. In 17:5 the disciples had asked for an increase in faith. At 17:7–10 faith was defined as an attitude of unqualified acceptance of responsibility, without a feeling of merit; 18:9–17 will expand on this theme.

God is indeed concerned about the disciples, but the disciples are re-minded that single-hearted devotion is required of them (cf. 2 Pet. 3:9). Is God merciful to the disciples in the face of their own weakness of faith? Verse 8 gives answers to this and the first question: (1) God will listen to the prayers of **his elect** and will avenge them speedily (cf. Isa. 13:22—14:1; 51:5). (2) The Son of humanity will have difficulty finding faith on the earth. The implied thought is: God must indeed be merciful, for God displays not wrath but patience, despite the fact that faith nearly runs out before the Son of humanity returns. In brief, the text contrasts divine and human fidelity. Before they question divine responsiveness to the suffering elect, it is incumbent on the people of God to take inventory of their own sense of commitment.

Besides the consolation offered to the believers, this passage is of christological significance. Christians are adjusting to the fact that their Lord is not winning a popularity contest. The closer the end comes in sight, the less recognition there will be of Jesus' credentials. That very fact, though, magnifies his credentials as the one who stands for the rising and the falling of many in the larger Israel of God (see 2:34).

Humility   Luke 18:9–14

Jesus' reply in 18:7–8 spoke of high spiritual demand in a context of consolation. The addressees in 18:9—**some who trusted in themselves that they were righteous and despised others**—are sufficiently indefinite and do not exclude the disciples. Since a Pharisee appears as one of the principal characters in the story, it is doubtful that the remarks were ad-dressed specifically to Pharisees. Not all Pharisees were like the man in the story, but the extreme commitment of a number in their ranks to petty concern for rules and regulations brought the entire sect under negative scrutiny. In any case, the Pharisee as understood in a negative sense lurks in everyone, and we should not evade the scrutiny of the text by casting stones at ancient Pharisees.

Preparation for the coming of the Son of humanity includes an under-standing of the basic principle of the Kingdom: The mighty will be brought low and the humble will be exalted (1:51–52 and 18:14). Jesus' contempo-raries and the church must recognize this fact. It is the faith of the lowly for which the Son of humanity will be looking. Those who pray (18:1) must pray in the proper spirit, if they are to hope for vindication (18:8; cf. Pss. 17:2; 34:6, 15–21). The prayer of the Pharisee follows the thought of Ps. 17:3–5. Psalm 34 shapes the prayer of the tax collector.

18:9. Trusted in themselves (that they were righteous; *dikaioi*) ex-presses the complacency of those who think that everything in them is in order before God. They think that they do not come under the stricture of Ezek. 33:13, for iniquity is not in them. But equally heinous is their attitude toward the "laity" of their time, who in the judgment of religious elitists were ignoramuses with respect to things divine (cf. Acts 4:13).

18:10. The liturgical stance of the two men is similar. Both stand and both address the deity directly: **God.** One offers a prayer of thanksgiving, the other a petition for mercy. Both use accepted forms of liturgy. Nor is the Pharisee to be criticized for thanking God that he was not rapacious. A psalmist prayed in similar fashion (Ps. 17:1–5). But this particular Pharisee is to be numbered among those who have a habit of being right in the wrong way, and his prayer soon deteriorates.

18:11–12. Instead of taking the high road of Deut. 26:12–15 and remaining on the level of thanksgiving, the Pharisee feeds on his own virtues and makes odious comparisons. He disclaims affinity with extortioners (cf. Luke 11:39), crooks, and adulterers and climaxes his self-glorification at the expense of another person's defects or notoriety. The Roman poet Horace said in a different context, "Yes, I have avoided censure, but deserve no praise for it." The Pharisee goes on to boast of his fasting (on Mondays and Thursdays), but fasting ought to go hand in hand with humility (cf. Ps. 35:13). His tithing is based on all his income, including garden herbs (see Matt. 23:23), far beyond the requirements of Deut. 14:22–23. With such trite reflections on morality he exceeds the psalmist's catalogues of virtue (Ps. 17:3–5) and in effect tries to bribe God (see Deut. 10:12–22).

18:13. The publican distanced himself from the Pharisee, perhaps to remain as inconspicuous as possible. Apart from the identity in stance, there is no similarity between this tax collector and the Pharisee. Not only does he not bore God with a long recital of his humility but he omits giving thanks that he is not like "those hypocritical Pharisees." Pharisees are also found among publicans who excuse themselves from responsibility by citing the hypocrisies of church members without making appropriate applications to themselves. The publican's prayer is that of the poor person in Ps. 34:6, 18, and is accompanied by gestures that suggest one who is deeply agitated by lamentation (see Homer *Iliad* 18.30–31, and cf. Luke 23:48). He describes himself with the odious label pinned on him by Pharisees—"sinner" *(hamartōlos).* Peter had used the same term about himself (5:8).

18:14. This man, like the elect of 18:7, cried to God and his prayer was immediately answered, for he went to his home with God's approval *(dedikaiōmenos,* "as a righteous person"), whereas the other failed to secure it (cf. Ps. 34:15, 17, 19, "righteous"). Because he walked the low path of the Kingdom, he went home exalted (cf. 1:51–52). Unlike Paul, who discusses the process of justification (see Romans 3), Luke describes the nature of the *recipients* of God's verdict of approval. The justified are the humble, those who recognize that no righteousness of their own can be so great that they would stand successfully before God with it (cf. 1 Cor. 1:27–29). Therefore they leave judgment to God. The Pharisee pronounced judgment on himself and for the moment seemed to win his case. Alas, baffler of his own prayers, he was in the wrong. The publican was wiser—he called on God to be both judge and defender. In Psalm 34 the poet states that the Lord's deliverance is open to the righteous. Luke 18:9–14 has defined the identity of "the righteous." But they are few (see 13:23–24), and the Son of humanity will not find many of this breed (see 18:8), for there are few who will be willing to take the risk that Jesus took in making the good news real by associating with people like this tax collector. Zecharias's word in 1:52 and Simeon's in 2:34 have received their commentary.

Faith of a Child   Luke 18:15–17
(Mark 10:13–16; Matthew 19:13–15; 18:3)

At 9:50 Luke had detoured from Mark's narrative. Now he resumes Mark's order of events, but with some adaptation. Like 9:43–48, this second recital of Jesus' acceptance of children is associated with the climactic events in Jerusalem (see 18:31–34). Luke clearly indicates that the death of Jesus will not be understood unless one has the faith of a little child, for the Passion of Jesus is the supreme illustration of the truth that the mighty and haughty are brought low and the lowly are exalted (1:51–52 and 18:14).

18:15. In his modification of Mark's account (Mark 10:13–16), Luke omits reference to Jesus' displeasure over the disciples and in place of Mark's first reference to "children" reads "infants" (*ta brephē,* also used in Luke 2:12, 16). Not only children but "even" infants were brought. The omission is in harmony with Luke's rather consistent removal of features that are unnecessarily embarrassing to the apostles, and the alteration is prompted by his interest in the theme of total dependence on God.

18:16. In his story of the Pharisee and the publican, Jesus put Pharisaic legal confidence under question. The publican laid himself open to the mercy of God. Precisely this attitude of receptivity is required for entrance into the Kingdom, and children, like birds and flowers (12:24, 27), are models of faith for the disciples; for faith in Luke is not intellectual assent but openness to divine generosity (see 17:11–19). The thought is in harmony with Jesus' instruction to address God with the familiar term "Abba" (see on Luke 11:2), and with the prophetic identification of Israel as the "child" of Yahweh (see Isa. 41:8; 42:1; 44:1, 2, 21; cf. Prov. 4:1).

At 11:52 "lawyers" were charged with blocking entrance to the Kingdom; here, disciples fall under rebuke. If Jesus is correct, theologians who think that the future of Christianity depends primarily on traditional formulations and their own perceptions of theology, with minimal input from those whom they refer to as the laity, require Peter's rooster.

18:17. So basic is the pronouncement that a solemn *amēn* (RSV: **truly**) prefaces the final saying. Entrance is possible only for those who come to God in the spirit of children approaching their parents (see 11:11–13), eagerly waiting to receive *(dechomai).*

Expediting for the Kingdom   Luke 18:18–30

Rid of Excess Baggage   Luke 18:18–27
(Mark 10:17–27; Matthew 19:16–26)

The two recitals in 18:9–17 focused attention on receptivity, distinguished from legal self-determination, as primary requisite for entry into the Kingdom. In 18:18–27 the last bulwark of the self-made religious person comes under attack, namely, material goods.

18:18. Mark's "a man" (Mark 10:17) is called **a ruler** in Luke's recital, perhaps to emphasize the larger civic responsibilities of which he is capable as a person of wealth. Matthew identifies the inquirer as a "young man" (Matt. 19:20) and therefore omits from Mark's record of the man's boast the words "from my youth." The man's manner of address and the nature of his request betray a basic misunderstanding. He views Jesus as a teacher of righteousness, who might be able to supplement what Moses had said. Moreover, he does not come like a child waiting to receive *now,* but in the future, and on the basis of his own performance. He was in error on the first count, for Israel has Moses and the prophets, and he should heed them (see 16:29). And he was wrong on the second, for the Kingdom of God is present, as well as future, reality (see 18:30).

18:19. Unlike Matthew (Matt. 19:17), Luke is not disturbed by Mark's phrasing of Jesus' question: **Why do you call me good?** This question, together with the affirmation **No one is good but God alone**, is not a disclaimer of personal goodness in the sense of moral rectitude. "Good" *(agathos)* in this context connotes extraordinary distinction. Any distinction possessed by Jesus must be viewed from the perspective of God, the Supreme Benefactor and ultimate exemplar of the good. To a Greco-Roman, that would especially mean uncommon concern for the welfare of human beings. Jesus renounces any shallow appraisal of his own person (see 11:27–28, where the focus is, as here, on God's word). Jesus has come to do the Father's will (see on 2:49). Everything has been handed over to him by the Father, and only one who understands the Father will understand the Son (10:21–22). Hence Jesus disavows any claim to special revelation beyond that of his own person as the embodiment and climactic demonstration of what had already found expression in Moses and the prophets (16:29). God is the Supreme Benefactor.

18:20. Jesus therefore reminds the ruler of **the commandments** given by God through Moses (see Deut. 5:16–20, and cf. Exod. 20:12–16). These are repeatedly endorsed by the prophets (see, e.g., Isaiah 5; Hosea 4). According to Deut. 30:15–20, obedience to these and other commandments would spell life for Israel.

18:21. The ruler's reply—**All these I have observed**—is to be taken at face value. Jesus recognizes the righteous who need no repentance (15:7). And there is no special virtue in confessing sins that one has not committed. But Greco-Roman auditors would catch more. Men and women of exceptional merit and distinction would on occasion be praised for manifestation of virtue "from their youth" (see on 2:41–52). This official desires to improve his reputation for extraordinary merit, and Jesus is an authority on what constitutes merit.

18:22. Jesus puts him to the ultimate test. The ruler had asked for further guidance. Jesus takes him at his word. He strikes first at the center of the man's security—his material possessions. Here the very issues of existence are determined (cf. Rom. 1:18–25). Sell all that you have and distribute it to the poor.

Caesar distributed bread and provided games for the Roman people. This official has opportunity for benefaction on a smaller but nevertheless spectacular scale. He had asked how he might inherit eternal life. Jesus equates this goal with having **treasure in heaven** (cf. 12:33–34). This means that he is invited to expose himself totally to God's verdict, without the support of material blessings. According to popular conception, wealth would be a sign of personal goodness (see Prov. 15:6). But even such self-denial is not enough. The ultimate decision must be made: **Come, follow me.**

Only a person of the highest distinction could make such a claim on another. Jesus is indeed "good," for he is the Great Benefactor. He comes as a giver, not as a demander, but his self-giving involves the strongest demand possible. Thus Jesus does not disclaim goodness but rather links his life and work with the One who is good. And his command is as absolute as any commandment of God. To be associated with him is to accept the most dangerous assignment, without command over anything that one can call one's own. The sincerity of all who claim to be interested in God is thus called into question by the way in which they respond to God's climactic self-revelation in Jesus (see Luke 6:46–49).

18:23–24. The ruler had expected something else. He did not anticipate a directive that went so contrary to all he had been taught to believe. Entrance into the Kingdom is indeed difficult, for it belongs to the poor (6:20).

18:25. This muscular proverb should not be numbed by mere appeal to size or by attempts to find a "Needle's Eye Gate" in Jerusalem. Jesus had a lively imagination and was fond of exaggerated pictures to make a point (see, e.g., 6:41). Try threading a needle when there is a knot on the thread. Well, says Jesus, a camel, despite its hump, will go through the eye of a needle before a rich man with his moneybags enters the Kingdom.

18:26–27. Those who heard the proverb grasped it—**Then who can be saved?** Verse 27 answers: It is God's doing, for the Kingdom is God's gift. And from the context it is clear that the faith of a little child makes possible the impossibility (18:15–17). Zacchaeus would know the answer, but only after he had seen and heard the generosity of Jesus, who communicated the love of a heavenly Parent (19:8). Paul learned it well (Phil. 3:7; 4:12). For the disciples, it was a repetition of an earlier warning (Luke 9:24–27; cf. 14:25–35).

Future Reward
Luke 18:28–30
(Mark 10:28–30; Matthew 19:27–29)

18:28–30. Jesus' response to Peter's question is a modification of the form in Mark (Mark 10:29–30). In Mark's account, what the disciple parts with is restored in parallel form. Luke replaces this idea with the more general **manifold more** (Luke 18:30). The Kingdom of God is present as well as future reality. In association with Jesus, disciples have much more than they previously renounced (see 6:20, and cf. 12:22–34). And **in the age to come**, that is, after the Son of humanity has returned, they will enjoy what the rich ruler longed to find but lost. Thus the Lord answers Peter with a further demand for faith. But the disciples dare not forget an earlier reminder of Jesus, that they are "unworthy servants," that is, "useless slaves" (17:10). For the Kingdom is *received,* not gained through shabby trade. And standard societal structures are not primary instruments for determining the identity of God's people.

FINAL PHASE OF THE JOURNEY
TO JERUSALEM
Luke 18:31—19:27

Sixth Prediction of the Passion
Luke 18:31–34

Jerusalem is the focal point in Luke's Gospel. In Luke 1 and 2 the city is mentioned repeatedly, climaxing with Jesus' visit to the temple (2:41–50).

The temple is mentioned in the third temptation (4:9). At Jerusalem, Jesus must carry out the exodus (see 9:31). At 9:51 the journey to Jerusalem had begun (see also 13:22; 17:11). And in 13:33 it was observed that no prophet perishes outside Jerusalem. The reminder of Jesus' destination is especially appropriate at this point, for the fate of Jesus involves the disciple in a call to decision that requires single-minded devotion, unhampered by misdirected concern about family or material possessions. Association with Jesus means readiness to part with standard status symbols or criteria of success.

Luke 18:31–34 presents the fourth of a series of predictions concerning the suffering of the Son of humanity (9:22, 44; 17:25). Other predictions, minus Son of humanity, were made in 12:50 and 13:32–33. This, then, is Jesus' sixth prediction of his Passion. Since the Passion story is about to be recited, 18:32–33 gives more details than the previous predictions. Another additional feature is the statement that the prophetic predictions about the Son of humanity will find fulfillment. The fate that ultimately befell Jesus was then understood in the light of such a passage as Isa. 50:6, in which is found Luke's additional note that the sufferer would be spat on. Hosea 6:2 appears to have offered the pattern for the emphasis **on the third day**; but Pss. 16:8–11 (see Acts 2:25–36) and 110:1 (Acts 2:34) are among the primary sources for Luke's interpretation of Jesus' resurrection.

18:34. Since the popular view of the Messiah did not include expectation of suffering, the disciples could not fathom Jesus' premonition of the fate in store for him in Jerusalem. As at 9:45, they **understood none of these things** (see also 2:50 and 24:16–21). Luke's variation in the phrasing of the last two clauses in v. 34 ("this saying was hid from them" and "they did not grasp what was said") points to his blend of early Christian proclamation with Jesus' own statements about his approaching death.

The RSV obscures the distinction in the clauses by the rendering **this saying.** The Greek *(to rhēma)* for this expression is used frequently in Luke in the sense of "this thing" or "this event" (1:37, 65; 2:15, 19, 51; Acts 10:37, "What happened," NEB). In brief, such an outcome as Jesus described lay outside the comprehension of the disciples. But Luke offers a theological interpretation. This thing or event was **hid from them**, namely, by God.

The second of the two clauses is correctly rendered in the RSV. Since the necessity of Jesus' death was hidden from the disciples, they could not understand **what was said.** But nothing is hidden that is not to be revealed, Jesus observed in 8:16–17, and knowledge of the mysteries of the Kingdom of God is granted to the followers of Jesus (8:10). Thus the motif of ignorance sets the stage for the enlightenment given by Jesus himself in 24:25–27. He is the authentic Teacher for Israel and the church. The church's emissaries are entrusted with the correct appraisal of the events that took place on Good Friday and Easter (see Acts 3:12–18); for what God conceals, God can also reveal.

Through this narrative Luke provides at least one solution for the problem of the disciples' earlier misunderstanding of Jesus compared to the continuing misunderstanding on the part of Israel's religious leadership. Disciples are spared the verdict: "seeing they may not see" (Luke 8:10). Their ignorance is viewed on a different level from that of the leaders who later rejected the apostolic proclamation (see Acts 28:25–27).

A Blind Man Sees

Luke 18:35–43
(Mark 10:46–52; Matthew 20:29–34)

Luke omits Mark 10:35–45, including the reference to the Son of humanity's death as "a ransom [redemption] for many." Although Luke includes references to God's ransoming intention (Luke 1:68; 2:38; 24:21), the death of Jesus is not the instrument of redemption. Redemption takes place through the totality of Jesus as God's gift to Israel and humanity. Not the death of Jesus as such, but the beneficence of God in raising him from the dead and the clemency that God extends to those who were responsible for his crucifixion make assurance of forgiveness possible for all who repent (see esp. Acts 2—3).

Luke's account of the blind man healed near Jericho, together with the account of Zacchaeus's conversion, climaxes his exposition of the Kingdom. Faith is the eyesight required to understand what God does in connection with Jesus. Disciples, as well as Israel in general, must approach Jesus as did this blind man. To sharpen this truth, Luke omits Mark's account of the request of the sons of Zebedee (Mark 10:35–45), reserving part of the passage for his recital at 22:25–27.

18:35. In Mark, the event takes place on the way out of Jericho (Mark 10:46). As shortly becomes apparent, Luke has his reasons for relating the story of Zacchaeus (not found in Mark) after this account, and therefore places the healing *before* Jesus' entry into the city.

18:36–37. The crowd proclaims that **Jesus of Nazareth is passing by.**

18:38. The blind man "sees" much more. This is the **Son of David.** The title is strongly messianic.

18:39–41. According to Isa. 35:5, sight will be restored to the blind in God's time of deliverance (see Luke 4:18; 7:22). The blind man recognizes in Jesus the fulfillment of this anticipated age, and the Davidic affirmation is in harmony with 1:27, 32, 69; 2:4, 11; 3:21; 6:3 (misunderstanding of the title will be taken up in 20:41–44). The blind man's request for removal of his blindness is a bold invitation to Jesus to validate his credentials as Messiah.

18:42. As in the case of the Samaritan leper (17:19), Jesus declares that the man's faith has "saved" him ("made him well"). Jesus is the one who gives sight to the blind, and he will aid the disciples to see (cf. 24:16, 31) the significance of his person as the link between God's past action in Israel and God's continuing activity in the Christian community.

18:43. Unlike the ruler who lacked such faith and refused to follow Jesus (18:22–23), the blind man is like the disciples who forsook all (18:28). And like the Samaritan (17:15), he glorifies—that is, praises—God. The words echo the response of the shepherds in 2:20 and anticipate the climax pronounced in 24:26. Isaiah prophesied the glory of the Lord which was to be "seen" (Isa. 61:1–5 LXX; 40:5; 58:8). Zechariah proclaimed the coming age as a time of light (Luke 1:78–79). The Kingdom is really present in the work and person of Jesus of Nazareth and those who earlier had discouraged the blind man (v. 39) now endorse the man's verdict (v. 43; cf. 19:37).

Again the phrasing echoes 2:20. If nevertheless Jesus goes to his death, let no one construe it as a collapse of messianic hope. Blindness remains in Israel, and her leaders who do not "see" must accept responsibility for the execution of the Messiah (see 18:32). Messiahship and ignominious death are not mutually exclusive.

Jesus Brings Salvation to the House of Zacchaeus

Luke 19:1–10

Luke's recital of the Lord's reception of Zacchaeus rounds out his exposition of the Kingdom and clears the way for proper understanding of Jesus' suffering and death about to take place in Jerusalem. The parable that follows (vv. 11–27) reinforces the major point made in this story: The Kingdom does not come accompanied by special apocalyptic effects. Salvation is its basic characteristic. The blind man pronounced Jesus Son of David and heard the verdict: "Your faith has saved you." The Kingdom now comes to Zacchaeus (for the name, see Ezra 2:9; Neh. 7:14), a Jew, but out of good standing because of his occupation.

19:2. Zacchaeus is described by the unusual term **a chief tax collector**, which suggests that he was an overseer in charge of collection of a variety of tolls. He would therefore be all the more despised by the native populace. Luke's account of the ruler (18:18–25) had stressed the hazard of wealth as a barrier to entrance into the Kingdom (see 18:25). By emphasizing that Zacchaeus was "rich" *(plousios),* he prepares the reader for the answer to the question: "Then who can be saved?" (18:26).

19:3–4. The observation that Zacchaeus was **small of stature** would not be mere descriptive detail for some of Luke's auditors, who would certainly recall that Jesus had spoken at 12:25 about the futility of attempting to add a cubit to one's stature (see also on 2:52). Zacchaeus's problem is overcome by the initiative of Jesus. His motivation for seeing Jesus differs from Herod's sign-seeking interest (9:9; 23:8).

19:5. It was not necessary for Zacchaeus to elevate himself, for Jesus knows who he is and calls out his name, without any suggestion in the text that he had made inquiry as to Zacchaeus's identity. Zacchaeus had to see Jesus, but Jesus was already on the search for him (v. 10). Jesus spoke: "Today I must *(dei me)* stay at your home." This is the thread of necessity that weaves Jesus' career (see 2:49; 4:43; 9:22; 13:16, 33; 15:32; 17:25; 22:37; 24:7, 26, 44). Far from being a restraint on freedom, necessity involved the recognition of unusual possibility. "Today," echoed later in v. 9, is the second major thread (see 2:11; 3:22; 4:21; 5:26; 13:32–33) climaxing at 23:43. Present encounter with Jesus spells Kingdom reality. Jesus had instructed his disciples to *remain* in the house where they were welcome (9:4; cf. 10:7), and his self-invitation to Zacchaeus's home indicates that Zacchaeus is a privileged recipient of the Kingdom (see also 24:29). As did the shepherds (2:16), Zacchaeus made haste in this hour of extraordinary opportunity, and **received** *(hypodechomai)* **him joyfully.**

19:6. This invitation, which is at the same time an absolution, marks the moment of conversion. Zacchaeus's joy is a fulfillment of the promise expressed in 2:10 (see also 1:14; 10:20; 13:17; 19:37; 24:41, 52).

19:7. As at 5:30, Jesus faces criticism for his action. But this time **all**—the general public, not scribes and Pharisees—**murmured** ("grumbled"). Their characterization of Zacchaeus as **a sinner** provides a stark background for the subsequent picture of the new Zacchaeus. Once a Pharisee stood in the temple congratulating himself on his tithes (18:11–12). Later a ruler had turned his back on the Kingdom when he was directed to sell all he had and give the proceeds to the poor (18:22–23). The fact that the people in general are scandalized by Jesus' action suggests that the Pharisees were not the only supporters of traditional values. Despite superficial appearances of popularity, Jesus, as events revealed, was out of touch with the mainstream. Too far out. Many a creative thinker after him has been amazed to discover that the general populace is reluctant to embrace even ideas that in the long run may be to its interest.

19:8. Zacchaeus addresses **the Lord** *(ho kyrios,* the community's term for Jesus as their recognized ruler) in words that demonstrate that humanity's impossibilities become God's possibilities (18:27), and that one is to have treasure in heaven (18:22). A king might speak of giving away half his kingdom (cf. Mark 6:23). Zacchaeus promises to give half of his possessions to the poor. In cases of extortion (see 3:14), the normal practice was to make restitution, plus 20 percent (see Lev. 5:16; Num. 5:7). Zacchaeus goes far beyond such expectation and binds himself to the law imposed on rustlers (cf. Exod. 22:1), who were liable to a fourfold penalty for theft of sheep. In the eyes of rabbis, such promises would be indicative of true repentance (SB 2:250). In Luke's recital he is a living definition of the word "repentance" (see 3:8). Thus Zacchaeus now lives up to his name, which means "righteous" or "pure" one, and becomes a living illustration of what Jesus repeatedly stated on the subject of wealth.

19:9–10. Jesus himself amplifies his earlier absolution with words that were originally aimed at the grumblers: **Today salvation has come to this house.** "Today" echoes v. 5. Salvation *(sōtēria)* in Luke includes release from the anxieties that hamper one's appreciation of God's outreaching love. Jesus, as the guarantor of God's concerned love, spells rescue for Zacchaeus, and the latter's repentance indicates that the circle is complete. His entire household is the beneficiary. According to Jewish thinking (see, e.g., Joshua 7), they were implicated with him in guilt, and with them they share the benefits of the Kingdom (cf. Acts 10:2; 11:14; 16:31; 18:8). Thus salvation also means assurance of God's desire that even the worst of sinners be included in God's family.

It was appropriate for Jesus to include Zacchaeus, for **he also is a son of Abraham** and contrasts with those who merely invoke Abraham as father (3:8; 16:24). Like the sheep, coin, and son (Luke 15), he had been lost, but now a cherished member of the family of Israel has been found. Jesus, the Son of humanity, will one day come in apocalyptic splendor at the end of history. In the present moment he, in total identification with the lot of humanity, comes as a shepherd, Seeker and Savior of the lost, Strengthener of the sick, Rescuer of the crippled, doing the task that the appointed shepherds of Israel were avoiding (see Ezekiel 34, and esp. v. 16). And what was done for a lost Israelite will be done for gentiles who are aliens in the commonwealth of Israel (Luke 7:1–10; Acts 10), "for we all are God's offspring" (Acts 17:28*). Expressed theologically, the story of Zacchaeus resolves the problem of apocalyptic through soteriology. The recital is Luke's literary magnet, and proclaimers of the text will find it worth their time to see how many of Luke's themes find expression in it.

It has been argued that the present tenses in v. 8 suggest Zacchaeus's "customary action" prior to his appearance before Jesus. But if such was indeed Zacchaeus's habit, it is difficult to explain Luke's emphasis on the grumbling by "all." The toll collector's kickbacks would certainly have encouraged a modification of their religious sensitivities.

The Kingdom—Present and Future

Luke 19:11–27
(Matthew 25:14–30)

19:11. In place of Mark 10:35–45, omitted after Luke 18:34, Luke presents the parable of the pounds. His editing of the material results in a contrast between the converted Zacchaeus and the rebellious people cited in vv. 11–27. Similarities to the story of the talents in Matt. 25:14–30 suggest that an original parable about trading has undergone modification in the instruction of the community. In its present context in Luke it climaxes the contrast between the ruler (18:18–25), who is representative of Israel's formalistic leadership, and Zacchaeus, who despite his lowly status in the eyes of traditionalists was found faithful in response to the Kingdom.

The parable also summarizes Luke's view of the two-phase Kingdom. Luke does not deny that the Kingdom is present reality, but he uses the parable to correct a misunderstanding. Jesus is near Jerusalem, but the Kingdom does not make its appearance now in the spectacular demonstration that will take place at the end of time. Thus Luke's recital anticipates the corrective issued in Acts 1:6–8 and is a further answer to the question raised in Luke 17:20. Jerusalem will be the site of consummation of the Kingdom in its first stage, but this will take place in the suffering, death, and resurrection of Jesus, a fact of which the disciples are ignorant (9:45; 18:34). Rescue of people like Zacchaeus exacts its toll, for it means crossing swords with an establishment and a mind-set that cannot tolerate such freewheeling practice, and it is only a matter of days before 2:35 finds fulfillment.

The parable in its present form contains allegorical elements, but there is no strict correspondence between characteristic features of earthly kings and those of Jesus as a royal figure. The king in the story bears marks of a tyrant. But unsavory characters have elsewhere been used as paradigms for truths relating to the Kingdom of God (see 16:1–8; 18:1–8). Money and rewards of cities are part of the scenario and appropriate to the royal theme. Auditors are expected to abstract from them the principles that govern relationships between themselves and the Lord of the People of God. The comments that follow represent an attempt to do justice to the meaning of the parable through application not explicit in the text, a procedure supported by unmistakable echoes of thoughts expressed elsewhere in the Gospel.

19:12. The hearers would be familiar with examples of rulers going to a distant capital to secure their positions. In 40 B.C.E., Herod the Great went to Rome to bolster his throne (see Josephus *Antiquities* 14.14.1–4) and on his return executed some of his opponents (*Antiquities* 15.1.2). But the activity of his son Archelaus seems to have suggested some of the more explicit detail in the story. His interest in the throne was challenged by the Jews, who sent a deputation to Rome. Philip, Herod's third son, supported Archelaus in his plea before Augustus, whereas Antipas, who had also gone to Rome, spoke out against Archelaus (see *Antiquities* 17 and *War* 2.2.1–3). On his return to Palestine, Archelaus deposed the high priest Joazar in favor of Eleazar.

The risks incurred by officials who left home were a subject of popular discussion. As Hiero of Syracuse told the Greek poet Simonides, a tyrant cannot feel at ease about taking a leave of absence, for he can have no assurance that the property he entrusts to others for safekeeping will be secure (Xenophon *Hieron* 12).

Jesus is like the **nobleman** *(eugenēs)* who **went into a far country to receive a kingdom and then return**. Between his first appearance and his return (see Acts 1:11) lies an indeterminate period of time, described in terms of a journey to a far country. Jesus does not take over the Kingdom, or kingly power, in terms of popular expectation at Jerusalem, but receives it from the Father (cf. Luke 1:32–33) by entering into his glory, as spelled out in 24:26. After a time he will return. Thus the Kingdom is an ongoing reality, but it will appear (v. 11) in a climactic phase at the end of history.

19:13. Whereas Matthew enumerates three servants ("slaves"), Luke begins with ten (cf. Luke 17:12) but brings three of them to the fore in the dialogue. In Matthew the slaves receive varying amounts, but the monetary value is considerable. In Luke's recital each receives one pound, (a *mina*), the equivalent of about several months' wages. This trifling sum makes more cogent the reference to "very little" in v. 17. The criterion of success is not to be based on varied endowment, with a one-for-one return, as in Matthew. Faithfulness and shrewdness, measured by varying returns on the original investment, which is the same for all, is the standard whereby the disciple is judged.

19:14–15. In these verses the contrast between Jerusalem's hostility and the faithful apostolic community is clearly drawn. As was the case with Archelaus, Jesus is rejected by many of his compatriots. But on his return, Jesus calls his disciples to account. Association with him does not spell automatic success any more than does invocation of Abraham as father (3:8). Faithfulness, as specified in 16:10, is the criterion.

19:16–17. Those who are faithful in **very little** *(elachistos)* are entrusted with much (cf. 16:10), here spelled out as **authority over ten cities** (cf. 22:30; 12:32). Thus the contrast between the trifling amount and the responsibility now entrusted to the slave points to the surpassing generosity of the King (see 18:30).

19:18–19. The second slave earned only half the amount of the other and is entrusted with commensurate authority. Neither slave congratulates himself, but only the first receives a special accolade from the Lord: "Well done, good slave!"★ *(agathe doule)*.

19:20–21. A third slave is chosen out of the ten as illustration of total failure. He took no chances, risked nothing. He was not as wise as "the sons of this world" (16:8). Given freedom to act, he lived in fear of his master, whom he viewed as a rigorous financial inspector. So he used his neckcloth, which ordinarily protected his back from the sun, as a vault.

Today one would say that he is typical of self-styled Christians who retreat from the world and involvement in the decision making that goes on around them; typical of those who are experts at predicting the past and confine the good news in a deposit box of tradition for fear they will incur the wrath of the Lord if they brave fresh frontiers of communication and creative enterprise.

19:22. The first slave was congratulated for being good *(agathos)*, but this man hears the opposite verdict: **You wicked** *(ponēros)*, worthless slave!

19:23. His own conception of the Master should have prompted him to gain a return on the investment.

19:24. Why the man with ten pounds should be interested in one more pound after being entrusted with ten cities is not clarified, but one can guess. Luke's point is that the faithless slave did not really recognize his master's true character and therefore lost what he had. Further capital is to be entrusted to those who have demonstrated creative use of the resources entrusted to them. The Kingdom of God is a burgeoning enterprise.

19:25. Those who "stood by" (v. 24) are quite surprised by the Master's order. So was Perillos when Alexander offered him fifty talents. "Ten will suffice," said Perillos. Replied Alexander, "Sufficient for you to receive, but not for me to give" (Plutarch *Moralia* 179F).

The rejoinder of the bystanders serves to introduce the principle expressed in the next verse.

19:26. The **one who has** is one who views his possessions as a trust from the Lord. The one **who has not** is one who functions in such a way that one would suspect he had been entrusted with nothing. Such is the condition of religious people who boast that they have a relationship with God but fail to bear good fruit (see 6:43–45). As did the other two slaves, the third man said "Lord" (v. 20), but it was as empty a liturgy as the rich man's "Father, Abraham" (see also the warning in 6:46). But to everyone who **has, more** will **be given** (see 6:36–38; 8:18). This is the principle of the plus. Divine beneficence never ends for those who learn to receive with responsibility.

No special punishment is meted out to the third slave. He is simply not entrusted with the program of the future. The Master will not permit the experience of history to be repeated. Mediocre, middle-of-the-road, play-it-safe disciples will not be allowed to retard progress in the New Age yet to dawn. Luke is not interested in details of the final judgment. Paul holds out more explicit hope that such people will be saved in respect to their persons but will lose much opportunity that might have been theirs (see 1 Cor. 3:15). It is a function of the good news to spare people such disappointment.

19:27. Here the citizens of v. 14 come back into view. Like Agag (1 Sam. 15:33), they are to be slaughtered before the king's eyes. This bloody description is not to be taken as a literal representation of events at the end of time but is again part of the scenery associated with ancient generals and kings. In Luke's recital it means that Jesus' presence in history is crucial. It was especially crucial for Israel, for much had been given to her. The language of 19:27 anticipates Jesus' lament over the city (vv. 41–44), and the auditor is prepared for the entry described in vv. 28–38. But there is a shaft of light in the gloom of this passage.

By sketching in darkest tones the just fate of those who rejected their appointed ruler, Luke permits a later act of divine clemency, which was displayed at Pentecost and through the apostolic proclamation, to shine more brightly. At the same time, Luke gives dramatic expression to his rise-and-fall theme (2:34) and offers his auditors a challenging backward look at his story about Zacchaeus. Zacchaeus was once in the category of these rebels, but he was rescued. In his case, mercy prevailed, but there are those whose fall is inevitable unless they heed the grave warnings of the story of the minas.

PART FIVE: THE MINISTRY OF
JESUS IN JERUSALEM

THE KING'S CLAIM
Luke 19:28—48

The Royal Procession
Luke 19:28—38
(Mark 11:1–10: Matthew 21:1–9)

19:28. The words **when he had said this** clearly indicate the relation between the preceding parable and Jesus' royal entry into Jerusalem. Earlier, Jesus had sent messengers to precede him (9:51; 10:1). Now, as the "journey" begun in 9:51 nears its end, he takes the lead, for he is the "Coming One" (cf. 7:19). Luke again takes up Mark's account (Mark 11:1), but with some variations. After the story of the entry he inserts a dialogue between the Pharisees and Jesus. In Mark the cleansing of the temple takes place on the day after Jesus' entry; in Luke, apparently on the same day. Luke omits Mark's narrative of the cursing of the fig tree and condenses Mark's chronology of the first part of the last week into a general statement (v. 47; cf. 21:37).

19:29. The village of **Bethphage** ("house of unripe figs") has disappeared. It was located on the southeast slope of the Mount of Olives. Closer to Jerusalem was **Bethany.** The meaning of this name is uncertain, but some interpret it as "house of the poor" or "house of the afflicted." The site is mentioned also in Luke 24:50; Matt. 21:17; 26:6; Mark 11:1, 11; 14:3; today it is called Azariyeh or Lazaiyeh, "the place of Lazarus."

To early Christian auditors the reference to the Mount of Olives would have been especially significant, for this was to be the locale of end-time events. According to Zech. 14:4, the feet of the Lord were to stand at this place and the mount would be split in two. "Then the Lord your God will come, and all the holy ones with him" (Zech. 14:5), and "the Lord will become king over all the earth" (14:9). This association may have been also in Luke's mind, for Zech. 14:21 declares that "there shall no longer be a trader in the house of the Lord of hosts on that day" (cf. Luke 19:45).

19:30. Throughout the proceedings Jesus appears as master of the situation. His prophetic powers are integral to the total picture. His approaching death is no tragic accident. He has been aware of the divine intention. Now his instructions concerning a **colt** lend further confirmation to the conviction that he proceeds with unmistakable design. To suggest, therefore, that Jesus had made previous arrangements with the owners of the colt is to miss the theological intention of the text. The observation that no one had ever ridden the colt heightens the impression of Jesus' mastery.

19:31–34. In the succeeding dialogue the RSV unfortunately obscures the wordplay in the original. **The Lord** *(ho kyrios)* **has need of it** (v. 31) would be the normal interpretation of the text. But in v. 33 the words **its owners** *(hoi kyrioi:* "masters") parallel the phrasing in v. 31, which by analogy can be rendered "Its master has need of it." Greeks loved such wordplay (see also Luke 10:42), and even an unsophisticated reader would have caught the double sense. The text suggests that Jesus is a sovereign *(kyrios)* who claims all property as his own.

19:35. Parallel to this stress on lordship is the use of the name **Jesus** (vv. 34–35). In 1:31–32 this name and the fact of Jesus' kingship are linked. Luke 2:11 had added the reminder that Jesus is the Anointed One and Savior. Luke's literary artistry in drawing attention to his infancy narrative through repeated stress on the word "Lord," and now with the name "Jesus," is supported by his clear echo of 2:14 in 19:38. It is not improbable that he was also conscious of Isa. 1:3, which states that the ass knows "its master's crib; but Israel does not know, my people does not understand." The context of Isaiah 1 would account for Luke's inclusion of the criticism made by the Pharisees (Luke 19:39) and Jesus' lament over the ignorance of Jerusalem (v. 42).

19:36. More pointedly than Mark or Matthew, Luke continues with the disciples as subject of the action. Like the servants of Jehu, who proclaimed their master as king (2 Kings 9:13), they spread their garments in Jesus' path (cf. 1 Kings 1:32–40).

19:37. As he was now drawing near *(eggizontos)* echoes v. 11 *(eggys)* and v. 29 *(ēggisen;* see also v. 41). In one sense the Kingdom has arrived, but the disciples are not yet aware of the somber truth expressed in the previous parable (vv. 12–27). As at 18:43, the participants give praise to God. In keeping with his stress on the witness-bearing responsibility of the disciples (see 24:48; Acts 1:3; 2:22; 10:39), Luke more specifically defines Mark's reference to the celebrants as a **multitude of the disciples**. The **mighty works** *(dynameis)* of Jesus are the measure of his royal benefactions, and the

reaction of his followers is in harmony with the message sent by Jesus to
John the Baptist (7:22).

19:38. John had asked at Luke 7:20, "Are you he who is to come?" The
multitude provides the answer with the cry in 19:38 (see on 13:35). Once
again Luke's literary artistry is obscured by the RSV. Mark (11:9) had
written, "Blessed is the one who comes in the name of the Lord," reproduc-
ing the wording of Ps. 117:26 LXX. Luke retains this part of the acclamation, but adds two words: **the King**. His sentence reads: "Blessed is the one
who comes, namely the King, in the name of the Lord."* Jesus is the
"coming one" of John's query (Luke 7:20). His royal credentials are in order.
The conclusion of Mark's recital (Mark 11:10) reads: "Blessed is the kingdom of our father David that is coming! Hosanna in the highest!" Luke
deletes the first part of this statement in favor of his simple reference to **the
King,** thereby preserving the perspective expressed in 19:11–27.

Luke does not deny that Jesus is a Davidian (see on 18:40) and a political
figure in his own right, but Jesus does not usher in the type of kingdom
expressed by the phrase "the coming kingdom of our father David." Nor
does he have the same interests as those of Caesar. In place of the words
"Hosanna in the highest!" Luke repeats, with some variation, the message
of the angels. Like the multitude, they gave praise to God. "Hosanna,"
meaning "God, save," would probably not have been understood by many
of Luke's Greco-Roman public. Significant is the change from "peace on
earth" (Luke: 2:14) to **peace in heaven**. As the Supreme Benefactor, God is
filled with utmost goodwill toward Jerusalem and toward the world. The
word "peace" *(eirēnē)* in this context not only communicates a vivid concept
of salvation (cf. 1:79; 10:5–6; 24:36), in the sense that nothing disruptive
stands between God and his people, but also prepares the reader for the
pronouncement in 19:42.

Lament over Jerusalem
Luke 19:39–44

19:39–40. Luke's reference to the Pharisees, his last in this Gospel, provides a cogent setting for the lament that follows. Their approach to Jesus is
respectful. And their concern is legitimate. They want no disturbance of the
delicate balance between their religious interests and Roman power. They
are typical of leaders who are allergic to demonstrations or what they term
"emotional outbursts"; they much prefer "orderly" discussion, preferably
under the adjudication of carefully selected committees, which practically
guarantee hardening of institutional arteries and obsolescence of the gospel.

Acts 4:13–22 will relate how Jerusalem's leaders attempted to gag Peter
and John, who were proclaiming God's beneficence in connection with
Jesus; but the disciples refused to be intimidated. In reply to the Pharisees'
request for a stop-and-desist order, Jesus uses a vivid Semitic expression (cf.

Hab. 2:11). So great is the crisis that, in the absence of any other voice, inanimate objects must cry out. The reference to stones crying out is filled with pathos, anticipating as it does the terrible doom predicted in v. 44.

19:41. Jesus felt the "sense of tears in mortal things" (Vergil: *sunt lacrimae rerum*), and as he comes within sight of Jerusalem he breaks into a lament (cf. Lam. 4:1). It is the weeping for the dead and for the fool whose understanding has failed him (see Sir. 22:11). The very syntax of the Greek throbs with the agitation of his heart. About two centuries earlier, the Roman general Publius Scipio Aemilianus also shared prophetic tears, but over Carthage, a city that only a short time before had been reduced to ruins, a testimony to his and Rome's military efficiency. As his gaze moved over what was once the Dresden of Africa, he pondered the possibility of his own city's destruction. And six centuries later Rome shared the fate of Ilium, Nineveh, Babylon, Persepolis, and Jerusalem.

19:42. Heedless of the truth expressed in such passages as 12:56–59 and 14:28–32, Jerusalem does not realize that the presence of Jesus had placed her at a crossroads of national destiny. The meaning of Jesus' earlier words, "From those who have not, even what they have will be taken away" (19:26★), finds tragic fulfillment: **Now they are hid from your eyes**. One who *will* not see *shall* not see (Isa. 29:10; Luke 8:10).

19:43–44. If, as is held by many, Luke wrote his book after the fall of Jerusalem (70 C.E.), some of his Greco-Roman auditors would have noted that Jesus' extraordinary credentials were ratified by the fulfillment of his prophecy. Similarly, Polybios (*History* 29.21) was impressed by the powers of Demetrios of Phaleron, who foretold the downfall of Macedonian power. A little more than fourteen centuries after the sack of Rome by Alaric the Goth and its plundering by the Vandal Gaiseric, a United States merchant named John Brown prophesied: "I . . . am quite certain that the crimes of this guilty land will never be purged away but with blood. I had, as I now think, vainly flattered myself that without very much bloodshed it might be done." His words found fulfillment at the outbreak of the Civil War, about two years after he was hanged for his part in the liberation of slaves.

Details of the disaster that followed in the year 70 C.E. recall descriptions in Isa. 29:3 and Ps. 137:9. The words **not . . . one stone upon another** are hyperbolic. Actually parts of walls and buildings were left standing. The phrase is simply a device to paint in bold lines the ruin of a great city. The words **because you did not know the time of your visitation** are a refrain of the first words. Israel knows how to predict the weather, but she does not know the critical moment in her history (12:56–59). Luke does not connect the destruction of Jerusalem with the death of Jesus, but he does affirm that if only Jerusalem had been more alert to his message, her awful fate could have been averted. But traditionalists had misled Jerusalem into thinking that there was peace when there was no peace (cf. Jer. 6:14), and they are out to destroy Jesus, the city's only hope (Luke 19:47). For Jesus is the manifestation of God's visitation *(episkopē)*. Zechariah had spoken of this visitation (1:68, 78) and the people had glorified God for it at the resurrection of the young man at Nain (7:16). Who knows what else Jesus might have done in Israel? As it is, all the magnificent displays of God's peaceful intention toward her are about to come to an end, and the glory will depart (cf. 1 Sam. 4:20–21; Jer. 16:5). God had kept his appointment with the city, but Jerusalem's power structure did not show up at the banquet (see Luke 14:15–24).

Cleansing of the Temple
Luke 19:45–46
(Mark 11:15–18; Matthew 21:12–13)

19:45–46. At the age of twelve, Jesus had claimed the temple as his proper province. As King of Israel his objective was reclamation of Israel for God. Mark lays stress on outreach to the gentiles (Mark 11:17). Luke omits this motif, for the temple, because of its disappearance in the year 70 c.e., could never serve the nations (see also Acts 7). Instead, Luke emphasizes the default of Israel's religious leadership, whose ancestors were severely castigated in Isaiah 9. There is to be no trader in the house of the Lord in the day anticipated by the prophet Zechariah (Zech. 14:21).

The temple is for prayer, for expression of dependence on God. No amount of sacrifices can substitute for self-dedication (see Isa. 1:10–17). Careless and venal authorities had permitted the temple to become a place for trading in livestock and pigeons, and on the side devoured widow's houses (see Luke 20:47). A non-Christian, Gaius Cestius, condemned the practice of grasping an image of Caesar after committing outrages on the reputations of fellow citizens (Tacitus *Annals* 3.36). But these religionists, like robbers who return to their hideout to divide their ill-gotten gains, use the temple as a place of refuge, a kind of bombproof shelter from the divine wrath (see Jer. 7:1–11). No mistake was ever so fatal.

Jesus Teaches in the Temple
Luke 19:47–48
(Mark 11:18)

19:47. Isaiah complained about prophets who taught lies and led the people astray (Isa. 9:15–16; cf. 29:13). In Luke's Gospel only Jesus appears as teacher. Now in the temple he daily does what Israel's leaders failed to do and gives proper instruction to the people. Liturgy is meaningful only when accompanied by an understanding of God's purposes and objectives for those who worship him. The **chief priests and the scribes** and leaders (**principal men**) of the people sense the rebuke. Enduring no curb of time-honored privilege, they seek to kill Jesus.

Undoubtedly they came up with the standard thoughts in such situations. Matters could have been discussed behind closed doors. There were orderly procedures, approved channels that Jesus could have followed. It was one thing for Moses to fill the ovens of Egypt with frogs, for Isaiah to parade naked for three years, and for Jeremiah to punctuate has sermons with the breaking of earthen flasks, but Jesus had gone too far in symbolic activism. Yet he succeeded in sounding a message for all time, that true religion is not merely a consolatory exercise for private satisfaction but is intimately connected with protest against distortion of divine interests.

Such was the effect of his powerful originality, so profoundly jarring his presence among them, that the authorities could come to only one conclusion: there was no longer room for both them and Jesus. The prophet of Nazareth had to go. So it had also been said about the prophet Jeremiah (Jer. 26:8). But Israel as a whole (see also Luke 21:38) has not renounced its right to the blessings promised to the fathers, and many **hung upon his words**. In the course of the apostolic mission Jesus will continue as the authoritative instructor of God's people.

At this point Luke omits Mark's reference (Mark 11:20–26) to the cursing of a fig tree by Jesus. In Luke's account Jesus speaks words of judgment but does not pronounce a curse on his beloved city. God's peace, despite its rejection by some, is repeatedly extended to Israel, and never more dramatically than after the crucifixion of Jesus (see Acts 2—4, and cf. 3:20; 10:36).

MISUNDERSTANDING
Luke 20:1—21:4

The Scribes
Luke 20:1–26

A Question about Authority
Luke 20:1–8
(Mark 11:27–33; Matthew 21:23–27)

20:1–2. Luke appears to allow a longer period than does Mark for the events recorded during the last days. According to 19:47, Jesus was teaching daily in the temple. On one of these days the recital recorded in 20:1–19 takes place *(kai egeneto)*. Jesus is questioned by members of the Jewish high court, the Sanhedrin, concerning his authority *(exousia)*. They want to know his credentials, for he lacks official recognition as a rabbi.

In Mark, the question arises relative to Jesus' protest against trade in the temple precincts; in Luke, the question is aimed at Jesus' activity as a teacher. Luke alters Mark's phrase "as he was walking in the temple" (Mark 11:27) to

as he was teaching the people in the temple and preaching the gospel.
Mark refers only to his "teaching" (Mark 11:18). Luke adds "telling the
good news," a favorite term in his Gospel, with emphasis on "the people"
(laos).

20:3–4. Such instruction, if earlier samples are any indication, would be
contrary to official guidelines and policy. Jesus counters with a question
concerning John's baptism. This is not an attempt to dodge the issue, but
simply a refusal to play into the hands of the opposition. Unless the
leadership face up to the basic problem raised by John, they could not
possibly understand Jesus' own conviction that he was sent by God to fulfill
what had been begun by John. The question deals with a vital theological
consideration. Was John motivated by God? If so, how can they conclude
that the message of Jesus conflicts with John's call to repentance?

20:5–8. The hierarchy betray their own hypocrisy. Their fear of the
people takes precedence over fear of God, and they plead the fifth amendment. Determined to charge Jesus with breaking the peace of Israel, they are
not interested in discussing the real issues, and *they* prefer to ask the
questions. Ancient Greeks loved this kind of repartee. When Ptolemy I
asked a grammarian who the father of Pelops was—mythologists were in
no agreement on the matter—the grammarian replied: "I will tell you, if
you first tell me who was the father of Lagos."

Martin Luther, when he attempted to engage his ecclesiastical superiors in
debate, encountered a similar refusal to that experienced by Jesus. In fairness
to authorities caught in such circumstances it must be granted that the
introduction of theological concerns might well put the continuation of
standard procedures into question and thus invite what in their judgment is
tantamount to anarchy. Be that as it may, anything Jesus might say would be
misunderstood, and if his questioners cannot grasp what the people had
long ago concluded (cf. 7:26), nothing would be gained by continuing the
discussion. Luke signals this point by a slight alteration of Mark's phrasing
(Mark 12:1). Mark has the following parable addressed in the main to the
inquisitors. Luke says that it was addressed to the people (v. 9), but of course
its bite was meant for the establishment (see v. 19). With some changes in
the script, the drama will be reenacted at a later date (see Acts 4).

Parable of the Vineyard   Luke 20:9–19
(Mark 12:1–12; Matthew 21:33–46)

20:9. Jesus proceeds to instruct the people *(laos)*. His parable, like the one
in 19:12–27, contains allegorical elements, but Luke does not appear to have
had in mind precise historical correspondence for each of the three slaves.
They are, rather, representative of a long succession of prophets. The picture
of Israel as a vineyard is derived from Isa. 5:1–7. As at 19:46, Luke omits

part of Mark's OT quotation. Not the quality of the vineyard but hostility toward the messengers is Luke's concern. His addition of the phrase **for a long while** is perhaps a way of indicating the interval between God's calling of Israel and the present fulfillment of the promises made to the fathers. It may also be a stylistic device to account for the various times in which the messengers were sent.

20:10–12. The three slaves are all treated with violence, but they all escape with their lives (in Mark the third slave is killed). In keeping with his artistic sensitivity, Luke reserves the climax for the third messenger and also omits Mark's reference to the murder of "others" who were sent.

20:13. Fine literary tact is apparent in Luke's further description of the owner's deliberation before sending out the last messenger. The actual dispatch is not mentioned, and the pathos is more profound than in Mark's phrasing, especially in the addition of the words translated **it may be** (*isōs*). The words **my beloved son** may echo the divine address at the baptism (3:22).

20:14–16. Both Luke and Matthew reverse Mark's sequence in their recitals of the fate of the son. He is first **cast . . . out** and then **killed** (cf. Heb. 13:12). The Lord answers his own question concerning the fate of the tenants and the vineyard. In Luke's account this can only refer to two things: the destruction of Jerusalem and the shift of responsibility for the good news from the custodians in Jerusalem to those Jews and gentiles who accept the message of salvation. At this point Luke inserts the words: **When they heard this, they said, 'God forbid!'** (*mē genoito*). The pronoun "they" refers again to the people (v. 9).

20:17. The addition of the dialogue in v. 16 helps bridge two patches of text in Mark (12:9–10). As they stand in Mark, it is unclear how the quotation of Ps. 118:22, which speaks of an exalted stone, ties in with the conclusion of the parable. In Luke, the response of the people permits a clearer explanation. Luke then cites Mark's quotation, but in abbreviated form, and in place of the omitted portion he introduces a pithy statement that echoes the note of judgment in v. 16.

The quotation from Ps. 118:22 appears also in Acts 4:11 and in 1 Pet. 2:7 as a messianic endorsement for Jesus. The figure is taken from procedures on construction projects. A stone with a flaw would be rejected by the supervisor. Jerusalem's theological experts disqualified Jesus from Israel's highest office, that of Messiah. But the early Christians knew that he was exalted (cf. Luke 24:26). Psalm 118:17 declares: "I shall not die, but I shall live, and recount the deeds of the Lord." And the same psalm (v. 26) contains the acclamation used in Luke 19:38. Luke's earlier correction of misunderstanding concerning the Kingdom (19:11) is here ratified. Jesus is the Coming One, the King, but first he must be rejected. After this comes the exaltation.

20:18. To reinforce this truth, Luke adds the words in v. 18, which may be derived from some Greek text of Dan. 2:44 (cf. v. 34) or Isa. 8:14–15, or even an unknown document. A rabbi once said: "Should the stone fall on the crock, woe to the crock. Should the crock fall on the stone, woe to the crock. In either case, woe to the crock!" (SB 1:877). Jesus is the point of decision. Response to him determines one's destiny.

20:19. Because Jesus had entered into scribal territory with this use of Scripture, the scribes are mentioned first. With the help of the chief priests (i.e., the ruling board of the Sanhedrin, see on 3:2) they would have arrested him on the spot, but their fear of the people was stronger than their outraged theological sensitivities (cf. 19:48). Theophilos would not fail to grasp the issues. Jesus was "framed" by the religious establishment.

Luke is clearly not anti-Semitic! Jewishness is not, in his judgment, defined in terms of Jerusalem's authorities. But it is questionable whether religious establishments since Luke's time have grasped the import of his recital. Until the institutional churches in their various forms recognize that God can well do without them in their present structural aspects, they must know that the Stone will ultimately crush them too. For Christianity is not to be equated with the continuance of any particular offices or structural forms. Extraordinary is the fact that the early Christian communities were authentic even in the absence of two primary features of traditional identity: circumcision and the priesthood.

A Question about Taxes

Luke 20:20–26
(Mark 12:13–17; Matthew 22:15–22)

20:20. Foiled in their attempt to get rid of the troublemaker in Israel, and determined to get as damaging a dossier as possible on the upstart from Nazareth, the hierarchy take a fresh tack. Unwittingly they implement Jesus' own prediction that he would be handed over to the gentiles (see 18:32). **The governor,** that is, the prefect (Pontius Pilate), will be taken into the dirty business. A slip of the tongue on Jesus' part will turn the trick. But the chief priests and the scribes cannot endure another debacle by tackling Jesus personally. Their experiences depicted in vv. 1–19 were already more than they could absorb.

Keenly aware of the seamy side of institutional practice, whether in state or in temple, Luke exposes a common tactic. These enemies of the future engage others, who could not be suspected of vested interest, to investigate Jesus. They would pretend **to be sincere** (*dikaios:* "upright"), that is, serious inquirers. Jesus has been teaching the people; let him now teach these pupils who feign interest in "the way of God" (v. 21). "Way" (*hodos*) is a favorite term in Luke's vocabulary. It refers not only to a set of truths but to behavior in harmony with religious affirmation.

20:21. We know that you ... show no partiality. All have their price, the spies say, but not you! You let the chips fall where they may. You tell it how it is. With such flattery they invite Jesus to his doom and themselves to Belshazzar's feast. Their question about payment of taxes to the emperor had a short fuse. Yes or no! It is the cheap trick often played by those who have no interest in probing the real issues, but only seek to retain waning power while ostensibly aiming to find the facts. "Damned if you do and damned if you don't." Should Jesus say "Yes," then his magnetic hold on the people would be broken. Taxes, in any event, are unpopular, but for a Jew to pay taxes to Caesar—this was the supreme indignity. Should he say "No," that would be the end of the matter, for Pilate would see to it quickly. Should he say neither yes nor no, he can be accused of *evading* the issue.

20:23–24. Jesus knows the game is rigged. He accepts the challenge and takes his interlocutors with him into the lions' den: "Show me a denarius." No sense in dancing around the issue. "Tiberius Caesar, Augustus, son of divine Augustus" reads the inscription on such a coin. Theology is what it's all about. The request is at the same time an exposure of their hypocrisy. They act profoundly concerned about God's loss of prestige through the domination of their nation by a foreign power, whose chief of state has his image incused on coins. Pious Jews abhorred graven images (cf. Deut. 7:5). But these hypocrites, affecting to come concerned about theological principle, just happen to have this denarius with Caesar's image on it. An alert spy would have said, "We don't carry them."

20:25. Since they have Caesar's coins in their possession, they should give them back: **render to Caesar**. If they have scruples about graven images, let them toss the scruples away by returning the coins. This, of course, they would not do, if they were numbered among some of their colleagues who are described as "lovers of silver" (*philargyroi*; cf. 16:14; 18:25; 20:47). Jesus' wit and profound sense of humor are here at their best, matched only by the profound moral sensitivity expressed in the clinching phrase, (**render**) **to God the things that are God's**.

Actually Jesus did not answer the question whether it was lawful to pay tribute to Caesar. Foolish questions, not to speak of motivation, do not deserve consideration (see Prov. 26:4). But his reply suggests that if Caesar's coins are used for normal business transactions and accepted for payment, as indeed they would be, for example in trading done at the temple, then their use in payment of taxes would not be incompatible with allegiance to God. If God doesn't mind, neither should they. The chief priests, on the other hand, will hand Jesus over to Caesar's representative (23:1), and the scribes will continue to take advantage of widows under a snug blanket of liturgy (20:47). All this in conflict with the reminder: "render to God the things that are God's."

The disciples will do better. Peter and John replied to the same authorities who sent these men: "Whether it is right in the sight of God to listen to you rather than to God, you must judge; for we cannot speak of what we have seen and heard" (Acts 4:19–20). Caesar will also learn his limit (see the Book of Revelation). Luke, who is at pains especially in Acts to show the quality of Roman justice, clearly understood the principle. God is not so insecure as to see in Caesar a threat to God's own claims (see also Rom. 13:1–7; 1 Pet. 2:13–17). On the other hand, God does not divide time with Caesar, as some versions of so-called two-kingdom theory suggest. Nor does Luke champion the idea of a left-hand and a right-hand mode of governance by God. What he does affirm is that Jesus is a politician in his own right, but not a nationalistic revolutionary. He is the One Name (Acts 4:12). And when authorities of any stripe challenge allegiance to the One Name, they discover who holds the chief seat of power.

Luke knows that the identification of Jesus as a King had raised eyebrows in Rome. This story should clear the air. "Down with the establishment" was not his theme song. There is nothing wrong with "establishment" as such. Establishment is necessary especially to protect the weak. The error lies with those who use power to serve their own interests and attempt to eliminate competition from the direction of truth. One who engages in critique of establishments, as does Luke, is not the menace. Those who cry peace when there is no peace are the real traitors. It is not Jesus but the chief priests and rulers who, in Luke's judgment, are in fact guilty of connivance with insurrection, for they will demand the release of one "who had been thrown into prison for insurrection and murder" (23:25).

20:26. The spies had failed to drive a wedge between Jesus and the people. They had received more teaching than they bargained for. Like an earlier audience in the temple (2:48), they were astounded by **his answer**. Like the lawyers and the Pharisees on a certain sabbath (14:6), **they were silent**. **Jesus, the wise one, confounds the foolish** (cf. Wisd. of Sol. 8:12; Sir. 20:1–8).

The Sadducees
Luke 20:27–44

A Knotty Problem   Luke 20:27–40
                                              (Mark 12:18–27; Matthew 22:23–33)

20:27. The Sadducees are the next victims of their own skulduggery. They are mentioned only here in Luke's Gospel. Their name is derived, with some probability, from the Zadok who was priest under David (1 Kings 2:35). In the Book of Ezekiel only the "sons of Zadok" are recognized as legitimate priests (Ezek. 40:46; cf. Sir. 51:12). The Sadducees emerge as a party during the Maccabean period (second century B.C.E.). Their chief interest was the preservation of priestly prerogatives, which included interpretation of the Law.

Against the Pharisees, who endeavored to update Moses through transmission of an oral law adapted to circumstances, the Sadducees appealed to the written law, with special emphasis on the first five books of Moses. Thus any interpretation imposed by tradition could be challenged by appeal to the primary source. It is improbable, though, that the Sadducees limited their canon to the Pentateuch, as was alleged by such fathers as Hippolytus and Epiphanius. They merely limited legal sources to the first five books of the Bible. In a sense they were constitutionalists of their time, whereas the Pharisees were more progressive in their interpretation of inherited tradition.

The Sadducees' refuge was status quo. They viewed with alarm what they criticized as "newfangled" doctrines of the Pharisees: the resurrection, future rewards and punishments, and the existence of angels and spirits (see Acts 23:8; cf. *Enoch* 15:6–9). The dialogue in vv. 27–39 revolves mainly about the first of these doctrines, namely, the resurrection *(anastasis)*, which finds no explicit support in the Pentateuch. In their behalf it must be said that their devotion to God was not dependent on eschatological recompense for fidelity.

20:28–33. According to Deut. 25:5–10, if a brother dies childless, a surviving brother is to take the widow, but not necessarily marry her, and beget children for his brother. The first child born of such a union is to bear the name of the deceased. A brother who refused to do this would fall into disgrace. Ruth 3—4 presupposes this custom. In the case propounded by the Sadducees, seven brothers in succession lived intimately with one woman, but not one child was born. With their question in v. 33: **In the resurrection, therefore, whose wife will the woman be?** the Sadducees hope not only to gain a trick on the Pharisees but at the same time deflate Jesus' image as a teacher. The problem is indeed most cleverly put. If there is to be a resurrection, the seven brothers must also rise. But then, to whom does the woman belong? Thus despite their own denials of the resurrection, they assume it for the sake of argument and put Jesus on the spot.

20:34–35. Luke omits the rebuke administered by Jesus in Mark's account (Mark 12:24), perhaps on the ground that the OT does not in fact say anything about social relationships after the resurrection. The basic error in their thinking, suggests Jesus, is a confusion between conditions that pertain on earth and those that will pertain in the age to come. In **this age**, people **marry and are given in marriage.** Such is not the case in the period after the resurrection. Moreover, the Sadducees imply in their trick question that *all* people are expected to rise. Jesus limits the participants in the resurrection to those who are **accounted worthy** (cf. 14:14). Thereby is demonstrated a basic relationship between God's final judgment and human responsibility to meet God's expectations as defined by Moses. The Sadducees through their denial of the resurrection invalidate such a serious view of moral responsibility.

20:36. As for the problem of raising up descendants for a brother, it is ridiculous, suggests Jesus, to cite Deuteronomy. Moses was concerned about surmounting the reality of death by ensuring the survival of a family name. The fundamental purpose of marriage, according to Moses, is to establish a posterity. But, says Jesus, there is no need for this when people **cannot die any more.** Not the parenthood of a brother, but the Parenthood of God is the crucial factor, and those who are **sons of the resurrection** (a Semitic expression meaning "share in the resurrection") are **sons of God.** Sadducees thought that the doctrine of the resurrection and specific laws of Moses were incompatible. Jesus' masterful reply, hammered out on their own anvil, shows that this is not at all a necessary conclusion.

Included in his argument is a further blow to Sadducean doctrine, for Jesus subtly takes issue with their denial of the existence of angels (cf. Acts 23:8). But Luke does not permit the argument to be weakened here by Mark's phrase that resurrected people "are like angels in heaven" (Mark 12:25). In place of the noun "angel," Luke has an adjective "angel-like" (*isaggeloi:* **equal to angels**), used only here in the NT. In contrast to Mark and Matthew, Luke includes the words **and are sons of God**, an expression that occurs only here in Luke-Acts, for Jesus is the Son of God par excellence. Its presence in this text therefore suggests awareness of a point made in another source from which Luke may be drawing. In the OT, "sons of God" is a term applied to beings ordinarily understood as angels (Gen. 6:2; Job 1:6; 38:7; Pss. 29:1; 89:6). In Luke's recital, the expression is used in a double sense, suggesting heavenly beings, or angels, as well as children of God (cf. 6:35, "sons of the Highest"*).

With his use of the adjective "angel-like," Luke avoids the suggestion that those who are resurrected will be angels. At the same time, he focuses attention on the expression "sons of God" as the category in which angels are to be understood. If resurrected people qualify as "sons of God," then there is no reason to deny the existence of the heavenly beings called "sons of God," or angels. Again, it is not Jesus or the community that has chosen the weapons of controversy, but when forced to the battle the representatives of the New Age are no amateurs in combat. We have here, then, a sample of the high-powered discussion that enlivened also many a debate within and outside the church.

20:37. Jesus could have rested his case, but he moves deeper into the Sadducees' own territory—the Pentateuch. Moses speaks of the Lord as **the God of Abraham and the God of Isaac and the God of Jacob** (Exod. 3:6). Thus **Moses showed**, or suggested, that the dead are to be raised. At Acts 3:13, Luke has Peter capitalizing on Jesus' line of argument.

20:38. If God stands in a relation to these patriarchs who were long dead when Exodus was written, they must in some sense be alive, for God is not a **God of the dead, but of the living** (cf. Isa. 26:19; Dan. 12:2; Ezekiel 37). As a psalmist, who thought like a Sadducee, wrote, there is no relationship with God in the grave (Pss. 6:5; 88:11). Jesus' inference is supported by Luke's editorial note, **for all live to him**, perhaps related to 4 Macc. 16:25: "knowing well that men dying for God live unto God, as live Abraham, and Isaac, and Jacob, and all the patriarchs"★ (cf. 4 Macc. 7:19).

A concise commentary on this passage is 1 Pet. 4:6: "From the human perspective, taking account merely of the body, the [Christian] departed are dead; but from God's perspective, taking account of the spirit, they are alive."★ Peter's verse rides on the confessional thought of 3:18: Christ was "dead body-wise, but was made alive spirit-wise."★

20:39. The Sadducees heard more than they bargained for, and the scribes are delighted at their discomfiture. Some years later a man named Paul would break up a meeting of the two parties by introducing the same topic defended here by Jesus (Acts 23:6–10). **Teacher, you have spoken well**, said the professionals.

20:40. Indeed, the amateur from Nazareth had not done at all badly, **for they no longer dared to ask him any question**, a phrase taken over from Mark 12:34 (see Wisd. of Sol. 8:12 on the wise man who confounds princes).

About David's Son—Counterproblem   Luke 20:41–44
                                              (Mark 12:35–37a; Matthew 22:41–46)

20:41. Once having taken the offensive, Jesus uses more artillery. Since Luke had recorded a modified version of Mark 12:28–31 at 10:25–28, he omits Mark 12:28–34, except for a portion of the last verse, and presents Jesus' query concerning Davidic sonship. Luke leaves the precise audience undetermined, but to include the scribes he deletes Mark's reference to the scribes (Mark 12:35, "How can the scribes say . . .?") and writes in a more general vein, **How can they say** . . .? "They" in this sense is colloquial. The question is not meant to deny the Davidic ancestry of Jesus. Luke is not in the habit of contradicting himself on themes to which he gives repeated expression (cf. 1:27, 32, 69; 2:4, 11; 6:3; 18:38–39; Acts 2:25–36; cf. Rom. 1:3). The point of the passage turns on the first word: "how." Is the Messiah a purely nationalistic figure or does he transcend David in a way not anticipated by the popular interpretation?

20:42. Psalm 110 is introduced as evidence. The fact that David's authorship of the psalm has been questioned does not invalidate the argumentation. Jesus is Messiah in his own right, but any counterarguments from his contemporaries based on the OT are legitimately met by sources generally accepted by them. Any assumption, though, that Jesus anticipated the results of modern scholarship and accommodated himself to the popular view of the authorship of the psalm is improbable. Twentieth-century concerns are not to be projected into the biblical text in such a way as to distort the primary interests of the writer.

In place of Mark's phrase "inspired by the Holy Spirit" (Mark 12:36), Luke refers to the general location of the passage, **the Book of Psalms** (see Acts 1:20, and cf. Luke 3:4; Acts 7:42). Luke may have thought that the more specific reference would assist some of his auditors to locate the passage more readily, but his two-volume work suggests no consistent practice on this score. Since the Sadducees are presumed to be included in the audience, it is also quite probable that Luke wished to avoid a phrase that might put the validity of Jesus' argument into question. More probably, Luke's theology of the Holy Spirit dictated the change.

Only Jesus and the disciples (and these only after Pentecost) are described as having something done to them or acting "in the Spirit" (cf. Luke 2:27; 4:1, of Jesus; Acts 1:5; 11:16; 19:21, of disciples). God or the Holy Spirit speaks "through the mouth" of prophets or of David (Luke 1:70; Acts 1:16; 3:18, 21) but they are never described as writing or speaking "in the Spirit," or as being "full of the Spirit," a common phrase applied to a number of persons in Luke's works. For Luke, the New Age ushered in by the arrival of Jesus and endorsed by Pentecost is the time of special endowment of the Spirit. Therefore the Holy Spirit can speak through the mouth of David and the prophets, but only Jesus and those associated with him in the history of salvation are "in the Spirit" or "full of the Spirit."

In Christian circles Psalm 110 was acknowledged to be messianic (cf. Acts 2:34; 1 Cor. 15:25; Heb. 1:13). For the theme, see, for example, Ps. 89:3–4; Isa. 9:7; 11:1–2; and *Psalms of Solomon* 17. In its original historical setting, the psalm expresses prophetic concern of an Israelite for his king (**my Lord**), who is addressed by God, **the Lord** (Yahweh).

20:43–44. Luke, who emphasizes the outreach of the gospel to the gentiles, uses this citation from Psalm 110 to stress the superiority of Jesus over any direct human descendant from David. The enemies are not the gentiles (as in Luke 1:71) but all who oppose God's elected Messiah. These would include the "citizens" mentioned in 19:14, whose downfall is described in 19:27 (cf. 19:41–44). Zechariah never dreamed that the "enemies" (Luke

1:71) might have their headquarters in Jerusalem. Israel does not know how the Messiah is David's son, for they have not pondered the fact that he is described as David's Lord. Hence they discredit Jesus, whom they measure in terms of criteria narrowly established by their own traditional thinking.

Gabriel in his announcement to Mary had declared that Jesus would receive "the throne of his father David" (1:32). But he also identified Jesus as "the Son of the Most High" (1:32) and as "the Son of God" (1:35). The Passion account will reveal the larger perspective from which the Davidic sonship is to be understood (cf. 23:46). The Sadducees, who deny a resurrection, will find it even more difficult to believe that Jesus is truly the Messiah (see on 16:31). Thus their narrow theological position and manner of interpreting the Scriptures invalidates even their own messianic hope. That Luke associates the question of Davidic sonship and resurrection is clear from Acts 2:24–36.

A Study in Contrasts
Luke 20:45—21:4

Beware of the Scribes
Luke 20:45–47
(Mark 12:37b–40; Matthew 23:1, 6)

This final sample of Jesus' public teaching climaxes the development of thought initiated by the recital of the entry into Jerusalem. The lines of kingship have been clearly defined. All that remains is the denouement. But the question of messianic credentials requires one last appraisal of Jesus' relationship to the destruction of Jerusalem and the events of the end time. There will be no city left for a son of David to rule. How then is Jesus David's son? And what is the disciples' role in the new Kingdom? The answer to such questions is the burden of 20:45—21:36.

20:45. Luke's view of the hazards of wealth prompts him to retain Mark's recital of Jesus' indictment of the scribes and the story of the generous donation by the widow (Mark 12:38–44). Closely related to crass messianism is ostentatious display and materialism. They are an invitation to the disaster about to be described in the apocalyptic discourse. Despite all the premonitions Jesus has of his death, he does not play it safe. In the **hearing of all the people** he makes his indictment of the scribes. It will be the seal on his death warrant. But his words are an address **to his disciples.** Luke's Jesus does not permit the community that bears his name to evade scrutiny by pointing fingers at Pharisees and Sadducees. Their sins are perennials, says Jesus, and the disciples must be vigilant lest they smother life in the New Age. Association with Jesus as Lord should not encourage them to jockey for position (cf. 9:46). But their memories would be short (see 22:24).

20:46–47. These verses in part echo 14:7–11, a passage that begins with the same warning. It is naive to think that Luke's record is overdrawn. The scribes have their clones throughout history. In a vein similar to the evangelist's recital, Epiktetos describes philosophers of his time who demand a "thousand benches" for their audience and put on "a fancy cloak, or pretty mantle, and mount their pulpit" (3.23.35). After delivering his sermon, the orator says, "The audience was much bigger today." His friend replies, "Yes, it was really crowded." The orator responds, "And they were quick to catch the points I was making." To this the friend answers, "Even a stone must give way to beauty!" (3.23.19).

Catering to mediocrity and using diplomatic speech that lacks prophetic clarity— this is the way to ecclesiastical success, declaims Erasmus in *The Praise of Folly* (32–33). And all of it under a facade of liturgical piety that bores God with long prayers.

The "long prayers" of the scribes probably are recited in behalf of widows who seek legal help. God, suggests Luke, would come to the aid of widows without such expenditure of ostentatious rhetoric. Widows' rights were a major concern in Christian communities (cf. Acts 6:1; 1 Timothy 5).

A prophetic tone is further apparent in the statement that they **devour widows' houses**, whose value is probably consumed in legal processes. Luke does not spell out details, but for this and similar injustices, all committed in the name of a law in which the scribes were experts, the prophets once called down fusillades of divine wrath (see Isa. 1:23–24; 10:2–3; 22:3–5; Ezek. 22:29–31; Zech. 7:10–14; Mal. 3:5; cf. Deut. 10:18; 24:17; 27:19; Ps. 68:5). Those who, like the scribes, are in positions of leadership will **receive the greater condemnation**, on the principle that to whom much is given of him will much be required (cf. Luke 8:18). The apocalyptic discourse in Luke 21 will relate how finely God's mill can grind.

A Poor Widow

Luke 21:1–4
(Mark 12:41–44)

21:1–3. The story of the poor widow contrasts ostentatious religion and true devotion, niggardliness and genuine beneficence. In a departure of wording from Mark 12:42, Luke at 21:2 describes the woman as "needy" (*penichra:* **poor**). At 21:3 Luke echoes 6:20 and uses the more customary term (*ptōchē*) which the RSV also renders **poor.** Before the woman threw in all that she had left, she was needy. Now she put herself into a beggar's status.

Luke's choice of terms is in keeping with what he has to say about the priority of the good news, which is sent to the "beggars" (*ptōchoi,* 7:22). The Kingdom belongs to a woman like this, and the scribes will learn it, but too late. Of faith that transcends material security Jesus has frequently spoken. This widow does what the ruler spoken of in 18:22 refused to do—she parts with her last resources and commits herself totally to God. Luke has two other sayings introduced by **truly** (*alēthōs*; 9:27; 12:44). The third is reserved for this woman.

21:4. Aristotle echoed a long line of sentiment when he wrote on the subject of benefactors: "One's generosity is to be evaluated in terms of one's resources. Generosity is not measured in terms of the amount given; it depends on the attitude of the donor. People who are truly generous give in proportion to what they actually have. It is possible, therefore, that a person who gives but little out of small resources is more generous than another" (*Nikomachean Ethics* 4.1.19). Herodes Atticus, a distinguished philanthropist of the ancient world, never surpassed the widow's record.

It would be a mistake for proclaimers of the text to exploit the widow's action in the interest of some stewardship program, for Jesus does not praise her action. Scribal teaching had indeed devoured this widow's house. Proclaimers, whether in mainline churches or on radio or television circuits, must therefore come to grips with the question of responsibility in dealing with the tender consciences of people who want to do the right thing in their relationships with God but in the attempt may well go beyond their means.

NEWS ABOUT THE END TIME
Luke 21:5–36
(Mark 13:1–36; Matthew 24:1–22, 29–35)

A major part of Jesus' instruction in the temple is his discourse on the fate of Jerusalem, on experiences of his followers as they carry on their world-wide mission, and on the windup of history. The overall theme is vigilant composure. It is customary to describe this section as an eschatological discourse because, as the first part of the word "eschatological" reveals, it is instruction about the last things (*eschata*) namely, the end of Jerusalem and of the world. The language in which eschatology comes to expression is commonly termed "apocalyptic," most of which is traditional, such as references to catastrophes and cosmic disturbances.

It is a basic error in interpretation to attempt to construct a timetable based on alleged correspondence of events in history with the vivid imagery used by such prophets as Ezekiel, Daniel, and the composer of the Book of Revelation in their descriptions of catastrophic developments. In other words, the imagery is not the thing itself. Those who exploit people's fears and claim either to know the precise end-time schedule or to be the one who ushers in the end are respectively termed false prophets and false messiahs.

Luke arranges and edits the discourse in such a way that Christians may retain their serenity amid the babble of alarmist rhetoric. Since the Hebrew Scriptures depict Jerusalem as the major locale of what God does in Israel's future, it is understandable that the question of her fate should be intimately connected with the fate of the entire world. The gospel message is just as critical for the world as it was for Jerusalem, for Jesus is the One Name. Because Jerusalem's destruction precluded fulfillment of her destiny as popularly conceived in the light of prophetic statement, it was all the more necessary that Jesus and teachers in the apostolic community should offer some guidance for understanding developments that had taken place. Luke's presentation is part of his effort to help Theophilos and others know the truth.

Luke has given no indication that Jesus left the temple at any time between the observation made in 20:1 and the recital beginning at 21:5. The second chapter of Luke's Gospel displayed Jesus speaking with wisdom in the temple (2:46–47), and there his last days before the arrest are to be spent. Therefore Luke omits Mark's note that Jesus went out of the temple (Mark 13:1), and he alters Mark's wording about the listeners' view of that splendid edifice. What the disciples had seen outside the temple is now referred to in their discussion within the temple. Since the instruction is public (see Luke 20:45, and cf. 21:37–38) and not, as in Mark, directed in private to a narrow circle (Mark 13:3), Luke omits the names of specific disciples mentioned by Mark.

The discourse falls into five main sections:

a. Verses 6, 8–11: warning about false messiahs and prediction of great disasters.
b. Verses 12–19: persecution of the disciples, and their witness.
c. Verses 20–24: judgment on Jerusalem.
d. Verses 25–28: cosmic disturbances and the coming of the Son of humanity.
e. Verses 29–36: warning about preparedness.

In keeping with his perception that the credentials of Jesus are not determined by observance of signs (cf. 17:20–21), Luke makes a number of significant alterations relative to Mark's account. This assessment is valid even if it could be demonstrated that Luke relied on other sources, or even wrote without dependence on Mark. Luke is chiefly interested in eliminating too intimate an association of end-time signs with the destruction of Jerusalem. He also aims to clarify the role of the mission to the gentiles in the context of apocalyptic hope. And through it all he absolves Jesus of the charge recorded in Acts 6:14, that he would "destroy this place."

Introductory Dialogue

Luke 21:6–7
(Mark 13:2–4; Matthew 24:2–3)

21:6–7. In response to Jesus' prediction of the destruction of Jerusalem (see also 13:1–8; 19:27, 41–44), the disciples ask, **When will this be?** They do not merely mean, "Tell us the time," but as their next question reveals, "What special effects (*to sēmeion:* **sign**) will take place about the time this is to happen?" Such an event, if it must occur, could mean only one thing—the Messiah would arrive! (This interpretation is clearly indicated by the subsequent information concerning false messiahs.) Luke shows that Jesus rejects such a sign (note the singular), and in the rest of the discourse uses the plural form (vv. 11, 25).

False Prophets, False Deliverers, and Great Disasters

Luke 21:8–11
(Mark 13:5–8; see also vv. 21–23;
Matthew 24:4–8; see also vv. 23–25)

Jesus avoids a direct answer to the disciples' question and issues a broad warning about false prophets and political disturbances (cf. Rev. 2:20; 12:9; 13:14; 18:23; 19:20; 20:8). Thus Luke 21:8–9 forms a general introduction to the more specific description that follows in vv. 10–11. Four major differences relative to Mark are apparent: (a) The addition of the phrase **The time is at hand!** (v. 8) as part of the false expectation. (b) The insertion of **first** (v. 9). (c) The alteration of "not yet" (Mark 13:7) to **not be at once** (Luke 21:9). (d) The omission of "this is but the beginning of the sufferings" (Mark 13:8★). With these changes, Luke succeeds in lengthening the interval between what the disciples might consider a sign and the actual arrival of the end of the end time. It is best, says Jesus, not to draw hasty conclusions.

21:8. The **many** who **come** in his **name** (v. 8) are not people who claim to be Jesus making his return. Rather, they claim to speak definitively for God but do not know whereof they speak, and they preempt the privilege of Jesus, who alone has the right in the end time to say **I am** *(ego eimi)*. They are, in effect, false prophets (cf. Acts 5:36–37) or deliverers without divine portfolio, or both. The expression "I am" *(ego eimi)* is used of God in the OT: Exod. 3:14; Isa. 43:10–11; 48:12; 52:6. It is applied frequently to Jesus in the Fourth Gospel: John 4:26; 8:24, 28, 58; 13:19; 18:5, 6, 8. In Luke 22:70 the phrase appears in a crucial context dealing with the question of Jesus' identity. Mark uses the phrase three times (Mark 6:50; 13:6; 14:62). The first of these is in a story omitted by Luke, who prefers the restraint of the account of the transfiguration to misunderstandings that Mark 6:45–51 might innocently encourage at the time Luke was writing.

The phrase clearly connotes claims that transcend normal human experience and is therefore appropriate in an apocalyptic context. Other false prophets will say, **The time is at hand** *(ho kairos ēggiken)*! This phrase is not equivalent to "The Messiah is here!" It means that some persons will under the guise of divine authority assert that the windup of history, as described in popular apocalyptic, is about to take place. In other words, the identity of the end-time Deliverer is to be dependent on spectacular cosmic events. Luke inserts the saying into Mark's material in order to emphasize the falseness of such a view, for throughout his Gospel he has demonstrated that Jesus' credentials are independent of the special end-time effects.

21:9. The word "and" *(de)* at the beginning of v. 8 is too strong. Luke's use of the conjunction *de* here is more like the colloquial "so." Prediction of wars and international unrest was standard in OT apocalyptic (Isa. 19:2; Jer. 4:20; Joel 3:9–14), and some of the language in Luke 21:10 reflects 2 Chron. 15:6. Such things come first, but it is erroneous to conclude that the end of the end time, with deliverance for God's elect, will follow immediately. Alfred Plummer cites Josephus *War* 6.5.3 in illustration of the type of misunderstanding that is here refuted. Greco-Roman poets and historians used portents as boilerplate to call attention to critical moments in history (see, e.g., Lucan *Civil War* 7.199–200; Tacitus *Histories* 5.13).

21:10–11. These verses do not form a separate paragraph, as suggested by the RSV. They complete the thought of v. 9 and form a pivot for transition to the second portion of the discourse. The disasters are described in most dire tones for maximum effect. One would think that ruinous earthquakes and **great signs** *(sēmeia)* **from heaven** would be sufficient indication that the end was imminent.

In the OT, war, famine, and pestilence are frequently linked as divine judgments (1 Kings 8:37; Jer. 14:12; 21:7; Ezek. 14:21). Earthquakes are mentioned in connection with the great Day of the Lord (Isa. 13:13–16, echoed at Luke 19:44; Hag. 2:6; Zech. 14:4; Rev. 6:12). There was thus good reason for the popular imagination to seize on such events, especially in connection with the judgment on Jerusalem, as a sign that the end was in the offing. Luke therefore appreciably heightens Mark's description in order to negate false conclusions that the end time follows a discernible timetable. The Kingdom in its final manifestation, it will be asserted in Luke 21:31, is near, but nevertheless indeterminate.

Persecution of the Disciples
Luke 21:12–19
(Mark 13:9, 11–13; Matthew 24:9;
10:17–21; 24:13)

21:12. At the end of Mark 13:8 the cosmic disturbances are viewed as "the beginning of the sufferings."* This phrase may have been taken by Mark's public as a reference to the "birth-pangs" of the Messiah" (cf. Rev. 12; Deut. 2:25; Jer. 6:24–26; Mic. 4:9). To avoid any ill-conceived conclusions, Luke eliminates the phrase and instead says, **before all this**, and then introduces the persecutions the disciples must undergo. The phrase "before all this" also replaces the word "first" in Mark 13:10, the thought of which is transferred to Luke 21:24, thereby giving greater coherence to Mark's sequence. The persecutions mentioned in Luke 21:12 echo those of 12:11, and the Book of Acts is the continuing commentary (Acts 18:12; 21:34; 23:10, 31–35; chaps. 24—26; see also 2 Cor. 6:5; 11:24–29).

21:13. As Phil. 1:12–14 testifies of the apostle Paul, the disciples will find in their persecutions an opportunity "to bear witness" *(eis martyrion).* (In Mark 13:9 the thought is that their testimony will spell judgment on the opposition; cf. Mic. 1:2.)

21:14–15. At Luke 12:11–12 the Lord had promised the disciples that the Holy Spirit would give them the proper words in a crisis. Great Benefactor that he is, Jesus bestows on the disciples whatever they need in the critical time. The thought echoes Exod. 4:15 and anticipates the experience of Stephen (Acts 6:10). See also Acts 3:12–26 and 4:8–13 on the eloquent boldness of Peter, and note the response of the community (Acts 4:23–31). He whose life had begun under the power of the Spirit (Luke 1:35) will continue his ministry through Spirit-endowed disciples, and the hostility he encountered will be theirs.

21:16. Since much of this hostility would come from their own relatives, Jesus had issued the stern requirement in Luke 14:26–27 (cf. 18:19–20; Ezek. 38:21–22). The deaths of Stephen (Acts 7:54–60) and James (12:1–2) provide gruesome commentary on the last item in the verse.

21:17. They would **be hated by all**. This does not mean that everyone would hate them (see Acts 2:47) but that they could expect hostility from any direction (cf. Acts 28:22).

21:18. Yet, in spite of all this, they receive assurance: **Not a hair of your head will perish** (cf. Acts 18:9–10; 27:34; 1 Sam. 14:45; 2 Sam. 14:11; and 1 Kings 1:52). These words echo the thought of 12:7 and are a promise of ultimate security.

21:19. Their bodies *(psychai)* they may and will lose but not their real selves (cf. Rev. 20:11–15, and see on Luke 12:5; RSV: **lives**; cf. 9:24; 12:4–5; 14:26; 17:33). In their **endurance** (cf. 8:15; 1 Pet. 2:20) they will **gain** them. Equanimity in the face of adversity was valued by Greeks (cf. Archilochos 67a, ed. by Diehl) and prized by Romans (cf. Seneca *On Tranquillity*; Horace *Odes* 2.3.1; 2:10.21–22). With this reassertion of a favorite theme, Luke replaces Mark's phrase: "But he who endures to the end will be saved" (Mark 13:13). The end does not come within the lifetime of all the disciples.

In the course of many decades, Roman administrators were to discover how firmly such words as these took root in the hearts of Jesus' followers.

Centuries later, a Greek general named Makryannis indirectly exposed some of the meaning of this text when he recollected actions taken against the Turks in a battle at Myloi during the Greek War of Independence (1821–27). Admiral de Rigny, who had forgotten some features of Greek history, had come to see Makryannis and asked him how he hoped to wage war from what appeared to be weak positions. Makryannis replied:

> These positions are indeed weak, and so are we, but the God who protects us has the power, and we shall test our fortunes at these same weak posts. And even though we are so few against the host of Ibrahim [the Turkish general] we take comfort in the thought that fortune has always found us few in number. From time immemorial to the present hour, all the wild beasts have taken up arms to devour us, but to no avail. They dine on us, but the yeast abides. And the few are determined to die and, once their decision is made, they win more often than they lose. Such is our situation here and we shall try our fortunes, the weak against the strong. (Translation of Makryannis, *Apomnemoneumata* [1957], pp. 205–6)

Judgment on Jerusalem
Luke 21:20–24
(Mark 13:14–17, 19, 10; Matthew 24:15–19, 21)

This section of "the little apocalypse" is almost completely rewritten by Luke, principally to eliminate the suggestion that the end of the end time is to be associated with the destruction of Jerusalem, whose military fortunes are described by Josephus (*War* 5–7).

21:20–22. Mark refers to a horrible desecration of the temple, "desolating sacrilege" (Mark 13:14), which is to precede its actual destruction. Mark's phrase *(to bdelygma tēs erēmōseōs)* is borrowed from Dan. 9:27, where reference is made to Antiochus Epiphanes, who erected a heathen altar in the Jewish temple (1 Macc. 1:54–59). Antiochus became a symbol of Antichrist (see 2 Thess. 2:1–12), a figure closely associated with events of the end time.

Since the destruction of Jerusalem had already taken place by the time Luke was writing his Gospel, Luke records Jesus' prediction in more explicit terms, specifying that **Jerusalem** is to be **surrounded by armies** (cf. 19:43; Rev. 20:9) and that **its desolation has come near** *(ēggiken he erēmōsis autēs)*. Thereby he makes unnecessary Mark's call for special wisdom: "Let the reader understand" (Mark 13:14). Also, by eliminating Mark's apocalyptic note he is able to reassure his own auditors that the credentials of Jesus were not invalidated by the nonappearance of the end of the end time in association with the destruction of the city. If anything, the destruction of the city endorses Jesus' credentials, for none but his enemies would deny that Jesus was, like Elijah, a man of God. But the fire that rained down from heaven fell not on Samaria but on Jerusalem (see 9:34; cf. 2 Kings 1:12).

Rome was not in the habit of provoking destruction of cities. If Josephus (*War* 7.5.2) is to be believed, when the conquering general Titus made a tour of Jerusalem's ruins, he was embarrassed to credit the destruction of such a beautiful and illustrious city to Roman courage, and he cursed the perpetrators of the revolt that had brought it on. "If only she had known the things that pertained to her peace" (Luke 19:42★). The enemy was within her walls, not on the outside.

And **all that is written** was fulfilled means that the Hebrew Scriptures provide the script and that some of Israel's history repeats itself (Plummer cites Lev. 26:31–33; Deut. 28:49–57; 1 Kings 9:6–9; Mic. 3:12; Zech. 11:6; 12:3; Dan. 9:26–27). At 4:19, Luke had omitted the reference to a day of "vengeance" in Isa. 61:2, for the inauguration of Jesus introduced the year of Jubilee. But the period of grace finally comes to an end for Jerusalem, and the reference to vengeance is now in order.

In Mark, the mission to the gentiles takes place between the resurrection and the destruction of Jerusalem. In Luke, the apostolic mission continues beyond the destruction of the city. Thus Luke opens the way for fresh interpretation and application of Jesus' apocalyptic discourse. Not the end would be near, as the false prophets claim (see 21:8–9), but the **desolation has come near**. More pointedly than in Mark's account, this desolation is viewed as judgment. The phrasing echoes Deut. 32:35 and Ezek. 9:1, and Luke adds the further note (Luke 21:22) that all is in fulfillment of the Scriptures (cf. Hos. 9:7; Jer. 5:29). Details in Mark 13:15–16 are omitted at this point, since they were used in Luke 17:31.

21:23. The woe pronounced on pregnant and nursing mothers repeats the thought of 19:44. Luke is at pains to emphasize that Jesus' earlier prediction in his lament over the city found horrible literal fulfillment in days that are but recent memory. The phrase **wrath upon this people** is a "tag" from 2 Kings 3:27 and replaces Mark's direction to pray that the flight may not "happen in winter" (Mark 13:18). The detail is unnecessary, since the destruction is, from Luke's perspective, a thing of the past. At the same time, he emphasizes more strongly than does Mark that the "wrath" applies to people in Judea, and at that specific moment in history. Those who rested their case in the Law find the curses of the Law pronounced to the letter. Deuteronomy 28:64 warns that Israel will be taken captive because of her transgression and scattered among all the nations (cf. Dan. 9:13). Luke 21:24, in keeping with the hermeneutics of the time, is the commentary on that oracle of the Lord.

21:24. The phrase **led captive** is dramatically illustrated on the Arch of Titus as well as on a coin that bears on its face the image of Vespasian and on the reverse a Roman officer with one foot on a helmet standing guard aside a palm tree under whose branches crouches a woman, the daughter of Zion, weeping over her defeat. Jesus had taught his followers a better way to deal with those who used power as a weapon (Luke 6:27–30), but very few listened. Eusebius (*Ecclesiastical History* 3.5.3) records that some members of the Christian community in Jerusalem heeded a prophetic warning and took refuge in Pella just before the outbreak of hostilities (cf. Luke 21:21).

The phrase **trodden down by the Gentiles** (cf. Rev. 11:2) is borrowed from Zech. 12:3 LXX. Since Mark's reference to the sparing of the elect (Mark 13:20; cf. Isa. 54:7) might suggest a hastening of the end, Luke deletes it and at this point introduces Mark's earlier reference to the gentiles (Mark 13:10), but with the modified phrase **until the times of the Gentiles are fulfilled**. For a related pattern of thought, see Tob. 14:4–5. Between the fate of Jerusalem and the actual arrival of the end lies the accumulation of responsibility for the gentiles.

The word *kairoi*, here rendered "times," means crises. Just as Israel met her time of decision, so the gentiles will be faced with theirs. God, the Supreme Politician, is no respecter of persons, establishments, or institutions. In Daniel, the various nations are assigned a "time" by God (Daniel 11; cf. 1QS 4:18) and then undergo judgment. Some of Luke's auditors may have thought of the vast missionary outreach to the gentiles during the interval (cf. Rom. 11:25).

Finally, in his rewriting of Mark 13:19–20 Luke modifies Mark's use of Dan. 12:1. Mark 13:19 reads: "In those days there will be such tribulation as has not been from the beginning of the creation which God created until now, and never will be." Since Jerusalem's destruction is not the climax of history, Luke preserves his stronger rhetoric for the end described in the succeeding paragraph (Luke 21:25–26). Moreover, in Daniel a resurrection of the righteous from their graves is discussed in association with the passage reproduced in Mark 13:19. Again Mark's presentation might give rise to misunderstanding and encourage the type of computation expressed in Dan. 12:11–13. Luke therefore discusses the anticipated deliverance in a subsequent consolatory passage (Luke 21:28–33), thus removing the end of the end time from any connection with any one particular historical event.

Cosmic Disturbances and the Coming of the Son of Humanity

Luke 21:25–27
(Mark 13:24–26; Matthew 24:29–30)

From consideration of Jerusalem's fate the evangelist now moves on to record Jesus' preview of "crises" that the world as a whole can expect.

21:25–26. Since false prophets have already come under discussion (see on 21:8), Luke omits Mark 13:21–23. He also omits Mark's specific reference: "But in those days, after that tribulation" (Mark 13:24), again to dissociate the signs of the end from the destruction of Jerusalem. As noted earlier, the distress of humanity is sketched in darker tones than in the earlier description of the fate of Jerusalem (Luke 21:19). In place of Mark's (Mark 13:24) citation of Isa. 13:10, Luke paraphrases the thought concerning cosmic disturbance (cf. Isa. 24:18–20; 34:4) and picks up Isaiah's (Isa. 13:7) description of the terror that overcomes humanity. **The roaring of the sea and the waves** appears to reproduce the thought of Isa. 17:12 (see also Pss. 46:4; 89:10; Wisd. of Sol. 5:22).

Luke's revision prompts the transfer of Mark's mention of stars to the beginning of the verse: **And there will be signs in sun and moon and stars.** Mark's description of falling stars is omitted, for Satan is the one who falls from heaven (Luke 10:18), and this was already taking place in the course of Jesus' earlier ministry.

Roman auditors of Luke's Gospel must certainly have taken pride in their tradition of unyielding discipline, which was evidenced especially by the Senate's steadfast resolution after Rome's disastrous loss of about forty-eight thousand infantry and six thousand cavalry at Cannae in 216 B.C.E. They would therefore have been impressed by the composed posture of Jesus' followers that is anticipated in the exhortation recited in v. 28, and they would note the contrast in Luke's description of a humanity that will be panic-stricken in **foreboding of what is coming.**

At the very end of the twentieth century, artist Ray K. Metzker notes that "people are seen today as wandering (if not lost) solitary figures subject to a labyrinth of fantasies, laboring under the imaginary quest for utopian freedom, afraid of their singularity, (individualness), dependent on the now and apprehensive of the future, stripped of charity, lamenting war but unable to live in peace" (*Chicago* Magazine [September 1985], p. 20).

21:27. Then, and only then *(kai tote),* will **they see the Son of humanity coming.** Luke's wordplay is apparent. The arrival of the Coming One (cf. 7:20) is the climax of an expectation that appears to have found support in Dan. 7:13 during early Christian pondering of the credentials of Jesus.

Luke always uses "cloud" in the singular (9:34, 35; 12:54; Acts 1:9), and his alteration of Mark's plural form (Mark 13:26) is of a piece with his other references (Luke 9:34, 35; Acts 1:9) to the "Shekinah," that is, the display of God's visible presence (cf. Exod. 34:5). Jesus, as the returning Son of humanity, does not simply come on clouds as a visitor from outer space. In a cloud he went up (Acts 1:9) and in the same manner he will return (Acts 1:11), endowed with full divine credentials. What chosen disciples experienced at the transfiguration (Luke 9:34–35) all humanity will observe at the end of the end time. Jesus entered into his glory through his resurrection (24:26), thus realizing the enthronement that the high priest endeavored to deny him (22:69); and **with power and great glory** he makes his climactic appearance. Thus Luke affirms the present reality of Jesus' kingship apart from the promised consummation but rejects any attempt to infer the time of the consummation through speculation based on signs.

The disciples had asked, "What will be the sign when this is about to take place?" (21:7). Jesus gives no one sign, only signs (v. 25); and these of such a nature that no prediction can be based on them, for they are common to human experience. All this does not mean that Luke denies an early arrival of the consummation. His primary interest is to discourage deduction about apocalyptic conclusions on the basis of particular historical events. Once this has been impressed, he is prepared to submit the Lord's reassuring consolation in v. 28 and its commentary in vv. 29–33.

Warning about Preparedness
Luke 21:28–33
(Mark 13:28–31; Matthew 24:32–35)

This section forms a unit, with v. 28 serving to bridge vv. 25–27 and 29–33. What the Lord announced to his own generation can now be pronounced to the Christian communities of Luke's time, for the signs have been dissociated from the destruction of Jerusalem. In the midst of international and cosmic disturbance the disciple need not lose heart. The Lord *will* return, and soon!

21:28. Your redemption is drawing near. The word for "draw near" *(eggizō)* has been frequently used by Luke of the Kingdom and of Jesus' approach to the city of Jerusalem (10:9–11; 18:35; 19:29, 37, 41; cf. 24:15). The term is appropriate here in contrast to the claims of the false messiahs recorded in v. 8. The Greek term for "redemption" *(apolytrōsis)* appears only here in Luke's two-volume work. A shorter form of this noun is used at 1:68 and 2:38. In 2:38 it is applied to Jerusalem. Perhaps Luke preferred the longer form, expressive of full and final deliverance, in order to preserve the distinction he has made between the fortunes of Jerusalem and the Christian community.

"Redemption," as used here, does not connote pardon for sin but rescue from tribulation and realization of the benefits that accompany God's defeat of all hostile forces (Luke 1:68–72; Rom. 8:23; cf. Eph. 4:30). Thus it is the climax of redemption understood as forgiveness of sins (cf. 1:77; 3:3; 24:47). According to Luke's teaching, God reaches out to gather the lost that they may share God's company (see Luke 15). This final deliverance is the realization of the promise expressed in 13:29–30 (cf. Acts 3:19–21).

21:29. Luke adds to "the fig tree" (Mark 13:28) **all the trees.** Through this amplification he avoids a limited association with Israel, whose judgment in prophetic writing is on occasion associated with the fig tree (cf. Jer. 8:13; Mic. 7:1).

21:30. Just as the fresh foliage in spring signals the coming of summer, so the disasters and cosmic disturbances signal the nearness of the end. **You see for yourselves** is Luke's addition. Disciples will need no one to inform them, as the false claimants attempt to do (v. 8). Luke believes in simplifying theology.

21:31. Like the phrase in 1:20, **these things** does not refer to *all* details in 21:25–27. In Mark 13:29 the subject of the verb in the concluding phrase is unexpressed, and the RSV attempts to supply it: "*he* is near." Luke 21:31 supplies the subject: **The kingdom of God is near** *(eggys)*. Far from being a sign of the absence of God's reign in connection with Jesus, the observed disasters are indications that the final phase of the Kingdom is about to make its appearance. The redemption is spelled out as the Kingdom of God in order to reinforce beyond the realm of contradiction that the Son of humanity does not return as the deliverer of one nation.

21:32. Now Luke is able to bring into focus the most difficult saying of all: **Truly** *(amēn)*, **I say to you, this generation will not pass away till all has taken place.** Luke knows well enough that Jesus' contemporaries had passed away at the time his Gospel was published. Was Jesus, then, mistaken? No, says Luke, his solemn statement was misunderstood. What Jesus said was that *this kind* of generation with whom he had to deal would not pass out of existence until everything took place. What was it that prompted Jesus to make such an indictment of "this generation"? It sought after signs (cf. 11:29–32). Very well, they shall have all the signs, but not the kind they seek, and in the meantime the gospel will go to the gentiles (cf. Acts 28:25–28).

It has been suggested that Luke identifies "this generation" with humanity in general, but this is improbable, for humanity obviously could not disappear before the end. That Israel should reject the witness of its own Messiah and his accredited apostolic messengers is a unique phenomenon requiring explanation, for its seems to call into question the credentials of Jesus. Luke therefore exploits the very problem as a proof of Jesus' ultimate success. In place of Mark's phrase "all these things" (Mark 13:30), Luke simply has **all.** This broadens the disciples' outlook to things beyond the signs already specified and is the climax of his instruction that the Kingdom comes "without observation" (17:20*). The Kingdom is among them in its first phase, and it will suddenly be among them in its final phase. Among other referents that have been suggested by commentators for the term "this generation" are the Jews in general and the contemporaries of Luke.

21:33. This verse forms a conclusion to the apocalyptic portion of the discourse and introduces the final admonition. The words of Jesus are said to have permanence in order to reinforce the point that the disciples' ultimate success in standing before the Son of humanity (v. 36) is determined by obedience to the word of Jesus (cf. 8:14–15; 13:22–30), and blessed are those who "hear the word of God and do it" (8:21).

Mark's statement (Mark 13:32) on the limitations of the knowledge of the Son (13:32) is completely eliminated, for everything has been delivered by the Father to the Son (Luke 10:22). Acts 1:7 is not in contradiction with this conclusion.

Concluding Admonition to Preparedness
Luke 21:34–36

The admonition in this section is similar to the instruction given in 17:26–37 (cf. 12:41–48).

21:34. The disciples are to be prepared at all times, for there is no single sign of the return of their Lord. **That day**, the day of the return of the Son of humanity, comes **suddenly** (cf. 17:24) and **like a snare**, that is, like a trap springing shut on its victim (Isa. 24:17–18).

21:35. The Greek for **it will come** *(epeiserchomai)* reiterates the thought of suddenness. The judgment that attends Jesus' return comes with climactic force and makes no exceptions. It is for **all.** Once more Luke reiterates his instruction that the return of the Son of humanity is to be dissociated from the destruction of Jerusalem. The phrase **all who dwell** is also used in Rev. 14:6.

21:36. Verse 8 introduced false messiahs who say, "The time is at hand!" Jesus, the true Messiah, says: **Watch at all times** *(kairos),* that is, "in any and every crisis." Watchfulness means to be on the alert against falling into temptation (cf. 8:13; 22:40, 46), that is, to be overpowered in the crisis, as was Peter during the trial of Jesus (22:54–62). **To escape all these things** means to survive the temptations, especially by making bold confession (12:9; 21:12–19). Then the Son of humanity will confess them before the angels of God (12:8) or, as the discourse concludes: They will **stand before the Son** of humanity. He who expects watchfulness from them has himself set the pattern, for the exalted Jesus remains the one who identified with humanity in all its frailty but accepted the hazard of that commitment.

TEACHING IN THE TEMPLE
Luke 21:37–38

21:37–38. Against the charge that Jesus had spoken traitorously about the temple (Acts 6:14; cf. Mark 14:58), Luke sets the pattern of Jesus' continuing instruction in the temple. Only obedience to the word of Jesus could save that edifice from the fate that awaits it. Israel's leadership must accept the major responsibility, for **all the people** were eager **to hear him**, as was evidenced by their arrival **early in the morning.** Jesus, the reservoir of wisdom, spells true security for those who love instruction (see Proverbs 1).

In this passage Luke chose a term that suggests his hero's dependence on the good will of others. Unlike Mark, who on occasion shows Jesus at home, Luke portrays a Son of humanity who has no permanent quarters (9:58). Presumably in this last week of his life Jesus found lodgings with friends (cf. Matt. 21:17), but Luke terms his temporary stay a bivouacking.

At this point a few manuscripts include the story of the adulterous woman, which is traditionally associated with the Fourth Gospel (John 7:53—8:11; see the RSV marginal note at John 7:52).

PART SIX: THE PASSION ACCOUNT

The Tale of Melibeus, by Geoffrey Chaucer, appears to be the first publication in English to note the fact of variation in recitals of the four evangelists. In this story Chaucer observes that "some of them say more and some say less / when they his Passion express. / I mean, of Mark, Matthew, Luke, and John; / but doubtless their sentence [meaning] is all one."

It is true that all four evangelists have one gospel to proclaim, and in this respect their meaning is one, but the "less" or the "more" that is a part of each evangelist's interest in the telling contributes to the distinctive character of each of the four Gospels. And this is especially true of the Passion narrative.

The principal function of Luke's account of Jesus' suffering and death, followed by the recital of his resurrection, is to prepare the evangelist's public for the message of clemency proclaimed at Pentecost and in the course of the apostolic mission.

To that end, Luke selects and arranges and modifies his sources. Jesus, the Great Benefactor, who went about "doing good and healing all who were dominated by the devil" (Acts 10:38*), accepts the dangerous course. Upright in all his ways, he dies in obedience to his heavenly Parent's purpose. But God invalidates the judgment. Against the background of history's most heinous crime Luke will show in the Book of Acts the astounding generosity of God, the Supreme Benefactor, who confirms Jesus as the One Name that supersedes all other claimants to saviorhood (Acts 4:12). Jesus is God's unique gift to all humanity. The various rhetorical tactics that Luke uses to achieve his overall literary strategy will surface in the commentary that follows.

THE PLOT OF JUDAS AND DISCOURSE IN THE UPPER ROOM

Luke 22:1–38
(Mark 14:1–2, 10–25; 10:42–45; 14:27–31;
Matthew 26:1–5, 14–29; 20:24–28; 26:31–35)

The most obvious departure from Mark in this section is the omission of Mark 14:3–9, the anointing in the house of Simon the leper. Luke recorded a version of this account in 7:36–50, and one of its main themes, concern for the poor, has received adequate treatment elsewhere in Luke's Gospel. Its inclusion at this point would have interrupted the close connection he wishes to establish between the resolution of the leadership (22:1–2) and the Satanic dimension in which that resolution is to be viewed (22:3).

Satanic Plot
Luke 22:1–6
(Mark 14:1–2, 10–11; Matthew 26:1–5, 14–16)

22:1–2. Luke does not make a strict distinction between the **Passover** and **the feast of Unleavened Bread.** The former marked the sacrificial rite, performed on the afternoon of the fourteenth day of the month Nisan (see Exodus 12). The period following this sacrifice and the eating of the Passover (which took place in the evening hours of the beginning of the fifteenth of Nisan) was designated the Feast of Unleavened Bread (Lev. 23:5–6). This feast continued for seven days (Exod. 23:15; Lev. 23:6). In popular parlance, the entire period, including the sacrificial rite, was **called the Passover** (cf. v. 7).

It is ironical that the religious leaders seek to kill Jesus about the time when preparations were made for the killing of the sacrificial lamb. Their plot was complicated by the popularity that Jesus enjoyed among the populace. Quiet efficiency, they hoped, would keep truth from taking to the streets. Instead, they all made the front page.

22:3. In their quandary **Satan** introduces himself as an ally. He had departed from Jesus "until an opportune time" (4:13). The Greek for "time" in 4:13 *(kairos)* is the same word used in 8:13 and 21:36. Jesus had warned his disciples to watch in time of temptation. Now Satan seizes his opportunity for the final showdown with Jesus and uses Judas, one of the Twelve, as his instrument to discredit Jesus once and for all. Let this carpenter from Nazareth know that one does not lightly turn down an offer of the kind Satan made to him in the desert (4:5–7).

Luke wants his public to know that the events which follow are to be seen in a cosmic dimension as a contest between demonic forces and God (cf. John 13:2; 1 Cor. 2:8). A related example of Satan's participation in the death of a righteous man is recorded in an apocryphal work, the *Ascension of Isaiah* 5.

22:4. For the first time, Luke mentions the captains, or temple guard, assigned to the Sanhedrin. It is an ominous note! Judas means business and his own quandary, **how he might** deliver *(paradidōmi:* "betray") Jesus into their hands, is the answer to their own (v. 2).

22:5. Jesus had also repeatedly warned his disciples about the proper use of wealth. Mammon now changes hands in the slimiest transaction that history shall ever record. To have betrayed Jesus on principle, and without fee, would have preserved for Judas some vestige of character. But lust for silver shriveled up his soul. More culpable, though, than Judas, were the religious leaders. Instead of seeking to save this wretched piece of humanity, **they were glad** to hear his proposal. As a religious leader put it two millennia later, when involved in challenge to constitutional security, "We don't have time for theology. We've got a crisis on our hands."

22:6. And he who had been warned to watch "at all times" (21:36) now sought **opportunity** (*eukairia:* "an appropriate time") **to betray him** (*paradidōmi:* see 9:44; 18:32; 20:20). The only stipulation was: **in the absence of the multitude** (cf. 22:2). This did not leave much choice. Night must see the doing of the deed (22:53).

Preparation for the Passover
Luke 22:7–13
(Mark 14:12–16; Matthew 26:17–19)

22:7. The fourteenth day of Nisan has now arrived. The lamb was **to be sacrificed** in the afternoon. Satan has marked his victim, but Jesus is in full control and heads with full knowledge toward that death which will set up a kingdom far outweighing all the petty kingdoms once offered him by Satan (Luke 4:5–6).

22:8. As one dispatching royal emissaries, **Jesus sent** *(apostellō)* **Peter and John.** Two only are mentioned, for this is a solemn apostolic mission (cf. 10:1). Since 9:51, the face of Jesus had been fixed on Jerusalem, and the messengers had been sent "ahead of him" (9:52). Now the final turn of that journey is to be taken, and messengers are for the last time sent on ahead.

The selection of Peter and John in the narrative is perhaps prompted by their presence together in 8:51 and 9:28 (cf. Acts 3:1–2; 8:14). Once they were witnesses of his extraordinary resurrection power (Luke 8:49–56) and then of his transfiguration (9:28–36). Moses and Elijah had spoken of the "exodus" (9:31) Jesus was to accomplish in Jerusalem. Now Peter and John are to make the initial preparations for that climactic event. At the same time, Luke points out that Jesus knows better than to entrust Judas with the final plans.

22:9. In keeping with his stress on the mastery of Jesus, Luke alters Mark's account, which shows the disciples taking the initiative (14:12). Their question (**Where will you have us prepare it?**) comes *after* Jesus' command. The Greek for "prepare" (*hetoimazō:* "make ready," v. 12) appears four times in this account (vv. 8, 9, 12, 13) and it is difficult to escape the conclusion that Luke sees in the events that follow the fulfillment of the announcement in 3:4–6, introduced by the cry: "Prepare the way of the Lord" (see also 1:17, 76; 2:31; 9:52).

22:10–13. This recital has some of the formal character of 19:29–33, and the stress on Jesus' detailed knowledge of apparently trivial circumstances heightens the picture of one in full command of the situation (see on 19:42). A woman with a pitcher would have been the normal expectation, hence the word **Behold** (*idou,* v. 10). Once there had been no room in **the guest room** (*to katalyma,* v. 11; see 2:7). Now Jesus himself secures one for a farewell banquet, but Luke omits Mark's use of the personal pronoun (Mark 14:14). Jesus has no place that he can claim his own (see on v. 37). The concluding sentence (v. 13) parallels 19:32.

The Passover Supper and Discourses
Luke 22:14–38

The New Covenant and Warning
about the Traitor
Luke 22:14–22
(Mark 14:17–25; Matthew 26:20–29)

22:14. At 20:19 the opposition was unable to take advantage of the "hour" to arrest Jesus. Now **the hour** has arrived (cf. 22:53), but in Jesus' own chosen time. This interpretation is signaled by Luke's alteration of Mark 14:17. Jesus did not "sit" **at table**, as the RSV renders, but "reclined" *(anapiptō).*

This Passover banquet climaxes a series of dinner parties (see on 5:27–39, and cf. 7:36–50; 11:37–54; 14:1–24). It is a feature of the Passover feast that Israel displays her deliverance from bondage by assuming the posture of freed people. Slaves ordinarily wait on those who recline (cf. 17:7–8; John 13:4), but this accepted social practice in the larger world to which Luke addressed his work does not mean that Jesus and his company were waited on by slaves.

In place of "the twelve" (Mark 14:17), Luke says that **the apostles** were **with him** (cf. Luke 17:5), anticipating the special instruction to be given to the apostles as chief servants in the new community. Luke revises Mark's order of events by presenting first the ritual of the Passover meal and then the announcement of the traitor. This rearrangement makes it possible for Luke to illuminate the meaning of the Last Supper in the light of the reaction of the disciples and Jesus' instruction on the themes of kingdom, service, and faith.

22:15. Since it was customary in some Greco-Roman social circles to converse on serious topics at banquets, Luke includes this kind of discourse material at this point. But since his narrative presents Jesus in the last hours of his life, the discourses function also as a farewell speech, a type well known in Jewish circles from Moses' speech to Israel recorded in Deuteronomy and an intertestamental work, *Testaments of the Twelve Patriarchs*. Greco-Roman circles were familiar with the convention from Plato's record of Sokrates's last conversations in the *Phaedo*.

Repeatedly Jesus had warned his disciples about his approaching fate (cf. 9:22, 44; 12:50; 13:32–33; 17:25; 18:32–33). Now in this solemn hour he tells them for the second-last time (for the final reminder, see 22:37). Since he will celebrate no more Passovers with them, he desires **earnestly** to eat **this passover** with them. Let them take note: death will make it his last one with them!

22:16. This verse explains Jesus' words. He had fasted in the wilderness before winning his skirmish with Satan (4:2). Now he is competing for the highest stakes. The Kingdom of God is about to reach a climactic phase. The Passover is the commemoration of Israel's exodus. From the perspective of Luke 9:31, Jesus has come to Jerusalem to "accomplish" (*pleroō*: fulfill) his exodus. The Passover comes to full meaning in the events about to take place on a hill outside Jerusalem.

22:17. In place of Mark's order, bread followed by wine, Luke presents first the words spoken about the wine ("cup" for the contents), so as to reinforce the thought expressed in v. 16. Jesus enters into the glory of his Kingdom only after his suffering (cf. v. 69 and 24:26). In the manner of a Nazirite (see Num. 6:1–4) he separates himself from the ordinary joys of humankind to devote himself totally to his task, the suffering that is before him. That will be his cup (cf. Luke 22:42)! Therefore he gives the disciples the cup out of which he would ordinarily have drunk and tells them to share its contents among themselves.

Since each one presumably had his own cup, this procedure must have made a profound impression. The variation in sequence, like that of the various versions of the Lord's Prayer, suggests that God's people need not be mired in slavish, repetitious liturgical patterns. Having broken away from their rule-regulation-oriented past, Christian communities manifested extraordinary liturgical creativity. To put it anachronistically, it was the age of the loose-leaf agenda. For Greco-Roman auditors of Luke's recital, the emphasis on thanksgiving would focus attention on God as the Supreme Benefactor. The Greek for "giving thanks" (the verb *eucharisteō*) is the source of our term "Eucharist" (cf. Acts 27:35).

22:18. Jesus accompanies his action with a solemn oath: **From now on I shall not drink of the fruit of the vine until the kingdom of God comes.** This celebration is a foretaste of the messianic banquet (see on Luke 13:22–29) and anticipates Acts 1:4; 10:41.

Confidence is the thematic note in Jesus' solemn utterance. A similar symbolic bit of self-denial was made by a seer who predicted Julius Caesar's victory over Pompey. Removing the wreath of office from his head, the seer said that he would not replace it until the outcome bore witness to the quality of his profession (Plutarch *Caesar* 47).

22:19. Jesus took a loaf of bread and, as he had done at the taking of the cup, "gave thanks." His words accompanying the distribution are the climax of his exposition of the meaning of the celebration: **This is my body.** With these words he explains that the Passover comes to full meaning in the events befalling his person. As the loaf was broken into pieces before their eyes, so he will shortly be destroyed. With the words **which is given for you** Jesus evidently means to say that he gives himself in behalf of his friends and that God is the ultimate instrument of the donation. Pauline thinking and later eucharistic debates are not to be read into Luke's use of the dominical words. For example, the term "vicarious" suggests a note of substitution that would go beyond Luke's simple terminology.

To give oneself is the ultimate in donation. Luke writes in the main for Hellenistic Jewish Christians and Greco-Roman auditors. The motif of self-giving is common in Greco-Roman documents in description of endangered benefactors. Of a certain Menas, for example, it is stated in a commemorative document that "he spares himself no expense or public service, avoids no personal inconvenience or danger, and gives no thought to any hazards threatening his own interest when he leaves on embassies in behalf of our city" (*OGI* 339.3–8; see *Benefactor*, p. 92). The expression "this is" is not of the same order as equivalence statements in 3:22; 4:34; and 6:5. The term is standard usage in definition of an action or statement and denotes "this means" or "this is to be understood as" (see BAGD, pp. 223–24, II.3).

When hereafter they celebrate the Passover—either following the Jewish calendar and forms or, from Luke's perspective, in the forms of observance that evolved in the Christian communities—they are to do it in remembrance *(anamnēsis)* of Jesus as the one who gave himself in their behalf.

22:20. This verse (once relegated to the margin in the RSV of 1946) is part of Luke's original text (as in the RSV of 1971). The New Age begins, and it is signaled here by the expression **new covenant** *(hē kainē diathēkē)*, a reference to Jer. 31:31. This is the counterpart of the "old covenant" that was made at Sinai (cf. Exod. 24:8; 2 Cor. 3:14). It is a costly covenant. God permits it to be made through the shedding of Jesus' blood, and therein lies the promise. God has a way to overcome what appears to be disaster. The loss of the temple, as prophesied by Jesus, will not be a major liturgical debacle. God gives assurance of how Jesus' disciples stand with God through the gift of Jesus. His death is not tragedy but a step to ultimate vindication (see Acts 2:36). Thus it is all done for the benefit of the People of God.

22:21. Jesus had said that he would be "handed over" (*paradidōmi*, **betrays**) into the hands of people (9:44; cf. 18:32; 22:4, 6). The deed has already been set in motion. And the hand of the traitor shares the Master's wine and bread (cf. Ps. 41:9). In brief, the suffering so often predicted is as close as the traitor himself. Set as this announcement is in the context of Jesus' declaration about the "new covenant," Luke's auditors could not fail to catch the main point—through Judas, Satan now confronts God.

22:22. But there is more to Jesus' word concerning the traitor. It is part of his final appeal and instruction to the apostolic circle. Jesus goes to his death **as it has been determined.** The Greek for "determined" *(horizō)* appears only here in the Gospel but several times in Acts (2:23; 10:42; 17:31; cf. Rom. 1:4) to define God's overarching providence and purpose in connection with Jesus Christ. Jesus goes to his death because he is obedient to his Parent (cf. 2:49) and must accept the full consequences of being identified with the divine purpose (cf. Luke 13:32–33; 22:42), which has always experienced frustration from within the loyalist encampment (see Stephen's recital, Acts 7).

Judas, who is not mentioned by name, is not compelled to betray Jesus. Jesus had warned his disciples (and Judas was certainly not excluded) about hypocrisy (12:1). And there is pathos in Jesus' self-identification as the Son of humanity. He shares the cloak of Adam with **that man**—who in Luke's time could be any person who puts a Christian community at public risk— **by whom he is betrayed.**

Through this solemn pronouncement of woe (cf. 6:24), which speaks to the Judas in everyone, Jesus makes his last appeal to a friend who violated not only the most sacred code of hospitality but rent the very fabric of his own soul. The betrayal has not yet taken place. Judas could still refuse to carry out his end of the bargain. God is not a slave of prophetic blueprints.

Final Instruction and Admonition   Luke 22:23–38
                                                        (Mark 10:41–45; 14:27–31;
                                                        Matthew 20:24–28; 26:31–35)

After the pronouncement on the traitor, there follow two disputes among the disciples. Their contrasting nature suggests the appalling lack of understanding that Jesus encounters in his chosen circle. Where were they when Jesus told the story about the hunt for the seats of honor (see 14:7–14)?

From an artistic viewpoint, the first question on the identity of the traitor permits an easy transition to the content of the second dispute, which provides Luke with the opportunity to present Jesus' own interpretation of his action and a correction of any misunderstanding respecting the political attitudes of the community. This intention of the evangelist is supported by the fact that he omitted Mark 10:41–45 at 18:34 but here presents a revised version of that account.

22:25. Luke suggests that the contrast made by Jesus between the attitudes of the **kings of the gentiles** and the prescription of service that he gives to the disciples should lay to rest forever the ghost of subversiveness. Such a charge, as brought in 23:2, was patently false. **Benefactors** renders a common Greek word, *euergetēs,* that served also as a title for rulers in Syria and Egypt (see, e.g., the prologue to Sirach). In many cases the title would conceal tyranny under extravagant expenditure. Luke is not discouraging the use of the term itself, but inappropriate attitudes that sometimes accompany the use of the term in high circles. Similarly, a South American theologian quite evidently did not wish to jettison the term "Christian" when he said that in his time the great hazard was rulers who called themselves Christians. Greeks made frequent use of the term *euergetēs* and, fond of puns, they referred to Ptolemy Euergetes II (Benefactor) as Kakergetes (Malefactor). (See also Plato *Republic* 344b–c.)

As indicated in my introduction to this commentary, the Greek language has many terms and modes of expression to convey concepts about people who are beneficial to others (see *Benefactor,* pp. 317–66). The English word "benefactor," as it has been used in this commentary, renders no single Greek expression but is an umbrella term for exceptional beneficent service or action. One who claims that Greco-Roman benefactors are unbecoming models to express New Testament Christology must look at the Septuagint version of Wisd. of Sol. 16:2, 11; Ps. 12:6; 56:3; 2 Macc. 4:2, to cite but a few. Hellenized Jews could not avoid making associations with current usage of the noun and cognates for the term used here by Luke. Naturally they would strip the metaphor of any negative associations. Even a string of bad popes or bishops no more invalidates usage of time-honored ecclesiastical titles than an experience with bad politicians excludes the use of the word "politician."

22:26. Disciples are not to contribute to the "sad et cetera of tyranny." The long history of search for office and attendant authoritarian control in the churches is a testimony to Luke's profound grasp of the relation between gorged egos of pompous men and the crucifixion of him who renounced all titles and kingdoms. Even more trenchant in its critique is the suggestion of this dominical word that secular institutions may well owe much of their exploitative and oppressive potential to the failure of religious institutions to recognize the part they play in abetting violation of the stewardship of power. As one modern observer put it, "If we can't face the flaws in our churches and ourselves, how can we expect society to right itself?"

Luke's forthright approach to reality, blended as it is with his profound conception of the power available for experience of a New Age, is the apostolic answer to those who delight in playing the game of "Ain't it awful?" without offer of hope.

In keeping with his earlier reminder that even the most faithful slave is still an "unworthy" slave (17:10), Jesus explains to his disciples that they are not to use their positions as avenues for self-aggrandizement (cf. 1 Pet. 5:3). If seniority is to be determined by age, then let the older be as the youngest. Since the younger members of Christian communities would recognize their obligation of obedience to the older members (cf. 1 Pet. 5:5), this is a striking invitation to humility. Leaders are to be open to the possibilities of service and not be anxious about their own prestige as authority figures.

22:27. Authoritarianism has established itself in history as a normal route to greatness. Jesus found a way to avoid such standardized mediocrity. He is in the midst of his followers **as one who serves** (cf. John 13), that is, as a waiter *(ho diakonōn)*. The saying echoes 12:37. "Serves" is related in its Greek form to our "diaconate." In Mark (10:44), the road to greatness lies through service. In Luke's account, Jesus says that the one who is "the greatest" (v. 26) should imitate Jesus through dedicated service. The reason for Luke's alteration of Mark appears to have its origin in disputes about leadership in the early Christian community. Peter was acknowledged as preeminent in the Jewish community, second only to James. But his credentials were apparently viewed with some suspicion in the Hellenistic community, and the problem of his denial had to be faced.

Luke's record of Jesus' words suggests that the church is to make service to the fellowship the primary criterion of greatness. Jesus' willingness to accept the Father's assignment, at great cost to himself, sets the pattern for their ministry. Since all their service pales into insignificance before his own, he above all is entitled to the title *Euergetēs*, or Benefactor (cf. Acts 10:38: "he went about doing good"). The prediction made at 1:32 was never rescinded. Leastness is the road to greatness (cf. 9:48), and through imitation of the Great Benefactor his followers will be benefactors to the world.

Imitation of the superstar is a recurring theme in Greco-Roman documents of recognition. In the decree cited in connection with the comment on Luke 2:52, the honorand Herakleitos is praised for having offered "his own way of life as a fine model for citizenship." In his autobiographical aretalogy, Antiochos of Kommagene presented himself as a model of piety for his children and their descendants *(Benefactor,* p. 349).

The entire discourse, as presented by Luke, is in harmony with the Lord's instruction in Matt. 23:8–10, where the disciples are admonished not to delight in the title "Rabbi" or "Father" or "Master." Just as Jesus does not invalidate the use of the term "benefactor" as such, so he does not preclude use of these titles but would very probably consider ridiculous the fuss made in books of etiquette on proper address of either ecclesiastical or civic dignitaries. He must be even more dismayed as he observes the problems of various churches in developing nomenclature for various functions in the church, while at the same time they seek to observe traditional views of ordination. When all are servants under one Father and Lord, there is no place for status-seeking. Servanthood is the only legitimate status in the Kingdom. And, as the ministry of Jesus attests, it is not a synonym for timorous passivity. Some of Luke's auditors who were familiar with Cicero's *Republic* (6.9–26) would have recollected Scipio Africanus's instruction to his grandson on the virtue of rendering service to humanity as an obligation of dedication to the state, without regard to personal glory.

22:28. Much of Jesus' ministry was spent in encounter with those who sought signs of his credentials (cf. 11:16). At 20:2 he was asked by what authority (the word is related to the term "those in authority," 22:25) he acted. His entire life had been a renunciation of Satan's earlier attempt to direct him along the path of normal status-seeking (4:6). Thus Luke does not violate his pattern of presenting Jesus' public ministry as one free from Satanic temptation (cf. 4:13 and 22:3). He accords due recognition to the Lord's conflict with a hostile establishment (cf. Acts 20:19). The disciples of Jesus have **continued with** him during the entire period of his ministry and they will share in the Kingdom about to be established.

22:29. The messianic banquet described in 13:22–30 and anticipated in 22:16 and 18 is to become reality. The Father has **assigned**, or "covenanted," a Kingdom for Jesus. These words are in harmony with Luke's earlier correction of popular hopes for the restoration of David's dynasty (1:32–33) and reflect the language of 2 Sam. 5:3, which states that the elders of Israel covenanted with David. Luke alters the thought of the OT passage and emphasizes that God, not Israel, makes the royal covenant with Jesus. The latter, in turn, "assigns" (the Greek *diatithēmi* corresponds to the Greek noun "covenant," *diathēkē*) the disciples as chiefs of state at the royal table.

In brief, Israel's royal hope can be fulfilled only in Jesus, and on God's terms. Once more the reversals expressed in the Magnificat come to the fore (1:52–53). Judas reclined at a table (22:21) that was only a foretaste of the messianic banquet, and he did not remain with Jesus in his trials. The greatness he sought would be forever denied him, for another would be chosen in his place to assume responsibility for one of the thrones (cf. Acts 1:16–26). Luke will not include Mark's references to the abandonment of Jesus by the disciples (Mark 14:27, 50).

22:30. The language of Ps. 122:4–5, with its stress on the house of David, appears to underlie the promise in v. 30. The **twelve tribes of Israel** are the community of believers gathered after Pentecost. The Christian community is in continuity with Israel (cf. 2:32; 3:6; Acts 3:25), linked by the Spirit under one Lord, the Messiah of Israel (cf. Acts 10). "Judging" *(krinō)* is the official function of those who sit on the thrones. In this respect they are like the judges of ancient Israel, who were sent from time to time to rescue God's people from their enemies. Thus the apostolic task is one of compassionate concern for people and of responsibility for their ongoing commitment to the Lord's purposes. In recognition of this fact, it is stated at Acts 16:4 that Paul and his entourage delivered the decrees passed by the apostles and elders who were at Jerusalem. The apostles function like the Senate at Rome. They are bureaucrats of the New Age, rewarded for their allegiance by the Great Politician. At the same time, the text sounds a wisdom motif: the suffering righteous are ultimately triumphant (cf. Wisd. of Sol. 3:8).

22:31. The thought is expanded in the personal address to Simon, significantly minus "Peter" (*Petros* means "rock"). The repetition of his name expresses the solemnity of the address (cf. 10:41). **Satan demanded** all of the disciples (the pronoun **you** is plural) for sifting, and he has been successful in one case (22:3). Mark 8:33 records a stern warning to Peter in connection with his confession at Caesarea Philippi: "Get behind me, Satan!" Luke had omitted the saying in his parallel recital (Luke 9:18–20), perhaps in order to give prominence at this point to Simon's misunderstanding of Jesus' role as the Messiah.

22:32. To learn the route of service is not easy, and Simon evidently revels in the privileges he has enjoyed as participant in special revelations (cf. 9:28). In any event, he did become a recognized leader in the early Christian community and his credentials must be reaffirmed, for he had denied his Lord. How was he different from Judas? Answer: His faith, his commitment, his loyalty did not give out completely, for Jesus had prayed for him. Those who stand, stand by the grace of the Master (cf. 1 Cor. 10:12). Although Jesus had to pray especially for Peter, all the disciples must realize they are no match for Satan without reliance on him who renounced all the kingdoms they find so difficult to renounce.

But one might still ask, Did Jesus fail to pray for Judas? This is a Western approach to problems that are of no interest to Luke. The evangelist is primarily concerned with the point that Simon's restoration to the community depends on Jesus, whose prayer in behalf of Simon is a sign or symbol of the larger service Jesus renders in behalf of all through his willing acceptance of the fate he endured at Calvary.

This warning, addressed to all the disciples and then especially to Simon, is a reminder to the total community. And Simon is to understand that judging the tribes means to **strengthen your brethren.** Certainly Peter's colleagues are included (see v. 31), but the plural term rendered "brethren," unless otherwise specifically qualified in a text, means "brothers and sisters," especially in reference to a religious community of mixed constituency (see BAGD, p. 16). Through Jesus' intercession Simon will be rehabilitated for service to the People of God (cf. John 21:15–19). And Acts 1:15–16; 2:29; and 3:17 show Peter carrying out the dominical directive.

22:33–34. Jesus' word of assurance is all the more vital, for he had said that anyone who denied him before people would be denied before the angels of God (12:9). Peter, who had once asked Jesus to depart from him (5:8), assures him that he desires his perpetual company. But soon **Peter** (now the "Rock-man," spoken ironically) would be guilty of the crime. Cocks like to crow at the dawning. So brief the time for Peter's fervent protestations to reach their melting point (v. 34; cf. vv. 54–62). Undoubtedly there were others like Simon who failed in a crisis, but strengthened by their brothers and sisters they would find fresh hope.

Luke is among those who do not apply the Lord's words to a given case with inexorable and judgmental logic. He had recorded memorable words on the subject of forgiveness (6:36–38). Even Judas could with tears of repentance have halted his headlong career toward destruction. Peter did shed them (22:62) and later became a fearless witness to his Master (cf. Acts 4:8–12, 19; 5:18; 12:3–11). The one fell, the other rose (cf. 2:34). For Peter did make good on his promise to follow his Lord **to prison and to death** (for his imprisonment, see Acts 5:19; 12:1–17). But there was that cock-crow! And he too made the front page.

22:35. Luke is ordinarily careful about observing correspondence between various parts of his writing. All the more remarkable, therefore, is the wording in v. 35: **When I sent you out with no purse or bag or sandals . . . ,** a clear echo of 10:4, which is part of the account of the sending *(apostellō)* of the Seventy (two). The Twelve were sent out earlier and with different specifications (9:3). The question, **Did you lack anything?** focuses attention on the disciples' peaceful and law-abiding intentions. They did not go out with purse or bag, for they did not intend to enrich themselves at the expense of others as did brigands and some itinerant preachers (see critique of greedy wizards by Apollonios of Tyana, *Life* 8.7). Yet they lacked **nothing.**

22:36–37. But now *(alla nyn)* the situation is different. To impress on his disciples the seriousness of the hour Jesus tells them to take up **purse** and **bag** (knapsack) and if necessary sell their mantles in order to purchase swords. In support of his directive he cites Isa. 53:12: **And he was reckoned with transgressors.** Some auditors of Luke's recital would catch a satirical tone in the directive. Israel's leadership is about to class Jesus as an outlaw, a revolutionary (cf. 23:2, 5, 14). He has exacerbated the religious establishment through his violation of custom (see, e.g., 5:8–11, 27–32;

6:11; 7:49; 11:53–54). He will be identified as a greater threat than Barabbas (23:25) and will finally be strung up between two brigands (23:33). Peter will feel the heat of association (22:54–62) and together with his colleagues will be subject to police control (see Acts 4:1–3; cf. 9:1–2). So let us look like outlaws, suggests Jesus. It is a prophetic maneuver, the saving grace of humor in the face of irresistible power.

There is still another perspective. Luke's only other use of the Greek *anomos,* here rendered "transgressors" (pl.), occurs in Acts 2:23, where Peter's audience is said to have "crucified and killed" Jesus "by the hands of lawless men," that is, through the Romans, who as gentiles do not know the Mosaic Law. Irony of ironies, the Messiah is delivered into the hands of Israel's occupying power.

The phrase **about me** is emphatic. At 12:50 Jesus said that he could not wait until his "baptism" was "accomplished," and at 18:31 he declared that "everything that is written of the Son of [humanity] by the prophets will be accomplished." By claiming the pending suffering as his proper goal, Jesus also claims the function of the Servant of the Lord (Isa. 53:12). At Acts 8:26–40 Luke will expand on the significance of all that happens here.

22:38. The disciples misunderstand the irony in Jesus' remarks and think that he actually intends them to secure swords. Unaware of the tremendous scope of the hour of truth that is about to dawn, they think in terms of a slight scuffle. At least the Master speaks of realities within their realm. No need for him to worry. They would handle it. And two swords should be enough! So impressed are they with their own prowess and preparedness for combat that they preface their display of arms with "Look" *(idou).* Jesus answers, **It is enough.** Case closed! They mean well, but there is no getting through their skulls this night.

AGONY ON THE MOUNT OF OLIVES
Luke 22:39–46
(Mark 14:26, 32–42; Matthew 26:30, 36–46)

In the preceding recital (vv. 14–38) the Lord tried to impress on his disciples the nearness of the struggle in which he was about to engage. Mark presents dialogue between Jesus and the disciples on their way to the Mount of Olives (14:26–31). Luke introduced part of it in connection with his presentation of events in the upper room, and omits the rest (Mark 14:27–28, 31). This makes it possible for him to submit the present section as a unit, in which the engagement of Jesus is probed to its depth. At the same time, by omitting the reference to Jesus going on ahead into Galilee after his resurrection (Mark 14:28), Luke avoids the need for recording a resurrection appearance in that locale.

22:39. Always Jesus moves with cohesive purpose and resolve. **As was his**

custom echoes 21:37 and suggests to Luke's public that despite his knowledge of the plot against him Jesus does not hesitate to meet his assigned responsibility. That this is Luke's intention is clear from his slight alteration of Mark 14:26. Instead of the comprehensive pronoun "they," Luke shows that Jesus takes the initiative and **the disciples followed him.**

22:40. Since Luke avoids the name Gethsemane, perhaps because some of his public might be puzzled by the additional place-name, he simply states, **when he came to the place.** Earlier, Jesus had taught his disciples to include in their prayers the petition: "Lead us not into temptation" (11:4). Luke considers the subject so important that he inserts the directive at this point (cf. Mark 14:32).

In the present context, "temptation" *(peirasmos)* bears special import, for Jesus has spoken of the nearness of the Kingdom (22:16, 18), and fiery trials were anticipated in the end time (cf. Zech. 13:9; Mal. 3:1–3; 4:1). The time of suffering endured by Jesus is the kind of moment that one finds described in apocalyptic works. The disciples, who were called to watch in every time (21:36), must now pray that they do not fall into the hands of Satan. The Son of humanity comes precisely in an hour like this—when they least expect it.

22:41. Jesus is the first to practice his own admonition. Having stressed the fact that all the disciples are directed to pray, Luke omits reference to Peter, James, and John (Mark 14:33), and in place of the phrase "going a little farther" (Mark 14:35) he indicates that there was at least **a stone's throw** between Jesus and the disciples. Thus his withdrawal from the disciples at this crucial moment is the second reminder in a very brief space of time that he will not long remain with them (cf. Luke 22:35–38). Ordinarily prayers were offered in a standing position (cf. 18:11, 13). The posture of Jesus is therefore an expression of profound humility and an indication of the depth of his inward struggle. Luke suggests in Acts 7:60; 9:40; 20:36; and 21:5 that the supplicatory gesture of Jesus was not forgotten.

22:42. Jesus does not go to his death with bravado. Luke does not recreate Plato's *Phaedo* in which Sokrates is portrayed as one who accepts his death heroically. Not sounded here is the Homeric tone in the story of Ajax, who prayed before the Trojan onrush, "If our fate be death, then give us light to do the dying" (*Iliad* 17.646–47). Nor does Luke suggest that Jesus' death is to be construed simply as a tragic miscarriage of justice. Rather, Luke's auditors are to understand that the death of Jesus is part of the Father's purpose. No other credentials are necessary. As in Vergil's Aeneid, in which his hero exclaims that he is "summoned by heaven" (*Aeneid* 8:533) to accept the role of leader in the war for Rome's future, this moment in Luke's narrative is one of consecration that grows out of the commitment announced at 2:49, in which all personal goals were subordinated to the interests of the heavenly Parent.

Without that purpose his death would be as the death of others. He had renounced an earlier cup (cf. 22:17–18) in order shortly to drink his cup of death (cf. Mark 10:38–39), but its contents are bitter. To the Father, his constant port of call (Luke 2:49; 10:21–22; 22:29), he now turns. **If thou art willing, remove this cup from me.** The words "art willing" *(boulei)* express deliberation. The verb *bouleō* is a bureaucratic term, cognate with a noun that means "senate" *(boulē)*. God deliberates and formulates a decision. Greco-Romans readily understood that a deity need only think or wish something and it would be done (cf. Homer *Iliad* 20.242–43; Pindar *Pythian* 9.67–68; Livy 1.39.4). Jesus asks whether the decision could be for removal of the bitter drink that awaits him. Sokrates refused even to think of evading the drinking of the hemlock. But the very agony that prompts Jesus to request his Father to explore a different way dramatically puts in sharp relief the spirit of complete obedience expressed in the concluding clause: **Nevertheless not my will, but thine, be done.** He has passed an initial test.

Once Satan had suggested that the criterion of divine sonship was divine protection (4:3–13). Jesus renounces the traditional criterion. One can appear to be repudiated even by God, and yet be the instrument of God's purpose. Paul learned well from his Master, and in the face of his refusal to avoid a showdown in Jerusalem his friends echoed the resolution of Jesus: "The will of the Lord be done" (Acts 21:14).

22:43. Luke had omitted Mark's earlier reference to ministration of angels at the temptation (Mark 1:13). Now, in this apocalyptic hour, **an angel** (in RSV margin) strengthens him for his remaining task (cf. 1 Kings 19:4–8, of Elijah; Dan. 10:18–19). The words **from heaven** accent the fact that God directs him on the present path (cf. 9:31).

22:44. The crucial responsibility that is his finds expression in the term "agony," which is a transliteration for the Greek term *agōnia,* which suggests anxiety over the issue of a great contest *(agōn).* The intensity of the struggle is emphasized by the observation that he **prayed more earnestly,** and that he sweated profusely. The simile, **like great drops of blood,** calls attention to the fact that he is shaken to the depths of his being, not that he actually sweated blood. The entire scene is reminiscent of 2 Macc. 3:14–36 and describes one who is dedicated wholly to the Lord.

To Greco-Roman auditors this scene would denote Jesus' entry into the most challenging crisis of his career. The divine purpose for all humanity depends on Jesus' fidelity. Greeks called such a time of challenge a "peristasis." Numerous public-spirited citizens, including especially heads of state and other administrators, receive accolades for their steadfastness in critical times. To cite but one, it was said of a priest named Akornion, who served at Dionysopolis, that he showed concern for the welfare of his city "by risking body and soul in every perilous circumstance" (*SIG* 762.38–39; *Benefactor,* pp. 78, 363).

As the margin in the RSV states, vv. 43–44 are omitted in some manuscripts, but the language is not foreign to Luke, and the thought is in harmony with other themes in the Gospel. Perhaps copyists thought that the description in these verses detracted from the divinity of our Lord. If such is the case, they not only missed Luke's point but also came close to misunderstanding the Gospel.

22:45–46. In a sense Jesus has already died a death. In the garden he has encountered the Enemy full force. Now he has only to complete the victory by suffering outside the garden. Like Caius Flaminius, who in 223 B.C.E. dismantled behind him the bridge over the river Po as he led his troops to face the enemy, Jesus is committed without reservation to the fulfillment of his task. So he "rose"—most appropriate in this context. He is now ready for the supreme confrontation. But he who had endured the profoundest agony imaginable finds his own companions sleeping. Once before in the presence of extraordinary revelation they had fallen asleep (9:32). It is clear that Jesus will receive no help from that source.

Misunderstanding from his closest friends is not the least of his burdens. Yet Luke protects the apostolic circle from further embarrassment. He omits Mark's reference to the rebuke directed at Simon Peter (Mark 14:37) and relates only one period of slumbering, instead of three as in Mark (14:37, 40, 41–42). Finally, he gives them an excuse. They slept **for sorrow.** It could not have been more than superficial, for sleep and grief are not bosom companions (cf. Ps. 6:6; Lam. 1:2). Instead of displaying a courageous alertness in harmony with their zealous offer at 22:37, they lapse into careless lassitude.

The total result is a scene of remarkable artistic, as well as theological, effect. Jesus' identity does not derive from the church's contemplation. Rather, it is God's action in connection with Jesus that brings the people of the New Age into being. But Jesus is a model for the People of God. As he successfully overcame his temptation, so Christian communities must be watchful if they are to be prepared for the coming of the Son of humanity (cf. 21:34–36).

Jesus is undergoing his peristasis, or crisis, and the disciples will not have long to wait for their own. The Book of Acts is replete with peristasis catalogues, and Paul brings the theme to eloquent expression in the well-known recital of his own perils in behalf of the gospel (2 Cor. 11:23–29).

THE ARREST

Luke 22:47–53
(Mark 14:43–49; Matthew 26:47–56)

22:47. Luke stresses that the arrival of Judas and his cohorts takes place while Jesus issues his warning about temptation (v. 46). Now in an hour

when all seems lost, the disciples will be faced with the choice of deciding
for or against Jesus, and Simon will in a short while illustrate the meaning of
Jesus' words. Judas had his instructions to betray Jesus without the presence
of a crowd (22:6). Now Luke writes, "Behold, a crowd . . ." The RSV omits
the interjection, with some loss of meaning. Judas has his crowd, but it
consists of chief priests, temple guard, and elders (v. 52). Judas now draws
near to betray Jesus with a fraternal kiss—the quenching of the last flicker of
light in his soul.

The "chief priests" in this account are of course not Caiaphas and Annas,
but other officers of the Sanhedrin.

22:48. Every syllable in the reply of Jesus carries its own freight: "Judas,
with a *kiss* are you betraying the Son of humanity?" Surely not this way, not
after all that I have said to you about hypocrisy! In Luke's story line, Judas
had also heard the words about the Son of humanity who was to be betrayed
(9:44) and then to return in glory (21:27). Does Judas dare to trifle in this
way with his own destiny? The curtain of silence rings down on what seems
to be a last invitation to a wretched soul who demonstrates the truth that the
One we ought to love the most is at the mercy of the things we ought to
love the least.

22:49–51. Just as the disciples displayed their incompetence after the transfiguration of Jesus (see 9:37–43), so the apostles now betray their total lack
of comprehension as they unveil their pitiful arsenal in this crucial hour. It
was wise of Jesus not to count on them. The best that one of their sword-
players could do was hack an ear off the high priest's slave. "Stop! No more
of this!" says Jesus, reinforcing his command with a repair of the damage.
Thus Luke emphasizes that Jesus is guiltless of intrigue. Greco-Roman
auditors would be impressed by Jesus' composure under pressure and by the
persistent quality of his beneficence. Jesus is truly a man of exceptional
excellence, one who combines word and deed in such a way that his counsel
in the Sermon on the Plain about loving one's enemies (6:27–30) cannot be
classed as starry-eyed impracticality. Jesus demonstrates what it means to
"turn the other cheek."

In v. 51 Luke uses a diminutive form of the term for "ear." This rhetorical
touch adds a note of pathos to the scene.

22:52–53. Should there be any doubt at all about Jesus' motivation, it is
dispelled by the succeeding words that he addressed to the leadership. Do
they actually think that he is **a robber**, or revolutionary brigand whom they
must capture with the help of **swords and clubs**? He had not hidden from
them: he was daily within their reach in the temple (cf. 21:37–38). Why did
they not take him there? The fact is, they themselves have been lured into
Satan's plot. Jesus had rejected Satan's offer of "authority" (on *exousia,* see
4:6; the RSV renders the same word as "power" in 22:53). The religious

establishment now accepts it. "This hour," **the power of darkness**, is appropriate for demonic designs (cf. John 13:20; Col. 1:13; Eph. 6:12). But any power they may have is of the heavenly Parent's permissive providence (cf. John 19:11). They are the real brigands (cf. Luke 19:27), who cloak evil behind a facade of religion. John the Baptist had spoken of the day that would "give light to those who sit in darkness" (Luke 1:79; cf. Acts 26:18). They voted for the night.

IN THE CUSTODY OF THE HIERARCHY
Luke 22:54–71
(Mark 14:53–54, 66–72, 65; 15:1; 14:55–64;
Matthew 26:57–58, 69–75, 67–68; 27:1–2, 59–65)

In keeping with his frequent presentation of contrasting scenes, Luke modifies Mark's order of events in order to depict the solemn confession of Jesus against the background of Peter's denial. Also he apparently considers it more probable that the judicial examination by the Sanhedrin took place not at night but during the day. On the other hand, he does not deny that the leaders held an informal meeting, for v. 54 clearly states that Jesus was led off to the "high priest's house."

Attempts to charge the evangelists with total distortion of Jewish legal procedure ignore elementary facts of life. When pressed to protect its own security, any establishment manages either to circumvent technicalities or to follow the letter with dispatch. The history of religion is filled with depressing evidence of that fact, and it is naive to deny it. A political scientist commented in reaction to an ecclesiastical committee's maneuverings to lay the ax to an officeholder who had fallen into disfavor with higher powers: "In political circles I know what the ground rules are. Here I can't lay my finger on the tactics."

Charges of anti-Semitism that have been made against Luke are libelous, for Luke is very fond of Jews. Of all early Christian writers, especially Luke is concerned to point out that it was not the Jewish people but their leaders who were the primary cause of ruin to Jerusalem. If the evangelists, three of whom are quite probably themselves Jews, are to be charged with anti-Semitism, then the prophets of ancient Israel were anti-Semitic, for the evangelists merely update the pattern of judgment pronounced in the OT. But anti-Semitism does display its ugly head when especially Christian readers of the Gospel think that "the Jews," not they, are under the evangelist's scrutiny. Seven million Jews have known the pain of such evil application of the text.

Nor is it fair to say that Jews, including Pharisees and the hierarchy of apostolic times, serve as whipping boys when contemporary sins, like those of Luke's or of a later time, are woven into the development or exposition of a biblical text. Sin is generic. Its basic structure, like that of language, comes to expression in a variety of forms. And patronage of Jewish sensitivities is itself a sign of anti-Semitism. Classics such as Luke's books elicit the interest that they do precisely because of their appeal to universal experience. Luke shows that Jesus was intensely patriotic (cf. 19:34–35). His only crime was a refusal to engage in what W. H. Auden termed the "worst human vice," namely, collective egoism.

Denial by Peter
Luke 22:54–62
(Mark 14:53–54, 66–72; Matthew 26:57–58, 69–75)

22:54–57. The arresting committee seizes Jesus. Paul would experience something similar (Acts 21:30). Peter is still a follower, but now **at a distance** (cf. Luke 23:49). Soon it will be determined whether he is wheat or chaff (see 22:31). Mark has the first remark of the maid addressed directly to Peter. Luke sketches the winnowing of Peter more dramatically. First he hears his exposure as an associate of Jesus before the group gathered around the fire. There the skin-saving disciple, resolved to keep a low profile, makes his first denial, exactly in the terms predicted by his Lord (v. 34).

22:58. The pressure intensifies. This time it is a man from the group (not the same woman as in Mark 14:69), and he addresses Peter directly. The woman had said, "This man also was with him" (v. 56). This man says, **You also are one of them.** Now it is not a matter only of being associated with Jesus but of being implicated with a band of suspected men. Peter's memory goes worse by the minute. And now, after disclaiming any relationship with Jesus, he renounces his own closest associates as he heads toward his own self-isolation. Denial of the community of believers is tantamount to denial of Jesus. In time of persecution this would be the real temptation.

22:59. Mark presents the third denial as taking place "after a little while" (Mark 14:70). Luke brings Peter closer to the hour of cockcrow with the phrase **after an interval of about an hour.** Again it is a man who speaks, this time identifying him, as the maid had done, to the assembled group. This identification of Peter as **a Galilean** introduces the incriminating suggestion that Peter is a dangerous revolutionary (cf. Luke 13:1–2).

22:60. Peter, acting more like a jellyfish than a "Rock-man," said, "I don't know the guy." Luke, who follows the Greek historian Polybios's principle (*History* 1.14) of giving due credit even to the enemy and merited censure to one's own side, does not hesitate to include this account that is so embarrassing to the church. On the other hand, he mercifully spares Peter from the terrible oath assigned him by Mark (Mark 14:71).

Peter, who had joined a group near a fire (Luke 22:55), has now passed through the crackling fire of temptation and hears the cock crow. (In Mark,

the cock expressly crows twice, see Mark 14:30, 72, thus heightening the
callousness of Peter.)

22:61. Somehow from the house Jesus was able to see Peter, who was in
the courtyard. Only one look from him, and Peter remembers **the word of
the Lord.** His memory would come back even better after Pentecost (see
his speeches in the early chapters of Acts).

22:62. Jesus had predicted Peter's denial, but he had also predicted his own
suffering and death. With sensitive economy and consummate art Luke
suggests that now it is all too clear to this disciple. So huge had been his fault
that **he went out and wept bitterly.** The k-sounds (cf. Homer *Odyssey*
1.46) in each of the five Greek words contrast with the p-sounds in Jesus'
prediction of denial (v. 61, *prin . . . phonēsai . . . aparnēsē;* cf. the mellifluous
l-sounds in *Odyssey* 1.56–57), and they sob forth one of the most poignant
sentences in literature. But even in this disastrous hour, his Lord did not
forget Peter, and now the sea must dry up to contain his sorrow. As the
sequel shows, this was the beginning of Peter's rehabilitation (cf. v. 32).
Peter was now indeed "a sinful man" (5.8), but he would see a living
definition of loyalty and constancy (24:34) after his bout in Satan's hour (cf.
22:3, 31, 53).

Mockery

Luke 22:63–65
(Mark 14:65; Matthew 26:67–68)

22:63–65. Luke's sketch of the movement from night to day in Luke 22
is a masterpiece of sensitive writing, and with his customary literary tact
Luke presents the scene of mockery, which incorporates ingredients in an
earlier prediction made by Jesus (18:32). Luke does not specify rank or status
of the participants. From Peter's experience it is clear that Jesus had prophetic powers. The demand for Jesus "to prophesy" stands therefore in
sharp contrast to the previous demonstration and points to Jesus' willing
acceptance of the humiliating path assigned him. But prophecy is more than
acumen to sort out future events. In its primary form, prophecy is the
ability to discern God's hand at work in the events of history. Jerusalem will
know that there was a prophet in her midst. In the year 70 C.E. there will be
no playing of blindman's buff.

Trial before the Sanhedrin

Luke 22:66–71
(Mark 15:1; 14:61–64; Matthew 27:1; 26:63–65)

22:66–68. The assembly of the elders (cf. Acts 6:12) is the Sanhedrin,
the high court of the Jews. To their first question, whether he is **the Christ,**
that is, the Anointed One or the Messiah, Jesus declines an answer. In

fairness to them it must be granted that most representatives of religious institutions expect clear and unambiguous adherence to traditional formal structures, and these officials have made up their minds about Jesus. Quite evidently their conclusions about the function of the Messiah do not square with his own understanding of messiahship. Therefore they would not believe him if he answered in the affirmative, and they would permit no cross-examination of the type expressed in 20:21–44. Instead, he speaks to them of the triumph of the Son of humanity. In this way he is able to affirm that the very road to messiahship lies along the unorthodox path of rejection and death.

22:69–70. In place of yes or no, Jesus expresses himself in terms of the outcome. The very events in which he is now engaged will make his identity explicit. Fragile human being, Son of humanity that he is, he will be identified by heaven itself as Christ and Lord. Acts 2:34–36 is the commentary on Jesus' reply. Where another would have seen only the bleakness of the unknown, Jesus beheld the splendor of promise. The outcome of the crucifixion will be the sitting at the right hand of God. And it will all happen within three days.

Luke does not say that they will "see" (Mark 14:62) the Son of humanity, for Jesus takes his seat at the right hand of God **from now on**, and this is hidden from the eyes of hostile people. Stephen, on the other hand, will "see," and the Son of humanity will arise to receive him (Acts 7:56). **The power** (*dynamis*) is that of God, not of the kingdoms of this world, nor of messiahship construed in nationalistic terms. Most carefully Luke refrains from expressing a *future coming*. Not end-time demonstration, but divine vindication, is Luke's main point. Thus the affirmation is in harmony with Jesus' earlier predictions of suffering in association with the self-identification of Son of humanity (9:22, 44; 18:31). In Luke 24 all ambiguity concerning the identity of Jesus is removed through the resurrection. The one who appears to be fragility itself, the Son of humanity, emerges as the victorious one. Therefore it is explicitly affirmed of him on the third day that he is the Christ (24:26 and 46).

22:70. The Sanhedrin glimpses its opportunity and asks, **Are you the Son of God, then?** At v. 67 Luke separated this specific identification from its conjunction with messiahship in Mark 14:61. Ordinarily it would not be arrogance to call oneself a son of God, for all Israelites were the children of God (see, e.g., Exod. 4:22; Deut. 14:1). But the affirmation in v. 69 suggests that Jesus understands more by the term. This One who styles himself a fragile human being asserts that "from now on" God grants to him the most privileged position of all. It is a claim to extraordinary power that the religious establishment cannot endure. Therefore they press their point.

From a literary perspective, Jesus' self-identification and their reaction are credible; for in Luke's account the term "Son of God" refers to Jesus' unique relationship with God, which is independent even of traditional associations with Davidic messianism (see on 1:30–35). In Luke-Acts the term "Son of God," in conjunction with the term "Lord," bears the main weight of Jesus' identity.

Even considered apart from his unique status, Jesus can lay claim to being a true son of God, for he is totally obedient to his Parent's assignment, and Luke wants the full burden of the judgment to fall at this point. Jesus was crucified, not because he was a nationalistic revolutionary or just another Galilean agitator of messianic hopes, but because he understood himself to be uniquely committed to carry out the divine will. There is no pleading of the fifth amendment possible. Yet the answer must be guarded, for the interrogators do not share with Jesus the same concept of sonship. As is usually the case in theological controversy, they were "talking past each other." But because the inquisitors have, as Luke suggests, prejudged the entire matter, he answers: **You say that I am.** "You" is emphatic. They must accept full responsibility for whatever assumptions they put into the question. On the other hand, he will not deny it: **I am** *(egō eimi).* Many would come and say, "I am" (cf. 21:8: "I am he!"). Only Jesus has the right to that solemn affirmation, and with this self-identification as the Son of God he tacitly affirms that one of the days of the Son of humanity has arrived (cf. 17:22).

22:71. So far as the court is concerned, the trial is over. On any sober assessment, Jesus has incriminated himself. But Luke's publics are invited to offer a different verdict. Jesus could have chosen Peter's road, but he took this path in order to find Peter. Significant is Luke's omission of the introduction of false witnesses who in Mark allege that Jesus would destroy the temple (Mark 14:58). Luke has an answer ready for what is tantamount to a charge of sedition, but preserves it for the Book for Acts, where he enters into the question at some length through Stephen's speech (cf. Acts 6:14, and see esp. 7:44–50). The Sanhedrin think they need no further witnesses. Peter will straighten them out on that score (Acts 3:15). For like Oidipous in Sophokles's tragedy, they pronounced a judgment that they never would have made had they not been blind to the truth (cf. Luke 11:33–36).

JESUS BEFORE PILATE AND HEROD
Luke 23:1–25
(Mark 15:1b–2, 11–15; Matthew 27:2, 11, 20–23, 26)

In this section Luke is apparently indebted to Mark but is also dependent on a source that linked Herod and Pilate. Of special interest is his stress on the threefold declaration of innocence (23:4, 14, 22). This is in accord with

Luke's repeated effort to clear Jesus in the eyes of Roman officials of any charge of anti-state activity.

Through references or allusions to Pss. 22; 31; 38; 69; and others, Luke establishes in this and succeeding portions of his narrative that Jesus is the classic upright sufferer and the Son of God par excellence.

Accusation before Pilate

Luke 23:1–5

(Mark 15:1b–2; Matthew 27:2, 11)

23:1. The whole company is the Sanhedrin (cf. Acts 23:7). Luke is well aware of the supportive closing of the ranks that takes place at top bureaucratic levels. To introduce first the charges made by the hierarchy, Luke alters "delivered" *(paradidōmi)* (Mark 15:1) to **brought** *(agō)*.

Through the abrupt entrance of Pilate into the narrative, Luke apparently intends to indict the religious leaders for turning to secular sources of power after running out of their theological capital in dealing with Jesus. At the same time, Luke's auditors, who have made previous literary acquaintance with Pilate at 13:1, know that the prefect will meet the leaders' expectations.

23:2. At 6:7 the scribes and the Pharisees were looking for grounds of accusation. Now it is the members of the high court who try to incriminate Jesus by permitting the introduction of fragments and distortions of statements made by Jesus. Hostility boils out of the manner in which they open their speech to Pilate: "We found this fellow [RSV: **this man**; *touton,* a one-word pronoun] upsetting our nation." Pilate will be more courteous (v. 4). Luke's recording of 20:21–25 revealed the lie in their accusation respecting tribute to Caesar. And, as was implied in 22:67–68, the hierarchy read their own anti-Roman nationalist hopes (cf. 23:19, 25) into the title "anointed one" (**Christ**). Their addition of **king**, a loaded word, was designed incrimination, amply refuted by the material presented in 19:28—21:38. But this is the way truth is twisted through appeals to fear and insecurity. In similar terms Ahab asked Elijah: "Is it you, you troubler of Israel?" (1 Kings 18:17). Later, Luke's narrative anticipates Paul's experience of false charges (Acts 25:7).

23:3–4. The brief dialogue between Pilate and Jesus is, in Luke's presentation, a brilliant literary gambit. Through his omission of Mark's reference to many accusations made by the chief priests (Mark 15:3), Luke also gives sharper prominence to Pilate's direct question and to Jesus' equally direct answer. With the secular authorities, dialogue was possible! The form of the reply, **You have said so**, lays before Luke's public a bald affirmation of Jesus' kingship made in the presence of the Roman prefect. But at the same time it shifts to Pilate the responsibility for determining the import of the question (cf. Luke 22:70).

Luke's manner of narrative suggests that Pilate is well aware that the antagonism toward the prophet from Galilee is related to Jesus' refusal to work within the system as defined by the religious leadership. The climax comes in v. 4 with Pilate's verdict in connection with what appears to be a most incriminating admission: "Not guilty!" The word "no" in the phrase **I find no crime** *ouden . . . aition)* **in this man** is in the emphatic primary position in Greek. (Here the expression "this man" renders two Greek words.) A high Roman official affirms that recognition of Jesus as a king was not incompatible with loyalty to Caesar! The "crowds" *(ochloi)* are mentioned to show that the fears of the hierarchy (22:6) were groundless. Jesus knew the fickleness of the crowd (cf. 8:4–15; 9:41; 11:24–30; 12:13–15, 54–59). Rabble-rousing was not his forte (cf. 9:57–62). But it is not necessary to conclude that all who were attracted by the proceedings were hostile to Jesus.

23:5. The accusations recited in this verse build a bridge to the introduction of Herod into the narrative. Emphasis is placed on the teaching done by Jesus. Luke had well documented the nature of that instruction. Jesus was no threat to Roman security. And Pilate knew that what he had heard was dust in the eyes of the jury. The hierarchy was in fact losing its grip on the people (cf. Acts 4:17; 5:28; 17:6; Mark 15:10), and charges of "confusing the people" reveal concern not so much for people as for vested interests now threatened by exposure to the truth.

History records that preservation of religious tyranny through appeal to public order and social stability is not a rare phenomenon. The more discerning have pointed out that many people become confused when they are told that they are being confused. Forming one's own judgment is the capital offense. Religious institutions that claim for themselves the right to protect faithfully their teachings by immunizing themselves against dissident instruction and activity are scarcely in a position to deny the same right to Caiaphas and his associates. They were certainly correct in their conclusions respecting the threat that Jesus posed to the maintenance of some of their traditions. Measured by the yardstick of time-honored institutional prudence, Caiaphas was justified by his procedures.

Judea means the land of Palestine. Mention of **Galilee** is part of the inflammatory propaganda, for Galilee was the hotbed of revolutionary uprisings. Mark refers to the accusations only in a general way (Mark 15:3–4) and does not explain why Pilate was prompted to inquire about Jesus' kingship. Luke not only shifts the accusations but spells out two of them explicitly, thereby offering suitable motivation for Pilate's question.

The RSV's rendering **from Galilee** obscures the precise Greek wording "beginning from Galilee," which Luke echoes at Acts 10:37. One of Luke's ploys in the Passion account is to edit information that comes from Jesus' adversaries, but in such a way that their essential misunderstanding is exhibited. At Acts 10:37–38, therefore, Luke corrects the erroneous perspective of Jesus' accusers. He was not disrupting the peace but was engaged in beneficent activity. And ultimately it is not from Galilee but from Jerusalem that the proclamation will go forth (Luke 24:47; cf. Acts 1:8); for the Christian communities, many with a goodly contingent of Jews, are in continuity with the center of Jewish religious thought and life.

Trial before Herod

Luke 23:6–12

23:6–7. A wily partisan politician, Pilate seizes the opportunity either to return Herod a favor or to have the latter owe him one. The fact that Pilate asks whether Jesus is a **Galilean** suggests that the governor has received no previous complaint concerning his prisoner. His question also provides an easy transition to Herod's role in the trial of Jesus. Psalm 2:1–2 is cited in Acts 4:25–26, and Herod and Pilate are equated with the kings and rulers mentioned in the psalm. Luke anticipates the later apostolic proclamation (Acts 4:27) through his inclusion of Herod at this point and at the same time secures the witnesses required by Jewish law. According to Deut. 19:15, a charge is to be sustained before two witnesses. Simeon and Hannah attested that Jesus is the Messiah (Luke 2:25–38); Moses and Elijah spoke of his exodus (9:30–31). Now two officials of state are to affirm his innocence in the face of false accusation. Paul experienced a parallel type of arraignment before Roman and Jewish officials (Acts 25:13—26:32).

23:8. Herod is typical of those who wish **to see** Jesus but are prompted in that direction by misunderstanding of his person. Unlike Zacchaeus, who wished to see who Jesus was (19:2) and then repented, Herod sought to see Jesus (9:9) but in the moment of truth echoed the mistake that religious leaders had made and demanded a sign (cf. 11:16, 29). Within the Passion account this reference to a sign is especially noteworthy. Jesus is in his very humiliation himself the sign (cf. 2:34). But some lessons are never learned!

23:9. Despite repeated prodding, Herod receives **no answer.** Jesus once again resists the temptation to secure his own safety (cf. 4:3–12). In the silence of Jesus some of Luke's public might have heard a tolling of judgment (cf. Rev. 8:1). Others would hear an allusion to Isa. 53:7 or the expression of a wisdom motif. According to Wisd. of Sol. 8:12, even the powerful will wait on the wise person to emerge from silence. Sirach 20:1 states that the wise person remains silent in the face of reproof that is uncalled for. The fool, on the other hand, "multiplies words" (Sir. 20:8). Diogenes Laertius (3.19) reports that according to one version of the story of Plato's appearance on a capital charge before a court at Aigena the philosopher uttered not a word as he awaited the verdict. Similarly, the sophist philosopher Timon, when he was charged with being a traitor, did not deign to speak a word in defense against the unfounded accusations (Diogenes Laertius 9.115). An epigrammatist put it bluntly: "There is no glory in outstripping donkeys."

23:10. The vehement accusations of **the chief priests and the scribes** lend sharpness to the verdict of innocence tacitly pronounced by Herod.

23:11. Incapable of grasping immense reality, this royal clown vents his frustration by joining with his soldiers in a round of buffoonery (cf. 18:32), climaxed by a mock investment ceremony, in which Jesus is arrayed in **gorgeous apparel** *(esthēta lampran),* the kind of garment worn otherwise in Luke's work by a heavenly messenger (Acts 10:30; cf. the two men in Luke 24:4). Luke does not inform his public about the color, and it is a cliché to say that it is not possible to determine all that Luke had in mind when he recorded this detail. Certainly he does not include Mark's hints about an enthronement scene. That imagery was therefore not of primary significance to Luke.

More probable is an allusion to the white toga worn by political aspirants (see Polybios *History* 10.5.1, cited in BAGD, p. 465). And some of Luke's auditors might well have thought in terms of Jesus' candidacy to Israel's highest office. But it is not important that a reader of a literary work be privy to all aspects of an allusion. If such were the case, most hymnody would be irrelevant and obscure as the liturgies of the Salii, those warders of ancient Roman rites. It is sufficient that the writer communicate clearly, and this Luke does. Once out of the public eye as a popular freewheeling prophet, Jesus is no longer a threat. Through this apparently munificent donation Herod mocks the poor sufferer's degradation. Indeed, in a brief space of time Jesus will be stripped even of this clothing (see v. 34). But Luke's public knows who the real person of excellence is, and God will clarify his political credentials in due time.

Pilate had sent Jesus to Herod (v. 7); now Herod returns him to Pilate. Thus he excuses himself from jurisdiction over Jesus. Besides, Jesus was popular in Galilee!

23:12. In any event, Herod and Pilate resolve a standing feud. Some auditors would infer that Ps. 2:2 had found contemporary expression; those who did not do so would hear an echo after exposure to Acts 4:25–27. The incident is one of many that display Luke's keen perception of the opportunism that infects much political activity in both secular and religious spheres.

Hitler's temporary pact with Stalin and the longtime support of South Africa by the United States are but two modern illustrations of the fact that contrived political solutions make bedmates of otherwise incompatible parties and ideologies when national and economic interests or egos are at stake. Rational and scholarly tempera-ment may be seen teamed up with the most erratic invention of scurrilous partisan tactics, as exhibited, for example, in some of the prefaces to books published during the Nazi terror.

Pilate Strives for Acquittal

Luke 23:13–17

23:13. Pilate now summons **the chief priests**—who had also appeared before Herod—together with **the rulers and the people.** This last group appears to be identical with the "crowds" (v. 4), but the term "people" in Luke-Acts frequently takes on a more technical sense, referring to Israel as a corporate entity. From Luke's Hellenistic perspective the "people" form a popular assembly as distinguished from the Sanhedrin, which is viewed as the primary legislative council. Acts 4:27 mentions the "peoples of Israel," apparently a reference to Israel's tribal structure. The "people" are included at this point in the Passion narrative to emphasize that Israel as a corporate entity must assume a large share of responsibility for the death of Jesus Christ, while at the same time hearing the verdict of innocence pronounced on him. On the other hand, Luke does not mean to imply that all individual Jews were hostile to Jesus. Throughout his narrative he has displayed their good will toward Jesus, and a "great multitude of the people" lament him on his way to the cross (v. 27).

23:14. Also, from Pilate's remark, **You brought me this man as one who was perverting the people**, it is clear that not all the individual people within the larger group known as the people of Israel were responsi-ble for handing Jesus over to Pilate. In his choice of the term, Luke is partly stimulated by the demands of the apostolic mission. Can Israel, understood as a totality, be forgiven for rejecting her Messiah? Or has God rejected Israel and turned eyes only to gentiles? Luke affirms availability of divine pardon for all in Israel who become their own jury and reverse the verdict pronounced before Pilate (Acts 2:21–40, see esp. vv. 38–39). In short, theological compassion, not anti-Semitic sentiment, directs the wording of his narrative.

Pilate announces before the leaders and the people of Israel that Jesus is clear of all charges made in his presence. For a second time Pilate says, "Not guilty!" *(outhen . . . aition).* Unlike Apollonios of Tyana, who vanished from Domitian's court (see Philostratos *Life of Apollonios* 8.5), Jesus remains at his post. This is not Nazareth (see 4:30)!

23:15. At this point Pilate attempts another tack. Between the lines the reader is to infer that Pilate is aware of the rising thirst for blood. "Look!" says the prefect, "this man has done nothing to deserve the death penalty" (cf. Acts 23:29; 26:31). In other words, Jesus may be disturbing the people, but it is not a capital offense. Pilate may mix Galileans' blood with their sacrifices (13:2) but he is still a Roman, and Romans have a strong sense of justice, mixed with a heavy dose of pragmatic savvy that made them masters of the Mediterranean for already eight centuries. Jesus is popular in Galilee. The Sanhedrin said as much (see v. 5). And Herod (whose alleged attempt to kill Jesus was reported at 13:31) considers him no threat. Why chalk up another excuse for Rome to check up on provincial administration in Judea?

23:16. I will therefore chastise him and release him, says Pilate. The chastisement to which he refers is equivalent to "teach him a lesson" *(paideuō)*. This was a light beating or whipping of the type administered to juvenile gangs and was accompanied with a severe warning (cf. Acts 16:22–24; 22:24). In other words, Jesus was to receive a suspended sentence.

23:17. This verse is correctly relegated to the RSV margin as a later copyist's attempt to explain the outcry for Barabbas. In keeping with his intention to show that Israel as a corporate entity is responsible for the crucifixion, Luke omits Mark's recital of the proceedings leading up to the request for Barabbas. Thereby he achieves a starker contrast between the innocence of Jesus and the suppressed anti-Roman stance of the hostile assembly.

The Sentence
Luke 23:18–25
(Mark 15:11–15; Matthew 27:20–23, 26)

23:18. In Mark, the crowds make their outcry at the suggestion of the chief priests. Luke includes the chief priests in the phrase they all cried out together. **Away with this man** echoes Isa. 53:8. The expression "this man" *(touton;* cf. 23:2) is uttered with contempt. The name **Barabbas** means "son (Bar) of the father (Abba)" and is not really a name but a description of relationship between himself and his father. The latter may have enjoyed special status as a leader in his community, with the honorific title "Abba!" At Matt. 27:16 (see the RSV margin), the original text may have included his real name, Jesus. If Luke knew of this tradition, he omits the name, perhaps out of reverence for the Lord.

23:19. The decisive moment has now arrived. For whom will Israel vote? For God's chosen candidate (see 3:22; 4:18) or for a partisan disturber of the peace? Luke sketches the specific crimes of Barabbas in order to contrast the verdict pronounced by Pilate and the evil choice of the people. Jesus was not anti-Roman. If there was any misled revolutionary sentiment, it lay on the side of his enemies. Luke stresses that the activity of Barabbas took place **in**

the city. Not Galilee (cf. v. 6) but Jerusalem is the locale of a huge reservoir of guilt.

23:20. Once more Luke indicates that Pilate was convinced of Jesus' innocence (cf. Acts 3:13).

23:21. The bloodthirst rises with the demand for crucifixion, the extreme penalty for rebellious slaves and revolutionaries. Certainly the political platform of Jesus was not reflective of this constituency.

23:22. Pilate repeats his earlier verdict, "Not guilty!" *(ouden aition)*, (v. 15). The form of the statement expresses surprise and indignation.

23:23. Raw power reaches a crescendo and Pilate assures himself a share of dreadful ignominy in history's most lamentable travesty of justice. The mantle of greatness had been handed to the prefect of mighty Rome, but he would have been better off never to have tried it on for size. Attempting to go down quietly in history as a clever administrator, he ended up embalmed in the Apostles' Creed.

Luke is well aware of how a dominant class can use the state as an instrument for continuing domination (cf. Acts 16:16–24). And his grasp of the scene conveys the thought that subjects or citizens must ultimately bear responsibility. It would be difficult to find any indictment of civic pressure expressed with profounder brevity: **Their voices prevailed.** And Luke's implied characterization of Pilate is far more devastating than Mark's appraisal: "wishing to satisfy the crowd" (Mark 15:15).

Throughout the narrative Luke portrays an official who puts on a garment of concern for justice that ill conceals the heavy-handed style of administration that later led to his summons to Rome on complaint of the Samaritans. In his *Embassy to Gaius* (38), Philo described him as "inflexible, merciless, and obstinate."

23:24–25. Luke recalls the dramatic possibility expressed at v. 19, and in v. 25 highlights for the last time the contrast between Jesus and Barabbas. In a tone of incredulity he concludes the trial with these words: **but Jesus he delivered** *(paradidōmi)* **up to their will,** meaning that, in accordance with the public specification of the sentence, Pilate ordered the execution to be carried out by crucifixion. Luke's publics could not fail to note the inverted echo of 22:42. And many of his auditors must have been struck by the odd fulfillment of it.

These two verses express two aspects of Pilate's decision as adjudicator. He meets their request for the release of Barabbas and satisfies their demand for the crucifixion of Jesus. A deft maneuver. The leaders of Israel put themselves in a compromising position by asking for release of a recognized criminal against the state. Pilate, in turn, can register the execution of Jesus as a justiciable action.

A superficial reading of Luke's account might suggest that Luke assigns responsibility for the death of Jesus to Jews so as to spare Rome. But Luke full well knows that Pilate is Rome at that time and place in history. Customary attempts to charge Luke with a pro-Roman bias must therefore be interpreted as a purchase at the expense of justice to Luke's perception of political realities. Moreover, they prejudice a fair assessment of Luke's attitude toward Jews and they are fatal to a profounder appreciation of Luke's literary texture.

The literary fact is that both Jerusalem and Rome are guilty of injustice in their treatment of Jesus, and Acts 3:13 is not to be read apart from 4:26. Luke's overarching theme is the beneficence of God. If the guilt of Jews in the crucifixion is in any way accented, Luke's intention is not to let Rome off lightly but to prepare his publics for the proclamation of forgiveness in the first chapters of Acts. No matter how great Israel's crime, God gives her a fresh chance.

Only from a superficial perspective does Rome appear to be white-washed, and it is to be observed that in the Book of Acts, Luke shows no reluctance to tell the facts about Roman administrative malpractice (see, e.g., 16:37; and 24:26, the portrait of Felix, who is on the take). Rome's liberal policies toward the many cults in the Roman Empire are so well known that they require no further comment. The picture of special interest groups preying on the concern of Roman officials for maintenance of an orderly society is in harmony with what is otherwise known about Roman policy. And anyone with elementary knowledge of partisan politics in major cities knows that Luke has recited truth.

THE CRUCIFIXION

Luke 23:26–49

Warning to the Women of Jerusalem

Luke 23:26–31
(Mark 15:21; Matthew 27:32)

23:26. Having described a scene of mockery in Herod's quarters (v. 11), at this point in his narrative Luke omits a parallel scene involving soldiers (Mark 15:16–20) and focuses on the theme of crucifixion. The subject of the phrase **as they led him away** is colloquially indefinite. Mark's identification of **Simon** as the father of Alexander and Rufus (Mark 15:21) was apparently helpful to the readers of that Gospel, but in Luke's time the sons may not have been prominent. The scene, though, is important to Luke, who emphasizes discipleship as willingness to identify with Jesus (cf. Luke

9:23; 14:27). Thus this Simon is a model for those of Luke's public who may be subject to harassment from religious quarters.

Verses 27–31 are peculiar to Luke. Luke's auditors would expect some lamentation over such an illustrious personage as Jesus. The evangelist therefore uses this occasion to incorporate a lament but with some revision of the conventional pattern of lamentation. In his eyes the death of Jesus is no tragedy. The tragedy lies on the side of Israel. Hence he carries out in this recital his theme of judgment (cf. 13:1–9; 19:42–44) and contrasts the innocent Jesus with guilty Jerusalem. At the same time, he is able to show that not all the inhabitants of Jerusalem shared the verdict.

23:27. Yet **the people**—that is, Israel—must hear the divine verdict on *their* verdict. Women were the principal participants in ancient funeral rites, and the dirge of these women, accompanied by beating of the breast, is a lament for one consigned to the dead. Some impetus for the inclusion of the description may have been provided by the prophet Zechariah:

> And I will pour out on the house of David and the inhabitants of Jerusalem a spirit of compassion and supplication, so that, when they look on him whom they have pierced, they shall mourn for him, as one mourns for an only child, and weep bitterly over him, as one weeps over a first-born. (Zech. 12:10)

But all the tears in Jerusalem could not wash out this stain of infamy.

Luke's recital also takes on added poignancy when it is recalled that a distinguished Roman poet expressed the importance of recognizing the divine hand in affairs of state. Celebrating the significance of piety for Rome's security, Horace (*Odes* 3.6.5–8) wrote:

> Only as servants of the gods can you expect
> to rule. With them all things begin,
> and theirs to say how they will end.
> Slighted, they drown our Italy in tears.

23:28–29. Jesus' stern prophetic warning, the third of his dirges (see 13:34–35; 19:41–44), is not a pronouncement of vengeance for the injustice being perpetrated. Rather, through their choice of Barabbas, Israel has chosen a road that will lead to certain ruin and has rejected him who was their real source of security (cf. 19:42). The words in v. 29 reproduce the content of 21:23. A public that was conditioned to understand blessing in terms of exceptional divine favor would be startled by this reverse "blessing" (i.e., *makarism*).

23:30. This verse includes a quotation from Hos. 10:8. The fact that this OT passage speaks of Samaria contributes an ironic note to Luke's narration about Jerusalem. In the context preceding Hos. 10:8 the prophet laments

Israel's predicament in being without a king (Hos. 10:3). Luke seems to sense the horrible parallel between that anarchy and Israel's crucifixion of their own last royal hope (cf. Luke 23:38). They had cut off their nose to spite their face. And they will cry to the mountains and hills to cover them. This is an expression of total disaster; death itself would be more merciful (cf. Rev. 6:16; 9:6). And their doleful plea is so unlike the festive cheer of those who celebrate the birth date of Augustus as the end of all regret they might have had for ever being born (see on Luke 2:4).

23:31. The prophecy is here explained in theological terms. Green trees are difficult to burn. Dry trees burn quickly. In the phrase **if they do this,** the word "they" is best referred to God (cf. 12:20). The meaning of the sentence is: "If God permits this to happen to one who is innocent, what will be the fate of the guilty?" (cf. 23:41).

The entire address by Jesus is a call to repentance. It is a reminder that the Passion history is not designed to evoke sentiment or resentment against those responsible for the death of Jesus. "Do not weep for me, but weep for yourselves" (v. 28). It was with deep insight that Luke portrayed Jesus as weeping over Jerusalem (19:41). This is the Lord's last audit of a city that Luke adjudges guilty of sad miscalculation. Now as the lamented one, Jesus expresses his last lament.

Crucifixion and Mockery
Luke 23:32–38
(Mark 15:27, 22–24, 29, 31–32, 36, 30, 26;
Matthew 27:38, 33–35, 39, 41–42, 48, 40, 37)

23:32. Peter had assured Jesus that he was prepared to go to death with him (22:33). Instead, two men who had been sitting in death row join Jesus in a common fate. The skin-savers stand off at a secure distance (23:49). On the significance of these two in association with Jesus, see on 22:37. Luke's thematic interest in the two *kakourgoi* will shortly be apparent. The Greek term for the RSV's "criminals" *(kakourgoi)* means "malefactors" or "people who do bad deeds," the opposite of "a person who does good," that is, "a benefactor" *(euergetēs).* Compare Pilate's question in 23:22. Jesus is the Great Benefactor. He is crucified between the two malefactors.

23:33. In place of the name Golgotha, which even Mark thought was in need of interpretation (Mark 15:22), Luke uses a Greek rendering meaning **The Skull,** so named perhaps from the shape of the hill. The expression **one on the right and one on the left** would suggest a picture of a king with two bureaucrats or cabinet members (cf. Mark 10:37). Politics is the theme of vv. 33–43, and the crucifixion between two malefactors is the first of three examples of public mockery of the Great Politician, the King of the

Jews (v. 38). At the same time the stage is set for further illustration of 17:34–37.

23:34. The prayer in v. 34 is in such harmony with the spirit of Luke's Gospel and his picture of Jesus that it is difficult to question its authenticity. Unfortunately, no conclusive judgment can be made on the basis of the ambivalent manuscript tradition. It has indeed been argued that the prayer was omitted because of a conviction that the destruction of Jerusalem was God's judgment for the crucifixion, but a similar omission does not appear at Acts 2:38–39, where forgiveness is proclaimed to Israel. It has also been stated (e.g., in the first edition of this commentary), that Stephen's prayer in Acts 7:60 suggested a parallel utterance for the passion account. But in view of the fact that Acts frequently echoes or builds on material expressed in Luke's Gospel it is more probable that Stephen's petition is modeled after the intercession made by Jesus. Moreover, the reference to ignorance in Luke 23:34 differentiates this passage from the one in Acts 7 and may well be understood as an anticipation of a motif that appears in Acts 3:17; 13:17; 17:30.

Of more interest is the disruptive role that the verse is alleged to play in Luke's narrative. A close reading of the verse in its immediate context and in the total narrative structure of Luke-Acts suggests that the allegation is not well founded. Verses 33–43 form a coherent unit, with malefactors *(ka-kourgoi)* as the key figures. Greco-Roman auditors of Christian persuasion would bring to their hearing of the narrative their own prior assumption that Jesus belongs in the category of benefactor *(agathourgos)*. They could not fail to observe that Luke's stress on the malefactors puts the true character of Jesus as the Great Benefactor into bold relief. At the same time, Jesus is treated as a malefactor, and this sets up the ironical moment. His tormentors at one level express all the correct judgments concerning Jesus. The position between two criminals is in one sense a climactic endorsement of Jesus' intimate association with sinners. It was his way of extending them salvation. Since salvation is a standard function of heads of state, Jesus is appropriately called God's **Chosen One** ("elect one," a conception that also underlay some Greco-Roman views of kingship) and **King** (vv. 35–36). Luke's own "correction" of the misunderstanding takes place through the inclusion of Jesus' intercession (v. 34). The pronominal referent appears to be left undefined by design. **They know not what they do.** If they really knew his identity as God's own great benefaction, they would not be identifying him with malefactors. Jesus' petition is itself a request for further beneficence—forgiveness for the participants in this judicial disaster. Luke's Greco-Roman public would recognize that one of the reasons for Rome's grip on empire was its reputation for clemency in partnership with

firmness. The Augustan poet Horace (*Odes* 3.4.65–66) celebrated this political virtue in these words:

> Might without prudence falls by its own weight,
> But might when tempered earns divine support.

Augustus rehearsed the point in his *Res Gestae* (Tablet 1.3):

> Frequent wars, civil and foreign, on land and on sea, I waged throughout
> the world. In victory I spared all citizens who begged for mercy. Foreign
> nations, where it was safe to grant clemency, I preferred to spare rather
> than annihilate.

Luke's public is well aware of Jesus' greater interest in the guilty. And Jesus'
prayer sets the stage for the specific declaration of amnesty pronounced at
v. 43.

In addition to the preceding considerations, it is to be observed that Jesus'
appeal to his Father offers the motivation for the ridicule cited in v. 35. Luke
appears to be conscious of Wisd. of Sol. 2:16–18★, in which the enemies of
the upright conspire to test the integrity of their prey: "They boast that God
is their father. Well, let us see if their claim holds up, and let us test it by the
outcome. If the righteous are really the children of God, God will certainly
come to their aid and rescue them from their oppressors. So let us put them
to the test with insult and torture. Then we can determine the quality of
their meekness and patience. Let us consign them to an ignominious death.
No need to worry, for their own words assure God's intervention."

As for the placement of the petition between the act of crucifixion and the
partition of Jesus' garments, had Luke put it after the latter, his auditors
might have thought that the ignorance was primarily associated with the
gambling. The present sequence, on the other hand, heightens the dramatic
impact. Besides the exhibition of ignorance as to Jesus' real identity, a
contrast between Tyche (Fortune) and the Father's plan comes into play. The
path of Jesus is one of carefully defined objective—long before this day,
Jesus had committed himself to his Father's purpose (2:49). The gamblers
worship at the shrine of Luck.

In addition to its value as a referent for Jesus' role as Benefactor, the
petition informs Luke's public that Jesus did not threaten his executioners,
as the condemned were accustomed to do. Instead, he accepted his death in
the manner expected of a faithful witness. In the *Martyrdom of Isaiah* (5:14),
for example, the prophet is praised for neither crying aloud nor weeping
when he was sawn apart. Sokrates (Plato *Apology* 39c) and Stoic philosophers (see, e.g., Epiktetos 1.19.8) display a related lack of vindictiveness in
gentile circles. In contrast, the psalmist cries for vengeance (Ps. 69:22–28;
see on Luke 23:46).

Luke's reference to ignorance, which will echo at Acts 3:17; 17:30, undoubtedly won cross-cultural appreciation from those who did not ponder
the fine points of law discussed by J. Duncan Derrett (pp. 148–54). (For the

Hebrew tradition see, e.g., Leviticus 4; Num. 15:24–29; Josh. 20:3–6; Job 6:24; 19:4; Ps. 19:12). In a notable protestation of ignorance, the author of a penitential psalm found in the library of Ashurbanipal confesses:

> The sin which I have done, indeed I do not know.
> The forbidden thing which I have eaten, indeed I do not know.
> (*Ancient Near Eastern Texts Relating to the OT,*
> ed. James B. Pritchard, 2d ed. [1955], p. 391)

Related thoughts are expressed by devotees of various deities in Asia Minor. William Ramsay (*The Cults and Bishoprics of Phrygia* [1895], p. 151, no. 48) cites an inscription found at Badinlar in which a repentant woman records her dedication of a monument after having been chastised for entering a sacred enclosure in a state of impurity. A devotee named Stratoneikos similarly expressed his repentance for inadvertently *(kata agnoian)* cutting trees in a grove sacred to Zeus and Artemis (Franz Steinleitner, *Die Beicht im Zussamenhänge mit der sakralen Rechtspflege in der Antike* [1913], no. 21). In Hellas concern over inadvertent sin finds expression as early as Homer. In Homer's *Iliad* (23.85–92), the shade of Patroklos informs Achilles that he accidentally slew the son of Amphidamos in a rage during a dice game.

23:34b. The mockery described in v. 35 is here filled out with words drawn from Ps. 22:18, which features humiliation of the righteous sufferer. Gambling for the prisoner's garments would be especially humiliating to the helpless sufferer. Jesus is like the homeless demoniac of 8:27, naked in his loss of all status, even of the one granted in jest by Herod (23:11). In Jesus' case the implication would be ominously clear: his career as Messiah is at an end. But Luke's auditors know that full regalia await the One who a few years earlier had pronounced superfluous all the trappings of a tawdry greatness (4:5–8).

23:35. Although Israel is implicated in the crucifixion, Luke preserves **the people** from direct participation in the mockery. The people were watching (cf. Ps. 22:7), certainly from curiosity, but perhaps with some respect (cf. Luke 23:48). The rulers, that is, the hierarchy, engage in the mockery (cf. Pss. 22:7; 80:6).

An auditor to whom the dramas of Aischylos were familiar would recall the words of Strength addressed to Prometheus, bound fast to a rock:

> Now revel there in ignorance!
> Rob from the gods for mortals of a day?
> Then let these earthling darlings ease your pain!
> False is the name the Gods have given you:
> INGENIOUS CONTRIVER. Ha!
> These bonds will test your skill.
> (*Prometheus Bound* 82–87)

Unwittingly the mockers reproduce aspects of the temptations recorded at Luke 4:1–13, 23, as well as features of the announcement made to the shepherds (cf. 2:11). Typical of the misunderstanding that Jesus encounters throughout his trial and suffering is the suggestion that he save himself if he is indeed the **Christ of God.** But they are ignorant of the fact that he who cautioned his own disciples about losing their life while attempting to preserve it (9:24) could not violate his own instruction, for he was among them as one who rendered service, the only route to greatness (22:27). Their further description, **Chosen One**, recalls the identification made by the voice from heaven at 9:35 (cf. Isa. 42:1). Implication: of what quality is the faith of him who called others to faith if he remains unrescued?

23:36. Soldiers now enter the act. Mark had earlier introduced them into his narrative (Mark 15:16–20). Luke reserves the recital of their mockery for this moment, since their horseplay related to Jesus as a royal figure. The honorable vocation of soldiery, whose duty is to maintain security and protect the weak against misuse of power, is smirched by these buffoons. Police brutality has a long pedigree. As the construction of the sentence reveals, Luke interprets their offer of very poor wine (*oxos;* RSV: **vinegar**) as a jest (cf. Ps. 69:21).

23:37–38. Satan had offered Jesus the kingdoms of the world (4:5–7). The soldiers now challenge Jesus to demonstrate his kingship by saving himself. They are stimulated by a description of the crime affixed above the victim's head. The wording itself is meant to be a jest: "The King of the Jews is This One," with the word "This" (*houtos;* cf. 23:2, 18) written contemptuously. For Luke this is of course a high point in his narrative. Jesus *is* the King of the Jews. His only crime was to be what he truly is, and the cross is the place of his enthronement, for greatness is won through renunciation of self.

Long Live the King

Luke 23:39–43
(Mark 15:32b; Matthew 27:44)

23:39. Luke is now prepared for his climactic definition of the Kingdom. One of the malefactors utters the third temptation. Jesus ought "to save" himself and the two hanging beside him. Again it is a misunderstanding. Jesus cannot do both. If the Messiah (**Christ**) is to be a benefactor who seeks and saves the lost (19:10), he cannot save himself, for it was his association with publicans and sinners that brought him into disrepute.

23:40. One of the malefactors expresses Luke's theology. Fear of God ought to prompt the other to ponder more deeply his fate. As at 13:1–9, superficial appraisal of circumstances is here put under critique. Also, the outlaw practices what Jesus enjoined at 17:3.

23:41. As a "hanged" (v. 39) malefactor, the recipient of the rebuke ought to know that a curse rests on him (cf. Gal. 3:13, a quotation of Deut. 21:23). Yet he shares the same fate with Jesus. But Jesus is innocent, while he and the other are guilty (cf. 2 Macc. 7:18). Jesus has not left his assigned path (**has done nothing wrong**, *ouden atopon*).

The malefactor's word **this man** *(houtos)* echoes the jest in the title. If Jesus suffers in this way, how fearful a thing it must be for a guilty person to fall into the hands of the living God! (Cf. 1 Pet. 4:17–18; Prov. 11:31 LXX.) The words are, of course, a reminder to the Israel of Luke's time to reevaluate her rejection of the King. Not one of Luke's auditors who had any Hellenic sensibility could fail to project into this text a story line from ancient Greece and hear the footpads of the Erinyes, those dread avengers of transgression. Coming from a condemned person aware of his wrongdoing *(kai hemeis men dikaiōs)*, the words are an exceptionally forceful declaration of Jesus' uprightness.

23:42. He now addresses the King, beginning with the name assigned by the angel (1:31; cf. 2:21). According to the angel's word, the Deliverer was to be called Jesus, and he would "reign over the house of Jacob forever." Through the malefactor's words Luke in effect endorses this association, introduces one of the most dramatic moments in this Gospel, and anticipates the declaration about the One Name at Acts 4:12.

Jesus, remember me when you come into your kingdom. The Kingdom does not come with "signs to be observed," said Jesus (17:20). And some would not taste death until they see the Kingdom of God (9:27). This man affirms the truth in an astounding demonstration of faith. It is to be recalled that at 2:11 the name Jesus is defined as Christ and Lord.

23:43. In answer to the indeterminate "when," Jesus answers with a solemn oathlike Amen, saying: **Truly** *(amēn)*, **I say to you, today you will be with me in Paradise.** To see such a future in an hour when others see no hope identifies Jesus not only as a true Jew but as one who is committed with total abandonment to his Father's purpose.

The word "today" *(sēmeron)* carries most of the weight. Not in some apocalyptic future, but in this hour the Son of humanity is to be affirmed in his reign, and one malefactor is "taken and the other left" (cf. 17:35). This "today" is the climax of many "todays" (cf. 2:11; 3:22; 4:21; 5:26; 13:32, 33; 22:34, 61), and especially of the encounter with Zacchaeus (19:5, 9). The malefactor will be "with Jesus" the Great Benefactor (cf. Phil. 1:23). This is the characteristic mark of Jesus' kingly activity—association with the lost. Jesus could have preserved some reputation for piety by an eleventh-hour reversal of his patronage of sinners. But he defies the expectations of unimaginative moralists and to the end affirms his mission to publicans and sinners. For of such is the Kingdom of God (cf. 7:28). The unknown malefactor will enjoy the most intimate association, for he will be with Jesus "in Paradise." He is taken and the other left (see on v. 33); one rises and another falls (cf. 2:34). So eloquently brief is also Luke's commentary on the search stories of chap. 15, whose thematic connection with the story of the repentant malefactor was noted in English literature first by Geoffrey Chaucer ("The Parson's Tale," 700–705).

"Paradise" (cf. 2 Cor. 12:3; Rev. 2:7) is a singularly appropriate word in the context. Its ordinary meaning is "garden" or "park" such as a king would have at his disposal (cf. 2 Chron. 33:20 LXX). The word appears frequently in Xenophon's descriptions of the royal properties located in Persia. To be with the king in his private gardens was an indication of singular status. In the intertestamental period the term was used of the realm reserved after death for the righteous (*Test. Levi* 18:10).

Luke's choice of the word "paradise" climaxes his interpretation of the Kingdom and explains the promise made at 22:29–30. Since the mention of paradise would bring to mind Adam's original home (see Gen. 2:8), recollection of Luke's association of Jesus with Adam in the genealogy (see Luke 3:38) would easily be made.

Luke brings his instruction on the Kingdom to full expression in the dialogue between the malefactor and Jesus, who is here recognized as the Great Benefactor who can dispense royal favors to the penitent. This is Luke's way of expressing how and why forgiveness takes place. Those who prefer Paul's more intricate approach to the divine mysteries will charge Luke with oversimplification. It is an irrelevant criticism. Nor does Luke's soteriology need shoring up from other parts of the canon. He does not use sacrificial terminology, and such imagery should not be imported into his presentation of the meaning of Jesus' passion and death. Jesus is King, for he is the obedient Son of God. And the genes show. His death is part of God's munificent permissive providence, and as God's viceroy Jesus issues a pardon that requires no legal rationale for validation. Such exercise of executive privilege is the ultimate in expression of saving action. So have emperors, kings, and presidents ever done. But Jesus did it in a moment when he was stripped of all the insignia of office (see on vv. 11 and 34).

Return to the Father

Luke 23:44–49
(Mark 15:33, 37–41; Matthew 27:45, 50–51, 54–56)

23:44–45. The final coming of the Son of humanity was earlier associated with cosmic disturbances (21:27). But repeatedly it had been affirmed that the Son of humanity must suffer and die (9:22, 44; 17:25). Luke's record of the darkness and the rending of the curtain therefore alerts auditors to the fact that in the moment of his deepest humiliation Jesus is indeed the victorious Son of humanity.

In his present enthronement, depicted by the dialogue between Jesus and the malefactor, the statement made before the Sanhedrin concerning the session of the Son of humanity at the right hand of God comes to fulfillment (22:29). Yet Luke does not follow the pattern of contemporary apocalyptic thinking and does not deviate from his implicit protest against the demand for signs. In keeping with his approach to the question of Elijah's role in events of the end time, Luke omits reference to Elijah (see, on the other hand, Mark 15:36).

The chief priests might have been impressed had Jesus made a spectacular descent from the cross as the darkness engulfed them. Luke rather follows the pattern set by ancient writers concerning people of exceptional merit, some of whom were rewarded with immortality. Aristophanes reports that the sun was darkened at the death of Aischylos, and a like phenomenon is recorded for the death of Alexander the Great (see BAGD, p. 757). During the first games that Augustus put on in honor of Julius Caesar's deification, a comet was visible for seven nights (Suetonius *Divine Julius* 88). Lucan depicts the encounter of Pompey and Caesar at Pharsalia as an event of cosmic interest, when the "sorrowing deity in heaven gave notice of the battle by the dimness and obscurity of the sun" (*Civil War* 7.199–200).

Some of Luke's auditors might well have caught an even more confirmatory note. The death of Jesus is one of three stages through which he accomplishes his destiny. Resurrection and ascension are to follow. In his *Metamorphoses* (14.815–16), Ovid shows Jupiter affirming the right of Romulus to ascend to the heavenly regions by obscuring the sky with dark clouds and terrifying the earth with thunder and lightning (for similar positive confirmation, see Pindar *Pythian Odes* 4.198–200).

Despite the fact that an eclipse is impossible at the time of the full moon, Luke employs the normal language used to describe an eclipse in v. 45 *(tou hēliou eklipontos)*. The debate concerning Luke's accuracy is similar to questions that have been raised about Horace's reference to a thunderclap in a clear sky (*Odes* 1.34.7), a phenomenon denied by Epicurus (6.99, 246–48, 400–401). Such rationalistic reading of Luke's text violates the main interest: the arrival of an exceptional moment in history and the death of an extraordinary personage are accompanied by unusual portents. At Acts 2:20, with its citation of Joel 2:31, Luke's auditors will find a further port of entry into the significance of this day that was a night.

The second portent is the rending of **the curtain of the temple.** Which of the numerous curtains that hung in the temple is the referent cannot be determined with certainty, but from a linguistic perspective it is probable that Luke refers to the one that would be most generally visible, the one hanging before the "holy place," and of which Josephus gives a detailed description (*War* 5.5.4).

Luke's public would receive a double message. In view of the prophecy uttered in 21:20–24 some would consider this the first installment of the destruction to overtake Jerusalem (cf. 21:20; 23:28–31). Israel had asked for a sign. Herod had demanded signs. All will get more than they bargained for. To others in Luke's publics the portent would suggest the radicality of the New Age. The people of God were authorized by the events at the crucifixion of Jesus to get along without traditional liturgical and bureaucratic structures. This change meant that Jews and gentiles could relate to one another in Christian communities without reference to standardized cultic practice. To be freed for creative expression and exploration of new ways to experience meaningful relationships with God and other people is itself part of the New Age salvation. The presence of Jesus is the measure and determinant of all Christian cultic practice.

23:46. Those among Luke's auditors who were especially familiar with the prophets of Israel would probably have thought of Amos 8, which celebrates God's concern for the poor and the oppressed with a display of special cosmic effects. The enemies of Jesus had sought the cover of darkness for their evil deed (22:53). Now they have darkness in full measure! But through it and the other portents God verifies the credentials of their victim and refutes the criticism that some had made of Jesus as being "a glutton and a drunkard" (7:34).

In contrast to the customary maledictions hurled at their tormentors by crucified evildoers, and in contrast to the curses expressed, for example, in Psalm 69, Jesus closes his ministry to humanity with a peaceful prayer from Ps. 31:5. This psalm sings of scorn heaped on the sufferer but also of confident trust in the Lord who delivers the faithful out of the hands of their enemies. At twelve years of age Jesus had affirmed his loyalty to his Parent (2:44). Faithful and pious to the end, Jesus grants total power of attorney as he entrusts his "spirit" *(pneuma)* to that same Parent for safekeeping (cf. Acts 7:59; Wisd. of Sol. 2:16). Some of Luke's public would more readily grasp the evangelist's artistic perception as they pondered the connections between this affirmation of fidelity, the declaration of commitment in 2:49, and the mockery at v. 35. And some among them must have found their appreciation enhanced by recalling that Vergil's Aeneas through the embrace of his mother Venus won the boon of crossing the barrier that separates the world of deity from that of mere mortals *(Aeneid* 8.615).

Significant is Luke's elimination of Mark's reference to the cry of dereliction (Mark 15:34). In Mark, the cry accents the moment when Satan apparently attempts to discredit Jesus through a lament that suggests God's rejection of one who is viewed by the mockers as a lawless person. Jesus refutes the demon, implies Mark, and overcomes him with his last breath. Luke, who emphasizes Jesus' return to the Father, records instead the prayer of peace, whose p-sounds in the Greek suggest composure (contrast Luke 22:62). As the citation of Ps. 16:8 at Acts 2:25 attests, God never lets Jesus out of sight.

If Lazarus upon his death was in paradise and in Abraham's bosom, it is certainly true of Jesus, implies Luke. And it is from this perspective that Jesus could speak to the malefactor about "paradise now." Indeed, Jesus triumphantly rides the crest of Satan's last temptation, exemplified in the mockeries (see on 4:9–13), and is the Son of God as declared before the Sanhedrin (22:70). The Greek word for **breathed his last** is carefully chosen. Verbatim *exepneusen* means, "He gave out his spirit." None of the evangelists uses the expression "He died." To the end, Jesus is in full command. He terminates his life under orders (cf. 4:29–30; 13:31–33).

No one ever grasped more clearly than Luke the fate of the innovator face to face with partisan political realities. A Florentine bureaucrat succeeded only in expressing it tediously:

> The innovator has as enemies all those who fare well under the old order and has lukewarm defenders in all who hope to profit from the new. This lukewarmness derives partly from fear of the adversaries who have the law on their side and partly from the incredulity of people who refuse to place any credence in the new development until they experience it personally. Hence it is that the enemies attack the innovator at every opportunity that presents itself. And they do it with such partisan zeal that the defenders resist so halfheartedly that they expose themselves and their leader to great perils. . . . This is why all armed prophets win and all unarmed prophets lose. . . . For people are by nature fickle and it is easy to persuade them about something. But it is another matter to maintain them in that persuasion. (Niccolò Machiavelli, *Il Principe,* chap. 6)

Jesus, who renounced the way of armed might (Luke 4:5–8), had carefully counted the cost. He did not make the mistake of the ill-fated tower builder and miscalculating general (14:28–32) described in one of his sermons, but steered straight for that bastion which was impervious to all other force except the power of the New Age. Satan, who had boasted that the religious and political establishments were in his pocket (see Luke 4:5–7), would discover that the obedience expressed this day was to generate a force no power on earth or in hell could stop. With Jesus, God had bred a new beginning. For Jesus proved that living need not be in vain (see on 2:4).

23:47. To Greco-Roman auditors the manifestation of Jesus' piety would be impressive. From a purely literary perspective, the inclusion of this saying (v. 46a) by Jesus prepares the way for the centurion's verdict in v. 47.

Lucan said of the day of Pharsalia: "How great these men, of whom the world took note; all heaven was attentive to their fate" (*Civil War* 7.205–6). A similar emotion finds expression in the description of the centurion who **saw what had taken place.** The birth of Jesus elicited the praise of shepherds (2:20); a Roman centurion is driven to similar response by his death. And wonder of wonders, it is a security officer who seconds the verdict of a malefactor (v. 41) by saying, "Certainly this man was upright"* (*dikaios* [RSV: **innocent**])!

For a Jew, to be upright or righteous *(dikaios)* means to be in harmony with God's law. The chief priests could therefore argue that Jesus was under the wrath of God. But this centurion reads the proceedings differently. He is another of a long series of witnesses who on that day pronounced a verdict of "Not guilty" when he said: "This was a genuinely upright person *(dikaios)*!" (On this rendering, see *Benefactor,* p. 345.)

The centurion's affirmation of uprightness at the moment of Jesus' death is equivalent to saying: "In his last hour this man thought only of his duty." So had Polybios, in diction that echoed numerous inscriptions, described the naval commander Margos at his death as one who had "fulfilled all his obligations *(panta ta dikaia)* to the common cause" (2.10.5). And he praised the illustrious soldier Lucius Aemilius as one who had "served his country to the utmost *(panta ta dikaia)*" in his dying moments (3.116.9).

Four centuries earlier, Plato *(Republic* 361e–362a) had one of his participants in dialogue speak as follows about the fate of a truly upright person: "One who is such will be scourged, be tortured on the rack, be bound, be blinded in both eyes, and finally, after suffering all this, be crucified." Jesus more than met Plato's definition of one who preferred to *be* upright *(dikaios)* rather than have merely a *reputation* for uprightness.

Jerusalem, for all her vaunted boast in the Law, is clearly in the wrong (cf. Acts 3:14; 7:52; 22:14). To Romans, uprightness was one of the principal marks of the national character, and Rome had likewise nothing to be proud of on this day. But the centurion salvages a bit of honor for his city with his reversal of a superior's judgment. It remains for the apostolic mission to echo his verdict throughout the world: "This man was in the right" (on the further use of *dikaios* in Acts, see 3:14; 7:52; 22:14).

Some of Luke's miracle stories end on a note of glorification (e.g., Luke 5:25; 7:16; 13:13; 17:15; 18:43; Acts 4:21). To Greco-Roman auditors, God's deed in Jesus Christ would be the supreme benefaction, and the centurion would be heard as describing Jesus in the manner of accolades for men and women of exceptional merit.

The RSV's rendering of *dikaios* as "innocent" does justice neither to the social-cultural context of Luke's narrative nor to his use of Psalms 22; 31; 38; and 69 in his depiction of Jesus as the upright sufferer. In his *Res Gestae,* Caesar Augustus notes that the Roman people recognized him with special honors because of his "piety and uprightness." (Latin text: *justitia, pietas;* Greek text: *dikaiosynē, eusebeia.*) This same combination appears in Luke's recital. Coupled with the affirmation of piety in v. 46 and with the special effects that accompanied the death of Jesus, the centurion's appraisal attests that Jesus is not to be measured by the traditional criteria that were sponsored by Caiaphas and associates.

Only one other centurion is mentioned in Luke's Gospel (7:2, 6). Of the latter, Jesus had said, "I tell you, not even in Israel have I found such faith" (7:9). The centurion at the cross was of that breed. Mark records a more explicit identification of Jesus as the Son of God (Mark 15:39). Luke attaches more importance to the Roman's appraisal of Jesus' true identity and takes care of the divine association in his record of Jesus' last prayer (Luke 23:46). It only remains for God to give the award to Jesus for his uprightness.

In the moment of ultimate conflict all the insults, lies, innuendos, pretexts, and evasions of Jesus' enemies proved useless. His unique individuality differentiated him from all that had ever lived on the face of the earth and demanded fresh definitions for what humanity had hitherto understood by defeat and victory. "Nice guys finish last," wrote a Hebrew poet (see Eccl. 8:14); it was another cliché for which Jesus again would find a refutation.

23:48. The crowds came to gawk and went home to pray. Luke's juxtaposition of the centurion's verdict and this response of the crowd reinforces his theme of repentance in the face of coming judgment. Like the publican in the temple (18:13), they beat **their breasts** in confrontation with the ghastly wrong done that day. In ordinary circumstances they would have been wailing. The description, stimulated perhaps by Zech. 12:10–14, is part of Luke's pronouncement of hope for Israel (cf. Luke 23:27–31). A criminal had secured executive pardon (v. 43). Israel will soon hear the apostolic absolution (Acts 2:36–39).

23:49. In contrast to the centurion and the crowds who now display some understanding, all of the male acquaintances of Jesus stood at a distance (cf. Ps. 38:11; 88:8; Luke 22:54). They treat him as a pariah, one to be shunned; and a man who is not even a relative must attend to his burial (v. 23:50). The women are mentioned almost as a separate group. They had been previously identified at 8:2–3, and Luke emphasizes that they **saw these things.** (The RSV obscures this point by making **all his acquaintances** part of the subject of the verb "saw" when in fact it is only the subject of **stood at a distance.**) As the primary witnesses from Galilee, these women are to play a leading role in the narrative of the resurrected Lord (see 23:55–56; 24:1–11). Only after his resurrection will the disciples and the women be able to endorse the verdict of the centurion and thus be witnesses to the world (24:47–48).

THE BURIAL OF JESUS
Luke 23:50–56
(Mark 15:42–43, 46–47; 16:1; Matthew 27:57–61)

23:50–51. The story of the burial is of such significance to Luke that he introduces it with "Behold" (omitted by the RSV). No relatives or disciples came forward to do the last honors, but Joseph of Arimathea had the nerve to do so. Joseph was a member of the Sanhedrin (**the council**). Like Zechariah and Elizabeth (1:6) and Simeon (2:25), he was *dikaios,* a **right-**

eous man (the adjective describes the excellence of his character and his fairness). The adjective **good** *(agathos)* emphasizes that he was known for his generosity.

Jewish auditors would be impressed by Joseph's reputation for upholding the Law of Israel and would therefore find his support of Jesus a climactic endorsement of his uprightness and innocence. To Greco-Roman auditors, accustomed as they were to laudations bestowed on judges who tried cases with equity, the combination of terms would suggest that Joseph is a person of exceptional excellence and merit. Since "Joseph" was such a common name, Luke cannot avoid mentioning his hometown **Arimathea**, but as a courtesy to his various publics he notes that it was a **Jewish town.**

Since Luke's use of the adjective "all" is part of his editorial vocabulary, it is inappropriate to see a contradiction between the statement in v. 51a and the apparently unanimous decision expressed at 22:70 (cf. 23:1).

Simeon anticipated the consolation of Israel (2:25), and Hannah (Anna) had spoken to those who were awaiting the redemption of Jerusalem (2:38). Joseph of Arimathea, who **was looking for the kingdom of God**, becomes in his person a forecast of the repentance of many in Israel (see Acts 6:7).

23:52. Yet Joseph does not hesitate to ask for the body of Jesus. Release of a crucified body could be secured only by special administrative action. Had Jesus been the anti-Roman revolutionary claimed by the hierarchy, Joseph would never have dared to make his request. Most carefully, Luke informs his own jury that Pilate never changed his mind about the character of Jesus. At the same time, he notes that the Kingdom is intimately associated with the fate of this body (cf. 22:18–19; 24:21–26). Whether Joseph himself considered Jesus to be the Messiah is not stated.

23:53. The reverence with which Joseph handles the body of Jesus contrasts against the earlier background of cruelty and mockery. Limited by time, for the sabbath is approaching, Joseph does the best he can. The ritual uncleanness incurred by his contact with the dead could be removed in the evening (cf. Lev. 22:4–7). Perhaps to avoid unnecessary objections from his colleagues, Joseph lays the body in a tomb **where no one had ever yet been laid** (cf. 19:30). Burial chambers would be considered contaminated by the body of one whom the detractors of Jesus would view as a criminal. But the fact is that we have no data on Joseph's motive. So far as Luke is concerned, the precaution was fortuitous, for great weight is to be attached in the community to the fact that Jesus died and was buried (1 Cor. 15:3–4). There is to be no doubt as to the identity of the one who comes out of that grave, and Luke underlines his description with three firm negatives. Nor is negligible the observation that it was **a rock-hewn tomb.** Thereby Luke's public is informed that the body is in a secure place and in the same breath is prepared for the information that a stone had been rolled in place at the entrance (24:2).

23:54. To allow more time for the preparations made by Joseph, Luke transfers Mark's note concerning the lateness of the hour (Mark 15:42) to the end of his story of the burial. **The sabbath** was about to begin on the evening of Friday, the day of Preparation for the sabbath. (In John 19:14 the day of Preparation is the day on which the Passover lamb was slain; cf. John 19:31, 42.)

23:55–56. Luke's arrangement of the narrative also allows a little time for the women to prepare spices, and he is at pains to note that **on the sabbath they rested according to the commandment.** Jesus did not teach his disciples disrespect of rules and regulations, when they did not interfere with human rights and well-being. In Mark, the women make their purchases on the morning following the sabbath (16:1). Luke emphasizes the careful observation of the women in order to establish the veracity of their later identification of the resurrected Lord. They **saw the tomb, and how his body was laid.** Thus they are witnesses of his death and burial, and shortly of the resurrected Lord, the triple ingredient of much apostolic proclamation (cf. Acts 2:22–36; 1 Cor. 15:3–4).

After a long series of episodes displaying many varieties of cowardice on the part of males, Luke must have found refreshing the courageous bearing of these followers who were stronger than their male counterparts. Certainly some of his Greco-Roman auditors must have recalled the brave Antigone, who defied Kreon, king of Thebes, and contrived to bury the body of her brother Polyneikes.

PART SEVEN: THE
EXALTED LORD

None of the Gospels records an account of the resurrection of Jesus such as we have in the apocryphal *Gospel of Peter* 35–42. The evangelists do relate the finding of an empty tomb and appearances of the risen Lord. Because of the numerous theological problems associated with the arrest and death of Jesus, and because of the pedagogical significance of his death for the faith and life of the People of God, the evangelists use more space for the telling of that story than they do for the narrative concerning the resurrected Lord. Luke's own recitation of the latter is the final preparation of his public for understanding the Lord's direction of the apostolic mission as recorded in the Book of Acts. The Endangered Benefactor is confirmed as the One Name.

EXPERIENCE OF THE WOMEN
Luke 24:1–11
(Mark 16:1–2, 4–8; Matthew 28:1, 5–8)

24:1. The women from Galilee (23:55) have scrupulously observed the sabbath period (see Exod. 20:10; Deut. 5:12–15) and proceed as early as the Law permitted to carry out their intention of anointing the body.

24:2–3. Luke contrasts the discovery they made (**the stone rolled away**) against the discovery they failed to make (**the body**). Whether the RSV's marginal reading "of the Lord Jesus" is to be retained in the text cannot be determined with complete confidence. The phrase is used in the Book of Acts (Acts 1:21; 4:33; 8:16) but is not necessary here, for the evangelist can make his point without it. His public knows that the body which was placed in the tomb is that of Jesus. And that body is not there!

24:4. In this time of their distress, **behold, two men stood by them.** The language is strikingly similar to that of 9:30. Luke had prefaced his account of the transfiguration with statements about the Son of humanity. He was to come in the glory of his Father and the holy angels. And there would be some who would not die before they had seen the Kingdom of

God. The transfiguration was not the inauguration of the Kingdom but a preparation for the understanding of the suffering of Jesus. Now, after his suffering, the glory with which he is to return has begun (cf. 24:26), and the women are among those who see the Kingdom of God.

As in the earlier account, two men—perhaps some thought of Moses and Elijah—make a glorious appearance (cf. Acts 1:10). But there is a difference. In the account of the transfiguration, Jesus has dazzling raiment, and Moses and Elijah appear with him "in glory" (Luke 9:31). Here the two men wear **dazzling apparel.** Thus the glory of Jesus receives only an indirect confirmation. That they are construed as heavenly messengers is apparent from v. 23.

Throughout the account of the appearances recorded in chap. 24, Luke adheres to his eschatological instruction. Jesus never appears in glorious fashion. That is to be reserved for his final coming (21:27). On the other hand, Luke took pains to associate the resurrection with the transfiguration in order to emphasize that the Kingdom is present reality even though the popular apocalyptic expectation is not satisfied. The word for **stood by** is used, among other passages, in 2:9 and 21:34 (cf. Acts 12:7; 23:11). In 2:9 it is rendered "appeared," in a context describing the glory of the Lord. The announcement to the shepherds affirmed that God's glory could be apparent in association with even so unspectacular an event as the placement of the newly born Messiah in a manger. Similarly the glory of God transforms a tomb into a throne room. In the second passage, 21:34, the word is used of the last day (cf. 1 Thess. 5:3).

24:5. The reaction of the women is typical of Daniel's responses to special revelations (Dan. 7:28; 10:9, 15). Through his careful use of apocalyptic type of language in this and the preceding verse Luke prepares his auditors for the pronouncement at v. 7 on the destiny of the Son of humanity. The question is a word of rebuke. If the women had listened to the words of Jesus, they would know that the tomb is not the place to look for him. New manuscript evidence since the first publication of the RSV suggests that the marginal reading "He is not here, but has risen," formerly regarded as borrowed by copyists from Matt. 28:6 (cf. Mark 16:6), is to be retained in the text. In view of Luke's emphasis in the Book of Acts on God's role in the resurrection of Jesus it is best (with Fitzmyer) to render the phrase: "He is not here. He has been raised" (Acts 3:15; 4:10; 5:30; 10:40; 13:30, 37).

24:6. Mark 16:7 records that the women were to announce to the disciples and Peter that Jesus had gone on ahead of them to **Galilee.** Since Jerusalem is the center of activity at the beginning and the end of his Gospel, and since the good news is to proceed from Jerusalem (Luke 24:47; Acts 1:8), Luke concentrates appearances of the risen Lord in Jerusalem. Therefore, instead of giving them a message, the two men remind the women of what Jesus had **told** them **while he was still** [with them] **in Galilee.**

24:7. Verse 7 reproduces the content of words recited at 9:22, 44; 17:25; 18:32–33. The last of these passages was addressed only to the Twelve and includes specific information not found in the earlier prophecies, namely, that Jesus "must be handed over" to the gentiles, who are here termed **sinful men.** The reference to crucifixion is a clearer description of the type of death Jesus was to undergo. This sentence is therefore of interest also as an example of the modification that a saying by Jesus might undergo in the course of transmission of the gospel.

Modern readers may be struck by the fact that Luke submits no proof of the resurrection based on the emptiness of the tomb, on remarkable signs following the resurrection (cf. Matt. 28:2–4), or even on appearances of the Lord. We ask whether a dead man can actually come alive out of a grave. Luke is more concerned about the identity of the one who came out of the grave. He must demonstrate that the resurrected Lord is Jesus! Hence the two men say explicitly that Jesus, while he was in Galilee, spoke to them of the fate of the "Son of humanity." Neither Matthew nor Mark includes a word about the Son of humanity in their accounts of the resurrected Lord. Luke considers the matter one of prime importance. Jesus said that the Son of humanity must suffer and die and then rise on the third day. The women had observed the death and burial of Jesus. Now they are confronted with the decision of faith, that God has actually reversed the verdict of those who were responsible for the crucifixion, itself a sign of apparent reprobation.

To Greco-Roman auditors, this emphasis on the fulfillment of Jesus' prophecy concerning his own destiny would have made a profound impression. It would have confirmed for them their impression of Jesus as a person of distinction, and one whom God has now immortalized because of his beneficence.

With the exception of Acts 7:56, this is Luke's last reference to Jesus as the Son of humanity. Henceforth his emphasis is on the identity of Jesus as the Christ (cf. Luke 24:26, 46 and often in Acts).

24:8–10. The women **remembered his words,** that is, they respond in faith, and rush to share the news with **the eleven** (Judas has decreased the number of the Twelve, cf. Acts 1:16–26), and **to all the rest** of the disciples.

Luke's rugged syntax in v. 9 troubled numerous copyists, but it appears that he endeavored to distinguish two groups of women in two separate acts of reporting, instead of one as in the RSV's rendering, so as to bring the apostles to the fore and emphasize that they were guilty of unbelief. The women who made the announcement (*apēigeilan,* v. 9) to the larger circle were Mary Magdalene, Joanna (cf. 8:2–3) and Mary the mother of James (perhaps the son of Alphaeus, cf. 6:15). The rest of the women, who were with these three, were reporting (*elegon,* imperfect tense) the news **to the apostles.** The term "apostles" is chosen specifically to stress the purpose for which the news is given, namely, for proclamation to the world (cf. vv. 47–49).

24:11. The apostles consider the report **an idle tale, and they did not believe** the women. Considering their own previous record of comprehension of Jesus' mission, this response was not only ungallant but foolish.

PETER'S UNBELIEF
Luke 24:12

24:12. Verse 12 is relegated to the margin by the RSV, but the content is important in view of the sequel and need not be considered an interpolation from John 20:3–10. Verse 24 says that other men had gone to the tomb, and v. 34 raises the question whether the Lord had appeared to Simon. Textual evidence for the inclusion of v. 12 is overwhelming. Of the women it was stated that they had observed only the absence of the body. Peter sees the "linen cloths" in which Jesus had been wrapped, and he goes off "wondering at what had happened."

Luke communicates here at two levels. Wonder is the standard reaction to a miracle, and the resurrection of Jesus is certainly to be classified as such. On the other hand, Peter's wonderment is not faith but its opposite. Like the rest who come under indictment at v. 41, Peter is guilty of unbelief. Clearly, evidence of the senses is not sufficient to help one grasp the reality of the resurrection of Jesus. Thus Luke prepares his auditors for the understanding that Jesus himself, through his exposition of the Scriptures, must be the teacher of the community (cf. vv. 32, 45). Well had Jesus said that unless Moses and the prophets were heeded, people would not believe (cf. 16:31), and that when the Son of humanity comes he will scarcely find faith on the earth (18:8).

TWO WITNESSES ON THE ROAD TO EMMAUS
Luke 24:13–32

24:13. Luke prefaces his most distinctive contribution to the Easter story with the words "And behold" (omitted by the RSV). The pronoun in the phrase **two of them** refers not to the apostles but to the larger circle of disciples. **That very day** underlines the fact that the events about to be recited took place on the third day specified at v. 7 (cf. v. 21). Once again **Jerusalem** is mentioned so that the auditor might not conclude that the first appearance of Jesus took place in Galilee. The precise location of the ancient village of Emmaus is not known. Modern Kulonieh, which lies in the direction of Joppa; or 'Amwas, near Latrun; and el-Qubeibeh, on the road to Lydda have been proposed.

24:14–15. The two disciples were not merely discussing what had happened but were "debating" with each other (cf. 22:23; Acts 6:9; 9:29). In this respect they are unlike the women, who simply reported what they had observed, and they need an umpire to resolve a disagreement that has been instigated by post-mortem inquiry, which in any case has never been known to bring a corpse back to life. At this moment **Jesus himself drew near.** The name is important, establishing the continuity between the Christ of faith and Jesus of Nazareth.

The verb "drew near" *(eggizō)* recalls the term used of the Kingdom of God (10:9, 11), of Jesus' earlier approach to Jerusalem (18:35; 19:29, 37, 41), and the apocalyptic redemption (21:28). The fact that he **went with them** suggests further the continuity between the activity of the resurrected Lord and his earthly ministry. He who was deserted by most of his acquaintances (23:49) does not abandon those whom he has chosen. Forgiveness is in process.

24:16. Despite the fact that it is Jesus himself, they do not recognize him. Luke's use of the passive verb, **were kept**, points to God as the agent. Similarly the disciples were kept from understanding Jesus' prophecy of his death (9:45; cf. 18:34), and the fate of Jerusalem was hidden from the eyes of her inhabitants (19:42). See also 2 Kings 6:15–20. Seeing Jesus after his resurrection is therefore more than a matter of ocular recognition. What the mind does not anticipate it does not believe, and in the absence of faith the eye is blind. Only Jesus, being filled with wisdom (2:40), was empowered in the opposite direction, and he will enlighten his followers.

24:17–18. Jesus inquires about the subject of discussion in this shooting war of words. In response the two men appear sullen. The RSV renders the Greek *skythrōpos* as "sad," but misses the point of this adjective, used only one other time in the NT (Matt. 6:16). It is the reaction of one who frowns indignantly, and the sarcasm in Cleopas's counterquestion explains the choice of the term: "You're putting us on. Every other visitor to Jerusalem knows what happened there, but you don't?" Little did they realize how right they were about his being a stranger in Jerusalem.

24:19. Jesus leads them on and asks, **What things?** Their reference to **Jesus of Nazareth** recalls 4:17–30. Well did they have cause, in view of the promises made at Nazareth, to anticipate the redemption of Israel (24:21). Writing for his Greek public, Luke phrases the first part of the description: "Who was a man, a prophet powerful in action and speech."* Jesus belongs to a class of people who deserve the highest respect and adulation.

People of speech and action were admired by the Greeks (cf. Thoukydides 1.139.4, of Perikles). The phrase is frequently found in descriptions of benefactors, especially those who are instruments of salvation to a beleaguered or oppressed city. At Acts 7:22 Moses is described as mighty in his words and deeds. Here the order is "deed" (cf. Luke 9:43; Acts 2:22) followed by "word" (cf. Luke 4:22, 36; 7:7). This is the sequence that Jesus recited in the instructions for John the Baptist (7:22), and Acts 1:1 picks up the theme. As Acts 10:38 affirms, Jesus is the Great Benefactor, who bestows his bounties on "all." The conjunction of "word and deed" is also applied to Paul in Acts 19:10–11. Paul uses the familiar formulation in a self-laudatory passage (Rom. 15:18) and in turn describes Christians as people who are to set excellence as their goal (Col. 3:17; 2 Thess. 2:17; on the theme and formulation, see *Benefactor*, pp. 339–43).

Jesus is a prophet greater than Moses. **Before God and all the people** (cf. 2:52) is a further testimony to the integrity of Jesus. The pandemic motif also echoes the message of the angels: "to all the people."

24:20. The phrase "all the people" of the previous verse contrasts with the chief priests and rulers, who cannot escape responsibility for the crucifixion.

24:21. The men do not deny the validity of their preceding description but complain that a further expectation of theirs (**But we had hoped** ...) is apparently not to be carried out, namely, the redemption of Israel. In Luke 1 and 2 this traditional nationalistic viewpoint finds expression (1:68, 74; 2:38; cf. 23:51; Acts 1:6).

The complaint made by the two disciples offers Luke opportunity to correct the traditional hope. Redemption indeed came for Israel, but the things that pertained to her peace were hidden from her eyes (Luke 19:42). Yet God will honor the divine word and Jesus will reign as successor to David through a worldwide mission (cf. 24:47; Acts 1:6–8, and see Isa. 11:10; Rom. 15:12). The men refer to **the third day** with a kind of expression of last hope fast fading away.

24:22–23. As their succeeding remarks show, the two men do not deny the possibility that Jesus may be alive. Their words about the women suggest how "two men" (24:4) easily become transformed into heavenly messengers (angels) in the course of tradition. They do not say that the women saw angels but that they had seen **a vision of angels.** And these angels asserted that Jesus was alive.

24:24. Some of the men from the circle of disciples also went to the tomb (cf. v. 12) and confirmed the report of the women, **but**—and this is the primary complaint—**him they did not see.**

Luke uses the dialogue and skepticism of these two men to sharpen the contrast between false expectations and apostolic instruction. Their comments also indicate that the disciples were not gullible and that the women did not make wild reports. Finally, it is to be observed, the empty grave did not awaken faith in the resurrection, but faith in the resurrection led to affirmation of the emptiness. But the chief purpose of the dialogue is to prepare the reader for the understanding that Jesus himself is the key to proper comprehension of the Scriptures.

24:25. Jesus criticizes the two men for not being quick enough **to believe all that the prophets have spoken.** The word "all" is important. They concentrated on the parts that promised deliverance for Israel (v. 21) and the prosperity of the golden Davidic age (cf. 1:32–33, 68–71) but overlooked the parts that spoke of the suffering experienced by God's chosen emissaries.

24–26. The phrase **was it not necessary** *(ouchi . . . edei)* repeats a dominant theme in the Gospel (cf. 2:49; 4:43; 9:22; 17:25; 19:5; 22:37). Not fate, but a Father's purpose watches over the destiny of **the Christ.** The latter term describes the Anointed One or the Messiah. Jesus says that one who would qualify for the office of Messiah must suffer and through that route **enter into his glory.** He himself was confident that God would deliver him, and God did (cf. Wisd. of Sol. 2:12–20). They should not expect to be able to see him, but they ought to believe in his victory over the opposition, for his resurrection was no improvisation wrought in disaster.

Worthy of special note is the fact that glory is here not associated with special apocalyptic effects, but with one who seems to be an ignorant tourist. His glorification began at the time of his suffering (22:69; 23:42–43); and, as Acts 14:22 teaches, disciples are not above their Lord in this matter. There is no concrete evidence for alleged expectation of a "suffering" Messiah in pre-Christian times. Luke's emphasis on the necessity of the suffering relates to the fact that God's representatives find no warm welcome. Acts 7 contains a résumé of the kind of treatment to which an emissary of God might be exposed and is also a sample of the kind of exposition used in the church to demonstrate the continuity between Jesus and the OT (see also Luke 22:37; cf. Deut. 18:15; Psalm 22; Isaiah 53).

24:27. With the phrase **concerning himself** Luke does not mean to say that Jesus called the attention of the two men to himself, but showed how the prophecies applied to the Jesus they had known.

24:28. The RSV rendering of the Greek, **he appeared to be going further**, is not quite accurate. Jesus "pretended to go on further" (cf. Mark 6:48; Job 9:11). Far from suggesting dishonesty on the part of Jesus, Luke indicates that Jesus longs to continue communication with these two disciples (cf. Rev. 3:20). But only those who desire his company will come to further realization of his identity.

24:29. As Lot did with two angels (Gen. 19:1–3), Cleopas and his friend urge their companion to accept the hospitality of their quarters. **The day is now far spent** (see on 9:12), and the reader would sense the tension. For the two men had said that it was now the third day (v. 21). They were not to be disappointed. Jesus **went in to stay with them** (cf. 19:5). Some of Luke's Greco-Roman auditors, familiar with the theme of the hero returning incognito, as in Homer's *Odyssey,* would be especially attentive to Luke's recital at this point.

24:30. The messianic banquet now takes place in their residence. Luke's recital in v. 30 does not reproduce the celebration of the Lord's Supper (note the absence of wine) but focuses primarily on the banquet scene in Luke 9. In chap. 9, Luke had associated the feeding of the five thousand (9:12–17) with the question of Jesus' messianic credentials and with the prophecy concerning the Son of humanity and his death and resurrection on the third day (9:18–22). As at the occasion of the feeding of the five thousand, the day is at its close, and the guests recline (9:14–15 "sit"; 24:30, **at table**). As on the earlier occasion, **he took the bread and blessed, and broke it, and gave it to** the disciples (cf. 9:16). These are the "signs" whereby the Hero is identified. In Homer's poem the stringing of the bow, which none of Penelope's suitors could muster, was the climactic moment.

24:31. Peter, after the feeding, had grasped something of the nature of Jesus' person and declared him to be the Christ (9:20). Here the eyes of the men are opened (cf. 24:16), and **they recognized** their guest, who had now become their host (cf. 5:27–32). Thus Luke affirms that the resurrection of Jesus is to be understood in terms of the fellowship he extends to the community, a fellowship that is in continuity with all his previous association with publicans and sinners, climaxing at the cross (cf. 23:43). It is not important that he is seen physically by the community. Therefore he vanishes **out of their sight** but remains visible to those whose eyes are opened. The language would be especially meaningful to Hellenistic readers who would associate the terminology with the return of gods or angels to the heavenly realms. (Wettstein cites Vergil *Aeneid* 9.656–58; see also 2 Macc. 3:34.) He has indeed entered into his glory (v. 26), that is, to be functioning in behalf of all humanity through the worldwide apostolic mission. If this is the case, the community need not be surprised that they do not see him. This is Luke's contribution to the problem of the resurrection.

24:32. After the disappearance of Jesus, the two men describe the great agitation (cf. Ps. 39:3) they had experienced while Jesus was interpreting **the**

scriptures (cf. 24:27: "all"). Their "burning hearts" is the first example of the fire that was to be cast down (12:49; cf. 3:26; Acts 2:3).

WITH THE ELEVEN AND OTHERS
Luke 24:33–43

24:33. The men lose no time in returning **to Jerusalem.** This news must be shared. They **found the eleven** and others who were associated with them (cf. v. 9) conversing about the events of the day.

24:34. Some were saying, "Has the Lord really risen?" Others asked, "Did he appear to Simon?" The latter perhaps was in allusion to the fact that Peter had only seen the grave cloths, not Jesus himself. The RSV, together with other versions and commentators, makes the verse a declarative statement, but then the subsequent verses (esp. v. 41) are incoherent, and vv. 11–12 are left suspended. If the statements are viewed as declarative, they are probably to be understood as confessional affirmations.

24:35. In response to the perplexity of the group, the two men recite their experiences. Their report falls into two parts: events **on the road** and recognition at **the breaking of the bread.** Thus the community is not dependent only on the personal witness of the two men, but primarily on the testimony of the Scriptures.

Reference to the breaking of bread is not incidental. The disciples are not to look for an extraordinary manifestation. Such anticipation can blind eyes to present reality. Not "Lo, there!" or "Lo, here!" Rather, "the kingdom of God is in the midst of you." So spoke Jesus (17:21). Through his continued reception of the poor and the outcast and those despised by an establishment that had forfeited its authority Jesus will show his continuing presence in the community (cf. Acts 4:23–31). This is in harmony with God's promise spoken through the prophet Ezekiel: "My dwelling place shall be with them; and I will be their God, and they shall be my people" (Ezek. 37:27). Especially significant is that prophet's prior statement: "My servant David shall be king over them" (37:24). God dwells with Israel through King David. Luke affirms that the Kingdom is reality in him who was crucified as the King of the Jews, and the resurrected Lord is this same Jesus who called sinners to his banquets.

24:36. Jesus himself now ratifies the words spoken by the two disciples. Before his death he had said: "I am among you as one who serves" (22:27). Now again he stands **among them,** the same one they had known before.

24:37. The language, like that of v. 5, contains apocalyptic overtones.

24:38. Why are you troubled? asks Jesus. Only once before was this description used in this Gospel, namely, of Zechariah at the appearance of the angel (1:12). Thus Luke again affirms that Jesus is indeed "in glory" but that this glory is possible without special apocalyptic effects. Moreover, his presence ought to be a consolation, not a source of fear (cf. 2:10). He comes to share his fellowship, not to destroy them in judgment.

Their **questionings** (dialogismoi), left unexpressed, are known to the Lord. They had experienced his penetrating understanding on an earlier occasion shortly after his second prediction of his suffering and death. At that time also they were ignorant of his meaning and were fearful (9:45), and they climaxed their misunderstanding with questions about greatness (v. 46). In their present stance they are like the opposition (cf. 5:22; 6:8). Jesus himself is the sign who was to be spoken against "in order that the questionings out of many hearts might be revealed" (2:35*). But the disciples ought to be the last to require such exposure, especially since they, like the women, have received the testimony of two witnesses (cf. Deut. 19:15).

24:39. Whether in the case of Jesus both his hands and feet were nailed to the cross cannot be affirmed with certainty, for procedures at executions varied. Nor is the point an issue in Luke's account. Attention is called to the hands and feet in order to establish the fact that the person they see before them is a genuine human being. Against false teachers who denied that Christ was really a human being, Luke affirms his corporeality. But recognition of corporeality does not necessarily spell faith. The disciples might have seen a genuine human being, but why did they not conclude that it was John the Baptist, to cite but one possibility (see Luke 9:19)? A further identification is therefore added: **It is I myself** (egō eimi autos).

Embedded in this phrase are the words "I am" (egō eimi). Jesus had warned that many would come and say "I am" (21:8), but only Jesus, who before the Sanhedrin himself affirmed "I am" (22:70), is the legitimate Messiah. This reply by Jesus is therefore strong christological affirmation and is accompanied by the directive, **Handle me**. The resurrected Lord is not a spirit, for he has all the components of a genuine body. Whatever metaphysical questions this passage may generate, the principal truth is that bogus prophets do not have nailprints.

24:40. Verse 40, assigned by the RSV to the margin, need not necessarily be considered a copyist's interpolation, notwithstanding its conformity to John 20:20 and apparent redundancy after v. 39.

24:41. Despite Jesus' words and demonstrations, the disciples still lack the faith to grasp what has happened. But Luke excuses them somewhat with the qualification that they **disbelieved for joy** (cf. Acts 12:14). It was a "sudden happiness beyond all hope." If what they hoped for turned out to be a dream, of all people they would indeed have been most miserable (cf. 1 Cor. 15:19). Those among Luke's auditors who were acquainted with Livy's recital of disastrous losses in the battle at Trasimeno (217 B.C.E.) might well have recalled that historian's account about matrons grieving for their husbands or sons. One died in her son's embrace after he had made a sudden appearance at the door. Another, after receiving a report of her son's death, was deep in grief, but at the sight of his return "died from too much joy" (Livy *History* 22.7.13).

24:42–43. The unbelief of the disciples helps motivate the final demonstration. In the presence of the company Jesus eats a piece of **broiled fish.** Acts 1:11 will similarly stress the corporeal nature of Jesus.

A comparison of the foregoing recital (vv. 36–43) with Mark 6:45–52 suggests that Luke omitted Mark's story at 9:17 so as to give force to its main features at the end of his Gospel. Mark locates the event at *evening;* Jesus appears as one who intends to *go past* the crew in the boat; the disciples think they see a *ghost;* and are greatly *troubled;* Jesus identifies himself with the words *I am;* and the disciples respond with further *astonishment.* All these italicized items appear in Luke 24:28–29, 37–41. In the account of the resurrected Lord the christological and apocalyptic issues raised in Mark's account are pertinent. Earlier Luke had concentrated these themes in the recital of the transfiguration (9:28–36). Mark's episode would therefore have been superfluous at that point.

PARTING WORDS AND ASCENSION
Luke 24:44–53

24:44. Having established his physical presence among them, Jesus now proceeds to affirm the continuity between his former words and subsequent experience. He identifies himself as the person to whom **the law of Moses and the prophets and the psalms** apply. To search for specific references to a Davidic figure or a suffering Messiah in each of these portions is to miss the point. All of Luke's specific and allusive use of the OT illustrates what he means in this passage. From Luke's perspective, the OT prewrites what the People of God in the New Age confess concerning Jesus Christ.

This appeal to such ancient writings would impress Luke's Greco-Roman public. Much of the respect enjoyed by Jews in the Roman world is traceable to their possession of such venerable documents. Appeal to these same documents was to some extent responsible for offering early Christians some opportunity to share in the liberal policies that Rome displayed toward Jews. The Book of Acts shows that some Jews aimed at discrediting followers of Jesus on this score.

24:45. The two disciples found their eyes opened (v. 31) at the breaking of bread. Now the rest of the company have **their minds** opened **to understand the scriptures.**

24:46. Once again Jesus speaks of **the Christ** in the third person (cf. v. 26). The form is similar to that used in sayings about the Son of humanity, and in neither case does the objective type of statement mean that the speaker is to be dissociated from the person described. Since this is the third recital in this chapter concerning the necessity of suffering and resurrection (cf. vv. 7 and 26), it is apparent that Luke attaches great weight to its content. Especially important is the phrase **the third day** (cf. 2:46; 9:22; 18:33; Acts 10:40). The story of the two men on the road to Emmaus confirmed that this was indeed the third day since the suffering had taken place. Christians, therefore, need not await a revelation of the Lord at some future time to validate the credentials of Jesus. He is validated on the third day and now assumes direction of his new community.

24:47. Repentance and forgiveness of sins should be preached in his name to all nations. These words echo 4:18 and constitute the *inference* to which one ought to be led by a proper study of the Scriptures, for no passage in the OT states this in so many words. But Jesus says, **Thus it is written.** That is, this is what the Scriptures have in mind, or this was their tenor. And the disciples are to begin **from Jerusalem.** Jerusalem was to hear the consolation of the Servant of the Lord (Isaiah 61).

To begin with Jerusalem means that the prophetic priority is recognized and that Jerusalem has opportunity to find forgiveness for crucifying the Messiah (Acts 2:22–40; 3:12–26; 10:42–43). They will have the chance to echo the words of Wisd. of Sol. 5:4–6 and thereby repudiate the folly exhibited at the crucifixion (see on 23:35):

> This was the one whom we made the butt of our ridicule
> and a byword of reproach. What fools we were!
> We thought his way of life was insane,
>   and the manner of his death without honor.
> How could he possibly be numbered among God's children,
> we asked, and his inheritance among the holy?
> It is obvious! We are the ones who went astray.
> The lamp of uprightness did not direct our paths,
> and the sun did not shine for us.*

The gentiles are included in the prophetic scope, for Israel is to be the light to the nations (cf. Isa. 42:6; 49:6; Luke 2:32). Jesus, in short, is the Great Benefactor who brings salvation to all who are repentant.

24:48. The disciples are not initiators of a new program. They are not developers of propaganda. Rather, they are witnesses (cf. Acts 1:8, 22; 2:32; 3:15; 5:32; 10:37–43) to God's own intentions including the beginning from

Jerusalem, expressed in the Scriptures. A witness is one who attests to truth and performance. Greco-Roman auditors would understand that the disciples are witnesses to a Person of exceptional merit. These disciples, who have observed Jesus' life and death and now his resurrected presence, are singularly equipped to testify to the truth of the Scriptures, for the latter have come to fulfillment (v. 44) in the person of Jesus. All is to be done "in his name" (v. 47).

An angel had proclaimed Jesus as the Christ (2:11). Jesus warned that many would come "in my name" saying "I am he!" and "The time is at hand!" (21:8). But there is only one name by which the Christ is to be identified—Jesus (1:31; 2:21), the sign that was spoken against (2:34). And in connection with his name, repentance and forgiveness, not apocalyptic speculation or nationalistic hope, is to be preached.

24:49. With a final **behold** Jesus says, **I send the promise of my Father upon you.** "Whoever receives me receives him who sent me," said Jesus (9:48). The sender is the heavenly Parent of Jesus, specifically called **my Father.** Gabriel had announced that Jesus would be not only son of David (1:32) but "Son of God" (1:35). The latter sonship dominates the final scene and is the answer to the question raised by the two men on the road to Emmaus: "We had hoped that he was the one to redeem Israel" (24:21).

As the Son of God, Jesus comes to rescue "all nations" (v. 47). The thought anticipates a speech in Acts: All humanity is the offspring of God (Acts 17:28), but Jesus, the Son of humanity, is distinctively so, and God chooses him to judge all humanity in righteousness. God has given assurance of this to all people by raising Jesus from the dead (Acts 17:31).

Along such route Luke synthesizes the national and the universal outlook of the prophets, for Israel is taken up into the single goal of repentance and forgiveness for all people, "beginning from Jerusalem." To expedite the disciples' mission Jesus will send "the promise" *(epaggelia)* of the Father. From Acts 2:33 it is clear that the Holy Spirit is meant (cf. Acts 1:4; Luke 3:16). Their ministry will extend his own (cf. 4:18–19), and they will not be left to their own resources. Their mission is not conceived in terms of standard political procedures. It is God's own innovative program, and they are to wait in Jerusalem until they are **clothed with power from on high** (cf. Isa. 32:15; Wisd. of Sol. 9:17). Theirs will be the politics of the New Age.

24:50. Without any suggestion of a long interval of time Luke pictures Jesus leading his disciples out to Bethany. There the events of Passion week had begun, and there he lifts **his hands** in blessing. Sirach 50 seems to have been in Luke's mind as he wrote vv. 50–52. Jesus resembles the high priest Simon, the son of Onias.

When this priest came out of the temple he was resplendent with glory

(v. 5). Of Zechariah it was said that the people perceived he had "seen a vision in the temple," but he could only sign the blessing (Luke 1:22). But after his muteness had disappeared, he blessed the Lord God of Israel (1:68–79) in words similar to the blessing recited by Simon (Sir. 50:22–24). Most appropriately Luke concludes his story with the gesture of a priest blessing his congregation. Through Jesus' word and deed all other blessings, including the *Benedictus* of Zechariah, receive a revised and fresh interpretation.

24:51. To bless *(eulogeō)* means to assure one of God's favor and support. Thus the disciples, who had stood afar off (23:49), now are brought near to God by the One who departs from them in order always to be near them.

According to the margin of the RSV, some copyists added the words "and was carried up into heaven," allegedly in reinforcement of the suggestion in Luke's narrative that the ascension took place on the third day. New manuscript evidence encourages retention of the reading in Luke's text. The ascension after forty days of appearances, recorded at Acts 1:9, would then mean the termination of such appearances. In any event, Luke's view of the ascension is not so much the physical removal of Jesus as his entry into "glory," that is, the repute he enjoys as the Ruler of the world and Director of all operations of the People of God.

Luke's view of the possibilities of governance by Jesus is not totally isolated from other human experience. Early explorers of the North American continent reported that the Central Algonkian Indian tribes appeared to carry out their "subsistence, religious, administrative, and military activities in the virtual absence of any sort of recognizable authority!" (Walter B. Miller, in *Readings in Managerial Psychology* [1964], 588).

As for the importance of Jesus' resurrection, Luke shows that it establishes the ascended Jesus as the one who was crucified, and at the same time it challenges the validity of any claim for a messianic deliverer whose appearance might be alleged after the removal of Jesus from visible association with God's people.

By raising him from the dead, God also reverses the charge *(krima)* that brought about his crucifixion. Resurrection, expected especially for "the upright" (see on 14:14), ratifies the centurion's verdict (23:47) and anticipates the proclamation in Acts 3:14; 22:14.

In the light of all that Luke has hitherto presented, the total recital would climactically suggest to Greco-Roman auditors that "benefactor" is the appropriate term to apply to Jesus. Luke will accentuate the point at Acts 4:9 and 10:38. Nor would special education be required for one to know the basic traditions that Diodoros of Sicily records concerning human beings, such as Herakles, Dionysos, and Aristaios, who were awarded immortality and eternal honor "because of their good services to humanity" (*Histories* 6.1.2).

In his *Metamorphoses,* Ovid recites the story of Romulus, first ruler of Rome, whose mortal body gave way to a beautiful form wearing a sacred robe (14.805–52), and Livy (*History* 1.16.5–8) records how he appeared to Julius Proculus, with instructions for the Roman people (see Alan Segal, in *Aufstieg und Niedergang der römischen Welt,* II, *Principat* 23.2: 13:47–48). Yet, despite some common features in such stories about benefactors who achieved immortal status, Luke's auditors would be conscious of a major difference. Luke's Jesus does not appear, as he did in the account of the transfiguration (9:29), in effulgent splendor.

As indicated in connection with the centurion's verdict (23:47), one who is really "upright" can, as Plato said, expect repudiation. But the same philosopher went on to say concerning a truly "righteous" person: "Whether the upright incur poverty, fall sick, or become victim to any other evil, ultimately things will redound to them, whether alive or dead, for good. Assuredly, deities do not ignore those who aspire to righteousness and who cultivate personal excellence so that, within the range of human power, they may bear God's likeness" (*Republic* 613a, b).

24:52. The words "worshipped him, and," in the margin of the RSV, are to be retained. Alexander the Great and others of exceptional merit received the kind of adulation described by Luke from their grateful publics, and the evangelist's Greco-Roman auditors would readily understand that Jesus is to be viewed as one who surpasses Alexander in claims to glory.

Jesus' blessing binds the disciples to their Lord in obedience, for they return **to Jerusalem.** Like those who were blessed by Simon son of Onias (Sir. 50:22–23), like the shepherds in the fields of Bethlehem (Luke 2:10), they experience **great joy** (see also 1:44, 47; Acts 2:46; 8:8; 13:52).

Certainly Luke's public would recognize that Jesus is here presented as one who has successfully accomplished his mission. The birth date of Augustus was heralded as a source of joy for the world (see *Benefactor,* No. 43.1–11). The resurrection of Jesus validates the assessment of Jesus that was made in Luke 2.

24:53. In grateful response the close associates of Jesus spend their time **in the temple blessing God.** To bless (*eulogeō*) God means that one gives thanks for benefits received. Luke began his Gospel with a series of events that took place in the temple. There Zechariah received the promise of the birth of John the Baptist. There Simeon had seen the light of the gentiles and the glory of God's people, Israel. There Hannah (Anna) had spent all her time and spoke to all who were awaiting the redemption of Israel. There Jesus had asked: "Did you not know that I must be in my Father's house?"

According to apocalyptic hope, "the righteous" would arise in the end time. The centurion's verdict—"this man was upright" (*dikaios*)—and the resurrection of Jesus together affirm that the end time is now reality.

Jesus had thought the unthinkable, dared the unbearable, and achieved the impossible. We only await the end of the end time, for with Jesus, the Great Benefactor, came the New Age.

THE HISTORIAN'S SUMMARY

Peter began to preach: I am now convinced that God has no favorites. God's heart is open to anyone, anywhere, who stands in awe of God and lives accordingly. You know the story that God dispatched to Israel. It told the good news of peace through Jesus Christ. He is Master of all.

That story went from one end of Palestine to the other, beginning from Galilee after the baptism that John proclaimed. It told that God anointed Jesus of Nazareth with the Holy Spirit and with power. It declared that God was with Jesus all the time that he lived as a benefactor, including the healing of all whom the devil was tyrannizing.

We can testify to all that he did throughout the land and also in Jerusalem. They hung him on a tree. But God restored his life on the third day and let him be seen—not by the entire nation, but by us whom God previously chose as witnesses. We ate and drank with him after his resurrection. And he ordered us to proclaim to the nation and to testify that God appointed him to be judge of the living and the dead.

All the prophets testify and declare that on his authority anyone who believes in him is entitled to forgiveness of sins. (au. trans.)

SELECTED BIBLIOGRAPHY

COMMENTARIES

For the General Reader

Ellis, E. Earle. *The Gospel of Luke*. Rev. ed. New Century Bible. Grand Rapids: Wm. B. Eerdmans, (1966) 1974. Based on the Revised Standard Version. Ellis pays constant attention to the function of form in the communication of meaning. Besides comments on words and phrases, Ellis discusses each section under one or more of the following categories: structure, teaching, and background. Expert use of Hebrew-language sources enriches this exposition.

Karris, Robert J. *Invitation to Luke: A Commentary on the Gospel of Luke with Complete Text of the Jerusalem Bible*. Garden City, N. Y.: Doubleday & Co., 1977. Designed for individual and group Bible study.

Plummer, Alfred. *A Critical and Exegetical Commentary on the Gospel According to St. Luke*. 4th ed. Edinburgh: T. & T. Clark, (1896) 1910. Especially valuable for the author's Greco-Roman references and his comments on Luke's style.

Schweizer, Eduard. *The Good News According to Luke*. Trans. David E. Green. Atlanta: John Knox Press, 1984.

Talbert, Charles H. *Reading Luke: A Literary and Theological Commentary on the Third Gospel*. New York: Crossroad, 1982. Features understanding of Luke in historical and cultural context.

For the Advanced Student

Brutscheck, Jutta. *Die Maria-Marta-Erzahlung: Eine redaktionskritische Untersuchung zu Lk 10, 38–42*. Frankfurt am Main: Hanstein, 1986. A model study of a small unit, but with sensitive awareness of the contours of Luke's total work.

Creed, J. M. *The Gospel According to St. Luke: The Greek Text with Introduction, Notes, and Indices*. London: Macmillan & Co., (1930) 1953.

Fitzmyer, Joseph A. *The Gospel According to Luke*. Anchor Bible Series 28 and 28A. 2 vols. Garden City, N.Y.: Doubleday and Co., 1981, 1985. Contains detailed bibliographies.

Marshall, I. Howard. *The Gospel of Luke: A Commentary on the Greek Text*. Grand Rapids: Wm. B. Eerdmans, 1978.

Schürmann, H. *Das Lukasevangelium:* Erster Teil. Herders Theologischer Kommentar zum Neuen Testament. Band III. Freiburg: Herder, 1969. Only 1:1—9:50 has appeared.

Wettstein, Jakob. *Novum Testamentum Graecum*. 2 vols. Amsterdam: Dommerian, 1751–52. Reprint, Graz, Austria: Akademische Druck, 1962. International quarry for references to Greek and Roman authors.

SPECIAL STUDIES

Only a few specialized studies of Luke's work are here listed. They will in turn direct their users to the vast body of literature available on Luke's two-volume work:

Brown, Schuyler. *Apostasy and Perseverance in the Theology of Luke*. Analecta Biblica 36. Rome: Pontifical Biblical Institute, 1969. Acute observations, especially on Luke's ethical perspective, with challenge to Conzelmann's understanding of "temptation."

Cadbury, Henry Joel. *The Making of Luke-Acts*. New York: Macmillan Co., 1927. A delightful study for the general reader, whom it takes into Luke's literary workshop. A classic in its own right. Cadbury's verdict of "general obscurity of plan" must be called into question, but much modern editorial criticism requires correction in view of his many insights and fertile observations well accompanied by sober judgment and fine historical discernment.

Cassidy, Richard J. *Jesus, Politics, and Society: A Study of Luke's Gospel*. Maryknoll, N.Y.: Orbis Books, 1978. Discusses the political and social stance of Jesus. For the general reader, with much supporting evidence.

Cassidy, Richard J., and Philip J. Scharper, eds. *Political Issues in Luke-Acts*. Maryknoll, N.Y.: Orbis Books, 1983. A series of ten essays by various scholars on political aspects of Luke's Gospel and the Book of Acts. A few Greek words here and there, but for the most part accessible to the general reader.

Conzelmann, Hans. *The Theology of St. Luke*. Trans. by G. Buswell. Philadelphia: Fortress Press, (1960) 1980. This English-language edition does not include the revisions available in the third German edition (Tübingen: J. C. B. Mohr [Paul Siebeck], 1960). A partial correction of Cadbury's verdict, but especially deficient in assessment of the role of chaps. 1 and 2 in Luke's Gospel.

Danker, Frederick W. *Benefactor: Epigraphic Study of a Graeco-Roman and New Testament Semantic Field*. St. Louis: Clayton Pub. House, 1982. Translations of selected inscriptions open up for the general reader features of the political-religious-cultural arena in which Luke's Gospel took shape. The detailed notes and index to discussion of passages in Luke-Acts will be appreciated especially by the advanced student. The bibliography in this work contains numerous works—especially those in the area of Greco-Roman studies—to which my commentary is partially indebted.

————. *Luke*. 2d ed. revised and enlarged, Proclamation Commentaries. Philadelphia: Fortress Press, 1987. Designed as an introduction to *Jesus and the New Age,* this work discusses the principal themes and topics in Luke's Gospel and shows the lines of continuity between the Gospel and Acts. Major contributions include a study of reversal motif and exploration of Luke's approach to accountability for the death of Jesus and its rationale in effecting salvation.

Derrett, J. Duncan M. *New Resolutions of Old Conundrums: A Fresh Insight into Luke's Gospel*. Shipston-on-Stour, Warwickshire, Eng.: Drinkwater, 1986.

Ellis, E. Earle. *Eschatology in Luke*. Facet Books. Philadelphia: Fortress Press, 1972. Twenty-five pages of solid study, with bibliography, on one of the most disputed topics in Lukan research. John Reumann's introduction, in ten pages, is alone worth the price of the booklet.

Farris, Stephen. *The Hymns of Luke's Infancy Narratives*. Sheffield: JSOT Press, 1985. A technical discussion of the origin, meaning, and significance of the hymns in Luke 1 and 2.

Flender, Helmut. *St. Luke: Theologian of Redemptive History*. Trans. by R. H. Fuller and I. Fuller. Philadelphia: Fortress Press, 1967. In critique of Conzelmann, Flender stresses the exaltation of Jesus as the consummation of salvation in heaven.

Jervell, Jacob. *Luke and the People of God: A New Look at Luke-Acts*. Minneapolis: Augsburg, 1972. One of the best resources for exploring the question of Israel's rejection of the gospel as depicted by Luke.

Keck, Leander E., and J. Louis Martyn, eds. *Studies in Luke-Acts*. Philadelphia: Fortress Press, (1966) 1980. A series of classic essays by seventeen scholars.

Kingsbury, Jack Dean. *Jesus Christ in Matthew, Mark, and Luke*. Proclamation Commentaries. Philadelphia: Fortress Press, 1981. A highly prized nontechnical discussion of Luke's Christology. See esp. chap. 4.

Krodel, Gerhard. *Acts*. Proclamation Commentaries. Philadelphia: Fortress Press, 1981. Luke's Gospel should not be read in isolation from Acts, and Krodel offers the general reader one of the most accurate guides to the evangelist's second volume. Included is a bibliography for study of Acts.

O'Toole, Robert F. *The Unity of Luke's Theology: An Analysis of Luke-Acts*. Wilmington, Del.: Glazier, 1984. A popular discussion of the dominant threads that go into Luke's literary tapestry.

Pilgrim, Walter E. *Good News for the Poor*. Minneapolis: Augsburg, 1981. For the general reader. Points to a new vision of intelligent discipleship in caring community.

Talbert, Charles H. *Literary Patterns, Theological Themes and the Genre of Luke-Acts*. Society of Biblical Literature Monograph Series 20. Missoula, Mont.: Scholars Press, 1974. Ingenious observations proposed for the advanced student.

Tannehill, Robert C. *The Narrative Unity of Luke-Acts: A Literary Interpretation*. Volume I: *The Gospel According to Luke*. Philadelphia: Fortress Press, 1986. A perceptive study of Luke as literature.

Tiede, David L. *Prophecy and History in Luke-Acts*. Philadelphia: Fortress Press, 1980. Nontechnical, but for advanced students of Luke's work. A diligent search for the roots of Christian faith in God's purpose as displayed in the OT.

INDEX OF ANCIENT AUTHORS
AND WRITINGS